FreeHand 7 Graphics Studio
the Comprehensive Guide

For Macintosh/Power Macintosh & Windows 95/NT

R. Shamms Mortier

VENTANA

FreeHand 7 Graphics Studio: The Comprehensive Guide
Copyright © 1997 by R. Shamms Mortier

Library of Congress Cataloging-in-Publication Data
Mortier, R. Shamms.
     FreeHand 7 graphics studio: the comprehensive guide/R Shamms Mortier. — 1st ed.
        p. cm.
     Includes index.
     ISBN 1-56604-679-3
     1. Computer graphics. 2. Aldus FreeHand (Computer file)
I. Title.
T385.M669 1997
006.6'869—dc21   97-16158
                                  CIP

First Edition 9 8 7 6 5 4 3 2 1

Printed in the United States of America

Ventana Communications Group
P.O. Box 13964
Research Triangle Park, NC 27709-3964
919.544.9404
FAX 919.544.9472
http://www.vmedia.com

Ventana Communications Group is a division of International Thomson Publishing.

President
Michael E. Moran

**Vice President of
Content Development**
Karen A. Bluestein

**Director of Acquisitions and
Development**
Robert Kern

Managing Editor
Lois J. Principe

Production Manager
John Cotterman

Art Director
Marcia Webb

**Technology Operations
Manager**
Kerry L. B. Foster

Brand Manager
Jamie Jaeger Fiocco

Creative Services Manager
Diane Lennox

Acquisitions Editor
Christopher D. Grams

Project Editor
Judith F. Wilson

Development Editor
Michelle Corbin Nichols

Copy Editor
Sarah O'Keefe, Scriptorium
Publishing Services, Inc.

CD-ROM Specialist
Adam F. Newton

Technical Reviewer
Brian J. Little,
Imagination Workshop

Desktop Publisher
Scott Hosa

Proofreader
Chris Riffer

Indexer
Richard T. Evans, Infodex

Interior Designer
Patrick Berry

Cover Illustrator
Elina Skrinak

About the Author

Shamms Mortier has written more than 500 articles (and produced their illustrations) over the past 10 years for a number of magazines, including *TV Technology, Computer Video, DTP Journal, Computer Graphics World, Web Techniques, Dynamic Graphics, Step-by-Step, 3D Design, Amazing Computing, Video Toaster User, Computer Shopper,* and *JumpDisk.*

He has beta tested products from dozens of internationally known developers over the years and has also written software documentation. He authored the complete graphics section of the *Maclopedia* (Hayden), and is working on (or has completed) a number of other books, including: *Desktop Videography* (Michtron Publications), *Web Publishing With Macromedia Backstage Internet Studio 2* (Ventana), *PageMaker 6.5 Complete* (Hayden), as well as 3D art and animation booklets (PIM Publications).

Eyeful Tower Communications—his design and animation studio—has served regional and national clients, including Thrifty Rent-A-Car, the University of Vermont, the State of Vermont, and ABC Television. Mortier has exhibited his computer and traditional artwork at several regional galleries and at national juried exhibitions. His animated film, *The Secret Dreams of Older Men*, was supported by a grant from the Boston Film and Video Foundation and the Vermont Council on the Arts.

Mortier has taught design, animation, mythology, and psychology courses at the college level for 15 years. He is also a professional jazz composer, performer, and recording artist with two CDs to his credit. He received support from the National Endowment for the Arts for a 1994 jazz ensemble tour of Russia.

R. Shamms Mortier, PhD
rshamms@together.net

Acknowledgments

I wish to thank the following individuals at Ventana, without whose efforts this book would have remained just a dream: Chris Grams, JJ Hohn, Michelle Nichols, Judy Wilson, Adam Newton, John Cotterman, Scott Hosa, Jaimie Livingston, Becky Steele, Diane Lennox, and Wendy Bernhardt. Each provided expertise and understanding, as well as a huge amount of patience, to a very challenging task. Thanks also are due to Sarah O'Keefe and Brian Little, whose suggestions helped to sharpen the edges of the book's contents. Thanks to all.

R. Shamms Mortier, PhD

Dedication

To all of the writers, artists, poets, musicians, and dreamers in the world, without whose vision and effort science and human communication would be impossible, and without whose struggle healing could not exist.

Contents

PART II

Mastering xRes

PART III

Mastering Extreme 3D

Mastering Fontographer

PART VI

Getting on the Web: Hands-On Exercises

Introduction

Welcome!

If you are a FreeHand user, or have experience or an interest in the other applications provided as part of the FreeHand 7 Graphics Studio suite of applications, your purchase of this book was a wise choice. Even if you are somewhat new to FreeHand, xRes, Extreme 3D, or Fontographer, this book can enhance your mastery of any or all of these products, and certainly increase your productivity all around. The FreeHand 7 Graphics Studio has all the tools you need to set up a true digital graphics studio. The applications cover vector drawing, bitmap painting, image processing, special effects, 3D object and scene creation, Web page authoring, font creation and editing, everything you need. This book touches upon all of these topics and more, suggesting ways that you can put each of the applications in the FreeHand 7 Graphics Studio to the best creative use.

What's Inside

There is a wealth of helpful material in this book, covering every application in the FreeHand 7 Graphics Studio. If you work through all of it, you will be able to master any project that comes your way.

- **Part 1: Mastering FreeHand.** This section covers everything necessary to become a master FreeHand user, starting with the installation and preferences settings. All of FreeHand's tools and techniques are discussed with suggestions of how to best use each effect. Before reading this section, you should work through the FreeHand documentation, including the tutorials. This section of the book will expand and deepen your FreeHand skills.

- **Part 2: Mastering xRes.** This section begins with the installation and preferences settings in xRes. From there, you are guided through the use of xRes's many painting tools and image processing capabilities. Before using this section of the book, you should work through all of the xRes documentation. You will find a wealth of information and tips on how to put xRes to work, allowing you to stretch your xRes creations far past what you would normally expect a bitmap painting application to do. This includes a thorough study of xRes objects, channels, and paths.

- **Part 3: Mastering Extreme 3D.** Your Extreme 3D work begins with an understanding of its installation and preferences settings, and then moves on to the uses of its tools and techniques. The book details the most creative uses of Extreme 3D's numerous tools and effects, and includes a thorough exploration of its animation capabilities as well. If you are an experienced FreeHand user new to 3D, you learn how to incorporate 3D output in your FreeHand documents. Before you read this section of the book, make sure you understand Extreme 3D's documentation.

- **Part 4: Mastering Fontographer.** Integrating customized or original fonts into your FreeHand documents opens up your creative options, especially for your headline elements. This section walks you through Fontographer installation and preferences settings, and then guides you through the steps to create and customize a font. It also includes information on how to install fonts on both Mac and Windows systems.

- **Part 5: Getting Down to Business: Hands-on Exercises.** Part 5 is really the creative core of the book. With more than thirty tutorial exercises, it demonstrates how to create a number of diverse graphics, using the components of FreeHand, xRes, and Extreme 3D in the process. If you diligently work through Part 5, your professional work with FreeHand, xRes, and Extreme 3D is guaranteed to be enhanced and deepened, and your confidence in using any of these applications will grow immensely. Whatever your level of expertise when you approach this section, your capacities to use the creative potential of all of the included applications will be increased.

- **Part 6: Getting on the Web: Hands-on Exercises.** This is a unique part of the book which guides you through the use of FreeHand, xRes, and Extreme 3D in the creation of ten different Web pages, each one with a different theme. The finished Web pages are also included on the CD-ROM for your perusal in both FreeHand format and also in Afterburner compressed format, which can be viewed in your browser.

In the next section, I'll give you ideas on how to best use all this information.

Preparing to Work Through This Book

This book has been designed to guide you through using each part of the FreeHand 7 Graphics Studio applications. The CD-ROM that comes with the book is packed with developer demos and hundreds of megabytes of file that reference all of the tutorials presented in the book (see the next section for a description of the CD-ROM contents).

This book is designed to help FreeHand users with different experience levels. Read the category below that best describes your experience with FreeHand to find out what you should do to make the best use of the information.

FreeHand Studio Power User

If you are a FreeHand power user, and also have experience with Extreme 3D, xRes, and Fontographer, then the best way to use this book is to go right to the tutorial sections. Pick out the tutorials that represent new ideas or options, and look them over. You can repeat them by following the step-by-step instructions. You might also want to store any of the CD-ROM images that interest you in your own library, for potential use in any projects you have in mind.

Even for the most advanced FreeHand professional, the included tutorials contain some very new perspectives on tasks and challenges. Your prior knowledge of the software documentation should make it a breeze to work through any of the tutorials. Also pay some attention to all of the appendices, as they contain expanded information on FreeHand utilities and other helpful applications. In addition, look closely at the chapter on animation, as it describes techniques most FreeHand and xRes users are not aware of: how to develop animations with 2D non-animation software. Professional FreeHand users should also check out the CD-ROM that accompanies this book, especially the FH7 folder. The FH7 folder contains FreeHand documents that have all of the tutorial elements in place. Those finished elements are copyright free, and can be used in your own FreeHand work if needed.

Professionals Who Have Upgraded to the Latest Versions

If you are a FreeHand professional who has just upgraded to FreeHand 7 Graphics Studio from a previous version of any of the applications, work through the sections of the book that best represent the applications you are upgrading. If you are an experienced FreeHand user, for instance, you will especially be interested in working through the FreeHand tutorials. They reference new ways to use the vintage tools, and act as creative introductions to the new items in FreeHand 7. If you have recently upgraded to Extreme 3D 2.0 from version 1.0, then you should work through all of the Extreme 3D tutorials. The same holds true if your xRes experience is based upon a version previous to version 3. You should also skim the up-front chapters, paying special attention to the "what's new" information.

Look at the content represented by the graphics in the Parts and Pieces folder on the CD-ROM first, to see if there are specific things you want to learn, and then go to the tutorial that guides you through that process. Your prior knowledge of the software documentation should make it a breeze to work through any of the tutorials. Pay some attention to all of the appendices, as they contain expanded information on FreeHand utilities and other helpful applications. In addition, look closely at the chapter on animation, as it describes techniques most FreeHand and xRes users are not aware of: how to develop animations with 2D non-animation software.

Professionals New to 3D Design

If you are familiar with FreeHand or xRes, but new to 3D design, you have a great treat in store. Not only is Extreme 3D a full-featured 3D application, but the 3D design section in this book is one of the most thorough discussions of 3D design in general you will find anywhere. The tools in Extreme 3D are represented (perhaps with different names and attributes) in all 3D applications. This means that if you work through these 3D tutorials diligently, you should be prepared to take on any other 3D application you come across. Most 3D designers work with a number of different 3D applications, allowing their project needs to determine which is best for the present task. If you are new to any of the applications the book focuses upon, read the application documentation before trying to work through the exercises in this book. This is especially important for Extreme 3D, if you are a newcomer to 3D art and animation.

If you don't have the time at present to work through the 3D tutorials, you may still be able to use some of the 3D rendered content in the Parts and Pieces folder on the CD-ROM. Your prior knowledge of the software documentation should make it a breeze to work through any of the tutorials. Pay some attention to all of the appendices, as they contain expanded information on FreeHand utilities and other helpful applications. In addition, look closely at the chapter on animation, as it describes techniques most FreeHand and xRes users are not aware of: how to develop animations with 2D non-animation software.

Intermediate FreeHand Graphics Studio Users

Be sure that you read and understand the documentation that ships with each of the FreeHand 7 Graphics Studio component applications before working through this book. This book's guided examples can advance your capabilities from intermediate experience to mastery. Pay special attention to those ideas and techniques that are new to you. Work through their tutorials, then work through them a few more times after changing some of the parameters. Save all of your work, and use your own examples as a way of expanding your familiarity and mastery of an application. Show the results of your efforts to others, and be willing to listen attentively to their feedback and critical remarks. Listening plays a large role in true learning.

FreeHand Users New to Web Design

You will want to go through the ten Web design tutorials in the book, and also explore posting a Web site built from a FreeHand document. Familiarity with Afterburner is a must, as is an understanding of how to surf the Internet. Contact your Internet service provider or webmaster to get the latest on any special requirements for posting your FreeHand Web pages (in most cases, there shouldn't be any). Learn how to tweak the FreeHand Web designs to get what you need. Read all of the associated material in the book on image mapping and incorporating URL targets.

Contents of the Book's CD-ROM

The book's CD-ROM contains the following items for your professional use and exploration:

- A folder of Parts that includes well over 100 drawing and experimental paintings that were created along the way as FreeHand, xRes, and Extreme 3D projects developed for the book.
- The Web-10 folder, which contains all of the 10 Web pages developed for the book, in both FreeHand and compressed formats.
- The xRes folder, which contains five extra xRes paintings.
- The Animguy folder, which contains three rendered frames of the Animguy animation in TIFF and GIF formats.
- The FH7 folder, which contains all of the FreeHand documents used in the book, as well as others not included.
- The Animz folder, which contains all of the animations mentioned in the book's animation Chapter 25.
- The Ex3D folder, which contains 32 Extreme 3D project files and associated renderings.
- The Rocks folder, which contains seven TIF renderings associated with the natural rendering exercises in the book.
- Other folders, which contain demo software from world-class developers.

System Requirements

Look at the separate chapters that deal with the installation of each of the four applications included in the book to find the details for what that application requires in terms of system software, RAM, and hard disk storage requirements. Assuming that you wish to install all of the four applications (FreeHand 7, xRes 3, Extreme 3D 2.0, and Fontographer 4.x), the following are the basic system requirements you will need.

Mac OS

You will need a Power Mac system (Extreme 3D needs a Power Mac) with at least 100 MB of storage space, 24 MB of RAM, a monitor and graphics system (built-in or card) capable of at least 16-bit color, and Mac OS 7.x. If you want to run any two applications concurrently, you should have a minimum of 48 MB of RAM. (You can certainly get by with less, but you will probably be dissatisfied with your system's performance.) If you plan to develop large graphics in xRes (over 10 MB), then you will need at least 50 MB of extra hard drive space to accommodate a scratch disk. The more RAM and storage space, the merrier. You will also need a CD-ROM drive.

Windows

You will need a Pentium system (Extreme 3D needs a Pentium) with at least 100 MB of storage space, 24 MB of RAM, a monitor and graphics card capable of at least 16-bit color, and Windows 95 or NT. If you want to run any two applications concurrently, you will need a minimum of 48 MB of RAM. If you plan to develop large graphics in xRes (over 10 MB), then you will need at least 50 MB of extra hard drive space to accommodate a scratch disk. The more RAM and storage space, the merrier. You will also need a CD-ROM drive. Windows NT users will require more RAM than Windows 95 users.

Conventions Used in This Book

When it is necessary to detail menu commands for any of the associated FreeHand 7 Graphics Studio applications, we will follow the convention of using the " I " sign to indicate hierarchical menu navigation. If, for instance, we are talking about using the FreeHand command that allows you to expand the stroke of a selected graphic, it might be necessary to tell you that the command is nested under the Alter path option in the Modify menu. To inform you where it is, we would say "choose to Modify I Alter Path I Expand Stroke." Most menu commands have keyboard equivalents, and many have associated icons in the Operations or Xtra Tools palettes.

The FreeHand documentation covers keyboard equivalents thoroughly, so we will not dwell on them in the book. We will, however, call your attention to the associated icons when possible, since this is a faster way of working than going to a menu command. If you are using FreeHand more than any other application, you will find it worth your while to remember necessary keyboard equivalents, since that's the fastest way to work. In general, you can get the job done quicker by working with keyboard equivalents (sometimes called "hot keys") first, using associated icons as a second option, and using embedded menu commands as an option when neither keyboard commands nor icons are available. The more you work with any single application, the more likely you are to opt for the use of keyboard equivalents to speed things up.

While FreeHand is supported on both Mac and Windows platforms, the screen shots for this book were taken on the Mac.

Are You Ready?

When a painting is finished and ready for showing, the artist feels a little torn by the prospect of allowing a work that contains so much of him/herself to leave the confines of the studio. It's like a piece of the self being removed for display. This book is a painting that has been worked upon and polished by many individuals, although it wears the author's name on the cover. Everything has been done to present you with the best creative ideas possible, so you can take the tools and create your own masterpieces.

There are tips and techniques included in this book that you will find nowhere else, and many a sleepless night has gone into the crafting of the book and the CD-ROM that accompanies it. It is a guarantee that the measure to which you work through the information presented here, your ability to push these software tools to the max in your own creative pursuits will be enhanced exponentially. FreeHand, xRes, Extreme 3D, and Fontographer are absolutely magical in their potential, and this book is a doorway that will allow you to use the tools to your best advantage. This book is a resource that should give you a wealth of creative ways to explore for years to come.

R. Shamms Mortier, Ph.D.
Eyeful Tower Communications
Bristol, Vermont
Spring 1997

Part I

Mastering FreeHand

Getting Started With FreeHand Projects

A journey of a thousand miles begins with the first step, and your journey into the powerful land of the FreeHand 7 Graphics Studio begins with the installation process. In this chapter, we will walk through the installation of FreeHand 7, as well as telling you what has changed from previous versions. In addition, we will look at setting up FreeHand 7 Preferences for documents, color, and maximizing the editing features. Generating reports, configuring your display, and importing/exporting elements are also included.

Installing FreeHand 7

The FreeHand 7 Graphics Studio comes on three CD-ROMs. One CD-ROM holds FreeHand 7 and xRes, as well as associated extra files. A second CD-ROM includes extra bitmap and clip-art files. A third CD-ROM contains Extreme 3D version 1, with an offer to upgrade to version 2 for a modest fee. The upgrade price tends to change, so contact Macromedia for details. Installation for both Mac and Windows systems follows the standard point-and-click conventions. The installation utility lets you specify where to install the applications and which files to include in the initial installation.

Tip

Although you can always leave extra files (those not needed to run the application) on the CD-ROM, it is best to install as many files as your hard drive space permits. This allows you easier access, and also cuts down on the time needed to develop a project. The wisest thing to do is to install everything possible, then preview what the actual files look like. From there, you can winnow out material you think will have no value for you.

Installing FreeHand 7 for Windows 95/NT

The minimum system requirements for installing FreeHand, xRes 3, and Fontographer (the three applications on the FreeHand 7 Graphics Studio CD-ROM) include:

- 486/50 MHz processor (Pentium strongly recommended)
- 26 megabytes of RAM (40 megabytes recommended)
- SVGA color (24-bit color recommended)
- Windows 95 or NT 3.51 or higher
- 65 megabytes of hard drive space (85 megabytes recommended for standard installation)
    Note: Extreme 3D 2.0 requires an additional five megabytes of disk space.
- CD-ROM drive

FreeHand 7 Graphics Studio RAM storage requirements for each component are as follows:

- FreeHand 7—12 MB
- Fontographer—6 MB
- Extreme 3D (version 1 or 2)—24 MB
- xRes—16 MB

To install the FreeHand Graphics Studio components from the CD-ROM, do the following:

1. Insert the CD-ROM into the CD-ROM drive.

2. In Windows 95 or NT 4, double-click the setup icon in the FGS7 folder (or run it from the Start menu in Windows 95).

3. Follow the prompts to customize the setup according to your needs, and to select the appropriate destination paths.

Installing FreeHand 7 for the Mac OS

The minimum system requirements for installing FreeHand, xRes 3, and Fontographer (the three applications on the FreeHand 7 Graphics Studio CD-ROM) include:

■ 68040 or higher processor (PowerPC strongly recommended)

■ 26 megabytes of RAM (40 megabytes recommended)

■ 8-bit color (24-bit color recommended)

■ System 7 or higher

■ 70 megabytes of hard drive space (90 megabytes recommended for standard installation)
    Note: Extreme 3D 2.0 requires an additional five megabytes of disk space. Also, Extreme 3D 2.0 runs only on a Power PC processor.

■ CD-ROM drive

FreeHand 7 Graphics Studio RAM storage requirements for each component are as follows:

■ FreeHand 7—12 MB

■ Fontographer—6 MB

■ Extreme 3D (version 1 or 2)—24 MB

■ xRes—16 MB

To install the FreeHand Graphics Studio components from the CD-ROM, do the following:

1. Insert the CD-ROM into the CD-ROM drive.

2. Double-click the setup icon in the FGS7 folder.

3. Follow the prompts to customize the setup according to your needs, and to select the appropriate destination paths.

What's New in FreeHand 7 Graphics Studio?

Each of the separate applications in the FreeHand 7 Graphics Studio, with the exception of Fontographer, offers new expanded features beyond those found in previous releases. These include:

- The MUI (Macromedia User Interface). The MUI ties FreeHand 7 applications together with the interface design of all other Macromedia products, making movement among diverse applications easier and more intuitive.

- MIX (Macromedia Information Exchange). MIX is based on common file formats included in all associated Macromedia products, so data can be easily ported from one application to another (and incorporated in Web page design). MIX formats include BMP, GIF, JPEG, PICT, Photoshop 3.0, PNG, TGA, TIFF, and xRes LRG.

- Complete cross-platform xRes integration, which lets you drag and drop and copy/paste all xRes and xRes LRG files from within FreeHand.

- Complete cross-platform Extreme 3D integration, which lets you drag and drop and perform copy/paste operations. Also, it has the ability to open Extreme 3D DXF in FreeHand.

- The ability to open and convert the Fontographer EPS files.

- The Trace tool, which translates bitmap data into vector data. The Trace tool generates full-color, fully editable line art.

- A new Links dialog box that centralizes user control over imported images.

- An improved Pen Tool, with a more natural feel.

- Multi-object blends and gradients between spot colors and along paths.

- Roughen and envelope distortion effects.

- A chart creation utility.

- A search and replace tool that allows you to find and modify any element that displays the selected parameter.

- New toolbars and tabbed, tear-off, dockable panels. Dockable panels are panels that snap into alignment.

- Integration with Photoshop, PageMaker, and QuarkXPress, with new color matching standards including high-fidelity color sets like Hexachrome.

- Macromedia Common Scripting (MCS) as a cross-platform feature.

- The ability to save FreeHand documents for use on the Internet, using Shockwave and Afterburner technology.

Tip

Most of these new features have been blended into the accompanying tutorials in the book.

Extra FreeHand 7 Goodies on the Application CD-ROM

There are a number of value-added items on the two FreeHand 7 Graphics Studio CD-ROMs, including:

- Over 300 megabytes of clip art in 36 categories
- A full working tutorial for FreeHand 7
- A FreeHand Shockwave installation directory
- Ten folders of templates (over 30 megabytes)
- Digital maps from the Magellan collection
- A loadable color palette with Web-safe colors (use this palette when creating Web pages, like the Web page tutorials in this book)
- ICC Profile Color offer for getting the same color output on printers, monitors, and scanners
- A number of demo Photoshop filters that can be accessed and operated within FreeHand for imported bitmap graphics. These include:

   Andromeda Software, Inc.
   Series 4
   Displaced texture mapping on the fly.
   http://www.andromeda.com/
   800-547-0055

   Chroma Graphics
   Chromatica
   Makes masking, recoloring, and edge blending a breeze.
   http://www.chromagraphics.com/
   888-8CHROMA

Cognicon
FreeD
Extract 3D models from 2D photographs.
http://www.cognicon.com/
info@cognicon.com
(e-mail preferred)

Digital Frontiers
HVS Color
Converts 24-bit images to 8-bit images with no visible loss in quality.
http://www.digfrontiers.com
800-328-7789

Extensis Corporation
Intellihance
Latest version of successful FreeHand effects add-ons.
http://www.extensis.com
503-274-2020

MetaTools
Convolver, Kai's Power Tools
Special effects for images including 3D transform, emboss, flare, neon, and more.
http://www.metatools.com
metasales@aol.com
(e-mail preferred)

Multi Media Marketing
HoloDozo
Special effects using Apple's QuickDraw 3D.
http://www.luxussoft.de/sw/plugs/holodozo/
+49-511-317221 (Germany)

Valis Group
Flo'
Manipulate an image by stretching the image through push and pull.
valisgroup@aol.com
(e-mail preferred)

Xaos Tools
Paint Alchemy, Terrazo, Typecaster
High-end paint filter effects and font-to-bitmap rendering.
http:// www.xaostools.com
415-487-7000

Setting up FreeHand Projects

A FreeHand project contains all of the elements in a document. The FreeHand documentation takes you through all the project settings options. This book assumes that you either are experienced with basic FreeHand project setups or that you have at least familiarized yourself with the documentation on these topics. Let's look at why you might want to consider certain setup parameters over others, and how certain options can influence the way that you work and the speed at which your projects get under way. If you need more detailed guidance on any of the topics not covered here, please refer to the FreeHand documentation that came with your software, and also to the online help in FreeHand.

Tip

Windows users can access the help both from the Question Mark icon in the main toolbar and from the Help menu. The Mac OS version of FreeHand has no Help menu, so the Question Mark icon is the only choice.

Setting FreeHand Preferences

When setting up a FreeHand project, this is your first stop. Both Mac OS and Windows users will want to choose File | Preferences to display the Preferences dialog. The Preferences dialog for Mac OS and Windows users covers the same settings and parameters, although each dialog obeys the generic conventions of the platform it is on (see Figure 1-1).

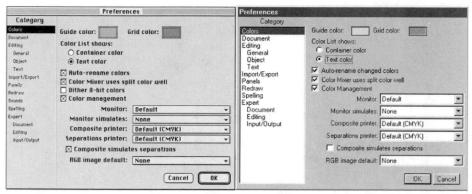

Figure 1-1: The Mac Preferences dialog on the left and the Windows Preferences dialog on the right appear a little differently, but cover the same topics.

As you click on a topic in the left-hand column, the associated parameters appear in the right-hand side of the dialog. These settings are applied to every project that is loaded into or created in FreeHand until you change the settings.

Tip

Remember, if you'd like more details about these preferences, please see the FreeHand documentation and the online help. The comments here explain why you might choose one preference setting over another, instead of simply duplicating the FreeHand documentation.

Colors

There are a couple of important items to consider when setting your color preferences (see Figure 1-2). The first is to make sure that your guide color is dark enough to see if you plan to use guides on your page. The default setting is far to light to be useful, and can cause eye strain when you spend long hours at the monitor. I use a dark blue setting (more on the use of guides later).

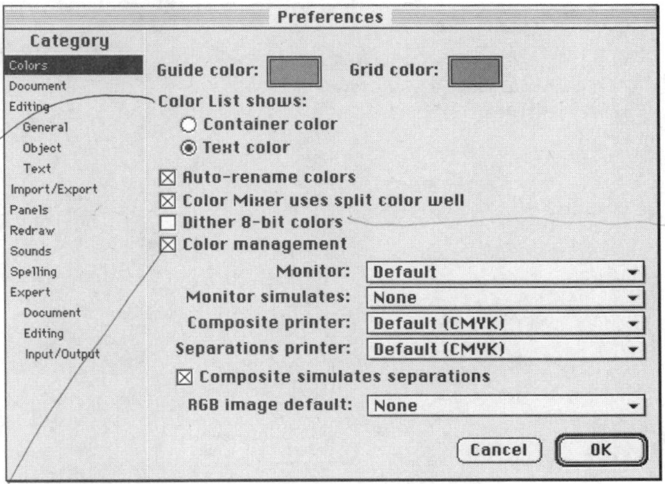

Figure 1-2: The Colors tab in the Preferences dialog.

In general, it's wise to leave the Color List set to reference the text color. When the screen page is small or the text block is small, it becomes difficult to drag and drop colors on the fill portions of text and not the strokes. Leaving the Color List set to reference the text colors helps.

By default, dithering 8-bit colors is off (Mac only), and should remain that way, especially if you are creating Web pages. 256-color palettes (8-bit) are best displayed as non-dithered on the Web, or dithered with external tools. In my experience, Web palettes dithered here can appear strange when placed online. The Color management option is best left on. This guarantees a closer match between what you see on your monitor and the printed output.

Document

I recommend that you leave the Remember window size and location and FreeHand 4 page placement options in their default settings of on and off, respectively (see Figure 1-3). The Remember window size and location option, when checked, opens the document in the same size window and at the same location as when the file was last saved. The FreeHand 4 page placement option, when checked, adds new pages at the lower left of the pasteboard, somewhat complicating the work area.

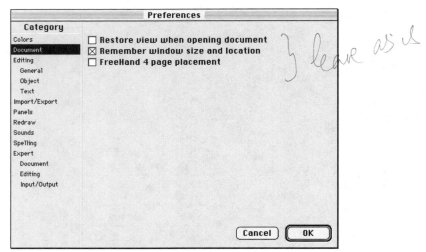

Figure 1-3: The Document tab in the Preferences dialog.

Consider turning off the third item, Restore view when opening document, in most cases. It's easier to allow the document to fit to the screen when you open it and adjust it from there, even though you may have saved it out when the view was either very tiny or zoomed in on one element on the page.

Editing

There are three subheads in this dialog: General, Object, and Text. Everyone works differently, so you will probably choose a different configuration than I do, but there are some items worth considering for all FreeHand design work.

General Editing

Consider the following settings for the general editing preferences (see Figure 1-4):

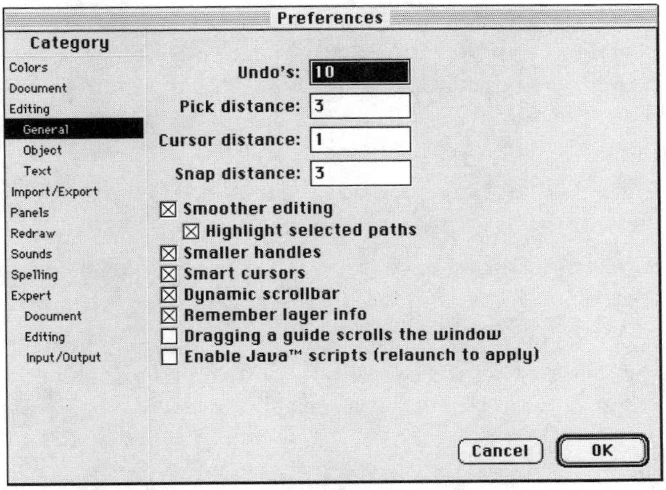

Figure 1-4: The General Editing tab in the Preferences dialog.

- **Undo Level**. Set this to 12 or 15 if you have enough RAM on your system. If you are working with a limited amount of RAM (less than 64 megabytes), consider reducing the Undo level to about 6 to conserve memory. The maximum setting is 100.

- **Pick Distance**. Can be set from 1 to 5, and determines how close, in pixels, the cursor has to be to an element to select it by clicking. Set this option low, at 1 or 2, if you dislike having an item selected that you didn't choose; a common problem when the screen gets overcrowded (which can happen often if you're not using layers).

- **Cursor Distance**. This controls how far a selected object will move (or be "nudged") when you use the cursor keys on the keyboard. Set this number low so that you can get fine movements not possible with mouse movements.

- **Snap Distance**. Use a setting of 3 (the range is 0 to 5). Snap Distance controls how close you can get to a grid, guide, or snap point before the item is magnetized to the grid, guide, or point.

- **Smoother Editing and Highlight Selected Paths**. If you create FreeHand graphics with a lot of paths, leave these checked.

- **Smaller Handles**. Leave this unchecked to use larger control point handles when modifying Bezier curve segments. If you are working with a 21″ monitor, you can probably see your selected graphics more clearly than those of us with 17″ and smaller monitors. In that case, checking this option might be a workable idea.

- **Dynamic Scrollbar**. Leave this on; without it, you have to stop scrolling the document to see a screen redraw.

- **Remember Layer Info**. Leave this on; it helps the editing process when you have to save a document and get back to it later, especially if you ungroup items originally on different layers.

- **Dragging a Guide Scrolls the Window**. Turn this off. There is nothing more irritating than having work scroll out of view.

Object Editing

Consider the following settings for the object editing preferences (see Figure 1-5):

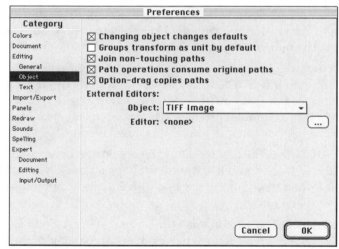

Figure 1-5: The Object Editing tab in the Preferences dialog.

- **Changing Object Changes Defaults**. Best left unchecked for most operations. There are too many times when you need to explore options with object strokes and fills.

- **Groups Transform as Unit By Default**. This option's usefulness depends on your style of work. I prefer leaving it on, since it allows a grouped selection to be transformed as a unit by any selected effects.

- **Join Non-Touching Paths**. Should remain off in most cases, unless you prefer that the computer make this choice for you.

- **Path Operations Consume Original Paths**. Leave this on, unless you plan to use paths involved in expand stroke, inset path, intersect, punch, or union operations over again.

- **Option-Drag** (Mac OS) and **Alt-Drag** (Windows). This useful item causes a selected path to be cloned when it is moved. Leave it on.

- **External Editors**. Select your favorite external editor for bitmaps. When you double-click a bitmap, this editor is loaded so that you can edit the bitmap.

Tip

Be careful when moving bitmaps when using FreeHand for the Mac. Holding the mouse down for too long will invoke the Image Editor, and you'll have to wait until its opened before shutting it down. A workaround is to first click on an empty part of the screen, and then reselect the bitmap before moving it.

Text Editing

Consider the following settings for the text editing preferences (see Figure 1-6):

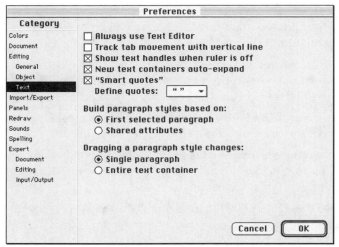

Figure 1-6: The Text Editing tab in the Preferences dialog.

■ **Always Use Text Editor**. This option has more to do with personal work habits than anything else. I prefer to leave it checked, as it makes text editing a distinct process, rather than embedding it in the FreeHand page.

■ **Track Tab Movement With Vertical Line**. This option has no advantages or disadvantages; it's your choice. When checked, a vertical line appears as tabs are dragged on the Text Ruler.

■ **Show Text Handles When Ruler Is Off**. The default is on. Since this is the way most text is displayed in other applications, there is little reason to turn it off.

■ **New Text Containers Auto-Expand**. The default is on, and I recommend that. Without it, you have to control the size of the text window manually.

■ **Quotes**. Customize the Smart Quotes item to fit the way you work.

■ **Build Paragraph Styles Based On**. This is an option that has no advantages or disadvantages; it's your choice. First selected paragraph: When checked, paragraph styles are based on the first paragraph in the selection range. Shared attributes: When checked, paragraph styles are based on the common attributes of the selected text range.

■ **Dragging a Paragraph Style Changes**. This is an option that has no advantages or disadvantages; it's your choice.

Import/Export

These options allow you to set how FreeHand saves the document or how FreeHand deals with placed EPS files (see Figure 1-7).

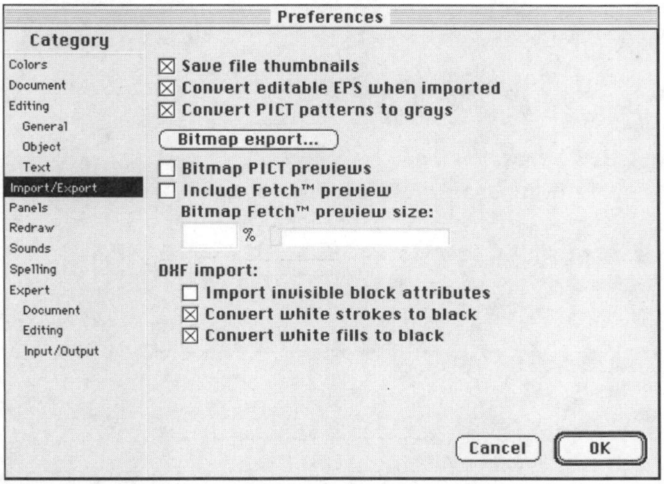

Figure 1-7: The Import/Export tab in the Preferences dialog.

- **Save File Thumbnails.** Check this to make viewing saved file content easier.
- **Convert Editable EPS When Imported**. Set this to on to allow for editing options for editable EPS graphics.
- **Convert PICT Pattern to Grays** (Mac OS only). This is on by default. It lets you see an approximation of a PostScript gray as a substitution for a PICT pattern, which helps you see what will be printed.
- **Bitmap Export**. Set the default bitmap export parameters you want to use, though this can always be changed on a case-by-case basis in the Options dialog of the Export window.
- **Include Fetch Preview** (Mac only). When checked, FreeHand includes an Aldus Fetch preview when you save or export the document.

- **Bitmap Fetch Preview Size** (Mac only). Adjust by percentage the size of the Fetch preview that is exported or saved with a FreeHand document.

- **DXF Import** (Mac only). Import invisible block attributes: When checked, DXF objects with invisible stroke and fill attributes are imported.

- **Convert White Strokes to Black** (Mac only). When checked, stroke color is converted from white to black.

- **Convert White Fills to Black** (Mac only). When checked, fill color is converted from white to black.

- **Bitmap PICT Previews** (Mac only). When checked, FreeHand saves AdobeFetch previews in bitmap PICT format rather than vector PICT format. Use this option for large FreeHand files to cut down the file size of exported or saved FreeHand files with a Fetch preview.

Panels

These options set the panel appearance and placement on the screen (see Figure 1-8):

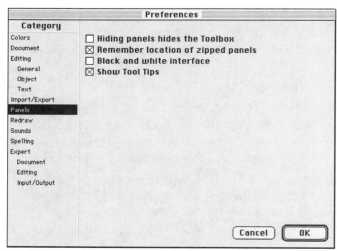

Figure 1-8: The Panels tab in the Preferences dialog.

- **Hiding Panels Hides the Toolbox**. When unchecked, choosing View | Panels hides all panels but the Toolbox. This is best turned off for most projects as it allows you a quick way to get more document view space.

- **Remember Location of Zipped Panels**. When checked, panels occupy two places on your screen: a zipped, stored location, and a different, unzipped location. Zipping and unzipping the panels causes the title bar and panel to appear in two different places. I suggest leaving this off.

- **Black and White Interface**. When checked, FreeHand's user interface uses black and white panels, icons, and toolbars. This option is useful if you are using FreeHand on a black and white monitor.

- **Show Tool Tips**. When checked, FreeHand displays short descriptions of tools and buttons called Tool Tips when you pause the cursor over a button for a few seconds. This is best left on until you have memorized all of the tool icons.

Redraw

Consider the following settings for redrawing (see Figure 1-9):

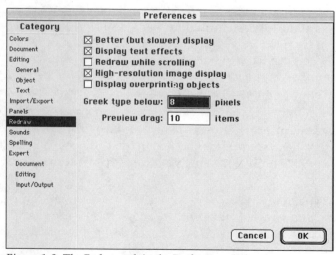

Figure 1-9: The Redraw tab in the Preferences dialog.

■ **Better (But Slower) Display**. When checked, the monitor displays as many colors as possible for graduated and radial fills. Unchecking this option limits the number of colors displayed and speeds document redraw. Deciding whether or not to turn this option on has everything to do with your trust in FreeHand output. I prefer to leave it off, because faster redraws allow me to be more creative. As an option, turn it on just before saving the document to see a better preview.

■ **Display Text Effects**. When checked, text on screen appears with high-light, inline, shadow, strikethrough, underline, and zoom text effects applied. There is no reason that I can think of to turn this off. I haven't noticed any appreciable increase in redraw speed with it off. This option is entirely dependent on your VRAM, processor speed (or video card speed), and the effect in question. Zooms can take a long time to redraw with slower processor speeds. When unchecked, text effects appear in print but not onscreen. It is usually preferable to see applied text effects on the viewable page.

■ **Redraw While Scrolling**. When checked, FreeHand redraws the document when you click a scroll arrow or scrollbar. When unchecked, FreeHand redraws when scrolling is finished. It's sometimes difficult to get the view you want if you have to wait for the redraw, so I would suggest leaving this option on.

■ **High-Resolution Image Display**. Check to display imported LRG and TIFF files at the highest resolution available. I suggest leaving this off until you want to (or need to) check the exactness of an LRG or TIFF graphic. This can happen when you need to see how a graphic is being overprinted with text. Otherwise, it's better to opt for faster redraws, and preview the graphics at a lower resolution. This is especially true when using high-resolution LRG files.

■ **Display Overprinting Objects**. When checked, displays small white Os in objects when Overprint is checked in their respective Inspectors. Good to leave on. It's for making sure your traps are set correctly, for the most part.

■ **Greek Type Below**. Sets the pixel size below which text appears "greeked" on screen. Unless you are trying to squeeze every bit of re-draw speed possible out of a FreeHand session, I would suggest leaving this setting low, perhaps at four pixels.

■ **Preview Drag**. Sets the maximum number of objects that preview when dragging. Though previewing a large number of objects slows redraw and requires more RAM, this option is more a matter of your work habits than anything else.

Sounds (Mac OS only)

Use the Sounds tab to set the sounds made by FreeHand when editing (see Figure 1-10). You can use built-in snap sounds or define your own. Set the sound for the following categories by selecting the sound from the pop-up menu next to the chosen category. To listen to the sound currently selected, click the Play button next to a category.

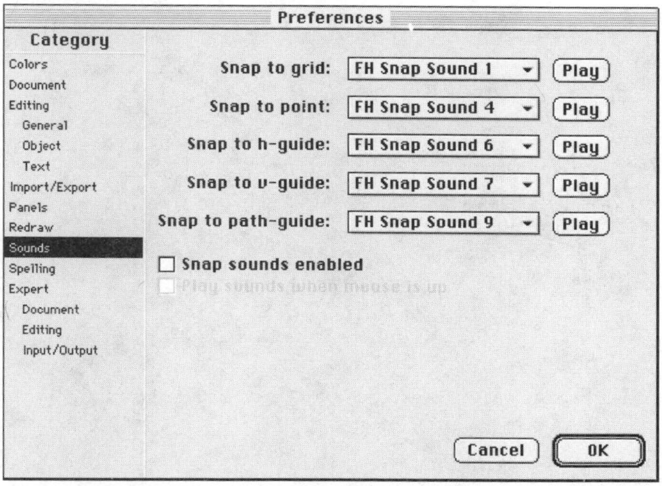

Figure 1-10: The Sounds tab in the Preferences dialog on the Mac.

- **Snap to Grid**. The sound activated when a point or object is snapped to the grid.
- **Snap to Point**. The sound activated when a point or object is snapped to a point.
- **Snap to H-Guide**. The sound activated when a point or object is snapped to a horizontal guide.
- **Snap to V-Guide**. The sound activated when a point or object is snapped to a vertical guide.
- **Snap to Path-Guide**. The sound activated when a point or object is snapped to a path-guide.

FreeHand can only use sounds installed in your system. To install a sound in your system, drag a System 7 sound to the closed system folder.

Tip

Personally, I enjoy working without those annoying little clicks and bird tweets that accompany editing choices, but the option to turn this feature on is there if it helps you work better.

Spelling

Consider the following settings for spelling (see Figure 1-11):

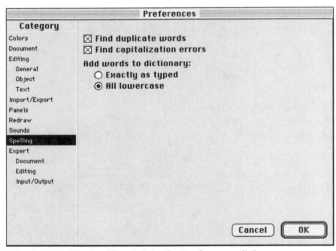

Figure 1-11: The Spelling tab in the Preferences dialog.

- **Find Duplicate Words**. When checked, the Spelling panel detects instances of words appearing twice in a row. I suggest leaving this option on.

- **Find Capitalization Errors**. When checked, the Spelling panel detects uncapitalized words following periods. I prefer to leave this off, as it introduces too many errors into creative text.

- **Add Words to Dictionary**. Exactly as typed or all lowercase. I prefer the second option because it helps to find more potential errors.

Expert

The following items should only be customized by experienced professional users familiar with FreeHand's precision controls.

Document

Consider the following settings for documents (see Figure 1-12):

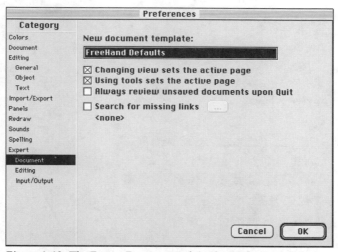

Figure 1-12: The Expert Document tab in the Preferences dialog.

- **New Document Template**. New documents are opened based on the template named in this entry field. This is a useful item if you find yourself using templates regularly.

- **Changing View Sets the Active Page**. When checked, moving to another page using the Page Before button, Page After button, or Command-Page Up or Command-Page Down sets the new page as the active page in the Document Inspector. This is a way of speeding up the process when creating multipage documents.

- **Using Tools Sets the Active Page**. When checked, using a tool on a given page activates that page in the Document Inspector. This option is a design decision that has to do with your work habits.

- **Always Review Unsaved Documents Upon Quit/Exit** (Mac OS/Windows). Check to review and save each open document when quitting or exiting the application. As a safety measure, I prefer to leave this option on.

- **Search for Missing Links** (Mac OS only). When checked, FreeHand searches the specified folder or volume (up to ten sub-folders deep) when a link to a graphic is missing or broken. If the graphic is found, FreeHand automatically relinks the placed graphic to the new location. Click the edit button to set the root folder or volume to search. This is a very handy option if you find yourself moving files and folders around on a regular basis. Use it every once in a while to connect the links.

Editing

Here, you can set the default line widths for all the Width pop-ups and determine the behavior of new object styles. Consider the following settings for editing (see Figure 1-13):

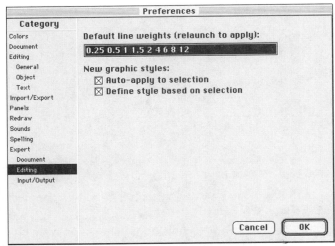

Figure 1-13: The Expert Editing tab in the Preferences dialog.

- **Default Line Weights**. Enter numbers in this field (separated by a space) to define the default line weights that appear in the Width pop-up in the Stroke Inspector. For fine-tuning a document, this is a wonderful option. The default widths in the Stroke Inspector seldom fit all of the projects you're working on, and entering your own choices can enhance the speed at which you work.

- **New Graphic Styles**. Allows you to auto-apply styles to Selection (when checked, object styles are applied immediately to selected objects) or to define a Style Based on Selection (when checked, selected objects define the style created). I usually prefer the first method, based on the way that I accomplish design tasks.

Input/Output

The Expert Input/Output tab allows you to set advanced printing and advanced file conversion options (see Figure 1-14):

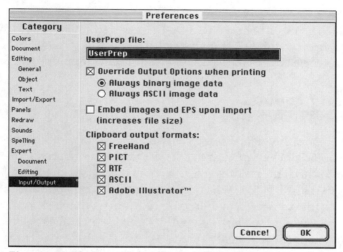

Figure 1-14: The Expert Input/Output tab in the Preferences dialog.

- **UserPrep File**. Enter a name in this entry field of the file you want to use as your UserPrep file. FreeHand ships with several UserPrep files designed to help customize FreeHand for high-end printing to specific output devices. Choose from the list of installed files containing PostScript code in the UserPrep file pop-up in the Print Setup dialog to modify printing to PostScript printers. Choose None to print without a UserPrep file. You will not need a UserPrep file when printing to most desktop printers. The UserPrep files are located in the UserPrep folder in the FreeHand application folder.

- **Override Output Options When Printing** (Mac OS only). If you select Always binary image data, printing will always be in binary format. If you select Always ASCII image data, printing will always be in ASCII format. Binary is the most common choice. You might want to select the ASCII image data output in order to be able to edit the ASCII data.

- **Embed Images and EPS Upon Import** (Increases File Size). When checked, FreeHand embeds imported LRG, TIFF, and EPS files instead of linking them to an external file. If you move files around a lot and don't want to bother with re-linking operations, check this option. Embedding increases the FreeHand document size by the size of each imported image, so make sure you have enough disk space.

- **Clipboard Output Formats**. Choose file types that FreeHand exports to the clipboard when you copy or exit. The default is to leave all of the options checked, which is a good idea for maximum options.

Generating Reports

Select File | Report. If you are doing cross-platform work, or if you plan to send a FreeHand document with native text to a service bureau, the most useful item to check in this dialog is the Fonts category (see Figure 1-15). This allows you to see at a glance what fonts are required for your document, and communicate that information to the correct sources. Other than that, always initiate a report when transferring your document to another facility, especially if the document is large. Print out the report and keep it on hand to answer any needed questions about the document's contents.

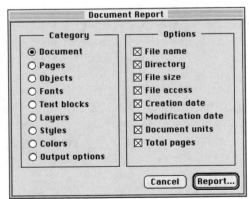

Figure 1-15: You can generate a report based upon any of the nine categories, each one of which has its own list of options.

Configuring the Display

The way that the FreeHand display looks on your monitor has as much potential for influencing the way that you work as any traditional workspace in your real-world design studio. The monitor display is, for all intents and purposes, a digital desktop, a table on which to spread your tools and papers. Keeping the tools you need in an arrangement that suits your personality is very important. Some designers prefer a minimum of tools within reach, while others are filed away in drawers until they are required. Other designers prefer to surround themselves with every tool imaginable, and actually look at the tool display from time to time to generate solutions and options. Which way do you work? Determining your most fruitful work habits, and then arranging your digital workspace to match, will give you a headstart as a digital designer. In order to master FreeHand, you must arrange the tools and palettes in a way that accentuates your designer's personality. Setting Preferences options, as we have already discussed, is one step in that direction. Arranging the FreeHand display options to your liking is another major step in that direction.

Viewing the Selection & Page Simultaneously

The View menu allows you to zoom in and fill the screen with the selected graphic and also to zoom out to see the entire page. In the midst of a design task, you may often find yourself having to constantly alternate between these two (and perhaps more) options. The best way to handle this is to use FreeHand's multiple view option. Select Window | New Window. In the original window, view the entire page (View | Fit to Page). In the second window, zoom in on your active object (View | Fit Selection). In a third window, you may want to zoom in to select a specific group of items. When you update or revise anything in one window, it is instantly updated in any additional window (see Figure 1-16).

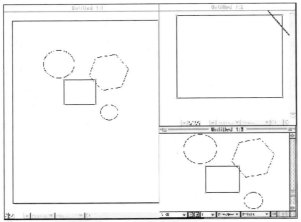

Figure 1-16: FreeHand allows you to design with multiple windows showing different zoom levels.

Preview & Keyline Options

You can toggle any FreeHand view between Preview and Keyline displays (see Figure 1-17). A Preview display shows all of the fills and strokes associated with the graphics and text in full color. A Keyline view shows only the object outlines.

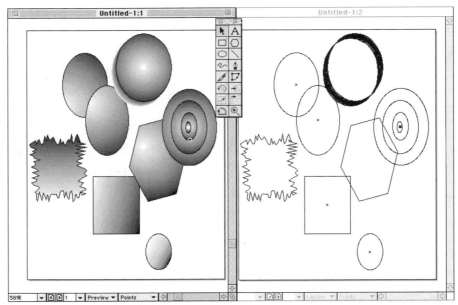

Figure 1-17: You can open Preview and Keyline windows side by side.

In traditional terms, the Keyline view acts like a mechanical layout, while the Preview represents a comprehensive layout (or "super comp"). Keyline views redraw lightning fast, and give you a better idea of how the elements in a composition balance one another. Full previews allow you to see how fill and stroke elements look. It's easier to manipulate shapes in keyline mode, and you can also see the center points of each object for centered placement.

Tip

A good way to work is to open a second document window. Make one window a preview, and the other a keyline. Now you have the best of both worlds.

Toolbars

There are three separate toolbars (see Figure 1-18), any of which can be toggled on or off from the Window | Toolbars menu: Main, Text, and Toolbox. The Main and Text toolbars are at the top of the page, and will be more welcomed by Windows users because they follow the Windows application convention more closely. If you turn them off, you still have access to their tools through menu commands, icons in palettes, and keyboard equivalents. This gives you more space for viewing a document. The Toolbox should be left selected, as it can be moved anywhere on the page at any time.

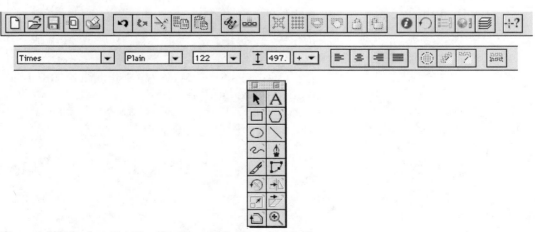

Figure 1-18: The three FreeHand Toolbars: Main, Text, and Toolbox.

Panels

Panels include Layers, Styles, Color List, Color Mixer, Halftones, Alignment, and Transform. Leave this selection checked on in the View menu, and turn the various palettes on and off as needed from the Window menu or from the Main Toolbar.

Info Bar

If you are doing exacting mechanicals, keep the Info Bar on so that you can see exactly where your cursor is located on the page. This also makes alignments easier to create and adjust.

Page Rulers

The two most common measurement types are points and inches. Use inches for graphic design work, and use points if your page is dominated by text. The Pica option is also useful, though not as popular as it once was except for newspaper work.

Text Rulers

Text rulers (see Figure 1-19) display when you select the Text tool, as long as you have not selected Always Display Text Editor in the Preferences dialog. The Text Ruler method of creating text has one advantage over the Text Editor method of placing text. You can define a measured area of the document by clicking and dragging the Text tool, just as if it were the Pointer tool. Remember that if it is important that your text block expands to accommodate the text you enter, you must select File | Text Preferences | All Text when you select Blocks Auto-Expand.

Figure 1-19: The FreeHand Text Ruler.

Grid & Grid Snap

Adjust the size of your grid to cover the page evenly if you are creating a tiled Web page, and turn Snap to Grid on. Then, simply clone a shape that has been sized to match the snap points, and move the clones so they cover the page. Snap to Grid is an excellent way to create tiled sections that butt up against each other without having to be manually tweaked. It is often preferable to use a dark color for Grid marks (set in the GridColor item in Preferences). Grids are used best in Keyline mode, where they are more visible.

Guides & Snap to Guides

Using guides on a page allows you to avoid the Alignment panel when the page has to show alignments of a large group of items. Use guides when the page has to display columned text, and drag the Text tool to take advantage of the guides. The advantage of using guides over grids is that guides can be moved. This allows you to create gutter spaces, and gives you more overall creative freedom in alignment and design. Turning the Snap function off allows placement of items that are free to ignore the guides, so it is a common practice to alternate the Snap function as the page design often requires both aligned and non-aligned elements. It is often preferable to use a dark color for Grid marks (set in the GridColor item in Preferences). Guides are used best in Preview mode, where they are more visible.

Snap to Point

Snap to Point is a very useful item to use when you are in Keyline mode. In Keyline mode, the center points of closed objects are displayed. Creating graphics like rays emanating from a central point or shapes that are to align on a center point is made much easier if you turn the Snap to Point function on. Turning on Snap to Point is also an aid in creating closed FreeHand shapes, since the endpoints can be easily snapped. The third way to use it is when you want to connect separate FreeHand or straight line segments together to form a shape. This allows you to draw partial shapes separately, instead of having to do them in one continuous line (for example, in the profile of a face).

The Document Inspector

The Inspectors panel is accessed by choosing Windows | Inspectors, and selecting one of the Inspectors. Clicking on the Document tab in the Inspectors panel displays the Document Inspector (see Figure 1-20).

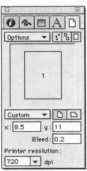

Figure 1-20: The FreeHand Document Inspector.

The Document Inspector features several attributes to make your creative page design life easier:

- Use the page move controls instead of the scroll bars to move the page in the viewscreen. Larger and more controlled movements of the page are possible than with the scroll bars.

- Set the bleed area of the document.

- Choose the page type, from A and B sizes to letter, legal, tabloid, or custom.

- Flip the page from Portrait to Landscape. This is an excellent way to aid the design of elements that have to align vertically in the Portrait mode, as the page can be flipped back to Portrait when your alignments are finished.

Saving a FreeHand Project

FreeHand projects can be saved as standard FreeHand documents, editable
EPS files (which you can open and manipulate in xRes), or as templates. The
best suggestion is to save your work both as a document and as a template
when finished. Templates provide accessible page designs that can act as
starting points for other page creations. Use the Output Options dialog to save
documents and templates to two separate folders, each marked appropriately
to avoid confusion.

To save a FreeHand project, choose File | Save or File | Save As, and deter-
mine where you would like to save the document.

Opening a Saved FreeHand Project

Documents and templates open automatically in FreeHand. If you saved out
the document as an editable EPS file, make sure that Convert Editable EPS
When Imported is activated in the Import | Export item in the Preferences
dialog, and you'll be able to nest page art within new pages easily.

To open a FreeHand project, choose File | Open, locate your stored docu-
ment, and select Open.

Tip

*A great way to use logo designs on a page is to save the original art out as an
Editable EPS file, even if the original art covered an entire FreeHand page. Once it
is imported, it can be resized to fit a new page area easily.*

Moving On

In this chapter, we have covered all of the ways to set up FreeHand projects,
from configuring the items in the Preferences dialog to paying attention to
how your screen display can be adjusted to suit your design needs. In the next
chapter, we will focus upon the creation of vector art.

2 Creating Vector Art in FreeHand

FreeHand offers you a number of different tools, each of which helps you create vector elements in different ways. Just as in the traditional arts you wouldn't use a pencil when a pen is called for, so you wouldn't use a straight line tool when a Bezier pen might do the job better in FreeHand. Knowing what the tools can and cannot do is half the battle in becoming a master vector graphic artist.

Lines drawn in FreeHand, whether they are connected back to themselves to form a closed shape or remain open, are called paths. A path has no resolution as such, meaning that no matter how close you zoom in on it, it remains at its maximum resolution, a line that indicates directional and curvature components. A path, therefore, is not like a line drawn in a bitmap application. A path in FreeHand is a vector, and can be thought of as a direction or a command that tells a line what to do and where to go. That's why we can say that vector art is resolution independent, because the vector doesn't care what resolution the screen or the printer is at. The direction it gives remains the same. It displays on the screen and prints on paper at the maximum resolution of the output device.

A bitmap line or shape addresses a certain number of pixels, and shows stair-stepping or aliasing when you zoom in close enough. This is why many digital artists prefer vector over bitmap applications, because they are not limited by pixels or resolutions. Your vector art can be rendered as a bitmap when exported as a bitmap graphic file, and then becomes subject to the resolution and pixelization common to bitmap art. Vector art is at first created, however, with none of those constraints.

Let's investigate the FreeHand tool options that allow you to create the elements that can contribute to a piece of vector artwork.

Creating Line & Shape Paths

Linear paths are called "open paths" in vector work, because they do not connect back to themselves. Open paths, or vector lines, cannot have a fill, but are made up entirely of a stroke, meaning a directional linear thickness or width. Strokes can have color and can be rendered as patterns in addition to solids. Shapes, on the other hand, are called "closed paths" because they do connect back to themselves (the first point and last point of a closed shape are joined as one), and this allows them to have color, gradient, pattern, and tiled fills.

Drawing Tools

FreeHand's drawing tools are accessed from the Toolbox, or from the keyboard equivalents that represent specific drawing tool icons in the Toolbox (see Figure 2-1).

Figure 2-1: The FreeHand Toolbox holds the icons that trigger drawing tool use.

 ### Using the FreeHand Tool
The FreeHand tool is best used when a free-flowing shape is required. Each time you release the mouse when drawing with the FreeHand tool, the line is finished. Clicking and dragging again produces a new line. Think of the FreeHand tool as a perfect way to draw hair, or lines that flow as a group, like waves of water. As open shapes, FreeHand lines can take on different strokes (see Figure 2-2), which can be set in the Stroke tab of the Inspectors palette (Windows | Inspectors | Stroke). To close a FreeHand shape, simply place the last part of the line you draw over the first point.

Figure 2-2: The FreeHand lines at the top have a 1-point stroke, while the group at the bottom has an 8-point stroke.

FreeHand lines, like any other open or closed lines, can also be set for a dashed or patterned stroke (see Figure 2-3). Just indicate the dashed quality or pattern in the stroke tab of the Inspectors panel.

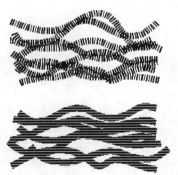

Figure 2-3: The top lines have a dashed stroke, while the bottom grouping has a patterned stroke.

Tip

Dashed strokes follow the direction of the line, like the cross beams on a railroad track, while patterned strokes remain in the same orientation throughout.

The FreeHand tool can be customized. Double-click on its icon to bring up the FreeHand Tool dialog (see Figure 2-4). There are only two options: Tight fit and Draw dotted line. Keep Tight fit toggled on, as this means that your FreeHand curves will be more closely drawn as you place them down. Draw with dotted lines in the special cases where that is what you want.

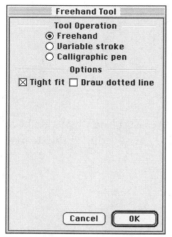

Figure 2-4: The FreeHand Tool dialog.

Using the Calligraphic Pen Tool

The Calligraphic Pen tool appears in the same area of the Toolbox as the FreeHand tool. To set the Calligraphic Pen tool, double-click on the FreeHand tool. Select Calligraphic Pen from the options, and then use the options that display in the FreeHand Tool dialog (see Figure 2-5). Unlike other line choices, Calligraphic Pen lines can be filled with colors, patterns, and gradients.

Tight fit is usually desirable, and Draw dotted line is only a special case choice. Auto remove overlap should be toggled on if you plan to fill the calligraphic lines with anything but black, and do some stylized penmanship (see Figure 2-6). The width is normally set to a Fixed size, but the Variable option gives more flowing results (try a minimum of 15 and a maximum of 30). Reasonable angle settings range from 30 to 50 degrees, but this can be explored on a case-by-case basis. To close a Calligraphic Pen shape, simply place the last part of the line you draw over the first point.

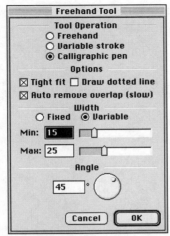

Figure 2-5: The FreeHand Tool dialog with Calligraphic pen (one mode of the FreeHand Tool) selected.

Figure 2-6: The top graphic was rendered with Auto remove overlap off, while the bottom graphic shows the results when it is toggled on. Each has the same gradient fill.

Watch what happens when you use the Modify I Split on a Calligraphic pen graphic that has Auto remove overlap turned on. A smooth line with no overlaps is the result. See Figure 2-7. Instant monograms!

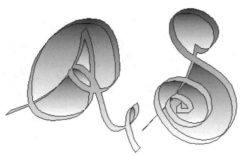

Figure 2-7: The result of using the Split command when Auto overlap is turned on for the Calligraphic pen art.

Using the Variable Stroke Tool
The Variable Stroke tool appears in the same area of the Toolbox as the FreeHand tool when Variable Stroke is selected as an option. To set the Variable Stroke tool, double-click on the FreeHand tool. Select Variable Stroke from the options in the Tool Operation settings.

This is also a special case of the FreeHand tool, and is especially for users who access FreeHand with a graphics tablet. It draws closed paths of varying widths in response to the pressure applied to the graphics tablet stylus. Use the Variable Stroke tool to draw pressure-sensitive paths that look like brush strokes. When used with a pressure-sensitive stylus, increasing pressure increases the stroke width. If you do not own a pressure-sensitive stylus, you can use the keyboard to vary the stroke width. To increase stroke width with the keyboard, Press 2 or] or the right cursor key. To decrease stroke width from the keyboard, Press 1 or [or the left cursor key. To use this tool without a graphics tablet is rather cumbersome. Using the Calligraphic pen tool with variable widths can produce somewhat the same results.

Using the Pen Tool
The Pen tool has no settings dialog. It lets you draw paths by placing a curve, a corner, or a connector, adjusting them as you draw. The Pen tool draws a curved path as a curve. With the Pen tool, you have exact control over the exact shape of the path. The Pen can be used in a point-and-click manner or by clicking and dragging. Paths are manipulated by adjusting control points.

Control points are points on a line that can be moved, and whose attached curves can be adjusted by manipulating the control point arms that extend outward from the points. If you need to add more control points to the Bezier line, simply click on Add Points in the Operations palette (Window | Xtras | Operations) with the line selected. To close a Pen shape, simply place the last part of the line you draw over the first point.

To:	Do this:
Place a curve point	Click and drag
Place a corner point	Click
Place a connector point	Control+click and drag (Mac) Alt+Click and drag (Windows)
Place the next point at a 45-degree angle	Shift+click and drag
Erase the most recent point	Delete
Close a path	Click the starting point

Tip

Use the Pen tool when you want to trace an outline around an element of a bitmap in order to mask out the surrounding area, or to fill it with an internal color, gradient, or pattern.

Using the Line Tool

The Line tool draws a line segment, a path consisting of just two points. You can constrain the line segments to 45-degree increments by holding down the Shift key as you draw.

To:	Do this:
Draw line segment at 45 or 90 degrees	Shift+click and drag
Draw line segment from center point	Option +click and drag (Mac) Alt+click and drag (Windows)
Draw line from center at 45 or 90 degrees	Shift+Option (Mac) Shift+-Alt+click and drag (Windows)

You can stretch a line and reorient its direction by simply grabbing one of its end control points and dragging it. By adding points to a selected line segment and bringing the first point to touch the last point (or vice versa), you can create a closed shape that can be filled.

Drawing With the Knife Tool

You wouldn't normally think of the Knife tool as a drawing tool, but it can be used quite effectively in the process of reshaping a graphic to create a new one. The Knife tool works only on strokes, so don't plan to cut a filled object in hopes of getting a new object that takes the fill into consideration. The moment you cut the stroke of a filled object, it loses its capacity for fills. This is because by cutting apart its stroke, it is no longer closed—and an open path cannot have a fill. The Knife tool offers you an easy way to create curved segments that can then be used as parts of a new graphic. This works especially well when an oval or circle is cut apart (see Figure 2-8).

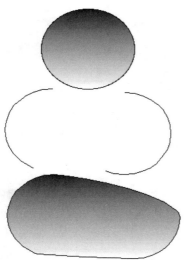

Figure 2-8: The Knife tool was used to cut the circle at the top into two pieces. The two pieces were then used to create a separate shape by stretching them and joining the ends.

Using the Bezigon Tool

I often refer to the Bezigon tool as the "polyline" tool, since for me, its use determines its name. It draws straight lines and arcs by placing curve, corner, and connector points. The Bezigon tool draws shapes easily because the program draws perfectly straight lines and applies automatic curvature to curves as you draw.

Draw a closed shape with the Bezigon tool. To place points, select the Bezigon shape you created. Click a button in the Object Inspector or use a modifier key to place a specific point type. There are three point icons in the center of the Object Inspector, under the Point type heading. They generate a curve point, corner point, and connector point (see Figure 2-9).

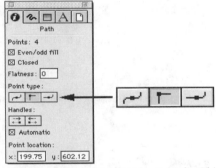

Figure 2-9: The three point icons in the Object Inspector. They generate a curve point, corner point, and connector point.

Curve points create an instant curve between any number of selected points on a bezigon object. They are the most effective when used on either a bezigon or polygon object. They can be used on other closed object types as well, but with far less dramatic effect.

To generate a polyline gradient painting, follow these steps:

1. Select the radial gradient fill option in the Fill tab of the Inspectors palette.

2. Use the Bezigon tool to create a series of angular shapes. To close the shapes, simply place the last point over the first one, and it will close automatically.

3. Select various points on each shape, and click on the curve point button in the Object Inspector, generating curves between the points.

4. Combine the bezigon shapes into a composition. See Figure 2-10 for an example.

Figure 2-10: When you introduce control point curves into a bezigon shape, the results are symmetries you would never have expected.

Creating a Gradient Line Drawing

A gradient line drawing is a unique way to use the Gradient Fill option to produce a customized media look in FreeHand.

1. Select your targeted graphic. The best ones to use should have internal fills involved.

2. Select Modify | AlterPath | Expand Stroke. Set the Width to 12, and the Miter limit to 5. Select OK.

3. Go to the Fill Inspector, and set the fill to Gradient (the default gray fill is OK).

4. Go to the Stroke Inspector and set the stroke to a 2 point black.

This method creates interesting spot drawings (see Figure 2-11).

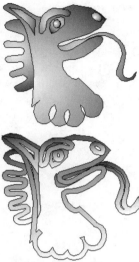

Figure 2-11: The top is the original graphic, transformed into the gradient line drawing below.

Drawing with Pattern Fills

You can use the Pattern Fills option in the Inspectors (Window | Inspectors | Fill) to create a series of filled shapes (leave stroke set to none). Use any tool you like, though the FreeHand tool seems preferable. The shapes can be joined together to create larger compositions (see Figure 2-12).

Figure 2-12: Compositions created with pattern filled shapes look stylized, and are best suited to large graphic backgrounds or a Web page.

Working With Primitive Closed Shapes

Primitive closed shapes (ovals, rectangles, and polygons) are often used as the literal building blocks in a composition (see Figure 2-13). They can always be altered by any of FreeHand's tools (see Figure 2-14). For example, you can add points to the shape by clicking on the Pen tool, then clicking on the shape's outline. Moving the new point allows you to stretch the shapes out.

Figure 2-13: The Ellipse, Rectangle, Polygon, and Line tools in the Toolbox.

Figure 2-14: Primitive shapes can be translated into more complex forms in FreeHand.

Editing Drawings

Drawings and their respective elements can be edited with both standard and unique methods. To understand the relative importance of the special copy and paste commands, it is important to start at the basics and go over the standard commands as well.

Standard Cut, Copy, Paste & Clear Commands

The standard word processor functions of cut, copy, paste, and clear apply in FreeHand as well. When deleting large areas of a composition or a whole page, it's wise to use the clear instead of the cut command. Cut places the deleted section on the clipboard, and if it's too large, this can use up your memory.

Special Copy & Paste Commands

In addition to the standard copy/paste routines many of us are familiar with from experience with word processors, FreeHand offers a series of special copy and paste possibilities that make the creation of vector graphics much easier.

Copy Attributes & Paste Attributes

If you select any graphic in a composition and choose the Edit | Copy Attributes, the stroke and fill attributes of the selected object are copied. You can then paste these attributes to any other object by selecting another object and choosing Edit | Paste Attributes. The copied attributes are pasted to the second object.

Duplicate

The Edit | Duplicate command copies the selected object, objects, or group to the screen with a little placement variance offset from the original object. If you select the duplicated objects and move, rotate, skew, mirror, or resize them (or any combination of these alterations), and then select the Duplicate command again without deselecting anything, the next duplicated items will be adjusted the same amount as the first, forming a chain of similar items. This effect has a lot of dimension, adding a 3D look to the resulting graphic (see Figure 2-15).

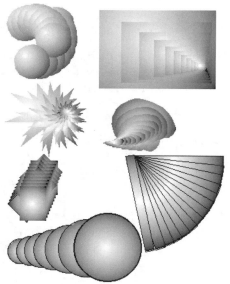

Figure 2-15: All of these graphics resulted from the duplication method described earlier in this chapter.

Clone

The best thing about cloning (Edit | Clone) an object is that the clone's dimensions fit over the selected object exactly. Resize the clone with the Scale tool and the Shift key held down to constrain the resizing, and then place the cloned image behind the original for instant concentric objects.

Paste Behind

Paste behind works as an adjunct to the Copy command. Whatever is in the clipboard is pasted behind the selected graphic on screen. Using this command with a text block in the clipboard creates very interesting background effects. This is one of the best ways to create a series of images behind a foreground selection.

Paste Inside

This is one of the star features of FreeHand as far as creating frames around graphic and pictorial content, including bitmap content. Simply select whatever content you like, and copy it to the clipboard. Select a graphic you would like to use as a frame, and place it over the content graphic (don't worry about alignment since you can move it later when it's inside!). Now select Edit | Paste Inside.

The content is now an internal part of the frame (see Figure 2-16). You can move the content around at any time, and even reshape it, simply by selecting the visible control points inside the frame.

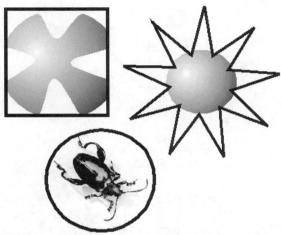

Figure 2-16: Anything can be pasted inside an active frame, from vector art to bitmaps. Once inside, the contents can be moved around until the frame clips the contents the way you like.

Using Strokes & Fills

A stroke in FreeHand means the border around an object. The stroke can be set to None, which gives the selection a softer appearance, in which the border of the graphic element blends in a more muted way with the page. In the case of the Line tool and the FreeHand tool, the resulting lines are nothing but strokes, with no fill possible.

Adding Strokes

Strokes are set in the Stroke Inspector (Window | Inspectors | Strokes). See Figure 2-17. If you configure the parameters of a stroke with no graphic selected, the stroke settings will be applied to all the graphics produced from that point forward until you reset the parameters. If you have an active selection while reconfiguring the stroke parameters, the stroke of that selection only will be changed accordingly.

Figure 2-17: The Stroke Inspector.

Modifying Strokes

You can drag and drop any color you like on a stroke, although it's better to drop the color onto the Color Swatch in the Stroke tab of the Inspectors palette. Strokes can be filled with patterns as well as solid colors (see Figure 2-18). You can either select one of the patterns in the Patterns list, or customize one for a unique stroke graphic.

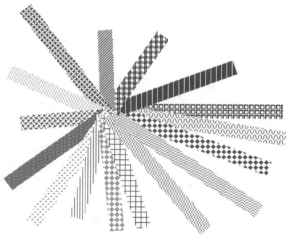

Figure 2-18: Strokes can be drawn with patterns as well as solids.

Use the patterned strokes for Bezier paths, and add yet another unique graphic option to your creative toolkit. Simply draw a path with the Bezier Pen tool. If you close it, the patterned stroke will frame the center. Use the curved point discussed earlier to smooth out the Bezigon angles (see Figure 2-19).

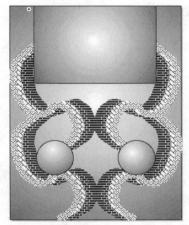

Figure 2-19: Patterned Bezigon stroke paths create interesting page design elements.

The Fractalize tool in the Operations palette is often applied only to closed shapes, but it works equally as well on stand-alone strokes (open shapes). Simply draw a stroke design (pattern fill it if you like), and click on the Fractalize operator until you achieve a design you like (see Figure 2-20).

Figure 2-20: Interesting symmetric graphics can be built from fractalized patterned strokes.

The width of the stroke can be set from the list of defaults, and also by simply typing in a number in the Width area box in the Stroke Inspector. Below the Width box are two rows of icons for caps and joins. Caps are end caps, the shape that the stroke ends will assume as long as it is an open shape (you can't see the end caps on a closed shape).

Joins (not to be confused with the Modify | Join command) represent the way that joined lines meet (selected from sharp, rounded, or beveled). See Figure 2-21.

Figure 2-21: From the top, these are the Join options set in the Stroke tab: Sharp, Rounded, and Beveled.

The Miter limit area is below the Join buttons. The miter limit is defined as the ratio of the length of the miter join to the stroke width. (The length of a miter join is the distance from the join's control point to the tip of the miter.) For example, if you set your stroke width to 4 points, and your miter limit to 2, then any time your miter is longer than 8 points, the miter join will automatically convert to a beveled join (8÷4=2). This function will remain esoteric and unused by the majority of FreeHand artists.

Below the Miter limit box is a pull-down list that contains a selection of dashed and broken lines. Any stroke can be drawn with your choice of these options. If No Dash is selected, the stroke will be solid. Below the pull-down list are Arrowhead options for either or both the start and end points of a line. If you select New you can design the arrowheads yourself.

If you think of strokes and fills as comparable operations and imagine that strokes have to be frames around a filled inside, then you're missing some very creative possibilities. If you set stroke width to 100 or more, the stroke becomes very heavy. Open lines drawn with that stroke setting take on the character of unique objects. Filling them with patterns emphasizes their weight even more. If you set the stroke width to 400+, even closed shapes drawn on the page can fill it completely without anything but the stroke being apparent.

What about gradient strokes? Impossible, you say. . . FreeHand has no gradient setting for strokes! No, FreeHand doesn't, but you can create them nevertheless. Not only that, but gradient strokes can help you create some of the most beautiful page and Web page backgrounds you've ever seen. Gradient strokes start as giant strokes as described above. Simply use giant stroke widths, and draw two strokes separated by space. Colorize each with a different hue. Use the same pattern for each stroke (different patterns will not blend). Shift-select both strokes and blend them. Amazing color ranges over the underlying patterns are the result. This is a class A act when it comes to creating FreeHand Web page backgrounds. The impression is that of a color engraved surface.

Designing Arrowheads

Why would you want to redesign an arrowhead anyway? Perhaps because in FreeHand, an arrowhead can be any graphic you would like to put at the end of an arrow's shaft. It could be a logo, which would make the graphic look like an emblem at the end of a branding iron. The shaft itself, when attached to a suitable graphic, is seen more like a "speed line," a line indicating directional movement. Because arrows can point in any direction, your graphic can also address whatever direction the arrow is pointing in, and provide instant rotation. Using an alternate graphic on the end of an arrow also allows you to create some interesting composite designs. Placing the alternate graphic at the feathered end of the arrow and leaving the arrowhead at the point gives you an instant way to generate a callout, making it appear as if the graphic is pointing to something else it is related to (another graphic, or perhaps a text block).

Selecting the New item in the Arrowhead list brings up the Arrowhead Editor (you can actually select it in both the start and end lists, giving you different customized arrowheads on both ends of a line). A menu of drawing and transformation tools is present in the dialog for designing the new arrowhead graphic. There is no reason to confine these graphics to standard arrowheads. You can even create a logo to place at the end (or start and end) of a stroke.

1. In your FreeHand document, create a text block that represents your logo with 72 point type. Make sure there are no closed letters (such as O or P). If you need closed letters, you'll have to redesign that letter so it is not closed completely. Convert the text block to paths.

2. Move the letters so they just touch each other, and click on the Union command in the Operations palette (Xtras | Path Operations | Union). This makes the letters one single connected shape. Copy the selection to the clipboard.

3. Open the Arrowhead Editor. Click on Paste In. This copies the logo type in the preview window (see Figure 2-22). You can move it around and even rotate and resize it. When it looks OK, click on New, and your new arrowhead logo is ready to design with (see Figure 2-23). The logo arrowhead, if selected in the arrowheads list in the Stroke Inspector, will appear at the end of any open stroke.

Tip

Increasing the size of the stroke with the logo arrowhead attached increases the size of the logo arrowhead.

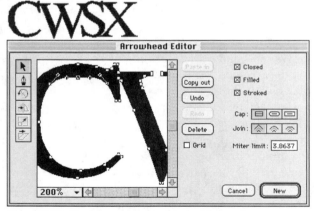

Figure 2-22: Design a new arrowhead with logo type.

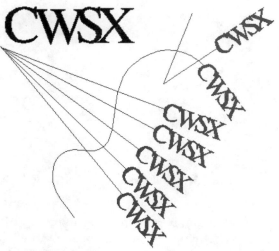

Figure 2-23: You can use the new logo arrowhead anywhere on the page.

Fills

Closed shapes may be filled with basic colors, gradients, patterns, or tiles. The Fill Inspector is the command center for fills. It features a pull-down list of options. The most common fills are basic colors. Patterns work the same way for fills as for strokes, as described above. The custom, PostScript, and textured fills cannot be seen on the screen, but only as output to a PostScript printer.

Gradient fills come in two flavors, graduated and radial. Graduated fills can be configured for logarithmic or linear tapers. In a linear taper, each color in the progression gets equal space, from one end to the other. In a logarithmic taper, the starting color band is very narrow, with each subsequent band growing larger, ending with a very wide band of the final color. Explore both to get a visual idea of how they differ. You can set the angle of the graduated or logarithmic fill, as well as dragging and dropping any number of color swatches in the color ramp (see Figure 2-24). Too many colors next to each other can result in linear banding, so unless that's an effect you want to create, keep the number of colors in any single gradient under six or so.

Figure 2-24: The radial gradient setting in the Fill Inspector.

Radial gradients make any round object look three dimensional, the most common use of the radial gradient option (see Figure 2-25). The lighter color is commonly the bottom color on the color ramp, and becomes the radial highlight color, so it is common practice to make it lighter than the rest of the colors. There is a Locate Center knob available for adjusting the placement of the highlight color.

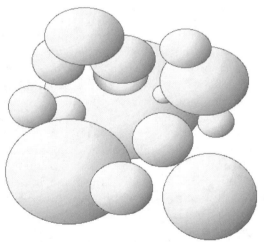

Figure 2-25: Radial gradient spheres make great bubbles and molecular objects.

The tiled fill is the most spectacular fill available in FreeHand (see figure 2-26). Any vector graphic on your page copied to the clipboard becomes available as a tiled fill. You cannot use bitmaps as tiled fills. We refer to tiled fills quite a few times in the tutorial sections of this book.

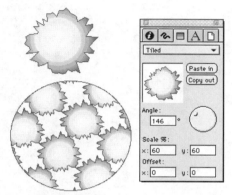

Figure 2-26: Tiled fills can be any vector graphic copied to the clipboard.

Always render tests of tile filled objects frequently, adjusting size, rotation, and offsets in the Tile Fill tab of the Inspectors palette until you get the result you're looking for. When you draw a new tile-filled object, you'll probably have to tweak the settings again to get things just right. Tile filled shapes with no strokes make great backgrounds for Web pages, and are just right for saving out as bitmaps to apply as material textures for 3D objects in Extreme 3D.

Tip

If you want to fill in the spaces between tiles in a tile-filled object, rotate the tile and create another object that uses the rotated tile fill. Remove the stroke from the second object, and place it over the first. This layering technique also adds more randomness to the fill in the original object.

Using Layers

If you have used layers in Photoshop, PageMaker, or any other application, you will find FreeHand's layers easy to master. Each FreeHand layer has four controls associated with it: a visible/invisible toggle, a toggle that changes the layer objects from fully visible to bounding boxes, a lock/unlock function, and a color swatch (see Figure 2-27). These are all to the left of the layer's name in the Layers panel. There are some general suggestions for using FreeHand's layers effectively.

Figure 2-27: The Layers panel.

The easiest way to use layers is to create a series of new layers first by selecting New from the pull-down list in the Layers palette. A good number to start with is six. Now create a number of filled shapes on your document. Click on a shape, and then click on the layer name in the Layers panel. The object is instantly moved to that layer. Do the same for the other shapes, moving them to other layers in the same manner. When elements of a document are moved to separate layers, they appear in front of the layers that are beneath them. This makes arranging objects in the stack much simpler than using the Arrange command. By simply clicking on an object and then on any layer that appears in the Layers panel, the object is moved to that layer instantly. Consider the following tips for using layers:

- If you have text and graphics on a page, use at least two layers to separate them, placing the text on a layer above the graphics (usually). As your compositions become more complex, use more layers to separate the components of one family of items from another.

- Use the color swatch function to color your layers so that you can instantly tell them apart. When you click on any object on the screen, its control points will be the same color as the layer color swatch.

■ If you have to do a lot of grouping of objects on any single layer on a page filled with objects on many layers, make the other layers invisible. This allows you to group objects as necessary without accidentally including objects on another layer.

■ Create a separate layer to leave production notes for the service bureau (make sure it is turned off before the job is printed). You can also create a layer to leave design comments to yourself or anyone else in your design group. Note that Guides are on their own layer.

Using the Object Inspector

The Object Inspector gives you a variety of controls over selected objects. The controls vary depending upon the type of selection. There are different object controls that appear for the selected object type. For instance, the only controls that appear when you select an Ellipse (Oval) are its related dimensions, which can then be altered numerically in the appropriate input boxes. Read the following table as "if the Object Type is . . . then the Object Controls offered are . . .".

Object Type	Object Controls
Open Stroke	Number of Control Points, Even/Odd, Fills (toggle enabling this causes overlaps in the shape to be transparent), Open/Closed control, Flatness setting (lower number causes smoother printing on a PostScript device)
Ellipse	Dimension and Position
Rectangle	Dimension, Position, and Corner Radius
Closed Path	Number of Control Points, Even/Odd, Fills toggle (this item causes overlaps in the shape to be transparent), Open/Closed toggle, Flatness setting (lower number causes smoother printing on a PostScript device)
Polygon/Star	Number of Control Points, Even/Odd, Fills (checking this item causes overlaps in the shape to be transparent), Open/Closed toggle, Flatness setting (lower number causes smoother printing on a PostScript device)
Open Bezigon	Number of Control Points, Even/Odd, Fills toggle (this item causes overlaps in the shape to be transparent), Open/Closed toggle, Flatness setting (lower number causes smoother printing on a PostScript device)

Object Type	Object Controls
Closed Bezigon	Number of Control Points, Even/Odd, Fills toggle (this item causes overlaps in the shape to be transparent), Open/Closed toggle, Flatness setting (lower number causes smoother printing on a PostScript device), Point Type, Handles Controls, Point Location (in XY coordinates)
Bitmap	Dimension Controls, Scale (% on X and Y axis), Transparency toggle, Image Source Editing, Link data

Tip

Use the Link Data button to bring up the Links dialog (see Figure 2-28), and select whether you want to embed the image in the document or leave it linked. Embedding increases file size, as the image will be added to the total storage "weight" of the page.

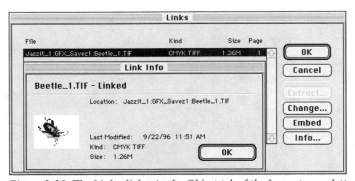

Figure 2-28: The Links dialog in the Object tab of the Inspectors palette as it references a selected bitmap on the page.

Reshaping Tips & Techniques

Any vector graphic can be infinitely reshaped, without ever being the worse for wear. Even graphics that become unrecognizable from their original shapes may provide a result that is exactly what you want. Vector graphics are always resolution independent until saved out as a defined bitmap.

Simplify

The Simplify command is activated by clicking on its associated icon in the Operations palette (Xtras | Cleanup | Simplify). Simplify removes control points based upon the degree setting in the associated dialog. Set the slider lower to remove a few control points, and set it higher to remove more control points.

Manipulating Control Points

Each time you click on Add Points in the Operations palette (Xtras | Distort | Add Points), you double the number of control points in a selected object. Always add points before doing a Fractalize operation (Xtras | Distort | Fractalize), or before reshaping the selection in the Envelope dialog (Extras | Distort | Envelope). In any of the operations mentioned, control points on an object always appear on the perimeter of the object. They are manipulated by moving them to a new location, which stretches the object out at that point, and by adjusting the control arms that jut out from the control points. Adjusting the arms changes the degree of the curve from that point to the next. Pulling the control levers out so they are longer gives you more perimeter between the control point and the next or previous control point.

Tip

> Add Points is great for rotoscoping a photo that contains an identifiable silhouette of an object (a teapot or an animal are good examples). Place an oval primitive on top of the photo, and click on Add Points five times. Now you can reshape the oval so it looks like the underlying shape in the photo. If needed, click on Add Points again to get the correct number of control points needed.

Tip

> If control point manipulation is new to you, practice by adjusting the control points on an oval after you add points to it. Try and reshape the oval into common silhouettes, like a bird or the profile of a face.

Common Object Transforms

The most common object transformation tools are Scale, Move, Rotate, Reflect, and Skew. In FreeHand, you can access any of these tools from the Toolbox, the Transform panel, the main Toolbar, or through keyboard equivalent keystroke commands. Although I prefer to use the Toolbar in most cases, there are times when the Transform panel comes in handy. The Transform panel has numerical controls as well as associated icons, so when an object needs to be transformed according to strict numerical guidelines, the Transform panel is the best option (see Figure 2-29).

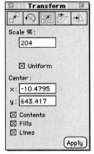

Figure 2-29: The Transform panel.

Tip

If you want the gradient or tiled fills to be resized or rotated along with the objects perimeter, be sure to check the Contents and Fills boxes in the Transform palette.

Arranging & Aligning Objects

Arranging objects means placing them in a needed order in an object stack, from front to back. This is accomplished through the Modify I Arrange command, or by using the required keyboard equivalents. Objects are arranged according to the layer they are on, so that sending an object to the back only affects its position on the layer it rests on. It will not be placed behind objects below it on lower layers. Arranging objects is one of the more frequent operations performed in any FreeHand project, and should be second nature to any FreeHand professional.

Aligning objects is accomplished through the Modify | Align command, associated keyboard equivalents, or by using the Align panel. Choosing Modify | Align just displays the Align panel. The Align panel has two pull-down lists, one for horizontal alignments and one for vertical alignments. Selections from both can be used at the same time. For example, you could align objects on their left perimeters and center them horizontally at the same time. Watching the preview in the Align panel always tells you what the alignment will look like beforehand. Use of the Align panel requires that at least two selections on the screen be activated at the same time (see Figure 2-30).

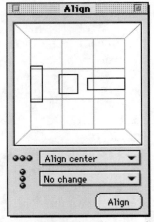

Figure 2-30: The Align panel.

Tip

Using the Align panel to align selections both horizontally and vertically on their common centers is very useful when you want to generate centered blends.

Gluing & Ungluing Objects

After composing a graphic that contains a number of elements created separately, it is useful to glue them together. That way, operations like resizing, rotation, skewing, and cloning let you duplicate work effortlessly. This also allows you to save the composite object in a less complicated fashion. All of the gluing operations are listed in the Modify | Combine menu, except for the Group and Ungroup commands, which are near the bottom of the Modify menu.

Grouping & Ungrouping Objects

Gluing and Ungluing are my terms for FreeHand's Grouping/Ungrouping operations. This is the most common way to glue objects together. Group works with any object selections, no matter how different they are from each other. Grouping works in a hierarchical consecutive order. That means if you group objects together, and then group other objects to the first group, you can undo the grouping step by step, reversing the process one group at a time (using the Ungroup function).

Tip

Remember that blended objects are automatically grouped, and you need to ungroup them in order to manipulate the separate components.

Join

Joining objects creates a composite path that acts as a single path. Any number of objects can be joined, but they must all be vector objects. The cue for color fill and stroke is taken from the bottom-most object. Gradient-filled objects can be joined, but they will lose their fill, and instead take on the fill of the lowest object in the stack that has a solid color. If the lowest object has no stroke, none of the joined objects will have a stroke. Split is the opposite of Join, though joined objects that have been split maintain their joined color fills.

Although gradient-filled objects lose their fills when joined to solid color objects, gradient objects maintain their fill when joined to other gradient objects. The final gradient is taken from that of the lowest object in the stack, and, like solid colored objects that have been joined, the overlapping areas are removed. Objects do not have to be touching to be joined, but the same fill rules apply (see Figure 2-31).

Figure 2-31: Joined objects that have the overlapping areas removed.

Blended Gluing

The blending operation (accessed from both the Operations palette and the Modify I Combine menu) is also a glue operation. Blended objects have to have compatible (on or off) stroke settings, and the fills must match (all must have color fills or gradients, but not a mixture of the two). Blended graphics are automatically grouped.

Union

Union, available in the Path operation, creates a single object from multiple selected vector graphic choices. It does, in fact, delete the original objects to create a new one. There can be a mix of gradient and solid fills, but the lowest object in the stack determines the fill for the new object. Union physically melds the original objects into a new path controlled by a single set of points (see Figure 2-32).

Tip

Use the Union operation to create a shadow for selected vector graphics, placing the new unified shape at the bottom of the stack under the original object but a little to the side. This works especially well when the unified object has a gradient fill, as this gives the shadow a more delicate muted look.

Figure 2-32: A union was performed on these objects, and the resulting shape was sent to the back of the stack to become a shadow.

Moving On

In this chapter, we have looked at a number of ways that you can enhance and alter your FreeHand vector graphics. We have also covered all of the vector drawing tools in FreeHand, and what they allow you to do best, as well as exploring the world of FreeHand paths. In the next chapter, we will focus on how to create and customize paths, and the uses to which they are best suited.

3 Using Paths

In this chapter, we will explore all the details of FreeHand paths. We will look at closed and open paths and their uses in creating sets of objects and effects. We will also investigate path modifications, text on paths, and setting graphics to follow a path.

Path is another name for vector. Paths are the core substance of vector graphics. They can be open like a line, or closed like a letter or shape. Paths serve as directional markers, forcing other FreeHand elements to follow their length and direction, thereby creating a final object.

Creating Closed Paths

The main tools for creating closed paths in FreeHand (paths whose first and last points coincide) are the Rectangle, Oval (or Ellipse), and Polygon tools. The Rectangle and Polygon tools have settings dialogs that can be used to alter their parameters and are accessed by double-clicking each of these tools. The Rectangle tool's settings dialog allows you to change the curvature of its corners, from a sharp 90 degree angle (a setting of 0 with the Corner Radius slider) to a perfect circular radius (a setting of 100 with the slider). See Figure 3-1.

Figure 3-1: The Rectangle Tool settings dialog allows you to shape the corner radius of the rectangle.

Double-clicking the Polygon tool brings up its settings dialog, where you can create both polygonal paths and star paths. If you choose to create a polygon path, you can control the number of sides it has (from 3 to 20). Star path controls are a bit more involved. The star path can also have from 3 to 20 sides, and it can also exhibit a perimeter that ranges from completely acute (producing a sharply spiked outline) to completely obtuse (creating a regular polygon). If the slider is set in the middle between acute and obtuse, true star-shaped paths result. As polygon and star paths are drawn on the screen, you can control their rotational angle with the mouse. See Figure 3-2.

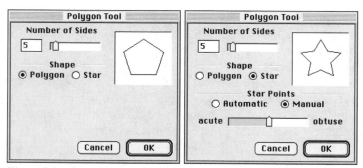

Figure 3-2: The Polygon tool can create polygon paths (left) and star paths (right).

Uses for Closed Paths

Tip

See the Nested Inline topic at the end of this chapter for a step-by-step way to create graphics to a path automatically, a process you will find described nowhere else outside of this book.

Opening Closed Paths

Closed paths, even those that are filled with colors or other fills, can be transformed into open paths by cutting across their vector boundary with the Knife tool. The fill will disappear when you do this.

Creating Open Paths

The main tools for creating open paths in FreeHand are the Line tool, the FreeHand tool (including its Calligraphic Pen and Variable Pen options), the Pen tool, and the Bezigon tool. An open path is a stand-alone vector. You can customize the stroke, giving it thickness, color, and a pattern. See the section in Chapter 2 on creating vector art for additional information, as well as how to configure the dialogs associated with open path creation.

An additional open path tool is not where you would expect it to be in FreeHand. This is the Arc tool (Window | Xtras | Xtra Tools). To use it to create a path, simply click and drag out an arc. Arc segments can be glued together with the Join command. The Arc tool addresses an open path.

Using Spiral Paths

The Spiral is a special type of path. The Spiral tool is in the Xtra Tools Toolbox (Window | Xtras | Xtra Tools). Double-clicking on the Spiral tool brings up its settings dialog. There are two spiral types, the standard spiral and the progressive spiral. The standard spiral maintains the same distance between rotations, whereas the progressive spiral increases the distance with each turn.

Here are some tips for using spiral paths:

- If you plan to use a spiral path as a path for text, use the Standard Spiral selection and Draw by Rotations, setting the Number of Rotation slider to 4 or less. Spiral text is hard to read at higher settings.

- Use the Draw from Edge setting when you want to place a spiral inside of other paths.

- For unique path shapes, connect the end points of a spiral together to form a closed path. If you fill it, the crossover sections will alternate between fills and no fills, provided you have Even/Odd Fill toggled on. This also makes an interesting inset path form (see Inset Paths at the end of this chapter).

■ If you are attaching text to a spiral path, use the text justification options. Justifying the text left will start the text at the spiral's center, which is generally undesirable because it creates too much unreadable text over-lap. Justify the text right in order to start it at the outer edge, giving you a lot more space for readable text.

Uses for Open Paths

One common use for an open path is to target it as a baseline for a text block. FreeHand open paths can be fine-tuned so that they follow the outline of a feature inside of a bitmap image, like mountains or even a face. The path then serves as a receptacle for a line of text. The second major use for an open path also involves text, but this time it's used as a text run-around line. This can also be applied to a curved feature in a bitmap, except this time the text would be a paragraph that used the outline as a guide to run around the feature. Run-around open paths are generally more vertical, while paths used as baselines for text tend towards the horizontal (see Figure 3-3). See the section later in this chapter on text paths.

Figure 3-3: Open paths used as a baseline for text (top) and as a text run-around shape.

Closing Open Paths

Open paths can be transformed into closed paths manually, by dragging the last point of the path over the first point. Another way to make an open path a closed one is to select the path and simply check Closed in the Object Inspector.

Modifying Paths

Paths, like other objects, respond to all modifications (resize, rotate, reflect, and skew). Path strokes can be altered in the customary manner.

Paths are shaped the same way as any other object. When they are selected, their control points are visible. The control points can be moved, and the control point handles can be used to modify the curves between control points.

In addition, there are a number of special commands listed under the Modify | Alter Path selection. There is also a set of options under the Xtras menu.

Altering Paths

To alter paths, you use the Modify | Alter Path menu, which contains the following useful options:

- **Correct Direction**
  The path direction is initially set by the order in which you place the first two points of a path, either from left to right (clockwise) or right to left (counterclockwise). Objects drawn with the Rectangle tool, Ellipse tool, or Polygon tool are drawn clockwise. When used on closed paths, the Correct Direction command sets the path direction to clockwise. Correcting the direction of a path does not alter its shape. Path direction is important when a path has arrowheads, is joined to another object, is blended, or has text attached to it.

- **Reverse Direction**
  Reverses the direction of one or more selected paths. Reversing the direction of the path does not alter the shape of a path. Use the Reverse Direction command when text attached to a path, a blend, or a subpath of a composite path does not work as expected because of a path going in the wrong direction. For example, text attached to a path might read upside down, or a blend might crisscross itself.

■ **Remove Overlap**

Removes redundant portions of a selected, closed path that crosses itself. The Remove Overlap command reduces the number of elements in a path without altering the path shape. Overlapping areas are converted into closed objects and composite paths as appropriate. Apply Remove Overlap to crisscrossing paths created using the FreeHand tool, the Variable Stroke tool, the Calligraphic Pen FreeHand tool, or the Expand Stroke command.

■ **Simplify**

Removes or adds points to a path to maintain the same shape using the optimum number of points for efficient editing and printing. When a path consists of a large number of points, use the Simplify command to remove excess points. Remaining points are moved to optimal positions along the path. In some cases, points are added to preserve the path shape. Simplifying a path generally makes editing and printing easier, because there are fewer points to worry about. Display is also faster when there are fewer points involved.

Tip

Simplify is useful when applied to objects created with the Trace tool or the FreeHand tool.

■ **Expand Stroke**

Applying Expand Stroke to an open path yields a closed path. If the original path was closed, inside and outside edges convert into subpaths of a composite path. Expand Stroke then fills each separate closed path. Here's an example:

1. Draw a circle and specify a wide stroke width.
2. To create a doughnut shape, use Expand Stroke to convert the wide, circle stroke into a composite path, with the large, outer circle filled black, and joined to the smaller, inner filled circle.

■ **Inset Path**

Expands or contracts one or more closed paths by the specified amount. When you use the Inset Path command, the selected path expands or contracts following the edge of the original path. Use Inset Path to create a larger or smaller version of a path at a distance from the original.

Applying Inset Path to irregular path shapes when scaling the path results in distortion relative to the original path. You can also use the Inset Path command to quickly create a contracted version of the original path to create a highlight blend or a hole.

Tip

Before using Inset Path, clone the selection. Use Inset Path as many times as you like to create concentric graphics. Before using it each time, clone the last inset graphic.

Altering Paths, Part 2

For more ways to alter paths, use the Xtras | Path Operations menu, which contain the following possibilities (these are also listed under Modify | Combine):

■ **Crop**
Crop operates like a cookie cutter on the selected objects. This feature takes two or more objects and crops the lower paths to the shape of the topmost path in the stacking order. See Figure 3-4.

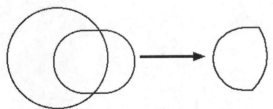

Figure 3-4: The result of a Cropping operation on two selected paths.

■ **Intersect**
Intersect creates a single path from the portions of selected paths that overlap, removing the remaining portions of the paths. The intersection you create inherits the stroke and fill of the backmost, selected path. See Figure 3-5.

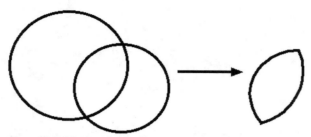

Figure 3-5: The result of an Intersect operation on two selected paths.

■ **Punch**
Creates a hole in selected closed paths, through which other objects are visible. For example, if a smaller circle overlaps a larger, selecting both and choosing Punch creates a doughnut shape, the center of which is completely open. See Figure 3-6.

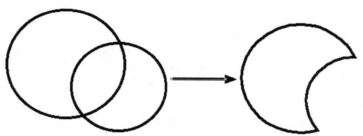

Figure 3-6: The result of a Punch operation on two selected paths.

■ **Transparency**
Using Transparency creates the effect that an object placed over another object is transparent. Transparency creates a new single path from the portions of selected paths that overlap, leaving the original paths. The original paths are retained as the new path is created from the intersection of the original paths, overlapping the originals. See Figure 3-7.

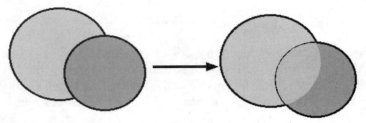

Figure 3-7: The transparent area is actually a separate path.

- **Union**

  Creates a single path from two or more selected, closed paths. Use Union to combine two overlapping paths and remove portions of the paths that cross over each other. If the selected path does not touch the other path, the created object is a composite path. Union is, in most respects, the inverse of Intersect. See Figure 3-8.

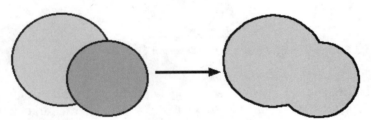

Figure 3-8: Union creates one path from multiple selections.

Text & Paths

Unless you convert a text block to paths in FreeHand, it remains an indicator of the various equations necessary to produce the type. Text blocks that are not converted to paths have limitations as to how and to what extent they can be modified. They cannot, for instance, be used as targets for FreeHand Xtra effects processing. What text can do is to use an external path as a guide and direction marker. Text can use a circular path, for instance, to bend itself around a circle. Paths can have transformative power over unconverted text objects.

Modifying Text Paths

The Text | Flow Inside Path command uses the selected path as a text frame for the text block. Select the path, then select the text and choose Modify | Flow Inside Path. The text is placed inside of the selected path (see Figure 3-9). The text can be moved around inside the path by using the Inset settings in the Object Inspector.

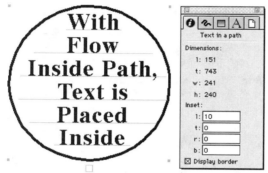

Figure 3-9: The text is placed inside the selected path.

Text is attached to a path by selecting it and the path, and using the Text | Attach to Path command. Attaching text to a path can target either open or closed paths. Once attached, the text can be manipulated and edited as always, by using standard text cursor methods or by adjusting the data in the Object Inspector (see Figure 3-10). The Detach from Path command undoes the attachment.

Figure 3-10: Text attached to a path.

If you need to create text on a path in FreeHand, then I strongly suggest that you become comfortable with the Object Inspector. The Object Inspector features powerful controls for altering and modifying text on a path (see Figure 3-11). These controls are not duplicated anywhere else. The Object Inspector allows you to align the text to the path using the text's baseline, ascenders, or descenders. Text can be oriented by rotation around the path (the default), or written vertically, and skewed horizontally or vertically. Left-right orientation can be adjusted as well.

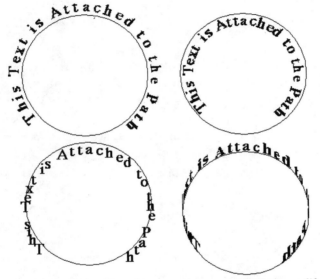

Figure 3-11: The Objects Inspector gives you controls for modifying the way that text is written to a path.

Working With Inline Graphics

Finally, you should know that the process can be reversed, and that the text baseline can act as a path for graphics. This feature is known as inline graphics, and it is easy to accomplish in FreeHand:

1. Create or select a vector graphic from your document. Make sure it is no more than 72 points high or wide. Copy it to the clipboard.

2. Select a path, and select Text | Attach to Path (see Figure 3-12). Now use the Paste command (Edit | Paste) to place the clipboard graphic on the path.

Figure 3-12: You can mix text and graphics on an Inset Path.

Now for some promised magic, simple to do and fascinating to view. There is no reason that you can't copy any inline graphic you create back to the clipboard, and then use it as an Inline graphic itself to create a more complex inline variation.

1. Create an inline graphic by writing a copied selection to a path as outlined in the inline graphics walk-through above (see Figure 3-13).

2. Copy the inline graphic to the clipboard.

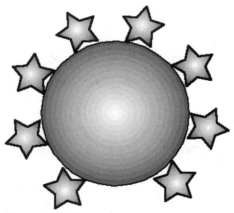

Figure 3-13: The original inline graphic.

3. Create another path, and choose Text I Attach To Path.

4. Instead of typing any letters to the path, use the Paste command or its keyboard equivalent to place as many of the copied graphics to the path as you like (see Figure 3-14).

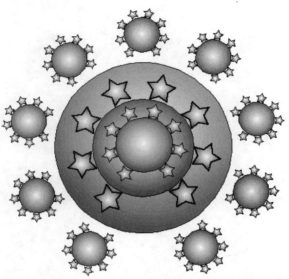

Figure 3-14: The nested inline graphics. Nested inline graphics are not only interesting, but the nesting process can continue further in the same direction and manner. Once placed on the path, graphics can be manipulated and centered by adding spaces between elements.

Moving On

We have explored paths thoroughly in this chapter. In the next chapter, we'll take a look at text and how to place it and modify it. FreeHand's ability to apply a number of special effects to text blocks will also occupy our attention, as well as text inlining and shadowing. We will also look at the Text Inspector and the Object Inspector and how they can be used to adjust your text blocks.

4 Working With Text

What is a core difference between FreeHand as a vector drawing application, and a desktop publishing application like PageMaker? After all, they both incorporate a number of tools and processes for working with graphics and text. A central difference is that as far as creation, modification, and enhancement tools are concerned, FreeHand excels at heading, display, or graphic-style type.

In this chapter, we will focus upon everything you always wanted to know about text, including how to place it and modify it. FreeHand's ability to apply special effects to text blocks will also occupy our attention, as will accomplishing such things as inlining and shadowing. We will also discuss the Text Inspector and the Object Inspector, and how they can be used to adjust your text blocks in discrete and global ways. It is vital that you prepare for this chapter by reading the FreeHand documentation as it relates to text, so that you best use the information presented here.

Text Tool Options

Sitting at the top right of the Toolbox, represented by the letter "A," sits the FreeHand Text tool. This is the doorway that opens all of the possibilities for text design and modification in FreeHand. Selecting it and then clicking on the screen does one of two things, depending on what you selected in the preferences. It either brings up a text ruler and a flashing cursor where you type in your text, or it brings up the Text Editor. The six major text origination commands (Font, Size, Style, Effect, Align, and Leading) can be addressed from the Text toolbar (Window I Toolbars I Text), the Text menu, or from the Text tab in the Inspectors palette (also called the Text Inspector, Window I Inspectors I Text). See Figure 4-1.

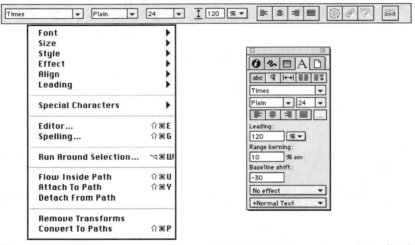

Figure 4-1: The Text toolbar, Text menu, and Text tab in the Inspectors palette offer different ways to create and modify text.

Although the Text toolbar offers the convenience of instant visual access to the text tools, it is missing some of the features available in the Text menu or the Text Inspector. The Text menu adds the capability to add special characters (end of column, end of line, non-breaking space, em space, en space, thin space, em dash, en dash, and discretionary hyphen). The Text menu also provides access to the Text Editor, Spell Checker, Run Around Selection, and Remove Transforms commands. The Text Inspector offers all of the features of the Text toolbar, and adds a more convenient numerical input area for leading, range kerning, and baseline shift commands. The Text Inspector, however, lacks the text-path features offered in both the Text toolbar and the Text menu.

So what is the best way to adjust your display for access to text features? The Inspectors palette should always remain on your display, because it offers you fast access to so many features with a simple click on a tab. You can't get rid of the Text menu, so it stays by default. If you need to conserve a little space to enlarge your page area, you could turn the Text toolbar off. If you plan to do a lot of text-path operations in your document, however, you have much faster access to these options in the Text toolbar than in the Text menu. If you plan to incorporate a good amount of text in your document, I would suggest having access to all three text items. If graphics will dominate your project, you can turn the Text toolbar off (Window | Toolbars | Text).

Special Effects

FreeHand offers you four text effects, each of which can add a bit of sparkle to a headline or callout on your page.

Tip

Be aware that you have to turn the selected text effect off in the Text Inspector after using it. If you don't, every text block you create will incorporate the effect as it has been set.

Highlight
The Highlight effect surrounds the text with a rectangular area of color (see Figure 4-2). The dialog allows you to set the flowing items:

- **Position**. Enter a positive number to shift the highlight box above the text baseline. Enter a negative number to shift the highlight box below the baseline.
- **Dash**. Select a dash effect to apply to the highlight.
- **Stroke Width.** Enter a number to set the vertical width of the highlight box. The width of the highlight box defaults to the size of the text.
- **Stroke Color.** Choose a color for the highlight from the pop-up.
- **Overprint.** Check to overprint the Highlight effect.

Double-clicking on the Stroke Color bar brings up another dialog where you can select whether the color is to be a process or spot color.

Tip

Be aware that these special effects do not *translate if you convert to paths, and are only useful if you plan to keep the text in its original font format.*

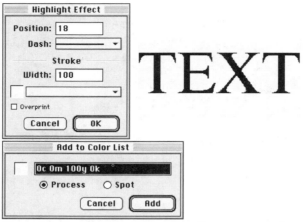

Figure 4-2: The Highlight Effect dialog allows you to set the parameters of all of the associated effect parameters.

Inline

Inlined effects may be thought of as stroked engravings, and offer much room for exploration. Selecting the Inline Effect option and choosing Edit brings up the Inline Effect dialog (see Figure 4-3).

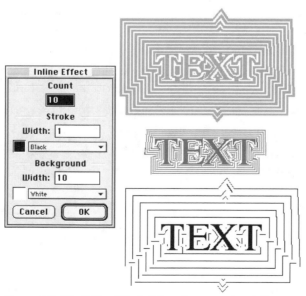

Figure 4-3: The Inline Effect dialog allows you to set the parameters of the effect.

Shadow & Zoom

The Shadow Effect creates a drop shadow. If you have no other alternative for creating quick and simple shadows with no interactive controls, you will appreciate this effect. I prefer converting the text to paths and using KPT Vector Effects ShadowLand, which offers much more variety (see Appendix C).

The Zoom effect creates a 3D-like extrusion of the type. As with the Shadow effect above, I prefer converting the text to paths and using KPT Vector Effects ShadowLand. The Zoom effect just doesn't offer the options that professional users need.

Figure 4-4 shows the results of the Shadow and Zoom effects.

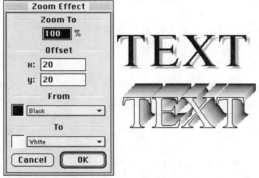

Figure 4-4: The Shadow effect (top right) and the Zoom effect (bottom right), and the Zoom Effect controls at the left.

Convert to Paths

Of all the text commands you are likely to use in FreeHand, this one will dominate over all of the others. It does what it says, and converts native text to editable vector paths. In order to apply Envelope and other effects to a text block, the text must first be converted to paths (see Figure 4-5). The other benefit of converting text to paths is that you need never worry about your service bureau or printer having the font that you have used in the document, since it is translated into a vector path object. This command is available in the Text toolbar and the Text menu.

Figure 4-5: The top font block remains in its original form, while its clone below has been converted to paths so that envelope effects can be applied.

The Text Inspector

The Text Inspector is only one part of the Inspector panel; the other Inspectors are Object, Stroke, Fill, and Document. The Inspectors panel should remain onscreen at all times, because it functions as an instantly accessible control center for most of FreeHand's operations. The Text Inspector holds the following controls in five sections (see Figure 4-6):

- **Text Character Inspector.** Font, size, style, justification, leading (space between lines), range kerning (by em percentages, the space between letters), baseline shift, effects, and styles panel style choices.

- **Text Paragraph Inspector.** Paragraph spacing, indent, Hang punctuation toggle (checks to place punctuation outside left and right paragraph margins), Hyphenate toggle (turns hyphenation on or off), and rules (allows you to apply a rule to the last line of a paragraph).

- **Text Spacing Inspector.** Horizontal scale (changes character width by percentage), Spacing percentages (enters the minimum, optimum, and maximum percentages of space between words). These values are the allowable deviation from the spacing of the font in use—as defined by the size of the font's space. Keep Together Selected Words toggle (checks to prevent selected words from breaking at the end of a line), and Keep Together n Lines, where n is the minimum number of lines allowed at a page break.

■ **Text Columns and Rows Inspector.** The Text Columns and Rows Inspector contains controls for setting the height/width, spacing, and rules of columns and rows, as well as the flow direction for text in those columns and rows.

■ **Text Adjust Columns Inspector.** The Text Adjust Columns Inspector contains copyfitting controls. Among these are: Balance (checks to distribute lines of text among columns in a selected text block evenly), Modify leading (checks to make sure the text fills the targeted column), Copyfit percentages (used to alter type size and leading proportionally to fit the selected text block), and First line leading (used to specify the distance from the top of the text block to the baseline of the first line of text, according to the leading specified).

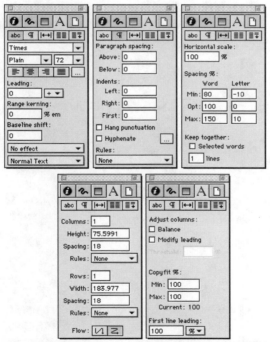

Figure 4-6: The five sections of the Text Inspector: Text Character Inspector, Text Paragraph Inspector, Text Spacing Inspector, Text Columns and Rows Inspector, and Text Adjust Columns Inspector.

The Object Inspector

The Object Inspector is the first tab in the Inspectors panel (Window I
Inspectors I Object). With text or a text block selected, the Object Inspector
displays the dimensions and inset values of the text block. If the text block is
converted to paths, the Object Inspector changes and lists the size and location
of the text graphic (see Figure 4-7).

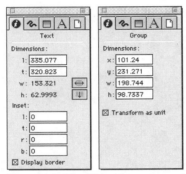

*Figure 4-7: The Object Inspector as it references unconverted text on the left, and text converted
to paths on the right.*

Tip

*If you are generating animation frames that require FreeHand text, use the Object
Inspector to control the text numerically for each frame, resulting in very smooth
animation files.*

Text Run Arounds

The Text Run Around Selection option wraps text around a selected object,
keeping the text away from the object by a specified distance. Select an object
and choose Text I Run Around Selection to set options. In the dialog, click the
first icon to remove text wrap from a selected object. Click the second icon to
apply text run around around a selected object. In the Standoff fields, enter a
positive value or a negative value to set the minimum distance between the
text and the selected object.

Tip

You cannot use the Run Around Selection command when a group or blend is selected. To wrap text around a group or a blend, draw a path around it and then set text wrap for the path. Alternatively, you can select objects in a group or blend and then set a text wrap.

One creative use for text run-arounds is around a drop cap:

1. Create a letter that is the first letter of a configured paragraph of text already placed on the screen. Convert it to paths.
2. Enlarge the letter to make it a drop cap for the text block.
3. Make sure the drop cap is at the top of the object stack. Select the drop cap and choose Text | Run Around Selection.
4. Remove the first letter of the text block, and move the drop cap into place over the paragraph, and watch as the letters move aside to accommodate it (see Figure 4-8).

Figure 4-8: A drop cap with run-around text.

Working With Styles

Use the Styles panel to create and apply graphic or text styles. If you edit a style later, FreeHand automatically applies the changes to all objects with the style applied. Why use Styles? Speed is the main answer. Applying a set style to a graphic or text selection is as simple as clicking on the style in the Styles panel while the graphic or text is selected (see Figure 4-9). That specific style is applied immediately. You can also drag and drop that style's icon from the list onto the selection.

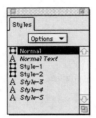

Figure 4-9: The Styles panel.

Style Types

There are two types of styles (Window | Panels | Styles): object and paragraph.

Object styles are listed in roman type in the Styles panel, with an icon that can be dragged and dropped onto any object on the document. Object styles can also be applied by selecting an object and then selecting a style name.

Paragraph styles are listed in italic type with an "A" icon that can be dragged and dropped onto text. Paragraph styles may also be applied by selecting a text block and then selecting a style to apply. The style applies to the paragraph or to the entire text block, depending on the selections made in Editing | Text preferences.

Creating & Editing Styles

Select the graphic or text that contains the style elements you want to have at hand. Choose New from the drop-down menu in the Styles palette, and a new listing that references those style attributes is added to the list of options.

Double-click any name in the Styles panel to rename. Select the style in the list and choose Edit from the Options pull-down menu to activate the Edit Style dialog (see Figure 4-10) where you can redefine every aspect of the style and write the changes back to that Style name in the list. If you apply a style to an object, then make further changes to the object, your "local" changes override the "global" dictates of the style. A plus sign (+) in front of a style name in the Styles panel indicates an overridden style. You can click the style name to reapply the original style and lose your changes.

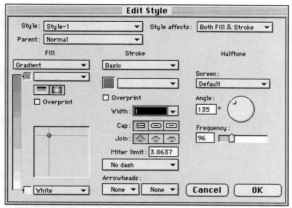

Figure 4-10: The Edit Style dialog.

Using Styles

Always keep the Styles panel on your workscreen, even if only in its rolled-up form. It is usually impossible to set up all of the styles you need in a document when you first begin designing it. You can add as many styles to the list as possible at the beginning, but be ready to add more as you work through a project, and to delete those you find you are not using. A great advantage in having alternate graphics and text styles in a list is that you can instantly preview what the page looks like with a change in the styles of one or more elements.

Moving On

In this chapter, we have explored the ways that text can be modified and altered as a component of a FreeHand document. In the next chapter, we will discover how to use FreeHand's color options, including the color models. We will also look at the uses of the Color Mixer and its association with the Color List.

5

Adding Color to Drawings

Color seduces the eye. Without color, the world would be less vibrant, and form and shape alone would compete for our visual attention. Color reproduction is still relatively expensive when the output is on paper, but absolutely expected in the new publishing worlds of the Web and multimedia CD-ROMs. In FreeHand, colors can be added separately to object strokes and fills. More often than not, an object's stroke, its perimeter frame, takes on a dark color, while the fill colors vary. Strokes are commonly rendered with a solid color; fills may be solid, graduated, or even color patterned. This whole scheme can be reversed, or customized according to your project's needs and your designer's eye. The fact remains, however, that color in FreeHand is thought of as having two separate targets (even if one is switched off): strokes and fills.

Choosing a Color Model Using the Color Mixer

Color models are processes by which colors are created or displayed. FreeHand's Color Mixer works with three main color models, along with tints and system colors. Each color model (or color "space") has a particular purpose. The main color models are:

- **CMYK (Process Color):** CMYK color is most commonly used in the print world, where cyan, magenta, yellow, and black inks are combined to produce other colors. If you are working on a project for process-print output (including all color inkjet and laser printers), stick with CMYK colors. Their range is somewhat limited, but what you see onscreen will look more like your final product.

- **RGB:** RGB is the color model used by all televisions, computer monitors, and other media that rely on the emission or transmission of light to produce color. In print, by contrast, the light is reflected from the page. RGB relies on the combination of red, green, and blue light to produce a wide range of colors. If you are working on a Web or multimedia project, RGB should be your primary color space, because it allows the widest range, or *gamut*, of colors.
- **HLS:** HLS color, sometimes called Lab color or HSB color, specifies colors by their hue, lightness, and saturation values (or hue, saturation, and brightness for HSB). This model was developed to overcome differences in the way certain video sources specify RGB color, thus allowing for more consistent color reproduction. For our purposes, the RGB and HLS color models are interchangeable.

HiFi Color

The new kid on the color model block is called High Fidelity Color, or more colloquially, HiFi color. Essentially, HiFi Color is an extension of the long-used CMYK standard. By adding more inks to the color model, printers extend the range of colors they can produce.

The current leader in HiFi color reproduction is PANTONE. Their HiFi color standard, called Hexachrome, consists of the standard cyan, magenta, yellow, and black inks, plus orange and green (for CMYKOG). The gamut of CMYKOG is tremendous—possibly surpassing even that of RGB—which gives you much greater flexibility in your color printing projects.

Hexachrome is supported by FreeHand, but may or may not be supported by your printer or service bureau. So before you dive in, talk to your vendor.

Use the Color Mixer (Window | Panels | Color Mixer) to build new colors, modify existing colors, and to switch from one model to another (see Figure 5-1). In addition, you can create a tint of a previously specified color by selecting the Tint button, or you can work with your computer's system color, by choosing either the Apple or Windows button. Think of it as your digital paint mixing station.

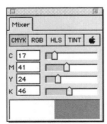

Figure 5-1: The Color Mixer.

System Color

The two system color models are handy if you're creating colors you know will be displayed only on a Mac OS or Windows machine, respectively. For Web or multimedia work, though, you're better off using RGB or HLS.

Apple Button: Displays the Apple color picker, where you can create a new color using Apple HLS (or HSL for the Mac) and Apple RGB models. (Note that Apple uses the designator HSL instead of HLS—they mean the same thing.)

Windows Button: Displays the Windows Colors panel, containing 48 basic colors.

Creating & Storing a Color Palette

I strongly suggest that before beginning any project you create a range of appropriate colors. For instance, if you plan to create an Independence Day poster, you can be almost certain you'll need a red, a blue, and a white. You may need other colors as well, but you can at least make a start—and using the Color List is a lot quicker and more reliable than redefining a color each time you need it.

FreeHand provides a single convenient panel for storing your project's Color palette—the Color List. Using the Color List, you can store your custom colors from the Color Mixer, apply colors to objects, name and rename colors, choose specific colors from a range of standard commercial libraries, select spot or process colors, and create portable color libraries for use in other FreeHand projects.

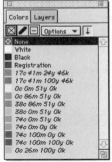

Figure 5-2: The Color List.

Building Custom Colors

Custom colors are colors that you create using the Color Mixer's CMYK, RGB, or HLS models. As stated earlier, the model you use will depend on your target output: CMYK for print, RGB or HLS for Web and multimedia jobs. If it's not already on your screen, open the Color Mixer (Window | Panels | Color Mixer), to begin creating your Color palette.

CMYK

Drag the sliders or enter precise values in the CMYK color model to create colors. CMYK color is based upon the *subtractive* method (all reflective color is subtractive). This means that you create white by subtracting or removing color. Combining all colors at 0 percent creates white, and combining all colors at 100 percent creates black. Certain colors, such as a strong, rich orange, cannot be reproduced in CMYK. If you need such a color, you want to look into using a predefined spot color ink to supplement your regular four-color process colors. It's easy to do, but be sure to consult with your printer or service bureau about their preferred setup.

RGB

Drag the sliders or enter precise values in the RGB color model to create colors. RGB is based on the *additive* method. The additive method creates white by adding or combining color. Combining all colors at 100 percent creates white, and combining all colors at 0 percent creates black. Colors created by transmitted light use the additive method, as on your computer monitor (which uses red, green, and blue phosphors).

HLS

HLS is also an additive process, where hue is an RGB color (such as orange, pink, or green), lightness indicates the blackness or whiteness of a hue, and saturation refers to the intensity of a hue.

Hue is determined by the position, in degrees, a color occupies on the color picker. You can enter precise values for specific colors or drag the color pointer around the color picker to create other colors.

Enter this degree:	To get this color:
0	Red
60	Yellow
120	Green
180	Cyan
240	Blue
300	Magenta

Lightness indicates how close the hue is to black or white. Moving the slider changes the lightness value for all hues on the color picker. Drag the slider or enter a value to change the lightness by specifying the percentage of black or white in a hue. At 0 percent, your colors all go to pure black, with no white present. At 100 percent, all black is absent and the colors fade to pure white.

Regardless of the model you choose, once your color is built, you should store it in the Color List. If you haven't already done so, open the Color List (Window I Panels I Color List). Drag your built color from the right side of the Color Mixer color well to the blank area at the bottom of the Color List. If you can't see any blank space, you can either open the panel a little further, or simply drop the chip on the Drop Box (the small box with a downward-pointing arrow, in the top right area of the Color List). When you drop the color chip, the color will appear in the list, with a name based on the method used to create it. Run through the following exercise to get the hang of the interface:

1. In the Color Mixer, select RGB. Drag the R slider all the way to the right. The R field will read 255, which is the maximum setting for any of the RGB primaries. The color chip will show a strong, bright red.

2. Drag the color chip to the Color List and drop it. You will see the color chip appear in the list, with the name *255r 0g 0b*. This is simply a translation of the primaries used to build the color. Note that the color name has three small dots just to its right. These indicate that the color is RGB (it's a visual reminder that the color shouldn't be used for print work).

3. Move back to the Color Mixer. Click CMYK. Notice that the color chip has darkened a bit. FreeHand recognizes that the CMYK model is unable to reproduce pure RGB red, and is substituting the nearest CMYK equivalent. The fields should show no cyan, 100 percent magenta, 74 percent yellow, and no black.

4. Drag the new CMYK chip to the Color List. Notice that the new color's name, *0c 100m 74y 0k*, reflects the fact that you used the CMYK model.

5. Now set the Color Mixer to HLS. You should see H=0, S=50, and L=100.

6. Drag the HLS chip to the Color List. You will see that the name assigned to the new color is *255r 0g 0b-1*, and that the little three-dot icon is back. This tells you that HLS works, essentially, with RGB colors.

7. Practice building a few more colors, until you feel comfortable with the range of each model and the interface.

Using Predefined Color Libraries

In addition to building your own custom colors, you have the option of specifying colors from a number of predefined color libraries—including PANTONE, Toyo, Trumatch, Dainippon, PANTONE Hexachrome, Munsell, and others.

Commercial color libraries use numbered color swatches to represent specific formulations of printing inks (to complicate matters, the inks may be either a specific, single-color ink, as with PANTONE, or a CMYK process specification, as with PANTONE Process). Your printer will pull out the ink that matches the number you specified (or mix the appropriate inks), and use that to print the appropriate plate. Thus, commercial color libraries are most useful for print.

However, if you're doing a Web site or a multimedia presentation for a client whose organization already has a set of specific colors (usually part of their corporate identity), you may find that the predefined libraries are a quick way to closely match the Web site to any existing printed materials. Just pick the designated color, and use it as you would any other.

To use the predefined color libraries, open the Color List's Options pop-up menu, and select the appropriate library. (The advantages and disadvantages of the various color libraries are beyond the scope of this book; normally, it depends on your printer, and possibly your location.) When the library window opens, just type the proper designator—which will vary with the library—into the field at the top of the window, and click OK. The color will be added to your Color List with the appropriate name.

In the list of predefined libraries, two names may catch your eye: Crayon and Grays. The Grays library is simply a series of shades of black, from 1 percent to 100 percent, and is of limited usefulness. The Crayon library is more or less what it sounds like. Like your childhood box of 64 Crayola crayons, the Crayon library lists a series of 62 colors (okay, so it's not *exactly* like the old box) and their names. Pick the one you want and it appears in the Color List. *Be warned:* Use these colors *only* for Web or multimedia work. They aren't built to match any printing specification, and your printer (commercial or desktop) won't have any use for them.

Tints

To create a color tint, select Tint from the Color Mixer. From the pop-up menu in the mixer, select a color (you will see that this menu mirrors the Color List—you could also drag a chip from the Color List into the Color Mixer's well). In the color ramp immediately below the menu, you will see a series of preset tints from 10 percent to 90 percent, in increments of 10 percent. You can drag one of these chips to the Color List to use it, or you may set your own percentage by using the slider. If you set your own percentage, be sure to use the color chip to the left of the slider to place the new tint in the Color List.

System Colors

To use the system color models, click the rightmost button in the Color Mixer. On Mac OS systems, you can use either Apple's RGB or HSL pickers, which operate almost identically to those in FreeHand. On Windows systems, you can choose from the list of preset colors. When you are finished, drag the new color chip to the Color List.

Altering Colors

If you build a particular color, say, Lemon Yellow, and later decide that it's too bright, you can easily change it. You can either build a new version in the Color Mixer, or drag the existing Lemon Yellow chip to the Color Mixer's well, and then modify the settings that appear. Either way, when you are finished, drag the new chip from the Color Mixer to the Color List, and drop it onto the existing Lemon Yellow color chip. The old chip is instantly replaced with the new one (this will also apply the new specifications to any objects in your document that you've colored with the old Lemon Yellow, so watch out).

You may also select Replace from the Color List's Options menu. This opens a dialog that lets you replace an existing color with a selection from a predefined library or another color currently on the list. Select the color you want and click OK to replace the old chip with the new one.

Warning

Don't replace colors from predefined libraries with your own colors. FreeHand will caution you against doing this if you try, because it might cause your onscreen work not to match your printed output. If you change a color that you've used as the basis for a tint (or for several tints), any tints are revised accordingly.

Renaming Colors

Once you've built (or selected) and stored your Color palette, you may want to rename the colors to suit your fancy. To do this, double-click on the existing color name in the Color List, and type the new name. Thus, the cryptic *255r 0g 0b* becomes the much more helpful *Bright Red*. You can also sort your list for easier reading. Either drag each color to the desired position in the list manually, or select Xtras | Colors | Sort Color List by Name.

Warning

Don't rename colors chosen from predefined libraries. Your printer needs the exact library color specification. If you rename a predefined color, your printer will be unable to determine what ink you want.

Applying Colors

In your FreeHand document, draw a simple square. With the square selected, choose the leftmost button from the Color List (the Fill control), and then pick a color from the list. Notice that your square is immediately filled with that color. Select the next button to the right, the Stroke control, and pick another color. Your square will be stroked appropriately. Finally, choose the third button, the Combination control, and pick a third color. Both the stroke and fill change to the new color. If you choose stroke and fill colors without an object in the document selected, the colors you choose become the new defaults and apply to each new object you create.

The Stroke, Fill, and Combination controls apply to any object you create in your FreeHand document. You also have the option of dragging the color you want from the Color List to the object and dropping it there. The object will assume the color for either its stroke or fill, depending on where you dropped the chip. However, when you're trying to drop a color chip on a half-point stroke at 50 percent magnification, this method can become tedious—it's often faster to use the Color List controls.

Spot vs. Process Colors

Using the Color List's Options menu, you can designate any color in the list as either spot (Make Spot) or process (Make Process). If you are working on Web or multimedia projects, you can ignore this setting. If your project is destined for a printing press, though, there's more you should know.

As I've said before, process, or CMYK, printing involves the combination of four inks to create specific colors. The CMYK range is limited, though. CMYK printing is also expensive—what if you just need one or two colors, like a red and a blue?

In this case, you can select a color from a predefined library (after checking with your printer to see which library to use), select its name in the Color List, and choose Make Spot from the Options menu. When your service bureau prints your file, they can make every object in a particular color print to a specific plate, which your printer can then use for that color.

If you choose Make Process, FreeHand assumes you want the selected color broken into C, M, Y, and K components for four-color printing, and will attempt to print it accordingly. Remember, though, that many colors cannot be reproduced in CMYK, so What You See may *not* be What You Get.

Spot and process colors are often best handled by a qualified service bureau. I can't stress enough that if you plan to have your project professionally printed, you need to get in touch with your printer or service bureau, or both, and have them talk you through the correct setup.

Custom Color Libraries

Now that you've created an entire library of custom-built colors, you may want to use it with other projects. No problem!

1. From the Color List's Options menu, select Export. Choose the colors you want in your custom library by pressing Shift-click, then click OK.

2. In the dialog box that appears, specify a name for your library (keeping the default .BCF extension), a name for the file to store it in, and any notes you wish to attach to it. (You can usually leave the Colors Per Column and Colors Per Row settings at their defaults.) By default, FreeHand will save the library in its Color folder. If you wish to store it elsewhere, click Save As and choose your location. Otherwise, click Save.

3. To import a custom library, choose Import from the Color List's Options menu, navigate to the folder where you stored the library, and double-click it.

4. Choose the colors you want to use by double-clicking them in the library window. You can choose multiple colors using Shift-click.

5. If you need to load other colors later, the custom library will appear in the Options menu.

Halftones

The controls in the Halftones panel (Window I Panels I Halftones) determine the halftone screen settings for a selected object, overriding the document-wide settings. Halftones are ways of representing continuous-tone art with a pattern of dots varying in size and angle of placement. This pattern is called a halftone screen. In photographic halftoning, each dot in the halftone screen is called a halftone dot. In digital halftoning, dots in the halftone screen are combined into halftone cells. Refer to Figure 5-3.

If you're working for print, keep reading. If not, this section most likely won't apply to your compositions.

Figure 5-3: The Halftones panel.

Tip

Black-and-white art is printed using black halftone dots, but color can also be reproduced. Spot color is created by applying a colored ink to a halftone screen. Process color is created by overlaying four halftone screens (one each for cyan, magenta, yellow, and black inks) at different halftone screen angles. This creates a "rosette" of color that fools the eye into seeing solid colors (examine your USA Today with a magnifying glass to get a better idea of what's going on).

Use the Halftone panel option to specify halftone screen settings that are different from the document-wide settings in the currently selected PPD (PostScript printer description) file. Settings made using the Halftones panel apply only to selected objects. Staying in very close contact with your print service or service bureau is extremely critical when it comes to halftone screening. If you use the Halftones panel to apply a screen angle or frequency to an object that uses a process color, all four process inks will use the angle and frequency you specified. This is not desirable. A workaround is to use a spot color for the selected object.

Settings in the Halftone Panel

Manipulate the settings in the Halftone panel to apply parameters to the selected object. Bear in mind that using this panel to apply specific halftone settings to specific objects will override any global options set in the Print dialog. The following settings can be modified:

Screen

This applies a halftone dot shape to the selected object. Select one of four halftone dot shapes:

- **Default:** Applies the default halftone dot shape specified by the currently selected PPD file.
- **Round dot:** Halftone dot shape is a circular dot. This is by far the most common dot.
- **Line:** Halftone dot shape is a line.
- **Ellipse:** Halftone dot shape is elliptical.

Angle

This sets the angle of the halftone screen when you drag the dial or enter a value. To use the value specified in the currently selected PPD file, clear the entry field.

Frequency

This sets the screen ruling of the halftone screen when you drag the dial or enter a value in lines per inch. To use the value specified in the currently selected PPD file, clear the entry field.

Tip

Unless you have professional experience in configuring halftone parameters, I strongly recommend that you either leave this matter to your printer or service bureau, or that you at least consult with them about the best approach for your project. Always get a color proof of your work to check the results of altered settings.

Moving On

In this chapter, we have discussed the Color Mixer and Color List panel operations, and suggested ways to conceptualize and use colors in FreeHand. This chapter concluded with a discussion about the halftone options available in FreeHand. In the next chapter, we will concentrate upon using FreeHand's awesome collection of effects, utilities, and tools.

6

Using the F/X Tools

In this chapter, we'll take a dedicated look at the F/X (effects) tools found in the Xtra Tools and Operations panel, as well as touching upon both the use of FreeHand styles and FreeHand chart creation. These effects allow you to infinitely vary the shape and look of selected graphics, often allowing you to emulate such things as water, fire, electricity, and fur. It is these effects which push FreeHand even further into maintaining its position as the best all-around vector graphics application on the market.

Xtra Tools

Many of the tools in the Xtra Tools panel can also be found in the Xtras menu. Access is a lot easier and quicker from the Xtra Tools panel, so it is recommended that you leave this panel onscreen during your work sessions, even if it is rolled up most of the time. The tools in this panel allow you to create a long list of variable and needed F/X.

Tip

The small button on the upper-right side of a panel is used to "roll up" (minimize) or expand the panel in the workspace.

3D Rotation

The 3D Rotation tool allows you to add a 3D look to a selected object or object group (see Figure 6-1). Always work with 3D Rotation zoomed in on the object (select View | Fit Selection). If the perspective doesn't come out exactly the way you want it to (as will likely be the case when you are constructing a 3D cube), you can always grab a control point and make the finer adjustments.

Tip

When you click on an object with the 3D Rotation tool, drag away from the object before finalizing your 3D Rotation. If you operate this tool at a little distance from the object, you will have finer control over the results. Move the tool slowly for the best control.

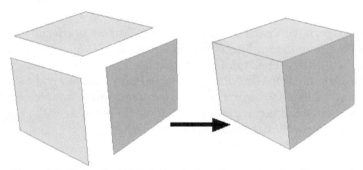

Figure 6-1: Using the 3D Rotation tool on three rectangles allows you to construct a 3D cube.

Uses for the 3D Rotation Tool

Consider the following tips for the 3D Rotation tool:

- Add dimension to a text block that has been converted to paths.
- Construct 3D cubes by working from cloned rectangles.
- Add a perspective plane to a page that fades into the distance.
- If you have a large number of cloned graphics on a page, 3D rotate some of them to give the composition more interest.

Fisheye Lens

The Fisheye Lens distorts the vector graphics it is placed over as if they were being seen through a thick magnifying glass. The Fisheye Lens applies a local distortion to the selected paths. This tool works equally well on singular selections or groups. You must select the targeted path first before dragging the lens over it. Multiple selections are also possible (see Figure 6-2).

Tip

The Fisheye Lens distorts in the direction of the major ellipse axis. Dragging out a horizontal Fisheye Lens ellipse over a selected graphic distorts the object horizontally, with a vertical ellipse distorting it vertically. Dragging out an even circle bloats the object equally on all sides.

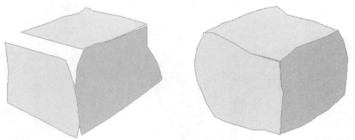

Figure 6-2: Here, the Fisheye Lens was applied several times to the cubic paths developed in figure 6-1.

Uses for the Fisheye Lens Tool

Consider these tips for using the Fisheye Lens tool:

- Distort a text block that has been converted to paths.
- Add crumpled looks to objects.
- Distort parts of photos that have been translated to vectors.
- Use the Fisheye Lens to create FreeHand animation frames to exhibit animated distortions.
- Use a concave setting to "dent" objects as if they were being struck by a projectile.

Smudge

Smudge adds a controlled blend to a selection that follows the direction and distance the mouse is dragged. Double-clicking the Smudge tool brings up its settings dialog, where you can set the ending stroke and fill target colors. A Smudge blend automatically fades to the set stroke or fill at the end point of the directional mouse drag. The starting color of a smudge is the stroke color of the selected object. If the object has no stroke, the fill color or gradient colors are used. Text needs to be converted to paths to accept a smudge (see Figure 6-3). Smudge will only work once on a selection, so don't attempt to smudge a smudge.

Tip

Using smudging on a text block that has been converted to paths often causes characters to be placed on the wrong level in the stack. After the smudge operation, ungroup the text block and move the misplaced characters to the back of the stack until the text block looks right.

Figure 6-3: A smudged text block.

Uses for the Smudge Tool

Consider the following tips for using the Smudge tool:

- Add 3D shadowing to selected paths.
- A smudge is a special case of a blend. Ungroup a smudged object and use the parts separately as cloned shapes with various colors. This works well when the initial shape has been gradient filled and has no stroke, because all of the ungrouped smudged parts will have separate and unique gradients.

Roughen

The Roughen tool adds points to a selected path and randomly distributes them away from the original path's location. Double-clicking the Roughen tool brings up its dialog. A High setting of 100 in the settings slider results in more rays emanating from the object, and is good for creating bursts and high-density splotches. Low settings create fewer extra points, deforming shapes into random silhouettes good for emulating rocks and water drop splashes. See Figure 6-4 for an example.

Tip

If you alternate the Roughen settings between a Rough and a Smooth 100 for the same object, the result is an object edge that looks almost like cross-hatching. This is impossible to achieve with any other vector tools.

Figure 6-4: Roughened with a Smooth setting of 1, these letters look enhanced with floral designs.

Warning! Repeated use of the maximum settings in the Roughen dialog on the same object will overload your system. No more than 32,000 points are allowed for a FreeHand object, and that limit can be reached very quickly.

Uses for the Roughen Tool

Consider the following tips for using the Roughen tool:

- Use a low Rough setting on a gradient circle to create rock forms, or even a swarm of meteors.
- Use high settings (75–100) and the Smooth option to create wispy dandelions.
- Create random scribbled frames by setting the fill to none in an object and using the Roughen tool at a Smooth setting of 1.

- Use a Smooth setting of 1 on a text block that has been converted to paths to produce ornate drop caps. Repeating this process a second time results in a jumbled graphic that is perfect for splashing surf.

Bend

The Bend tool is used to curve paths inward or outward from the point where the mouse is clicked. Starting Bend operations outside of the selection causes the mouse click to act as the magnetic point for all reshaped elements (see Figure 6-5).

Tip

Starting in the center of the selection with the Bend tool preserves bilateral symmetry.

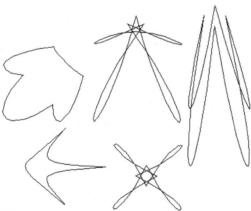

Figure 6-5: These patterns were all created from a circle with the Bend tool.

Uses for the Bend Tool
Consider the following tips for using the Bend tool:

- Use the Bend tool with a setting of 1 to create a flower-like pattern from a circle. Click the mouse outside of the circle and draw it into the circle before releasing it.
- Create elements to act as borders and spot graphics.

Operators

There are 18 operators in the Operations panel. Note that the Operations panel is *not* the Xtra Tools panel, and the two should not be confused. The selections in the Operations panel are also called Operators. See Figure 6-6.

Tip

Some of the operators also deal with paths, and those that do are also covered in Chapter 3.

Figure 6-6: The Operations panel.

Create PICT Image (Mac OS Only)

 Use the Create PICT Image tool to convert any image drawn or placed in FreeHand into a bitmap PICT image. You can control color depth, dithering, anti-aliasing (1–4), and image resolution.

Tip

Stay away from 300 and 600 dpi resolutions unless you have hundreds of mega-bytes of RAM on your system. Even medium-large graphics set at this dpi level will choke all but the most powerful Mac OS box.

Fractalize

There is no settings dialog for this tool. To use it, click the operator, and the results appear. Fractalize causes a four-point symmetry to be applied to the selection each time it is clicked (see Figure 6-7). This results in squarish patterns, while continued clicking doubles the symmetries involved.

Tip

Don't use more than four or five clicks, because the result beyond that is a jumbled mess that is too chaotic for most any uses.

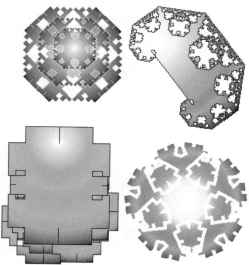

Figure 6-7: The Fractalize tool excels at symmetrical designs.

Uses for the Fractalize Operator

Consider the following tips for using the Fractalize tool:

- Use Fractalize four or five times on a straight line to generate interesting embroidery patterns.

- Use it four or five times on concentric grouped shapes for symmetrical designs.

- Generate cityscape designs. Start with a grouped series of 12 rectangles of different sizes that overlap, and use Fractalize five times.

- Use it five times on a star shape. The points on the star indicate the level of fractal symmetry, so that a five-point star produces a design with five-point symmetry.

Trap

Use the Trap tool to generate overlapping, overprinting objects to compensate for any slight potential misregistration of printing presses. The Trap Xtra works on objects with basic strokes and fills only, though most trapping is done by Strokes. To use traps on text, always convert your text to paths first.

Tip

You should always consult your printer for recommendations on trapping before generating traps, unless your professional experience dictates otherwise. 99 percent of FreeHand users should stay away from this tool and allow print and service bureau professionals to handle trapping.

Blend

You can think of blends as directional gradients with an attitude. A blend considers every aspect of the personalities of the targeted members between, or among, which the blend is created. It then creates a series of objects that bridge the distance from one selected member to the other. If we think of the selected paths from which a blend will be created as parents, then the string of graduated objects between these original members can be though of as their children. Actually, there is an analogy in animation terms that also serves quite well. The central frames in an animation are called keyframes, and the frames that are created to take you from one keyframe to the next are called "in-betweens." In a blend, the new graphics that are created between the original selections are truly in-betweens, a string of sequential paths that inherit the personality of both the source and target paths.

This is an important analogy. Once you understand it, you will see why the Blend tool is an excellent way to generate real animation frames for a FreeHand animation sequence. A guided tutorial that walks you through a real FreeHand animation using the Blend tool is included in Chapter 25 of this book.

Uses for the Blend Tool

Consider these tips for using the Blend tool:

- Use a spiral path and a blended ellipse to create a spiraling conch shell. Use Blend to Path, and adjust the components as required.

- Create parts of a fantasy machine with the Blend operator, and connect the pieces together.

- Blend one letter into another. Ungroup the results, and use each element as a frame in an animation.

Creating Multimember Blends

Blends can have more than two initial characters (or "keyframes" if you prefer). Blends can have as many initial nodes as your project needs, or that your RAM can handle. The only stipulation is that the initial paths chosen as the blend nodes must have a good degree of similarity. They must all have strokes and fills of the same type. For example, you cannot have one member with a gradient linear fill and another in the blend chain with a radial gradient fill. You cannot have one member with a stroke, and another with no stroke. You can, however, have members that each have a radial gradient fill whose center is in a different place. You can have members with strokes of different colors or different widths, as long as they all either do or don't have strokes. The shape of blend members and the number of control points in those shapes may vary. Blends do not work on grouped paths.

Any number of keyframe members can participate in a blend chain, as long as the above conditions are observed. Figure 6-8 shows some examples of blend operations.

Note: Always have the Object Inspector onscreen when you create a blend. It contains a control for setting the number of steps (in-betweens) in the blend chain. This number always defaults to 25, unless it is set otherwise in the preferences. The more steps in a blend chain (up to 256 are allowed), the smoother the resulting graphic. Try using the 3D Rotate tool on separate keyframe members of a blend. You can create very interesting perspective shapes by using this small alteration.

Figure 6-8: Blends can be smooth if Stroke is turned off, or with Strokes on can generate a pen and ink look.

Joining a Blend to a Path

This is one of the most elegant blend operations, pushing your creative blends to the limit. Create a blend and then create a path. Select both the blend and the path. Choose Modify | Combine | Join Blend to Path. Your blend follows the shape of the selected path. Use this feature to create intricate parts of a larger structure, in compositions that emphasize both mechanical and organic topics (see Figure 6-9).

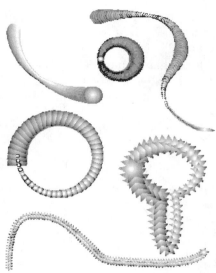

Figure 6-9: Blends that are joined to paths greatly increase the variety of blended objects that you can create in FreeHand.

Set Note Tool

Use the Set Note tool to attach labels or notes to objects. This is an important feature for including project notes, especially when your document is part of a group design project, and you want to relate conceptual data to a co-designer. To use the Set Note tool:

1. Select an object.

2. Choose Xtras I Other I Set Note, or click on the Set Note icon in the Operations palette.

3. Enter a name in the Object Name field and a note.

Names can have up to 26 characters. Notes can contain up to 254 characters. If multiple objects are selected and Set Note is applied, the name and note entered attaches to each of the selected objects. To view notes, select the object and choose the Set Note Xtra.

Tip

Use Set Note with Find & Replace Graphics to search for objects with names to find and replace several objects or object attributes.

Envelope Tool

Envelope effects are sometimes known as "rubber sheet effects." This is because of how they work. Envelope effects place control points around a selection, and allow you to push and pull on the control points to reshape the selection. FreeHand's Envelope operator does just that, but it lacks options. You could just as well generate more control points around the selection on the main screen, and do what is needed without calling up this operator.

For more variable Envelope warping, investigate the VectorShape operator in the VectorTools FreeHand plug-in application from Extensis Corporation (see Figure 6-10). See Appendix C for a full description of VectorTools.

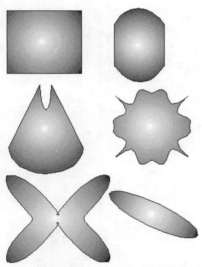

Figure 6-10: The rectangle on the upper left was used as the basic shape to generate all of these other shapes with the VectorTools VectorShape FreeHand plug-in from Extensis. See Appendix C.

Add Points Tool

The more control points a path has, the more opportunity for smoothly altering its shape. The Add Points tool is the opposite of the Simplify tool. A good way to work when you need extra control points is to click on Add Points as many times as you need to (though more than three clicks is seldom required). After altering the selected shape, use the Simplify operator to remove the extra control points, without affecting the new shape in the least.

Creating Charts From FreeHand Graphics

 The Chart tool is used to create and edit charts and create or remove pictographs from existing charts (see Figure 6-11).

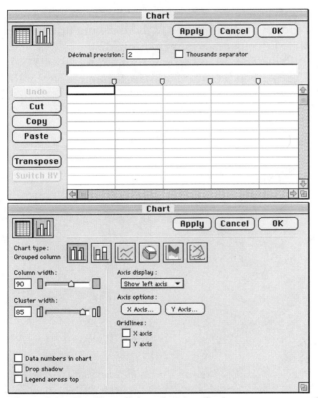

Figure 6-11: The Chart dialog, showing the data entry areas at the top and the style component area at the bottom.

Creating & Editing Charts

Instead of having to create your charts in an external application, FreeHand gives you all of the necessary tools to create and edit customized charts. You can even modify your charts later on using any of FreeHand's Xtra Tools or operators to add special graphics effects.

To create a chart:

1. Click on Chart tool in the Xtra Tools palette.

2. Click and drag a marquee. This positions and sizes the chart and opens the Chart dialog.

3. Enter data in the Chart dialog and select the type of chart.

4. Click OK. The chart is rendered to the screen.

You can edit the chart by selecting the chart and double-clicking the Chart tool in the Xtra Tools panel. Use the Chart dialog that is displayed to edit the chart. The chart can be enlarged, scaled, rotated, or moved and still be edited as a chart. Once ungrouped, however, the chart permanently becomes a graphic and you can no longer edit it using the Chart tool. A chart as a graphic does have advantages, however, if you need to make graphic modifications.

Adding Chart Pictographs

Grouped and stacked column charts can have pictographic elements (see Figure 6-12). A pictograph is your own symbolic graphic, used to replace the standard color bars in the chart. A chart concerning finances, for example, might show stacked coins representing the data.

1. Select and copy, or import, any object.

2. Select one of the columns in the chart.

3. Choose Xtras | Chart | Pictograph. The Pictograph dialog appears.

4. Click Paste In, and the copied object appears in the preview area.

5. Check Repeating to cause the columns to be composed of stacked copies of the object.

    Partial objects are used to represent values that are not whole increments. Leave Repeating unchecked to cause the object to appear as one object, scaled to fill the space occupied by the column.

6. Copy Out returns the object to the clipboard.

Tip

Take advantage of the Chart Pictograph function to personalize charts you include in your FreeHand documents. Use gradients for color or symbols that represent what your data is about.

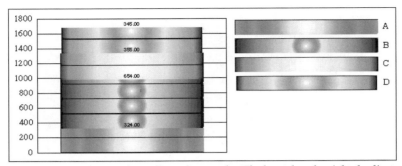

Figure 6-12: A chart with gradient pictographs. The legend at the right duplicates the pictograph content as a key to understanding the data.

Moving On

In this chapter, we have investigated the use of the Xtra Tools and Operators palettes and have explored the styles and chart creation. In the next chapter, we will look at how to work with textures and bitmaps in FreeHand.

7

Working With Textures & Bitmaps

FreeHand has all of the necessary tools to aid you in creating an infinite variety of textures. In the digital arts, the term "texture" refers to a graphic pattern used to enhance and support other elements in the design. In vector design, textures are used as backdrops for entire pages, and sometimes as smaller interesting spot art that supports the concept or theme of the FreeHand project. In Web page design, textures are most often used as a Web page background, and Web textures commonly repeat, or tile, to the page. In 3D applications, textures are translated into materials that are wrapped on 3D objects. This gives the objects more believability and character. Using FreeHand, you can develop textures for FreeHand projects, for Web page backgrounds, and for materials intended for 3D objects in Extreme 3D. In this chapter, we will explore all of FreeHand's texturing capabilities, including the creation of vector and bitmap composites, and also the application of textures to selected text blocks.

To create textures in FreeHand, you must be able to use a number of tools and processes. Some will be more important than others in specific projects and design challenges. If your experience with FreeHand's tool options and how they function needs to be enhanced, please read or re-read Chapter 2, Chapter 3, Chapter 5, and Chapter 6 in this book. The material that follows in this chapter will assume that you are experienced with FreeHand's tool, or that you have read, worked through, and understood the listed chapters.

Texture Types in FreeHand

FreeHand is a vector drawing application, so the primary texture types FreeHand addresses are textures created with its drawing tools, operators, Xtras, and utilities. FreeHand also allows you to place and augment bitmap art, and even to reconfigure that art with Photoshop-compatible filters. This allows you to create and augment interesting bitmap textures as well.

In the arts, a "composite" is a piece of work that is created by combining a variety of items, each of which has its own individual personality. Traditionally, the two main areas of composite art have been the collage and the montage. The collage is defined as a work that can combine any number and variety of 2D media and 3D elements. The montage is defined more narrowly as a composite of photographic images. Neither of these terms holds completely when it comes to developing composite artwork with the computer, because a computer art composite may contain photographic, graphic, and digitally sculpted 3D elements. Until the theorists and academicians work out a new term for general use, we will stick with the term composite for now.

Vector Composites

A vector composite is a piece of FreeHand art whose elements are created completely with FreeHand's vector drawing tools, or whose elements are all vector art imported from another source (like a library of vector images). Sometimes, bitmapped images that have been translated to vector art are also used in a vector composite (see the section on the Trace tool at the end of this chapter).

In order to develop vector composited art in FreeHand, you need to master all of FreeHand's options, especially the following tools and techniques:

- Creating shapes and adjusting their attributes. This means you should also have a good working knowledge of how the Object Inspector works on shapes.

- Using the Envelope tool, or an external plug-in envelope function. This allows you to easily reform shapes.

- Add Points and Simplify tool. This allows you to control the modification of shapes more effectively.

- The Transparency tool. This is a vital operation when using large shape blocks to form a texture with personality.

- The Text | Convert to Paths function. If your texture is to contain alphanumeric elements, you should be well aware of the functionality of this step.

- Aligning and arranging selections in the stack. Absolutely required in order to compose the final texture art.

- Working with tiled fills. This operation in the Fill Inspector is essential for the development of a wide range of textures.

- Saving your work out to various file formats. A FreeHand composition may remain a FreeHand composition when displayed by various means, and it might require a translation to another format. You should know when to make this decision, and how to make it happen.

- Other tools and techniques as required. Obviously, this is a catch-all phrase. It means the more you know about FreeHand, the more creative options you'll have, and the happier your design life will be.

Tiled Vector Composites

Tiling is one of FreeHand's strongest options. Tiling is accomplished with the controls in the Tiled option in the Fill Inspector (Window | Inspectors | Fill). Simply select or import a graphic, and copy it to the clipboard. Deselect it, and open the Tiled option from the list in the Fill Inspector. Click on "Paste in," which places the graphic you copied onto the preview window. Below are controls that allow you to alter the graphics angle, scale (X and Y separately by percentage), and offset (X and Y separately by pixels). Do a test render with a primitive closed shape to see the tiles. Adjust the controls as needed, and you're ready to tile a closed shape.

Tip

Make sure you deselect the original object before using the Paste In command, or you may get an error telling you that you can't tile an object into itself.

Figure 7-1: The Tiled option in the Fill Inspector.

Here are some tips for working with tiles:

- Try removing the stroke from rectangular tiles if they don't seem to draw the way you would like. This can make them butt up against each other better.

- If you resize and/or rotate the tile in the Fill Inspector, use the Copy Out command to recopy it to the clipboard and make the reconfigured tile available for other purposes.

- You may have to adjust the offset of the tiles or the scale for each new object you draw. Different shapes require specific tiling parameters.

- Be careful that your tiles don't get so complex that they interfere with the text and graphics placed over them.

- Remember that tiles copied from the FreeHand page are transparent where the background shows through. This allows you to place a tiled surface over a multicolored background, or layer the same tile with different sizes or colors over itself.

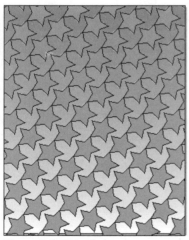

Figure 7-2: This tiled texture was created by placing the tiled star over a gradient backdrop, layering both together as a composite.

Tip

You cannot use bitmaps as tiled components.

Use tiled textures for any texture project need, but especially for Web page backgrounds. They can work as material textures for some 3D purposes, with the strongest being tiled ground planes. If they're not overly busy (complex), they can be used for printed page backdrops as well.

Non-Tiled Vector Composites

Tiled graphics are perfect symmetries. That is their beauty, but it may also be the very aspect that makes them unsuitable for specific purposes. Sometimes, mechanical perfection is the wrong message for a specific project theme. When that is the case, it's better to consider other texture options.

One option might be to take a graphic and change it each time it's pasted down, so that a more random look is achieved.

Figure 7-3: A more random look is achieved when you alter the graphic on a backdrop each time you paste a clone in place. Larger graphics can be used as mortises (frames) for text blocks.

Transparencies as Textured Backgrounds

When simple is better, try developing a background that consists of multi-colored rectangles that overlap. Select each overlapping pair in turn, and use the Transparency tool with a setting of 85 percent to make the overlaps transparent. This will give you more colors. The effect can be stunning without intruding on the copy placed over the texture. This texture can also be saved out and applied in a 3D environment to a ground plane, or even to simulate a stained glass window.

Figure 7-4: Transparent rectangles provide a basic but useful background texture option.

Bitmap Composites

Bitmap composites are usually associated with bitmap painting applications, like xRes or Photoshop. FreeHand, however, is also an excellent environment for creating bitmap composites, since you can crop and frame the bitmaps and even apply filter effects inside of FreeHand. A bitmap composite consists mainly of bitmap components, although graphic frames and other supporting elements may also be vector related.

Tiled Bitmap Components

Though you can't use the Tiled option in the Fill Inspector (Window | Inspectors | Fill) to incorporate bitmaps, you can tile them by hand. All that's required is a knowledge of the cloning, grouping, and vector tiling processes in FreeHand.

1. Import and place two bitmapped graphics. Size them so the two can be used horizontally across the page. Group them.

2. Clone the group and move the clones below the originals. Repeat this process until the bitmaps fill the page.

3. Draw a spiral one-eighth the width of the page, set its stroke to 6 points, and color it white (the page color). Set its fill to white as well. Copy it to the clipboard.

4. Use the Tiled Fill Inspector to develop a tiled fill from the spiral. Draw a rectangle that uses the spiral tiled fill over the bitmapped tiles, muting them out.

Tip

Though we have suggested a spiral, you can explore any shape you like to cover and mute the bitmaps.

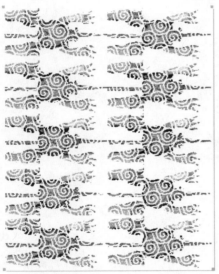

Figure 7-5: The tiled bitmap has been covered with a tiled vector spiral whose fill and stroke are the same color as the page.

Non-Symmetrical Tiles of Bitmap Composites

This is the easiest way to use bitmaps. Just import a bitmap, clone it as needed, and resize each of the clones. Don't worry about proportionate resizing. Squash some on the horizontal, and others vertically. The idea is to wind up with one image in a variety of altered shapes. It would be your choice whether to use a tiled screen over these images.

Tip

If you use a logo bitmap as the graphic in this example, you can create very interesting corporate logo backgrounds for your Web pages.

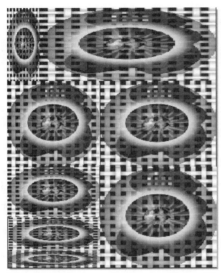

Figure 7-6: A composite screen with one bitmap cloned and resized.

Creating Bitmap Line-Screens

The problem with using bitmaps as a textured background is that they are often too attractive, and dominate the page, making it hard to look at other content. The solution is to mute them. Do the following to create a line-screen to mute a bitmap you have imported and placed on the page.

1. Draw a filled horizontal shape with the Calligraphic Pen tool about an inch long. Don't make it too straight, but curve it. Set the stroke to None and make the fill a light blue.

2. Rotate it 45 degrees to the left. Copy it to the clipboard.

3. Use the shape as a tile, adjusting its size and rotation as you like.

4. Draw a rectangle over the bitmap. Notice that the tiled pattern mutes the bitmap's contents, but still allows enough of it to be seen to evoke a degree of interest.

Tip

This technique works best when the bitmap has highly defined content and large identifiable elements. To mute the underlying bitmap further, layer another screen over the first with a different sized tile.

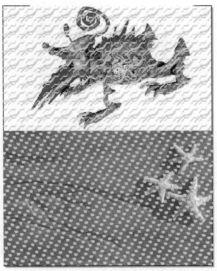

Figure 7-7: Screens mute bitmap content without making them completely indecipherable. The top bitmap is overlayed with two differently sized tiles.

Translating Bitmaps Into Vectors Using the Trace Tool

The FreeHand Trace tool transforms a bitmap into a vector graphic. Complex bitmaps take time to translate, and bitmaps that are large may severely tax your system at translation time. The positive aspects of bitmap to vector translation include less disk space needed to store the graphic and being able to use all of the vector modification tools to reconfigure the graphic. On the downside is the fact that complex bitmaps may not appear in the same way as vector drawings as they did as bitmaps; color loss or color modifications are the most common problems. Each bitmap is a separate case, and only experience and exploration will give you the mastery and confidence you need to use this tool effectively.

The Trace tool is very straightforward. Import a bitmap, select the Trace tool, and draw a rectangle around the portion of the image that you need to translate into a vector drawing. That's it. Wait for the tool to do its work, and delete the bitmap. Of course, you can always move the bitmap to the side if you need it for further reference.

When the vector tracing is complete, there's still one more task to do . . . simplify. The Simplify operator attempts to maintain the object shape while lessening the number of overall control points. This makes it display quicker and print faster, but may also alter the content. Simplifying is a "lossy" process. When you select the new vector object and click on Simplify, its settings dialog appears. The dialog has one slider, with a range of 0 to 10 in hundredths. Higher values tend to reshape the selected shape more radically. A good range to explore is 3 to 5 in most cases. Any vector graphic or path can be simplified.

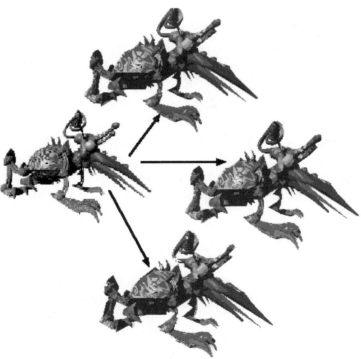

Figure 7-8: The original bitmap is the figure on the left. Different Simplify settings were applied to test the results. The top translated vector image has 0 simplification, the middle image a setting of 3, and the last image a setting of 10 (maximum).

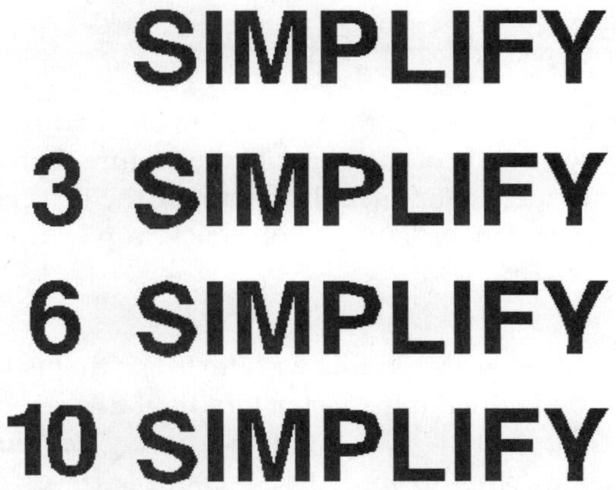

SIMPLIFY

3 SIMPLIFY

6 SIMPLIFY

10 SIMPLIFY

Figure 7-9: Simplify can also be used on text converted to paths. The top line is the original text, while below are path-converted examples showing the effect of the Simplify tool at settings of 3, 6, and 10 respectively. Curved letters show the extent of the effect.

If you need to simplify components of the vector translation and not the whole image, select the components before applying the Simplify tool (Option-Select on the Mac or Alt-Select in Windows). If you use the Trace tool on a block of unconverted text, it will be immediately converted and ungrouped at the same time, saving you the ungrouping operation.

Using Textures in Projects

Using textures in your FreeHand work is the rule rather than the exception. When you look at all the variable options that FreeHand offers for texture design, placement, and modification, it is difficult not to use textures in some part of your FreeHand projects. Textured headlines, for instance, can speak more clearly about the context of your page than color or gradients alone can manage. Of course, a FreeHand project that includes too many different textures can also detract from the message or content of a page, and in some cases turn readers and viewers away.

In the following section, we'll explore the use of textures as a part of a text block, and also as a background for other page elements. There is no ultimate rule for integrating textures in any specific project, except that the more radical the effect or look you're using, the more space it needs to be appreciated. A page can stand a dozen subtle effects, but one or two radical graphic approaches is usually the limit.

Text Blocks

Textures can enhance text in three ways: the text can be filled with a texture, making it appear as if it were made of the material the texture represents (more common with wood, metal, and metallic textures), the text can sit on a textured backdrop, or the text can be "cut out" of a backdrop texture.

Texture as a Fill

There are two main ways to use textured fills with text. The first is to design a fill with the Gradient option in the Fill Inspector. Gradient fills, especially those that use dark and light variants of a single hue (gray, gold, blue, copper, orange) are common when it comes to emulating metallic surfaces. If you add some rotation to the gradient fill, the metallic character is emphasized.

Figure 7-10: A gradient-filled texture used on text can appear metallic.

The second method is to use a tiled texture inside of the letters. This gives the letters the same personality that the tiled texture invokes.

Figure 7-11: The text block can be a target of tiled texturing.

Texture as a Backdrop

A texture, bitmap, or vector can be used as a backdrop for text. The only stipulation to keep in mind is that the text has to be read, so make the text pop out of the backdrop. This can be done by altering the color of the stroke or the entire text block. Sometimes, adding a drop shadow to the text does the trick. The only hard and fast rule is to make the text readable.

Figure 7-12: Textured backdrops add interest, especially to headline text. Sometimes, readability is enhanced if you hang the text out of the background a bit.

Text Cut-Outs

You can literally cut the text out of a backdrop by using the Punch tool, or you can fill the text with the page color and give it a black stroke to make it look as though it's cut out.

Tip

Use of the Punch tool requires that the text (the top object) not be a group. If it is, you will have to ungroup the text and do the punch letter by letter.

Figure 7-13: The text can be punched out of the backdrop.

Printed Page Textured Backgrounds

Using FreeHand to create textured backgrounds for print media relies on your capabilities as a designer and how you craft a total project. Other than the restrictions placed upon you by budget (for color printing as an example), by your client (for example, hates the color red), or by your own designer's personality, textured backgrounds for print media can vary as widely as the sky. All of the techniques recounted here can apply, and each can be varied to suit your specific project.

Web Page Textured Background Constraints

Web page design is another matter. Until new broadcast and Internet bandwidth possibilities emerge (and many will in the first quarter of the next century), Web pages have limitations in resolution and palette requirements. See the chapter in this book on color and design, and especially all of the data on Web design. Web browsers have palette requirements that place restrictions on the design of Web pages. The safest bet is to keep a copy of the Netscape palette on hand, and use it as a color format when you design your Web work. A copy of the Netscape palette ships with FreeHand. Web page backgrounds are video media backgrounds, so a knowledge of what video displays require is important. Keep your colors a little less hot by toning them down from a 100 percent saturation (use a 90 percent saturation component). Other than that, surf the Web and take notes on what you like and what you dislike, and use that as an initial guide for your designs.

External 3D Object Maps

If you plan to use FreeHand to design textures that can be used as material components for your Extreme 3D work or textures that can be used as 3D backdrops and/or as object textures, explore how they translate to 3D before getting involved too deeply in a 3D project. A texture that looks good in 2D on the printed page or even on the Web may be less than impressive when seen as a component of a 3D environment. Get to know your 3D application and how it handles textures, and what options are involved. Extreme 3D users should read everything in this book, and work through all of the tutorials that deal with assigning and editing materials in Extreme 3D before designing texture maps for Extreme 3D projects.

Moving On

In this chapter, we have explored how textures can be created and applied in FreeHand, how to incorporate and modify bitmap textures, and also how to use the Trace tool to convert bitmaps to vectors. In the next chapter, we will look at the uses for different file formats in FreeHand.

8

Importing, Exporting & Saving Files

F ile formats abound, with several hundred in existence at this point. FreeHand supports a distinct set of file formats, each one with a dedicated purpose and with specific attributes. The file formats addressed by FreeHand are the most common ones used when creating and saving your FreeHand projects for use in print media, multimedia applications, and Web projects. It is important that you understand what file formats to use for a specific task. In this chapter, we will also look at the differences between opening a file and importing it, and between saving and exporting.

Graphic File Formats

It is important for you to know about the file formats that FreeHand addresses, so that you can make the best choice in accordance with your project and needs. The following sections discuss which file format you should consider and why you should care about any specific format.

Save/Save As

If you use the Save or Save As command (File | Save or File | Save As), FreeHand offers only three options: FreeHand Document, FreeHand Template, and Editable EPS.

Tip

The Save As command is used when you save the document for the first time, or if you have reason to save it under a new name to another location. The Save command is used when you are updating the presently named file.

- **FreeHand Document**. Use this save option if you want to store all of the panel settings along with all of the other elements, both on the FreeHand page and outside of it. This allows you to send the FreeHand document to a service bureau, or to open it again when it needs to be revised or updated.

- **FreeHand Template**. Use this option when you have designed a document consisting of areas for text and graphics placement rather than content. This allows you to design mechanicals for such projects as monthly newsletters, brochures, and other tasks that have to be regularly updated while using the same general layout and look.

- **Editable EPS**. An editable EPS is a special EPS format that can be opened and edited in FreeHand, and then saved as EPS without exporting again. An editable EPS file can also be modified in xRes, and includes the entire FreeHand document rather than just a selected element.

DXF

FreeHand can only import DXF images. DXF is a two-dimensional vector graphic file exchange format used to transfer files between 3D editing applications, or between 3D editing applications and vector drawing applications. Most 3D editing applications, including Macromedia's Extreme 3D, support DXF format.

BMP

FreeHand can import and export BMP images. BMP is the Windows standard format for bitmap graphics. BMP is capable of supporting an alpha channel. To set BMP-specific options, click More in the Bitmap Export Defaults dialog when exporting a BMP. The BMP export options include:

- **8-bit Uncompressed**. Check to export BMP images in 256 colors without any compression.

- **8-bit Compressed**. Check to export BMP images in 256 colors and compress the BMP on export.
- **16-bit**. Check to export BMP images in thousands of colors.
- **24-bit**. Check to export BMP images in over 16 million colors.
- **32-bit w/Alpha**. Check to export BMP images in over 16 million colors and include an alpha channel.

Tip

To set resolution and anti-aliasing when exporting, click Options in the Export dialog to open the Bitmap Export Defaults dialog.

EPS

FreeHand can import and export EPS graphics. EPS is a format that is ideal for use in professional printing. An EPS can contain vector graphics, bitmap images, or both. EPS is the best file format for preserving prepress-ready color.

Tip

Multiple Pages: When you choose an EPS format, each page exports as a separate EPS file. Specify export of all pages or a range of pages in the Export dialog.

Editable EPS is a special EPS format that can be opened and edited in FreeHand, and then saved as EPS without exporting again. To save an editable EPS, check Include FreeHand document in EPS when exporting.

EPS Export Types
FreeHand exports four types of EPS file formats:

- **Generic EPS**. This is a basic EPS format with no preview attached.
- **Macintosh EPS**. This is an EPS with a PICT preview attached.
- **MS-DOS EPS**. This is an EPS with an embedded TIFF preview for use on Windows-based computers.
- **Photoshop EPS**. This is the best EPS format for opening or importing into Photoshop.

GIF

FreeHand can import and export GIF files. GIF (Graphics Interchange Format) is a bitmap format developed by CompuServe to easily transfer graphic files online. GIF is an 8-bit (256 color) format that uses LZW compression to make bitmap files smaller—about half of their original size. The GIF format uses the 256 most representative colors for the image so that the final images have small file sizes, but good image quality.

GIF images are also capable of having one of its colors defined as transparent, so that when the GIF is placed over another image, either online or in a bitmap editing application, the bottom image is seen through areas defined as transparent. In FreeHand, this transparency is similar to using an "alpha channel" (a separate, 256 gray-levels channel used for image masking). GIF images may contain completely transparent or completely opaque areas; partial transparency is not supported. Because of its small size, high quality, and ability to include transparency, GIF is an ideal format for use in the development of web pages.

FreeHand GIF Export Options

To set resolution and anti-aliasing when exporting, click Options in the Export dialog to open the Bitmap Export Defaults dialog. To set GIF-specific options, click More in the Bitmap Export Defaults dialog, when GIF is selected as the export type.

- **Interlaced GIF**. Check to create an interlaced GIF. Interlaced GIF images redraw progressively on screen by drawing every other line of pixels and then filling in the gaps. Use Interlaced GIF images on Web pages for faster display since there is less initial data to transfer before part of the image appears.

- **Transparent GIF**. Check to create transparency in the exported GIF based on the color found in the top left corner of the GIF file.

HPGL

FreeHand can import and edit HPGL graphics. Hewlett-Packard Graphics Language, or HPGL, is a vector graphic language used to print to plotters.

JPEG

FreeHand imports and exports JPEGs. JPEG (Joint Photographic Experts Group) is a highly compressible bitmap graphic format. It is used most often in non-print media work, since it always manages to "lose" a few pixels from the original (it is called a "lossy" format). JPEG compression ratios are decided at the time you export to the format, presenting you with a slider that determines compression versus quality. Higher compression settings produce lower-quality images, and lower compression produces higher quality with larger file sizes. For multimedia use, it's best to create JPEG files that are higher quality with less compression. For Web use (at the present), lower quality images (a compression ratio of around 70 percent) work fine.

To set resolution and anti-aliasing when exporting, click Options in the Export dialog to open the Bitmap Export Defaults dialog. To set JPEG-specific options, click More in the Bitmap Export Defaults dialog. Configure the settings as follows:

- **Image Quality**. Enter the percentage of quality to maintain when exporting as JPEG. Higher numbers create a better image with less compression. Lower numbers create rougher images with more compression.

- **Progressive JPEG**. Check to save as a Progressive JPEG, a format that is optimized for transfer speed. It is ideal for use in creating Web pages. Progressive JPEGs load a blocky, extremely low-resolution image at first, and then gradually "focus."

PICT (Mac only)

FreeHand imports and exports PICT files (Mac only). PICT is a Macintosh format that can include both bitmap and vector graphics. When exporting a PICT from the Export menu, FreeHand exports your image as an object-oriented (vector) PICT at 72 dpi. To rasterize your FreeHand image as a bitmap-based PICT, use FreeHand's Create PICT Xtra, found in Xtras | Create.

PNG

FreeHand can import and export PNG images. PNG is a bitmap graphic format designed to offer lossless, well-compressed storage of bitmap graphics for display and transfer on the Web. PNG can contain an alpha channel. To set resolution and anti-aliasing when exporting, click Options in the Export dialog to open the Bitmap Export Defaults dialog. To set PNG-specific options, click More in the Bitmap Export Defaults dialog, when exporting a PNG. PNG Export Options include:

- **8-bit**. Check to export PNG images in 256 colors.
- **16-bit**. Check to export PNG images in thousands of colors.
- **24-bit**. Check to export PNG images in over 16 million colors.
- **32-bit w/Alpha**. Check to export PNG images in over 16 million colors and include an alpha channel.
- **48- or 64-bit**. Check to export PNG images in 48- or 64-bit color depth, yielding an image with an extremely high number of colors.
- **Interlaced PNG**. Check to create an interlaced PNG. Interlaced PNG images redraw progressively on screen by drawing every other line of pixels and then filling the gaps.

Targa

FreeHand can import and export Targa images. Targa is a bitmap graphic format developed by Truevision, Inc., and it is widely used in professional video editing. Targa can support 16-bit, 24-bit, and 32-bit color and can contain an alpha channel. To set resolution and anti-aliasing when exporting, click Options in the Export dialog to open the Bitmap Export Defaults dialog. To set Targa-specific options, click More in the Bitmap Export Defaults dialog when exporting a Targa image. Targa export options include:

- **8-bit**. Check to export Targa images in 256 colors.
- **16-bit**. Check to export Targa images in thousands of colors.
- **24-bit**. Check to export Targa images in over 16 million colors.
- **32-bit w/Alpha**. Check to export Targa images in over 16 million colors, and include an alpha channel.
- **Compression**. Check to compress Targa images upon export.

TIFF

FreeHand can import and export TIFF images and can transform imported TIFF images. TIFF (Tagged Image File Format) is a bitmap graphic format widely used in commercial printing. When you export an object or document as a TIFF image, FreeHand rasterizes the FreeHand document. Use the Bitmap

Export Defaults dialog to set options. To set TIFF-specific options, click the More button in the Bitmap Export Defaults while exporting as a TIFF. The TIFF specific options are:

- **8-bit**. Check to export TIFF images in 8-bit color.
- **24-bit**. Check to export TIFF images in 24-bit color.
- **32-bit with Alpha**. Check to export TIFF images in 32-bit color with an alpha channel.

xRes (LRG)

FreeHand can import and export LRG images and can transform imported LRG images. xRes LRG is a bitmap graphic format for quickly opening and editing large bitmap files in Macromedia xRes. Uncheck the High Resolution Image Display checkbox in the Redraw | Preferences to greatly increase redraw speed when using LRG files. This also applies to TIFF files.

Tip

Do not embed LRG images when importing, but link them instead. Since LRG images tend to have very large file sizes, embedding them can cause FreeHand to redraw very slowly, and may even cause system crashes.

Click More in the Bitmap Export Defaults dialog to set LRG-specific export settings:

- **24-bit**. Check to export 24-bit color.
- **32-bit with Alpha**. Check to export LRG images in 32-bit color with an alpha channel.

The Macromedia Information Exchange (MIX)

MIX Xtras enable FreeHand and other Macromedia applications to import and export additional file formats. Add new MIX Xtras to FreeHand as they are developed. Always check the Macromedia Web site for the latest developments.

The MIX Xtras that ship with FreeHand are automatically installed when you install FreeHand. To install new MIX Xtras, place them in the System\Macromedia\Xtras folder. The present MIX formats include: BMP, GIF, JPEG, Photoshop 3.0, PNG, Targa (TGA), TIFF, and xRes LRG.

Importing Files

The Import command imports a graphic file created from another application or from an earlier version of FreeHand.

To import a file, choose File | Import and simply find and select the file to import, and click Open. When importing HPGL and DXF graphics, FreeHand displays an additional dialog for setting format-specific options. Use the import cursor to position the upper left corner of the graphic and click the mouse button, and the object imports at its default size. You can also click the mouse button and drag the import cursor to scale the graphic as you place it.

You can also convert an editable EPS when imported. Just check this option in the Import dialog. When checked, FreeHand converts imported EPS files to paths if the EPS file contains vector graphic information. For DXF Import, you may want to select the Import Invisible Block Attributes box. When checked, DXF objects with invisible stroke and fill attributes are imported. White strokes are converted to black if the Convert White Strokes to Black option is checked. If you check Convert White Fills to Black, the fill color is converted from white to black.

Managing Links

Select Edit | Links Management to open the Links Management dialog to make changes to the way imported graphics behave. The Links Management dialog describes the file name of the linked or embedded graphic, and displays the path location of the selected graphic. You can also use the Links function to search for missing links, graphics that have been moved from the location they were at when used in a FreeHand document. FreeHand can be configured to automatically search a folder and its subfolders for the missing linked graphics.

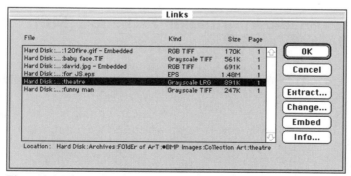

Figure 8-1: The Links Management dialog allows you to re-establish document links.

How to Use the Links Management Dialog

Bring up the FreeHand document that has elements linked to it that have been moved to other disk locations (missing links). Open the Links Management dialog (Edit | Links Management).

The Links Management dialog lists all of the graphics files on the page of the document you are looking at: its name, file format, size, and the FreeHand document page it is embedded on. The Location data at the bottom of the dialog displays the present location of the graphic. Do one or more of the following:

- Click on Extract to extract an embedded graphic to a file and create a link to the new file.

- Click on Change to open the Change dialog and re-establish a broken link or change the link.

- Click on Embed to embed the selected, linked graphic.

- Click on Info to display the selected graphic's name, location, size, type, and modification date, as well as the preview (if available).

Importing a PDF document

FreeHand can open documents saved in the Adobe PDF (Portable Document Format) format, the standard developed by Adobe for use by its Acrobat line of products. For more information on the capabilities and limitations of the PDF, consult the Adobe Acrobat product specifications.

To open a PDF document, select File | Open. Multipage PDF documents open in FreeHand as multipage documents. Each page has the same size and orientation as the original PDF document. PDF Import does not provide automatic font substitution. If a font specified in the PDF file is not present on your system, FreeHand's Missing Font dialog appears and asks you to select replacement fonts.

Supported Fonts

FreeHand's PDF Import Xtra supports all font formats allowed by the PDF format. These include PostScript Type 1, PostScript Type 3, and TrueType fonts. FreeHand displays any font in a PDF document if that font is installed on your system. For more information about the types of fonts PDF supports, please consult the Adobe Acrobat documentation.

PDF creation tools sometimes output PDF documents that separate single or partial lines of text according to their differing font attributes. When FreeHand opens a PDF file, the document may contain a large number of individual text boxes. This is a normal occurrence resulting from the manner in which the PDF creation tool structured the original PDF document. If you want to, you can combine these individual text blocks in FreeHand using traditional text manipulation methods.

Supported Graphics

The PDF format supports RGB, grayscale, and monochrome bitmaps. FreeHand can modify these bitmap images just like any placed or imported bitmap image. Depending on the structure of the original PDF document, an entire page may appear as a single object with the graphic elements pasted inside. Select the page with the Selection Arrow and choose Edit | Cut Contents to release the graphic elements. EPS images in a PDF document open as editable objects.

Exporting Files

When Save File Thumbnails is checked, FreeHand documents are saved with a preview embedded. This thumbnail preview is displayed in the Open, Import, or Links Info dialogs. These are Export dialog options:

- **Convert PICT Patterns to Grays**. When this item is checked, a Pattern fill or line converts to a PostScript tint that approximates the darkness of the original PICT pattern.

- **Export EPS with Color Previews**. When this is checked, FreeHand includes a color bitmap preview when exporting an EPS graphic. That preview is used as a low-resolution placeholder when that EPS is placed back into FreeHand or into another application.

- **Bitmap Export**. This sets default options for exporting in bitmap formats.

- **Bitmap PICT Previews**. When checked, FreeHand saves Adobe Fetch previews in bitmap PICT format rather than vector PICT format. Use this option for large FreeHand files to cut down the file size of exported or saved FreeHand files with a Fetch preview.

- **Include Fetch Preview**. When checked, FreeHand includes an Adobe Fetch preview when you save or export the document. Bitmap Fetch preview size allows you to adjust by percentage the size of the Adobe Fetch preview that is exported or saved with a FreeHand document.

Using Alpha Channels

Use alpha channels to export bitmap images with complex masking and transparency for use in bitmap editing applications. An alpha channel is a layer of a graphic that defines which areas of the graphic are transparent and which areas of the graphic are opaque. Using alpha channels, you can quickly define an outline or edge of an object created in FreeHand. This is especially useful if you are creating a graphic for a Web page, or for use in multimedia or video where you want to see a background graphic through areas of an image. FreeHand can export the following formats with an alpha channel: xRes LRG (32 bit), TIFF (32 bit), TGA (32 bit), PNG (32 bit), BMP (32 bit).

How to Create an Alpha Channel

When exporting a bitmap format that supports alpha channels, check Include Alpha Channel in the Bitmap Export Defaults dialog to automatically create an alpha channel on export of the selection. This alpha channel is a mask, or outline, of all the objects on the FreeHand page. When the image is opened in an application that supports alpha channels, the edges of objects in the image can be easily defined.

Tip

The formats must be exported as 32-bit to support alpha channels. Access bit depth options by clicking the More button in the Bitmap Export Defaults dialog.

Exporting to a PDF Document

To export to a PDF document, select File | Export and choose PDF as the format. Click Options and select the settings in the PDF Export dialog.

- **JPEG Compression Level (Color Images)**. Available levels of compression are Maximum, High, Medium High, Medium, Medium Low, Low, and None.
- **Image Compression: Grayscale**. Set JPEG compression level for grayscale bitmap images in the exported PDF document. Available levels of compression are Maximum High, Medium High, Medium, Medium Low, Low, and None.

- **Pages: All**. Export all pages in your FreeHand document to a PDF document.

- **Pages: From-To**. Export a range of pages from your FreeHand document to a PDF document. Enter the beginning page of the range in the From box, and the ending page of the range in the To box.

- **Compression**. The compression level of your color and grayscale images greatly affects the file size and the quality of printing for the PDF. Images at higher compression levels create smaller file sizes, but the images print with lower quality. Little or no compression yields larger documents that print with higher quality. When designing a PDF document for print, choose little or no compression. When designing a PDF document for on-screen viewing, choose higher levels of compression. The screen is kinder when it comes to viewing compressed files than the print media are.

Click OK to close the PDF Export dialog, and click OK in the Export dialog.

The PDF format does not support the following in FreeHand:

- A page larger than 3240 x 3240 will be clipped to fit the maximum PDF page size.

- Custom, Textured, and PostScript fills are not supported by the PDF format.

- Custom and PostScript strokes are not supported by the PDF format, nor does the PDF format support arrowheads.

- Alpha channel transparency is not supported by the PDF format.

- The EPS format is not supported by the PDF format. If an EPS has a TIFF preview, FreeHand exports the preview instead of the EPS file.

- Text effects do not export to the PDF format.

- PDF does not support overprinting. Overprinting applied to objects is turned off when exporting to PDF.

- When it finds any incompatible object, the PDF Export Xtra displays a cautionary dialog upon completion of export.

Why & When to Save to Specific File Formats

As we said at the start of this chapter, each graphics file format has a use and a purpose, and each of the graphics file formats that FreeHand addresses should be chosen with an awareness of its purpose and use in mind. Consider using one or more of these formats for the following reasons:

- **DXF**. DXF is the standard format for CAD (Computer Assisted Design) applications, sometimes called drafting programs. If you need to port your FreeHand work to a CAD application, DXF is the best option. The DXF format that FreeHand addresses is sometimes called 2D DXF. There is also a 3D DXF format used in 3D modeling and animation applications. Although FreeHand does not support 3D DXF, you can usually import 2D DXF into a 3D application, where it can be used as the basis for extrusion techniques to create 3D models.

- **BMP**. BMP is the standard for Windows bitmap graphics. It is not as complex a format as TIFF, but is in general use for low-end to medium-end graphics work. Use the BMP format to export your FreeHand work to applications that use BMP graphics.

- **EPS**. EPS is a vector format, and as such is resolution independent. You are usually asked what resolution you would like to have the EPS file appear at by the application you import an EPS graphic into. Use EPS graphics in any application that allows its importation, when you want the graphic to come in at a very high anti-aliased quality.

- **GIF**. As long as the Web remains in its present condition as far as bandwidth capabilities and display options (which will change radically in the next 15 to 25 years), the file formats that address a Web page continue to be GIF and JPEG. GIF is the dominant file format used on the Web. Interlaced GIF displays quickly at a low resolution, then progressively gets clearer. GIF is also a Web animation format. Restrict GIF files to Web uses.

- **HPGL**. If you have an HPGL plotter, or plan to export your FreeHand graphics to an HPGL plotter or another plotter that uses the HPGL language, export your FreeHand documents in HPGL.

- **JPEG**. As long as the Web remains in its present condition as far as bandwidth capabilities and display options (which will change radically in the next fifteen to twenty-five years), the file formats that address a Web page continue to be GIF and JPEG. Use JPEG for anything but high-end print-to-paper tasks. Use it at a lower compression setting when you want a higher quality graphic. Never use it at 50 percent compression or below, unless you are looking for chaotic output.

- **PICT**. As BMP is to Windows, so PICT is to the Mac. It is a lower quality format than TIFF, but serves most medium-end uses as far as multimedia is concerned.

- **PNG**. This is a fast rising format that threatens to challenge GIF for Web dominance, but probably not for some years to come. Use it as an alternate format for Web graphics, since most browsers now support PNG. PNG is capable of much higher-quality images than GIF, and may even supplant JPEG for Web uses.

- **Targa**. If your targeted application uses Targa hardware, write to the Targa format. This format has fallen into disuse in the last few years, but is still a high-end option. Its use is centered upon video and multimedia, and it is included as a standard import format by most bitmap painting applications.

- **TIFF**. Always save your selected FreeHand graphics as a TIFF file, even though you may need to save them to other formats as well. This is especially true when you want to save only selected elements on a page as a bitmap export. TIFF is a very high quality format, meaning that everything about the image is placed in the file. FreeHand TIFF files can be exported at 72, 144, and 300 dpi. Choose TIFF for high-end printing uses.

- **xRes**. If you want to port your image to xRes and edit it, save it in the xRes LRG format. This is best when the image being saved is very large (like a whole page of FreeHand interwoven graphics), since the LRG format lets you edit large images in xRes, which is resolution independent and quicker.

- **PDF**. PDF is a strong commercial file format when it comes to developing documentation for software and transmitting content files over dedicated intranets. How much alteration PDF will go through in the next years is not known at the moment. There is also a PDF plug-in available for browsers that allows you to open PDF files online, so you might want to embed a URL in a page that has a PDF document in your FreeHand Web page.

Moving On

In this chapter we have covered all of the file format issues that FreeHand users should be aware of. This completes Part 1 of the book. The next chapter begins Part 2 of the book, Mastering xRes, starting with xRes installation and preparatory remarks.

Part II

Mastering xRes

9 Setting Up xRes 3

In this chapter, we will detail the installation procedures for xRes. Also listed are the feature improvements xRes 3 offers over previous versions. In the second half of the chapter, we will look at the xRes preferences, and also cover the ways that you can customize the xRes workspace to your liking.

Installing xRes 3

xRes is normally installed when you install FreeHand. Just follow the installation procedure outlined in Chapter 1.

xRes Requirements for Windows Systems

xRes requires installation on a Pentium. If you are installing it on a Windows 95 system, it requires a minimum of 12 MB of RAM (18 MB recommended). For Windows NT 3.51 or higher, you will need a minimum of 16 MB of RAM (32 MB recommended). For Preview, you will need an SVGA monitor. The application requires 10 MB of hard disk space, 500 MB of free disk space for a swap file, and a CD-ROM drive.

   If you are going to use the RipLink feature (described below), you will need another 2 MB of hard disk space and an additional 4 MB of RAM.

xRes Requirements for Macintosh OS Systems

Installation on a Macintosh OS machine requires either a PowerPC with a minimum of 16 MB of RAM (20 MB recommended), or a 68040 system with a minimum of 12 MB of RAM (16 MB recommended). You will also need System 7.5 or later, an 8-bit monitor (24-bit for preview), 10 MB of free hard disk space, 500 MB of free disk space for a swap file, and a CD-ROM drive.

To optimize xRes' performance, set your Disk Cache to 32K, turn virtual memory off, and enable the Modern Memory Manager. All these settings can be adjusted from your Memory control panel.

If you are going to use the RipLink feature (described below), you will need another 3 MB of hard disk space and an additional 5 MB of RAM. You will also need the Helvetica font installed in your System folder.

New Features in xRes 3

xRes 3 offers many advances over previous versions. Note that it does not offer 100 percent compatibility with your Photoshop files in the following data.

- Open Adobe Photoshop files. Opening Photoshop files in xRes preserves the attributes of the original file. Each layer of the Photoshop file translates to an object layer in xRes and maintains the same transparency, position, order, and composition as in Photoshop. The background of each object is also imported, and translated as an alpha channel for transparency and effects manipulation.

xRes does not:

- Open grouped layers from a Photoshop file.
- Open Photoshop files saved in the LAB or multichannel mode.
- Open saved duotone files (it opens them as grayscale images).
- Open files with all of Photoshop's applymodes (it will attempt to convert the applymode to blend, with varying results).
- Acquire EPS files with the new PS RipLink feature acquire interface. Encapsulated PostScript files are automatically rasterized. This establishes another bridge between xRes and FreeHand.
- Create Image maps for the Web. This includes the capacity to define hot spots for URL targeting. New anti-aliasing controls for the Pen, Lasso, and Ellipse tools are provided.
- Display of the object's name in the Channels palette.

- A reset control in the dialog boxes to force them to return to their default settings. Mac OS users access this feature by pressing Option and clicking Reset. Windows users press Alt and click Reset.

- Recall of last four files for opening.

- Drag and drop (Mac OS only). Drag and drop bitmaps to and from other drag and drop–enabled applications.

- xRes as the in-place bitmap editor for FreeHand (xRes is activated when you double-click on a bitmap image in FreeHand). Although you can tell FreeHand to select another bitmap editing application from the list of bitmap programs installed on your system, xRes maintains the deepest correspondence with FreeHand as far as file formats are concerned. For this reason, it is the default bitmap editing application for FreeHand.

xRes Goodies on the Application's CD-ROM

There are a number of value-added extra components on the installation CD-ROM, including the following:

- **Artbeats WebTools 7 MB Demo (Mac OS and Windows).** WebTools is a cooperative effort between Artbeats™ and stat™ media who have combined their libraries of buttons, decorative bars, icons, sounds, and seamless tiles in a CD-ROM for Macintosh and Windows users. The actual product contains over 600 MB of data and also incorporates a TurboSearch™ browser for quick viewing and installation of the files on your hard drive. Graphic formats include GIF, PICT, JPEG, and BMP. Sound formats include AIF, AU, and WAV. The demo contains a collection of bars, buttons, tiles, icons, and extras.

- **FASTedit/LRG (Mac OS only).** A demonstration version of FASTedit/LRG for the Macintosh. Total Integration's FASTedit™/LRG is the latest in the series of award-winning FASTedit Technology™ based products. An Adobe Photoshop plug-in module, FASTedit™/LRG provides a gateway between Photoshop and Macromedia xRes by allowing you to toggle between both applications. You can stop translating LRG files before you bring them into Photoshop because FASTedit/LRG eliminates the need to translate. This Photoshop plug-in module allows you to open portions of LRG files in Photoshop and edit, append, and resave the section back into the original image. When your finished editing, the changes are inserted seamlessly into the original image. Additionally, you can save the FASTedit portion as a working file, re-edit it later (even days later), and, when ready, insert it into the original file.

- **Xaos Tools demos (Mac OS only).** Demos for Terrazo, Paint Alchemy 2, and Typecaster.
- **Extra fonts (Mac OS and Windows).**
- **Palettes (Mac OS only).** Included is a Mac systems palette and the vital Netscape palette for developing xRes Web pages.
- **Chromatica (Mac OS only).** Color translation application.

ChromaPalette™ lets you create xRes color effects in seconds. You can extract all the colors from an image and apply them to another—including fractals and textures. ChromaPalette is the perfect tool for artistic exploration and technical recoloring where a broad color range is necessary. Chroma–Color™ is used for masking, recoloring, and edge blending. You can quickly and easily mask objects within images and recolor complex areas. No need to depend only upon the Magic Wand and Lasso tools. ChromaColor enables you to choose new, realistic color, keeping all the detail and subtle nuance of the original image. This version of Chromatica is a fully functional demo program. You can install the software and explore all its features, but you cannot save your work. To enable the save capabilities, you must buy the software. When you purchase the commercial version, you receive the Chromatica CD-ROM, which also includes:

- 1,000 free Chromatica Palettes
- Fred's Sample Fractals
- Chromatica Electronic Manual
- PhotoNavigator™ 1.0.1 (Extensis Corporation)

INSTALLING CHROMATICA

1. Locate the Chromatica Installer on your xRes CD-ROM and double-click on the installer icon to start the installation.
2. In the main install window, click "Select Folder" and choose your xRes Plug-ins folder.
3. After selecting your Plug-ins folder, click "Install" to continue.
4. You are now ready to enjoy Chromatica. Simply run Macromedia xRes, and choose one of the Chromatica plug-ins from the "Effects" menu.

A Power Macintosh is recommended for optimum performance. Next best is a Macintosh with an FPU. Allocate as much memory as you can to Macromedia xRes. Chromatica is compatible with a wide range of applications that support the Adobe Photoshop plug-in standard including Macromedia xRes. As Chromatica enables complex masking, recoloring, and edge blending tasks, it requires that you work in Direct Mode. Certain xRes tools, such as Magic Wand, are also unavailable in xRes mode for the same reason.

- **Image maps (Windows only).**
- **240 MB of images (Windows only).**

Setting xRes Preferences

The first thing you will want to do in xRes is to set all of the preferences that affect your setup and your project needs. Most of the preference settings, except those that require a new path (like redefining where plug-ins are located), take effect without the need to restart xRes.

General Preferences

The General Preferences dialog (File | Preferences | General) includes the more common items you'll want to access.

Consider the following settings for the options on the General Preferences dialog (see Figure 9-1):

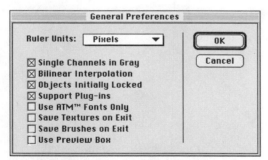

Figure 9-1: The General Preferences dialog.

- **Ruler Units.** Select Inches or Centimeters (whichever you prefer) for desktop publishing work and select Pixels for Web page work.
- **Single Channels in Gray.** Leave this checked. It allows you to see the single channels of a graphic (RGB or CMYK) as a grayscale image, which makes it easier to edit. Turning this option off makes editing difficult because separate channels are seen in the color they represent ("R" for instance in an RGB setup is seen in shades of red).

- **Bilinear Interpolation.** Leave this checked. It allows xRes to do higher-quality image transformations when effects are applied.

- **Objects Initially Locked.** Leave this checked. It locks the background object in a stack so it cannot be accidentally moved.

- **Support Plug-ins.** Yes. Leave it checked. You always want to support plug-in filters. (Why would xRes even ask this question?)

- **Use ATM Fonts Only.** Leave unchecked. You want to have access to all of your fonts.

- **Save Textures on Exit.** Leave unchecked, though your work habits may decide the opposite. I like the textures to be in their default mode when I restart xRes.

- **Save Brushes on Exit.** Leave unchecked for the same reason as above. Each project is different, and requires a new brush approach. The only reason to save either textures or brushes is when you quit to come back to a project the next day, and want to continue where you left off. In that case, just check these items at the end of an xRes session.

- **Use Preview Box.** This should be left checked. It allows you to see and use the Preview box in the Shape Inspector (Window I Inspectors I Shape) dialog (see Figure 9-2).

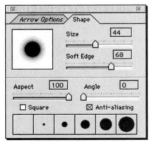

Figure 9-2: The Shape Inspector, showing the Preview box in the upper left.

Memory Preferences

Use the Memory Preferences dialog (File I Preferences I Memory) to set up the location of xRes swap disks, and to set the number of Undo levels you want.

Consider the following settings for the Memory Preferences dialog (see Figure 9-3):

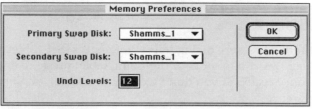

Figure 9-3: The Memory Preferences dialog.

- **Primary and Secondary Swap Disks.** If you have only one hard drive, or just want to use a single drive as your swap disk, then both of these selections will remain the same. If you have more than one drive, set up a different primary and secondary swap disk. xRes needs swap disks to handle file transfers when transformations are taking place.

- **Undo Levels.** Be careful of setting this too high. On average, xRes needs about 20 MB of system memory to initialize Undo operations, and higher settings require more memory (after all, all of those Undo levels have to be stored). If you are working with very large files, decrease the number of Undo levels.

Set Plug-in Folder

The Set Plug-in Folder dialog (File | Preferences | Set Plug-in Folder) allows you to tell xRes where to find the plug-ins it uses. We suggest that you leave the default, the xRes plug-ins folder, because xRes has a number of unique plug-ins available. If you have Photoshop plug-ins you want to use in xRes, then load them into the xRes plug-ins directory. You could also place an alias (Mac OS) or a shortcut (Windows) for your plug-ins into the xRes directory, getting the best of both worlds.

Tip

Do not place Photoshop-only plug-ins or aliases/shortcuts to them into your xRes plug-ins folder. These plug-ins are designed to work in Photoshop only.

Tablet Pressure Preferences

The Minimum Tablet Pressure dialog (File | Preferences | Set Tablet Pressure) (see Figure 9-4) allows you to set your digitizing tablet pressure on a slider-scale ranging from 1 to 255. If you don't work with a tablet, don't bother setting this preference.

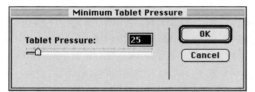

Figure 9-4: The Minimum Tablet Pressure dialog.

Monitor Gamma Preferences

There are color discrepancies between your RGB monitor and a CMYK output device, and between your monitor and RGB film recorders. The Monitor Gamma dialog (File | Preferences | Monitor Gamma) allows you to adjust the monitor so you can see a little closer to what you are going to get in either case. As monitors age, color correctness deteriorates, so it's best to check this dialog every once in a while.

Consider these settings for the Monitor Gamma dialog (see Figure 9-5):

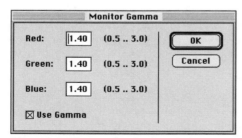

Figure 9-5: The Monitor Gamma dialog.

- **Red, Green, Blue settings.** Numeric input areas for adjusting the color values to an even gray. RGB to CMYK values (so you can trust the RGB monitor color as far as CMYK printer output) usually means setting each color at 1.6 to 2.0. For RGB output (like an RGB film recorder), the settings normally range from 2.0 to 2.4. The entire Gamma correction settings range from 0.5 to 3.0. Adjustments are seen on the screen as a gray level setting.
- **Use Gamma.** This checkbox starts the Gamma correction process.

Black Generation Preferences

The Black Generation dialog (File | Preferences | Black Generation) (see Figure 9-6) allows you to adjust curve for Start, Ink Limit, and Gamma settings of the "K," or Black, printing plate. Unless you have the required knowledge and experience to do this, leave it alone.

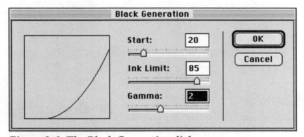

Figure 9-6: The Black Generation dialog.

CMY to RGB Table/RGB to CMY Table

These color lookup tables (File | Preferences | CMY to RGB Table and File | Preferences | RGB to CMY Table) (see Figure 9-7) provide exacting CMY to RGB and RGB to CMY conversion. This is an advanced setting for experienced color professionals only. The documentation guides you through the process, though color conversion is best left to those working on the print output.

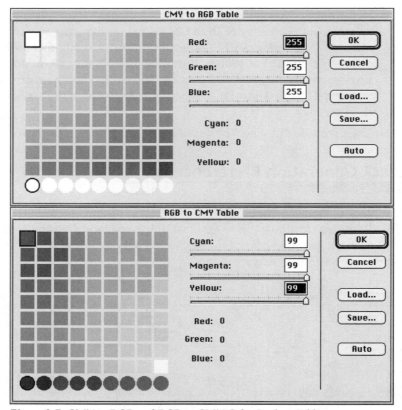

Figure 9-7: CMY to RGB and RGB to CMY Color Lookup Tables.

Printing Inks

The Printing Inks dialog (File | Preferences | Printing Inks) (see Figure 9-8), together with the Gamma Correction and CMY/RGB Color Lookup Table settings previously mentioned, allows you to get an exact match (or as close as possible match) between your RGB monitor and your CMYK printer. The xRes documentation walks you through the entire process. Again, your level of professional experience with color printing will determine whether you should do this yourself or leave it to printing professionals when your design work is complete.

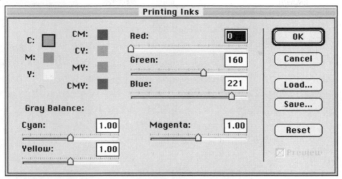

Figure 9-8: The Printing Inks preferences dialog.

Setting up the xRes Display Screen

Your xRes display screen is your digital 2D art table. Setting it up to reflect the way that you work, so that your creativity can flow without the frustration and irritation that comes with misplaced or wrongly placed tools, is vital. Various ways of managing the components of the display can be configured and activated in xRes.

Arrange Panels

Being able to arrange your panels (Window | Arrange Panels) answers a great need for the xRes artist. In the midst of a furiously paced project, after shuttling palettes and panels over the screen so you can get access to a tool or to the workspace, chaotic placement of xRes elements is almost inevitable. One journey to Arrange Panels fixes it all. The screen, and your creative world, is put back in order again, and you're ready to continue on with the creative process.

Central Palettes

xRes arranges its central palettes into three groups (Window | Palettes): Tool, Brushes/Textures, and Swatches Picker. All are movable to allow you to customize the look and feel of your workspace.

Tools Palette

The Tools palette, or Toolbox, is the palette (Window I Palettes I Tools) you will use the most, since it contains all of the activity-oriented tools you will need in your project (see Figure 9-9). Photoshop users will have little or no problem with the tools; they are the standard tools used by digital artists all over the world. Place the Toolbox in a separate place on the screen, so it is always accessible. Standard placement is on the left of the work area.

Figure 9-9: The xRes Tools palette.

Brushes/Textures Palette

You will probably want to keep the Brushes/Textures palette (Window I Palettes I Brushes or Window I Palettes I Textures) rolled up, because unrolled, it takes up the full height of your display screen (see Figure 9-10). This is the second most important palette that you will use. I suggest placing it at the top of your display, so it is always accessible, and so it unrolls in an expected manner when you need it. One tab represents all of the xRes brushes (an extensive list, as we shall see), while the second tab lists all of the texture swatches as visible thumbnails.

Swatches/Picker Palette

The Swatches/Picker palette (see Figure 9-11) is your color selection tool represented as two alternate types (Window I Palettes I Swatches or Window I Palettes I Picker). Keep it handy, but rolled up. Click on the swatch area at the bottom of the Toolbox to open it.

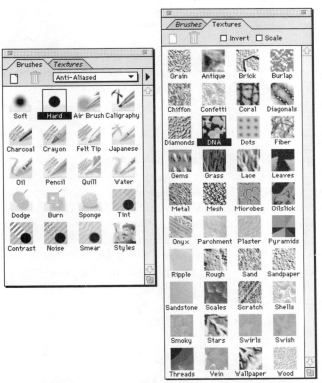

Figure 9-10: The Brushes and Textures tabs of the Brushes/Textures palette.

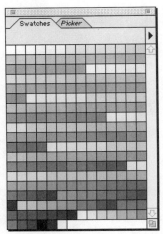

Figure 9-11: The Swatches/Picker palette.

Inspectors

The term "Inspectors" is familiar to FreeHand users, although these panels don't really resemble the Inspectors found in FreeHand. Tool Options and Shape (Window I Inspectors I Tool Options/or Window I Inspectors I Shape) are two tabs of the same panel.

Tool Options

Many tools in the Toolbox bar offer settings in the Tool Options dialog (Window I Inspectors I Tool Options) (see Figure 9-12). By far the most important Tool Option dialog box is that connected to the Gradient tool. This is one of xRes' most expansive tools, and one that no other bitmap painting application possesses. We will look at it in detail later in this book. Access to the Tool Options dialog for the Gradient tool has to be primary, so keep the Tool Options window handy and accessible. Some of the tools in the Toolbox have no options, and most have just a simple toggle or slider for one setting option.

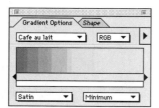

Figure 9-12: The Tool Options window, showing the Gradient Options.

Shape Inspector

The Shape Inspector (Window I Inspectors I Shape) controls the size of the Line, Brush, and Eraser tools, so if you find that you need to change these sizes frequently, keep the Shape Inspector (see Figure 9-13) handy.

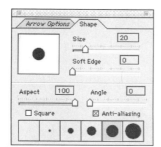

Figure 9-13: The Shape Inspector for the brushes.

Info Inspector

To conserve space on your display, you may want to hide the Info Inspector (Window I Inspectors I Info) until you need it (see Figure 9-14). It shows the position of the cursor, and also lists the RGB and CMY color components of every pixel you pass over.

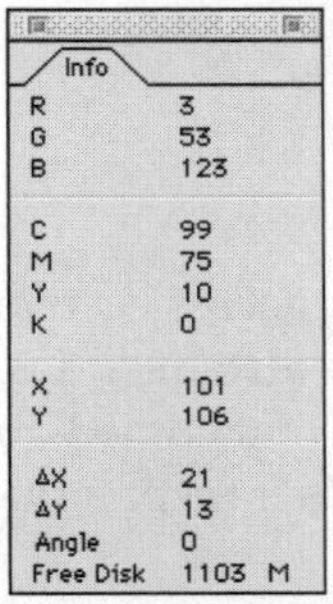

Figure 9-14: The Info Inspector.

Windows

The Objects, Channels, and Paths windows display as a a palette with three tabs (Window I Objects, Window I Channels, or Window I Paths). The most important tab to keep in view is the Objects window. In xRes, objects are addressed on layers, so Photoshop users might call the Objects window the Layers palette. In fact, imported Photoshop art that is layered comes into xRes separated according to object layers, and is visible and can be manipulated here.

Objects

In xRes, as in Photoshop 4, all copy/paste operations place the pasted graphic on a new layer. In xRes, it's called an object layer. In the Objects window (Window I Objects) (see Figure 9-15), you can move the layers in the stack at any time, drop them into place on the background, or leave them as is for saving in the xRes MMI format. Keep the Object Layers window in view, so you can manipulate the stack as needed.

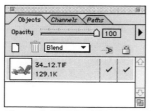

Figure 9-15: The Objects window.

Channels

In the Channels window (Window | Channels), you can access each of the RGB or CMY channels independently (see Figure 9-16). xRes also includes alpha channel masks as part of the Channels list. That means that copied objects can be used in an object layer on a project with backgrounds transparent or opaque.

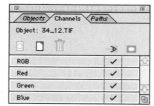

Figure 9-16: The Channels window.

Paths

Paths in xRes are vector selections. You can create them, copy them, and use them to create interesting stroke and fill in an xRes project. We will explore paths in more detail later. You can also create clipping paths in xRes, so that paintings exported to other 2D applications will show transparent areas everywhere but inside the xRes clipping path. Since the Paths window (see Figure 9-17) is in the same palette with the Objects window, which we have suggested is vital to keep in view, paths will be highly accessible as well.

Tip

FreeHand users! Make sure you install the xRes Paths Export Xtra to your FreeHand Xtras folder. This allows you to export FreeHand paths to xRes, a very valuable feature.

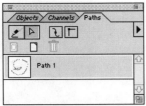

Figure 9-17: The Paths window in the palette.

The Mask Window

In order to conserve space on your display, hide the Mask window (Window | Mask) until you require it (see Figure 9-18). You can think of xRes masking as a way of having more automated control over the Wand operation in the creation of a marquee. Make sure you read, follow, and understand the tutorials on masking in the xRes documentation. We will delve into some creative masking techniques in the next chapter.

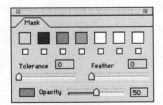

Figure 9-18: The Mask palette.

Selecting xRes Work Modes

The two xRes work modes are Direct and xRes (Modify | Work Mode | Direct or Modify | Work Mode | xRes). Choosing one or the other, or moving between them, has everything to do with how you set up your xRes projects. Images can be translated from Direct to xRes work mode and back.

What Is the Direct Work Mode?

Direct work mode (Modify | Work Mode | Direct) is designed for your normal image needs, as long as the image you're working on is less than 10–20 MB in size and contains less than 10 objects. Items functional in Direct mode that are not available in xRes mode include: actions on pixel data, no post-processing, required Magic Wand tool, Bucket tool, dropping objects, enabled dropping selections enabled, and indexed 256-color mode enabled.

What Is the xRes Work Mode?

xRes work mode (Modify | Work Mode | xRes) is for projects larger than 10–20 MB in size, and projects that contain more than 10 objects. In xRes mode, you act on representative "tiles" of data, not on pixels. xRes work mode is known as "resolution independent" because you are working on a proxy of the image in order to speed up processing.

Tip

xRes mode works more smoothly and faster if all of the object layers have been translated to the xRes LRG format first.

Working With xRes Files

There are discrete differences between opening and importing files, and between saving and exporting in xRes. These differences are detailed below.

Saving Files

xRes allows you to save work (File | Save or File | Save As) in MMI, LRG, TIFF, PICT, Photoshop 3, ScitexC, JPEG, EPS, Targa, BMP, GIF, and PNG file formats. The two most important for you to have familiarity with are the MMI and LRG formats.

The MMI format (Macromedia Image) is used to save all works in progress, whether Direct or xRes projects. MMI files are fairly small, and point to the associated object layers in the LRG format (so your object layers should be saved as LRG files from the start). All associated filter operations for the LRG object layers are also remembered in the MMI file.

Any imported graphic can be translated to a LRG file simply by importing it as such. You are presented with a file dialog that allows you to save the image as a LRG file, before it is placed in its own object layer in the project. When you work in xRes mode, all open and imported images are immediately converted to the LRG format. LRG formatted images respond much quicker to editing operations in xRes.

Exporting Files

To save out multiple-object layered document files in formats other than MMI, you must use the Export command (File | Export). Otherwise, unless you drop all of the layers into the background, the saved file will not contain any of the object data. Exporting the image in xRes mode automatically renders the file with all of its layered data. xRes exports can be saved at different zoom levels from the Save dialog. Zoom level options are 1:1, 1:2, 1:4, 1:8, 1:16, 1:32, and 1:64. Lower zoom levels do not represent lower resolutions, but do represent less pixel data. xRes files saved for use on the Web can always be saved out at the 1:32 or 1:64 ranges, while files for print media use the higher zoom level ratios (1:1 being the highest).

Importing Files

xRes can import (File | Import) LRG, TIFF, PICT, Pshp 3, ScitexC, JPEG, EPS, Targa, BMP, GIF, and PNG file formats. MMI files must be opened, rather than imported.

Opening a Saved xRes Project

If you are opening an xRes project (as opposed to an image file), it will be in MMI format (File | Open). It will open quickly because the MMI file contains only markers to where the object (LRG files) are stored and any image processing applied to the object. No matter what format you save your project files to for display or publishing, always save out an MMI file as well. You never know when you might want to create a variation of the project.

Warning

If you move the LRG files that are part of an xRes project saved in MMI format, they will not be found! Leave your LRG files in place, at least until the project is complete and exported as a finished piece. The best idea is to create a separate folder that holds all of your LRG files for works in progress, and perhaps for all LRG files even after the project they are involved in is finished. Removable media, like ZIP disks, are great for this purpose.

Acquiring Files

xRes can acquire data (File | Acquire) from your scanner. It can also acquire data as part of the PS RIPlink operation.

Moving On

Having covered the installation procedures for xRes in this chapter, we will look at how you can utilize xRes to perform its major task: creating and modifying bitmap paintings.

10

Creating & Modifying Bitmap Paintings

A 2D bitmap painting and image processing application, xRes has advanced features that help the digital artist create novel image effects. xRes is also a vital integrated part of FGS Graphics Studio, acting in concert with the other FreeHand components to shape projects that pass among all of the FreeHand applications before they are finished. xRes artists can shape content for both FreeHand and Extreme 3D, as well as accept content from both. The tutorial projects in this book emphasize the integrated role xRes plays in the Graphics Studio concept.

Creating Selection Shapes

You can use xRes tools to work on an entire electronic canvas at once, but xRes also contains a familiar range of tools that help the digital artist cordon off smaller areas for specific changes, while the rest of the design is protected from alterations. In general, these tools are called marquee or selection tools. Mastering the creation and use of the selection tools in xRes is a vital part of mastering the software.

Marquees

The term marquee comes from the fact that once an area is defined with a selection tool, an animated dashed line surrounds the selection, rather like the animated lights that surround the display on a theater marquee. Selection marquees are used by xRes artists to separate areas of a digital painting in order to work only on that section, without altering neighboring elements. Selection tools are also a vital part of image processing applications, of altering and retouching digital photographs to enhance or add elements or to remove unwanted features. Mastery of the marquee tools is a vital part of all xRes work. Beyond that, since all of the FreeHand Graphics Studio applications feature their own marquee tools, learning to use them in any single application advances your understanding in the other applications.

Tip

You can remove elements from any marqueed selection by holding down the Command key (Mac OS) or the Control key (Windows) while drawing over the selection you want to remove elements from.

The Lasso

The Lasso's name is associated with its use. With this tool, you surround selected areas of the object (like a lasso), and you also are forced to draw the marquee in a continuous manner. The best way to use this tool, however, is to avoid trying to draw in one continuous line.

Hold down the Shift key as you draw with the Lasso tool. If you release the mouse button while still holding down the Shift key, the drawing stops its progress, but does not end the session. Instead, it just pauses the operation. This allows you to pause as well, to take a breath, instead of being forced to finish outlining an area in one continuous (and often arduous) motion.

Tip

With the Shift key still held down, moving the mouse and clicking it from point to point allows you to draw a shape that combines FreeHand curves with line segments. This is exactly what you need when outlining forms in a photograph that are meant to be separated from the surrounding areas.

There is only one checkbox listed in the Lasso Options tab of the Tool palette. It allows you to toggle anti-aliasing on or off.

Tip

After completing a selection marquee, holding the Shift key down will allow you to draw others in addition. This is useful when you need to operate on several areas of a page at the same time. Clicking any selection marquee tool down on an area of the page outside of the marquee removes all active marquees on the page.

Ellipse Tool

The Ellipse tool works by clicking and dragging an oval around the targeted graphic, or around any part of the page.

Tip

The Ellipse and Rectangle tools draw from a corner by default. To draw from the center, hold down the Option key (Mac OS) or the Alt key (Windows) while dragging the shape.

Rectangle Tool

The Rectangle tool works by clicking and dragging a rectangle around the targeted graphic, or around any part of the page.

Tip

The Ellipse and Rectangle tools draw from a corner by default. To draw from the center, hold down the Option key (Mac OS) or the Alt key (Windows) while dragging the shape.

Practicing Your Marquee Skills   Here's a good exercise for working with marquees, and one that you can actually use to develop an xRes project.

1. Create a blank document in xRes.

2. Select the Ellipse l or Rectangle tool. Draw a shape. Now, with the Shift key held down, draw another shape that intersects with the first one. You will see that the shapes combine to form a single shape. Repeat this action until the marquee shape looks interesting to you.

3. With the marquee active, select Edit I Fill. The Fill dialog appears.

4. You can select to fill the marquee selection with either the background or foreground color. Select the foreground color, and set Opacity to 50 percent. Click on OK. The marquee is filled with a 50 percent tint of the foreground color.

5. Change the foreground color by selecting another color from the Swatches palette. Draw another elliptical marquee, so that part of it overlaps the color tint area you just created. Go to the fill dialog again, and select a 30 percent tint of the new foreground color. Click on OK. The new tint is painted in, and, where it overlaps the first tint, the transparency shows through a muted portion of what is covered. Repeat this process until you have created an arrangement of multiple transparent tints (see Figure 10-1).

Figure 10-1: A finished graphic composed of transparent marquee tints.

Tip

A finished graphic that follows the above guidelines can itself be imported as a separate object layer for a photo or another work in progress. It can be used as a tinted screen to mute any underlying art.

The Wand

The Wand tool is a special case of the Marquee tools. It has its own settings dialog in the Tool Options palette (see Figure 10-2).

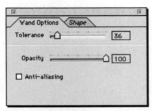

Figure 10-2: The Tool Options Inspector showing the Wand settings sliders and anti-aliasing checkbox.

The Wand tool allows you to place a marquee around areas of your work that have the same color values. Just click it on one example of the targeted color, and the area marked by that color is selected. The Wand tool options are controlled by two sliders. The first is the Tolerance slider. A lower setting means that fewer adjacent pixels to the chosen color will be selected. A higher setting means that similar colors are also selected. Moving this slider all the way to the right guarantees that everything on the page will be selected.

The second slider controls opacity, with settings of 0 to 100. Opacity controls the strength of any effects that will be applied to the selection. Usually, this should remain at 100 percent. The check box at the bottom should remain checked in most cases, since it allows the selection border to be anti-aliased, producing smoother results.

Path Selections

The function and operation of xRes paths will be second nature to experienced FreeHand users. Path selections are controlled in the Paths window (see Figure 10-3). Paths are created in much the same way as a selection using the Lasso tool—with the Shift key held down, allowing you to create selections that combine curved and straight line segments. The difference is that path selections also have control point modifiers, so the selection can be changed after it is created.

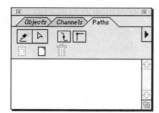

Figure 10-3: The Path window.

Creative Options in the Select Menu

Selections can also be altered and manipulated from the listings in the Select menu.

■ Using a selection tool to outline an area of your work and "floating" it from the Select menu choices allows you to effectively clone that area. Floating it places the clone as a new object on its own object layer, where its opaqueness can be changed. This gives you one way to create quick montages built from elements already present in your artwork. When you have placed the cloned floater where you want it, use the Select I Drop Object command to paste it back to the background layer.

■ The Inverse command is the most important to determine what the selection is. One good way to use it is to hold down the Shift key after activating it and draw areas that will be removed from the original selection. Use the Invert command a second time to see how the original selected area has been affected. Using the Invert command twice in a row in this manner allows you to fine-tune the original area selected, removing parts of the image from the selection that your original outline covered by mistake.

Tip

You can also invert a selection by using the Invert button on the toolbar.

■ The Select I Feather command gives you control over the ways that a selected area pasted back to the background layer will blend into that layer. Especially if you are creating a montage, you will want to set a Feathered option to the selection. Hard-edged montage elements have no character. You can experiment with the Feathering settings (they range from 0 to 128), but a setting of 50 is a good place to start. When the selections are photographic, feathering produces high-quality vignettes of the selected graphic elements when they are pasted back to the background.

Tricks With Mobile Selections

Empty selections, marquees without graphic content, can be copied and pasted to object layers just like marquees that surround content.

1. Draw a lasso selection around a blank area of a page background.

2. Copy it to the clipboard.

3. Paste it, and it comes back on its own object layer.

4. Fill it with color or a texture. Now on its own object layer, it can be moved anywhere on the page (and even off of the page).

5. Use any selection tool to draw another selection inside of the object layer selection, and color or texture it as well. Now you have a selection within a selection. This same technique can be used to put a label on a floating bottle, or to provide similar project solutions. Everything remains movable until (or if) you export it as a graphic file.

Bitmap Painting

Bitmap painting is different than using vector tools to draw in FreeHand. Bitmaps are made up of pixels, and pixels determine resolution, at what size a graphic looks good and sharp. Zoom in closely on a vector drawing and the detailed area looks larger and just as sharp. Zoom in on a bitmap painting or photo, and the zoomed in area looks unrecognizable and lumpy.

The resolution that you draw at is determined by the output you plan to support. Magazine output can demand artwork that prints at 2400 dpi and much greater. To work at these bitmap levels requires hundreds of megabytes of RAM, and very high resolution monitors. Film recorders, like the ones that record single frame sequences for major motion pictures, demand very high-end output as well. After all, a movie screen is pretty big, and small details loom large when projected on a screen. Television, on the other hand, at least in its present NTSC format, demands a resolution of only 72 dpi. This is small enough so that desktop systems with the right hardware are quite able to create graphics for national broadcast media. The Web is also a 72 dpi medium. The new Digital High Definition formats on their way will require higher resolution standards, meaning higher-resolution bitmaps, but nothing as radically high as either print or film recorder resolutions.

What does this mean to the animator? It means that applications like xRes have a very long life ahead, because there will continue to be venues that will be open to creative input from digital artists and animators who work on desktop workstations, from small studios, or right from their home. Broadcast media, multimedia enterprises, and Web pages can easily be enhanced with bitmap art produced on desktop systems. With a little hardware enhancement to the right desktop system, even magazine resolutions can be achieved.

Bitmap painting involves the same process as any other art form, placing your visions and ideas in a suitable medium so they can be shared and appreciated by an audience. To this end, it means mastering the tools that an application has to offer. In an application like xRes, with so many tool options, mastery of the tools means pushing them beyond what the documentation defines for them, combining tool usage, and discovering new ways to shape your ideas. This book is filled with new approaches for utilizing the tools in xRes, FreeHand, and Extreme 3D, but it makes no pretense of covering all of the bases. Your time and effort is essential. All of the tutorials and exercises presented in this book are just doorways to new realms of creative possibility, and not finalized ends in themselves. To be an artist, traditional or digital or a combination of the two, is to continue to explore "what if." What if I use this tool in this way, what if I place this color here, what if I push this effect where no artist has gone before? Take that attitude as you look through this book and as you explore xRes painting options, and you will succeed beyond your wildest hopes as a digital artist.

xRes Painting Tools

It is expected that you have already examined and worked through the xRes documentation that outlines the basic tool usage for the painting tools, as we will not duplicate the basics here. Of the seven tools in Figure 10-4, all but the Eyedropper are discussed. This is because the use of the Eyedropper in selecting colors is basic, and needs no expanded coverage. The other painting tools, however, have infinite potentials for xRes painters to explore.

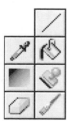

Figure 10-4: The seven essential xRes painting tools: Line, Eyedropper, Fill Bucket, Gradient, Stamper, Eraser, and Brush.

Line Tool Magic

Although the Line tool has no options of its own in the Tool Options palette, that is not completely true. The Shape Inspector gives you some interesting options with the Line tool.

1. Click on the Line tool.

2. In the Shape Inspector, set the size of the Line tool to 100, the maximum, and set the Soft Edge slider to zero.

3. Click and drag the mouse cursor a tiny amount on the screen, about one-sixteenth of an inch or so.

4. Perfect filled circles! You have forced the Line tool to become a filled circle generator, something it was not designed to do.

5. The Size slider in the Shape Inspector does not hint that it can be altered past the maximum amount of 100 indicated by the slider. Click in the numeric area and change the 100 to 200, or any number between 100 and 500. Now do the same operation with the Line tool, and you will draw larger filled circles.

6. Push the Size slider up higher, and you can generate instant color fills for the whole page.

Tip

Be careful to reset the Size slider to more standard settings before using other painting tools.

Sepia-Toned Images With the Fill Bucket

The Tool Options palette allows two sliders to affect the way the Bucket works. The first is the Tolerance slider. It controls the boundaries of a fill. Lower settings force the fill operation to end when it meets the edge of another color. Higher tolerances will push the fill past other colors. The highest settings will force the fill operation to address the entire workspace. The Opacity slider tells the fill operation what the tint of the fill color is to be, on a range from 1 (no opacity) to 100 (full opacity). You can use these sliders to create instant sepia-toned photos by doing the following.

1. Import a digital photo that would look interesting as a sepia-toned print.

2. Click on the Bucket tool. In the associated Fill Options, set the Tolerance slider all the way to the right. Set the Opacity slider to 25 percent.

3. Select a sepia color from the Swatches palette. Click the Bucket tool on the photo. The result is an instant sepia-toned print. Selecting other colors will apply tints in those colors.

Eraser Painting

The xRes Eraser tool should be thought of as an alternate paintbrush, in addition to its role as an element removal tool. It erases everything to the texture that is set in the Brush Options palette, using the background color. It can be used as a muting device to create blended graphics.

1. Fill the background with a dark blue color.

2. Click on a non-dark blue color, and on the Brush tool.

3. Use the Wax Crayon brush from the Brushes palette. Select the Wallpaper Texture from the Textures palette. Move the associated Texture slider in the Tool Options palette to 100 percent, while setting the Concentration and Flow to 30.

4. Use different colors to paint textured patterns to your dark blue background.

5. Make sure your selected background color swatch in the Toolbox is set to white. Select the Eraser tool, and erase over the painted textures in a ray design emanating from the upper right hand corner of your image. Notice that the texture remains, but that it is blended to white. When the image looks finished, stop to appreciate your work. For an example, see Figure 10-5.

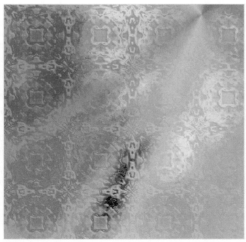

Figure 10-5: Following the above example, you can create interesting ray paintings with the Eraser tool.

Tip

Remember that the Shape Inspector controls the softness and extent of the Eraser as well as the Brush.

Stamp Fun

With the Stamp tool, you can clone elements in an image and create interesting composite montages that incorporate those elements.

1. Select an image that has interesting elements for creating a cloned composition, and open it.

2. Create a new xRes document, and size it as large as or larger than the image you opened previously.

3. Copy the image you opened, and selecting the new document, paste it in. It is brought in on its own object layer.

4. Click on the Stamp tool. Hold down the Option key (Mac OS) or the Alt key (Windows), and click with the Stamp tool on the image in the object layer. Click at a point in the center of the image area you want to clone.

5. Move the object layer aside with the selection arrow so you can see the blank background.

6. Set up a brush that you would like to paint with. The Oil Painting Brush is a safe bet. Set its options in the Tool Options palette, and set its brush size in the Shape Inspector.

7. With the Stamp tool selected, use it to paint a clone of the object layer into the background. Wherever you start to paint, the cloned image will start from the center point on the object layer you set previously. You can always reset this point and continue painting, bringing in new cloned elements. You can also import other images and set a stamp point on them, introducing new elements into your stamped painting. When you're finished, delete the object layers and save out the new painting. See Figure 10-6 for an example.

Tip

Remember that the Stamp tool only clones from one object to the same object in xRes mode.

Figure 10-6: A finished stamped painting allows you to experiment with cloned image elements.

Mastering the Tool Options Palette

Every new painting tool you select reconfigures the same Tool Options palette. A basic understanding of the Concentration, Flow, and Texture sliders is imperative, and from your acquaintance with the xRes documentation, it is assumed that you understand what these settings do. To master the Tool Options dialog, however, you also need to understand the items listed under More Options for each of the painting alternatives (see Figure 10-7). Most sliders range from 1 to 100, with higher settings enhancing the selection to a greater extent.

Figure 10-7: The Brush Options palette showing the More Options extended controls.

Different brushes will bring up one or more of these controls. They are listed as follows:

- **Smoothing:** Controls the anti-aliasing of the brush stroke. Higher settings will slow down your brush strokes, so the suggestion is to set this to a value between 30 and 50 for the best compromise between anti-aliasing and speed.

- **Spacing:** High settings cause the brush to skip as you draw it across the digital canvas faster, an effective way of reproducing paint drips at the start or end of a brushstroke.

- **Blackness:** The higher the Blackness settings, the more the medium will look as if the color is bleeding into it, causing it to darken. Raise the Blackness level when you want the color to affect the backdrop more.

- **Bleed:** This is an effect that results naturally from watercolor painting, because everything is very wet, and colors bleed into each other. It can happen in oil painting too, and is known there as "wet on wet" painting. Raise the Bleed level to increase this effect.

- **Fringe:** High Fringe levels leave little shreds at the edge of the brush, great for emulating shavings and waxy shreds.

- **Tips:** The number of Tips ranges from 1 to 32. Tips relate to bristles and hairs. If you want to show these artifacts, raise the Tips setting.

- **Tip Spacing:** This allows you to control the amount of space between tips so they show better. Raising this number also increases the width of the brush accordingly.

Special Painting Techniques

If you use xRes regularly, you will be able to invent hundreds of your own painting techniques. Here are a few examples I have discovered along the way.

Painting With Mixed Media Brushes

In traditional painting, a watercolor artist works in watercolor, and an oil painter in oils. With xRes, there is no reason to limit yourself to these looks alone. It can be quite effective to use alternate brush modes in the same work, since each has a separate personality that might lend itself to a separate element of your painting. Some examples that I have found effective are:

- Watercolor backgrounds with oil foregrounds. This emphasizes the foreground elements, and does the opposite with backgrounds.

■ Dark-textured airbrushed backgrounds with 100 percent texture, and oil foregrounds. This is like painting on an embroidery.

■ Japanese Sumi backgrounds and Ribbon Calligraphy foregrounds, to create a Zen-like atmosphere.

Painting With Textured Gradient Overlays

This is another technique you might like to explore. The idea is to use the Gradient tool to create semi-opaque overlays on the initial layer of a painting. Just set the Type to either Satin or Folds in the Gradients Options. Select Blend as your first Gradient Fill, and then change it to Minimum for two more gradient overlays. This works best with colors that are not too dark, like medium browns. The composite has a cloth look with futuristic patterns.

Painting With Multiple Textures

Look at the textures in the Texture palette. See if you can design a painting that uses the look of the texture as an object. Explore the Sand texture for painting a beach, and use the Coral and Brick Textures to shape a house on it. The idea is to break with the standard way of looking at textures to embellish objects, but to use them as objects.

Creating Your Own xRes Textures

Don't pass up learning how to perform this xRes option. Creating your own texture library can greatly enhance and personalize all of your xRes work. Just follow these steps.

1. Select an image that has interesting potential texture elements from your image library. Stock photo images are a good choice.

2. Open the image in xRes. Place a rectangular marquee around an area of interest, copy it, and paste it to its own object layer.

3. Notice that it appears in the object layer stack in the Objects Window. Click and drag it from the Objects palette to the Textures palette. When the naming dialog appears, give it a unique name.

That's it! You can now paint with your own texture. Textures are stored as 256-level gray images, so don't expect to see a color representation of your new texture as you paint. Figure 10-8 shows an example of a texture painting.

Figure 10-8: There's nothing quite as thrilling as painting with your own textures.

Tip

Remember to set the Save Textures on Exit item under General preferences if you want to use your texture for other projects.

Enhancement Techniques

To finalize your xRes creations, you may need to use one or more of the basic image editing options. Although the xRes documentation details the general uses of these options, here are a few suggestions about their extended use.

Editing Tips

You are already familiar with these basic editing commands after having read the xRes documentation thoroughly, but here are a few things to remember.

■ **Resize:** Instead of using the Modify | Resize command to resize objects, use the Resize tool. It's easier and faster, and you have visual control over what you're doing.

- **Rotate:** Perform rotations after any necessary resizing operations for better image control.

- **Slant:** Try slanting a circular selection, and then resizing it. Interesting image warps can be created in this fashion.

- **Crop:** Do not attempt to crop an object layer separately from the document. Everything below will respond to the cropping procedure.

- **Cut/Copy/Paste/Duplicate/Clear:** Don't confuse Cut and Clear. Cut removes an object and places it on the clipboard. Selecting Paste will paste it back on a new object layer. Selecting Clear gets rid of it with nothing written to the clipboard. Copy places the selection on the clipboard, so it can be pasted at any time. Duplicate clones it immediately on the screen for image processing, and places the clone on a new object layer.

Using Filter Effects

Tip

See Appendix B for filter effects that are useful for xRes animated output.

Rather than use a lot of words to describe what can only be appreciated visually, look at the figures that demonstrate what the xRes-native filters do. Each filter contains a settings dialog, so the examples represent only one possibility for each filter.

Tip

There are no suggested settings for any of these filters, since each setting produces a result that may or may not be suitable for your specific need. The best suggestion is to explore the filters, acquainting yourself with the ways in which alternate settings affect the filtering of the image. Each designer will find a list of favorite settings over time and use.

Sharpen

There are three Sharpen filters: Basic, Luminosity, and Unsharp Mask. Figure 10-9 shows an example of each filter.

Figure 10-9: The Sharpen filters as applied from left to right—Basic, Luminosity, and Unsharp Mask.

Blur

There are four Blur filters: Simple, Gaussian, Radial, and Motion. Figure 10-10 shows an example of each Blur filter.

Figure 10-10: The Blur filters as applied from left to right—Simple, Gaussian, Radial, and Motion.

Noise

There are two Noise filters: Add and Add HLS. Figure 10-11 shows an example of each Noise filter.

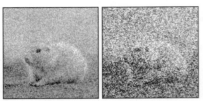

Figure 10-11: The Noise filters as applied from left to right—Add, and Add HLS.

Distort

There are five Distort filters: Cylinder, Fisheye, Ripple, Wave, and Whirlpool. Figure 10-12 shows an example of each Distort filter.

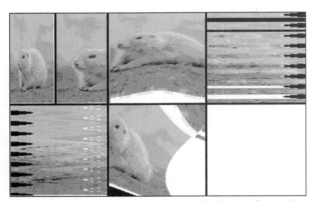

Figure 10-12: The Distort filters as applied from left to right—Cylinder, Fisheye, Ripple, Wave, and Whirlpool.

Stylize

There are nine Stylize filters: Colorize, Diffuse, Emboss, Find Edge, Glowing Edge, Mosaic, Posterize, Solarize, and Tint. Figure 10-13 shows an example of each Stylize filter.

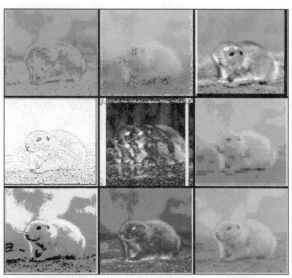

Figure 10-13: The Stylize filters—Colorize, Diffuse, Emboss, Find Edge, Glowing Edge, Mosaic, Posterize, Solarize, and Tint.

Working With Text

When you click on the Text tool, xRes presents a standard text dialog for configuring a text block (see Figure 10-14). You can select the style, size, and pixel border dimension, before typing in your text.

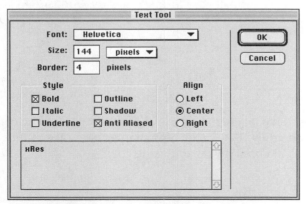

Figure 10-14: The xRes Text Tool dialog.

The text block is written to a separate layer, so that all of the image effects filters and utilities that can be used on a graphic object can be used on the text block. The most spectacular results can be achieved by brushing textures on a text block (see Figure 10-15). No other painting application and no plug-in filter offers more texture variance or quality than xRes does in this area. Just drop the text block into place when the texturizing process has been completed.

Tip

If your text consists of multiple object layers, be sure to use the Drop command on the layer immediately above the background layer first, and move upward in a linear order from there.

Figure 10-15: Text created in xRes can be texturized like any graphic, which can help you create some of the most spectacular text effects imaginable.

Moving On

In this chapter, we have taken you on a tour of the ways that you can create and modify bitmap art in xRes. In the next chapter, we will continue our xRes journey with a look at object layers and using color.

11

Working With xRes Objects

In the first part of this chapter, we will explore the creation and use of xRes objects, and emphasize that their mastery is vital in order for you to use xRes to the best advantage on your images. In the second part of the chapter, we will dwell on the use of various color modes and options in xRes.

Using Object

xRes objects can be equated with Photoshop layers with a few exceptions. Unlike Photoshop, you cannot drag and drop selections between documents. Otherwise, many of the conventions of working with layers in general apply. Objects can be restacked in the Objects window (actually, the Object tab in the Objects/Channels/Paths window). See Figure 11-1. All of the xRes effects can be applied to an object, and the object can then be composited back to the background.

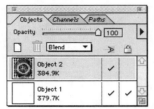

Figure 11-1: The Objects window.

Object layers can be adjusted for transparency/opaqueness, assigned image effects, resized, rotated, skewed, drawn on, textured, colorized and tinted, stamped, gradient filled, transformed into a texture, and saved out separately from the document they are nested in. You need to master layer use to take full advantage of xRes's creative potential.

Creating a New Object

Click on the New Object icon at the left of the Objects window to add a new object to the top of the stack. The object is blank and opaque, and takes its color from the presently set background color.

Instant Tint Tests

Here's a way to develop a use for xRes as a photographic utility that tests various tints on an image.

1. Open an image to work on. Choose one that has a good amount of color.

2. Use the New Object icon to add six new objects to the image.

3. With the Bucket, color each object a different hue.

4. Make all but one of the colored object layers invisible by unchecking the View toggle (it's the column under the Eye icon in the Objects window). Adjust the transparency level of the remaining one to 30 percent. Now you can check how your image will look with a 30 percent overprinting (a 30 percent Gel) of that color. Do the same with the other colored objects. This would be a good way for photographers to test out various lens filters against an image, and perhaps a way for art directors to show their clients what the effects of a tint on an image might be. See Figure 11-2.

Figure 11-2: The left image is the original, while the right image displays a 30 percent overlay of color using the object concepts discussed.

Progressive Disclosure Overhead Presentations

"Progressive disclosure" is a term used by instructional pros that means that data is disclosed one step at a time, showing how something progresses from one fact to another. Progressive disclosure is often used in overhead transparency and video slide presentations. With the Visibility/Invisibility feature in xRes, you can easily create progressive disclosure art for overheads or video.

1. One by one, create all of the bulleted points that are to display as separate images (all the same size), and save the images.

2. Create a new document, and fill the background with color or a muted texture.

3. Open (don't import) all of your bulleted data images. Use the Wand tool to select only the text, and not its background.

4. One by one, copy each data image to the clipboard and paste it on the new document you colored previously. Each data image will come in as a new object.

5. Adjust the bulleted data so that it lines up and is in the order you require from top to bottom.

6. If your presentation is a video slide presentation, you can plug your system into a suitable projector and do the rest live (always risky, but doable). Start with all of the data invisible, and as you need it to support your talk, make that point visible. The other alternative would be to print out overhead transparencies of each data slide in the stack, and simply flip them into position as needed, progressively disclosing the data.

Modifying Layers

The column under the Eye icon in the Object window can be used as mentioned above to make each object visible or invisible. Making specific objects invisible allows you to preview the interaction of various object combinations.

If you click in the column under the Lock icon for the object you want to affect by checking the Lock toggle, you will no longer be able to move, resize, rotate, or skew that object.

You can move objects in two ways—which may be thought of as horizontally and vertically. You can change their position in the object window (vertical, top to bottom movement), and you can alter their position in the document window (horizontal, side-to-side movement):

- To move objects to different top/bottom positions in the object window, simply drag their icons in the Object window to a new position. Preview your actions by viewing the document window.

- Use the Arrow tool to move your objects around in the document window. Move them until their corner control points are visible if you want to resize or otherwise manipulate them. They can be moved completely off the workspace.

To remove an object from the object window, simply click on it and drag it with the mouse, placing it over the Trash Can icon at the top of the Object window.

Importing Objects

Importing a graphic makes it an object in xRes terms if you already have an active image on the screen. If you want to keep the new graphic separate from the one already on screen, open it, don't import it. An imported graphic comes in as an object superimposed upon the selected image already on the screen.

Rendering Objects

All files render automatically when they are saved or exported to any file format except MMI, whether you're in Direct or xRes mode. The Render command is available to xRes mode documents. It renders the selected objects, effectively removing all undo operations to that point. This clears out the undo buffer, and makes overall operation move faster. xRes documents should be rendered every once in a while to clear the undo buffer. Once the undo buffers are cleared, however, operations performed on separate objects are cleared as well. The only format that preserves all of the data in its original form, including object undos, is the MMI format.

Dropping Object Layers

Dropping object layers in place moves them to the background, the first object in the stack. You can move the first object to another position, thereby altering the target to which a selected object is dropped, though this is seldom suggested except to explore the possibilities. In xRes mode, you cannot use the Drop command on an object.

Warning

Always drop objects in the stack starting with the one directly above the background layer and working upward to the highest member. To do otherwise guarantees unexpected results.

Saving Object Layers

Objects can be saved as separate images at any point in an xRes session. They can be saved to any of the image formats that xRes supports, and the original image file need not be altered (as long as you don't save the image with the same name in the same location as the original image file).

Why and When to Save an Object as an Image File:

- When the object has been altered, but may be altered more. This allows you to have a visual record of various states of the image.

- When you want to save it to an image format different from its original format, perhaps a file format for use on the Web (JPEG, GIF, or PNG).

- When you are building a sequence of altered files for animation frames.

Controlling the Opacity of an Image

Each object can be altered by adjusting the Opacity slider that sits at the top of the Objects window. The slider ranges from 0 (completely transparent) to 100 (completely opaque). If the object is a masked selection, so that the object background is transparent, that transparency will hold true for the object in the stack. A series of stacked objects with transparent backgrounds will just show the objects, and the transparent backgrounds will show the objects beneath. In this way, the objects behave like a multi-plane animation camera, making it possible to move any of the layers in the stack to achieve a different composite view. Add to this the fact that the Opacity slider can be used to make all opaque objects transparent to any degree, and you begin to gain a large amount of respect for the sheer power of the objects concept.

Opacity & Animation Frames

You can adjust the opacity of any object in xRes and export the composited graphic to a file without altering or damaging the object stack. This is because all exported graphics are rendered as layered composites. This allows you to move transparent graphics around, object by object, in order to gain new see-though groups of images. Then the new composite can be added to a sequence of similarly named files (as for example: Frame001.TIF, Frame002.TIF, Frame003.TIF, and so on). These frames can be used later in animation editing applications.

Opacity as Fog & Haze

If you need to create a fog or haze effect over a graphic, simply place a blank or suitable colored object over the graphic, and adjust the Opacity slider so that the image underneath shows through only as much as you would like it to. Then save out the composited result. If the "fog" object is painted with a misty airbrush look, the fog or haze effect will look that much more real (see Figure 11-3).

Figure 11-3: The cityscape has a "fog" object added, hazing out the image content.

Text Transparency Effects

If text is on the top object, it too can be made semi-transparent to whatever graphic is underneath (see Figure 11-4). It's as simple as moving the Opacity slider, without applying any time-consuming effects. Of course you could also stack a number of semi-transparent layers of text, making those lowest in the stack a bit harder to read. This would be great for a mystery video title, or even for the printed cover of a book.

Figure 11-4: The lettering was placed on a top object layer, and its opacity diminished to 50 percent.

Blending Mode Options

There is a pull-down list in the middle of the Object window that allows you to set blending mode variations for the selected object layer. Each of these choices affects the way that the object selected interacts with the layers below it. This is the beating heart of the object operations, its major reason for existence. It allows you to combine the objects in a stack in infinite interactions, each one with a new look. You can choose to assign the following mode to any image layer, although assigning them to the background layer will do nothing.

The background layer has by definition no layers below it to make any compositing effect visible. You choices are: Blend, Add, Subtract, Difference, Multiply, Minimum, and Maximum. Pictures speak louder than words when it comes to gaining some awareness of what each of these compositing functions does and how they differ. Take a look at Figure 11-5.

Figure 11-5: "A" is the background object, while "B" is an object above it. The first row is set to 100 percent Opacity, and the second row to 50 percent. The seven columns represent Blend, Add, Subtract, Difference, Multiply, Minimum, and Maximum.

Tip

FreeHand users can compare these compositing effects to the Transparency Operator in FreeHand. You might even want to import a few composited xRes graphics into FreeHand and use the Trace tool to transform them into vector art, just to compare the two methods.

xRes Color Modes: When & Why

We appreciate color even when the content of a page is less than what we're looking for. All around us, colors blaze and whirl, catch us off guard, invite, allure, demand. Some colors shout, and others whisper, but all colors have a voice that won't take no for an answer. People who work with color as their primary concern in the arts are known as colorists. In working with color, in being attracted and overwhelmed by it, we all become colorists. xRes is an ultimate colorist's playground, offering all of the magic that color has to offer in the digital medium, and then some.

xRes offers you the possibility of working in four distinct color modes. These are selectable from the Modify I Color Mode menu. Each of these modes has a targeted use, and when needed, you can switch back and forth among them.

CMYK Color Mode

This is the standard mode for printing in color, so desktop publishing users usually stay with this mode. The computer tries its best to emulate the colors on screen that match what you see on paper, but it is not a battle that can be won completely. This is because no matter what anyone tells you, three does not equal four (or more). The computer generates color with three color guns that handle and mix RGB (red, green, and blue) signals. Printing presses work with at least four color plates, abbreviated CMYK (cyan, magenta, yellow, and black or K). Red is not magenta. Blue is not cyan. Green is not yellow. And there is no black color gun on a monitor. CMYK works as an additive color process, so all of the rules about which color inks to mix to get which other colors are perfect for CMYK theory and practice.

In the attempt to try to adjust the RGB signals to compensate for what is demanded by CMYK printing operations, we have come to incorporate dedicated color management systems (CMS) technology. There are a number of world-class color management systems available from major industry color houses. You probably have a few on your system, especially if you operate any level of desktop publishing enterprise or if you use professional desktop publishing software. A good CMS utility tries to match RGB reality with CMYK demands, and tries to adjust what you see on your monitor along the way. Even the best CMS, however, is like the well-tempered scale. In our appreciation of the 12-key music system, we have traded off the fact that some notes can never be exactly the pitch that harmonics demand, but we gain the capacity to play in many keys. A good CMS is like a well-tempered clavichord.

To make matters even more interesting and complex, CMYK is not the whole story when it comes to printing. CMYK color is also known as process color, because separate CMYK plates are used to overlay the colors to produce the final color document. Printing plates can also handle spot colors, inks mixed to specific colors, and applied to select spots on the page. Other newer technologies are also coming into play, like Hexachrome technology and more. This makes it even more difficult for the computer to answer the demands of the modern printing press, though the attempts continue at a furious pace. Contact a professional printing facility to learn more about the details and when and where to use Hexachrome and Hi-Fi color schemes.

Work in CMYK mode whenever your output is targeted for print, whether that means a high-end printing house or a local or regional service bureau (and it's sometimes hard to distinguish them anymore). If you do elect to do work with xRes, or any other application, for print purposes, establish a close working relationship with your print professional. Do not get involved with issues like color trapping on your own, but instead learn from and work with the experienced printer. In many cases, it's worthwhile to save out a separate CMYK version of a document, even when your present needs are for RGB or other output. That gives you the opportunity to have a version available should a demand arise for quick print-to-paper output.

Tip

Unless you enjoy unpleasant surprises, never send out a CMYK job for print unless you have a chance to preview the color output as a proof first. An off-press proof (AGFAproof, Chromalin, and so on should be pulled), but you should also request a press proof.

RGB Color Mode

The computer lives with an RGB heart. The computer is a cousin to the television, only with the capacity for higher resolution display (until the coming HDTV standards take hold). Computer art is television art, and was not meant to emulate the paper art process originally. The computer is the perfect medium for video and multimedia art, because these are both television media, though the computer monitor is far ahead of the standard TV monitor in display resolution. With the new film recorder technologies, the computer is also perfect for movie art, as long as your system and peripherals are powerful enough to handle it. In a few years, 24-bit RGB video will be the expected medium and color mode choice for transmission on the Web, but we have to be cautious about doing that at the moment. The RGB mode is a subtractive process when it comes to mixing colors, so if that befuddles you in a project, do the project in CMYK mode (or at least mix your colors in a CMYK context) and translate to RGB afterward.

In xRes, select the RGB mode if your output is targeted to video or multimedia use. If you are just exploring digital art media, RGB is also the suggested environment. Although you can generate interesting channel paintings (see Chapter 15) in CMY mode, staying in RGB for channel work is the best way to learn to live in the computer's own neighborhood.

Grayscale Color Mode

Grayscale is an indexed color mode with the color saturation set to zero. This removes any hue, and leaves only the elements. Most paper book publications consider color too expensive for illustrations, so if you are designing or illustrating a book, you will likely develop your art using grayscale, or at least translate your color art into grayscale along the way. Most magazine art, however, is in color these days, so the demand for grayscale art is declining from what it was just a few years ago. You would either translate your art to grayscale if your output is a standard non-color laser printer, or the printer would do it for you. It's always safer for you to translate it first, because some colors are "seen" by the printing process in ways that cause problems in the output. Reds, for instance, print too black, and blues not black enough. Translating the art to grayscale on your own allows you to tweak the tones yourself before printing commences.

Tip

Always consider heightening the Gamma level, the overall brilliance of the image, before printing a grayscale piece. Without this, grayscale art has a tendency to print too dark, even though it may look perfect on your screen.

Indexed 256-Mode

Indexed color mode allows each color in a picture to be targeted to a specific color slot, one of 256 such slots. Colors in the picture that are not represented by a specific color slot are created by dithering between colors that are represented. Dithering is a term that indicates that a color is produced by using intermixed dots of two colors, allowing the eye to see a third color. Indexed colors have color lookup tables, and you can edit the colors in any color lookup table. This means of the 256 colors, you could have 200 variants of red and 56 variants of green, but no blues. Altering a color lookup table also allows you to create interesting image effects. Both Mac OS and Windows systems have their own system palette of 256 colors, but they are not equal. The Mac OS has an actual 256-color system palette, while Windows has a 216-color palette, reserving 40 colors exclusively for Windows use.

When it comes to displaying Web pages on a browser, not knowing this fact can lead to unpleasant results. If you don't design with the indexed palette in mind, displays can alter the colors of the intended graphics. This is why the Netscape Navigator browser, the most popular, has its own color palette. The Netscape color palette is included on the Mac FreeHand 7 CD-ROM, and can always be downloaded online from hundreds of free sources. *Always* use the Netscape palette, an indexed color palette with 216 colors, so Mac and Windows users can share the same colors, when you're designing a Web page. Users (surfers) with 24-bit displays never run into this problem, since they have enough color choices to see Web art as the designer intended. Many surfers, however, are using monitors that can display only 256 colors, so it is for their benefit that the Netscape palette exists.

Modifying Color in xRes

Under the Modify | Color menu, xRes offers you a list of color modification effects. Most have associated control dialogs, but some do not.

Inverting Colors

Invert (Modify | Color | Invert) has no control dialog. It simply creates a negative range of colors in the selection that you specify. See Figure 11-6 for an example.

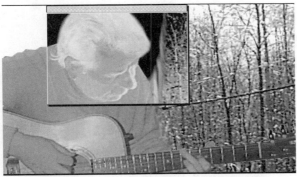

Figure 11-6: The selected area has been modified with the Invert command.

Enhancing the Brilliance of a Color

Levels (Modify | Color | Levels) does have a control dialog with movable threshold points. More importantly, it contains a Gamma Setting modifier. Use this control to alter the overall brilliance of the image, necessary for many printing output devices (see Figure 11-7). A small preview area allows you to preview any alterations in the settings immediately.

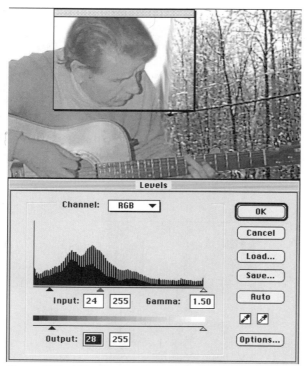

Figure 11-7: Adjusting the Gamma setting in the Levels dialog allows you to enhance the brilliance of the image.

Adjusting the Color Brightness of Channels

The Curves dialog (Modify | Color | Curves) allows you to adjust the color curves (color brightness levels) in each separate channel or the composite channel (see Figure 11-8). This is a good dialog to visit after you have created a channel painting to adjust the levels in the channels. This command has an interactive dialog and a real-time preview area.

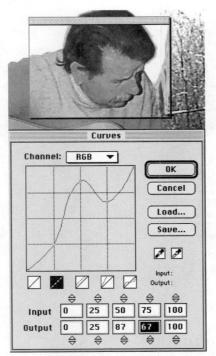

Figure 11-8: The Curves dialog allows you to adjust and customize the color curves in each channel.

Modifying the Contrast & Brightness of Color

Modifying contrast and brightness (Modify | Color | Brightness/Contrast) is a very important color modification dialog, and one that you will visit many times over in the quest to achieve the most perfect image. It has an interactive control dialog and a preview area (see Figure 11-9).

Figure 11-9: Brightness and contrast adjustment is often necessary.

Modifying the Hue or Saturation

Hue and saturation changes (Modify | Color | Hue/Saturation) can be interesting image effects, and may be needed to get the palette of an image just right. This command has an interactive control dialog and a preview area (see Figure 11-10).

Figure 11-10: Changing the hue of an image can create new uses for the image in overall page design.

Balancing Colors

Color balance (Modify | Color | Balance) is often necessary in photos to achieve the right flesh tones and also to correct the anomalies caused in the color of the image by lighting conditions. This command has an interactive control dialog and a preview area (see Figure 11-11).

Figure 11-11: It's easy to alter the color balance in the image with the interactive controls offered in this dialog.

Equalizing Colors

Equalization (Modify | Color | Equalize) in the color palette is something handled automatically without user-controllable input in xRes. This command does not have an interactive control dialog.

Selective Fine-tuning Color Palettes

This control (Modify | Color | Selective) allows you to add more ranges of colors to each channel's output. It is best used in conjunction with the Hue/ Saturation command. This command has an interactive control dialog and a preview area (see Figure 11-12).

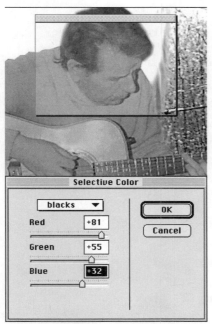

Figure 11-12: Use this command along with Hue/Saturation to fine-tune the color palette.

Modifying the Color Index Table

This is the place to alter any of the color swatches in the color lookup table (Modify | Color | Color Index Table), if the image is in 256-color mode (see Figure 11-13). It is extremely important when working on Web pages. It's also where you want to go to load in alternate 256-color palettes, like the Netscape palette or Mac OS/Windows-specific palettes.

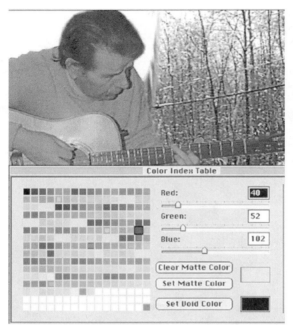

Figure 11-13: xRes makes it simple to alter the colors in the color lookup table, and to load and save new indexed color palettes.

Altering Black Ink in CMYK Images

GCR means Gray Component Replacement and UCR stands for Under Color Removal (Modify I Color I GCR/UCR). Altering the black (K) component in a CMYK image is best left to professionals at the printing end, but if you want to explore the possibilities, this is the place to go (see Figure 11-14).

Figure 11-14: This dialog allows you to alter the black ink component in a CMYK image.

Working With Channels, Paths & Masks

In addition to all of the creative alternatives made possible in xRes because of its object tools, you can also alter and manipulate images by interacting with channels, paths, and masks. Each of these attributes is unique, and combines its power with xRes' other creative features.

Channels

What are channels? A channel is a storage area set aside to keep track of all of the color information in an image. When you work in RGB mode, there are separate channels set aside for the red, green, and blue image components. When you work in CMYK mode, the channels represent cyan, magenta, yellow, and black (K). These are called an image's primary channels. Secondary channels also may exist for the image. These are non-primary channels like alpha channels, which store intermediate channel operations for overlays and other special effects. Certain file formats can contain alpha channels, while other formats disregard them when you save the image.

If you work in indexed 256-color mode or grayscale mode (each has a 256 color palette), you will have only one channel, which represents the entire range of color or gray level choices. This is because indexed 256 and grayscale modes have associated color or gray level tables. Each color onscreen must be one of the 256 colors in the color table, or it must be represented by a dithered compromise between color table colors.

Working With the Channels Window

The Channels window can be torn off of the Objects/Channels/Paths window, and placed separately on the screen. This allows for easier access to its features.

Channel Gradient Painting

To create psychedelic effects, select separate RGB or CMYK channels of an image, and apply the same gradient fills, but from different directions (see Figure 11-15). The palette you originally chose (perhaps the Sunrise palette) will be radically altered in the final composite image. This is because you have changed the levels in each of the channels, so that instead of the range of reds targeted in the color palette you chose, a separate range has been overlayed with the other colors. Explore this technique, and record the steps to those experiments that produce unique results.

Tip

When working with channels, it is important that you remember that each object has its own channels that can be modified separately from other objects. Each object can have up to 32 channels.

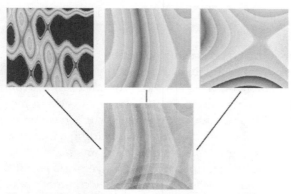

Figure 11-15: Gradient channel painting produces graphics no other technique can generate.

Composite Channel Backgrounds

This effect also takes advantage of the Gradient Fill options. There is no other way to create backgrounds that compare to these for sheer complexity and transparent overlays.

1. Create a new page, 400 x 400 pixels at 72 dpi.

2. Click on the Gradient tool, and in the Gradient Options, set the gradient for an RGB Rainbow Satin Blend.

3. In the Channels window, click on the green channel, thereby masking out the others. Draw a gradient line of any length and direction you like in the work area for the green channel. A gray gradient appears.

4. Repeat the same procedure for the blue and red channels, each time selecting a different length and direction of the gradient control line as you draw it.

5. In the Channels window, click on the RGB channel to preview your results.

This technique produces excellent Web page backgrounds and the printed page, while also generating unique textures for 3D applications. In the object stack, compositing a channel painting is very helpful, since it can give the other object layers a more creative space to rest upon.

Adding & Subtracting Channels

You can perform other image processing operations on channels by adding and subtracting them from each other, and more, by accessing the commands in the Modify | Calculate menu. This is a more complex process calling for a lot if exploration and taking notes along the way, but it can add immeasurably to your ability to perform digital retouching of images when called for. New alpha effects channels can be added at any time. Adding a line of white text to an alpha channel and using the Float command, for instance, allows the text to be masked from all of the other primary channel layers and to cut through all of them in the final channel composite. Any primary channel can be duplicated to emphasize its contribution to the final color composite.

You can think of the Calculate commands as producing a channel palette, as compared to a color palette. The possibilities are truly infinite, because the calculations can keep writing the results back to the same target channels. The Calculate commends are:

- **Duplicate:** Creates a clone of the selected channel, and places it in the channel window. Use this command when you want to explore alternate effects options for a channel. You can turn each duplicated channel on or off to see how it composites in the final result when you select RGB or CMYK.

- **Darker/Lighter:** This allows you to intermix the lightness or darkness of two channels with each other, placing the lighter or darker pixels from the source to the target channel. This is an operation worth considering when you want to remove a channel from the window, but keep its effects involved in the channel composite.

- **Blend:** This operation fuses two channels together according to your settings, determining the percentage of each that will make up the new channel. Use this command when it's important to see how one channel might suffice for two at different blend percentages. It's a good idea to do a series of different percentage blends and compare their effect on the composite before selecting the one that looks best.

- **Composite:** This is a rather complicated operation. It's comparable to the Blend option, but takes its percentage values from yet a third alpha channel that tells the command how the selected channels should be composited. As you become more familiar with the application of alpha channel effects, this operation will become more a important alternative.

- **Add/Subtract:** Channels can be added or subtracted, with all of the pixel values being considered in the mix. Try this when compacting the channels window is important.

- **Multiply:** Channels that are multiplied together always result in a destination channel that is darker than either. The resulting alpha channel is perfect as a drop shadow for the objects. Commonly, the Multiply command would be used on anything but the background channel, but this is something for you to explore.

- **Brightness:** This makes a channel uniformly lighter or darker on a scale from -128 to 128. This is one of the most used commands in the Calculate set, because it's something you will want to explore quite often.

- **Difference:** This command calculates the absolute difference between two selected channels, and writes out the result as a separate destination channel.

Paths

FreeHand users are going to love this xRes attribute, because it allows you to work with path controls that are common to FreeHand. Paths are an alternate way of creating selections in xRes. You would choose a path over a FreeHand marquee for several reasons:

- Your familiarity with manipulating path controls in FreeHand might be the deciding factor.

- Path controls allow more fine-tuning and shaping of a selection than other marquee creation alternatives.

- Paths can take on strokes and fills, while other marquee selections are limited to fills.

The Path window has controls for creating and editing paths, including adding curved or corner control points (see Figure 11-16). Paths can be copied, duplicated, saved, and otherwise manipulated (rotated, resized, and so on). Paths can be used as marquees for masking operations, and also as painting guides. To transform a path into a marquee, use the Select | From Path command.

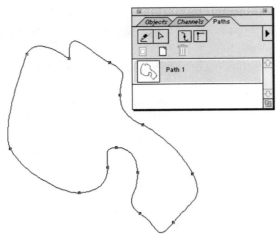

Figure 11-16: The Paths window gives you control over path creation and manipulation.

Clipping Paths

A clipping path can be used to select only one part of an image, making the parts outside of the path transparent. Clipping paths are commonly used in PageMaker and QuarkXPress for masking non-rectangular bitmap images. Selecting the Make Clipping Path command from the fly out menu in the Paths window performs this operation. Then it's just a matter of saving the file (TIFF is suggested).

Painting With Paths

This is a unique painting method not immediately apparent when working with paths in xRes, and leads to interesting abstracted graphics:

1. Import a bitmap that has content you would like to transform into a painting. A face image is a good choice.

2. Use the Path pen to draw outlines around the features in the image that are to be translated. You can draw as many paths as you like, and they can be closed or open paths.

3. When finished, use the control handles to adjust the shapes as needed, so that the paths conform to the features in the image as closely as possible.

4. Select your brush and the options required to render the image according to the look you want to achieve (the Calligraphic Ribbon brush is a good starting point).

5. Select all of the paths that make up the image, and select Edit I Stroke. The brush style you configured will automatically draw itself on the screen, following the exact outline the paths have laid out.

Tip

A perfect subject for this technique is bird photos. The results are likened to fine Zen masterpieces if you use either the Calligraphic Ribbon brush or the Japanese Bamboo brush.

Masks

There are several techniques for creating masks in xRes. The one most used is to draw or create a selection area, with any one of the tools we have covered so far. Everything inside the selection area can be modified with the tools and effects at your disposal. Everything outside of that area is masked, and cannot be modified until the marquee is removed or unless the Invert command is used. Commonly, the marquee tools, Magic Wand tool, and the Pen tool are sufficient for generating masks.

Using the Mask Window

The advantage of using the Mask palette in developing selections is that you can choose any or all of seven colors in your document, all with a variable degree of tolerance, to create the selection (see Figure 11-17). Creating a selection from a group of color components often results in smoother selection masks than using the Wand tool.

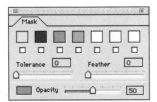

Figure 11-17: The Mask palette.

Creating an Automatic Color Mask

When you have an image that needs to be masked, but has too many colors to allow the use of the Wand tool effectively, use the Mask window to automatically generate the mask.

1. Use the Eyedropper tool to fill up to seven color swatches on the Mask palette with colors from the document that you would like to include in the mask. A checkmark will appear under them as you do this.

2. Set the Tolerance and Feathering sliders in the Mask window. Unless you would like to extend the selection into the non-selected area with a visible halo, a feathering of about 5 is common. The tolerance depends upon the range of colors in your document. It's a good idea to start at about 50, and adjust the slider up or down depending upon the preview of the selection as it is generated.

3. Choose Select | Auto, and the selection is generated.

Using FastMask Mode

For the artist new to the digital arts, this may be the most natural way to create a selection, since it uses the more common painting tools as mask (selection) creation devices. Use of FastMask mode is extremely intuitive.

1. Open an image that you would like to add selection effects to.

2. Define a brush style. The Oil Painting brush is a good choice here, as is the Magic Marker.

3. Click on the FastMask function, the red oval, at the bottom of the Toolbox. The screen will be overlayed with a transparent red tint. Use the white color in the foreground/background swatches on the Tool palette to paint away areas of the red overlay where you do not want the mask to be. Use the black swatch to paint in (or touch-up) areas of the image you do want the mask to be. The nonmasked area becomes a selection, though it can be inverted as a protected area as well.

Tip

The opacity of the mask overlay is set in the Mask window. Consider setting it to 40 percent, so you can see where it is, but also can see through it to the objects on the screen.

Moving On

In this chapter, we have thoroughly explored object operations, and how their usage helps to create astounding image composites. We also delved into the uses of color and Color Modes in xRes, and fully explored the uses of channels, paths, and masks. In the next chapter, we will begin our explorations of Extreme 3D.

Part III

Mastering Extreme 3D

12

Installing & Configuring Extreme 3D 2.0

Extreme 3D 2.0 ships with the FreeHand 7 Graphics Studio. Version 2 of Extreme 3D offers more speed and more versatility over version 1.0.

Installing Extreme 3D

Version 2.0 comes on a separate CD-ROM along with the other components of the FreeHand 7 Graphics Studio. Place the CD-ROM in your drive. Extreme 3D installation starts automatically from the CD. Installation for both the Mac OS and Windows follows the installer script. Just follow the installation instructions and specify where the application should be placed when prompted, what your serial number is, and so forth.

Extreme 3D 2.0 Requirements for Windows Systems

The following are the system requirements for Extreme 3D versions 1.0 and 2.0:

- Pentium processor
- If installing under Windows 95: 16 MB of RAM minimum (24 MB recommended)
- If installing under Windows NT 3.51 or higher: 16 MB of RAM minimum (32 MB recommended)

- For 24-bit preview: SVGA monitor
- 20 MB of hard disk space
- CD-ROM drive

Installing Extreme 3D 2.0 does not upgrade Extreme 3D 1.0. If you want to keep Extreme 3D 1.0 on your machine, install Extreme 3D 2 into a different folder.

Extreme 3D 2.0 Requirements for Macintosh OS Systems

The following system requirements are for Extreme 3D versions 1.0 and 2.0, but note that version 2.0 requires a Power PC system:

- Power Macintosh
- 16 MB of RAM minimum (24 or more MB recommended)
- System 7.5 or above
- 8-bit monitor (24-bit for preview)
- 20 MB of disk space
- CD-ROM drive
- Modern Memory Manager setting in the Memory Control Panel must be on

Installing Extreme 3D 2.0 does not upgrade Extreme 3D 1.0. If you want to keep Extreme 3D 1.0 on your machine, install Extreme 3D 2 into a different folder.

New Features in Extreme 3D 2.0

Extreme 3D 2.0 provides a number of new features and enhancements. This includes faster rendering times, enhanced effects features, and a list of new supported file formats.

New Web Features

Extreme 3D now supports several 2D file formats useful for exporting Web-ready images, including:

- GIF89a (still and animated, transparent and interlaced)
- Progressive JPEG

- PNG
- xRes LRG for the new Shockwave imaging plug-in
- Several 3D file formats are also supported by Extreme 3D for creating 3D worlds and images. These include:
  - VRML 1 & 2
  - Apple's 3DMF (Windows users also have access to 3DMF files)

You can also incorporate VRML 1 and 2 features in Extreme 3D models, such as attaching Anchor, Inline, and Texture URLs to objects within the Object browser. Extreme 3D's uniform and adaptive smoothing features are uniquely suited to creating highly optimized objects and worlds for the Web. Use these features to quickly change object resolution for VRML level of detail support. VRML worlds built with Extreme 3D are fully compatible with VRML browsers such as Netscape's Live 3D, SGI's Cosmo, or Intervista's WorldView. Extreme 3D files can also be exported as 3DMF files for Web use.

Cross-Platform Formats

Extreme 3D now supports a number of cross-platform bitmap 2D file formats. These files can be both imported, for use as texture maps and backgrounds, and exported, for use in other applications, including Macromedia studio applications. The bitmap file formats that Extreme 3D supports are:

- BMP
- GIF
- JPEG
- Photoshop 3.0
- PICT
- PNG
- Targa
- TIFF
- xRes LRG

Extreme 3D now supports import of two vector-based 2D file formats. These files are especially useful for importing profiles designed in professional illustration programs for use as defining geometry for Extreme 3D models. You can now drag and drop profiles from FreeHand 7 directly into Extreme 3D. The vector-based file formats that Extreme 3D supports are:

- FreeHand 4, 5, and 7
- EPSF

Extreme 3D has further optimized its ability to work with other Macromedia studio applications by implementing a number of its features as extensible Xtras:

- All file import and export filters
- Materials
- Lights
- VRML (export only)
- 3DMF

New Tools

The Toolbox provides two new tools: the Metaforms tool and the Particle System tool. Apply any of Extreme 3D's materials and use any material animation features with metaforms and particle systems to create a wide variety of new effects.

- Use the Metaforms tool to create blobby or organic forms that can be animated, like clay models, to break into pieces or flow together.
- Use the Particle System tool to create complex models like leaves on a tree or behavior-based animations such as floating bubbles, exploding fireworks, and falling rain.

Lights & Materials

All of Extreme 3D's lights and materials are now listed as Xtras. This means that a wide variety of new functions can be incrementally added to Extreme 3D over time without requiring you to upgrade. Instead, you will be able to check Macromedia's Web site for new lights and materials and download them. Check the site often to download new Xtras. If you are a developer, you can write lights and materials Xtras that Extreme 3D can use.

- Transparency and Luminosity have been added to solid materials, such as Organic Magic, and texture map materials, such as the Mondo Map material. You can also choose to invert bump maps used in Mondo Map materials to create new effects.

- Designing new materials that use transparency and luminosity is easier because you can see these effects immediately in the Materials browser preview window.

- With version 2.0, you can define all the standard material properties, including the new properties of transparency and luminosity, as colors rather than simple gradient steps. By using actual set color values, you can create a much wider variety of material looks.

- The Plastic material and Texture Map material have been combined into one default material. Look for Generic+Texture in the Materials browser if you want to create a simple texture map or solid material. This is the most basic material texture.

- Ambient lights, lights that illuminate all sides of an object, are now available as a separate light type in the Light browser. The Ambient light settings created using Global Effects in version 1.0 Extreme 3D files are applied to the default Ambient light in the version 2.0 Lights browser.

- Spotlights and Distant lights now provide you with more control over the shadows they create. You can use the new Shadow Resolution and Shadow Fuzziness properties to create softer shadows and to optimize memory usage.

- Another addition to Spotlights is a control for enhancing dust shadows and/or light rays. Use these features to achieve more customized lighting effects with Extreme 3D 2.0's improved volumetric lights.

Rendering Changes

A number of enhanced rendering features have been added to version 2.0, all of which make the application more useful for high-end project needs.

- Extreme 3D's renderer has been completely re-written to take advantage of floating point processing capabilities found in the Power PC. This means that Extreme 3D 2.0 for Mac OS is a PowerPC-only application.

- The Extreme 3D renderer now supports transparency in shadows. You can choose to have any material that has a transparency value render that transparency in the shadow of the final rendering. Use this feature to achieve effects usually found only in ray tracers. Extreme 3D can produce effects such as light casting shadows through venetian blinds or lamp shades, but at speeds much faster than comparable effects rendered with ray tracers.

- Gamma correction is now available as a final render setup option. Adjust gamma according to your final output medium needs, and eliminate the need to do gamma correction as a post-processing step.

- Pre-multiplied alpha for film and video output is still available and standard alpha has been added as an option. Use standard if you want to use output images as mattes for compositing in post-production.

QuickDraw 3D on the Mac OS

Extreme 3D 2.0 is completely compatible with Apple's QuickDraw 3D. By using QuickDraw 3D, you can take advantage of hardware acceleration to increase interactive rendering speeds. This provides you with fully rendered scenes while you are previewing animations or scene building. All animatable parameters can be previewed in real-time with QuickDraw 3D, including scaling and moving texture maps, and moving objects.

Extreme 3D's own internal renderer is still available. With the QuickDraw 3D extension on, you can choose to take advantage of the improved transparency rendering of QuickDraw 3D in one window and view your work in 32-bit shaded mode with the Extreme 3D 2.0 internal renderer in another window.

New Improved Help Access

The online help now supports a Help pointer, which provides context-sensitive help in the workspace. A comprehensive index has also been added to the Help screen. Other online additions include electronic documentation built into the help application that supplements the printed documentation. These include overview, how to, reference, and troubleshooting.

Other 2.0 Improvements

A collection of other new and enhanced features that don't fall within the previous categories mentioned include the following:

- Use the new Collect Files feature to collect all the texture (*.TEX) files for a scene. Move them from the Material folder to a folder of your choice. This reduces the number of texture files that you accumulate in the Material folder, makes it easier to archive scenes and their associated texture files after a project is completed, and supports multi-user production by making it easier to transfer complete files to other users without having to supply all of the original bitmap textures.

- You can quickly create complicated arrays and multiple linked duplicates with the new Duplicate Special feature. Create windows in a skyscraper or a spiral staircase in a single step.

- The Score has two features to facilitate customizing score organization and display. Use the hierarchy expand and collapse arrows to hide properties that are otherwise exposed using the filters alone. Sort objects into layers in the Layers browser and then use the new Selected Layer object filter type to further organize and manage the Score.

- A Find All capability has been added to Edit/Find dialog boxes.

Information for Extreme 3D 1.0 Users

Older Extreme 3D 1.0 files are upwardly compatible with Extreme 3D 2.0's new features. Version 1.0 files open in version 2.0 without the need for conversion. Some changes to lights and materials, however, may alter aspects of your lighting or materials designs. You might see differences in Ambient lights, shadows, or mapping.

Here are some suggestions for recreating Extreme 3D 1.0 looks in Extreme 3D version 2.0:

- **Ambient lights:** There is now a default Ambient light in the scene. It can be edited in the Lights browser like any other light. The ambient settings you made in Extreme 3D 1.0 using Global Effects are automatically stored in this light and can be edited using the 2.0 Lights browser.

- **Materials:** Materials no longer have individual Ambient settings to control each material's response to the Ambient light. Use the new 2.0 luminosity property in any material to control the effect of ambient light on a per-material basis.

- **Spotlights:** Extreme 3D 1.0 files containing Spotlights that used dust fall off, if read into Extreme 3D 2.0 with the Use Dust Fall Off check box unchecked. To render these Spotlights correctly, open the 2.0 Light editor for each such Spotlight and check the Use Dust Fall Off check box.

- **Shadows:** Some shadows may look different in 2.0 from 1.0 files. Use the new 2.0 Shadow Resolution control in Distant lights or Spotlights to approximate, or improve, the look of shadows created in Extreme 3D 1.0 files.

■ **Fog:** In Extreme 3D 1.0 the fog color was added to the background color or image. Extreme 3D 2.0 handles layers of transparency better, but this makes the version 1.0 functionality impossible. In Extreme 3D 2.0, if the fog transparency is not pure white, the fog is assumed to be completely opaque. This is because the background is infinitely far away, and even a little opacity becomes opaque if it is thick enough. When the transparency is pure white, the fog color is added to the background (as it was in Extreme 3D 1.0). This is done separately for each color channel R, G, and B. So if blue is 1.0 (255) but the others are less than that, just the blue channel of the background will be visible behind the fog. It is recommend that you do not use fog with an orthographic view. If you have an Extreme 3D 1.0 file that used fog in orthographic perspective, you must choose a different perspective. You might also need to increase the Fog Depth value in order for your file to render in Extreme 3D 2.0 as it did in Extreme 3D 1.0.

■ **Mapping types:** All objects in version 2.0 now have a default mapping type. For objects using texture maps, the default mapping style is intrinsic; for all others it is projective. For example, if you apply an Organic Magic material to an object, its default mapping style is projective, creating a solid material look. If you change your mind and apply a Mondo Map material to the object, its default mapping style is intrinsic, mapping the texture map to the object's surface.

Solid materials, such as Organic Magic and Tiles, can now be used either as solid materials or like texture maps. To use a solid material like a texture map, change the object's mapping type to intrinsic in the Objects browser. Because solid materials in Extreme 3D 1.0 didn't pay attention to the mapping type set for an object, some solid materials in existing files might look different in Extreme 3D 2.0. Objects with solid materials that were saved in Extreme 3D 1.0 with a mapping type other than projective can be corrected by explicitly setting the objects' mapping type to projective in Extreme 3D 2.0. To change the object's mapping type, select it and go to the Info page of the Objects browser.

■ **Alpha options for mapping:** The existence of surface alpha option works differently. In Extreme 3D 2.0, areas outside the map use the surface color and its properties. If the tile flag is set, or if the map covers the whole object, the existence of surface alpha option looks the same in Extreme 3D 2.0 as in Extreme 3D 1.0.

■ **Mapping of endcaps:** Mapping of endcaps is improved in Extreme 3D 2.0. This means that some Extreme 3D 1.0 files might not display texture maps in version 2.0 as they did in version 1. You can use the Texture

Placement tool to adjust the mapping. This will be especially necessary for tiled texture maps.

- **Mapping improvements:** The algorithm for creating bumps in the Mondo Map material has changed. Bumps look more realistic in Extreme 3D 2.0. If a bump appears less obvious, you can increase it to get the bumps to match their look in Extreme 3D 1.0. A Stripes pattern on a spherical object or a Cubic pattern on a cube object will appear as a solid color until you change the offset value. Also, because the cylindrical pattern of stripes relies heavily on the number of polygons on a drawing, it may appear chunky if the number of polygons is low. To smooth out the stripes, increase the number of polygons.

  The way that the Organic Magic material calculates bumps and pattern and bump transitions has been improved. Extreme 3D 1.0 files that use the Organic Magic material will look different in Extreme 3D 2.0. You can adjust the material settings to re-create the look achieved using Extreme 3D 1.0.

- **Gamma correction and pre-multiplied alpha:** In Extreme 3D 1.0 all files were saved by default using pre-multiplied alpha and no gamma correction. Extreme 3D 1.0 files are imported with these settings.

Extreme 3D Goodies on the Application's CD-ROM

The CD-ROM used to install Extreme 3D also lists a number of added items which can be integrated with the application. These include:

- A number of "Learning Extreme 3D" short training movie files are included on the CD-ROM. It is essential that you view these if you are new to Extreme 3D, and especially if you are new to 3D applications in general. They cover all of the necessary basics, and give you a jump start in mastering the software. These learning movies cover everything, including lights, material, and special effects.

- Over 20 MB of 3D models from ViewPoint and Zygote

- 160 MB of Wraptures (a trademarked brand name) textures in 22 categories

- Over 70 MB of fonts in TrueType and Type 1 formats

For examples of the kinds of images and movies you can create with Extreme 3D, see the Gallery Viewer in the Gallery folder on the Extreme 3D CD, or the Gallery in the Extreme 3D section of Macromedia's web site at http://www.macromedia.com.

Setting Preferences

To set up your Extreme 3D environment for your project needs, you have to attend to several components of Extreme 3D. Setting the global preferences options is the place to start.

Extreme 3D preferences are listed in the Edit menu instead of the more standard File menu. They include Geometry, Animation, Views, Files, Network, and 3D Acceleration. All of these settings appear under separate tabs in the Preferences dialog.

Geometry

Select Edit | Preferences, and select the Geometry tab to display the geometry preferences (see Figure 12-1). The geometry settings affect editing controls and parameters for 3D objects. The defaults should be left alone for most users. Users with a need for a high degree of precision (mechanical engineers, CAM users, and others) might want to adjust the Nudge factors, and especially the Fit Tolerance factor. On the other hand, users whose projects require a lesser degree of mechanical exactness (cartoonists, logo animators, multimedia producers) may find it to their advantage to adjust the settings in the other direction, allowing for a greater degree of movement for commands that address display precision and fit tolerances. If you don't know where you fall in this regard, we suggest you leave these settings at their default positions until you need to change them.

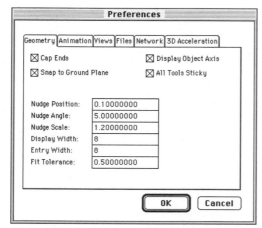

Figure 12-1: The Geometry tab of the Preferences dialog.

Animation

Select Edit | Preferences and choose the Animation tab to display the animation preferences (see Figure 12-2). Under the Play Animations Using choices, select the Bounding Box Render Style alternative as you develop the animation. This allows you to see the animation at a faster pace, close to that of its real frame rate playback speed. When the animation reaches its final phases, you can click the Currently Selected Max Render Style mode alternative to get a better preview of how the 3D volumetric elements are interacting in the scene.

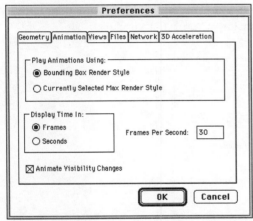

Figure 12-2: The Animation tab of the Preferences dialog.

As for the Display Time In option, that's purely a matter of choice and what is important to each animator. Displaying frames is vital if you are trying to have certain things occur at certain frames, to comply with the frame rate settings. For instance, if you wanted an event to take place two seconds into the animation and the frame rate setting playback speed were set to 30 fps (Frames Per Second), then the action should occur at frame 31. If you choose seconds, then the global time an animation takes is of more importance. For example, if your production manager or client is asking you to develop a five-second logo spin for a commercial, you will want to make sure that your animation matches the time exactly, with the proper movements and freezes.

Visibility changes deal with animation tracks that control whether and when a selected object is visible in a scene. Visibility changes would include a spaceship suddenly appearing through a space warp field, or food disappearing from a plate. Visibility changes do not fade objects in and out, but make them pop in or out, and are comparable to what is called a "cut" in video terms. Leave the Animate Visibility Changes option off until your animation is completed, then turn it on, and go back to the animation controller, where you can decide which objects will appear or disappear at what point in the animation timeline.

Views

Select Edit | Preferences and choose the Views tab to display the views preferences (see Figure 12-3). The Create New View for New Window option defaults to on and should be left that way. This adds a New View item to the Views browser, allowing you to instantly jump to that view.

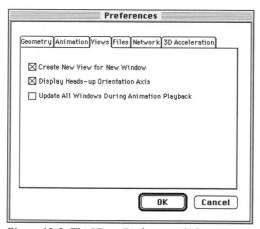

Figure 12-3: The Views Preferences dialog.

The Display Heads-up Orientation Axis option should also be left on in its default position. This displays a helpful view axis on the screen, which can help you to rotate the view back to its normalized state if things get turned around (which they often do in complex computer animations).

The Update All Windows During Animation Playback option is best left off. The only reason to turn it on would be to preview which animated view is best when an animation is complete. Animators often include several views of the same animation in a final movie. This allows you to do less work to get more variety in the playback, and also to consume more time when you need to stretch things out without resorting to boring animation loops.

Files

Select Edit | Preferences and choose the Files tab to display the files preferences (see Figure 12-4). The Import Text option brings in text from a PICT (Mac OS only), DXF, EPS, or FreeHand file as a separate object. The default is off. If you use many non-Extreme 3D text files, or plan to, turn this on.

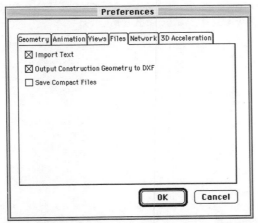

Figure 12-4: The Files tab of the Preferences dialog.

The Output Construction Geometry to DXF option includes the working plane and construction geometry (except construction points) with other geometry in any scene that is exported as a DXF file. This is useful only when the working plane and construction geometry are needed for reference when working with the DXF file, which they seldom are. The default is off, and should remain that way.

The Save Compact Files option compresses an Extreme 3D file when it is saved according to a prioritized formula. Compact files save the geometry, but some levels of geometry information are not saved, and instead are rebuilt the next time you open the file. It takes longer to open a file that has been saved with the Save Compact Files option selected, but the file size is smaller. The default is off. The main reason for turning this on would be if you were doing all of your 3D work in Extreme 3D, or if your disk space was getting a bit tight. In that case, saving some disk capacity might be a good trade-off.

Network

Select Edit | Preferences and choose the Network tab to display the network preferences (see Figure 12-5). For file sequence naming, Windows users will want to check the first option (Name####.ext Convention), while Mac OS users will probably select the second one (Name.#### Convention). This will set the right conditions for platform conventions. If you have to select one convention for both Mac OS and Windows uses, opt for the Windows convention, as Windows is less forgiving when it comes to file names.

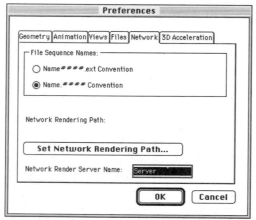

Figure 12-5: The Network tab of the Preferences dialog.

The network rendering options in this dialog are for those fortunate enough to have a render farm (separate systems used for rendering that are networked to one main control system). Use these options to specify your network rendering path and server.

3D Acceleration

Select Edit | Preferences, then choose the 3D Acceleration tab to display the 3D acceleration preferences (see Figure 12-6). Check the Use Dedicated 3D Acceleration Board option if you have hardware installed that is used to accelerate rendering.

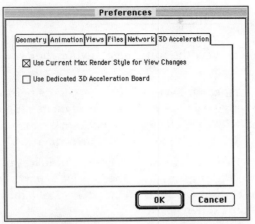

Figure 12-6: The 3D Acceleration tab of the Preferences dialog.

View Settings

All of the following customizing options are accessed through selections in the View menu. Each has its own set of parameters, as detailed in the following listings.

New View

New View (View | New View) creates a new view by duplicating the current view. The new view then becomes the current view and is named after the view it duplicates. To help avoid confusion, a number is appended to the end of the new view's name in the Views browser's list of views. To change the name of the view, enter a new name in the Views browser's text entry field while the new view is selected and press Enter. Use the Views browser to change the view settings of the new view to those you want. To recreate the view that is available upon opening Extreme 3D, choose View | Home before selecting New View.

Perspective

Extreme 3D 2.0 allows you to view the edit screen in your choice of perspective (View | Perspective), including:

- **Very Wide:** (View | Perspective | Very Wide)—Very wide perspectives exaggerate the outer edges of a selection, especially when it is animated. They should be used with care, since they tend to make the viewer think she/he is hallucinating. They are great for dream sequences.

- **Wide:** (View | Perspective | Wide)—This choice is a little less radical than the Very Wide option, and is great when the graphic is part of an animated scene that shows the camera following in back of a moving element, like a car speeding down a road.

- **Moderate:** (View | Perspective | Moderate)—This is the most common choice, adding just enough image deformation to make an animated scene interesting, with very little warping effect on the images involved.

- **Narrow:** (View | Perspective | Narrow)—This option adds no perceptible warping to images in a scene, but does allow a realistic perspective. Its most common use is for static images, such as a magazine graphic.

- **Orthographic:** (View | Perspective | Orthographic)—This option should only be used in the design phase, since it produces a distorted perspective when used on the finished graphic.

- **Custom:** (View | Perspective | Custom)—This option comes into play when you use the view controls to alter the perspective on your own. When designing 3D objects, always use the Orthographic option, because this gives you straight-on views, which help you see what the dimensions and measurements are really about. Select any of the other options when you are ready to render the scene to give it more interest (see Figure 12-7).

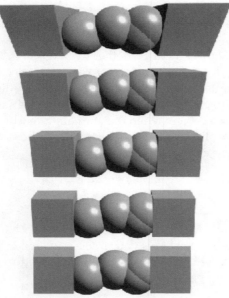

Figure 12-7: Shown are the results of alternate Perspective settings: Very Wide, Wide, Moderate, Narrow, and Orthographic.

Tip

Note that the wider the perspective is set, the wider the scan of the scene, and the smaller the separate objects become in the distance. As objects draw close with wider perspectives however, they loom large and become distorted.

Fit to Window

Fit to Window (View | Fit to Window) attempts to fit the selected object to the window, making it as large as possible. It's helpful to invoke this after zooming in for editing, to get things back in view. It also works when multiple objects are selected to bring them all into view. In this case, use Edit | Select All, and then View | Fit to Window.

Camera Alignment

Camera alignment (View | Align Camera), whether to an object or to views, are animation controls. Aligning a camera to an object keeps the selected object as the center of attention, no matter where it goes or what it does. Aligning the camera to views allows you to create an animation in which the same actions are seen from a different selected view when the animation reaches a certain frame in the sequence. Before aligning the camera to views, those views have to be created first.

Setting up Rendering

Render Style (Object | Render Style) allows you to select the rendering for the editing process, while Render Setup (Render | Final Render Setup) gives you control over the final rendering parameters.

Render Style

The Render Styles, from low to higher detail, are accessed by Object | Render Style | Bounding Box, Wireframe, Hidden Wireframe, Faceted, Faceted Wireframe, Smooth, or Shader. Depending upon what stage your 3D work is at, you should consider different render styles. Bounding Box is the fastest, but shows no detail. Use it to preview animations, and to place objects in approximate positions on the screen. Starting with Smooth, you get a good idea about object dimensions and reflections. The Shader gives you a 32-bit draft mode look at the object. The various wireframe and faceted styles present more detail, but lack the finer features of Smooth and Shader. Use Smooth and especially the Shader option to give you the best previews of how the final render will look.

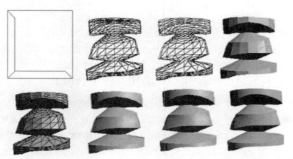

Figure 12-8: Here is an object showing the different rendering styles, from top left to bottom right: Bounding Box, Wireframe, Hidden Wireframe, Faceted, Faceted Wireframe, Smooth, Shader, and Final Render.

Final Render Setup

The Final Render Setup dialog (Render | Final Render Setup) allows you to shape the quality of the finished graphic or animation (see Figure 12-9). This can be done at the start of your session and be considered as a project preference, or you can intervene at any time to change these settings before the final rendering. It is suggested that you use a low 2x2 setting until the final rendering is ready, because this provides faster feedback when rendering the scene to the screen as a test. Final renders, even at low settings, show all lights, shadows, and textures. For the best final renderings, select the highest quality, 8x8. Consider the following settings for final render setup:

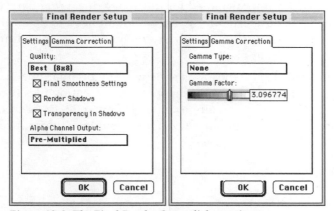

Figure 12-9: The Final Render Setup dialog options.

- **Final Smoothness Settings:** Leave this unchecked until the very final rendering to save time. If this option is not checked, final render uses the Interactive Render Settings for uniform and adaptive smoothing. Because each object can have its own surface smoothness setting, different objects in the same scene may have slightly different resolutions.

- **Render Shadows:** Leave this off until the very final rendering to save time. When Render Shadows is selected, the final rendering includes shadows, which are calculated for each light source listed in the Lights browser that has its Shadows check box turned on. Calculating shadows increases rendering time; a rule of thumb is to multiply the rendering time without shadows by the number of lights with shadows on to get the rendering time with shadows.

- **Transparency in Shadows:** Leave this off until the very final rendering to save time. When Transparency in Shadows is checked, shadows in the scene are calculated based on the amount of transparency in each material. Materials that are at least 50 percent transparent (transparency at 50% gray, for example) are transparent to light, which means that light can pass through the material's surface. If the material is less than 50 percent transparent, the light does not pass through the material, so it casts a shadow on the surface where the light hits it. When Transparency in Shadows is on, each pixel is checked for transparency during rendering, so rendering requires more time.

- **Alpha Channel Output:**
  - **Pre-Multiplied:** This is the default, and should remain selected in most cases. This is the type of alpha rendered by Extreme 3D. It retains aliasing calculated for the image during rendering, so it may be the preferred format if you don't need to do additional editing or compositing with this image in an image editing or digital video application.
  - **Standard:** This is the alpha style used by popular image editing applications. Use this option only when creating files in a file format that supports alpha channels (either 32- or 64-bit). File formats that do not have alpha information may produce aliased (jagged-edged) images.

- **Gamma Correction:** Optimizes the rendered image so that the colors look best when viewed in the intended delivery method, such as film, video, or print. There are four gamma types:

  - **None:** No gamma correction is applied.

  - **Punch Up:** The highlights of the image are compressed to improve the contrast between dark and light areas. Use this for print.

  - **Video:** The default Gamma Factor is 2.2, which is the correct value for NTSC gamma correction. With this setting, colors are compressed so that they display correctly and don't oversaturate on an NTSC display. Use this for video work, multimedia, and display on the Web.

    - **Film:** Imitates color correction for film. Use this for film output.

- **Gamma Factor:** Determines the amount of correction that will be applied to the rendered scene. Consider exploring different settings for a few frames of a final render, and check the output.

Design Planes

Extreme 3D offers you both working and ground planes as design aids. Although you can toggle both of these on as initial preferences, you will probably toggle them off and on throughout the design session as needed.

Working Plane

Toggle the working plane on when you need an onscreen guide to design objects (Object | Show Working Plane). The working plane is a design grid. It can be oriented to the view, the world, or the ground plane. Orienting it to the view is the most common option, since this presents it full face in every view. Select the Auto Working Plane to View option. By default, the working plane is red when selected. Double-clicking on it allows you to resize and reshape it.

Tip

The working and ground planes can be used as a perspective indicator in all views after setting them up in the ³/4 View.

Ground Plane

The ground plane is useful for placing objects on a common level, and for orienting objects to a common surface (Object | Show Ground Plane). The ground plane is a defaulted design and placement grid that cannot be altered in any way. It cannot be mapped, but can serve as a guide for the placement of a rectangular ground object.

Global Effects

You can set Global Effects as a preference at the beginning of a session, or toggle it on later for preview rendering (Render | Global Effects). There is one Global Effect: Fog. You can set its color, transparency, and depth. Depth is a relative number, and sets the distance at which the fog is at 70 percent. A setting of 1 would cause the Fog to start almost from the eye, and so obliterate most objects. A setting of 100 would emulate a distant mist. The default setting is 10, a good place to do a test render. Fog can only be seen in final renders (see Figure 12-10).

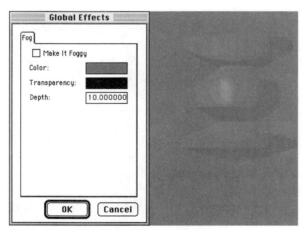

Figure 12-10: The Global Effects dialog.

Set Background Options

Depending upon your need to see a background even during the preview phase of your work, Set Background Options (Render | Set Background) can be set as an initial preference or left for later rendering checks. The dialog is simple, offering either a color or a graphic to be loaded (see Figure 12-11).

Figure 12-11: The Set Background dialog.

Tip

Create a series of gradient backgrounds in xRes, and store them in a separate folder for background use in Extreme 3D. Use the xRes gradient effects options.

Window Setup

Window Setup (Window | Window Setup) is one of the first things you should do when setting up your project preferences at the start of a session. The Window Setup dialog allows you to set the Image Size, Max Render Style, and Interactive Renderer Type of your project (see Figure 12-12). Select a size from the pop-up list, or determine a custom size in the secondary dialog.

Figure 12-12: The Window Setup dialog.

Tip

Although you can set up the working window at any point in a session, we highly recommend that you set it at the start for the type of project you are creating. The size of your window will influence your 3D design habits.

Four-View Setup

Four-View Setup (Window | Four View Setup): by default, Extreme 3D opens up with one window, allowing you to change the view as needed from the View menu. Some 3D designers prefer to have multiple views on screen all of the time, so they can check their scenes from different angles as they work. The positive part of doing this is that you'll make fewer trips to the View menu, and wait less for the redraws that accompany a view change. The liability is that you will have less workspace for design and manipulation. Four-View Setup places four equally sized windows on your display (see Figure 12-13). One of the views shows the Preview rendered setting as a default, while the other views are Wireframes.

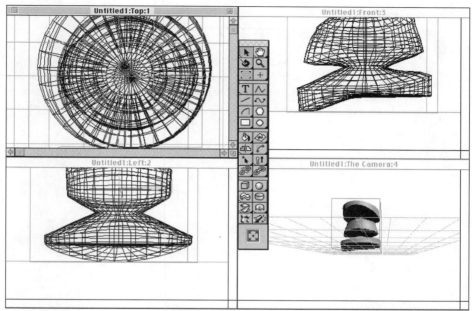

Figure 12-13: The standard Four-View Setup.

Tip

> *One way to have the best of both worlds is to use the Four-View Setup, but to shrink three of the views radically, and expand the last one for design comfort.*

Saving an Extreme 3D Project

Use the File | Save and File | Save As options to save the Extreme 3D project in Extreme 3D format with all of the geometry, lighting, and materials intact. You can also export your work as DXF, Extreme 3D Tracks, Swivel 3D, 3DMF (text and binary), VRML, and the following single-image graphics formats: BMP, GIF, JPEG, PICT, PNG, Targa, TIFF, and xRes LRG. No matter what else you do, always save the project out as an Extreme 3D file first, so you can come back to it and edit the contents if you want to. Refer to Chapter 8 for more details on file formats.

Moving On

This chapter has covered the installation procedures for Extreme 3D, as well as how to go about setting all of the necessary parameters for Extreme 3D project management. In the next chapter, we will explore how to create and modify 3D objects in Extreme 3D.

13

Creating & Modifying Objects

In FreeHand and xRes, an object is any element in the file, be it a FreeHand path or an xRes brushstroke. In Extreme 3D, an object is closer to a real-world object, a shape with a 3D appearance and a possible texture. The whole idea in Extreme 3D is to place one or more objects in a 3D scene and to render and save the resulting rendering as a picture or an animation.

Rendering and saving out a single-frame 3D scene allows Extreme 3D output to be easily reused with xRes and FreeHand. xRes and FreeHand can be used with Extreme 3D by providing 2D and bitmap and vector art that Extreme 3D can use as a background or to texture 3D objects. The basic form in FreeHand is the point and the line, in xRes it is the 2D plane represented by the graphic surface, or "canvas." In Extreme 3D we move everything up one dimensional notch, moving from XY to XYZ, the third dimension. Then Extreme 3D allows us to incorporate the fourth dimension, time, as the basis for creating animations.

Importing

There are thousands of free 3D objects in every format imaginable that you can download from the Web. Just surf around, and you're sure to find at least a dozen good 3D sites a day. There are thousands of other 3D objects in every format available on CD-ROM libraries, and most ask just pennies a model.

Thousands more models are available on the CD-ROM that accompanies every major 3D application (Extreme 3D has two directories of 3D models from Acuris and ViewPoint on its own installation CD-ROM). If that isn't enough, everyone who has spent the necessary learning time with the 3D application they own and use has at least a few models of their own in storage, and many are given to friends and peers.

Except for major films with a fat budget for computer animation, very few computer graphics 3D projects create all of their models from scratch. Why should they? There are just too many high-quality 3D models available to keep reinventing the wheel. Besides, even if two 3D animators import the same 3D model of a chair from the same source, they will probably wind up with two very different models by the time they render an animation. This is because most 3D models that are imported are also edited and crafted with the unique signature of the computer artist and animator in charge. As an Extreme 3D artist and animator, you have to be able to import, edit, and place externally available 3D models, as well as having the knowledge and expertise to create your own from the ground up.

Import Types

In addition to models saved in the Extreme 3D format, Extreme 3D 2.0 can import other formats, including: DXF, EPSF, FreeHand, Swivel 3D, and 3DMF. FreeHand and FreeHand EPSF "models" are of course just vector outlines that have to be modified to become 3D objects. The inclusion of Swivel 3D is a nod to the history of Extreme 3D, as Swivel 3D is not a major modeling format of choice, though there are a lot of Swivel 3D files still floating around.

The two major importable file formats are DXF and 3DMF (QuickDraw 3D models). DXF is important in the same way that NTSC TV is important; it's outmoded, but there's so much of it in existence that it will take years for it to be replaced. 3DMF files are created with applications (like Extreme 3D) that write out models based upon Apple's 3D Metafile format, in either ASCII or Binary form. 3DMF files continue to go through evolutionary new phases, and may become one of (if not *the*) major 3D object file formats around. All major 3D applications, on both Mac OS and Windows platforms, support the DXF format. Many also support the 3DMF format, with numbers increasing each year. This makes it vital that you know how to import and use both DXF and 3DMF 3D objects in your Extreme 3D compositions.

Primitive Objects (Cone, Sphere, Cube)

A "primitive" object is one that is always available from inside an application, so that it does not have to be created each time it is needed. 3D applications normally have a library of primitives, because they can be used as building blocks to form more complex objects, and also because they can be edited or deformed to create more interesting 3D forms. Extreme 3D is no exception to this rule, and offers three primitives: sphere, cube, and cone. Placement is simple. Just click on the appropriate tool (see Figure 13-1), and drag the mouse on the screen. When you release the mouse button, the 3D form is placed in the workspace.

Figure 13-1: The three primitive tools in the Extreme 3D toolbox.

Tip

If you are new to 3D applications, the best project to assign yourself is to build a anthropomorphic (or "human-like") form made completely from 3D primitives.

Figure 13-2: One example of a simple 3D human form, created in Extreme 3D.

Tip

> *For more complex object creation tutorials with Extreme 3D, see the projects sections in Chapters 19 to 25.*

3D Creation Tools

Extreme 3D's tools for creating 3D objects are essentially the same as those found in almost every 3D application. They may have different names, or work a little differently, but the same tools are found everywhere. Extreme 3D is an excellent 3D application in its own right, and because of the similarity in tools, it is a perfect training ground for working in 3D in general. It is far more intuitive to learn with than almost any other 3D application, making it perfect for integration into the classroom.

Like all of the tools in the Toolbox (see Figure 13-3), the 3D creation tools are accompanied by descriptive text that pops up at the bottom of the workscreen whenever you pass the mouse over a Toolbox icon. Although we are including some brief rundowns on tool operations, we suggest that you refer to the Extreme 3D documentation for more detailed descriptions of these tools and processes.

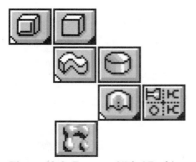

Figure 13-3: Extreme 3D's 3D object creation tools.

The Tools

Use these tools from the Front View. Watch the instructional lines at the bottom of the screen after you click on a modeling tool. They walk you through the process each time.

Lathe

The Lathe tool spins a form on an axis to create a 3D shape. Use it to sculpt symmetrical objects like wine glasses, table legs, and other forms that look as though they were turned on a lathe. Import or draw a profile, closed or open. Draw an axis in any direction (stay in the Front View all of the time). Select the profile and Shift-select the axis, and the 3D lathed object appears. Refer to Figure 13-4.

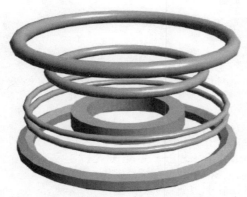

Figure 13-4: This is one object, not six. It was built all at once by simply drawing a series of 2D closed shapes and lathing them around a common axis.

 Extrudes (Beveled & Unbeveled)

The Extrude tool pulls a profile along a straight line to create a form that has depth. Use it to create blocks, coins, and other 3D forms from simple profiles. The Bevel Extrude tool pulls out from the standard Extrude icon (see Figure 13-5). Double-clicking on it gives you its control dialog, with checkboxes for three options: Bevel Front, Bevel Back, and Hard Edged (Chamfered) Bevel. The first two are normally checked by default.

 Tip

Unlike some other 3D applications, lathed and extruded forms in Extreme 3D can be built from groups of unconnected objects. Four symmetrically placed squares, for instance, could be multiple selected, and extruded at the same time to produce four table legs exactly the same length.

Figure 13-5: These perfectly cloned chamfered cylinders were constructed by using the Bevel Extrude tool on four equal circles.

 Sweep (or Path Extrude & Pipe Extrude)

The Sweep tool allows you to follow a line or curve in space with a 2D shape, closed or open, creating a form whose cross-section is the 2D shape, and whose length and angles match the line or curve. Items like railroad tracks, twisted tubes, and meandering tunnels all are built with the Sweep tool. Like extruding and lathing, you can also assign more than one shape at a time to the curve. It has a settings dialog that allows you to select the object or the path as the location of the finished form, and also allows for user input on the number of sections involved (more sections equal a smoother form, but slower rendering and more memory for storage). Refer to Figure 13-6.

Figure 13-6: This convoluted form is the result of sweeping a warped shape on a curved path with the Sweep tool.

Skin

When I was young, my friends and I used to get together to build model airplanes. We would get a kit that contained a balsa wood skeletal structure, and diligently wrap the structure with a skin of light paper, completing the fragile form. The Skin tool in Extreme 3D works in much the same way, wrapping forms with a digital skin to complete a 3D shape. The forms can be any open or closed 2D shapes, and they can be set at different angles. Forming objects in this way forces you to think in terms of polygonal cross sections beforehand, especially since the 2D structures need not be of the same polygonal type. For example, circles can be skinned to squares. Refer to Figure 13-7.

When you are setting the 2D structures for a skinning operation, there are some things you should think about:

- The same form can be cloned and resized to create a smooth form that pinches or expands in the skinning process.

- Skinning between a smooth 2D shape (an oval, for example) and a sharp cornered shape (a polygon) introduces creases partway toward the sharp cornered shape.

- Placing unlike 2D shapes at angles to each other in the skinning process emphasizes the creases between them.

- Skinning from an open to a closed shape will only close the 3D form at the last step. Clone the closed shape and move it away from the original closed shape to force the open shape to close earlier in the skinning process.

- Introducing angles between the 2D structures should be done by using clones that separate the source and target polygons, and slowly introducing them at gentle angles between the two. Otherwise, instead of an angled 3D object, you will create one that has an oblique end plane.

- Always work in Orthographic perspective in the Front View when doing skin modeling.

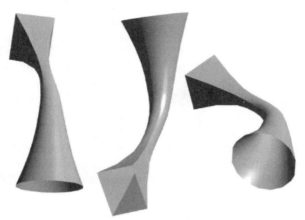

Figure 13-7: A skinned 3D object created from a mixture of oval and rectangular shapes in three views. The end caps were removed so you can see inside.

Cross Section

This tool is a cross between extruding and skinning. It pulls an object along a path, but the path represents the closed polygonal cross-section of the object. The object pulled along the path is the other cross-section of the object, perpendicular to the first one. No other 3D application offers this tool. See Figure 13-8 for an example.

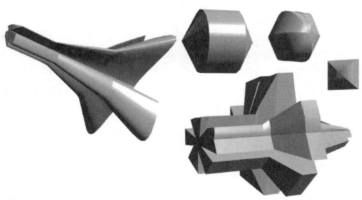

Figure 13-8: A selection of objects formed with the Cross Section tool.

Tip

Use the Cross Section tool to model things like machine parts whose shapes change dimension along an extruded path.

Metaforming

Metaforming is also known by another name: blobby modeling. Certainly metaforming sounds classier than blobby, but the tool is generically the same. Metaforming is a class of skinning, allowing both open and closed shapes to be used as the building blocks. The skin formed between shapes (as many shapes as you like at whatever angles) tends to look more organic, so metaforming is often used to model human and animal parts. It's also a great way to create landscape features like rocks. Refer to Figures 13-9 and 10.

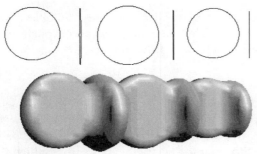

Figure 13-9: A simple metaform created from six circles.

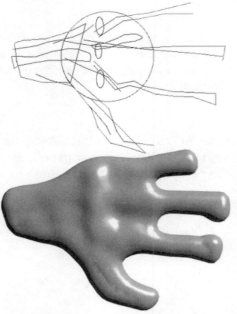

Figure 13-10: A more complex metaform, emulating a living foot or hand. Notice that metaformed objects seem to allow the underlying structure to show through.

Tip

For more believable metaformed objects, use a combination of open and closed shapes. Make sure to keep distance between parts you don't want to "web" together.

Cloning With a Click

Extreme 3D allows you to clone and duplicate profiles and objects without ever going to a menu command. The three tools that accomplish this—2D Mirror, 3D Mirror, and Offset—all have different uses.

2D Mirror
This tool creates a flipped clone of the 2D shape or 3D object you select in the same plane as you are working in. This would, for example, allow you to create one butterfly wing, and then create the other one as its flipped mirror image. All that's needed is for you to specify the axis across which the mirror cloning will occur, which for our butterfly wing example would be a straight vertical line.

3D Mirror
This tool is somewhat complex. It also creates a mirror image of a selection, but uses the plane you are working in as the axis for the mirrored clone. You could take an object of a building, for instance, and 3D mirror it so that the clone is placed in back of the original image.

Offset
Extreme 3D's Offset tool is similar to FreeHand. It places a cloned shape (it works on 2D shapes) on the inside of the first shape, with both shapes centered on each other. The resulting shape is perfect for creating extruded objects with holes in them.

2D Profiles

All of the modeling techniques we have looked at use 2D profiles, open and closed, as the building blocks to form 3D objects. Extreme 3D's 2D profiles are essential in sculpting believable 3D elements.

2D Closed Primitives

The Ellipse, Regular Rectangle, and Polygon are the three 2D closed primitives in Extreme 3D. Each plays a vital role in conjunction with one or more of the modeling techniques. The Circle and Square primitives are special cases of the Rectangle and Ellipse, accessed by a pull-out option from both the Rectangle and Ellipse icons. By using any of the sculpting tools in conjunction with a 2D closed primitive shape, the following objects can be created.

Ellipse

The Ellipse and Circle primitives can act as a root form for a series of 3D shapes, using the following techniques:

- **Lathing:** Lathing an ellipse produces egg-like shapes when the lathing axis is internal, and donuts when the lathing axis is external.
- **Extruding:** Extruding an ellipse creates cylinders.
- **Sweeping:** Sweeping an ellipse produces elliptical tubes.
- **Skinning:** Skinning an ellipse also creates elliptical tubes.
- **Cross Sectioning:** Cross-sectioning an ellipse creates either cylindrical shapes or ellipse-convoluted cylinders, depending upon the other cross-section path.
- **Metaforming:** Ellipse used in metaforms lend smooth curves to the surfaces.

Rectangle

The Rectangle and Square primitives can act as a root form for a series of 3D shapes, using the following techniques:

- **Lathing:** Lathing a rectangle with the axis internal to the rectangle creates angular cylinders, depending upon the number of sides. If the axis is external to the rectangle, the result is a donut shape with straight sides.

- **Extruding:** Extruding a rectangle produces elongated cubic volumes.

- **Sweeping:** Sweeping a rectangle generates a rectangular tube.

- **Skinning:** Skinning a rectangle results in a curved rectangular tube if the skinning path is curved.

- **Cross Sectioning:** Cross-sectioning a rectangle produces rectangular elements in the object, with the final shape also dependent upon the second cross-section.

- **Metaforming:** Rectangles used in metaformed objects smooth out their corners, but still leave the impression that the underlying structure is angular (like bone).

Polygon

The Polygon primitive can act as a root form for a series of 3D shapes, using the following techniques:

Tip

3D objects built from regular polygons take the number of sides of the polygon into consideration. Use the Object Control palette, described below, to alter the number of sides in the selected polygon.

- **Lathing:** Lathing a polygon with the lathing axis internal to it produces a cylinder with altered radius dimensions, that conform to the shape of the polygon.

- **Extruding:** Extruding a polygon creates a sharp-angled cylinder.

- **Sweeping:** Sweeping a polygon creates a tube with angled sides.

- **Skinning:** Skinning a polygon creates an angled tube that follows the curves of the skinning path.

- **Cross Sectioning:** Cross-sectioning a polygon produces an object, at least one cross-section of which follows the polygonal shape.

- **Metaforming:** Polygons used in metaforming emphasize the angular skeleton of the underlying structure.

2D Open Primitives

These consist of the Polyline, Line, Spline, and Arc. 2D open primitives are the core ingredients in forming modeling paths, and are used more rarely as structural ingredients in a model. When used as structural ingredients, they form open 3D objects with no thickness. If they are closed in on themselves, however, so the last point is joined to the first, they form closed 2D shapes that are very useful in acting as modeling ingredients as well as paths.

Polyline
Open polylines can be used as paths to create angular objects. When closed, they are useful in creating walls, angular containers, and barriers of all kinds.

Line
The line has little or no use in most 3D modeling skeletons, except in metaforming, where it can be used as one element that combines with other open and closed shapes. As a path, however, lines are used to help model 3D objects that need perfect linear extrusion, like legs to tables and other straight elements.

Spline
The spline is the most useful Path tool for creating 3D models. It is especially valuable as a path in performing sweeps. When closed in on itself, it is a useful form in creating curved surfaces of every type, especially glasses and other utensils.

Arc
The arc, like the spline, is useful as a path. Because of its symmetry, it is useful in creating objects and object elements whose symmetry is an important feature, leaning more towards mechanical rather than organic parts. When closed in on itself, it can be used to create bowls and other symmetrical containers.

Modifying Objects

As Yogi Berra said, "It ain't over till it's over," and that holds as true for modeling a 3D object as it does for baseball. Even after you have sculpted the initial object, there are a lot of options you can introduce to change the model's shape globally or selectively.

Duplicate Special

Duplicate Special (Object | Duplicate Special) creates arrays, cloned arrangements of a selected shape that are generated all at one to give you perfect symmetrical groups. The Duplicate Special command is perfect for creating objects like a Rubik's cube, and also for generating things like spiral staircases. See Figure 13-11.

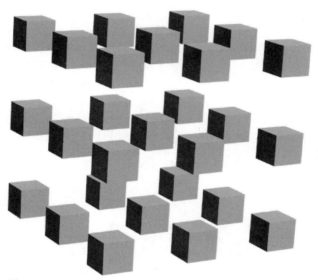

Figure 13-11: This array of cubes was created with the Duplicate Special operation. The cubes were cloned three, above, three below, and three to the side of the original.

The Spiral Staircase

Using the Duplicate Special command, it's possible to create 3D objects that would otherwise be very difficult to create. Do the following (refer to Figure 13-12):

1. Draw a rectangle that represents a stair tread seen head-on in the Front View.

2. Duplicate it, and rotate the clone so that it is 30 degrees off center from the first stair. Move the clone above the first stair, and link them together.

3. Open the Duplicate Special dialog, and type **8** in the Duplicate With Link box. Click on OK. Your staircase is finished and ready for texturing and rendering.

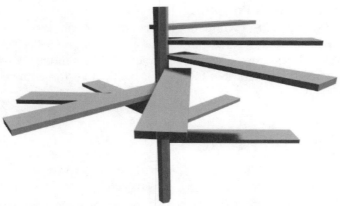

Figure 13-12: The basic spiral staircase, modeled with the Duplicate Special command.

2D Modifications

Because 2D objects are the building blocks of 3D objects, it's important to consider how they might be modified before 3D modeling.

Join Profiles

There are times when no single open shape tool will suffice for creating a final 2D shape as a basis for a 3D object. The Spline, Polyline, and Arc tools can all be combined using the Join Profiles operation (Object | Join Profiles). Linear segments are joined as one continuous object, which can be closed as the final step. See Figure 13-13.

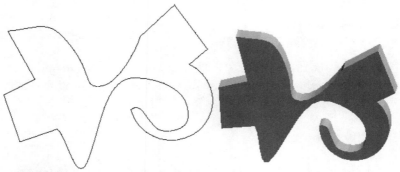

Figure 13-13: The shape on the left was used as a template to create the Extruded 3D object on the right. The template has spline, arc, and polyline elements, all of whose profiles have been joined.

Fit Polylines/Smooth Polylines

Polylines create open lines whose angles are sharp. It would be nice to have a command to round out the angles, which is exactly what Fit Polylines (Object | Fit Polylines) does. Smooth Polylines (Object | Smooth Polylines) produces a curved segment that follows the original vectors more closely. See Figure 13-14.

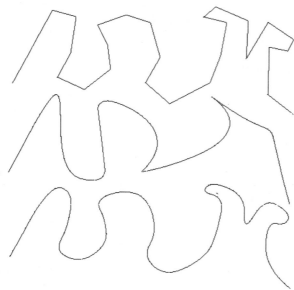

Figure 13-14: The sharp angles of the polyline segment at the top were rounded to the shape below with the Fit Polylines command. Below that is the same shape smoothed with the Smooth Polylines command.

Working With Geometry

In Extreme 3D, the selected 3D object is said to have a "geometry," to be made up of a series of polygons or wire meshes that can be modified to create new shapes.

Simplify Geometry

The Simplify Geometry command (Object | Simplify Geometry) makes the surface geometry of the selected object, whether it's a 2D shape or a 3D object, accessible for editing. Use Simplify Geometry as a first step to reshape an object. To actually edit the shape, you have to open its geometry.

Open/Close Geometry

Opening an object's geometry makes its control points visible. Control points can be added to the object when its geometry is open, and they can be manipulated to reshape the object. See Figures 13-15 and 13-16.

Figure 13-15: Here is a scene with one of the objects ready for geometry modification, showing its associated control points.

Figure 13-16: The object has had its geometry modified.

Why Use Layers?

Now stop and think for a moment. What are layers used for in FreeHand and xRes? They are used to place objects in front of or behind each other in the stack, right? But a 3D application has no layer stack as such. If you want to move an object in front of or behind other objects, you simply drag them there in a 3D space. Extreme 3D has layers to make your design life easier. Layers are used to make hiding and selecting objects much easier. If you have 10 objects in a scene, and place each on a different layer, you could hide or show that object with one click in the Layer palette.

It gets even better if you have only two layers for the ten objects, placing some on one layer and the rest on the other. That way, you could show, hide, and select all of the objects on any one layer in a flash. You can also move objects to different layers.

Warping Objects

 As long as a selected object is simplified first, allowing editing and control point placement, it can also be manipulated by any of the five warping tools: Twist, Bend, Taper, Stretch, and Skew (see Figure 13-17). Look at the examples in Figure 13-17 to see what is possible.

Figure 13-17: The tower object from Figure 13-16 has been modified by each of the five warping controls (left to right): Twist, Bend, Taper, Stretch, and Skew.

The Objects Window

You must, you absolutely must, *always* have the Objects window (Window | Objects) on your workspace. Because you can control object position, scale, rotation factors, texture mapping types and tiling, and texture flipping, all to eight decimal point accuracy, you won't move objects to the wrong space constantly. In 3D work, accuracy in positioning and scaling is an absolute necessity. Depending upon manual controls alone over these factors, especially when the scene gets complex, is not worth the effort. Move your objects into a proximal position manually, but always use the capacities of the Objects window to fine-tune your efforts.

Special Modifications

You might think that at this point, after looking at all of the ways that you can manipulate and modify your selections, that there would be nothing left to mention of any importance in those areas. Not so. The three topics that follow can give you even more creative alternatives for finessing your objects.

Cutting Holes

Extreme 3D offers an elegant and intuitive solution for cutting holes in an object. There are really two steps. One is to select the "drill" and the targeted object. The next is to take the "knife" and cut away what the drill has left behind. *Always* work in Orthographic perspective when doing a drilling operation so you can see exactly what the results will be.

A 2D closed surface is used as the drill to create a trim curve (the cut elements) and a Trim tool (knife) is used to cut away the sliced surface. The other option is to intersect two 3D objects, and use the Intersection tool to allow one object to cut another. Either way you slice it, you can cut into objects to develop more shaping control. Refer to Figure 13-18.

Figure 13-18: A circle and the letter "S" were cut into the big sphere. The small sphere was placed in the large one for viewer interest, and to emphasize the cuts.

Separating End Caps

Normally, when you create cylindrical objects, end caps are put in place. If the cylinder is to be used as a solid piece of steel, end caps will suffice. But if you want it to emulate a tube, end caps have to go. Just use the command Object | Separate End Caps, select the end caps, and delete them. Refer to Figure 13-19.

Figure 13-19: Two objects, one with end caps on and the other with them removed.

Tip

Instead of removing the end caps, you could simply move them aside. If you extruded them, they could be used as hatches or manhole openings in an animation.

Fillet Tool

A fillet is a rounded corner that displaced a sharp corner. The radius of a fillet can be set in the numerical listings at the bottom of the workspace. Larger fillets produce large radii for the curves. See Figure 13-20.

Tip

After a fillet takes place, you must select all of the line segments that make up the profile and join them, since the curves are separate line segments until joined back to the profile.

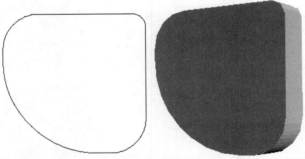

Figure 13-20: The profile on the left started as a rectangle. Fillets of different sizes were applied to its corners, and the profile was then used to generate the 3D form on the right.

Applying Object Textures

An object without a texture is like a human being without a personality. All it does is take up space with nothing meaningful to contribute to the scene. 3D art is built upon textured objects.

Mastering the Materials Browser

The Materials browser (Window | Materials) should remain on screen at all times, especially after your objects have been sculpted (see Figure 13-21). A huge library of textures ships on the Extreme 3D CD-ROM, and many more can be developed from your own graphics sources. Assigning a material (texture) to an object is simple.

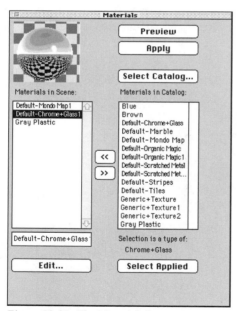

Figure 13-21: The Materials browser.

1. Load whatever materials resources you have from the Material Presets on the Extreme 3D CD-ROM into the list on the right.

2. Click on a selection, and click the left pointing arrow to move the selection to the list on the left.

3. Click on a selection in the left-side list, and use the Assign button to assign it to a selected object. Or, click on the Edit button to make changes to the texture, and then assign it to a selected object.

Texture Types

There are a number of materials presets that can be categorized into different material types. What differentiates these types is how many and what parameters they contain that are open to editing.

A material with nothing but a color swatch, as an example, cannot have anything edited but its color. Most of the texture types contain many parameters that can be edited, each of which affects the color. These parameters may include the following, depending upon the material you select:

- **Surface Color:** Set any color you like.
- **Surface Bumps:** Will the surface look bumpy or smooth?
- **Surface Bump Patterns:** These are mathematical patterns that produce bumps from organic looking to mechanical.
- **Surface Bump Height:** Make the bumps high for asteroids, and not so high for fabrics.
- **Specular:** What is the size and strength of the highlight?
- **Roughness:** Rough surfaces absorb light, and are used for materials like cloth and old woods.
- **Specular Color:** What is the color of the Specular highlight? Set it here.
- **Index of Refraction:** Different materials react to light in different ways. Select from air to diamonds and beyond.
- **Bump Map:** Same as Surface Bump Patterns, except some materials have bump mapping set in a separate tab.
- **Bump Pattern Scale:** How much of a surface spread will the bumps consume? Choppy seas have smaller bump patterns, while rolling hills seen from a plane have larger bumps.
- **Bump Height:** Bump height reacts to shadows, and higher bumps cause more shadowing on a surface.
- **Invert Bumps:** Invert the bumps for effect for an alternative.
- **Texture Map and Intensity:** Will a graphic be used to map the surface? If its intensity is set high, it will look like a photo, but if low it will blend more with the other surface features.

■ **Specular Map and Intensity:** Will a separate texture be used as a Specular texture map? The results will be a texture that is apparent only where there is a highlight.

■ **Roughness Map and Intensity:** Will a separate texture map be used to emulate the roughness of the surface? If so, you will see its effects more than the image.

■ **Transparency Map and Intensity:** If a texture is used as a transparency map, the places where it is dark will make the surface less transparent than where the map is lighter. A strange effect.

■ **Luminosity Map and Intensity:** If you want the image to glow unevenly, wrap a texture map to the luminosity settings.

■ **Environment Map and Intensity:** Extreme 3D is not a ray-tracing application. This means that if you want objects to show that they are reflecting the world they live in, they have to be told what world to reflect. Using a texture map as an environment map does just that.

■ **Organic Map Pattern Complexity:** Organic mapping is done with a mathematical algorithm and not a bitmap texture, so there's never any pixelization of the texture, no matter how close you zoom in. The pattern can range from simple striations to complex whirls and swirls.

■ **Organic Map Material Proportions:** If the proportions are large, they won't look as interesting as they would if set to medium and smaller, which gives more life-like organic detail.

■ **Organic Map Pattern Transition (Blends):** The patterns can blend in a number of ways, from edges to internal blends. Experiment.

■ **Organic Map Bump Transition (Blends):** The bumps can look craggy or smoothed out, depending upon the look you're aiming for.

■ **Organic Material 1 and 2 (6 controls):** Organic textures mix two materials, each of which has separate transparency, luminosity, roughness, and color controls.

■ **Marble Colors (4 Color and Band Widths):** This is a procedural texture (an algorithm). Select four colors and set the amount of proportional space they consume on the surface.

■ **Marble Surface (Specular, Transparency, Roughness, Luminosity):** Set all of these options for the way the Marble surface reacts to a light source.

■ **Marble Effects (Vein Pattern and Turbulence):** Set the veins to a complex pattern and turbulence for close-ups, but less so if the camera will remain in the distance.

- **Stripe Pattern (Planar, Cylindrical, Spherical, and Cubic), Edge Sharpness, and Material Proportions:** Stripy patterns are good for cloth materials, and also for clothes. On other surfaces they look stranger (which might be exactly what you want).

- **Stripe Warp (Turbulence, Turbulence Scale, and Blend):** Change the stripes to swirls, a great option when developing a material for wood.

- **Stripe Material 1 and 2 controls:** Stripes are made from two separate materials, each of which has to be configured separately.

- **Tile Pattern:** Cubes, Checks, Dot, Sphere, Brick, Grid, Hexagonal Grid, Triangles, Triangular Grid. Tile floor and walls are the main recipients of this material. Choose the pattern and size it for the object.

- **Tile Material 1 and 2 controls (Color, Specular, Roughness, Transparency, Luminosity):** Tiles are made from two separate materials, each of which has its own personality as a target of lights in the scene.

Using Your FreeHand & xRes Art

Any material that uses a texture can be the target of your unique graphics. In the section of the book on xRes, we mentioned several methods for developing texture maps for Extreme 3D. In general, keep your personal texture maps small for objects you will have in the view but won't zoom in on. Make them larger when zooming in is a prerequisite in an animation. Use colorful backdrops for your Extreme 3D animations, developed in xRes and FreeHand.

Texture Placement Alternatives

The most important texture placement controls are in the Objects window under the Info tab. Here, there is a check box for making the textures tile to the object, while the size of the tiles is controlled from the numerical input boxes below the workscreen. Size your tiles to fit their use in the scene, previewing the renders regularly. You can also flip your textures on the X or Y axis, by checking these items in the Info tab of the Objects window. The most important texture control in this palette is listed under Mapping Types. Mapping types include default, spherical, cylindrical, projective, cubic, and intrinsic. Match the Mapping type to the object targeted for the texture as closely as you can. Textures wrap very differently depending upon this choice. Intrinsic mapping allows you to use the mapping controls in the Tool palette, so you can perform magic like wrapping a label to an object.

Tip

Be sure to read and work through the Wine Bottle labeling tutorial in the tutorial section of this book to see how intrinsic mapping can be used.

Mastering Object Linking

There are no group/ungroup functions in Extreme 3D. Instead, objects are glued together in different ways by selecting and applying a linking type. All of the linking types are applied by clicking and dragging a line from one object to another. The source object is the child, and the target object becomes the parent. Children objects obey parent objects when movements occur in an animation. As we look at the linking types, it might be helpful if you looked at the simple humanoid we constructed at the start of the Extreme 3D part of the book. Using that figure will make our descriptions of linking types clearer. Use the figure to experiment with linking type assignments. If you haven't created the figure, you may want to do so now.

Linking Types

There are five linking types in the Toolbox. The one that stands alone, and looks like a broken chain, breaks any link that has been set up. The next four represent: Free link, Lock link, Ball joint, and Watch link.

- Free link is used when you want the child to move on its own, except to follow the parent when the parent moves. Free links could be used to connect an orbiting satellite to a planet, so that as the planet revolves, the child object moves with it. The child object would also be free to revolve on its own axis.

- Lock links attach the child to the parent, and allow no separate movement of the child. You would use a Lock link to attach a fender to a car.

- Ball joints links are essential in animating creatures. Ball joints allow the child freedom of movement and rotation, except at the object's center point where it is attached to the parent. Arms, legs, and other body parts work with Ball joints. Ball joints have a vital hierarchy. Feet are attached to lower legs, then lower legs to upper legs, then upper legs to hips, and hips to torsos. The torso, by the way, in the human figure is usually the hone and last link point for all other body parts. Alien constructions may vary.

■ Watch links are commonly used to attach the camera to an object in the scene, so in the animated sequence, the camera always remains centered on the targeted actor.

Center Point Manipulation

When you simplify an object's geometry, you will see a small control point that is colored green. This is the center point, and it is very important when creating linked objects, especially Ball joints. The center point is moved to a place on the object before a Ball joint link is initiated that will be the fulcrum around which that object rotates. The center point for the upper arm, for instance, is at the point where the upper arm attaches to the torso. As long as the center points of Ball joint linked objects are placed correctly, natural movement can occur without a hitch.

Moving On

In this chapter, we have investigated all of the ways that objects can be created and edited in Extreme 3D. Now it's on to Lights and Particle Systems in the next chapter.

14 Controlling the Scene

After we create and place our 3D objects in a scene, what else can we do to enhance the way the scene appears? As it turns out, there are a number of additional techniques and operations that we need to master in order to take advantage of Extreme 3D's capabilities, so that we can achieve the best renderings possible. The primary way to enhance a scene is by modifying the lighting. How lights play against the objects in the scene can alter the perceived context radically. Another alternative that Extreme 3D allows is the addition of timed object elements via a particle system, making such effects as crackling fire, flowing water, and even meteor storms possible.

Lighting the Scene

Too often, lights in a 3D scene are handled as an afterthought, purely to make all of the textured models you worked on for so long visible. But lights can do much more than that with just a little thought and planning on your part. Lights can add tremendous emotional impact to a scene, and give the viewer an instant indication, a hint, what your animation is really about. Lights are another important consideration when it comes to telling a story, no less vital than the characters and their textures, the object environment, and the background. In addition to reading this chapter, you'll need to work through the Extreme 3D documentation that deals with light types, placement, and alternatives.

Mastering the Light Editor

The Lights browser (Window | Lights) is where Extreme 3D allows you to add and edit lights, and when they no longer serve your design, delete them (see Figure 14-1). The first control mechanism you will notice in the Lights browser is the Light Pointer. This is an interactive device that allows you to point your light at the scene. The narrow end of the Light Pointer represents the direction the light is pointing. You can drag and rotate the larger end of the pointer to change the direction the light is coming from. Clicking on Update Scene instantly changes the scene to demonstrate the new light direction (Omni and Ambient lights do not have a direction, so the Light Pointer does not affect them). As you move the Light Pointer, the numbers in the Orientation fields are updated. These numbers are expressed in degrees relative to the current view. You can create backlighting by moving the pointer so that the large end is partially hidden. You can also change the orientation of the current light by directly editing the numbers in the Orientation fields. In addition, to adjust the position of the light, use the Arrow tool to drag the light icon visible in the workspace.

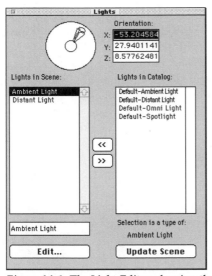

Figure 14-1: The Light Editor, showing the Light Pointer device in the upper left of the browser.

The Lights in Scene list, in the Light Editor Light Editor, shows the available lights in the current scene. Ambient Light and Distant Light are listed in new documents by default. The Default-Distant Light can be renamed, but it is the only light that cannot be deleted. To create a new light, copy or duplicate a light that is selected in the workspace or in the Light Editor Light Editor.

To edit a light's attributes, click its name in the Lights in Scene list and click Edit, or double-click the name. The Light Editor window appears, displaying the options for that type of light, either Distant, Ambient, Spot, or Omni light. You can also copy a light from the Lights in Catalog list on the right and edit its values. To move a light into the scene, select it in the Lights in Catalog list and click the left double-arrow button to move it to the Lights in Scene list on the left (exactly the way the Materials browser entries work).

Change the name of the selected light by typing a new name in the field below the lights list, at the bottom of the browser. When you've set the light attributes, click Update Scene to redraw the scene in the workspace using the newly defined light. Light settings affect both the objects in the workspace and the preview in the Materials browser. You can copy any light from the Lights in Scene list to the catalog by clicking the right double-arrow button. This means the new light is available for other projects in the future.

The Lights in Catalog column on the right of the browser displays the complete list of available light types in the current lights catalog. In addition to default light types, the catalog also contains any lights that you have customized and moved into that catalog. To copy a light from the catalog to the Lights in Scene list (the list on the left), select that light and click the left double-arrow button. A copy of the light will appear in the Lights in Scene list.

Tip

It's a good idea to copy two additional Distant Lights and at least one Spotlight into the Lights in Scene list at the very start of a project. You can switch them off, but they will be available when needed for editing.

Light Types

There are four basic light types in Extreme 3D: Ambient, Distant, Spot, and Omni.

Ambient Lights

These are lights that illuminate all sides of an object in a scene. In general, Ambient Lights are the most common light source. They can be turned off when using other light types to achieve more dramatic directional light effects. They have the following editing controls:

- **Light Switch**: Turns the light on in the scene. You can turn the light off without losing its settings.

Tip

The Light Switch can be animated, suddenly causing a scene to lighten or darken.

- **Color**: Shows the color of the current light. To change the light color, click the color chip. This opens your system's Color Picker dialog box, in which you can select a new color.
- **Intensity**: Controls the brightness of the light. Change the intensity of a light by typing a value between -20 and +20 in the numeric field. The higher the number, the brighter the light. A negative light subtracts light from the scene, making objects darker. An intensity of 1.0 is normally too much light and saturates the scene to pure white. Start with a value of .2 and adjust from there.

Distant Lights

Distant Lights provide you with more control over the shadows they create. Use the new Shadow Resolution and Shadow Fuzziness properties to create softer shadows and to optimize memory usage. Their control dialog offers the following options:

- **Light Switch**: Turns the light on in the scene. You can turn the light off without losing its settings.

Tip

The Light Switch can be animated. One use for an animated Distant Light might be to show the lighting effects of a far off explosion on objects.

- **Color**: Shows the color of the current light. To change the light color, click the color chip. This opens the System Color Picker dialog box, in which you can select a new color.

- **Intensity**: Controls the brightness of the light. Change the intensity of a light by typing a value between -20 and +20 in the numeric field. The higher the number, the brighter the light. A negative light subtracts light from the scene, making objects darker. An intensity of 1.0 is normally too much light and saturates the scene to pure white. Start with a value of .2 and adjust from there.

- **Source Radius**: Determines the size of the source of the light. A radius of 90 degrees creates a hemispheric source of light. The size of the Distant Light source radius is seen most directly in the specular highlights of the objects on which the Distant Light falls.

- **Cast Shadows**: When Cast Shadows is selected, a shadow is cast by this light. (Render Shadows must also be selected in the Final Render Setup dialog box for shadows to be rendered.)

- **Shadow Resolution**: A shadow is represented as an image whose resolution is determined by the image size and the shadow resolution. The image size is equal to the area that contains all the objects in the scene. The shadow resolution determines the distance the light has traveled through that area as represented in pixels. The number of pixels entered for Shadow Resolution is squared to define the two-dimensional area the shadow will cover. The limit is 2,048 pixels. This lets you control the amount of resources that are dedicated to rendering the shadow. A low number might result in shadows that have very obvious pixels. A very high number results in shadow with extreme detail. High shadow resolution takes longer to render and consumes more memory than low resolution. You can use low shadow resolution to save rendering time or create shadows that are not the focus of the scene.

- **Shadow Fuzziness**: Controls how distinct the shadow image is. As the value increases, the shadow's image is blurred more when rendered. A low fuzziness value will result in a crisp, defined shadow. Because fuzziness is the number of pixels to blur, higher resolution shadows that use more pixels appear less blurry than low resolution shadows at the same fuzziness factor (see Figure 14-2). Use low resolution shadows and higher fuzziness values to decrease rendering times.

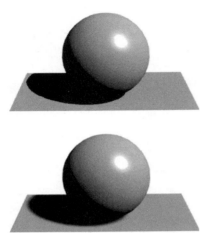

Figure 14-2: At the top, shadows were generated with no fuzziness, resulting in a lot of jaggies. At the bottom, fuzziness at 80 percent was added, creating a higher quality rendering.

Spotlights

Spotlights provide you with much more control over the shadows they create. Use the Shadow Resolution and Shadow Fuzziness properties to create softer shadows and to optimize memory usage. Another addition to Spotlights is a control for enhancing dust shadows or light rays. Use these features to achieve better lighting effects with Extreme 3D's improved volumetric lights. The following controls are available in the Spotlight editing dialog:

- **Light Switch**: Turns the light on in the scene. You can turn the light off without losing its settings. Turn off lights to speed up test renders.

Tip

The Light Switch state can be animated. Use it to do things like turning flashlights on and off, or controlling the rays emanating from a robot's eyes.

- **Color**: Shows the color of the current light. To change the light color, click the color chip. This opens the system's Color Picker dialog box, in which you can select a new color.
- **Intensity**: Controls the brightness of the light. Change the intensity of a light by typing a value between -20 and +20 in the numeric field. The higher the number, the brighter the light. A negative light subtracts light

from the scene, making objects darker. An intensity of 1.0 is normally too much light and saturates the scene to pure white. Start with a value of .2 and adjust from there.

■ **Source Radius**: Sets the beginning radius of the light cone, which determines the size of the light and dust cones.

■ **Cone Angle**: The angle of the light and dust cones. (Set the radius for the cones on the Dust Cone tab.) The maximum angle is 120 degrees (plus or minus 60 degrees around the light's axis).

■ **Cone Fuzziness**: The fraction of the cone of light that is softened or fuzzed. A value of 0.5 softens half of the radius of the cone from the outer edge inward. A value of 1 softens the whole cone of light.

■ **Use Light Fall Off**: When checked, the fall off distance is calculated.

■ **Light Fall Off Distance**: This is the distance, in units, at which the light is at half intensity. The light intensity continues to decrease as the distance increases.

Tip

Make sure your background is dark enough to show the spotlight cone. Dark blue to black, or a very dark bitmap backdrop are suggested.

Spotlights can also create effects such as visible dust cones. The options on the Dust Cone tab of the Edit dialog are used to create and control these effects:

■ **Render Dust Cone**: When this option is selected, a visible dust cone is calculated for this light. After setting up the dust cone, turn this option off to speed up rendering while working on other parts of the scene. All dust cone properties are retained when this option is disabled. Be sure to turn it back on before rendering for final output.

■ **Dust Brightness**: Sets the overall intensity of the glowing dust. Keep Dust Brightness below 1.0 in most cases.

■ **Use Dust Fall Off**: When checked, the dust cone's fall off distance is calculated.

■ **Dust Fall Off Distance**: This is the distance, in units, at which the dust cone is at half intensity. The intensity continues to decrease as the distance increases.

■ **Dust Turbulence**: Gives an uneven and smoky character to the dust.

- **Turbulence Scale**: Determines the relative size of the wisps of dust in the air.

- **Turbulence Contrast**: Determines the brightness contrast of the turbulence. A low value produces dust clouds composed of shades of gray that are close in intensity. A high value produces dust clouds that are high in contrast; that is, the intensity ranges between black and the color of the light.

- **Cast Shadows**: When Cast Shadows is selected and Render Shadows is selected in the Final Render Setup dialog box, a shadow is calculated for this light.

- **Cast Dust Shadows**: When this check box is checked, shadows for the dust are rendered. Dust shadows increase rendering time.

- **Shadow Resolution**: A shadow is represented as an image whose resolution is determined by the image size and the shadow resolution. The image size is equal to the area that contains all the objects in the selection. The shadow resolution determines the distance the light has traveled through that area as represented in pixels.

- **Shadow Fuzziness**: Controls how distinct the shadow image is. As the value increases, the shadow's image is blurred more when rendered. A low fuzziness value will result in a crisp, defined shadow. Because fuzziness is the number of pixels to blur, higher resolution shadows that use more pixels appear less blurry than low resolution shadows at the same fuzziness factor. Use low resolution shadows and higher fuzziness values to decrease rendering times.

- **Dust Shadow Enhancement**: Amplifies the effects of dust shadows and light rays in a dust cone when dust shadows are on. There are four options:

  - **No Enhancements**: No enhancements are added.

  - **Enhance Shadows**: Makes the dust shadows more visible and defined.

  - **Enhance Light Rays**: Makes the shafts of light created by a spotlight with dust more visible and distinct. This is especially useful for enhancing shafts of light that are passing through small holes in an object.

  - **Enhance Both**: Enhancements are added to both shadows and rays.

Omni Light

The Omni Light features the following controls:

- **Light Switch**: Turns the light on in the scene. You can turn the light off without losing its settings.

Tip

The light switch state can be animated. Omni light switch animations are useful for demonstrating lightning flashes.

- **Color**: Shows the color of the current light. To change the light color, click the Color chip. This opens the system's Color Picker dialog box, in which you can select a new color.

- **Intensity**: Controls the brightness of the light. Change the intensity of a light by typing a value between -20 and +20 in the numeric field. The higher the number, the brighter the light. A negative light subtracts light from the scene, making objects darker. An intensity of 1.0 is normally too much light and saturates the scene to pure white. Start with a value of .2 and adjust from there.

- **Use Light Fall Off**: Enables the use of the Fall Off distance.

- **Light Fall Off Distance**: This is the distance, in units, at which the light is at half intensity. The light intensity continues to decrease as the distance increases.

Lighting Tips

Consider the following tips for adding lighting to your 3D creation:

- If more than one light is casting a shadow on an object, make the lights come from noticeably different directions, and color them a little differently.

- Shadows set to maximum hardness usually look very unnatural in a scene. As a rule, move the Shadow Softness slider about halfway up or more.

- Consider turning Ambient lights off in the final scene renderings to emphasize the effects of other directional light sources.

- It is suggested that you stay away from using dust cones when the objects in the scene have a lot of detail, unless you are zooming in on the detail. Dust cones compete with any object content for attention.

Your First Particle System

Extreme 3D's particle system allows you to add arrays of objects that each have predetermined "life spans" to a scene, so that they decay over time. This leads to all sorts of effects possibilities, from natural animated elements like water, fire, lava, smoke, and insect swarms, to more concrete object arrays like falling leaves and meteor showers. Generate this basic Extreme 3D particle system exercise as follows.

1. Using any of the modeling tools, create the shape you want each particle in the system to have. To begin this exploration, it is suggested you use a small rectangle. You may extrude it slightly or just use the profile shape.

Tip

All particles in the particle system have the same shape. To create a particle system that has particles of different shapes, create more than one particle system. To generate small single polygon particles at render time, use a construction object or profile as the initial shape. Smaller particles animate more effectively to create various effects.

2. Select the Particle System tool from the Tool palette.

3. In the workspace, select the rectangle to use as the particle shape.

4. Define the particle system's initial position by clicking in the workspace.

The new particle system assumes this position and inherits its orientation and particle size from the orientation and scale of the original object. The original object is no longer related to the particle system object.

Creating a Meteor Storm With the Particle System

As stated previously in the introduction to this section, the Particle System tool creates a collection of shapes or polygons that evolve over time. Anytime you want to create objects in an animation that have swarming capabilities, that is, that seem to appear and then decay over a set time period, the Particle System tool is the one you need. Here is an interesting example, further enhancing your knowledge of the particle system. Do the following to create a meteor storm animation (see Figure 14-3):

1. Create a small meteor by using the Sphere tool to draw a sphere, then simplify it, and open its geometry to warp it. Close the geometry when you are done.

2. Follow the steps for creating a particle system using the meteor as the shape for all particles.

3. Select the meteor particle system in the workspace and open the Objects browser.

4. Choose the Particle tabs in the Objects browser and set the following properties to the values indicated. Leave other properties at their default values.

5. Set the Particle Rate to 100 (this increases the number of meteors to 100).

6. Set Source Radius to 7.0 (this enlarges the area that the leaf particles emanate from).

7. Set the Cone Angle to 90 (this determines how much the leaves fan out from their original position).

8. Set the Particle Lifespan to 2 seconds (this keeps each meteor in the particle system animating for two seconds before disappearing).

9. Set the Angular Velocity to 270 (this makes the leaves roll as they animate so they don't all face the same direction).

10. Choose Animate | Animation Controls and set the Current Frame to 120 frames or 4.00 seconds.

11. Click Play on the Animation Controls to play the animation. Tweak it as necessary.

12. When the particle system achieves the look you want, click Stop on the Animation Controls.

Figure 14-3: As you can see from these frames taken from the meteor storm animation, the objects change position and size over time.

Particle System Tips

Consider the following tips for creating any particle system project:

- The rule of thumb in creating particles is that complexity is inversely proportional to quantity. 3D shapes are more complex than 2D profiles, and some 3D shapes are more complex than others. Keep the number of particles down when working with 3D elements.

- It's a good idea to move the camera around in a particle animation that lasts over two seconds, to prevent the magic from becoming boring.

- When possible, consider using several differently colored Distant Lights for lighting your particles. This allows them to catch various lights at different angles, increasing the magic.

- Shorten the lifespan of particles meant to emulate natural effects like fire and other robust effects, and the particles will look more dynamic.

- Variety is the spice of life. It is better to generate three or four overlapping particle systems (if your RAM is up to it), each with slightly different shapes. That way, uniformity won't destroy the effect. If the particles have a very short lifespan, however, you don't have to be concerned with this.

- Use tiny red or orange colored particles as a stream of gases emanating from the exhaust nozzle of a space ship, or even from the fiery nostrils of a dragon.

Moving On

In this chapter, we explored all of the facets of lighting a scene, and controlling all of the parameters of Extreme 3D's four lighting types. We also delved into the Particle System, and showed how it could be used to create a swarm of animated meteors. In the next chapter, we'll move on to Extreme 3D animation.

15

Animating in Extreme 3D

Unlike xRes and FreeHand, Extreme 3D is a true animation application. It was designed both for generating animations and for developing graphics for publishing. Animation was not a major concern or avenue of general communication for most publishers until the development of interactive multimedia and writable CD-ROM technology. This was followed by the development of Web publishing, which incorporates animation as a tool for communication and enlightenment as well as glitz.

Initially, the use of animation in television commercials provided the framework for how and when to use animation for the Web. The major use seemed to be flying logos, an animation category that has become almost a separate art on its own. Flying logos, simply described, involve putting your personal symbols or company logo in motion, which theoretically makes it more attractive and eye-catching than allowing it to sit in one place. Flying logo animations are done more because "everybody's doing them," or because the technique is fun and available, than for any direct marketing reason. Animation, especially on the Web, is another way to make what you're doing stand out from what your neighbors or the competition is doing, so it's a good medium to incorporate.

The rules of the animation game are evolving; the standard animation techniques used for film are no longer the only way digital animators design or conceive of movement. Because of the Web and multimedia technology, a whole new area of animation that requires no recorded frames at your end is alive and well. This is interactive animation, 3D worlds that users can maneuver around and live in. In a sense, this is animation with a billion story lines, because each user decides how to move, and when and where to go. Interactive and standard animation techniques are both folded into Extreme 3D.

Animation Interface

Tip

Before reading this section, you must complete reading the documentation on animation. This section was not designed to replace the Extreme 3D documentation, but rather to point out important considerations in creating and controlling Extreme 3D animations.

Extreme 3D allows you to develop animated movies from your 3D designs that involve all of the commonly understood standard techniques developed for and by animated films, and also gives you a few digital extra added features along the way. There are two Extreme 3D control screens that you must be able to use effectively to develop your animations: the Animation Controls and the Score.

Animation Controls

The Animation Controls (Animate | Animation Controls) can be thought of as an extended VCR-like interface (see Figure 15-1). It contains the standard VCR controls for playing, stopping, recording, and starting an animation, and a few new features as well. You can also jump to any frame in a sequence to preview it for rendering. Also included are controls for forcing the playback to loop from start to finish over and over until stopped, and to "ping-pong" the animation (to continuously play it from start to finish, and then backwards from finish to start). All of these features are very helpful when previewing an animation to see where some editing might make the piece look better and tell the story more effectively. There are also input boxes in the Animation Controls for entering how many frames the animation is to have, and its frames per second (FPS) playback rate. A separate input area is provided to initiate the preview display of any selected frame in the sequence.

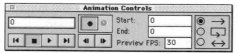

Figure 15-1: The Animation Controls.

Using the Animation Controls to Format a New Animation

Do the following to use the Animation Controls to design a new animation. Do this before any objects are placed on the screen.

1. Enter the Start and End values in the proper boxes. The start frame is normally frame 1, and the end value represents the last frame in a sequence. If you want to develop a 30-frame animation, the start number would be 1 and the end value 30.

2. Enter the frame rate (FPS). Animations will play back at this frame rate if the viewing system can handle it, or as close as possible if it can't. The lowest frame rate you should consider is 15 FPS. Standard video playback is at 30 FPS. Higher frame rates should be avoided.

Tip

The only place where low FPS rates should be considered (2 to 5) is when you want to show an animated slide show, composed of frames that are either text oriented, or that don't need to show the movement of elements.

The size of an animation is an important consideration if you plan to play it back from a disk on your system or someone else's system. A quarter-screen size for your animation will almost certainly play back at a 30 FPS rate on PowerPC or Pentium systems; larger screen sizes may play back more slowly. Animations recorded to video will always play back at the full 30 FPS rate.

3. Enter the number 0 in the Current Frame field, if it isn't there by default already.

4. Draw a sphere on the screen in the upper left corner.

5. Change the current frame to 10, and press Return (Enter). Move the sphere to the middle of the screen. Change the current frame to 20 (press Return/Enter), and move the sphere to the right of the screen. Change the current frame to 30 (press Return/Enter), and resize the sphere so that it just about disappears.

6. Select the Playback button. The sphere should start at the left and move to the right and almost disappear. Repeat this same procedure with multiple shapes onscreen at the same time to get a better feel for developing animations in this manner.

Animation Paths

When you generate an animation, like the one described above, you also create a path on which the object is animated. That path is normally invisible. To make it visible, select the animated object, and go to Animate I Animation Path I Show. The animation path becomes visible. You can edit the path by moving its control nodes like any other splined profile. Just open its geometry, and the control points become visible. Adjust them as necessary, and close the geometry. See Figure 15-2.

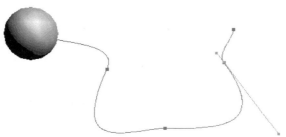

Figure 15-2: The animation path can be edited by opening its geometry and adjusting the control points.

You can also use the same animation path to create 3D objects! Refer to Figure 15-3. Select the object attached to the animation path, and choose Animation I Animation Path I Convert Path to Profile. A cloned profile of the path is placed over the path. This can be used as a profile in a sweep or skinning operation to create an object that conforms to the path. When the original object is animated, its movements will follow this exact object. Uses for this feature include:

- Creating an object that moves through a tunnel (the tunnel can be a semi-transparent tube, or the camera can be set to follow the object through an opaque tunnel by using the Watch Link feature described in Chapter 14).

- Creating an object that moves along a rail (trains are the obvious object choice).

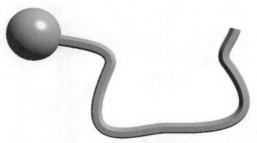

Figure 15-3: The animation path has been cloned to create a profile, and the profile used to create a tubular object that the object will be attached to in the animation.

Score

Absolutely everything in your Extreme 3D scene can be part of an animation: objects' scaling and movement, textures, lights, and more. Once you have set the length of the animation in the Animation Controls, open the Score (Animate | Score). Here, you will see every component of the scene listed by name, and all of its elements listed under it. To use the Score effectively, do the following:

1. Open the Score, and select All Objects and All Tracks from the object filter and track filter drop-down lists. Set the view range to 5 frames.

2. Click on an object in the workspace. You will see it highlighted in the Score list window. Under it you will see all of the object attributes that can be animated (see Figure 15-4).

3. Select Scale. Go to the Animation Controls and type the number 10 in the Current Frame field (press Return/Enter). You can now change the object's scale for that frame. Double the object's size, meaning that the object will grow in size from the start of the animation to frame 10.

4. Use the Playback button in the Animation Controls to preview the animation.

Tip

For previewing animations, you should consider setting the object render style to Wireframe in the Object menu. This will allow you to view the preview at a faster speed, so you can pay attention to movements and not to object detail.

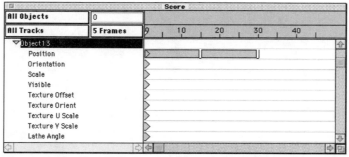

Figure 15-4: A view of the Score with an object and its animatable attributes listed.

Creating Animation Paths From Splines

This is one of the best uses of the Score. By following these steps, you can create animation paths from any profile:

1. Draw a profile on the screen. Use any of the tools to accomplish this, either as an open spline of line, or a rectangle, oval, or polygon.

2. Click on the Cone tool. With the profile still selected, move the mouse until the first point of the cone you will create matches a point on the profile. You will see the mouse cursor change to an open rectangle. Create the cone at that point.

3. In the Animation Controls, set the current frame to 30, and set the number of frames to 30.

4. Open the Score, and make All Objects/All Tracks visible from the filter pull-down lists. Select the cone on the screen, and look in the Score for its highlighted name. Under its name is an attribute called Position. Click on it.

5. On the screen, select the profile.

6. Select Animation | Animation Paths | Convert Profile to Path.

7. Press the Playback button in the Animation Controls. The object will follow the new animation path.

Tip

Use this method of path animation when the path has to be designed first in order to follow a complex set of directions.

Keyframe Animation

Keyframes are points in an animation that allow you to set the animated object to a position in space, or to modify it in some way so that at that frame the exact action occurs. In Extreme 3D, it's best to develop a path animation first, then use the keyframe feature to control the animation at specific points.

1. Create a 30-frame path animation, using the techniques described earlier.

2. Select the object, and input the number "10" in the Current Frame field of the Animation Controls (press Return/Enter). Resize the object to one-third of its original size.

3. Set the current frame to 20. Resize the object to twice its original size.

4. Preview the animated playback. At frame 10, the object reaches it smallest size, and at frame 20, its largest size. At frame 30, it shrinks back to its normal size. Frames 10 and 20 are keyframes, targeted frames that tell the object to be exactly equal to whatever changes you have scripted for that frame.

Interactive Options

The types of animation we have covered so far are useful in creating animated movies, to display in whatever medium you select. Animated movies in the QuickTime (Mac OS and Windows) and AVI (Windows) formats can be recorded to video with the right equipment, placed on an interactive CD-ROM so they play back when a hot spot is selected, given to friends and associates on a disk for their viewing pleasure, or played back on your own screen. With the right movie plug-ins in your Web browser application, you can view movie files on the Web. There are other ways to generate scenes, however, that leave the animation up to the viewer.

There are two important file formats that allow this to happen, and both are available as file format saving options in Extreme 3D.

QuickDraw's 3DMF

The first is 3DMF files, a format created by QuickDraw 3D, an Apple software package available for both Mac OS and Windows platforms. When loaded in, QuickDraw 3D object files can be rotated and zoomed in on in a 3D environment. 3DMF files are very useful for industrial designers and architects, because they allow an object to be interactively turned and zoomed from any angle. QD3D operates at the system level, effectively building 3D construction into the OS. Designs can be shared and appreciated in 3D, with textures applied. There are also 3DMF plug-ins available for your Netscape browser that allow you to view 3DMF files online without downloading them. 3DMF files are better used for objects as opposed to whole scenes.

VRML

The second interactive animation format is where the real excitement comes in: Virtual Reality Modeling Language (VRML). VRML is transforming the Web into a repository for real-time 3D browsing, with no disk space required for animation files. A VRML 3D world is traversed according to each viewer's needs, so no two animated journeys are ever the same. VRML files are better suited to whole scenes than to objects. After creating your Extreme 3D scene, save it as a VRML file. Anyone with a VRML-capable viewer, or a VRML-capable browser, can journey through the scene as if they were inside of it. VRML will continue its upward evolutionary pace, and may become the animation context of choice in the future, leaving other kinds of animation behind. The newer approaches to VRML and QuickDraw 3D are on the verge of incorporating both keyframe and path animation inside of the VRML environments.

Moving On

This chapter was devoted to looking at ways that animations can be created and controlled in Extreme 3D. We looked at both Animation Controls and Score operations and dialogs, focusing upon how their use controls every aspect of animation creation. We also delved into the association between splined paths and animation paths. Finally, we also looked at interactive animation alternatives, including QuickDraw 3D and VRML. In the next chapter, we'll look at Extreme 3D's rendering alternatives.

16

Rendering Your Creations

In this chapter, we will explore the ways that you can customize the rendered pictures or animations you will create in Extreme 3D. We will also look at other settings that influence the look of both final and preview renderings, and how they can be modified.

As you create your picture or animation, you will want to render various frames along the way to make sure everything is progressing as you want it to. These text renderings are usually at lower settings than the final rendering of your project. When everything is in place, and your art or animation is ready to be rendered in its final version, Extreme 3D checks on a number of settings to determine the rendering quality and options. These settings are taken from the Final Render Setup dialog (Render | Final Render Setup).

Final Render Setup

The Final Render Setup dialog (Render | Final Render Setup) offers you the opportunity to control all of the necessary parameters for achieving the highest quality renderings possible in Extreme 3D (refer to Figure 16-1). Adjust any of the following options as needed to get the best renderings:

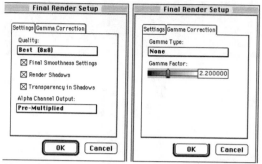

Figure 16-1: The two tabs of the Final Render Setup dialog.

The Final Render Setup dialog includes settings for the following:

■ **Quality:** Four quality options that affect the sharpness of the final image by adjusting anti-aliasing (that is, by setting the number of times Extreme 3D calculates each pixel in the image). Quality affects the entire rendered scene: Lights and shadows are anti-aliased as well as objects. The four Quality settings are: Low (1x1), Good (2x2), Better (4x4), and Best (8x8).

As the quality gets better, Extreme 3D breaks some pixels into subpixels and then calculates the sharpness of each pixel. The increase in rendering time depends on the type and complexity of materials used, the level of detail in the scene, and other factors. The greater the number of calculations, the more accurate the image, and more calculations increase rendering time.

Use the Low or Good Quality setting to develop the animation, and higher settings to preview rendering.

■ **Final Smoothness Settings:** When Final Smoothness Settings is selected, final render uses the Final Render Settings specified for each object in either the Adaptive Smoothing or Uniform Smoothing dialog box. (All objects, except polymesh and polylist objects, use either Adaptive or Uniform Smoothing.) If this option is not checked, final render uses the Interactive Render Settings for Uniform and Adaptive Smoothing. Each object can have its own surface smoothness setting, so objects in the same scene may have a slightly different resolutions.

■ **Render Shadows:** When Render Shadows is selected, the default, the final rendering includes shadows, which are calculated for each light source listed in the Lights browser that has its Shadows toggle turned on. Because the scene is rendered once for each light, calculating shadows roughly multiplies the rendering time by the number of lights with shadows on. Depending on the material used, rendering time can be a good bit longer with shadows turned on.

Leave Render Shadows off until the final render checks.

- **Transparency in Shadows:** When Transparency in Shadows is checked, shadows in the scene are calculated based on the amount of transparency in each material. If the material is less than 50 percent transparent, the light does not pass through the material, so it casts a shadow on the surface where the light hits it. The light color is combined with the transparency color. If the color is still above the 50 percent threshold, the light passes through the material. When Transparency in Shadows is on, each pixel is checked for transparency during rendering, so rendering requires more time.

- **Alpha Channel Output:** The following two options are included:
  - **Pre-Multiplied:** This is the type of alpha rendered by Extreme 3D 1.0. retains aliasing calculated for the image during rendering, so it may be the preferred format if you don't need do additional editing or compositing with this image in an image editing or digital video application.
  - **Standard:** This is the alpha style used by popular image editing applications, so use this option when you need to do additional editing or compositing with this image. Use this option only when creating files in a file format that supports alpha channels (either 32-bit or 64-bit). File formats that do not have alpha information may produce aliased (jagged-edged) images.

- **Gamma Correction:** Gamma correction optimizes the rendered image so that the colors look best when viewed in the intended delivery method: film, video, or print.

- **Gamma Types:** There are four gamma types to consider:
  - **None**: No gamma correction is applied.
  - **Punch Up**: The highlights of the image are compressed to improve the contrast between dark and light areas and generally improve the image for print.
  - **Video**: The default Gamma Factor is 2.2, which is the correct value for NTSC gamma correction. With this setting, colors are compressed so that they display correctly and don't oversaturate on an NTSC display.

- **Film**: Imitates color correction for film.
- ■ **Gamma Factor:** This setting determines the amount of correction that will be applied to the rendered scene. Experiment with this setting for the intended delivery system to see what works best.

Displaying Polygon Faces

When you modify an object (reshape it or cut into it), you may need to change a display option to make the object appear correctly onscreen by altering the display of Polygon faces (Render | Display Polygon Faces). If an object is initially made as a lathed object with end caps, and you remove the end caps, some of the polygons on the inside (that is, the back-facing polygons) are not displayed. From some viewing angles this can make it look as if part of the object is missing. Selecting Back Faces or Both should allow you to see the parts that appear to be missing.

The display options are Front Faces, Back Faces, and Both. In Extreme 3D, front-facing polygons are those whose normals point towards you, and back-facing are those whose normals point away from you. A polygon "normal" is a line drawn perpendicular from the center of the polygon.

Tip

If you plan to do a lot of editing in a project, it's best to select Both in the Display options at the start for each object you create.

When you import a model from another program, the normals may be oriented opposite to the way they are oriented in Extreme 3D, so the model may not appear correctly in Extreme 3D. Select the object and choose one of the other Display Polygon options until the object displays as required.

You must select each child object in a linked hierarchy and apply a Display Polygon Faces setting individually. Here is what each of the display options does:

- ■ **Front Faces:** Draws only the surfaces of an object that are facing the viewer. This holds even if you are oriented to the back of the object, since you are viewing the front-facing polygons (the light-reflecting surfaces are pointed toward you).

- ■ **Back Faces:** Draws all the surfaces of the 3D object that are facing away from the viewer (for example, the surfaces on the inside of a closed object).

Tip

Make sure that Back Faces is selected if you use the cutting operation on the object and can see inside of it.

- **Both:** Draws all the objects' surfaces, regardless of whether or not they are visible onscreen. This option takes the longest to render, but is my default choice.

Tip

If an imported model doesn't look right, even after trying various display options, try selecting the model and using Object | Control Points | Reverse Ordering option. This will reverse the order of all the control points in the model, thereby reorienting the normals.

Smoothing Types

Smoothing is a technique that allows an object to look more detailed as it is rendered. There are two smoothing types available in Extreme 3D: Uniform and Adaptive. Each accomplishes the task of smoothing the edges of a 3D object in different ways.

Uniform Smoothing

In Uniform Smoothing, objects are defined and edited as smooth curves. The Uniform Smoothing dialog box lets you control how the display polygons are sampled from the spline-based geometry and precisely control each object's rendering speed and quality. Uniform Smoothing samples the surface of a model into a gridwork of evenly spaced polygons. This dialog box sets the number of gridwork divisions (that is, the number of polygons) that are drawn between the object's control points during rendering. The greater the number of subdivisions, the finer the mesh and the smoother the rendered object. Objects with a finer mesh take more time to render.

To apply smoothness setting changes to specific objects, select the objects, choose Render | Uniform Smoothing, and click Update. Apply smoothness settings to the child objects of a selected parent object by pressing the Option (Mac OS) or F3 (Windows) key when you click Update. To use the Final Render settings for the final render, you must also select Final Smoothness Settings in the Final Render Setup dialog box. If Final Smoothness Settings is not selected, Extreme 3D uses the Interactive Render settings for the render.

When rendering the object, consider these smoothness settings:

- **Final Render Settings:** Applies the resolution specified in the Row and Column subdivisions entry fields when the final object is rendered. To use the Final Render Settings values for the final render, you must also select Final Smoothness Settings in the Final Render Setup dialog box. If Final Smoothness Settings is not selected, Extreme 3D uses the Interactive Render Settings values for the final render.

- **Interactive Render Settings:** Applies the resolution specified in the Row and Column subdivisions entry fields to the scene currently in the workspace.

For objects farther away from the camera you can frequently afford lower settings than for objects near the camera, so scenes will render faster.

Tip

For most projects, a Smoothness setting of 4 in both the row and column areas is sufficient. If you are doing work for national broadcast media or the movies, higher settings may be necessary.

- **Render Edges Sharper:** If this option is checked, Extreme 3D bases the rendering on the object's actual surface geometry rather than the approximation used for the polygon mesh. This gives objects with corners sharper edges.

Adaptive Smoothing

Adaptive Smoothing samples the surface of a model into polygons by concentrating more polygons in areas where the surface bends or changes direction rather than in broad or flat expanses of surface. The slider determines, on a relative scale from 0 to 1.0, how this polygon weighting is calculated. The value 1 gives the smoothest possible surface rendering but takes more time to render.

To apply Adaptive Smoothing changes to specific objects, select the objects, choose Render | Adaptive Smoothing, and click Update. To use these settings in the final render, you must also select Final Smoothness Settings in the Final Render Setup dialog box. If Final Smoothness Settings is not selected, Extreme 3D uses the Interactive Render Settings values for the render.

When rendering the object, consider these smoothness settings:

- **Final Render Settings:** Applies the resolution specified on the slider when the final object is rendered. To use the Final Render Settings values for the final render, you must also select Final Smoothness Settings in the Final Render Setup dialog box. If Final Smoothness Settings is not selected, Extreme 3D uses the Interactive Render Settings values for the final render.

- **Interactive Render Settings:** Applies the resolution specified on the slider during model creation on the workspace.

- **Render Edges Sharper:** If this option is checked, Extreme 3D bases the rendering on the object's actual surface geometry rather than the approximation used for the polygon mesh.

Tip

Use Adaptive rather than Uniform Smoothing to improve the appearance of an object that has curves or twists, such as one that has been bent with the Bend tool. Adaptive Smoothing increases the number of polygons in the areas where the object bends the most.

Rendering Options

Extreme 3D allows you to render your creations to a number of different destinations. You can render to the screen, to a disk file, or to a connected network (a "render farm") of multiple computers.

Final Render to Screen

Final rendering to the screen (Render | Final Render to Screen) is an option worth considering when you want to either grab the image off of the screen with a suitable utility, or save it to a file path after rendering. The output appears in the active window. Final Render to Screen automatically uses the best render style possible, regardless of the scene's current Max Render Style. Consider doing at least a few renders to the screen when ready to save an animation. This allows you to check the details of texture placement and the smoothness settings. After the image is rendered to the screen, you can use the Export command to save it.

Render to Disk

Render to Disk (Render | Render to Disk) renders the current scene to a file. Check the options selected in the Final Render Setup and Window Setup dialog boxes, which also affect rendering. The Render to Disk dialog (see Figure 16-2) includes the following options:

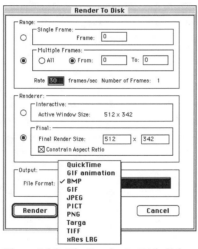

Figure 16-2: The Render to Disk dialog.

■ **Range:** This specifies the number of images to be rendered. These values are displayed in seconds rather than frames if the Display Time In option on the Animation tab of the Preferences dialog box is set to Seconds. If you want to render a single frame, the frame number specified in the Frame field is rendered. This value defaults to the current frame number, but can be changed by entering a new one. Selecting Multiple Frames means a series of frames is rendered. To render an entire animation, select All. To render a designated section, specify the start and end frames of that section by frame number in the From and To text fields.

The Frame Rate should be a frame rate that is lower than the current default rate (set in Preferences), to render fewer frames for the sequence. This is a good way to do test renders for scene blocking and object relationship. The Number of Frames field displays the total number of frames that will be rendered.

- **Renderer:** Select either Interactive or Final. Interactive rendering is faster and better for previews. The Final renderer uses the options specified in the Final Render Setup dialog box (see Figure 16-1).

  - **Interactive:** The size of the rendered image is determined by the current window size as specified in the Window Setup dialog box. This size is displayed in the Active Window Size field. To make changes to this or any of the other display-only fields, close this dialog box and choose Window Setup from the Window menu. The maximum window size is 2048 x 2048 pixels.

  - **Final:** Final Render Size field allows you to specify an output image size for output files that is different than the current active window size. The height and width fields accept values in pixels. The maximum size for images is 8192 x 8192 pixels. There is one exception: the maximum size for PICT images is 4090 x 4090 pixels.

  - **Constrain Aspect Ratio:** Computes the height and width of the high-resolution output image based on the height and width of the active window. If you provide a value for height or width and press the Tab key, the other value is automatically calculated. Aspect ratio should be determined by the image size required by the final medium (multimedia, video, or print).

    If the aspect ratio is not maintained, the screen display of the render may make the image look disproportional when rendering an image that is larger than the screen size. The rendered image will be correct.

- **File Format:** Specifies the output file format. You can render movies, still images, and single frame sequences in any of the following:

  - **Movies:** The movie formats create an animation that is contained in one file. Movie formats cannot participate in network rendering: AVI (Extreme 3D for Windows only), QuickTime (Extreme 3D for the Mac OS only), and GIF Animation (animations for the Web).

  - **Single Image and Sequence Formats:** These image formats are Macromedia Exchange image file formats: BMP, GIF, JPEG, PICT, PNG, TIFF, Targa, and xRes LRG.

- **Render:** A Render Progress counter appears that indicates which frame is being rendered and how much of the total rendering is completed. To stop rendering, press Command-period (Mac OS) or Escape (Windows).

- **Submit Job:** Adds a task for network rendering (see below).

Enable Network Rendering Mode

The network path has to first be set in the preferences. You cannot use network rendering to create QuickTime movies. Submit Job in the Render to Disk dialog adds a task for network rendering. It creates a folder in the location specified on the Files page of the Preferences dialog box. When the computer is in Network rendering mode, all submitted jobs are rendered and stored in this folder. You can use network rendering to create images in any of the 2D Macromedia Information Exchange formats (BMP, GIF, JPEG, PICT, PNG, Targa, TIFF, and xRes LRG). All of these formats, except PICT, allow you to use both Windows and Macintosh systems to collaborate on a single network rendering job.

The Network rendering mode (Render | Edit Network Rendering Jobs) opens a dialog box that shows you the status of the network rendering system and lets you modify the order of jobs listed in the queue. The dialog contains the following options:

- **Jobs:** Contains a list of jobs in the job queue and the percentage of completion for each one. If a job fails because there was not enough RAM on the system that attempted to process it, the minimum RAM requirements for the job appear in this space. Frames are automatically resubmitted, and they will be submitted only to systems that meet the minimum memory requirements.

- **Set Priority:** Allows you to edit the order of jobs in the queue list. The first job in the list has the highest priority as a scheduling task. To change a job's priority, select it and click one of the Set Priority buttons:

  - **Highest:** Moves the selected job to the top of the list.

  - **Lowest:** Moves the selected job to the end of the list.

  - **Up:** Moves the selected job up one space in the list.

  - **Down:** Moves the selected job down one space in the list.

- **Errors:** Allows you to manage jobs that have stopped due to rendering or crashed system errors. Set the parameters as follows:

- **Retry:** Schedules tasks in the selected job that have errors for reprocessing.

- **Skip:** Omits tasks in the selected job that have errors. Corresponding frames will be missing from the final output.

- **Delete Job:** Deletes the selected job. Completed frames are saved.

■ **Server Systems:** For computers in Network rendering mode, this option contains the status of servers on the network (that are pointing to the same network rendering path). Any computer that participates in network rendering is a server. The server names that appear in this list correspond to the Network Render Server Name listed on the Network page of the Preferences dialog box. Make the Network Render Server Name a unique name for each computer so you can easily identify which computers are working on network rendering jobs. Set the Server parameters as follows:

- **Stop Server:** Stops the selected server and takes the machine out of server mode.

- **Stop Task:** Stops the task that the selected server is processing. This task is then flagged as an error and must be either retried or skipped. The Stop Task command is useful if you need to stop a network rendering job and manually reschedule it.

- **Refresh:** Reads the current status of the network rendering system and updates the window. Since rendering is going on all the time, the dialog box updates only when it is initially displayed or when you click Refresh.

- **Done:** Closes the dialog box.

Moving On

In this chapter, we focused on rendering in Extreme 3D. We also looked at the three rendering destination alternatives: screen, disk, and render farms (networked systems), including setting render server parameters. That completes Part 3 of the book. Part 4, on Fontographer, starts with the installation of Fontographer.

Part IV

Mastering Fontographer

17

Installing & Configuring Fontographer

Fontographer allows you to create and edit fonts. You can import EPS files created in FreeHand and xRes as elements to build a new font library. The version of Fontographer that ships with the FreeHand 7 Graphics Studio is 4.1.5 (Mac) and 4.1 (Windows). In this chapter, we will guide you through the Fontographer installation process, copyrights, updates, and the materials on the Fontographer CD-ROM. This will be followed by a detailed look at setting all of the preferences, and also installing fonts on both Mac and Windows systems.

Installing Fontographer

Fontographer's installation procedure is very straightforward. Just follow the installer script that comes with the FreeHand 7 Graphics Studio CD-ROM.

Installing Fontographer 4.1 for Windows

Fontographer is included on the FreeHand 7 Graphics Studio CD-ROM. The following are the minimum system requirements:

- 386 or higher processor (I strongly recommend a Pentium system)
- Windows 3.1, 3.11, NT, or Windows 95

- 5.5 MB of hard drive space
- VGA video capability
- 6 MB of RAM minimum

If you want to print PostScript files, you will need either a HP driver dated after September 1993 or the Adobe 3.01 PostScript driver.

To install Fontographer, double-click on the Fontographer installer on your CD-ROM and then follow the instructions. Your Fontographer sample fonts will be automatically placed into the same folder as the Fontographer application during the installation process. To select only those options you want installed, select the Custom Installation option.

The first time you run Fontographer, it will display a Personalization dialog. Look for the 21-digit serial number, which will allow you to use Fontographer. If the serial number is not typed correctly, Fontographer will not run. Be sure to include the dashes. Please retain the registration card with your records; you will need the information for technical support or if you install Fontographer on a different machine. You might try writing the serial number in the manual or staple the card to the inside of the user's manual. The serial number is all you will need to personalize your new software, or contact Macromedia technical support if you run into complications.

If you are using pressure-sensitive tablets with Fontographer, then be sure you have the most recent versions of the software drivers. Call technical support (415-252-9080) to ensure that you do. Make sure you have your serial number on hand.

New in the Windows Version

The following items are new additions and updates in the Windows version of the software:

- PFM files generated from Adobe Standard Encoded fonts now have correct widths for all the characters in the Windows 3.1 character set.
- Print Sample Kerning Pairs now has correct spacing of the kerning data.
- A problem with importing metrics data from AFM files which have parentheses in the notice string has been fixed.

Installing Fontographer 4.1.5 for the Mac OS

Fontographer is included on the FreeHand 7 Graphics Studio CD-ROM. The following are the minimum system requirements:

- Mac Plus or better is highly recommended, with a Power Mac being the best bet

- System 7
- 5.1 MB hard drive space
- 6 MB of available RAM

To install Fontographer, double-click on the Fontographer installer on your CD-ROM and then follow the instructions. Your Fontographer sample fonts will be automatically placed into the same folder as the Fontographer application during the installation process. To select only those options you want installed, select the Custom Installation option.

If you run into any problems when installing Fontographer, try again after restarting with the extensions turned off. When the installation is complete, you can reactivate the extensions.

The first time you run Fontographer, it will display a Personalization dialog. Look for the 21-digit serial number, which will allow you to use Fontographer. If the serial number is not typed correctly, Fontographer will not run. Be sure to include the dashes. Please retain the registration card with your records; you will need the information for technical support or if you install Fontographer on a different machine. You might try writing the serial number in the manual or staple the card to the inside of the user's manual. The serial number is all you will need to personalize your new software, or contact Macromedia technical support if you run into complications.

If you are using pressure-sensitive tablets with Fontographer, then be sure you have the most recent versions of the software drivers. Call technical support (415-252-9080) to ensure that you do. Make sure you have your serial number on hand.

New in the Mac OS Version

The following items have either been added or revised in the Mac OS version of Fontographer:

- Fontographer 4.1.5 for the Mac OS will open database files created in the new Fontographer version 4.1 for Windows. Mac OS bitmap files (.bmap) format NFNT will no longer contain an incorrect maximum character width of 255, eliminating the resultant problem of extremely long text fields in 4D.

- Problems with keymap printing have been resolved, and all lines will now be visible on a StyleWriter.

- Print Sample Kerning Pairs now has correct spacing of the kerning data.

- A problem with importing metrics data from AFM files that have parentheses in the notice string has been fixed.

Power PC Users

The Power PC-native Fontographer application is much faster than the 68K version. You can open fonts, perform CPU-intensive operations, and manipulate huge paths with unprecedented speed. When you run the installer on a Power PC-based system, it will automatically install Fontographer for the Power PC. If you experience a problem using Fontographer for the Power PC (a crash, a network copy detection error, or an extreme slowdown), remove all of the non-Apple system extensions using the Extensions Manager and restart. Commonly, an extension will be the source of all such troubles. If you really need the offending extension, contact the vendor to see if there is a later version that will run safely on the Power PC with Fontographer.

Fontographer Copyright Issues

Before you import a font and alter it, you might want to consider the following potential copyright issues. This is especially true if you have plans to market the font, or to use it in some commercial way.

- Call the maker of the font and ask for any details you may need in the font's licensing agreement. See the Copyright Notice field in Fontographer for the name of the copyright holder. You must treat a font as you would any other software licensing agreement.

- If you are creating a commercial PostScript font, you need to acquire a unique ID number from Adobe Systems.

- To find out whether a font name has been used or is copyrighted, check Tim Ryan's Typeface NameBase. The NameBase lists font names, designers, dates of creation, and originating foundries, as well as information regarding who owns and distributes the fonts at this time. He has compiled information on over 20,000 fonts. Tim can be contacted at: SourceNet, 1728 North Moorpark Road, Thousand Oaks, CA 91360. Phone: 805-494-7123, Fax: 805-497-3790.
  AOL: SOURCENET@APPLELINK.APPLE.COM

- Call the Software Publishers Association (800-388-7478) for legal advice on these issues.

Fontographer Updates

Fontographer may have been updated by the time you read this book. If so, go to one of the following online sources to get the latest information:

- America Online: Keyword: Macromedia, select Software Library, Product Updates.

- On the Web: http://www.macromedia.com/software/fontographer/updates.html.

- Tech notes are also available 24 hours a day via Macromedia's MacroFacts service at 800-449-3329 or 415-863-4409.

- CompuServe: Enter "go macromedia" and leave a thread for tech support in the software support area. You'll also find tech notes in the Technotes area and updates in the library.

- AOL: Enter Keyword "Macromedia" to leave a thread for tech support in the software support area. You also can browse the Technotes area and the library section for information and updates.

Fontographer Goodies on the Application's CD-ROM

In addition to the Fontographer application, the following support material is included on the application CD-ROM:

- **AltSys PC Font Access 1.0:** This is a free font utility program for PC fonts generated from Fontographer. PC Font Access allows you to open .TTF (PC TrueType) files and .PFM (PC Type 1) files to change a large number of fields that are too subjective for Fontographer to know what good values are (for example, the width of the upper double underline bar). After you have tweaked these fields, you can then save the files with the new values (and a new filename so as to not overwrite your original font), thus customizing the font.

- **AltSys Style Merger 1.0:** This is a small utility that makes one font family out of up to four fonts. Their base names must be the same.

- **Sixteen Sample Fonts:** These are included for your exploration and use, and come from various professional font houses.

Setting Preferences

There are four pages in the Preferences dialog (File | Preferences): General Preferences, Editing Behavior, Point Display, and Windows and Dialogs.

General Preferences

The top section of this page in the Preferences dialog (see Figure 17-1) contains the options for the Undo command. The default number of Undos is 8, which should suffice in most instances. Increase this number only if you have enough RAM to handle it. On a 32 MB RAM system, you should be able to safely operate with the Undo level set to 15. The next two toggles should be left on; they allow the application to delete Undos if you run low on memory and notify you before this takes place.

The next two items in this Preferences dialog allow you to select whether to use the font's encoding or the system's (Mac OS or Windows) encoding. Select the system's encoding. Encoding is the ordering of the font's characters. Even though you can set the general parameters here from the two options, you can also select from more encoding options from the Encoding pop-up in the Font Info dialog (Element | Font Info). Preferences encodings determine the encoding before you start a project, whereas the encodings listed in the Font Info dialog are assigned after a font is loaded in.

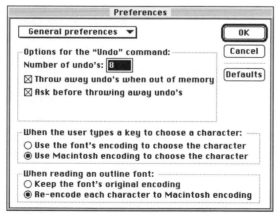

Figure 17-1: The General Preferences page in the Preferences dialog.

Editing Behavior

The Editing Behavior tab on the Preferences dialog (see Figure 17-2) allows you to control em and pixel unit behavior. Unless you are an expert font designer, leave the settings at their defaulted position. Also listed are controls for snap-to-point and active path options. In their default positions, they will satisfy 99 percent of Fontographer users.

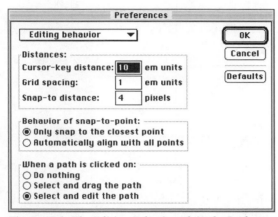

Figure 17-2: The Editing Behavior tab in the Preferences dialog.

Point Display

You create and edit font characters by drawing Bezier curves and adjusting the associated control points and arms. In the Point Display tab (see Figure 17-3), you can customize how the control points and line elements are displayed to suit your designer's personality. There is no need to go through all of the options represented here, because each check box alters the preview display, where you can see what your choices entail.

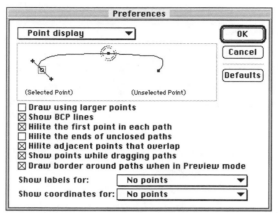

Figure 17-3: The Point Display tab of the Preferences dialog.

Windows & Dialogs

In the Windows and Dialogs tab (see Figure 17-4), the default values for the display of data in all windows and dialogs in Fontographer should remain checked as the defaults indicate. If any of these items disturb the way that you work, you can explore altering them as you go.

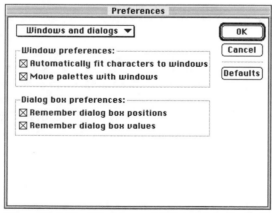

Figure 17-4: The Windows and dialogs tab in the Preferences dialog.

Hint Parameters

Hints improve a character's outline definition so that it is clearer on the screen and prints better. Fontographer assigns hints by default. There is no reason that you should alter the Hints parameters, unless you see some problems in the font display or printout. Even then, you might want to seek assistance before adjusting these settings yourself. The Hint Parameters dialog (Hints | Hint Parameters) is where this is accomplished (see Figure 17-5).

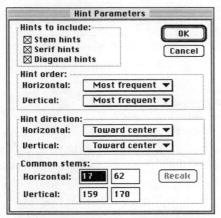

Figure 17-5: The Hint Parameters dialog.

Opening a Fontographer Project

A Fontographer project is a font set. Opening a project presents you with that font set displayed as editable characters, as seen in Figure 17-6.

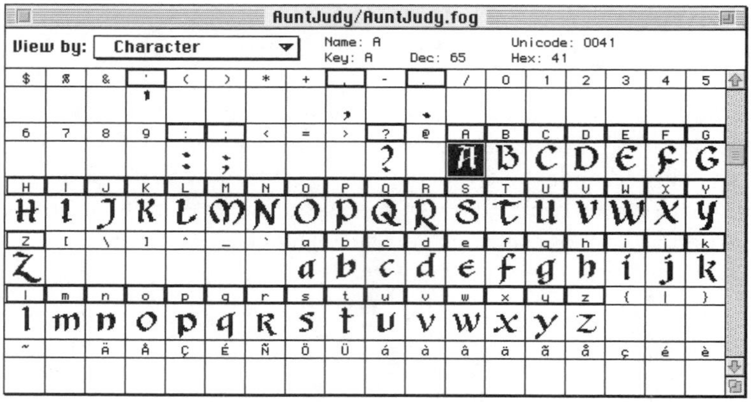

Figure 17-6: The Font display indicates that a Fontographer project is open.

Saving a Fontographer Project

Saving a Fontographer project can mean two separate things. The first is to simply save the altered or new font to the Fontographer folder, or another folder of your choice. The second level of saving the Fontographer font set is to actually embed it in your system so it is available for all applications that address fonts.

Installing Fontographer Fonts Under Mac OS

Depending on the type of font you are installing, the instructions are slightly different for installing a font on a Mac OS system.

Installing PostScript Fonts in System 7.1 or Later

1. Select both bitmap and PostScript files from the folder where you stored the completed Fontographer fonts.

2. Drag and drop both files on the closed System folder.

Installing TrueType Fonts in System 7.1 or Later

1. Drag and drop the suitcase file from the folder where you stored your completed Fontographer font to the closed System folder.

2. A message asks whether you want the fonts stored in the Fonts folder. Click OK.

Installing Fontographer Fonts on a Windows System

Depending on the type of font you are installing, the instructions are slightly different for installing a font on the various Windows machines.

Installing PostScript Fonts in Windows 3.x or Higher or Windows 95 With Adobe Type Manager 2.x

1. Find the ATM Control Panel icon, and double-click it.
2. Click the Add button.
3. Scroll the directories listings until you find the folder where you stored your completed Fontographer font and select it.
4. Click the Add button to install the font.
5. Click the ATM Exit button, and restart Windows.

Installing TrueType Fonts in Windows 3.x or Higher

1. Open the Windows Control Panel.
2. Open the Fonts panel.
3. Find your Fontographer font in the appropriate directory, and select it.
4. Click OK to install the font.

Installing TrueType Fonts in Windows 95

1. Open the Windows Control Panel.
2. Select File | Install New Font to display the Add Fonts dialog.
3. Find your new or edited Fontographer TrueType font in the directory where you stored it.
4. Make sure that the Copy Fonts to Folder box is checked, and then select your Fontographer font. It will be added to the System folder. Restart Windows 95.

Removing Installed Fonts

There are times when your font directory becomes too full, or perhaps when some of the fonts installed no longer serve any purpose. When these conditions occur, there is a way to remove selected fonts.

Removing Fonts From the Mac OS (System 7.1 or Higher)

1. Open the Fonts folder in the System folder.

2. Drag both the bitmap and PostScript files (if it's a PostScript font) into the Trash.

Removing PostScript Fonts With the ATM Control Panel in Windows

1. Open the ATM Control Panel.

2. Select the font you want to remove.

3. Click Remove, and exit ATM.

4. Open the WIN.INI file with Notepad.

5. Find the section header for PostScript, LPT1, or whichever port you had selected when you installed the font.

6. Find the font by its DOS file name and remove that line from the table.

7. Find the line near the beginning of the table that reads "Softfonts=x", where x represents a number. Adjust the number to reflect the font(s) you removed.

8. Exit and restart Windows.

Removing TrueType Fonts in Windows

1. Open the Control Panel.

2. Open the Fonts panel.

3. Select the font you want removed, and click Remove. If you want to remove it permanently, click the Delete Font File from Disk check box.

4. Press Enter and restart Windows.

Moving On

In this chapter, we have covered the installation of Fontographer. We have also discussed how to configure the settings for a Fontographer project session, and how both Mac and Windows users can remove fonts from their system. In the next chapter, we will look at how Fontographer can be used to edit an existing font or to create a new one.

18

Working With Fonts

Fontographer allows you to customize any TrueType or PostScript fonts you may encounter. Before editing a font on your system, however, be sure you understand the copyright information included in Chapter 17. If you create your own fonts for display or marketing purposes, you may want to secure your own copyrights. Check with the U.S. Copyright Office, and also the names and addresses provided in the Copyright Information section in Chapter 17, to do so.

Tip

This chapter will not repeat all of the excellent Fontographer details from the documentation. We expect that you have already worked through that documentation before doing the guided exercises listed here.

The Fontographer Font Folder

The 16 Fontographer fonts included in the Font Samples folder are for your exploration in Fontographer. They cannot, however, be used for commercial display or marketing purposes in any form, as they are all copyrighted. If you do develop an interesting customized version of any of these fonts, please contact the developers to seek their permission and guidance. Customizing copyrighted fonts does not alter their copyrighted status.

Encoding Pop-up in Font Info

Select Element | Font Info to display the Font Info dialog where the various Encoding options can be configured. See Figure 18-1.

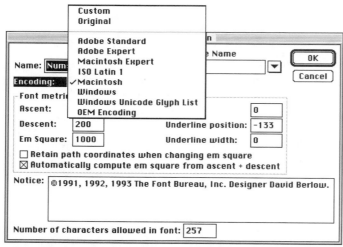

Figure 18-1: The Font Info dialog, showing the Encoding options in the pop-up list.

The Encoding options listed here are meant to give you more definitive choices, and include the following:

- **Custom:** This encoding allows for the custom naming of characters. Custom character naming is used widely by people who design non-Roman fonts.

- **Original:** This encoding is useful when opening fonts with strange encodings such as Sonata (a music symbol font), Carta, or Zapf Dingbats.

- **Adobe Standard:** This is the Adobe default encoding. It includes 16 symbol characters as a part of the font.

- **Adobe Expert:** This encoding is only useful for the creation of expert font sets. If you have no idea what this means, stay away from this encoding option.

- **Macintosh Expert:** This encoding is only useful for the creation of expert font sets for the Mac OS. If you have no idea what this means, stay away from this encoding option.

- **ISO Latin 1:** Select this encoding option if you are designing a font for Sun workstations. It is preferable for most UNIX systems.

- **Macintosh:** This is similar to the Adobe Standard Encoding option, but is especially designed to be compatible with the Mac OS's keystrokes.

- **Windows:** Gives you the option of creating a Windows 3.1 PostScript or TrueType font, with the added option of selecting Windows 95.

- **Windows Unicode Glyph List:** This gives you access to the full character set for Windows 95. The added OS/2 option gives you access to the full OS/2 character set.

- **OEM Encoding:** This is a standard encoding vector that lists character names and unicodes.

Tip

The safest general options: Mac OS users should select either Macintosh or Adobe Standard encoding. Windows users should opt for Windows encoding.

Customizing a Fontographer Font

Using one of the included Fontographer fonts, we will walk through customization procedures in Fontographer. Do the following:

1. Open Fontographer, and use the Open Font command (File | Open Font) to load in the GoodCityModern.fog font file from the Font Samples directory in the Fontographer folder.

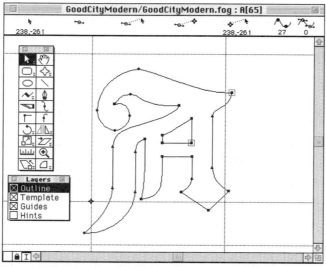

Figure 18-2: The GoodCityModern font as it appears in Fontographer.

2. Double-click on the letter A to bring up its editing window.

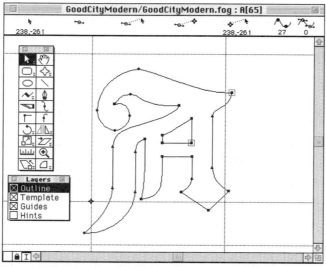

Figure 18-3: The letter A is accessed on its own editing window.

3. Grab the top control point of the letter by selecting it with the selection arrow, and pull it to the top of the guide line. It will snap into place when it meets the guide line.

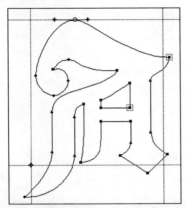

Figure 18-4: The top control point is moved up.

4. Using the same method, pull the right control arm of the same point to the right, until the curve meets the right guideline. The curve will snap when it meets the guide.

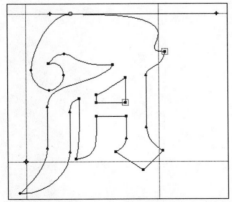

Figure 18-5: The control arm is moved to the right, widening the top of the letter.

5. Double-click on the Multigon tool (under the Hand icon) to access its settings dialog. Configure the following settings: Star, 7 sides, Automatic Star Points. Click on OK to close the dialog and accept the settings.

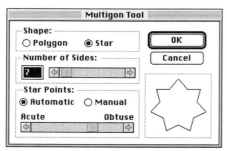

Figure 18-6: The Multigon settings are adjusted.

6. With the Multigon tool still selected, place the mouse cursor in the center of the part of the letter you widened, and click and drag to create a seven-point star.

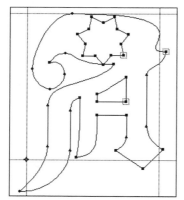

Figure 18-7: A seven-point star is added.

7. Use the Oval tool to draw a circle inside the seven-point star.

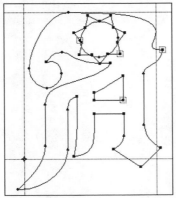

Figure 18-8: A circle is drawn in the star.

8. Select the star and circle (use Shift-select to get all of the parts), and copy them to the clipboard. Close the letter A, and open the letter B by double-clicking on it. Widen the top of the B to accommodate the star-circle graphic, and paste it in. You will have to nudge the graphic into place by using the arrow keys.

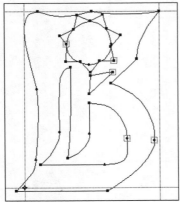

Figure 18-9: The letter B now contains the same graphic as the A.

9. Repeat this same operation for all of the letters that you would like to use as a common typeface. When you are finished, select Windows | Open Bitmap Window. Answer OK when the system asks if you would like to create bitmaps for the font. Type in the sizes 24,48,72 as indicated in Figure 18-10. Click OK.

Figure 18-10: Generate bitmap files for the font.

10. When the bitmap dialog appears, use the Pencil tool to outline the letter as shown in Figure 18-11. Close the dialog when finished. You will have to repeat this step for each bitmap required.

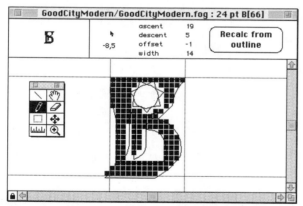

Figure 18-11: Outline the bitmap version of the letter to expose the graphic.

11. Select File | Save As, and save your .fog font to a folder with a new name. Close the current file, and open the saved newly named font. Select Generate Font Files, which will translate the .fog font file to a file your system can use (see Figure 18-12). Select your computer choice and the format you want. The bitmap sizes should already be listed. Select the folder where the font is to reside. Click on Generate.

Tip

You may want to output the font to a non-system folder and transfer it to the system fonts folder as a later step. This is a safer way to operate.

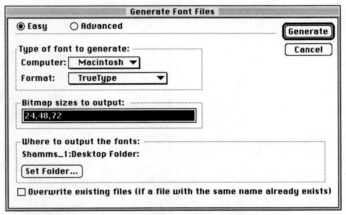

Figure 18-12: Generate the font in the format you like.

12. Use the information provided in Chapter 17 to place your font in the proper system fonts directory or folder.

Using Your Customized Font in FreeHand

Although we used the GoodCity Modern font as an example of customizing a font in the above exercise, do not use it in a FreeHand project. Customized fonts used in your personal projects should not be copyrighted fonts like GoodCity Modern. The following material is presented as an example only, and not to indicate that you have the right to use the customized GoodCity font in your FreeHand projects. To use a customized font in FreeHand, do the following:

1. Open FreeHand 7. Select your custom font from the font menu, and, with the Text tool selected, type in an A and a B.

2. Convert to paths. Ungroup the letters, and use the Fill Inspector to add new fills to the star graphics (I used gradient fills, but anything will work). Regroup the letters.

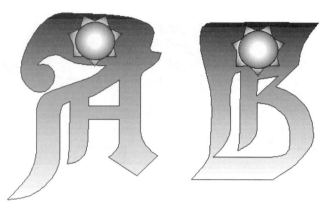

Figure 18-13: All of the letters in your customized font are available to you in FreeHand 7.

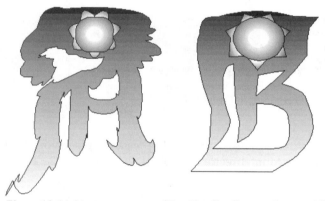

Figure 18-14: You can use any of FreeHand's effects tools to modify the customized text. Here we've used the Bend Xtra on the A and the Fisheye Lens on the B.

Using Your Customized Font in xRes

Although we used the GoodCity Modern font as an example of customizing a font in the above exercise, do not use it in an xRes project. Customized fonts used in your personal projects should not be copyrighted fonts like GoodCity Modern. The following material is presented as an example only, and not to indicate that you have the right to use the customized GoodCity font in your xRes projects. Your customized font characters can be saved out as graphics files. If you save your font characters out as EPS files in FreeHand, you can import them into xRes.

Select the xRes font dialog and use the customized font (the areas where the graphics were placed will be filled). xRes does not address the font with overlayed graphics, so using exported FreeHand files is best. Refer to Figure 18-15.

Figure 18-15: Once imported into xRes, the customized letters of the font can be targeted for xRes effects, like these gradient fills.

Using Your Customized Font in Extreme 3D

Although we used the GoodCity Modern font as an example of customizing a font in the above exercise, do not use it in an Extreme 3D project. Customized fonts used in your personal projects should not be copyrighted fonts like GoodCity Modern. The following material is presented as an example only, and not to indicate that you have the right to use the customized GoodCity font in your Extreme 3D projects. You can also use Fontographer fonts in Extreme 3D. Use the xRes filtered version of the customized font letters as texture maps in Extreme 3D. Refer to Figure 18-16.

1. Locate the xRes filtered font graphic, and import it into Extreme 3D as a bitmap in one of the materials settings.

2. Apply the bitmapped font graphic to a suitable 3D object.

Figure 18-16: The same xRes filtered version of the customized letter can be used as a texture map in Extreme 3D.

Creating a New Graphic Font

Graphics fonts can be used to store logos and clip art in a font format, making it simple to develop fonts that provide instant access to these graphics with a keystroke. The drawing tools in Fontographer should be very familiar to you as a FreeHand artist, with any lack of understanding being addressed by your thorough reading of the Fontographer documentation. The same process is used in Fontographer to create either a new font or a new set of graphics symbols. We are choosing to guide you through the graphics option because it is very important to your ability to transfer what you create in Fontographer to FreeHand, xRes, and Extreme 3D creations. Having already walked you through the customization of a font, the graphics option should balance your understanding and appreciation for Fontographer as an integral part of the FreeHand 7 Graphics Studio.

To create a new set of graphics symbols, do the following:

1. Open Fontographer. Select File | New, which displays a new font window.

2. Double-click on any empty area. Use Fontographer's drawing tools to draw any symbols you like, and close the drawing window. Do this for as many symbols as you can, filling the empty areas with your graphics.

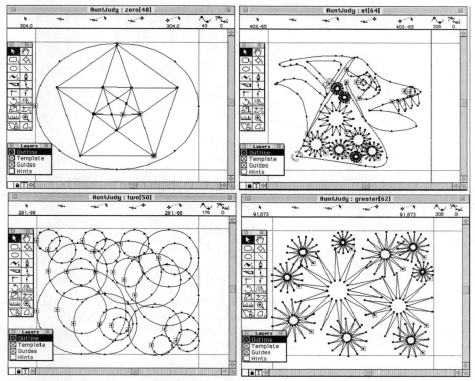

Figure 18-17: Draw your symbols for each of the empty keystroke content areas you want to fill.

3. Create bitmaps for the font the same way you did for the customized font exercise.

4. Generate the font files in the same manner that you did for the customized font exercise. Use the new symbols in your FreeHand documents.

Does this exercise give you any ideas for adding customized graphics as components of a font file?

Figure 18-18: Each of these four symbols was placed in FreeHand with a single keystroke, because they are part of a saved Fontographer PostScript 1 font. Once in FreeHand, gradient fills and strokes were added, and FreeHand effects can be used to customize the shapes further.

Bitmap to Vector Translations

There is one more technique that Fontographer offers that is important for transferring files back and forth among the FreeHand 7 Graphics Studio applications: the translation of a bitmap picture file (not to be confused with a bitmap font image) in the vector format that Fontographer can embed in a keystroke area. The process is straightforward. Refer to Figure 18-19.

1. Copy a bitmap graphic to the clipboard in FreeHand, xRes, or Extreme 3D.

2. Open Fontographer, and create a new font. Double-click on a keystroke area, activating the editing window. Select Edit I Paste, and the graphic on the clipboard is pasted to the Template layer of the Fontographer edit window as a grayed-out graphic. Move the image into whatever orientation is needed.

3. If the image needs to be scaled, choose Element I Transform and input the selected reduction in percentage numbers.

4. Click on the Outline layer, and select Element I AutoTrace. That's it. Your vector image is ready to edit in Fontographer.

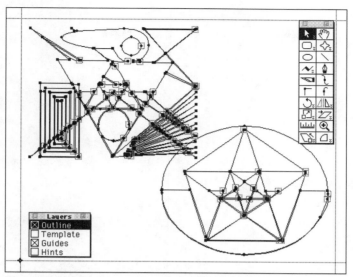

Figure 18-19: This image was copied to the clipboard from FreeHand and imported into Fontographer, where it was resized and autotraced.

Moving On

This chapter centered on using Fontographer to edit and create fonts for FreeHand and xRes projects. We also looked at how a customized font can be used in FreeHand, xRes, and Extreme 3D, and explored bitmap to vector translation. In the next chapter, the first in Part 5, we move on to a series of dedicated tutorials that guide you through the integration of FreeHand 7, xRes 3, and Extreme 3D 2.0.

Part V

Getting Down to Business: Hands-On Exercises

19

Text FX

FreeHand 7 offers several new options when it comes to giving your selected text block a more personalized look. The range of modifications runs the gamut from subtle to radical, satisfying every possible design need. Altered text is most often used when a headline needs to stand out, but there are other uses as well. Customized text can be used to blend more logically into a document theme, or even to emulate the feeling of a historical period or an emotional moment in a story. Altered text can even be seen as a pure graphic form when used in a collage composition, so that its form becomes more important than its ability to act as a verbalization to be read. To begin to explore FreeHand's unique options for creating text blocks, take a look at the following five diverse techniques: 3D Embossing, Hollywood Titling, Reflected Text, ElectroText, and BubbleText.

3D Embossing

3D Embossing adds interest to headlines when applied to a text block and can also make your selected graphics look more contemporary, even when you use clip art or graphic fonts as the root elements.

Tip

If you prefer to see what the finished elements look like in FreeHand before trying to create your own versions, you can use the accompanying CD-ROM to load the 3D Emboss Project and all of the tutorial elements into FreeHand so you can more easily work through this example. You may also find some of the elements in the Parts and Pieces folder. Especially for the less experienced FreeHand user, this may offer an enhanced way of learning the processes involved.

Embossing Text

Embossed text has a carved appearance, much like that achieved with a wood block carving. Using a 3D look in a 2D project makes the selected text block stand out on the page.

Step #1: Create a Set of Squares

Use the Rectangle tool in the Tool palette to draw a rectangle one inch wide and one inch deep. Use the drag-and-drop functions of the Color Mixer to color it a bright CMYK red (0, 100, 100, 0). Duplicate it seven times, so there are a total of eight squares on the screen. Align them all on the same baseline by selecting all of them with the Pointer tool, and using the Align Bottom function in the Align panel.

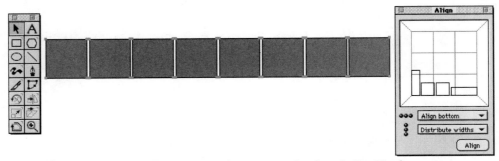

Figure 19-1: In the first step, eight duplicated squares are placed on the FreeHand page.

Step #2: Add the Text Block

Create a text block with the Text tool that reads "3D Emboss" using Helvetica Bold 72 points. Convert it to Paths. Duplicate the text block, and move the duplicate out of the way for the moment. Ungroup the original text block.

Figure 19-2: Create a text block that reads "3D Emboss."

Step #3: Move the Lettering over the Squares

One by one, use the Pointer tool to move each letter separately over one of the red squares, so that about half of the lettering height extends over the top of the square. When the move is completed, Shift-select all of the letters. Use the Align panel to set the horizontal alignment to Align Bottom and the vertical alignment to No Change.

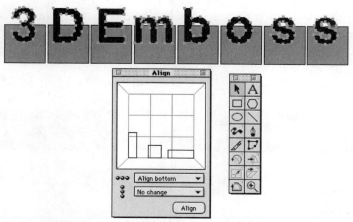

Figure 19-3: Move the lettering over the squares as illustrated.

Step #4: Change the Color of the Letters

With all of the elements of "3D Emboss" selected, use the Color Mixer to drag and drop a solid CMYK yellow (0, 0, 100, 0) on the letters. See that there is no stroke assigned to these selections.

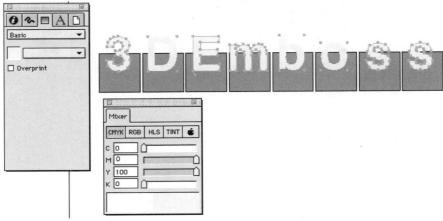

Figure 19-4: Change the fill color to yellow.

Step #5: Blend the Color of the Letters

Open the Operations panel. Click in an empty area of the screen to deselect everything. With the Pointer tool still chosen in the Toolbox, Shift-click on the "3" and the red square it rests upon. Click on the Blend operator in the Operations panel, causing the red square and the number "3" to blend.

Figure 19-5: A blend is applied to the letter and the rectangle it sits upon.

Repeat the same blending procedure outlined in step five for each of the letter/square pairs. The "D," "b," and "o" have holes in them, and will not take a blend until you split them, and discard the holes.

Figure 19-6: Each of the letters is blended with the rectangle it sits upon.

Step #6: Add a Linear Stroke

Select the whole graphic, and set the Stroke Inspector to a one point black stroke. This adds a linear stroke over each of the blended parts.

Figure 19-7: A linear stroke adds a carved look to the text block.

Step #7: Place the Letters From the Other Text Block on Top

Select the duplicated text block you set aside, ungroup it, and, after assigning a bright CMYK red fill and no stroke to the letters with the Color Mixer, place each of the letters over their counterparts on the 3D graphic.

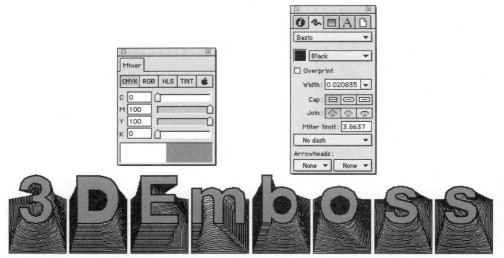

Figure 19-8: The finished 3D embossed text block should resemble this example.

Embossing Shapes

This technique works just as well with shapes other than text. Let's take a look at how it can be applied to a text symbol font (these are from the DeniArt Hieroglyphics 3 set, but you can use any symbols you desire, since everything is converted to a path).

Step #1: Add the Symbols

Use the Text tool to place your symbols on the page.

Figure 19-9: The same technique can work wonders on your symbol fonts. This hieroglyphic font is from DeniArt Systems, and comes in Mac and Windows flavors.

Step #2: Create an Oval for the Background

Convert the text block to paths, and ungroup the symbols if you plan to work on more than one ~~more than one~~. One at a time, and fill it with a bright yellow hue, giving it a one point black stroke. Create an oval about the same size as the symbol, and color it blue with a one point black stroke.

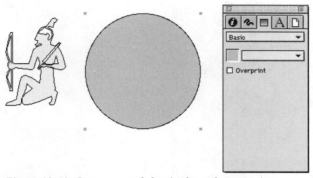

Figure 19-10: Create an oval that is about the same size as your chosen symbol.

Step #3: Blend the Symbols & the Oval

Blends work only on non-grouped selections. Clone your graphic. If it is a graphic that has holes in it, use the Split command to break it apart. Delete the extraneous matter so that you have just a silhouette for the cloned result.

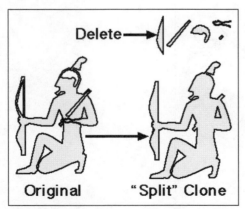

Figure 19-11: If you have any "holes" in your selected graphic, they should be thrown away after you split the object apart, as this example shows.

Take the silhouetted clone and place it over the oval. Make sure some of it extends beyond the top of the oval. Select both the symbol and the oval, and click on the Blend tool in the Operations panel.

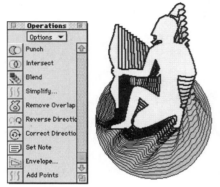

Figure 19-12: The symbol is then blended with the oval.

Step #4: Place the Original Shape on Top

Clone the original shape again, and place this clone over the silhouetted graphic on the blend. Your embossed symbol is finished.

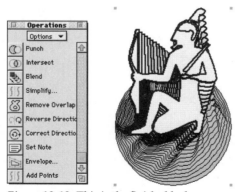

Figure 19-13: This is the finished look.

The underlying shape and its color play a large part in determining the final look of the graphic, as illustrated in Figure 19-14.

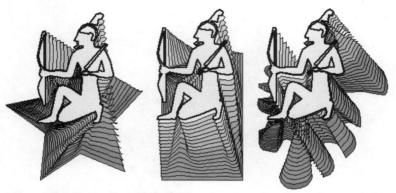

Figure 19-14: By varying the underlying shape, a series of variations result from the blend operation.

Other Shape Variations

Let's look at another variation. Draw any shape you like (the one illustrated is a seven-pointed star drawn with the Polygon tool). Place a silhouetted clone in the center of the shape, so that none of it extends beyond the perimeter. Blend the two. Place a clone of the non-split original over the shape, and group everything. Blend it.

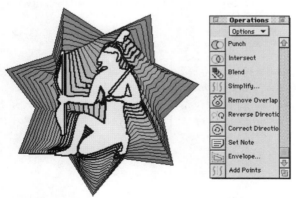

Figure 19-15: By placing the symbol in the middle of the shape and blending it, a whole new look is achieved.

For another variant, try this. Follow all of the steps in the previous example, only set the stroke of both the silhouette and the shape to None. This produces less of a 3D and more of an extruded shadow effect.

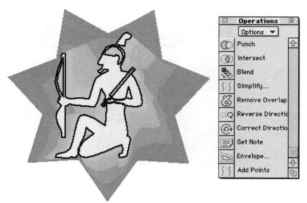

Figure 19-16: The blend with no strokes.

Hollywood Titling

This technique produces Hollywood titling, like that used for 50s gladiator movies. First, we'll use FreeHand to create the lettering, and then we'll add a 3D extrusion in xRes. Then, the graphic will be ported back to FreeHand, so it can be used as part of a page layout. Finally, we'll look at the same process with the help of VectorFX from MetaTools, a FreeHand-specific plug-in.

Tip

If you prefer to see what these finished graphic elements look like prior to creating them yourself, use the accompanying CD-ROM to load the Colossus Project and all of the tutorial elements into FreeHand so you can more easily work through this example. You may also find some of the elements in the Parts and Pieces folder.

Using FreeHand & xRes

In order to achieve certain effects, it is often necessary to port a graphic back and forth amongst various Graphics Studio applications. In this example, we demonstrate this by moving between FreeHand and xRes.

Step #1: Add the Text Blocks

Create a text block that reads "COLOSSUS" in all caps in a bold serif typeface. Place it in the center of your workspace.

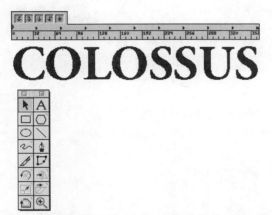

Figure 19-17: The beginning text block is placed on the page.

Step #2: Set the Gradient

Convert the text to paths. Apply a multicolor CMYK gradient. Set the gradient as follows: separate the color ramp into three sections, with more space allocated to the two outermost sections. Set the four color pots to Dark Blue (100, 100, 0, 0), Dark Blue (100, 100, 0, 0), Yellow (0, 0, 100, 0), and Dark Red (0, 100, 78, 36). Select Graduated and Logarithmic, and set the angle to 90 degrees. This gives the text a colorful shimmer. Apply the fill to the text (see Figure 19-18).

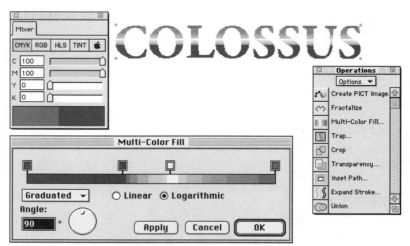

Figure 19-18: A multicolor fill adds a shimmer to the text.

Step #3: Enlarge the Text & Simplify It

Enlarge the text to about three times its original height.

Figure 19-19: The text is then enlarged vertically.

Make sure the Operations panel is still open. Select Simplify from the Operations panel. Apply a setting of 10 to the text. This creates a blocky text look, rather like ancient Greek.

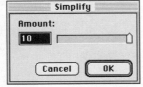

Figure 19-20: A "Simplify" effect at a setting of 10 is applied to the text.

Figure 19-21: This is the result of the Simplify effect.

Step #4: Add a Stroke to the Text

Add a two-point stroke to the text by selecting Modify | Stroke. This opens the Stroke Inspector. Select the Stroke option (the squiggly line), and make sure basic and black are selected. Select 2 Points from the drop-down menu. The stroke is added to the text block.

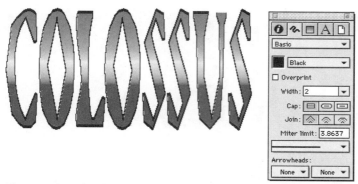

Figure 19-22: The black stroke causes the text to pop out more.

Step #5: Add Perspective

Open the Xtra Tools panel. Select the 3D Rotation tool from the Xtra Tools panel. Adjust the 3D look of the text until it is smaller at the top than the bottom. This makes it look like a large building observed from the ground.

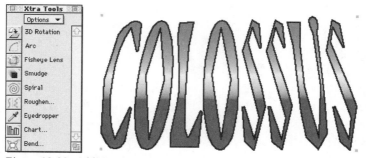

Figure 19-23: Adding perspective makes the text more dynamic.

The text block is now ready to port to xRes, so a 3D extrusion can be added. Save the text as a TIFF file at 300 DPI in the Export dialog in FreeHand, making sure that only this text block is exported (and not the whole page).

Step #6: Import the Graphic Into xRes & Select It

Import the graphic into xRes, and place it in the center of your workspace. Select the area around the graphic with the Wand tool, causing the graphic to be outlined with a marquee, and then choose Selection | Invert. Now the graphic is selected. Choose Edit | Clear, and all that remains is the marquee.

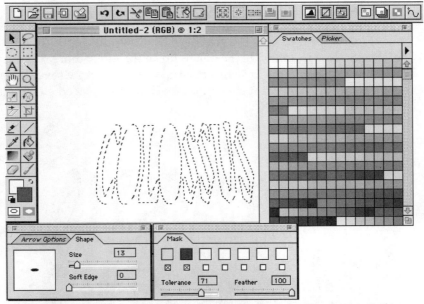

Figure 19-24: When you clear the imported graphic in xRes after selecting it, the marquee surrounding it remains.

Step #7: Add a Mystical Gradient in xRes

Select the Gradient tool in xRes, and from the Gradient Options tab on the Tool Options panel, select the Mystical gradient from the pop-up list. Apply this gradient as a linear fill by holding down the mouse button and moving from the bottom of the marquee to the top and then releasing it. The Mystical gradient is applied. Turn off the marquee.

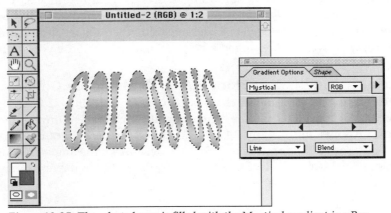

Figure 19-25: The selected area is filled with the Mystical gradient in xRes.

Step #8: Import the Graphic Again

Now import the graphic again, and deftly place it over the Mystical gradient, making it appear to give the graphic a shadow-like depth. To remove some of the shadow from inside the O's to make the effect more real, just draw a white shape inside the O's with no stroke. You can now save the graphic as a TIFF again, and import it back into FreeHand as a placed element in a page composition.

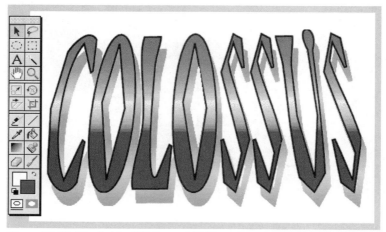

Figure 19-26: The finished Hollywood Titling effect.

Using VectorFX, MetaTools' FreeHand Plug-in

If you own VectorFX, a FreeHand plug-in from MetaTools, you have one more option for creating Hollywood titling effects for your text blocks. This one creates spectacular 3D images, as if they were generated in a 3D program. However, all of the art is vectorized, meaning that it is resolution independent (there will never be any jagged edges, no matter how close you zoom in).

Step #1: Add the Text Block & Apply a Multicolor Gradient

Create a text block as before that reads "COLOSSUS" in a 72 Point bold serif face in all caps. Place it in the center of your workspace. Convert the text to paths. Apply a multicolor CMYK gradient fill, exploring your own color choices. Select Graduated and Logarithmic, and set the angle to 90 degrees. This gives the text a colorful shimmer. Apply the fill to the text. Enlarge the text to about two times its original size.

Figure 19-27: The initial text block with a multicolor gradient fill.

Step #2: Use the KPT VectorFX 3D Transform Plug-in

With the text block selected, use the KPT VectorFX 3D Transform plug-in (Xtras | KPTVectorFX | 3D Transform). When the VectorFX interface comes up, set the X rotation to -41, the Y rotation to -36, the Z rotation to -12, Extrusion to 72 points, perspective to 100%, highlight color to dark blue, and ambient color to light blue. Click on the check mark to apply the 3D effect.

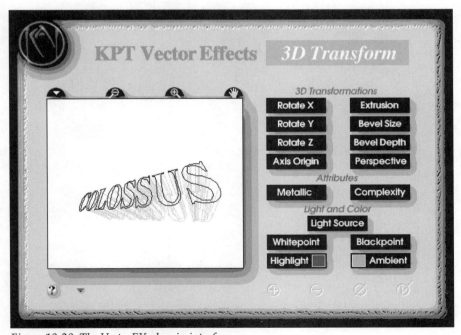

Figure 19-28: The VectorFX plug-in interface.

Figure 19-29: A gradient 3D extrusion is added to the text block by VectorFX.

Figure 19-30: Using the same VectorFX plug-in, and altering the rotation, perspective, beveling, and other settings, can help you create a variety of alternative 3D colossus effects.

Using Extreme 3D

Another way to achieve the same effect is to use Extreme 3D as the initial application, and then to port the results as a TIFF file into FreeHand for placement in a composition.

Step #1: Add the Text

Make sure the view is set to front. Click on the Text tool in the Toolbox, and then on the screen at the place you want the text to start from. Type in the word "COLOSSUS" in Times Bold, one inch high (remember that the text dialog is brought up by double-clicking on the Text tool, where fonts and sizes can be set). Press the return (Enter) key, and your text will appear on the screen.

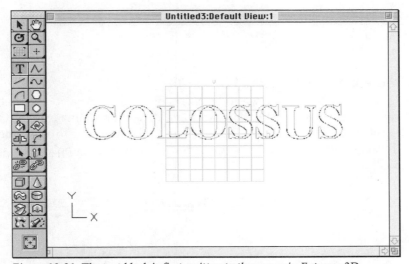

Figure 19-31: The text block is first written to the screen in Extreme 3D.

Step #2: Extrude the Text

Change the view to Three-Quarters ¾. Click on the Extrude tool in the Toolbox, and draw a line from the text block diagonally to the lower right to assign a depth to the text. Release the mouse when the depth meets your needs.

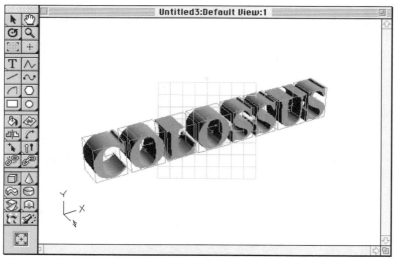

Figure 19-32: The text block is extruded along a drawn axis line.

Step #3: Apply a Material to the Text

Open the Materials browser and click on the Default-Scratched Metal material. Bring it to the list on the left by clicking on the left pointing arrows. Change the color of the material to a light blue and the roughness to a dark blue in the Edit Materials dialog at the bottom of this browser, and apply the material to your text.

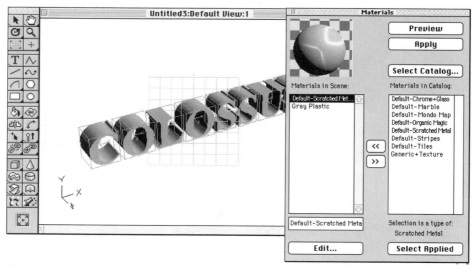

Figure 19-33: The text block changes color to signal that a material has been applied to it.

Step #4: Render the Graphic

In the Final Render Setup, choose Best (8x8) from the Settings tab, then, from the Render menu, select Final and Render To Screen. Save the render as a TIFF file, and import it for use in a FreeHand composition.

By manipulating the view Trackball in the Views browser, and also altering the perspective zoom settings, you can create any number of variations of this 3D Hollywood titling effect. When satisfied with your renderings, export them as 24-bit TIFF files, and import them into FreeHand as needed for page compositions. For even more variety, try assigning different textures to your object, and also change the type style at the start.

Figure 19-34: Any number of variations can be created in Extreme 3D by simply rotating the object in space before rendering it.

Reflected Text

Text reflected on a surface adds more reality to a FreeHand composition. It also adds viewer interest, so when reflected text is used appropriately as part of a message, viewers tend to dwell on the content of the message longer. Let's look at how a reflection effect can be created in FreeHand, in xRes, and in Extreme 3D. When the effect is created outside of FreeHand itself, save the results as a 24-bit TIFF and import it into FreeHand for placement.

Tip

If you prefer to see what these finished graphic elements look like prior to creating them yourself, use the accompanying CD-ROM to load the Reflection Project and all of the tutorial elements into FreeHand so you can more easily work through this example. You may also find some of the elements in the Parts and Pieces folder.

Using FreeHand

Use and mastery of the FreeHand Reflect tool are the most important components of this technique. This technique can be used effectively on images and text.

Step #1: Add the Letter

Use the Text tool to write the capital letter "A" on the screen. Make it Helvetica Bold 72 point.

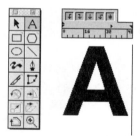

Figure 19-35: The letter A created with the FreeHand text tool.

Step #2: Add Color & Stroke to the Letter

Convert the letter to paths, and use the Color Mixer palette to assign a CMYK cyan fill (100, 0, 0, 0) and a 1.5 point black stroke to the letter.

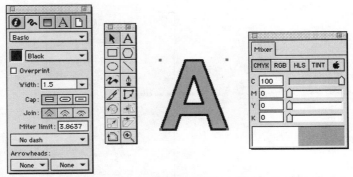

Figure 19-36: The letter with a fill and stroke added in FreeHand.

Step #3: Rotate the Letter & Add Color & Stroke

With the letter selected, clone it. This pastes a copy of the letter directly over the original. Use the Reflect tool in the Toolbox to rotate the cloned letter so that it rests beneath the original at an angle of 180 degrees. Use a CMYK light blue (15, 0, 0, 0) to fill the cloned copy, and set the stroke to None.

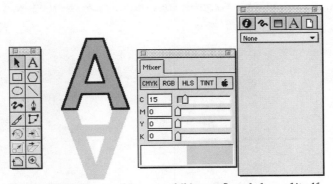

Figure 19-37: The graphic now exhibits a reflected clone of itself.

Step #4: Add a Horizon Line

Draw a two point straight black line with the Line tool, and place it in back of the letter. This line acts as a horizon line or table edge.

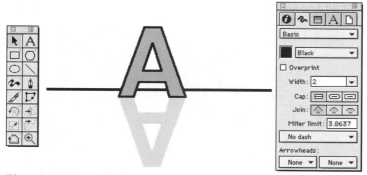

Figure 19-38: With the horizon line added, the reflected effect seems more identifiable.

Step #5: Add a Smudge

Reflected images often take on a blurry effect, due to the refractive components of the surface the original image sits upon. Double-click on the Smudge tool in the Xtra Tools panel to bring up its settings dialog. Set the fill and stroke colors in the Smudge Tool dialog to CMYK white (0, 0, 0, 0). Accept the settings and close the dialog. With the reflected letter selected, click on the Smudge tool. Place the mouse over the bottom of the reflected letter, and drag it down about the height of the letter.

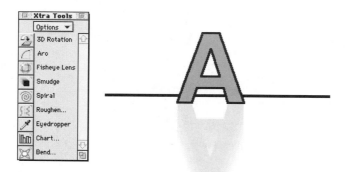

Figure 19-39: With a smudge added, the reflection is less mechanical.

Step #6: Stretch the Letter

It is also common for the reflected image to be a bit wavy, due to other components of light and the reflective surface. Select the smudged reflection. Use the Envelope tool in the Operations palette to stretch it out as illustrated. Click Apply to preview the changes, and, when you're satisfied, OK to accept them.

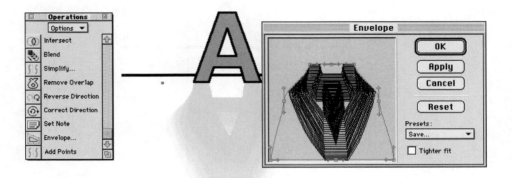

Figure 19-40: The Envelope tool adds warping to the reflection.

Step #7: Customize the Smudge Settings

Select the Smudge tool's settings dialog again by double-clicking on it in the Xtra Tools panel. Change the fill and stroke colors to a solid CMYK black (0, 0, 0, 100).

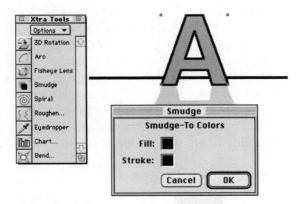

Figure 19-41: The settings in the Smudge Tool dialog can be customized.

Close the dialog by clicking on OK. With the original letter selected, click and drag the Smudge tool cursor from the letter a little to the upper right, just to give it some dimension. The reflected letter scene is complete.

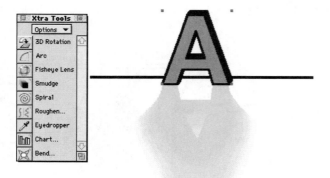

Figure 19-42: The effect is complete and accomplished entirely in FreeHand.

Using xRes

You can create reflective effects and apply them to bitmap images in xRes. The results can then be saved as a TIFF file, and exported to FreeHand for use in a composition.

Step #1: Apply the Gradients

Click on the Gradient tool, and in the Gradient Options tab of the Tools Options panel set the gradient to the Blue Range gradient in the list, Pinch, CMYK, and Blend. Use the rectangle marquee to select the bottom half of the screen, and apply the gradient with the Gradient tool by clicking and dragging the mouse in the rectangular marquee from the bottom center to the upper right on a diagonal path. After you release the mouse, the gradient is painted (Figure 19-44). Using the same technique, apply the Sunrise gradient (Sunrise, Line, CMYK, Blend) to the upper half of the painting (Figure 19-45).

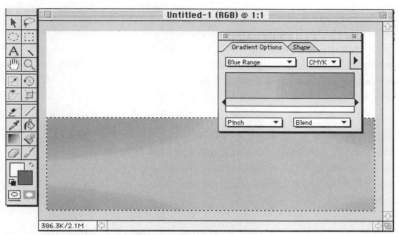

Figure 19-43: The bottom half of the painting will show a gradient surface by using the suggested technique.

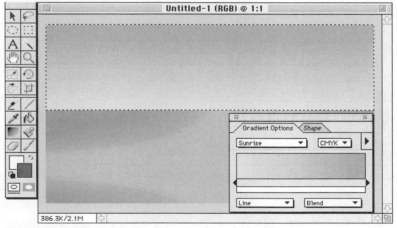

Figure 19-44: The Sunrise gradient completes the backdrop.

Step #2: Add a Text Block

With the Text tool, create a text block that says "Reflections" in a Helvetica typeface. Center it as shown in Figure 19-45. Duplicate it and flip it vertically, placing it below the original with just a hair of space between them (this shows the surface has a glossy thickness). With the cloned reflection selected, use the Opacity slider in the Objects panel to set the percentage at 50.

Step #3: Add a Wave Distortion

Place a rectangular marquee around the reflection, and go to Effects I Distort I Wave. Set an amplitude of 3 and a wavelength of 20 to distort the reflection. Apply the distortion. Save the image to disk, and import it into a FreeHand composition.

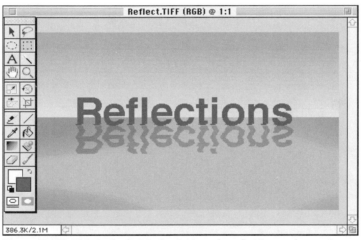

Figure 19-45: This is the finished painting of a reflective surface and a text block.

Using Extreme 3D

Reflectivity is handled very differently by a 3D application like Extreme 3D. In ray-tracing 3D applications, you can make surfaces reflective, so that anything placed upon them naturally reacts to produce a reflection of itself. However, Extreme 3D is not a ray-tracing application. Instead, it allows you to map images to surfaces, and you can attain some interesting reflective effects by doing it. Here's how to accomplish reflectivity in Extreme 3D.

Step #1: Add & Extrude a Text Block

In Three-Quarter view, create and extrude a text block. It can say whatever you like. Open the Materials window, and use the Select Catalog button to find the Brass Preset folder in the Extreme 3D folder and load it in. Select the Smooth Brass material, and bring it to the active materials list on the left by clicking on the left pointing arrows. Assign the Brass Smooth material to the text block. Render the text block at the highest settings (8 x 8), and save the rendering to disk.

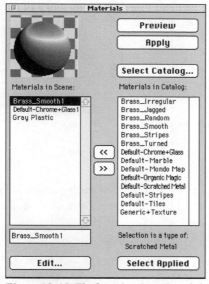

Figure 19-46: The lettering is assigned the Smooth Brass material, rendered, and exported to disk as a 24-bit TIFF file.

Step #2: Add a Sphere Under the Text Block

Create a sphere under the text block. In the Materials browser, place the Default-Chrome + Glass material in the active list at the left by selecting it from the list on the right and clicking on the left pointing arrows. Click on Edit. We are going to add the rendered letters as the reflection map for this material. Click on the Environment preview, and then on Load. Find the saved letters you rendered, and select the file. This now becomes the reflection map for the Default-Chrome + Glass material. Apply the Default-Chrome + Glass material to the sphere.

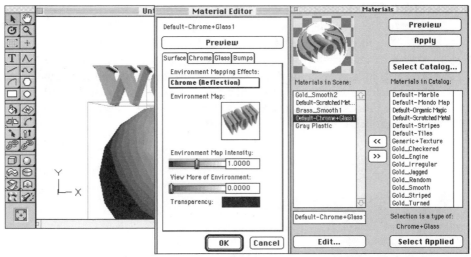

Figure 19-47: Use the Edit Materials dialog to load in the saved text block graphic you just rendered. This is now the reflection map for any Default-Chrome +Glass material in the scene.

Step #3: Add Additional Spheres

Place the text block in the center of the scene, and create a number of randomly sized spheres in the space around the text. Apply the Default-Chrome +Glass material to all of the spheres. Render the scene at high resolution (8 x 8), and export the rendered scene as a TIFF file, which can later be incorporated into a FreeHand page composition.

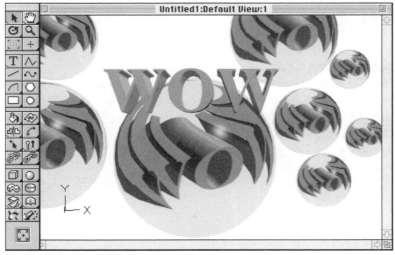

Figure 19-48: The finished Extreme 3D reflective text graphic.

ElectroText

This effect gives the impression that the text block has had a very shocking experience, and is still vibrating electric energy. It can be created in both FreeHand and xRes with slightly different looks.

Tip

If you prefer to see what these finished graphic elements look like prior to creating them yourself, use the accompanying CD-ROM to load the Electric Project and all of the tutorial elements into FreeHand so you can more easily work through this example. You may also find some of the elements in the Parts and Pieces folder.

Using FreeHand

Attaining this effect in FreeHand couldn't be simpler. All it really requires is a familiarity with the Bend tool in the Xtra Tools palette.

Step #1: Add the Text

Use the Text tool to create a text block that reads "Electric," and convert it to paths.

Figure 19-49: The initial text block.

Step #2: Bend the Text

With the text block selected, go to the Xtra Tools palette. Double-click on the Bend tool, which brings up its dialog. Set the slider all the way to the right, for a setting of 10. Select OK in the dialog to set the slider.

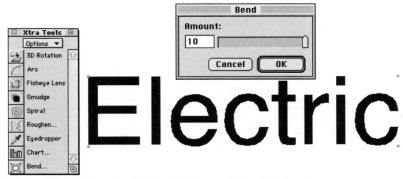

Figure 19-50: Set the Bend slider all the way to the right to 10.

With the Bend tool and the text block still selected, hold down the mouse button and move the cursor about a quarter inch to the upper right. You will see the text block respond to the bend tool as the lettering changes. ElectroText works well as a headline, or when you want to pop some text out of a paragraph in a radical manner.

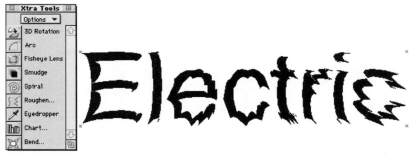

Figure 19-51: The shocking result.

Using xRes

xRes bitmap plug-in effects are perfect for creating electric looks, especially the Effects | Distort | Ripple filter.

Step #1: Create the Text Block
Create a text block that says "Electric" in sans serif bold caps.

Step #2: Add the Ripple Effect

Bring up the Ripple filter dialog by selecting Effects | Distort | Ripple. Set the amplitude to 3 and the wavelength to 9. Apply the effect to the text.

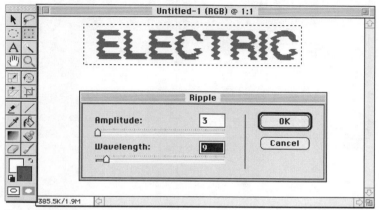

Figure 19-52: It's simple to get an electric type effect with xRes's Ripple filter.

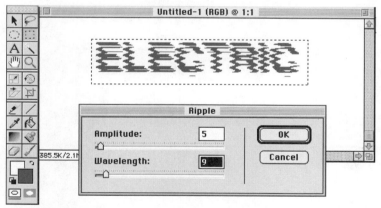

Figure 19-53: By adjusting the amplitude and wavelength settings, you can achieve different electric effects, but in general, you'll want to keep both settings fairly low.

Step #3: Add a Glowing Effect

Both the Ripple and Wave distortion filters create electric-like warps on a text block, as long as the settings are kept to the left of the sliders. Using Effects | Stylize | Glowing Edge produces an effect like an electric or neon sign. Just set the sliders to 4.5 for the amount and 2 for the radius. The Diffuse filter at a setting of 5 transforms the text block into a storm of charged particles.

Figure 19-54: The Glowing Edge filter creates ElectroText like a neon sign.

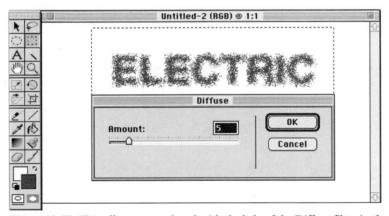

Figure 19-55: This effect was produced with the help of the Diffuse filter in the Effects menu.

BubbleText

Using the technique described here, you can create text wrapped on a sphere or even non-spherical shapes. You can do this with words or single letters. If you decide to do it with single letters, you can place the lettered spheres next to each other to form a word for a unique headline effect in a FreeHand document. The BubbleText effect can be generated in FreeHand, xRes, and Extreme 3D. Each application adds its own special attributes to this text look.

Tip

If you prefer to see what these finished graphic elements look like prior to creating them yourself, use the accompanying CD-ROM to load the BubbleText Project and all of the tutorial elements into FreeHand so you can more easily work through this example. You may also find some of the elements in the Parts and Pieces folder.

Using FreeHand

If you decide to create this effect in FreeHand, you will be using the Fisheye Lens effect in the Xtra Tools panel as the central tool. The settings of the Fisheye Lens tool are controlled in its Fisheye Lens dialog, which is accessed by double-clicking on the tool's icon. The settings range from -100 (concave) to +100 (convex). We will be using this tool at the maximum convex setting, +100.

Step #1: Add the Text

Use the Text tool to create the word "WOW!" in a sans serif bold face. Convert it to paths, and place it at the bottom of your workspace.

Figure 19-56: The initial text block is written to the screen.

Step #2: Add a Sphere

Use the Ellipse tool to draw a circle on the screen (hold down the Shift key to constrain it to a circle). The diameter of the circle should be about equal to the width of the text. Using the Fill Inspector apply a radial gradient with three CMYK colors to the circle: Blue (top- 100, 100, 0, 0), Red (center- 0, 100, 100, 0) and Yellow (bottom- 0, 0, 100, 0). Move the Locate Center crosshairs to the upper left. Your circle should look like the one illustrated below.

Figure 19-57: A sphere with a radial gradient is added separately as the next step.

Step #3: Make the Text Bulge

Use the Fisheye Lens tool in the Xtra Tools panel to completely encircle your text, and make the shape of the lens as circular as possible when dragging it. Constrain the oval to a circle by using Option+Shift, and drag from the center of the text.

Figure 19-58: The Fisheye Lens tool is used to give the text a convex bulge.

Make sure the text is in the front of the stack (Modify | Arrange | Bring To Front), and place the text over the gradated circle. Resize the text until it looks as though it belongs with the circle, and is imprinted on it.

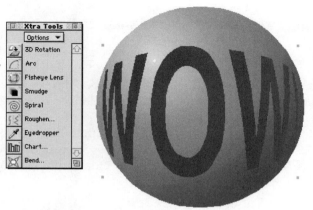

Figure 19-59: The text is placed on top of the gradient sphere.

Another variation of this process is to wrap single letters on spheres that are colorized differently, and then to string them together to form a festive headline.

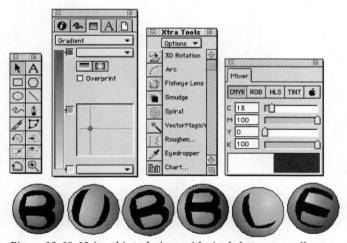

Figure 19-60: Using this technique with single letters to spell out a word is effective for headlines in FreeHand.

Although this is a simple technique, it is very effective when you want to create text headlines that differ from the norm, and have some dimension. You can vary the coloration of the text and its background sphere to achieve zillions of unique results.

Using xRes

xRes ships with a special Macromedia edition of MetaTools's Kai's PowerTools, which has to be installed separately, and we will make good use of the KPT filter effects (KPT 3.0 ME) in generating BubbleText. The KPT filter we will use extensively here is the one called Spheroid Designer, so if applying this effect and working with the Spheroid Designer interface is new to you, you may want to gain some degree of familiarity with it first. What Spheroid Designer does best is to create a textured sphere that appears to have its texture mapped on a 3D surface, which is just perfect for our BubbleText project.

Step #1: Create the Sphere

Create a circle with the circle marquee tool in the xRes Toolbox. Select Effects I KPT 3.0 ME I KPT Spheroid Designer to open its settings dialog. Click on the downward pointing arrow to bring up the Presets menu textures, and select one that you like from the list. Leave everything else at its default level. Click on the check mark icon to apply the texture inside your circular marquee.

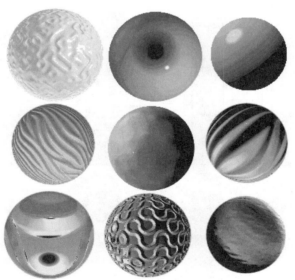

Figure 19-61: The KPT Spheroid Designer effects plug-in can help you create thousands of unique 3D spherical textured surfaces. Here is a small example.

Step #2: Add the Text Block

Create a text block that says "3D" and size it so that it fits with the textured sphere you just created. Place it on top of the textured sphere. Choose Selection | Drop Objects to paste the text to the sphere.

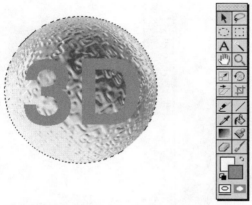

Figure 19-62: The text is placed over the sphere.

Step #3: Use the Glass Lens Plug-in

Select the ball with the text on it (use the Wand tool on the backdrop, and then choose Selection | Inverse). Select Effects | KPT 3.0 ME | KPT MetaToys f/x. This will warp the entire selection. Use the default settings and apply the warp.

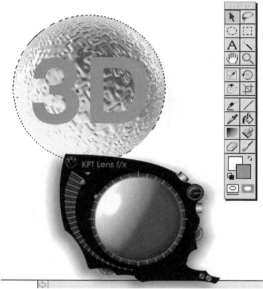

Figure 19-63: The KPT MetaToys interface looks like a magnifying glass.

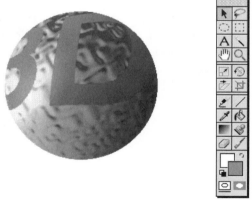

Figure 19-64: The sphere and text are bonded together as a 3D object.

Using Extreme 3D

In Extreme 3D, the image of the text block, saved out as a TIFF file, can be used as a texture map that automatically marries itself to the selected object. Any saved graphic file, whether it contains a picture of text or an image, can be used to texture a 3D object in Extreme 3D. The Default-Chrome + Glass material must be chosen as the basic material applied to the object.

Step #1: Create the Sphere

In Extreme 3D, create a sphere that fills your workspace from the Front View. Open up the Materials browser, and select the Default-Chrome + Glass material from the list on the right. Move it to the active list on the left by clicking on the left pointing arrows. Select it from the list on the left, and click on Edit at the bottom of the palette. When the Edit window opens up, you will see an Environment Map preview under the Surfaces tab. Click on it.

Step #2: Add a Graphic

Select a graphic that you have saved out to disk, text or not, and load it into the environment preview window. This graphic or environment map now becomes the texture for the object it is applied to. Apply this texture to the sphere.

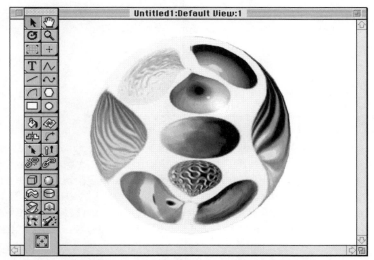

Figure 19-65: We have used the graphic from Figure 19-62 as the assigned environment map that textures this sphere. Any graphic you have saved on file can be mapped to a 3D object in Extreme 3D.

Any of the textured objects saved from xRes or Extreme 3D can be imported into FreeHand and placed in a page composition. Illustrated in Figure 19-66 is an example of a FreeHand page that is composed of many of the examples we worked through in this chapter.

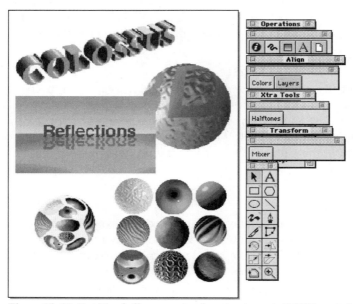

Figure 19-66: FreeHand allows you to place any imported TIFF created in xRes and Extreme 3D as a page element.

Moving On

In this chapter we have covered five diverse text block projects: 3D Embossing, Hollywood Titling, Reflected Text, ElectroText, and BubbleText. In addition to guiding you through ways these effects can be produced in FreeHand, we have also looked at variations that can be created in xRes and Extreme 3D to be imported into a FreeHand project later. In the next chapter, we'll move on to creating useful things and objects in FreeHand, xRes, and Extreme 3D.

20 Things & Objects

The FreeHand 7 Graphics Studio allows you to create representations of any form or object you desire, and fosters their creation with vector, bitmap, and 3D tools. Using graphical representations of an object in a FreeHand document can happen in several ways. Among the most popular are spot graphics, items that point to a specific portion of the text, or pure graphic ornaments. The world we see is made up of countless objects, some of which we classify as organic and others as not. You can create drawings and paintings that emulate real-world objects by using the options and tools contained in the FreeHand Studio 7 applications. To begin to explore FreeHand's unique options for creating things and objects, take a look at the following five diverse examples: Snowflake, Child's Block, Butterfly, UFO, and Castle.

Snowflakes

Snowflakes are altered hexagonal shapes. Snowflakes, like people, come in infinite varieties, though snowflakes are all related to the six-sided star. Snowflake Bentley, the early twentieth-century scientist who was the first to catalog snowflake shapes, was a Vermonter who lived not far from where I do today. In this project, you will learn to create fractal-based objects and designs.

Tip

If you prefer to see what these finished graphic elements look like prior to creating them yourself, use the accompanying CD-ROM to load the Snowflakes Project and all of the tutorial elements into FreeHand so you can more easily work through this example. You may also find some of the elements in the Parts and Pieces folder.

Using FreeHand

Snowflakes are fractal shapes, meaning that their smaller parts are clones of larger parts. You can achieve a fractal effect in FreeHand by placing cloned copies of the larger shape within the boundaries of the original shape.

Step #1: Create a Star

Double-click on the Polygon tool. In the dialog that pops up, select six sides and Star. Set the Star Points slider halfway betweew acute and obtuse.

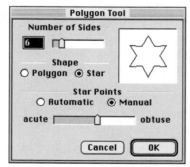

Figure 20-1: A six-pointed star is configured in the Polygon Tool dialog.

With the Polygon tool selected, draw a six-sided shape on the page, covering half of the top of your page. Set the fill color to a CMYK Blue (50, 0, 0, 0), and the stroke to a 1.5 point black.

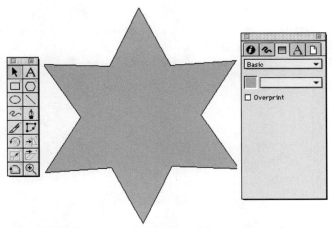

Figure 20-2: A six-pointed blue star is drawn on the workspace.

Step #2: Add the Control Points

Click on the Envelope tool in the Operations panel. When the dialog pops up, select Apply and OK without doing anything else. You have just added more control points to the star. Click on Add Points in the Operations panel. You have doubled the control points on the perimeter of the star.

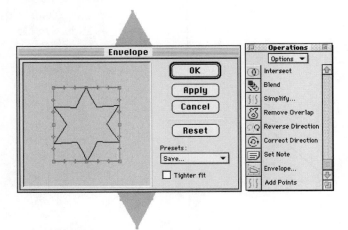

Figure 20-3: Opening FreeHand's Envelope tool automatically adds points to a selected shape.

From each point of the star, count down to the third control point. The star has six points with two sides connected to each point, so we are talking about twelve control points altogether. Move each of these control points away from the star, so that the figure is altered as shown in Figure 20-4.

Figure 20-4: The basic six-pointed star shape with extended points.

Step #3: Copy & Resize the Star Shapes

Clone the shape. This places a copy of the shape over itself. Select that copy and resize it (with the Shift key held down to constrain it) to about one-sixth of its original size. Use a fill color of White so you can see it against its blue parent, and place it on one of the arms of the shape as shown in Figure 20-5.

Figure 20-5: The white cloned shape is placed on an arm of the larger blue shape.

Duplicate the small shape until you have six of them, and place each in the same position on the arms of the larger star shape. Exactness is not important. Just use your eye.

Figure 20-6: All of the duplicated smaller white shapes are placed in similar positions on the arms of the larger blue shape.

Make one more duplicate of the small star shape, and with the Shift key held down, use the Resize tool to make it approximately 50 percent smaller. Make another five duplicates of this smallest star, and place each between the arms of the large star. See the accompanying illustration in Figure 20-7 for placement.

Figure 20-7: Six smaller white shapes are added and placed closer to the center of the large blue shape.

Step #4: Cut Away the Star Shapes

Now it's time to cut each of the 12 smaller star shapes away from the large star shape. Select each one in turn, and Shift-select the large star. Use the Punch command to cut the small shapes out of the large star.

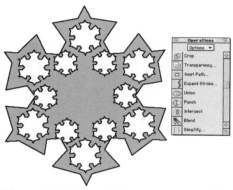

Figure 20-8: The small shapes are cut out of the large blue shape with the Punch command.

Bring up the Polygon dialog again by double-clicking on the Polygon tool. The dialog has retained the settings from the last use. Move the Star Points slider about one quarter of the way across, so it is set nearer to acute than to obtuse, and select OK.

Draw this new shape in the center of the star shape on the screen. After it is placed in the center of the larger star, use the Punch command to cut it out of the larger star.

Figure 20-9: The new star shape is cut out of the center of the larger shape with the Punch command.

Step #5: Reduce, Duplicate & Group the Star Shapes

Reduce this entire shape to one third of its original size with the Scale tool (hold down the Shift key). Duplicate it six times, and create a larger six-pointed star with each of the six shapes as a component. When your composition is balanced and complete, group all of the separate elements together as one entity.

Figure 20-10: The new shape is composed of six of the previous shapes.

One variation on this theme is to place the snowflakes against a cool wintry backdrop. Use the Gradient Fill option to color a rectangle with a blue to white gradient, from a dark CMYK blue (100, 0, 0, 42) to white. Double the blue swatches in the gradient bar, place one slightly below the other, and set the rotation of the gradient to 270 degrees. This gives you a gradient that is dark at the top and white at the bottom. Color the snowflakes with a white fill and set stroke to None. Clone the snowflakes, resize them in a random manner and place them against the blue backdrop. Group the elements in the graphic.

Figure 20-11: The completed Snowflake composition in FreeHand.

Using xRes

xRes allows you to apply effects to the snowflake design, so that the resulting graphics appear even more dynamic when imported into FreeHand.

Step #1: Add the xRes Whirlpool Effect

Import the finished snowflake developed in the FreeHand tutorial above into xRes as a TIFF file. Bring up the Whirlpool dialog. Set the slider at 50, and apply the effect. The snowflake has a more dynamic appearance, as if it were whirling in space. Export the graphic to FreeHand as a TIFF for use in a FreeHand composition.

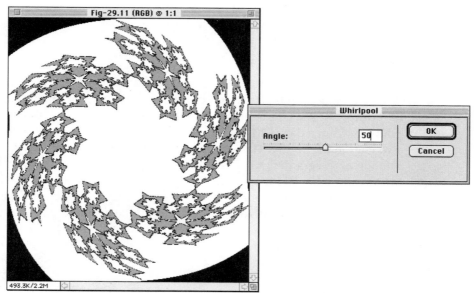

Figure 20-12: The xRes Whirlpool effect reshapes the snowflake into a more dynamic form.

Using Extreme 3D

Images can be transformed into object textures in Extreme 3D in many of the Materials browser dialogs, one of which is the Default-Chrome + Glass option in the Materials browser list (refer to the Reflection project in Chapter 28). When you save a TIFF image of the snowflake from xRes or FreeHand and import it as a texture map into Extreme 3D, it produces interesting effect maps on object surfaces. It doesn't matter what the shape is.

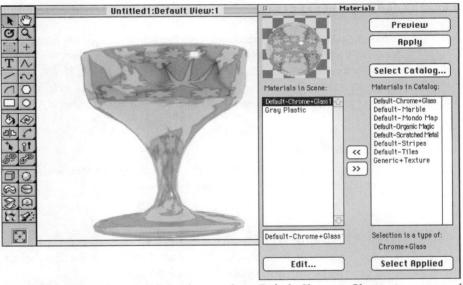

Figure 20-13: Here, the snowflake has been used as a Default-Chrome + Glass texture map, and applied to a lathed 3D shape in Extreme 3D.

Child's Block

A child's block is an identifiable object the world over. As such, it becomes a good object on which to place text for headlines. A child's block is both a useful and playful graphic element when added to a FreeHand composition.

Tip

If you prefer to see what these finished graphic elements look like prior to creating them yourself, use the accompanying CD-ROM to load the Child's Block Project and all of the tutorial elements into FreeHand so you can more easily work through this example. You may also find some of the elements in the Parts and Pieces folder.

Using FreeHand

FreeHand is not a 3D application, so perspective squares have to be created and moved into place as the sides of a 3D block. This technique produces perspective letters on the visible faces of a cubic block. If you use just one letter to a side, the finished graphic will look more like a child's block. This project teaches you to create a 3D surface as a base for text.

Tip

You will need MetaTools's KPT VectorFX plug-ins to complete this part of the tutorial, which have to be installed separately.

Step #1: Create the Square Elements

Create a square. Clone it twice. Move all three squares apart. Select all of them, and give them an eight point light blue stroke.

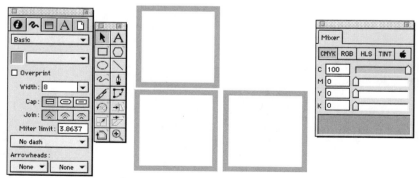

Figure 20-14: Start with three squares, each representing a face of the 3D block.

Step #2: Use 3D Rotation for the Sides

Use the 3D Rotation tool in the Xtra Tools panel to adjust each of the blocks so they have a loose resemblance to three sides of a perspective block. Don't worry about perfection yet.

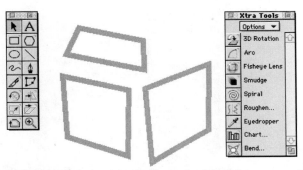

Figure 20-15: Perspective starts to take shape when you manipulate the rotation planes of the squares.

Step #3: Adjust the Control Points

When a graphic has been manipulated with the 3D Rotation tool, its control points can be moved separately, though this is not the only way to access the control points. Move the front and side faces so that their control points match up on the side that connects them.

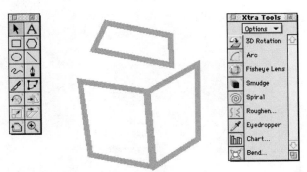

Figure 20-16: Moving the control points on a selected rectangle makes it appear that the shape has perspective.

Step #4: Make the Block Look Like a 3D Object

Select the remaining face, and, by moving its control points, adjust it so that it forms the "top" of the perspective block. You can then tweak any of the control points until the block looks correct.

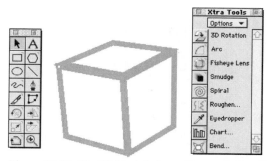

Figure 20-17: The 3D block is formed by carefully adjusting how the three separate faces contact each other.

Step #5: Add Gradient Fills

Now we'll add a gradient fill to each side. Use the Fill Inspector to add a three-color gradient fill to the left side of the block. Set the colors as CMYK black (0, 0, 0, 100), dark red (0, 0, 100, 15), and shaded yellow (0, 0, 100, 15) as shown. Turn the Angle dial so that the gradient has the yellow appearing at the upper right corner of the block's left face.

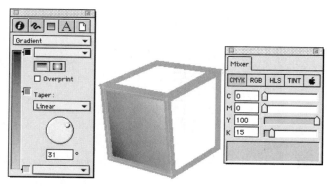

Figure 20-18: Adding a gradient makes the surface look as if it was being affected by a light source.

Step #6: Adjust the Gradients

Set the same gradient on the other two faces, rotating the gradient so that the yellow is used at the corner where all three faces meet. Select all three faces, and group the block.

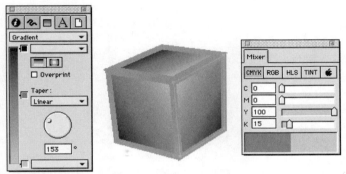

Figure 20-19: Adjusting the gradient for each face gives the block the look of a 3D solid.

Step #7: Create & Color the Letters

Create the letters A, B, and C (caps, Helvetica Bold). Convert them to paths and ungroup them. We are going to place the letters on the block in perspective. Resize the letters so that they look as if they are the right size for the block. Exactness is not important here…not yet anyway. Color each letter a solid yellow with a one point black stroke.

Figure 20-20: The letters are sized for placement on the sides of the block.

Step #8: Use KPT VectorFX

Select the letters one at a time, and use KPT Vector Effects 3D Transform to adjust the rotation and perspective of each letter so it "fits" on one side of the cube. Extrude each letter to 100 points before you apply the effect, then move the letter into place. You may have to adjust its size a bit.

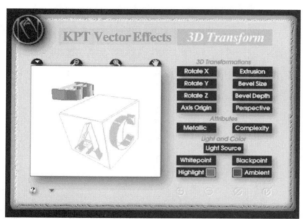

Figure 20-21: KPT VectorFX is critical to add a believable 3D extrusion to selected type.

Step #9: Start Building an Arch

By simply cloning the blocks and rotating them so their edges touch, you can build an archway.

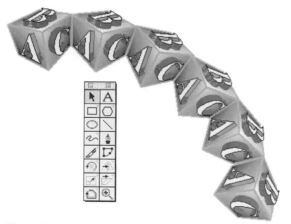

Figure 20-22: An interesting archway is composed of cloned blocks rotated into position.

Step #10: Clone & Rotate

After grouping the blocks in the half arch, clone them. Then, rotate the cloned half arch and group it with the first one.

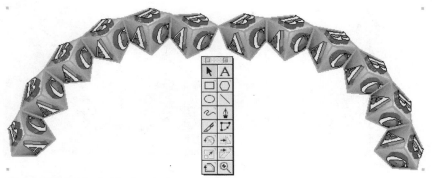

Figure 20-23: The finished archway.

Step #11: Build an Archway Variation

Clone the arch, and resize the clone to about half its size. Select both arches, and use the Align panel to center one on the other, by selecting Align bottom for the horizontal alignment and Align center for the vertical alignment.

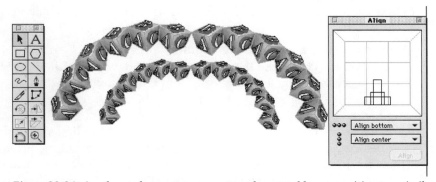

Figure 20-24: Another archway arrangement can be created by compositing two similar designs.

Step #12: Use Symbol Fonts in the Process

Using a dingbat or a symbol font, there is no limit to the unique graphics you can create utilizing this same method. This symbol is from the Hieroglyphics Volume 3 font set from DeniArt Systems.

Figure 20-25: Utilizing this same technique with symbol fonts can create attractive 3D borders and other graphic elements in FreeHand.

Using xRes

Because xRes has many more texturizing options than FreeHand, you might find it worthwhile to design the 3D block in xRes, import it into FreeHand, and place the letters or symbols on it there. Designing the underlying 3D block in xRes will allow you to tap into xRes's wealth of unique gradient textures. Here's how to use the xRes texture variants in creating a 3D block.

Step #1: Build a Side of the Square

Select the Lasso tool from the xRes Toolbox, and, while holding the Shift key down to constrain the drawing to straight lines, draw the right side of your cube. Give it a perspective look by making the back edge smaller than the front edge.

Click on the Gradient tool in the Toolbox when your first side of the cube has been created with a marquee, and go to the Gradient Options tab of the Tool Options palette. Select the Metal Burst gradient from the list, and a Folds shape. Select CMYK and the Blend option. Place the Gradient tool cursor in your marqueed shape, and click and drag from lower left to upper right.

Figure 20-26: The gradient adds an interesting fill to the side of the square.

Step #2: Build the Other Two Faces

Complete the other two faces of the square, adding the gradient to each in the same manner as the first side.

Figure 20-27: The square is complete, and the folded texture gives it a 3D textured appearance.

Step #3: Create Variations on the Theme

By exploring different gradient variables in the Gradient Options tab of the Tool Options palette, you can create thousands of different 3D cubes. Save the ones you like to disk as TIFF files, and import them into FreeHand. Place lettering or symbols on them, using the same methods as described in the FreeHand Child's Block tutorial, and overlay the FreeHand graphics on selected xRes cubes.

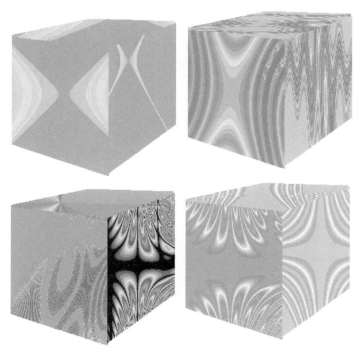

Figure 20-28: Unlimited options are available when you tap into the gradients in xRes for creating believable and unique textures.

Using Extreme 3D

When you create a child's block in Extreme 3D, much of the 3D work is already done for you. Merely selecting the Block Primitive tool from the Toolbox assures you that the block will be a perfect cube, without any need for you to tweak the faces. All that remains is deciding upon the texture in the Materials browser and adding the letters. Then the results can be exported to FreeHand as a saved TIFF file.

Step #1: Use the 3D Primitive Cube

Make sure you are working in the front view. Create a 3D block and place it in the Extreme 3D workspace (use the Cube Primitive tool in the Toolbox). Use whatever material you would like to add texture to it (from the Materials browser). Use the Default Mondo Map, and select the defaulted Clouds material in the Material Editor.

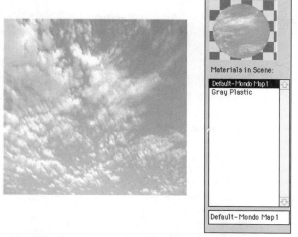

Figure 20-29: The textured 3D block is quickly ready for lettering.

Step #2: Create an Extruded Text Block

Select the cube and hide it. Create the text block "3D," and extrude it to give it a little depth. Lock-link the letters together as one unit. Use the Materials browser to apply a desirable texture to the text block. Move the lettering into place on the front face of the cube so that it is embedded partially in the cube, and lock-link the letters to the cube. As an option, you could duplicate the lettering and place it on every cube face, linking it to the cube each time.

Figure 20-30: The lettering is extruded, textured, and placed on the front of the cube.

Step #3: Adjust the 3D View to Render

The child's block graphic created in Extreme 3D has one distinct advantage over the same graphic created in either xRes or FreeHand itself: Once you create the 3D object and link the lettering to the cube's surfaces, it can be turned in real 3D space, rendered, and saved to disk as a TIFF file. When ported to FreeHand for placement, there is no need to fudge the various 3D viewpoints. They will look perfectly natural. The appearance of these cubes in FreeHand, when placed there as part of a page composition, will be photo-realistic. The FreeHand and xRes ways of accomplishing this same task, however, may give you alternate looks desired for a specific project.

Figure 20-31: You can turn the Extreme 3D child's block object in 3D space and even assign alternate perspective zooms, rendering each view as you go.

Butterfly

You can create both stylized and representational organic forms in any of the three FreeHand applications: xRes, Extreme 3D, or FreeHand itself. Each environment will foster the development of specific graphics looks suitable for that environment. The same item created in FreeHand has different visual properties than one created in xRes, and Extreme 3D gives the object its own stamp as well. There is no single way that is best for all situations, because it depends upon what the project you are working on demands: vector, bitmap, or 3D photorealism. This project demonstrates exactly what this means to the designer.

Tip

If you prefer to see what these finished graphic elements look like prior to creating them yourself, use the accompanying CD-ROM to load the Butterfly Project and all of the tutorial elements into FreeHand so you can more easily work through this example. You may also find some of the elements in the Parts and Pieces folder.

Using FreeHand

Creating the Butterfly drawing here assures you that you can print the graphic without jaggies (as long as you print it from FreeHand, and not as a graphic saved as a bitmap).

Step #1: Create a Colored Square

Using the Rectangle tool in the Toolbox with the Shift key held down, create a two inch by two inch square. In the Color Mixer, create a 50 percent CMYK yellow (0, 0, 50, 0), and drag and drop it on the square.

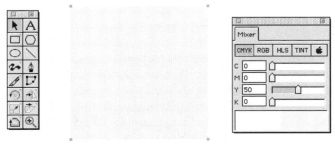

Figure 20-32: The butterfly is born within this initial square.

Step #2: Draw the Wing Pattern

With the Shift key held down and a black fill color selected in the Fill, draw a series of random filled black circles in the yellow square. Select everything, and copy the graphic to the clipboard (Edit I Copy). Move the square aside.

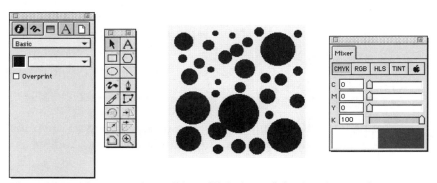

Figure 20-33: The pattern that will later fill the butterfly's wings is created.

Step #3: Begin the Wing Shape

Draw a black filled circle three inches in diameter.

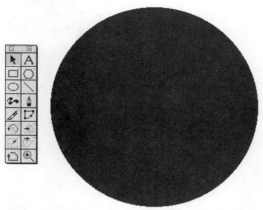

Figure 20-34: The wing shape begins with this circle.

Step #4: Use the Envelope Operator

Make sure the circle is selected. In the Operations panel, click on Add Points one time to add more control points to the circle. Click on the Envelope tool in the Operations panel.

Step #5: Shape the Wing

Try to reshape the envelope approximately as illustrated. It doesn't have to match the illustration perfectly. You are shaping the butterfly's wing, so use your experience as a guide. If you like, you can also use a photo as an example. When you are satisfied, click Apply, and then OK to leave the Envelope dialog.

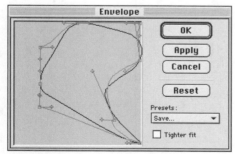

Figure 20-35: Shaping the wing in the Envelope dialog.

Step #6: Finish the Shape

Your butterfly wing should look something like Figure 20-36.

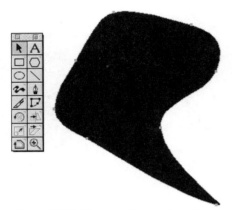

Figure 20-36: The wing is now shaped.

Step #7: Fill with a Tiled Pattern

Go to the Fill Inspectors panel, and select Tiled from the list of choices. The butterfly wing will temporarily disappear. When you click on Paste In, the preview area and the selected wing are filled with the black dotted pattern developed earlier and saved to the clipboard.

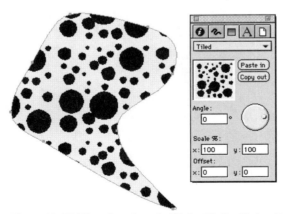

Figure 20-37: The wing shape is filled with the tiled pattern created earlier.

Step #8: Create the Second Wing

With the wing selected, use the Stroke Inspector to add a 1.5 point stroke to the wing. Clone the wing, which pastes a copy directly over the original. Click on the Reflect tool in the Toolbox, and rotate the duplicate wing in an opposite orientation to the original. Move it into place and group both wings together.

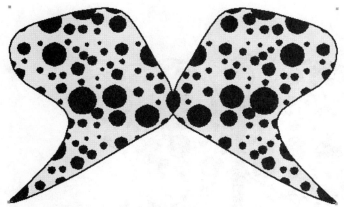

Figure 20-38: The two wings are in place and grouped.

Step #9: Draw the Body

Use the Ellipse tool in the Toolbox to draw a black, slender body, and again to draw each of the bulbous eyes. When everything is in place, group everything created so far.

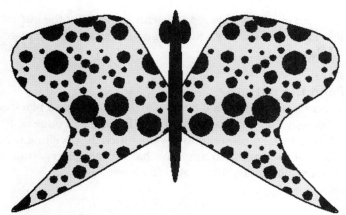

Figure 20-39: The body joins the wings.

Step #10: Draw the Legs & Feelers

Use the Line tool in the Toolbox with a two point stroke to draw the legs, configured as illustrated. Group everything. Double-click on the FreeHand tool in the Toolbox to bring up the FreeHand dialog. Configure it as: Calligraphic pen, Tight Fit, a fixed width of 0.12, and an angle of 90 degrees. Use the FreeHand tool to draw the feelers, which completes the drawing.

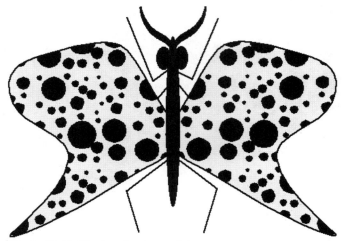

Figure 20-40: The drawing is complete.

Using xRes

Instead of the hard chiseled edge of the vector drawing of the butterfly we created in FreeHand, we can use xRes's unique media tools to create a softer and more subtle butterfly.

Step #1: Paint the Butterfly

Select the Japanese Brush from the Brushes palette, and use a black color from the Swatches palette. Set the brush to a size of 8 and a soft edge of 10 in the Shape tab. Draw a loose representation of the butterfly, dwelling more upon the smooth flow of the lines then upon mechanical symmetry. Your drawing may or may not resemble that illustrated in Figure 20-41.

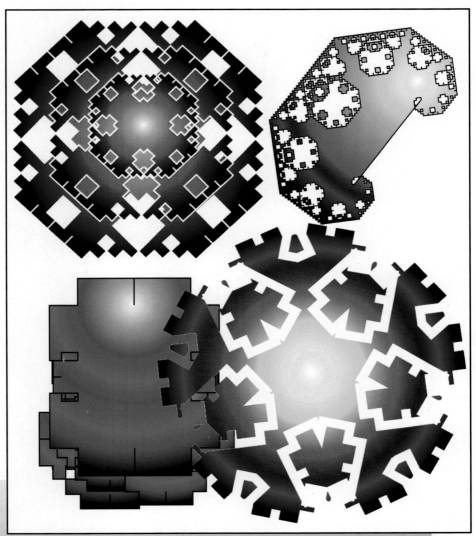

These designs display the power of the Fractal Operator in FreeHand 7.

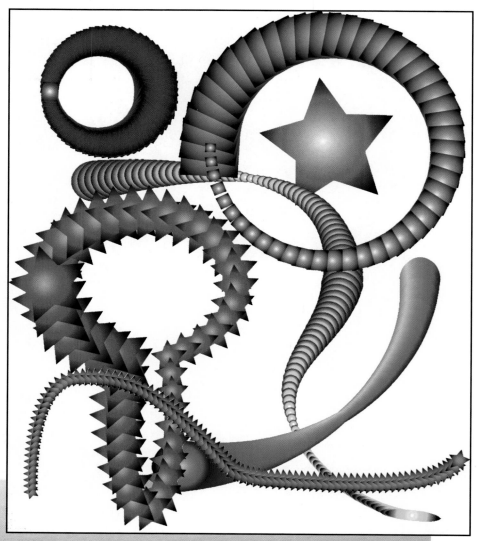

FreeHand 7 offers you the opportunity to assign blends to a Path, opening the way for intricate designs.

This plate shows the quality of FreeHand 7's ability to control pattern blends.

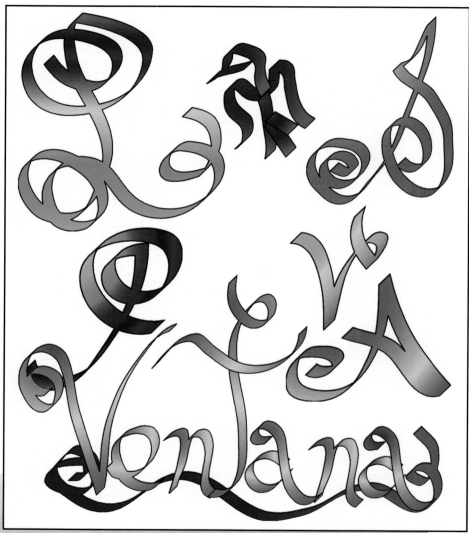

Using the Calligraphy Tool with the Overlap function on creates type styles that stand out from the page.

These are four frames from an animation developed in xRes with the Fisheye filter.

Creating a drawing in FreeHand is a step-by-step process, as shown by this progression of drawings.

The burger was built from elements in FreeHand, xRes, and Extreme 3D, then composited in xRes.

FreeHand, xRes, and Extreme 3D can be used to design and render interesting medieval fortresses.

XRes allows you to fill gradient areas with patterns like Satin and Folds, resulting in high-quality images.

These candles were designed and rendered in Extreme 3D, from the wax candle to the brass holder, and including the flame and smoke.

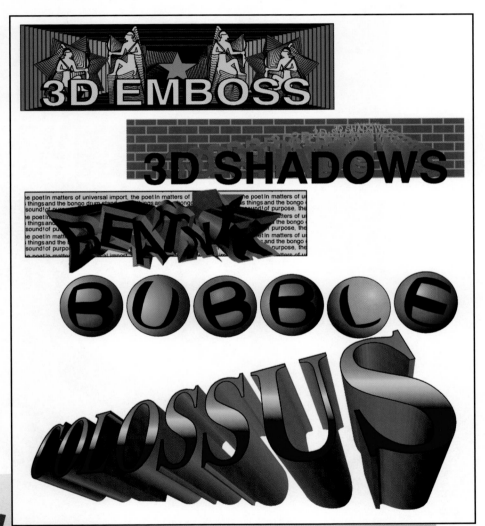

With FreeHand, you can create a barrel of special effects looks for text. These are just a few examples.

From fuzzy type to extruded 3D characters, the FreeHand 7 Graphics Studio allows you to do it all.

XRes offers a number of image enhancement tools for altering bitmaps.

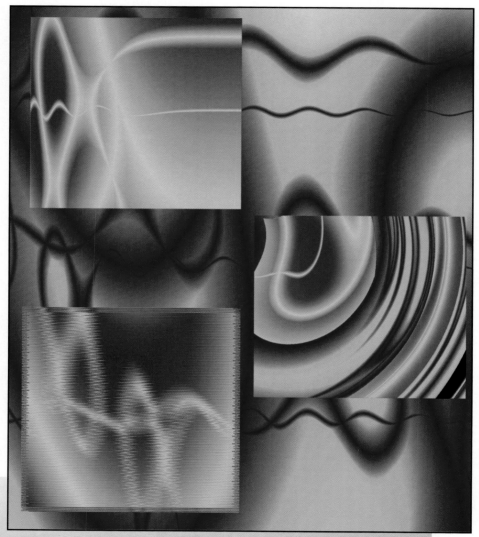

The areas showing a blue hue show the xRes distortion effects: Cylinder Distort, Whirlpool, and Ripple.

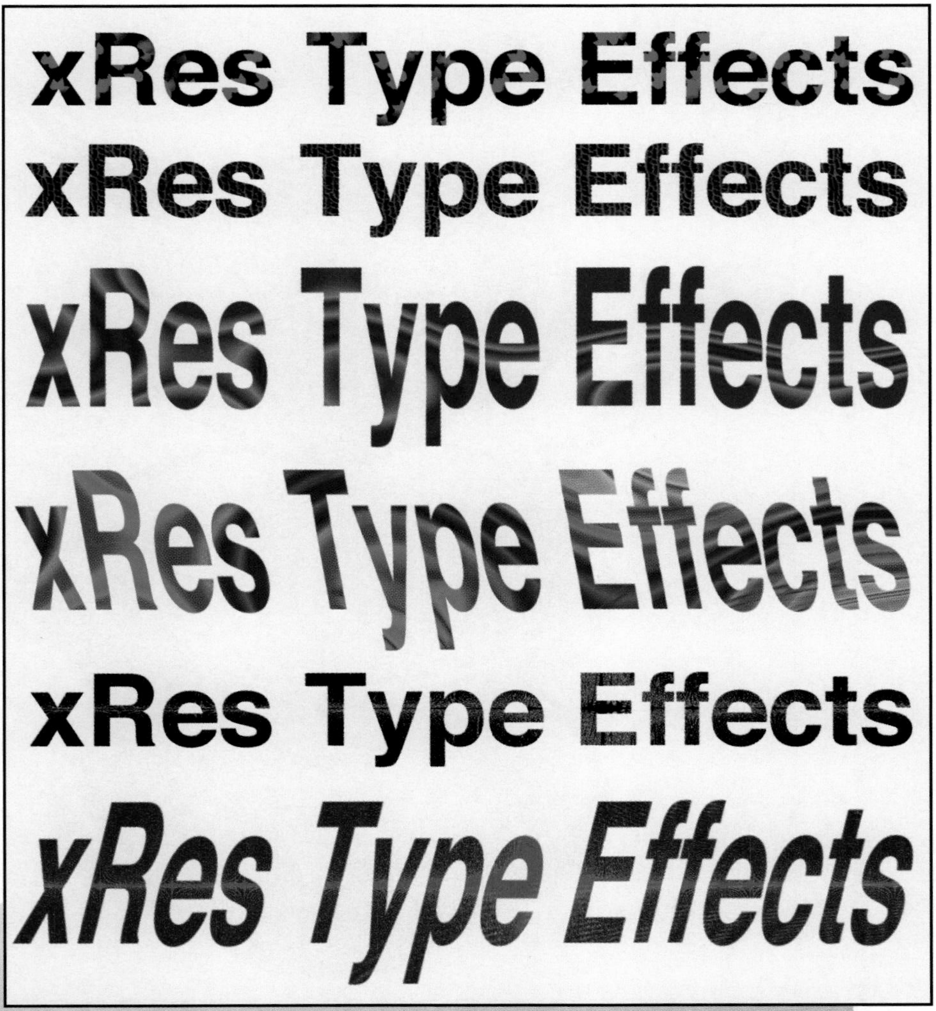

xRes Type Effects

xRes Type Effects

xRes Type Effects

xRes Type Effects

xRes Type Effects

xRes Type Effects

XRes is also a full-featured text effects generator.

Alphabet soup, anyone? This figure shows the progression of a rendering in Extreme 3D, from an empty bowl to a full one. All of the elements were designed and rendered in Extreme 3D.

The label on the bottle was developed in FreeHand, colorized in xRes, and applied to the bottle in Extreme 3D.

From top left to bottom right, these four images of nature were developed with xRes, Extreme 3D, and FreeHand.

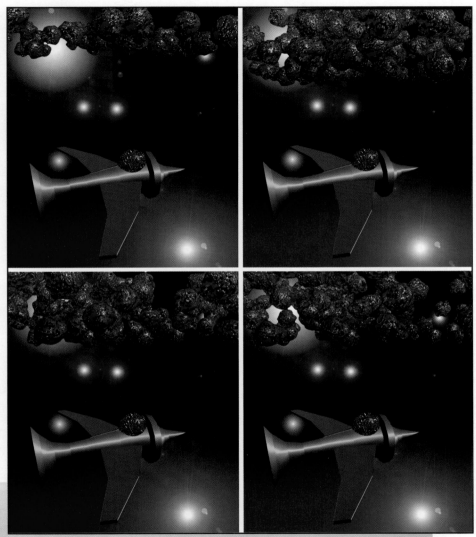

The meteors floating above the spaceship in these frames from an animation were generated with the Particle Effects tool in Extreme 3D.

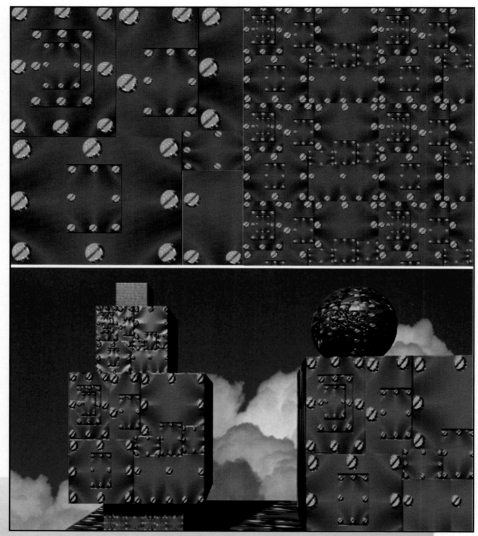

The top metallic textures were painted in xRes, then they were imported as Materials in Extreme 3D and used on these shapes.

This figure was sculpted and textured in Extreme 3D. You can find him on the Web tutorial called "Family."

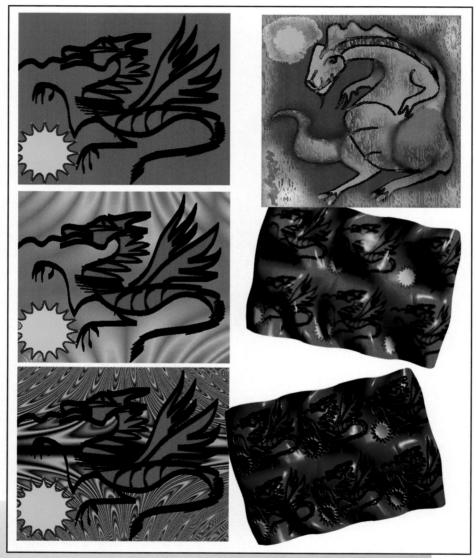

The dragon was first drawn in FreeHand, then ported to Extreme 3D as a texture. It was also used in FreeHand as a Tiled fill. Another dragon, at the upper right, was painted in xRes.

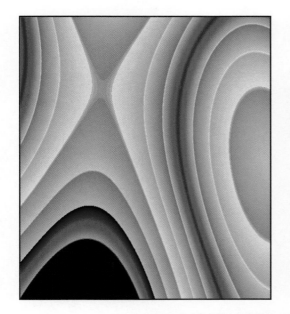

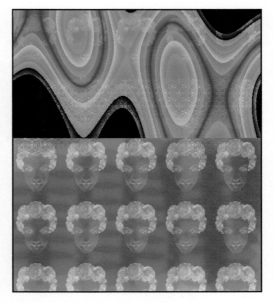

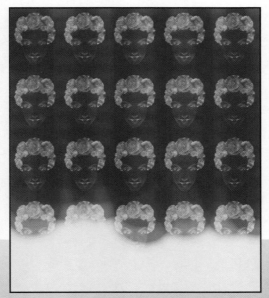

In xRes, you can paint separate graphics on any of the three channels to create a channel painting.

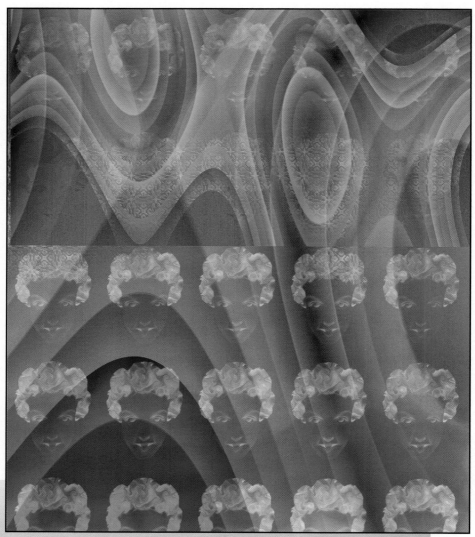

The combined channels shown as separate paintings in Color Plate 23 resulted in this xRes painting.

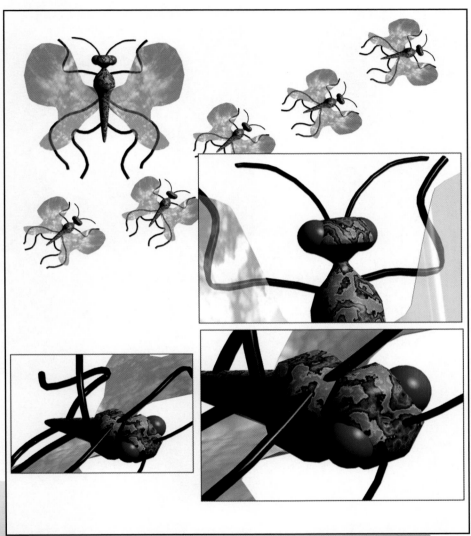

These flying insects were modeled and textured in Extreme 3D.

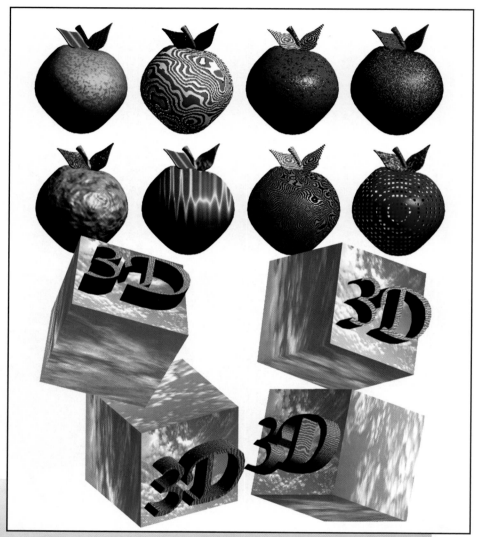

T he apples at the top were texture mapped with a variety of Extreme 3D materials. At the bottom, the cubes were mapped with clouds and attached to an extruded text block.

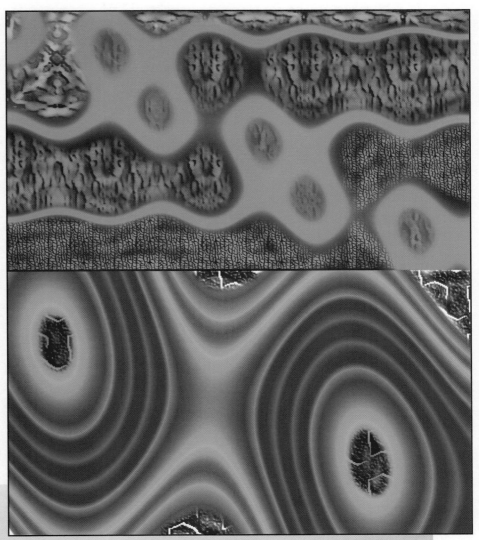

These textures display the gradient and texture capacities of xRes. Look at Color Plate 28 for an example of how they can be used as texture maps in Extreme 3D.

T hese Extreme 3D objects are texture mapped with the textures developed in xRes, shown on Color Plate 27.

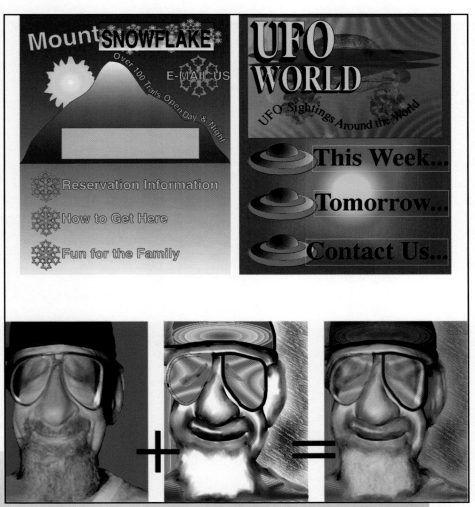

The top shows two of the Web page designs covered in this book. At the bottom is an xRes-enhanced transition, from a photo, to an xRes painting, to a blend of the two.

Four of the Web page designs covered in this book.

Four of the Web page designs covered in this book.

The Art Studio, a digital painting by the author. This painting was composited in xRes from Extreme 3D and xRes elements. Fractal Design Poser was used for the figures.

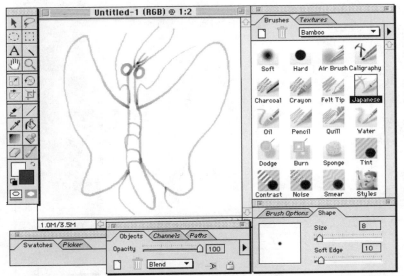

Figure 20-41: Keep your drawing as free-flowing as possible, while still representational enough to give the idea of the butterfly.

Step #2: Color in the Shape

Use the Wand tool to select the entire graphic (click on the white space, then choose Selection I Inverse). Color the shape with muted pastels for the body. To paint in the wings, use a Coral texture with the airbrush. Set the Brush Options at a concentration of 25, a flow of 60, and a texture of 30. This applies a texturized feel under the paint. Now use a soft smear brush with a concentration set to 40 to blur all of the outlines around the wings and body for a more muted effect. Save the graphic as a TIFF for later placing in FreeHand.

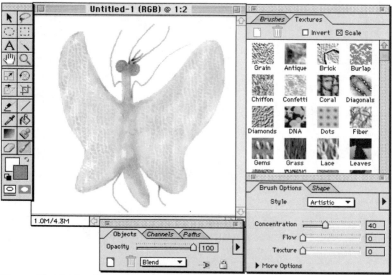

Figure 20-42: The finished muted butterfly.

Using Extreme 3D

If the media tools in xRes can produce what might be called a soft muted butterfly, then we might say that Extreme 3D allows us to produce very hard mechanical insects. 3D graphics excel when it comes to harder-edged artwork, so let's see how we can develop a whole new butterfly machine look with Extreme 3D.

Step #1: Draw Half of the Butterfly Body
Use a front view and an Orthographic perspective. Click on the Spline tool, and draw one-half of the silhouette of the butterfly's body.

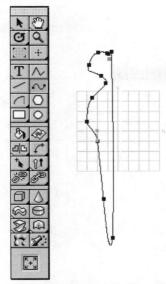

Figure 20-43: The splined outline configures half of the body.

Step #2: Lathe the 3D Shape

Click on the Lathe tool, draw the lathing axis as a vertical line along the right side of the shape, and watch as the 3D body attains its shape. Assign the default marble texture to the body.

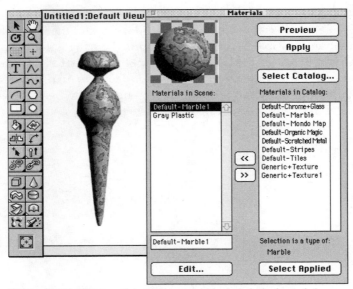

Figure 20-44: The completed 3D textured body is lathed into being.

Step #3: Create & Place the Eyes

Create two red eyes by texturing two duplicate spheres with a red plastic material with a yellow specular highlight. Place the eyes so they are embedded in either side of the head, and lock-link all three objects.

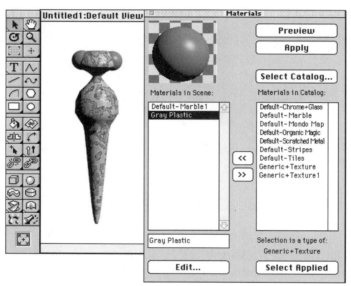

Figure 20-45: The eyes of the butterfly are now in place.

Step #4: Create the Wings

Use the Spline tool to create the outline of the wing, and then extrude it the smallest amount possible. Without some depth, the wing will not be able to take on a texture. Assign the Default-Generic+Texture material to the wing. Edit the generic material so that it has the cloud texture map, and set the Transparency of the material to about 50 percent (you are free to select another texture material if you desire). Copy and paste the wing, and use the 2D Mirror tool to move the second wing into place.

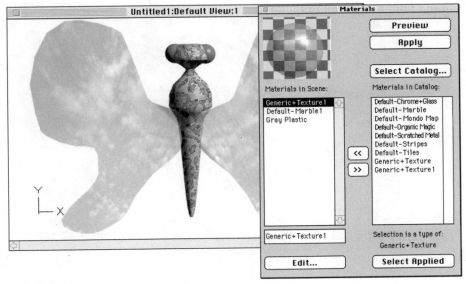

Figure 20-46: Our butterfly now has its wings.

Step #5: Create the Legs & Antennae

The legs will be modeled by using Extreme 3D's Sweep tool. Draw three paths for the six wings. You can curve them as you like, since we are looking for more character than exactness in our mechanical butterfly. A small circle is used as the shape drawn along these paths by the Sweep tool, and each of the three legs will be duplicated so that there will finally be three pairs of legs across from each other. Draw one more splined element for the antennae, and sweep a small circle along it. Assign a black Default-Generic+Texture material to these parts.

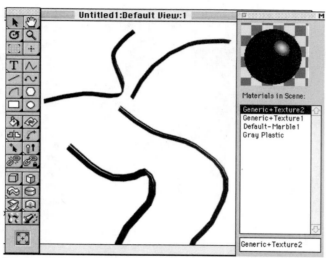

Figure 20-47: The legs and antennae are created by sweeping three small circles along three separate splined paths.

Step #6: Complete the 3D Butterfly

As a last step, place the legs and antennae where they belong, duplicating their opposite pairs. Lock-link everything to the main body. Your new mechanical butterfly can be rendered from any viewpoint, and the renderings saved to disk as TIFFs for import into a FreeHand composition.

Figure 20-48: The final butterfly shape can be used to create a swarm of different renderings.

UFO

UFOs remain a dominant curiosity for computer graphic artists and animators the world over. This is both a multicultural phenomenon and a designer's dream. UFOs are, after all, so interesting to model. They also teach us how to use various modeling tools in whatever application we use to shape them. FreeHand, xRes, and Extreme 3D have different tools and techniques that can provide us with comprehensive modeling skills when we take on a UFO project.

Tip

If you prefer to see what these finished graphic elements look like prior to creating them yourself, use the accompanying CD-ROM to load the UFO Project and all of the tutorial elements into FreeHand so you can more easily work through this example. You may also find some of the elements in the Parts and Pieces folder.

Using FreeHand

This FreeHand project will sharpen your skills when it comes to reshaping basic design elements, and requires a mastery of the Bend tool.

Step #1: Create Four Ovals

Use the Ellipse tool in the Toolbox to create four ovals as illustrated in Figure 20-49.

Figure 20-49: The four basic design elements from which the UFO will take shape.

Step #2: Add the Control Points

Select the top shape. Go to the Operations panel and click on Add Points twice. The oval has four default control points. When Add Points is clicked on the first time, this is doubled to eight, and the second click gives it 16.

With the Pointer tool selected in the Toolbox, we are going to delete some of the bottom control points. Select the bottom control points and press the Delete key to remove them, which alters the shape. The top shape illustrated is the original oval; the bottom one is what we want the final oval to look like. Of the 16 control points, we will delete 6, leaving 10. The bottom center control point is not deleted; it provides a curve control to the bottom of the oval.

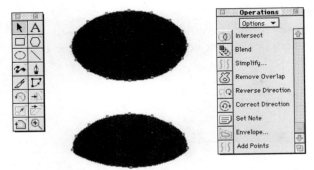

Figure 20-50: Adding these control points allows us to reshape the ovals.

Step #3: Apply the Gradients

The final ovals now have color and gradients. The second and fourth from the top are color filled with a CMYK green (86, 0, 53, 0). The first and third have two different gradients applied. Apply the gradients by selecting each oval separately and using the Fill Inspector.

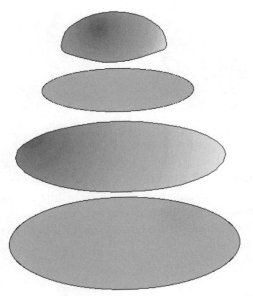

Figure 20-51: Color gradients give the UFO parts dimension.

Step #4: Use a Radial Fill

The illustration shows the gradient fill applied to the top altered oval. This is a radial fill as indicated. Look at the colors involved. You don't have to duplicate them exactly.

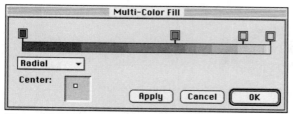

Figure 20-52: Mastering the gradient fill is essential.

Step #5: Move & Group

After the color fills and gradients have been applied to the shapes, move them into place and group them to create the composited graphic.

Figure 20-53: The finished ship.

Step #6: Create the Glow Silhouette

Make a duplicate of the UFO, and move it below the original. Then modify it by joining, splitting, and grouping it, exactly in that order. This allows us to assign another color to the silhouette. Assign the CMYK light blue (49, 5, 0, 0) fill color to the duplicate image.

Figure 20-54: The shape is the beginning design for a glow.

Step #7: Add Energy Rays

With the duplicate image selected, click on Union in the Operations panel, and then click on Add Points four times. Click on the Bend tool in the Xtra Tools panel, and click-drag the cursor upwards from the center of the duplicated graphic until you generate spikes from the affected control points.

Figure 20-55: The Bend tool adds rays of energy to the glow.

Step #8: Complete the Graphic

Select the duplicate graphic and resize it so it is about one quarter as large as the original UFO. Duplicate it. Enlarge this new duplicate, making it about twice as large as the original UFO graphic. Send it to the back of the image stack, and color it a CMYK white (0, 0, 0, 0).

Select the blue duplicate and the white duplicate, align them on the same center, and blend them. Place the original UFO graphic in the center of this electro-glow.

Figure 20-56: The completed UFO with its energy field.

Using xRes

xRes offers gradient options for bitmap fills that are perfect for a project like this. The gradients mimic metallic surfaces, and can be forced to shape themselves in ways that look like no known material.

Step #1: Create the Silhouette

We begin by using the Ellipse tool to draw the entire silhouette of the ship. This is constructed of two overlapping ovals (hold down the Shift key to draw the second one).

Figure 20-57: The ship's silhouette is constructed from two ovals.

Step #2: Add a Color Gradient

Use the Magic Wand tool to select the shape. Click on the Gradient Fill tool, and set the parameters of the gradient in the Gradient Options tab as follows: Cobalt Blue, Satin, CMYK, and Blend. Click and drag the cursor about one-half inch in the center of the shape. You should see a gradient fill that resembles that in Figure 20-58.

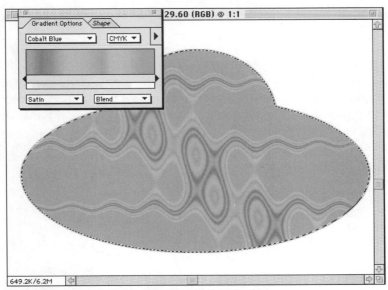

Figure 20-58: A swirling gradient is added to the ship.

Step #3: Separate the Parts

Now use the Lasso tool with the Shift key held down (constraining it to a Polygonal selection) to separate the top half of the ship, the bridge, from the bottom part. You may have to experiment a few times to get a smooth curvy separation, as shown in Figure 20-59.

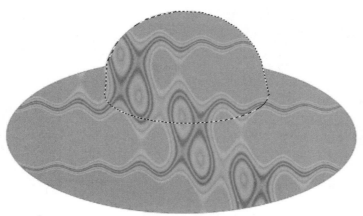

Figure 20-59: The top part of the UFO is separated from the bottom part by a marquee.

Step #4: Alter the Coloration

Click and drag the Gradient tool cursor about one-quarter inch in any direction inside this new marquee, giving the top section its own gradient fill. With the marquee still set, use the Brightness/Contrast dialog (Modify | Color | Brightness/Contrast) to change the settings to a brightness of -50 and a contrast of 100. This further separates the top part of the ship from the bottom.

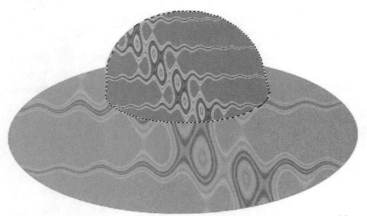

Figure 20-60: The top and bottom parts of the ship are now separated by a different gradient and brightness levels.

Step #5: Create an Eye with KPTools

Use the Spheroid Designer from Kai's Power Tools 3.0 (a limited version of which is included on the FreeHand CD) to place an eyeball in the center of the top part of the UFO. You can customize the gradients further if you like by using the Wand tool to add gradients within gradients. When done, your ship should resemble the one shown in Figure 20-61.

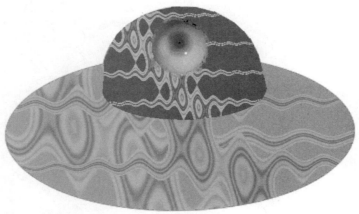

Figure 20-61: The finished xRes UFO.

Using Extreme 3D

When you need a more mechanical look to a graphic, especially something as hard edged as a UFO, you might want to develop it in full 3D with Extreme 3D. By "hard edges," I mean an object that is so clear in its rendering that subtlety (also called "softness") is lost. This will also allow you to turn the object in space until you have just the right view, which can then be rendered and saved as a TIFF file for placement in a FreeHand document.

Step #1: Create Two Circles

Create two circles in the top view, one slightly larger than the other. Center the smaller one within the larger one. In the front view, move the larger one below the smaller one.

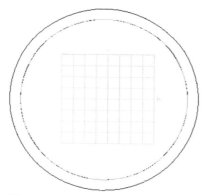

Figure 20-62: The two circles from the top view.

Step #2: Skin the Circles

From the front view, use the Skin tool to create a surface between the two circles. This will be the body of the ship.

Figure 20-63: The ship's body is constructed with the Skin tool.

Step #3: Create the Control Center

Draw a sphere, and place it in the center of the body of the ship. With both shapes selected, choose Object | Align | Position to center the two shapes. Lock-link the shapes together.

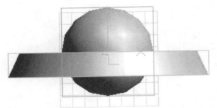

Figure 20-64: The two main parts of the ship are in place.

Step #4: Create the Light & Legs

Now we want to create a light at the top of the UFO, and four sets of "legs" for it. For the light, simply create another small sphere and embed it part way at the top of the object. For the legs, extrude a small square on a straight path for the rods, and attach a sphere at the bottom. Mirror this arrangement, and lock-link the composition. Duplicate the leg part four times, and move the duplicates into place around the base of the UFO.

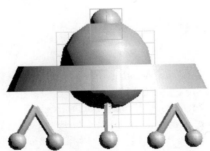

Figure 20-65: All of the separate elements have been constructed.

Step #5: Link Everything Together

Move the four sets of legs up, and embed them in the bottom of the body of the UFO. Use the Materials browser to assign colors and textures to the ship. Use Red Plastic for the top light, Scratched metal with a gold color for the body and the "balls" on the feet, and Chrome and Glass with your choice of texture for the main sphere. Lock-link all of the parts to the control sphere of the ship. Render and save it as a TIFF, and have fun incorporating it into a FreeHand composition.

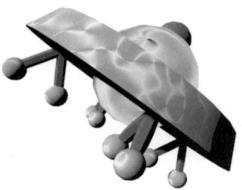

Figure 20-66: The finished and textured Extreme 3D UFO.

The Castle

Structures of every kind are favorite subjects of computer graphics artists. The material they are constructed with, whether wood, stone, or brick, is one of the reasons they are so interesting to create. FreeHand, xRes, and Extreme 3D especially offer options that make the creation of a structure and its background a very interesting project. In this project, you will learn to both create and texturize a castle-like structure.

Tip

If you prefer to see what these finished graphic elements look like prior to creating them yourself, use the accompanying CD-ROM to load the Castle Project and all of the tutorial elements into FreeHand so you can more easily work through this example. You may also find some of the elements in the Parts and Pieces folder.

Using FreeHand

FreeHand offers exacting tools when it comes to emulating stone materials, and a complex structure can be built up in FreeHand piece by piece.

Step #1: Begin With Two Rectangles

Create two rectangles, one small and light gray, the other larger and darker gray, and center them on each other. Set stroke to None for each.

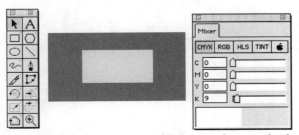

Figure 20-67: First, center two filled rectangles on each other.

Step #2: Blend the Rectangles

With both rectangles selected, click on the Blend tool in the Operations panel. We are going to combine the colors of one block with the next.

Figure 20-68: Select both rectangles and blend them.

Step #3: Clone to Create an Array

Clone the block as many times as needed to create a grouping on a background rectangle. Resize the blocks to give them a random appearance horizontally, but use the Align palette to make each column of blocks flush left (set horizontal to No Change, and vertical to Align Left). Group this construction.

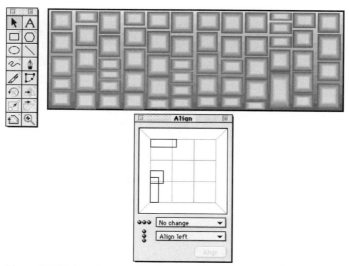

Figure 20-69: Create a graphic that contains columns and rows of the blended rectangle, with the columns matching up and the rows staggered.

Step #4: Use the Fisheye Lens Tool

We'll use this graphic to create several variations. With each variation, the original should be cloned so it remains intact for future use. With a working clone selected, use the Fisheye Lens tool in the Xtra Tools panel within the rectangle's borders six or seven times to warp the blocks. Do not allow the Fisheye Lens tool to warp the large rectangle's borders. Select None for the rectangle's strokes. Copy the texture to the clipboard.

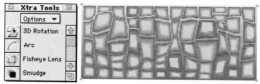

Figure 20-70: The Fisheye Lens tool is used to warp the internal blocks.

Step #5: Create a Snake

Draw an undulating closed snake shape with the FreeHand tool. With the shape selected, go to the Fill Inspector, and select Tiled. Click on Paste In, and your snake shape will develop instant scales.

Figure 20-71: One variant for this texture is to use it to emulate snake scales.

Step #6: Create the Basic Castle Shape

Clone four of the large rectangles, and using the Resize and Rotation tools in the Toolbox, construct a composition as illustrated in Figure 20-72.

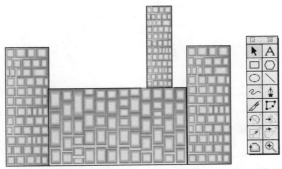

Figure 20-72: The rough components of the basic castle are put in place.

Step #7: Create Cut-away Elements

Draw a small red rectangle and clone it 20 times. Place the small red rectangles over the block structure as shown in Figure 20-73.

Figure 20-73: The small rectangles will be used to cut away parts of the underlying shapes.

Step #8: Complete the Castle

Select all of the red rectangles, and fill them with white. Select the ones used as windows, and give them a half-point stroke. Group all the elements of the castle as one graphic.

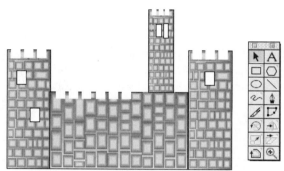

Figure 20-74: The castle is complete.

Using xRes

Now we'll use xRes to craft a backdrop for the FreeHand castle graphic. This section will teach you how to create a background that matches the theme of a FreeHand graphic, so the two can be grouped together to form a complete picture. xRes has a collection of diverse media tools that allow us to easily create any thematic graphic desired for a background.

Step #1: Import the FreeHand Castle

Begin a new page in xRes, making it 600 x 600 pixels at 72 dots per inch (dpi). Use the Sunrise gradient (Sunrise, Line, CMYK, Blend) to fill the page from bottom to top. Open the file in which you have stored the final castle illustration from FreeHand (you can also find the completed FreeHand castle saved as a TIFF file on the accompanying CD-ROM: Castle.TIF).

Use the Wand tool to select the background wherever it appears, and then use the Inverse Selection option to select only the Castle. Once it is selected, choose Edit | Copy. Click on the page with the Sunrise gradient, and select Edit | Paste. The castle should now be floating over the background as a separate object.

Figure 20-75: The castle graphic from FreeHand is now floating above the gradient backdrop in xRes.

Step #2: Add Darker Strokes to the Towers

Click on the Burn tool in the Brushes tab of the Brushes and Texture palette, and then on the Brush tool in the Toolbox. Use the brush to paint a darker overlay on the right sides of the towers. This adds 3D depth to the castle.

Figure 20-76: The Burn Brush is used to add darkened surfaces to the castle, emulating an incoming light source.

Step #3: Add the Sky & Ground

Make the castle object invisible by turning off visibility in the Objects tab in the Objects palette. Paint a large red sun on the backdrop, and use the Airbrush with its Dark Textured mode to add a colorized Mesh Texture that acts as the ground. Paint some wispy airbrushed (with no texture) clouds in the sky. Make the castle visible again, and move it until it looks right in the composition.

Figure 20-77: The castle now sits on a backdrop complete with sky and ground.

Step #4: Complete the Composition

Finally, use a Nature Styles brush to add some greenery around the base of the castle, and drop the castle object layer into place. Save the graphic as a 24-bit TIFF, and import it into FreeHand to include in one of your compositions.

Figure 20-78: The Nature Styles brush is used to add some shrubs in the foreground for the final element.

Using Extreme 3D

If your castle has to be seen from different angles in a composition, then the easiest thing to do is to create it in Extreme 3D so you can manipulate the viewpoint. This will guide you through a basic castle structure in Extreme 3D. You can use it as a basis to make it as complex as you desire.

Step #1: Build a 3D Wall

Select the Cube tool, and create five cubes to your workspace. Draw a rectangle beneath these cubes to act as a wall, making it as long as the cube spread and about six times as high. Extrude the rectangle out about the depth of the cubes. Lock-link the cubes to the castle wall. Assign a marble texture to the finished wall. Set it aside.

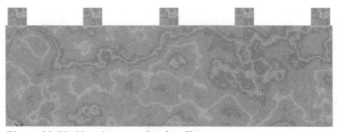

Figure 20-79: Here is a completed wall.

Step #2: Draw a Tower Outline

Draw an outline with the Polyline tool that can be lathed into a castle tower (Figure 20-80).

Figure 20-80: The outline of the tower.

Step #3: Lathe the Completed Tower Elements

Use the Lathe tool to complete the 3D tower base. At the top of the tower, construct a cylinder with a cone on top of it. Color the Cone red, and apply a marble material to the cylinder. Make sure the group is centered, and lock-link it.

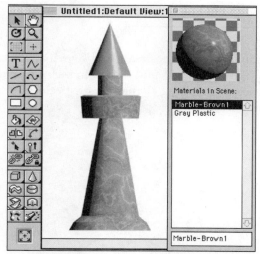

Figure 20-81: The completed 3D tower with its red cone top.

Step #4: Duplicate the Parts to Get the Finished Object

Use the Duplicate function to get the four walls, and also for the towers. Move everything into place and lock-link it. Now you can turn it in space to get just the right view. When the view is the way you want it, render it as a TIFF file and import it into FreeHand as one element in a composition.

Figure 20-82: The finished castle in Extreme 3D.

Moving On

In this chapter, we have guided you in the creation of five diverse objects: Snowflake, Child's Block, Butterfly, UFO, and Castle. In the next chapter, we will look at the exciting prospect of using all manner of special effects tools in FreeHand, xRes, and Extreme 3D.

21

Special Effects

In this chapter, we'll take a look at some important special effects (sometimes called FX) that you can achieve in FreeHand. In a couple of cases, we will also demonstrate how the graphics developed with these effects can be ported back and forth to either or both xRes and Extreme 3D for incorporation in other projects. The whole idea of special effects comes from the use of computer graphics in films, especially the use of computer animation to do things that are too dangerous, expensive, or impossible to achieve in the physical world. In comparison, the special effects we will look at in the FreeHand Graphics Studio applications might seem rather tame, but they are no less special to FreeHand users who haven't had these capabilities before (or who haven't had any guidance creating them). We will look at five different effects: displacing graphics with other graphics ("Punching"), using spiral text paths, shatter effects, creating splatters, and configuring transparent graphics.

Punchout

You can craft logos and symbols for use in a FreeHand heading in a standard way with lettering and graphics, or construct them from unexpected elements that offer more interest to the audience. One of these ways is to construct them out of "negative space," so that they appear as a cutout, stencil, or hole. Both FreeHand and Extreme 3D offer options to this method.

Tip

If you prefer to see what these finished graphic elements look like prior to creating them yourself, use the accompanying CD-ROM to load the Punchout Project and all of the tutorial elements into FreeHand so you can more easily work through this example. You may also find some of the elements in the Parts and Pieces folder.

Using FreeHand

It is vital to have the ability to remove parts of a graphic when you need to in order to create certain text and graphics looks. FreeHand offers this capability through the Punch and Join command.

Step #1: Create Five Gradient Rectangles

Adjust the gradient colors in the Inspectors Fill so that the top color is a bright CMYK Red (0, 100, 100, 0), and the bottom color a deep CMYK Purple (50, 100, 0, 0). Use the Rectangle tool and draw a rectangle 1 ¾" wide by 3 ½" tall. Clone this image four times, so that you have a total of five equal rectangles. Round the edges. Set them in an equally spaced row, and align them at the top.

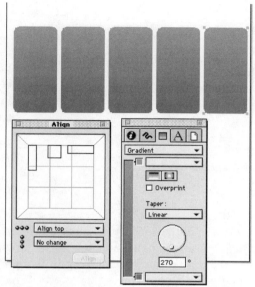

Figure 21-1: Five gradient round-edged rectangles begin the exercise.

Step #2: Design & Place the Cutter

FreeHand allows you to cut one polygon with another. The last polygon constructed becomes the cutter shape. Go to the Fill Inspector. Make the fill color blue, so the cutters you create can be distinguished from the gradient filled rectangles that will be cut. Deselect the existing shapes. With the color set to a solid blue (100, 0, 0, 0), draw a rectangle sized 1" wide by 1 ¾" tall, and a circle with a 1" diameter. Place these over the first gradient filled rectangle. The object is to place them so that when they cut away the parts of the rectangle, the letter "P" will be the result. Refer to Figure 21-2 for placement.

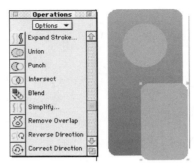

Figure 21-2: Use shapes with a different color for "cutters."

Step #3: Make the First Cut

Select the blue rectangle, and then (with the Shift key pressed) select the gradient rectangle below. Go to the Operations panel and select the Punch operator. The blue rectangle cuts away the underlying area of the gradient rectangle. Repeat this same procedure with the blue circle and the gradient rectangle. The result will be the letter P.

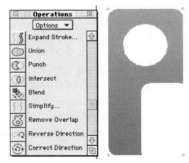

Figure 21-3: The result of the first cutting operation is the letter P.

Step #4: Continue the Cuts

Use similar blue shapes over the other gradient rectangles to design the rest of the letters to spell out the word "PUNCH."

Figure 21-4: Now cutters are placed on the other rectangles.

Figure 21-5: The result of the cuts is the word "PUNCH."

Step #5: Create a FreeHand Shape

A variety of cut paper effects can be achieved with similar tools. Using the FreeHand tool in the Toolbox, draw a closed shape that resembles the one illustrated.

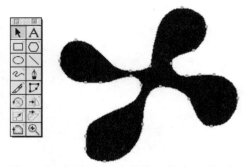

Figure 21-6: The initial shape to be fractalized.

Step #6: Fractalize the Selection

With the object still selected, click on the Fractalize tool in the Operations panel six times. This transforms your original shape into a series of connected fractal squares. Select the collection of squares and group all as one object.

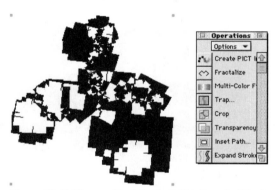

Figure 21-7: The result of six fractalizations is this shape.

Step #7: Clone & Group

Clone this shape three times, and using a very close zoom, rotate and connect the four shapes so that you have a final graphic that looks something like the illustration. Group all four patterns as one.

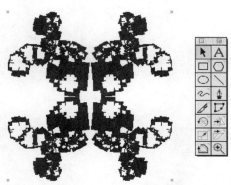

Figure 21-8: A group of fractalized clones is created.

Step #8: Continue the Clones

Repeat this same procedure again, creating three clones of this group, and then rotating each so that the resulting pattern resembles this one. Clone this pattern, and set the clone aside.

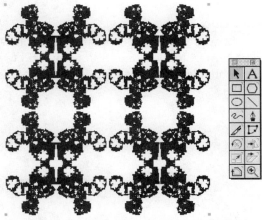

Figure 21-9: Expanding the cloned group further creates this pattern.

Step #9: Join the Shapes

Place a purple rectangle behind this pattern, and Shift-select the pattern followed by the rectangle. Use the Join command, and allow the pattern to be punched out of the rectangle.

Tip

Join works on grouped objects the same way that Punch works on non-grouped objects.

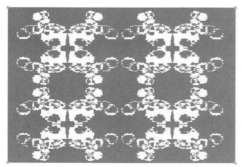

Figure 21-10: The cloned fractalizations are cut out of the backdrop.

Step #10: Duplicate & Group

Using the same procedures as outlined above, clone the pattern three times and construct a four-part pattern from the clones. Use a Basic fill to fill each of the four patterns with a different color. Select all four and group them as one pattern.

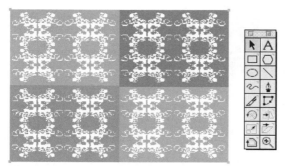

Figure 21-11: This grouping is made from duplicating the graphic in figure 21-10.

Step #11: Copy & Use as a Tiled Pattern

Use the Text tool to create a line of text. Copy the four-colored pattern rectangle. Select the text, go to the Fill Inspectors, and select the Tiled option from the list. Click on Paste In, and the colored pattern will be used as a pattern fill in the text.

Figure 21-12: The fractalized group can be used as a tile pattern inside letters.

Step #12: Simplify the Text

Go to the Operations panel and click Simplify. In the settings dialog that pops up, set the slider to 7, and click OK. This adds a squarish look to the text.

Step #13: Achieve a Colorful Variation

The white space in a punched-out graphic is transparent to anything underneath. For a colorful variation, draw a rectangle and use the Gradient Fill option in the Fill Inspectors to fill it with a three-color radial gradient: dark blue, red, and yellow. Place the punched graphic over it to achieve a colorful variation.

Figure 21-13: Setting the combined graphic text block against a gradient backdrop allows the holes to makes the gradient visible.

Using Extreme 3D

If you are interested in having your cutouts appear in a more photorealistic 3D manner in a FreeHand document, then you might be interested in creating them in Extreme 3D. Extreme 3D offers you the capability to accomplish this technique in a fast and intuitive way with the Projection/Trim method.

Step #1: Draw a Splined Shape

In an orthographic right view, draw a shape with the Spline tool like that shown in Figure 21-14. Duplicate it and move the clone four screen inches to the left in the front view. Line up the bottoms of both shapes.

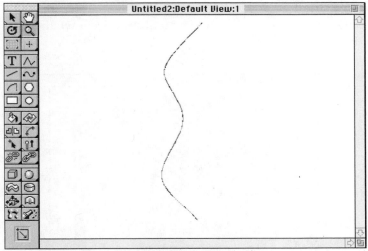

Figure 21-14: The initial curved spline shape.

Step #2: Build a Skinned Shape

From the front view, use the Skin tool to create a 3D structure between the two shapes, and assign any material you like to it. Go to the top view to move it back one screen inch, and return to the front view.

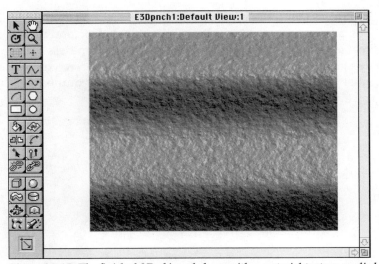

Figure 21-15: The finished 3D skinned shape with a material texture applied.

Step #3: Create an Alphanumeric Graphic

Create a letter or number with the Text tool, and size it relative to the illustration in Figure 21-16.

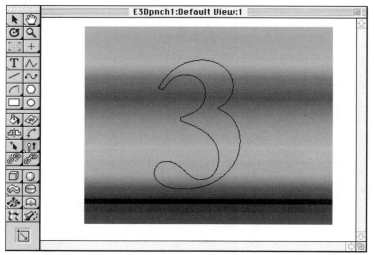

Figure 21-16: Place the number in the center of the skinned surface from the front view.

Step #4: Project & Trim

Use the Project tool function to cut the surface with the number or letter you are using as a cutter. Save the finished graphic to disk, and import it for use in a FreeHand project. Remember that you can get limitless 3D perspective with this graphic by simply turning it in 3D space before you render it. Also remember that you can use any splined shape or text outline as a cutter with this procedure.

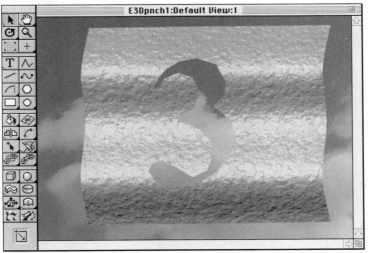

Figure 21-17: The finished example shows the surface cut by the graphic, with a background in place.

Spiral Gyrations

FreeHand's Spiral tool offers you the capacity to create some unique graphics easily, making it simple to connect text to a spiral path. Because you can use the spiral's control points to vary its shape infinitely, you possess limitless options for developing unique text spirals. In most other projects in the tutorial sections, a FreeHand example is followed by either or both an xRes and an Extreme 3D example. In this case, this important effect can be achieved only in FreeHand because of the unique nature of the tools involved.

Tip

If you prefer to see what these finished graphic elements look like prior to creating them yourself, use the accompanying CD-ROM to load the Spiral Gyrations Project and all of the tutorial elements into FreeHand so you can more easily work through this example. You may also find some of the elements in the Parts and Pieces folder.

Step #1: Use the Spiral Tool in the Xtra Tools Panel

Click and drag to place a spiral on the FreeHand page. Allow the spiral to consume about half of the page as shown.

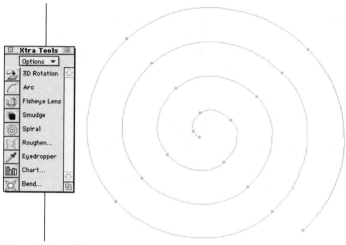

Figure 21-18: The initial spiral is created.

Step #2: Place Text on the Spiral

Click on the Text tool. Select Text | Attach to Path (with the spiral still selected). Notice that a flashing cursor now appears at the center of the spiral. Set the text to Helvetica 48 point, and begin typing. You can type any message you desire. It will follow the spiral-shaped path.

Figure 21-19: Text is added to the spiral path.

Step #3: Color the Text

Drop a Red CMYK color on the text (0, 100, 100, 0).

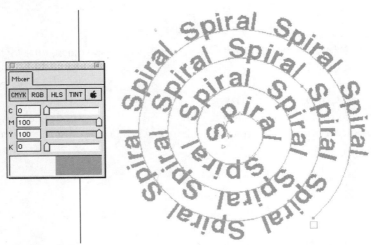

Figure 21-20: The text on the spiral path is colored.

Step #4: Reshape the Spiral

Each of the blue rectangles on the spiral is a control point that you can move and reshape with its handles. Grab one of the control points on the spiral and move it, forcing the attached text to move with it. Reshape the spiral (and therefore the attached text) by moving a number of the control points. Stop when you are satisfied with the new design.

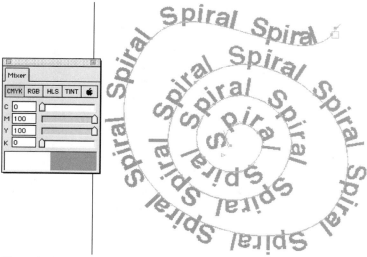

Figure 21-21: Moving the spiral paths control points moves the elements attached to the path.

Step #5: Convert to Paths

Convert to paths. Notice that the blue spiral path disappears, leaving just the text. You can now add a stroke to the text. Add a one point black stroke.

Figure 21-22: When the assigned text is converted to paths, the spiral path disappears.

Step #6: Create a Text Shadow

Select Edit | Duplicate. Notice that a duplicate copy of the spiral text is written to the screen. Select the duplicated copy, remove its stroke, and color it a light CMYK Gray (0, 0, 0, 20). Place the gray text behind the red text. The red text gains an instant shadow.

Figure 21-23: You can duplicate the spiraled text for shadow effects.

Step #7: Create Another Spiral

You can also apply spiral textures to another graphic. Double-click on the Spiral tool in the Xtra Tools panel to bring up its settings. Select the first spiral option at the top, Draw By Rotations, Number of Rotations 22, Draw from Center, and the right-handed spiral option. Draw a spiral. Set its stroke to one point white (use the Stroke tab in the Inspectors).

Step #8: Stack the Spiral on the Text

Move the spiral to the front of the stack. Group the spiral. Use the Text tool to write the word SPIRALTALK. Place the white spiral over the text, and resize the spiral so that its lines cover the length of the text block.

Figure 21-24: A spiral texture can be added to text.

Step #9: Create a Spiral Graphic Texture

Using the same idea over a graphic is also interesting. Draw a rectangle, and set its fill to a blue radial gradient. Draw a spiral over it, group the spiral, and set the spiral's stroke to one point white. Now click on the Roughen tool in the Xtra Tools panel and move the mouse slightly to the right. The spiral's edges roughen, creating another alternate effect over the graphic.

Figure 21-25: Interesting textures can also be created by using the spiral as one of the elements.

Shatter

There may come a time when you want to show a graphic or a headline being smashed or shattered in a FreeHand project. When that time arrives, use this example as a way of understanding how it's done. Shattering is especially effective when you want to add something to a headline that will shock your audience, adding chaos and mystery.

Again our example is involved with FreeHand alone, and especially relies on your capacity to master the Knife tool (a tool not duplicated in either xRes or Extreme 3D). Shatter effects can be created in xRes and Extreme 3D by the simple method of creating the parts of the shatter in the initial construction phases. This is not the same as taking a clear cohesive text block and cutting it apart. Mastering the use of the Knife tool in FreeHand can be compared to learning to draw with the knife, a unique process.

Tip

If you prefer to see what these finished graphic elements look like prior to creating them yourself, use the accompanying CD-ROM to load the Shatter Project and all of the tutorial elements into FreeHand so you can more easily work through this example. You may also find some of the elements in the Parts and Pieces folder.

Step #1: Set the Knife Tool's Parameters

Double-click on the Knife tool in the Toolbox, bringing up its settings dialog. Set the options as illustrated, choosing Straight, a width of 4, and with both items checked under Options.

Step #2: Create the Text

Using the Text tool in the Toolbox, create a word that reads "BUSTED." Make it Helvetica, Bold, 72 points in all caps.

BUSTED

Figure 21-26: The initial lettering is placed in the workspace.

Step #3: Add Stroke & Fill
Give the text a CMYK fill color of bright red (0, 100, 100, 0), and a two point black stroke, using the Fill and Stroke Inspectors.

Figure 21-27: Stroke and color are added to the lettering.

Step #4: Configure the Smudge Tool
Double-click on the Smudge tool in the Xtra Tools panel to bring up its settings dialog. Place a 100% CMYK black color in the fill and stroke swatches (0, 0, 0, 100). Ungroup the letters in the text block.

Step #5: Cut the Letters Apart
Click on each of the letters in turn, and with the Knife tool in the Toolbox, click and drag a cut across them. Use a random approach, or follow the illustrated example. On letters with a hole (the "B" and the "D"), be sure to cut across the holes. After cutting the "B" and the "D," you must select Modify | Split to complete the separations.

Figure 21-28: The letters are cut with the Knife tool.

Step #6: Move the Letter Segments

Move each of the cut pieces apart, and rotate each piece randomly. Do not move the elements too far apart, nor rotate them too radically, since we still want to have some sense of the readability of the word when we're through.

Figure 21-29: The parts are rotated to show the force of the breakup.

Step #7: Use the Smudge Tool

Then, using the Smudge tool in the Xtra Tools panel, add 3D depth to each cut part. You'll have to select each part separately (use the Pointer tool). Move the Smudge tool just a slight amount to the upper left in each case by clicking in the cut part and dragging the mouse.

Figure 21-30: A smudged shadow is added.

Step #8: Create a Projectile

To add a touch of 3D realism, add a projectile created in Extreme 3D to the graphic. In Extreme 3D, use the Cone primitive to draw a cone on the screen in orthographic front view. Then open its geometry, and reshape it like a projectile. Save it out and composite it with the "Busted" graphic in xRes. Save it to disk for later import into a FreeHand project.

Figure 21-31: The "Busted" graphic with the Extreme 3D projectile added.

Splatters

Splatters can be used as backgrounds for headlines and important text, as well as just placed for visual interest. We will look at both FreeHand and xRes as the applications that can create them.

Tip

If you prefer to see what these finished graphic elements look like prior to creating them yourself, use the accompanying CD-ROM to load the Splatter Project and all of the tutorial elements into FreeHand so you can more easily work through this example. You may also find some of the elements in the Parts and Pieces folder.

Using FreeHand

The main tool to use in FreeHand to create splatters is the Bend tool.

Step #1: Draw Two Circles

Draw two circles filled with different colors, blue on the left and red on the right, with about two inches between them. They should have the stroke set to None in the Stroke Inspector. Select both circles.

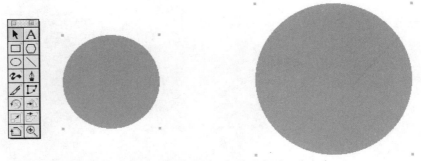

Figure 21-32: We start with two differently sized and colored circles.

Step #2: Blend the Circles

Click on the Blend tool in the Operations panel to create a blend between the two circles.

Figure 21-33: The circles are connected with the Blend tool.

Step #3: Create a Spiked Look

With the blended circle graphic still selected, click on Add Points in the Operations panel four times in succession. This adds more control points to the graphic. Click on the Bend tool in the Xtra Tools panel. Move the mouse to the center of the blended graphic. Click and hold in the center, and drag the mouse about three inches in any direction until you see spikes protruding from the graphic. Release the mouse button.

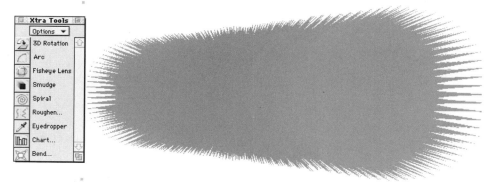

Figure 21-34: The Bend tool produces spiked extrusions.

Step #4: Place Text Against the Splatter

If you place text against the splattered graphic, it looks like an emphatic statement from a comic.

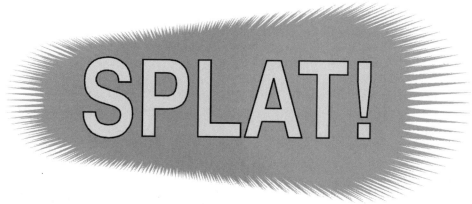

Figure 21-35: A caption is set against the splattered graphic.

Using xRes

Achieving a similar effect in xRes produces a softer splat, which we might poetically call a Splotch.

Step #1: Paint & Color the Shape

Paint a freeform shape with the Lasso Marquee tool. Select a Textured Airbrush, and choose the texture named "Rough." Set the Airbrush controls at full for concentration, flow, and texture. Use a combination of brown and green colors, and spray the textured colors within the boundaries of the marqueed shape.

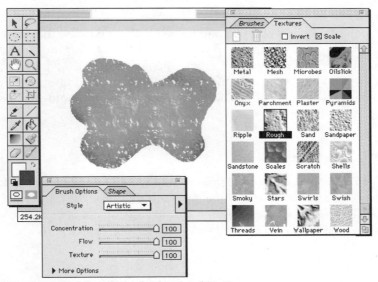

Figure 21-36: The initial splotch painted in xRes.

Step #2: Add a Drop Shadow

Invert the selection, making everything but the shape selected. Set the Airbrush controls at no texture (move the slider all the way to the left). Use a black color to add a drop shadow to the right and bottom edges of the shape. Turn off all selections and save the graphic to disk as a TIFF file. You can import and place this more organic-looking splotch in a FreeHand document. If you need other looks for an xRes splotch, it's simple to vary the shape and the texture of similar designs.

Figure 21-37: The finished xRes splotch.

Transparencies

Transparent graphics and text add viewer interest because they add an edge of mystery to a page, whether in print or on the Web. FreeHand, xRes, and Extreme 3D all contain tools that target graphics, text, or drawings, for transparency. Here's how to use each of these applications to add transparent elements to a FreeHand composition. Each of these applications handles transparency very differently.

Tip

If you prefer to see what these finished graphic elements look like prior to creating them yourself, use the accompanying CD-ROM to load the Transparency Project and all of the tutorial elements into FreeHand so you can more easily work through this example. You may also find some of the elements in the Parts and Pieces folder.

Using FreeHand

In FreeHand, transparency is automated when you select two items on the page that overlap, and click on the Transparency tool in the Operations palette. You can set the percentage of transparency from 0 to 100 percent, with the lower settings producing more believable transparent regions.

Step #1: Draw the Initial Shapes

Use the Text tool to create the word "Transparent" in the workspace. Color it red. Draw two overlapping rectangles over it, coloring them green and yellow.

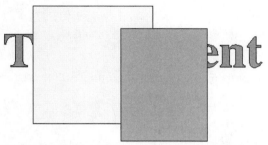

Figure 21-38: The initial placement of the three elements should look something like this.

Step #2: Use the Transparency Tool

Select one rectangle and then the text block. Click on the Transparency operator, bringing up its settings dialog. Set the slider to 15 (slide it left), and click OK. Transparent letters are written over the rectangle. Do the same thing with the second rectangle and the text. In order for the final results to look real, you will also have to perform this operation with the two rectangles selected together.

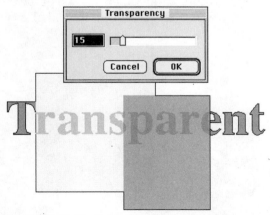

Figure 21-39: The Transparency tool creates transparent regions according to the percentages set.

Tip

Transparencies in FreeHand actually create separate re-colored graphics of the elements that look transparent. You will have to group the entire region if you want to reposition it; otherwise, everything will move separately. FreeHand's Transparency operator creates a reordered stack of graphic elements.

FreeHand transparent graphic elements are wonderful for creating overlapping collage looks and also the feel of glass.

Another FreeHand Variation

Here's an interesting little project that uses your knowledge of transparency generation in FreeHand to create "Light Through a Window." Light actually refers to the word "Light," but you can alter the elements of this example as you see fit to get limitless variations.

Step #1: Create the Text & the Hexagon Group

Create the word "Light," and convert it to paths. Configure the Polygon tool so that it will generate a hexagon, and create an arrangement of hexagonal shapes like those illustrated in Figure 21-40. Color fill each of the hexagons in a random manner, so that they appear like parts of a stained glass window.

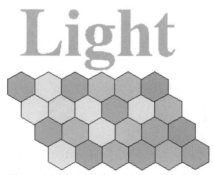

Figure 21-40: The elements you create to accomplish this example should appear something like this.

Step #2: Create the Transparent Overlap

Move the text in back of the hexagon arrangement. Select a hexagon that overlaps the text, and shift-select the text. Use the Transparency tool with a setting of 15 to allow the text to show through the hexagon. Do this for every hexagon that overlaps a portion of the text.

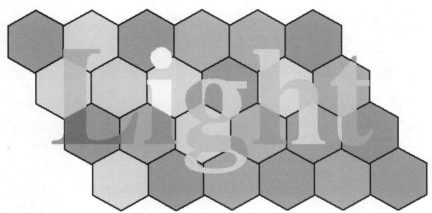

Figure 21-41: Your finished transparent project should look something like this.

Group everything as one graphic. Using your own variations on this theme and incorporating it into a FreeHand project should allow you to create very unique elements that stand out and attract attention.

Using xRes

Configuring a transparency in xRes has everything to do with your ability to manipulate object layers. The slider on the Object tab is the main tool to be mastered.

Step #1: Make an Arrangement of Multicolored Squares

Create a text block that reads "LightFX," and copy and paste it twice.

Each of these text blocks is automatically placed on a separate object layer until it is dropped into place, so it can be moved freely. Color each of the text blocks differently, and move them over the blocks.

Adjust their transparency by manipulating the slider in the Object tab of the Object/Channels/Path palette. Notice if you move them over each other, you get multiple layers of transparency. When everything is in place, drop all object layers into one. Save to disk, and import into a FreeHand document for use.

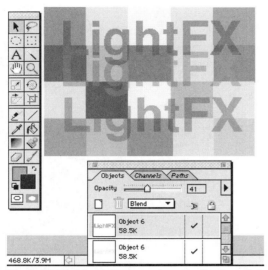

Figure 21-42: New lettering automatically comes into xRes on a separate object layer that can be moved on its own and can be made transparent according to the slider settings.

Using Extreme 3D

Extreme 3D uses an ingenious and simple method to make objects transparent. This is called alpha channel mapping, and it utilizes a grayscale slider with 256 possible levels of transparency, from completely transparent to completely opaque. The darker you set the slider, the more opaque the selected object; the lighter the slider is set, the more transparent the object becomes. Rapid 3D transparent compositions are possible using this technique.

We are going to create a series of transparent 3D spheres over a 3D text block, each sphere texture mapped in a unique fashion. This technique could be used as a visual enhancement in a FreeHand document, or the spheres could be placed over a background photo or graphic in Extreme 3D itself before porting the rendering to FreeHand. The variations are truly limitless when you consider that the arrangement can also be rotated in 3D space before rendering.

Step #1: Create the Text

Create a text block that reads "My Logo." You can actually use a splined drawing of your logo if you create it first, but the text block will do for this example. Lock-link all of the letters to the "M." Extrude it a little so it will accept a texture, and assign a red plastic material to it. Go to the top view and move it back about one screen inch, and return to the front view.

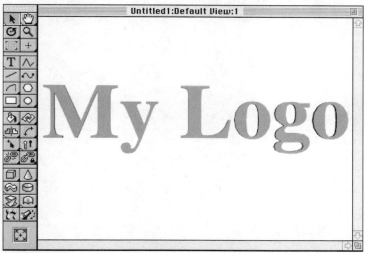

Figure 21-43: The text block is the first element added to this composition.

Step #2: Create the Spheres & Edit Their Material

In the front view, create five randomly sized spheres, and place them so that they overlap each other and the text. They can actually intersect the text if you prefer. Assign a different material to each sphere.

Now for the most important consideration. Edit the transparency of each sphere's material. You'll have to experiment a bit to get a feel for what looks right, but generally, moving the transparency slider in the Material Editor about one-third of the way to the right is a good place to start. Materials that are very complex may need more transparency, and those with simpler looking textures may need less. The object is to be able to see the text block (and read it) through the overlapping spheres.

Figure 21-44: It's better to have a background against which the transparent objects can be noticed, though a solid color would also work.

Moving On

If you have diligently worked through this chapter, you have mastered five important effects offered in the FreeHand Graphics Studio applications: displacing graphics with other graphics ("Punching"), using spiral text paths, creating shatter effects, configuring splatters, and mastering the use of transparent graphics. In the next chapter, you will learn how to create decorative graphics, and how to use them to spice up your FreeHand documents.

22

Decorative Elements

The FreeHand graphics you need to complete a page may have little to do with exact content, but more with the overall design concept. Decorative graphics run the gamut from photorealistic to painterly and abstract, depending upon how you want to get the overall feeling of the message across.

In general, harder-edged subjects work well with harder-edged decorative elements. A page about computers, for instance, is less likely to be decorated with leaves and more likely to incorporate electronic symbols and mechanical graphics. A page advertising computers in autumn, however, may benefit from a border of leaves.

The decorative elements you use on a page have everything to do with the targeted audience the page is meant for, whether as a brochure or mailer or as a Web page. Here are a handful of examples of decorative themes, showing how they can be crafted in FreeHand, and also (in certain cases) xRes and Extreme 3D. In this chapter we will learn to create patriotic and oriental fabric looks, native Southwestern designs, urban elements, and a holiday candle.

Patriot's Bunting

Whether it's to advertise a sale on the 4th of July or to post a notice concerning an upcoming visit by a congressperson, a graphic representation of bunting is a useful decorative element to know how to create and place in a document. By simply applying alternate fills to the bunting examples, you will learn how to create a wealth of decorative fabric looks for your FreeHand documents.

Tip

If you prefer to see what these finished graphic elements look like prior to creating them yourself, use the accompanying CD-ROM to load the Bunting Project and all of the tutorial elements into FreeHand so you can more easily work through this example. You may also find some of the elements in the Parts and Pieces folder.

Using FreeHand

Creating bunting in FreeHand requires a mastery of using graphics on a path and tiled fills, as well as a working knowledge of the Calligraphic Pen tool. Extremely complex effects can be achieved by altering the graphic elements explored in this project, the kind of results that will make your audience ask "how did you do that?"

Step #1: Draw a Star

Bring up the Color Mixer and create a CMYK color with the settings 99, 0, 0, 30. This makes a teal blue. Drag and drop the color to the swatch area of the Fill Inspector with Basic selected. Use the Rectangle tool with the Shift key held down to create a two inch by two inch blue teal–filled square.

Deselect everything by clicking once on an empty part of the screen with the Pointer tool. Double-click on the Polygon tool to bring up its dialog, and configure the settings as illustrated in Figure 22-1 for a star with five points and the Manual slider moved to the halfway point. Click OK to close the dialog. Draw a star about one-half inch in diameter. Set its fill color to white, and give it a one point black stroke. Copy the star to the clipboard.

Step #2: Paste 13 Stars Around the Circle

Use the Ellipse tool with the Shift key held down to draw a circle about 1.5 inches in diameter. With the circle selected, choose Text | Attach To Path. This turns the circle into a path ready for text.

If you select Edit | Paste or its keyboard equivalent (Command-V on the Mac or Control-V in Windows) with the circle path selected, copies of the star will be pasted around the circle from the clipboard. We want to get a total of 13 stars around the circle, which may mean you will have to resize the circle to get the proper spacing. Place 13 stars around the circle using this method.

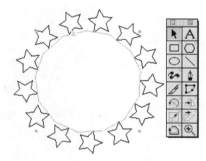

Figure 22-1: Thirteen stars are pasted around the circular path.

Step #3: Place the Stars Over a Blue Field

Once you have the 13 stars arranged around the circle, use the Scale tool in the Toolbox to reduce the size of the star group so it fits within the bounds of the blue square, and place it there.

Figure 22-2: The white stars are placed over the blue field.

Step #4: Create Concentric Star Circles

Use the Clone command to copy the selected star circle in the square. Reduce it so that it fits in the first circle. Repeat this process again, so that you wind up with three concentric star circles in the blue square. Select all of the elements, including the square. Use the Align panel with vertical and horizontal settings of Align Center to center everything. Click on Align. Group all of these elements into one graphic.

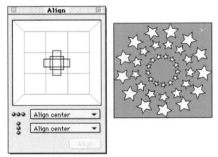

Figure 22-3: Three concentric rings of stars are centered in the blue field with the help of the Align palette.

Step #5: Draw a Wavy Shape

Use the Pen tool in its click-and-drag mode to draw a closed wavy shape, using the illustrated example in Figure 22-4 as a guide. Fill color it with a CMYK bright red (0, 100, 100, 0) and set its stroke to a 1.5 point black.

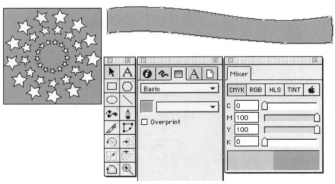

Figure 22-4: A red wave is drawn next to the star field.

Step #6: Place the Waves

Clone the red wavy stripe twice, and move the elements into place as illustrated in Figure 22-5. Group everything as one graphic. Copy the grouped graphic to the clipboard (Edit I Copy).

Deselect everything, and go to the Fill Inspector. Bring up the Tiled fill type from the list, and click on Paste In. Set the X and Y scaling percentages to 50. A thumbnail version of the flag graphic appears in the preview window. This means that any shape you draw will be filled with this tiled graphic, as long as Tiled is selected in the Fill Inspector.

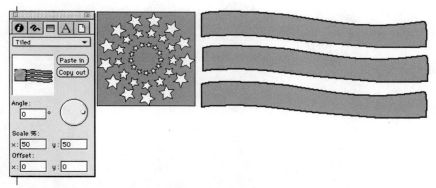

Figure 22-5: Three waves are positioned next to the star field, then the whole arrangement is copied to the clipboard for access in the Fill Inspector.

Step #7: Configure the Calligraphic Pen

Double-click on the FreeHand tool in the Toolbox, bringing up its settings dialog. Configure the settings as illustrated, choosing the Calligraphic Pen setting with a Tight Fit option, a width of 9, and a angle of 90 degrees. Click on OK to accept these settings.

Step #8: Draw With the Tiled Fill

Using the FreeHand tool in the Toolbox, draw your buntings. They will be automatically filled with the flag pattern. Notice that the tiled fill remains in the same orientation, even though the border shapes differ.

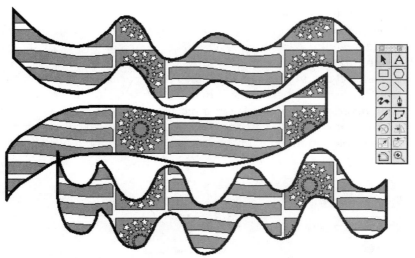

Figure 22-6: Using the FreeHand tool automatically assigns the tiled fill to the lines.

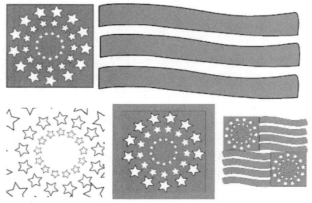

Figure 22-7: You can develop limitless variations on this theme.

Figure 22-8: The tiled graphics can be used to create a variety of compositions.

Using Extreme 3D

When you save out your bunting creations, they automatically become available as texture elements in Extreme 3D. There, you can use them to compose 3D scenes and export the renderings back to FreeHand for placement. Let's use the bunting graphics just created in FreeHand as texture elements in Extreme 3D.

Step #1: Create the Spheres & the Materials

Use Extreme 3D to create dimensional graphic elements for use on your FreeHand pages. Create two spheres for placement on the Extreme 3D workspace. Create two Chrome+Glass materials by selecting the material from the right hand list in the Materials browser and moving it to the left.

Step #2: Use the Bunting Art

Use a different Bunting tile graphic for the Environmental Map in each Chrome+Glass edit screen, and assign these materials to the two spheres. Render and save to disk as a TIFF file for incorporation into a FreeHand document.

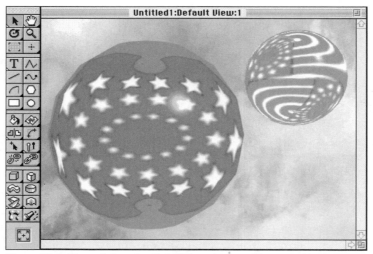

Figure 22-9: By applying the tiled fill bunting graphics as an Environmental Map in the Chrome +Glass material in Extreme 3D, unique objects can be created for placement in a FreeHand document.

Oriental Designs

Of all of the designs and symbols that remind us of the ancient Orient, the dragon remains one of the most dominant. The dragon has come to symbolize both strength and good luck. Here's how to design graphics in the FreeHand Graphics Studio applications with the dragon in mind.

Tip

If you prefer to see what these finished graphic elements look like prior to creating them yourself, use the accompanying CD-ROM to load the China Silk Project and all of the tutorial elements into FreeHand so you can more easily work through this example. You may also find some of the elements in the Parts and Pieces folder.

Using FreeHand

This is a perfect exercise for attaining complete mastery over the tiled fill.

Step #1: Configure the Calligraphic Pen

Double-click on the FreeHand tool in the Toolbox, bringing up the settings
dialog for this tool. Configure it as illustrated, choosing Calligraphic Pen,
Tight Fit, a fixed width of 5, and an angle of 90 degrees.

Step #2: Sketch a Dragon

Using the Calligraphic FreeHand tool you just configured, draw an abstract
Chinese dragon. Use the illustration as a guide, or follow your own instincts.

Figure 22-10: Use the calligraphic pen to sketch out a dragon.

Step #3: Complete the Dragon Art

Draw a bright CMYK red (0, 100, 100, 0) rectangle around the dragon using
the Rectangle tool in the Toolbox. Move the rectangle to the back of the image.
Remove any stroke from the rectangle (Stroke Inspector set to None). Group
everything drawn so far. Using the Ellipse tool in the Toolbox with the Shift
key held down, draw a bright CMYK yellow (0, 0, 100, 0) circle in the lower
bottom of the red rectangle. Give it a 1.5 point black stroke.

With the yellow circle still selected, go to the Operations panel and click on Add Points twice. This gives the circle a total of 16 control points. In the Xtra Tools panel, click on the Bend tool. Place the cursor in the center of the circle, and click and drag upwards to produce spiked rays emanating from the sun symbol. Select everything and group it. Choose Edit | Copy to copy the graphic to the clipboard.

Figure 22-11: Place the dragon on a red rectangular backdrop, and add a yellow sun.

Step #4: Create the Tiled Texture

Deselect everything by clicking on an empty part of the page with the Pointer tool. Go to the Fill Inspector, and select Tiled from the menu. Click on Paste In, and a thumbnail of the graphic saved to the clipboard appears on the preview window. Any shape you draw will now be filled with tiled images of this graphic.

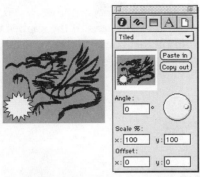

Figure 22-12: The dragon becomes a tiled texture.

Step #5: Draw With the Tiled Texture

On an empty part of the page, draw a rectangle, using the Rectangle tool in the Toolbox. Notice that it is tiled with the dragon graphic.

Figure 22-13: The tiled dragon fills any new shape you draw.

Step #6: Configure Alternate Tile-filled Shapes

The rectangle can be resized to accommodate the fill more precisely by using the resizing and repositioning capabilities in the Fill Inspector to adjust the placement of the graphic. Resize the graphic to 50 percent on the X and Y axes, by typing those figures into the X and Y scaling boxes in the Fill Inspector.

Set the tiled rectangle aside. Draw an oval shape, and then a star shape. Notice that the same tiled dragon pattern textures all of the shapes you draw. The same would hold if you used it to fill text converted to paths.

Figure 22-14: The tiled dragon can be used as a fill for any shape, and also as a texture for text blocks.

Using xRes

Bitmap fill options are more extensive than those found in a vector graphics application like FreeHand. This is even more true if xRes is the bitmap application. We've already explored some of those options in other examples, and porting the dragon graphic to xRes will allow us to investigate them more thoroughly.

Step #1: Import the Dragon Tile Created in FreeHand Into xRes

Use the Wand tool to select the red background that the dragon rests on. Shift-select all of the corners where the background appears. Now click on the Gradient tool in the Toolbox. In the Fills palette, notice that there are several options to select from.

The most important processes when it comes to applying gradient backgrounds are the use of the color spectrum list and the selection of the gradient type. Select any spectrum member you are interested in exploring, and select a type (Satin and Folds stand out as very unique to xRes). Drag the cursor in the graphic in any direction you prefer, and watch as the texture is painted into the backdrop.

Save the graphic to disk when you have something you're satisfied with, and import it into FreeHand as an element on a page.

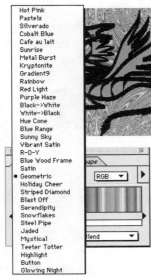

Hot Pink
Pastels
Silverado
Cobalt Blue
Cafe au lait
Sunrise
Metal Burst
Kryptonite
Gradient9
Rainbow
Red Light
Purple Haze
Black->White
White->Black
Hue Cone
Blue Range
Sunny Sky
Vibrant Satin
R-O-Y
Blue Wood Frame
Satin
● Geometric
Holiday Cheer
Striped Diamond
Blast Off
Serendipity
Snowflakes
Steel Pipe
Jaded
Mystical
Teeter Totter
Highlight
Button
Glowing Night

RGB

Figure 22-15: This pop-up list of textures is only the start of the process. You can also create and save your own.

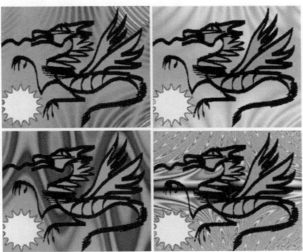

Figure 22-16: There is no limit to the unique backdrops that you can apply to a picture in xRes.

Step #2: Explore the Art Brushes

In addition to the xRes texturizing options, you may also want to explore the oriental art brushes. These are listed under the Japanese brush, and include Bamboo, Sumi, and Rising Sun. Each has a different effect on the way that watercolored blurry edges and textures are applied to a painting. One good way to explore on your own is to use a photograph as copy, trying to emulate the contents in a minimalist fashion. You may even want to redraw your dragon using one of these brushes or a combination of them. xRes also includes a Watercolor brush and its own Calligraphy brush for soft-edged graphic effects.

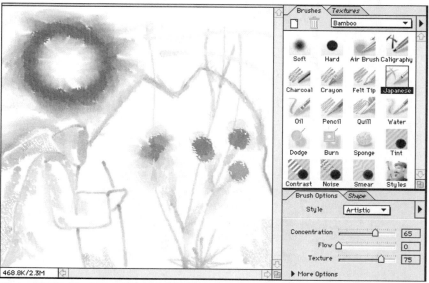

Figure 22-17: The Japanese brushes in xRes are perfect for creating a Zen-like graphic—a much softer look than that usually produced by computer art.

Figure 22-18: You may even want to redraw the dragon using the Japanese brush effects.

Using Extreme 3D

Fabrics have folds and textures of their own. We can design folded fabric objects in Extreme 3D, and apply our dragon texture to them from the Materials browser.

Step #1: Create a Stack of Splined Lines

Go to the top view in Extreme 3D, and create a curved line (use the Spline tool) that has three or four waves in it. Go to the front view and move the line down to the bottom of the page. Create another line and do the same thing, except this time moving it a little higher on the page. Do this until you have seven or eight curved lines.

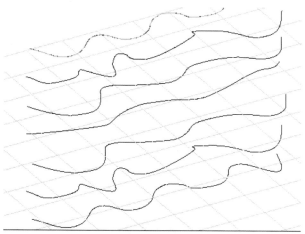

Figure 22-19: Create a stack of splined lines as the first step.

Step #2: Skin the Lines

Click on the Skin tool, and join all of the lines to form a skinned object, the basic 3D fabric.

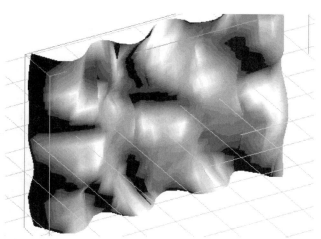

Figure 22-20: The surface is built from the splined curves with the Skin tool.

Step #3: Explore the Material Options

From here on in it's a matter of your exploration. You can assign any material type to the object that you like, as long as you apply the dragon texture map to the Surface tab in the Materials Editor for that material.

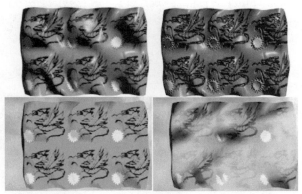

Figure 22-21: Depending upon the types of mapping applied to an object that has a texture applied to it, the looks can range from plastic to silk to carved surrealism and beyond.

Tip

Many different materials in Extreme 3D can accept a texture map, and some accept several types for different kinds of mapping.

Southwestern Mosaic

What are the forms and colors that detail the soul of the Southwestern United States? Southwestern form is reflected in the use of the square and the rectangle more than other forms, which can be seen in the shapes of the Native American living spaces. The color palette of the Southwestern U.S. reflects its geography, geology, and climate—red, orange, yellow, brown, and blue turquoise. Keeping these observations in mind, let's explore the development of graphics that emulate the character of the Southwest in FreeHand, xRes, and Extreme 3D.

Tip

If you prefer to see what these finished graphic elements look like prior to creating them yourself, use the accompanying CD-ROM to load the Mosaics Project and all of the tutorial elements into FreeHand so you can more easily work through this example. You may also find some of the elements in the Parts and Pieces folder.

Using FreeHand

The principal FreeHand tool used in the development of the graphics in this exercise is the Fractalize tool. With it, the designs we're looking for will fall gently into place.

Step #1: Draw Rectangles & Squares

Draw five squarish rectangles stacked on each other, resizing them smaller as you go. Use the Align command or panel to center them on each other horizontally and vertically. From largest to smallest, make their colors turquoise, brown, orange, yellow, and red. At the very top of the stack, place four purple squares at the corners. Select all of the elements and group them. See Figure 22-22 as a reference.

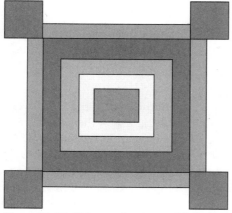

Figure 22-22: This exercise starts with five centered rectangles in a stack, accompanied by four purple squares.

Step #2: Fractalize the Grouping

Go to the Operations panel and click on Fractalize twice, resulting in the illustration displayed in Figure 22-23.

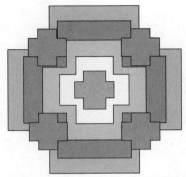

Figure 22-23: The Fractalize tool is used to create this graphic from the previous one.

Step #3: Finish the Tile

Clone the group, and resize the clone so that it's about 25 percent larger than the original. Place the cloned group behind the original group. Draw a yellow rectangular shape that is placed behind all of the others.

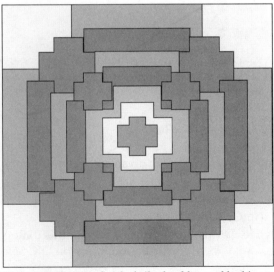

Figure 22-24: Your finished tile should resemble this one.

Step #4: Clone & Align

Use the Clone and Align functions to get a composite graphic that contains four of these tiles grouped together. Save the graphic to disk as a TIFF file, and as a potential element in a FreeHand project.

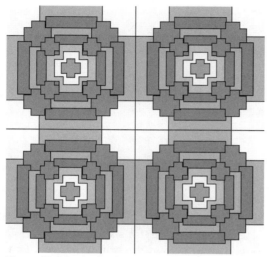

Figure 22-25: The final grouping of mosaic tiles.

Using xRes

The Southwest has an established sacred tradition that centers around sand painting. Here is how to translate your FreeHand graphic into a sand painting graphic.

Step #1: Render the Graphic in xRes

Import your FreeHand mosaic graphic into xRes. You may have to resize it to fit the dimensions of your new page. If so, do so by bringing up the Resize Object dialog.

Step #2: Texturize the Graphic

Next, go to Effects | Stylize | Diffuse, and set the slider of this dialog to 3. The graphic will instantly display the transformation. Click on OK. Select the

Sandpaper texture, and apply it to the yellow areas only (use the Magic Wand tool to select these areas). That's it! Save it to disk as a TIFF for incorporation into a FreeHand project.

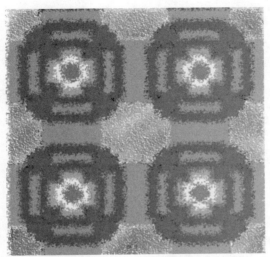

Figure 22-26: The mosaic sand painting graphic rendered in xRes.

Using Extreme 3D

Now for some 3D fun! Since we have both the FreeHand and xRes mosaic tiles saved as TIFF files, let's use Extreme 3D to tile a floor ("ground plane") with them.

Step #1: Render the Mosaic Tiles to the Ground Plane

Draw a large rectangle that will act like a table for the mosaic tiled material. Extrude it so it will accept a texture. Use the Default Mondo Map material for it, and edit it. Under the Clr (Color) tab, load in the Mosaic texture you saved to disk. Click on the Intrinsic Texture Placement tool in the Toolbox, and in the data entry area at the bottom of the screen, adjust the size of the tiling until you get what you want. A good place to start is a size of 50 percent for both the X and Y values.

Figure 22-27: The mosaic tiles are rendered to the plane.

Step #2: Add a Bowl of Oranges

In a 3D scene, it's always best to add addendum objects of interest when possible, so we'll add a bowl of oranges to the table. Create the bowl by lathing a splined shape. Create the oranges from four spheres mapped with the Vinyl-Orange material (set the Jagged Swirls in the material's Edit dialog to 0.9 to give the orange some texture). Map the mosaic tile to the bowl with the Mondo map. Use the views to move all of the elements into place. Place the oranges in the bowl, and the bowl on the table. Lock-link the oranges to the bowl in case you need to move elements later on. Render, and save to disk as a TIFF file for incorporation into a FreeHand project.

Figure 22-28: The finished rendering looks good enough to eat.

Urban Elements

We could choose any number of items to represent the urban environment, but we'll stick to just two: shiny metal/rusty metal and graffiti on a brick wall. The city has a metallic heart. This example will look at a wall and graffiti in FreeHand, and then travel to xRes for shiny metal and Extreme 3D for the rusty metal for texture mapping, and finally suggest that the finished renderings be ported back as a TIFF file for placement in a FreeHand project.

Tip

If you prefer to see what these finished graphic elements look like prior to creating them yourself, use the accompanying CD-ROM to load the Brickwall Project and all of the tutorial elements into FreeHand so you can more easily work through this example. You may also find some of the elements in the Parts and Pieces folder.

Using FreeHand

This exercise will test your capabilities to use both tiled textures and the Rotate tool.

Step #1: Create the Brick Color Swatch

Bring up the Color Mixer and the Fill Inspector. In the Fill Inspector, select Gradient from the list. Create a dark red CMYK color (0, 100, 100, 37) in the Color Mixer palette. Drag and drop a swatch of this color on the top of the black color pot, replacing the black. Place another swatch of the red about one-quarter of the way down on the right side as illustrated.

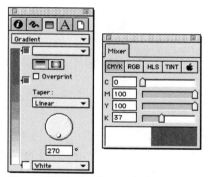

Figure 22-29: Configure the brick color swatch.

Step #2: Create the First Brick

Using the Rectangle tool in the Toolbox, draw your first "brick." It should be one inch wide and one-half inch tall. It will be automatically filled with the red to white gradient from the Fill Inspector. By default, it will have a one point black stroke around it. Go to the Stroke Inspectors, and change the stroke to 1.5 point.

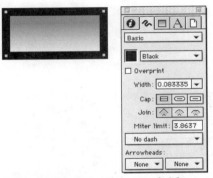

Figure 22-30: Create the parent brick.

Step #3: Create a Brick Group

With the brick still selected, use the Duplicate command to copy the brick in a multiple fashion. You will need eight bricks across and six down, for a total of 48. Place them in a loose configuration as shown.

Bring up the Align panel. Select the top row of bricks by either shift-selecting each brick in the top row in turn or using the Pointer tool to group-select them. In the Align panel, set the horizontal to Align Top and the vertical to Distribute Widths. Click on the Align button. Group the bricks in the top row. Repeat this process for each of the six rows of bricks.

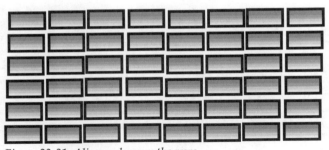

Figure 22-31: Align and group the rows.

Step #4: Make the Grouping Symmetrical

Select all of the bricks. In the Align panel, set the horizontal to Distribute Heights and the vertical to Align Left. Click on Align. You now have a perfectly symmetrical arrangement of bricks.

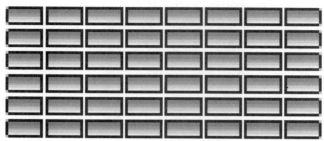

Figure 22-32: The grouping is now symmetrical.

Step #5: Adjust the Groups

Group rows 1, 3, and 5. Group rows 2, 4, and 6. You now have two groupings of bricks. Move the rows 2-4-6 group so that it is centered on the rows 1-3-5 group as shown. Select each group and ungroup it, so that you now have each row grouped by itself. In the Align panel, set the horizontal to Distribute Heights, and the vertical to No Change. Click on Align.

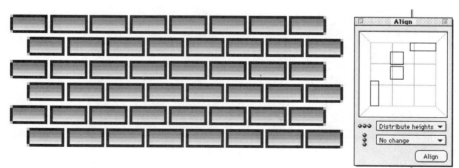

Figure 22-33: The wall looks more natural with a little adjustment.

Step #6: Create the Cutter Shapes

Using the Stroke and Fill Inspectors, set the stroke to None and fill to Basic. Using the Rectangle tool in the Toolbox, draw two blue rectangles as shown. Make sure that they even out the left and right edges of the brick wall by lining up on the bricks.

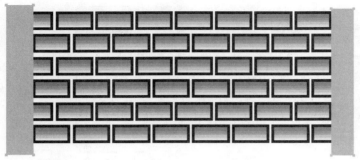

Figure 22-34: The cutter shapes are placed in position.

Step #7: Cut Away the Unwanted Areas

Shift-select each of the six rows of bricks and the left blue rectangle. In the Operations panel, click on Punch to cut away and even up the left side of the bricks. Repeat this process for the right side, using the blue rectangle on the right to punch away the overhang.

Figure 22-35: The wall is evened up with the cutting operation.

Step #8: Create a Believable Perspective

Create a CMYK color in the Color Mixer palette whose settings are 13, 22, 59, 0. Drag and drop this swatch in the swatch area of the Basic Fill Inspector. With the Rectangle tool, draw a rectangle on top of the brick wall that exactly matches the brick wall dimensions. With this new rectangle selected, choose Modify | Arrange | Send To Back to move it behind the brick wall. Group everything into one graphic.

With the brick wall grouped and selected, use the 3D Rotation tool in the Xtra Tools panel to give it some perspective. After clicking on the tool, click inside the brick wall and drag the mouse until the right perspective is achieved.

Figure 22-36: The perspective of the wall is adjusted.

Step #9: Give the Wall Depth

Click on the Pen tool in the Tool panel. Click and release to add the points of a rectangle that defines the depth of the wall. Color the new rectangle with the CMYK settings 13, 22, 59, 29. Group everything as a single graphic. Save the graphic, and open xRes. Import the graphic to a new xRes screen.

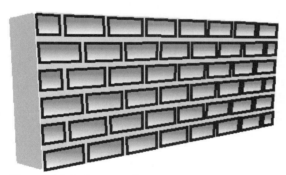

Figure 22-37: The 2D wall now appears with 3D depth.

Using xRes for Graffiti

Now let's add some graffiti.

Step #1: Create the Graffiti

Select New again, and select the Magic Marker pen. Write out a phrase. Use the Magic Wand tool to select only the magic marker text. Copy it to the clipboard, and click on the screen that has the brick wall graphic on it.

Figure 22-38: Write out a phrase with the magic marker pen.

Step #2: Texture the Wall

Select Edit | Paste, and the text will come in on a separate layer, and can be moved around. Select Edit | Duplicate with the text layer still selected, and a clone of the text will appear on its own object layer. Color the top text layer text red, and the text beneath blue. Place the text on position on the wall, with the blue text protruding just a little from the red text.

Select the "mortar" on the wall (use the Wand tool), and use xRes Airbrush to spray a 100 percent Rough texture onto it. Do the same for the "bricks." This gives the mortar and bricks dimension. Select Object | Drop Objects, and the text and wall will be married together. Save out the graphic as a TIFF file for importation into a FreeHand project.

Figure 22-39: The finished graffiti wall.

Using xRes for Metal

The metal look we will work with here emulates the surface of a well oiled machine, and might even suffice as RoboCop's body armor as he cleans up the urban environs. Metal is one of the characteristic looks of urban environments, and can be used to fill a text block heading as well as to act as the material for various graphic elements.

Step #1: Create the Basic Elements

Draw a screw head with a notch in it. Use a textured brush to give it a little character, and place a slight shadow on the lower right side. Duplicate the object so you have a total of eight screws. Each will be on a separate layer.

Open up a separate screen and use the Rectangle Marquee tool to draw a rectangle. Select the Gradient tool, and set it to Jaded/Folds/RGB/Blend in the Gradient Options palette. Hold down the mouse button, and drag the cursor from the upper left to the lower right of the marquee. Copy this filled rectangle to the clipboard. Click on the page with the screw heads on it, and make it active. Select Paste, and the rectangle will come in as a new object layer on this page.

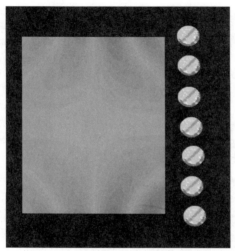

Figure 22-40: The basic elements of our metallic texture are shown here.

Step #2: Designing the Initial Screw-Plate

Move the rectangular plate to the bottom of the stack in the Object Layers palette. Place the screws in position. A little misalignment is actually good here, as it will add more viewer interest later. Drop all of the objects so you have just one layer. Crop out everything but the plate with the screws. Save this graphic as a TIFF file and close all the windows.

Figure 22-41: The finished basic screw-plate.

Step #3: Configure the Arrangement

Configure a new page, and import the screw-plate about a dozen times. Resize some smaller, rotate some, and then go about the challenging task of making an interesting composition of the elements you have. You may have to move some of them to new positions in the object layer stack to achieve what you want. Think of this as a 2D Rubik's Cube. When you are finished, save the results to disk as a TIFF file. You can use this graphic as a background for a FreeHand page, or as a material texture in Extreme 3D.

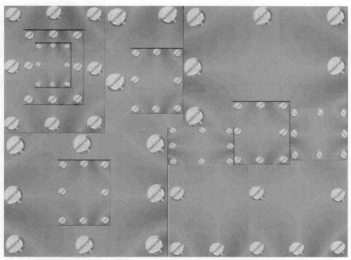

Figure 22-42: A composition consisting of a collection of screw-plates, grouped and saved as a separate texture from xRes.

Figure 22-43: Used in Extreme 3D as a material texture, the screw-plates emulate the mechanistic aspects of urban life.

Holiday Graphics

Whether it's the newspaper flyer that advertises a Thanksgiving Day sale, a Mother's Day card that arrives from across the country, or a Web page devoted to researching the real meaning of holiday icons, visuals play an important part in displaying the symbols and signs that mark the religious and secular holidays. Designers are aware that much of their work centers upon these times of year, as do the creative challenges needing to be solved. The FreeHand creative suite of applications can be a big help in crafting holiday messages in unique ways.

Tip

If you prefer to see what these finished graphic elements look like prior to creating them yourself, use the accompanying CD-ROM to load the Pumpkin Project and all of the tutorial elements into FreeHand so you can more easily work through this example. You may also find some of the elements in the Parts and Pieces folder.

Using FreeHand

Halloween is a great time for graphic designers and desktop publishing professionals. It is full of identifiable visual symbols that play a part in plays at the local high school, book illustrations, masked gatherings, and even product displays. The dominant visual symbol of Halloween is the carved pumpkin. Just like cutting a real pumpkin, you can use FreeHand's cutting tools to carve your digital artwork.

Step #1: Create the Initial Pattern

Create a pattern of 18 vertical rectangles, alternating between deep CMYK orange (0, 68, 100, 0) and a lighter orange (0, 18, 100, 0). Do not group the bars. See Figure 22-44.

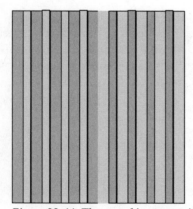

Figure 22-44: The pumpkin starts with this pattern.

Step #2: Use the Fisheye Lens Tool

Click on the Fisheye Lens tool to activate it, and click and drag the mouse to draw an oval shape inside the rectangular vertical stripes. Release the mouse button and the Fisheye Lens tool does its work. Group all of the bars that make up the pumpkin.

Figure 22-45: Use the Fisheye Lens tool to create the pumpkin's 3D shape.

Step #3: Create the Cutter Shape

Use the Polyline tool to draw a cutter shape around the pumpkin. You may want to do this in two segments. If so, do not use the Group command to join the segments, as a grouped object cannot cut another one. Instead, use the Union command from the Operations panel.

Figure 22-46: The cutter is in place.

Step #4: Cut the Shape Out

Select the background bar group, and then Shift-select the cutter shape. Click on the Punch command in the Operators panel and the cutter does its job. You now have a pumpkin shape and colored graphic. Use the Polyline tool to create black-filled eyes, nose, and mouth shapes, and put them in place on the pumpkin.

Figure 22-47: The facial parts are in place, giving the Great Pumpkin a personality of its own.

Step #5: Finish & Place the Elements

Use the Polyline tool to draw a filled stem on the head and place the eyeballs where they belong. Group everything and save to disk as a resource for a future FreeHand Halloween project. As an option, you can export this drawing to xRes and give it some gradient fills to emphasize its 3D appearance.

Figure 22-48: The finished Great Pumpkin as a FreeHand drawing.

Using xRes

St. Valentine's Day is equated with softer, more muted, graphics, a look that is seldom identified with computer output by the public. For either commercial illustration purposes or your own expression of caring for a loved one, you may want to use FreeHand to produce a card for this occasion. FreeHand is great when it comes to setting the needed type for an enterprise like this, but xRes is better when it comes to developing a muted electronic painting to accompany the text. Art developed in xRes can easily find its way back to a FreeHand page as a saved graphic.

Step #1: Paint Half of a Heart Shape

In xRes, select New, and create a page of 300 x 300 pixels at 300 dots per inch (dpi). Make the background a deep red. Select the Oil Painting brush, and set its shape to a size of 5 and its soft edge to 65. The brush will draw multiple lines. Draw half of a heart shape on the left edge of your workspace in a CMYK pink (0, 50, 0, 0).

Figure 22-49: Half of a stylized heart is drawn in the workspace.

Step #2: Create Three Centered Heart Shapes

Use the Wand tool to select the red backdrop, and then invert the selection so only the graphic has a marquee around it. Copy and paste the graphic. The pasted copy will be on its own object layer. Flip the cloned object horizontally, and move the cloned object until it forms a symmetrical shape with the original. Drop the object so that the second object layer is removed.

Use the Wand tool and invert the selection again, so that now the completed heart has a marquee around it. Copy and paste it, and resize the copy to about two-thirds the size of the original. Do this one more time, resizing the second copy to half. The result should be three centered heart graphics as illustrated in Figure 22-50.

Figure 22-50: The finished heart graphic has three centered heart shapes.

Step #3: Add a Muted Color Backdrop

Select just the heart shape with the Wand tool. Compose your own gradient made up of about eight striations of pink and light blue, and call it "My Heart." Save it. Set the Fill Inspector's gradient options to read My Heart, Satin, CMYK, and ADD. With the Gradient tool, drag the mouse over the graphic twice, from left bottom to right top. The resulting graphic should resemble something like that in Figure 22-51.

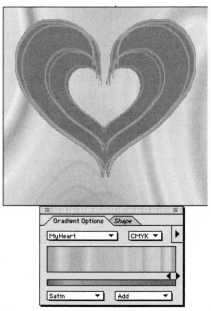

Figure 22-51: The heart shape with the gradient backdrop.

Step #4: Add the Jewel

As a final touch, we will add a jewel to the center of the heart shapes. Draw a circular marquee at the center of the composition. Select the Effects | KPTools 3 | Spheroid Designer. Select the Red Plasma sphere, and click on the check mark. Your jeweled heart can be saved out and imported to a FreeHand composition, where you can add whatever text you feel is appropriate.

Figure 22-52: The jeweled heart.

Using Extreme 3D

The winter solstice, and all of the worldwide celebrations that mark it, is the time that the world turns again towards light. The candle, lamp, and light bulb all symbolize this event. But there is little reverence for the light bulb and the non-electric lamp has been superseded as both a symbol and a technology. The candle, however, even after thousands of years of history, magically maintains its symbolic power. As such, it is still used to denote both hope and mystery for a wide variety of occasions. The candle remains a powerful visual symbol, and a graphical component whose use will never be exhausted. Extreme 3D is the perfect environment in which to create a candle.

Step #1: Create the Candle

We'll model a candle first, and then some supporting cast members. For the candle, simply use the Lathing tool to rotate a vertically oriented rectangle around its Y axis to start.

Remember that a candle is made of wax, and wax, especially when it gets hot, does not maintain its even symmetrical shape. In order to emulate this characteristic attribute of wax, we will have to deform the candle object a little. Select the object, and then open its geometry. Now simplify its geometry. You are presented with dozens of control points that can be used to warp and resculpt the candle object. Explore their movement in all views, and when satisfied that the candle looks sufficiently "wax melted," select Object I Close the geometry.

Assign the default Gray Plastic material to the candle, adding a light yellow-green color and a light blue specular highlight. Move the Transparency slider in the Edit material dialog about one-fifth of the way to the right to give it some translucency.

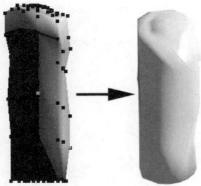

Figure 22-53: Move the control points on the open geometry of the candle to reshape it to look more waxy.

Step #2: Add the Wick, Flame & Smoke

For the flame, draw a curvy profile and use the lathe function to sculpt it in 3D. Color it orange, and give it a 20 percent transparency. Flames have smoke, and Extreme 3D offers you smoke materials in the Presets folder. Load the Smoke materials, and select the Smoke Wisp material. Sculpt a smoke object with a primitive cone. Turn it upside down, and open its geometry to give it some random curviness. Set it in place on the flame. Lock-link everything to the candle at this point.

Figure 22-54: Wick, flame, and smoke are added to the candle.

Step #3: Add the Candle Holder

Now for a candle holder. Draw a profile of the bowl of the holder, using the Spline tool in the front view. Click on the Lathe tool, select a vertical axis, and generate the bowl. For the handle, draw a curvy splined path using your imagination. Draw a small circle to use as the shape, and select the Sweep tool to pull the circle along the path. Add any additional ornaments as you desire. Lock-link the handle to the bowl.

Figure 22-55: The finished candle holder with a brass material assigned to it.

Step #4: Finish & Render the Candle & Holder

Put the candle in the holder, and double-check the alignment from all views. Render as you please from as many angles as you like. Import the graphic to a FreeHand composition the next time you need to use a candle as an ornament or an important design element on a page.

Figure 22-56: The candle and the holder can be seen from different vantage points.

Moving On

In this chapter, we have learned to create diverse ornamental graphics, including patriotic and oriental fabric looks, native Southwestern designs, urban elements, and a 3D holiday candle. The next chapter will present nature at her best, with the creation of fire, water, and earth graphics.

23

Creating Natural Elements

Computer graphics was known early on as a medium in which "hard" mechanical art could be accomplished with ease. Reflective chrome spheres set over a checkerboard plane, fine-edged machine surfaces remaining believable in close-up views, and other examples used computer graphics as a medium of choice to emulate the human-constructed environment. But linear, hard-edged reality is only one facet of the world we live in, and a minor one at that. Despite the march of technology, we are still immersed in the world of curves and chaos, of natural symmetries that elude the mechanistic view of life. So to become more accepted as a real artist's medium, computer graphics have been forced to evolve in softer and gentler directions, zeroing in upon hazier realities, like the world of the leaf, the cloud, and the ever-changing waters.

Mandelbrot's theories of fractal dimensions and chaotic reality brought us a huge step closer to this reality. The concepts of fractals and chaos quickly moved computer graphics away from the dominance of the static line and toward the direction of the chaotic curve.

Although mathematically chaos and fractal dimensions concern themselves with somewhat different descriptions of how the world works, we can risk combining both theories in a unified whole. This allows for a short and under-standable description of what fractal dimensions add to our perception of the "real" world, and how that is transferred to more believable computer graphics. The chaotic part of the process of perceiving informs us (as if we didn't know it intuitively) that what makes a subject believable when we perceive it is its chaotic elements, its variance from pure mechanical symmetry. For instance, if you render a ruffled sheet on a bed, it will seem more "real" than a perfect rectangle with no folds. We witness the real world as dented, crumpled, and bruised, and all of that has to be taken into consideration when we want to develop "believable" computer graphics.

The simplest way to describe fractals is that they are *self-replicating forms*. For example, as we look at a leaf on a tree, and as we come closer to the leaf, the patterns of the leaf start to resemble the patterns of the overall tree itself. Coming even closer with a microscope reveals that patterns in the leaf at microscopic levels resemble the patterns of the whole leaf. This awareness has had a major effect upon 2D and 3D computer graphics, allowing programmers to mathematically describe small fractal patterns that can than be used to produce realistic pictures of the larger forms of the natural world, like trees and mountains. This chapter deals with both chaos and fractals as devices for creating natural elements. Knowing how to use chaos, or randomness, in a design makes the art seem more connected to nature. In a sense, to create natural elements, you have to go beyond the very thing computer art is so good at, which is being so coldly exacting and symmetrically perfect.

Earth & Stone

Your FreeHand text may need either a background to rest on, or a supplemental graphic or ornament to point out an important phrase. Earth and Stone graphics can add observer interest and provide needed elements in an illustration. Variations of these elements can be created in FreeHand, xRes, and Extreme 3D.

Tip

Use the accompanying CD-ROM to load the RckScn.FH7 Project and all of the tutorial elements into FreeHand so you can more easily work through this example. You may also find some of the elements in the Parts and Pieces folder.

Using FreeHand

The primary tools that must be mastered in order to create the natural effects in FreeHand include Fisheye Lens, Smudge, and Roughen in the Xtra Tools palette, and Fractalize in the Operations palette. Other tools will be accessed depending upon the desired effect, but these are the main ones.

Step #1: Create a Loose Shape

Use the Bezier Pen tool to create a randomly curved closed shape. Fill it with a 30 percent CMYK black (0, 0, 0, 30). Set the stroke to None. We will transform this shape into a rock.

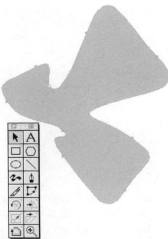

Figure 23-1: A gray, curved, closed shape is the first element in the design.

Step #2: Warp & Clone the Shape

With the shape selected, click on the Fractalize operator. This reshapes the selection while adding points to it. Adjust the points in any manner you desire, trying to add more randomness to the shape. Use the Fisheye Lens to make the shape more oval. Clone the resulting shape twice. Use CMYK gray fills of 30 percent, 50 percent, and 75 percent on the three shapes. Set their strokes to None.

Figure 23-2: Now we have three similar shapes filled with different grays.

Step #3: Create a Rock Composition

Rotate two of the shapes so they are different from each other, and group them. This creates one "rock." Now clone the rock several times and resize the clones randomly. Place the resized shapes in a composition that seems interesting to you, and group it.

Figure 23-3: The finished rock grouping.

Step #4: Create a Tree

Double-click the FreeHand tool to customize the settings. Select Calligraphic Pen, Tight Fit, Variable Width (5 to 9), and an angle of 135 degrees. Draw a loose tree form.

Figure 23-4: The basic tree shape is drawn.

Step #5: Add Complexity to the Tree Shape

Clone the tree form twice, and reduce the size of the clones to about half. Rotate each of them in a different direction, and place them as branches on the main tree. This is how to use fractal theory as a part of your drawing. Group the elements of the tree into one. Place the tree behind the rock, and group the composition.

Figure 23-5: Fractal branches are added to complete the tree.

Step #6: Add Grass & a Moon

Use the Calligraphic Pen with the same settings, and at a 15 percent gray fill with a one point black stroke, to add some grass in the foreground. Make it random and wispy in clumps. Use the Oval tool to draw a circular moon or sun behind the tree, with no fill and a one point black stroke. Group everything. As one last touch, add an oval under the base of the composition. Give it a 15 percent gray and no stroke. The vignette is complete, and can be used as a spot drawing as needed. You can always color these parts differently, though this composition works well as grayscale art, resembling a Zen landscape painting.

Figure 23-6: The finished FreeHand composition.

Using xRes

The textured fills in xRes can be used to create a similar theme, but with a very different look. xRes offers its natural textures library, and the ability to sharpen bitmaps with Luminance controls.

Step #1: Create Five Rocks

Use the Lasso tool to draw a rock outline in the workspace. Click on the Airbrush, and select the Textured option. Set its Concentration and Flow to 35 percent, and set the Texture slider to 100 percent. Choose a texture that appeals to you, and spray it into the marquee. Choose another texture and spray it, giving the shape two blended textures. Sharpen the Luminosity of the textured graphic to a setting of 5, giving the graphics a definite pen and ink look (Effects | Sharpen | Luminosity). Export this shape to a file as a TIFF. Repeat this process until you have five separate rocks on file.

Figure 23-7: Five rock shapes are painted and textured.

Step #2: Compose the Rocks

Open each of the rocks separately in its own window (use "Open" and not "Import"). Open a new window that is large enough to hold the finished composition, about ten times the size of the largest rock. One by one, use the Wand tool to select only the rock and not its background. Copy it to the clipboard, and use the Paste command to place it within the new blank area. It will come in on a separate object layer. Do this with all five rocks.

Once all of the rocks are in the new graphic area on their own layers, you can move each around separately. Before moving any of them, add a bit of definition to their edges with a black Airbrush. If you don't do this, they will all blend into one blob when layered against each other. All you need is a thin black outline around each. Since each appears on its own object layer, you can move the layers under or on top of each other in the Object Layers palette. Explore their relationship with each other until you achieve an interesting composition. Drop all of the layers into one, and save this out as a new graphic.

Figure 23-8: The completed composition of textured rocks.

Step #3: Create a Tree

On a new page, 400 x 400 pixels, use the Calligraphy Brush with the Gift Wrap option to draw a simple tree shape. Use the Styles Brush with the Hav option to spray leaves on it. Save out the tree as a separate graphic.

Figure 23-9: The completed tree is painted using the Calligraphy/Gift Wrap Brush and the Styles/Hav Brush.

Step #4: Combine the Rocks & the Tree

Leave the tree graphic on the screen and open the rocks graphic. Use the Magic to select the backdrop, and then invert the selection so only the rocks are selected. Copy them to the clipboard, and paste them into the tree painting. Move them into position where they appear best, and drop the rocks graphic on the tree page. You should have something similar to the graphic illustrated in Figure 23-10.

Figure 23-10: The rocks and the tree are in place.

Step #5: Add the Orb

Use a new document (400 x 400 pixels) to paint a 15 percent gray circle in the upper left corner of the page. Go back to the tree and rocks composition, and select only the graphic (Wand and then Invert). Copy it, and paste it as a separate object layer over the orb. Move it until satisfied, and then drop it into place. Congratulations! Your xRes rendition of the theme is complete, and can be imported into FreeHand as a spot graphic.

Figure 23-11: The finished composition.

Using Extreme 3D

The same theme carried out in Extreme 3D is going to have a very different look. Remember that 3D graphics are more hard edged by nature than vector or bitmap 2D graphics. There are times when this may matter for the overall FreeHand page you are trying to create. Trees created in a 3D application by hand are usually much more stylized, or symbolic, in character than those created in vector or bitmap applications. This tree will be more mystical, like the tree that held the golden apples of Greek myth.

Step #1: Create the Main Tree Form

Draw a shape in the Top view. It can be any shape you like, as long as it is closed. Create five duplicates of the shape, sized from large to small. Place them in a line so that a curve is formed in the Front view. Use the Skin tool to connect them so they form a 3D object.

Figure 23-12: A series of 2D shapes is transformed into a 3D object with the Skin tool.

Step #2: Duplicate the Shape & Add Complexity

Duplicate the shape three times. Resize the duplicated forms to 70 percent, 50 percent, and 20 percent, and combine them with the original shape to form a singular object as illustrated. Duplicate the smaller shapes twice more, and construct a tree sculpture that you find interesting, perhaps resembling the one illustrated in Figure 23-13. Lock-link the smaller shapes to the larger one. Use a wood material from the Wood Presets to texture the whole graphic.

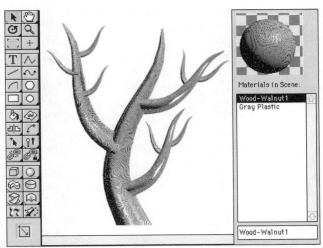

Figure 23-13: The basic shape is duplicated and a more complex shape is formed.

Step #3: Add a Chaotic Element

Duplicate the entire object. Rotate the duplicated object so that it looks different than its parent, and lock-link it to the original object.

Figure 23-14: The tree now has twice the breadth, and needs a trunk to be complete.

Step #4: Add the Trunk

Use the Spline tool to add a shape from the Top view that will be used to skin the trunk. The Top view is useful, because you can size the shape according to your view of the tree (in Orthographic perspective). Go to the Front view, and duplicate the 2D trunk profile three times. Spread these profiles out, enlarging them a little as they move downward. Use the Skin tool to create the trunk. Lock-link both main branches to the trunk.

Figure 23-15: The trunk is added to the tree. The black stripe is put there on purpose; it represents a part of the tree that has an elongated crevice for chaotic interest.

Step #5: Add the Golden Apples

Now we'll add some unusual fruit to the tree. Load in the Gold materials from the Presets folder, and select the Gold-Jagged listing and add it to the list on the left (Materials in Scene). Create a small sphere, and this material is applied to it. Place the gold spheres randomly as fruit on the tree.

Figure 23-16: The tree blossoms with golden fruit.

Step #6: Add the Rocks

Since gold is the theme of this composition, let's add gold rocks to the base of the tree. Add a sphere to the scene. Open its geometry, and simplify it. Pull on the Bezier control handles to reshape it and make it more irregular. Close its geometry, and duplicate a few more resized and rotated clones, placing them at the base of the tree in a random composition. Add the Gold striped material to the rocks.

Figure 23-17: The rocks add more stability to the bottom of the graphic.

Step #7: Add Some Leaves

A tree needs leaves during the time its fruit is ripening, even when that fruit is golden apples. Click on the Spline tool and draw the outline for a clump of leaves, and give it a little depth with the Extrusion tool so it will accept a texture. For a texture, bring the Mondo Map to the list on the left, and click on Edit to customize it. Set the color to a deep green, the Roughness texture to the Clouds map (and the slider all the way to the right), and the Bump texture also to the Clouds map (with the slider also set all the way to the right). Accept the changes, and apply this map to your extruded leaf object. Duplicate the leaf object at various places on the tree. The mystical tree of golden apples is complete. Save it to disk for incorporation into a FreeHand project.

Figure 23-18: The tree is completed with the addition of foliage.

Clouds & Fog

If we define chaos as something that obstructs clarity and symmetry, then fog is an agent of chaos. Fog and other kinds of haze obscure clear vision, and this adds mystery and suspicion to what we see. Clouds are a perfect example of fractals, because they can be generated by duplicating one shape and overlaying the clones in a randomized fashion.

Tip

Use the accompanying CD-ROM to load the Cloudz.FH7 Project and all of the tutorial elements into FreeHand so you can more easily work through this example. You may also find some of the elements in the Parts and Pieces folder.

Using FreeHand

Blending and transparency applications form the core of the FreeHand tools used to accomplish this exercise.

Step #1: Create the Background

Draw a rectangle that fills the FreeHand workspace. Fill it with a linear gradient that ranges from light CMYK blue at the top (15, 0, 0, 0) to white at the bottom.

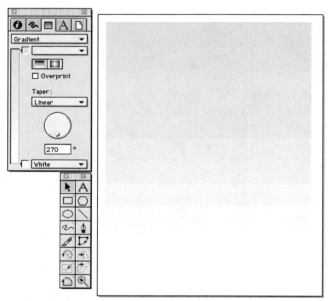

Figure 23-19: Create the background first, and fill it with a blue to white gradient.

Step #2: Draw a Cloud

Use the FreeHand tool to draw a closed, billowy cloud shape at the top of the screen. Give it a white fill and set the stroke to None. Clone this shape, and enlarge the clone so it is about 30 percent larger than the original. Move the larger shape in back of the original shape (Modify I Arrange I Move Backward). Set the fill color of the larger shape to the same CMYK blue as the background (15, 0, 0, 0). Click on the original white cloud shape, and Shift-click on the larger blue cloud shape. With both selected, click on the Blend tool. You should see a cloud whose edges fade into the background.

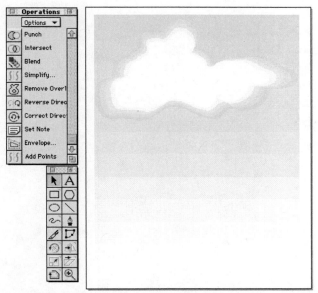

Figure 23-20: The finished cloud fades into the haze of the background.

Step #3: Create More Clouds

Select the blended cloud, and use the Clone command (Edit I Clone) to create three more clouds. Resize each of them 50 percent smaller, and flip one horizontally. Now you can place them in a grouped composition.

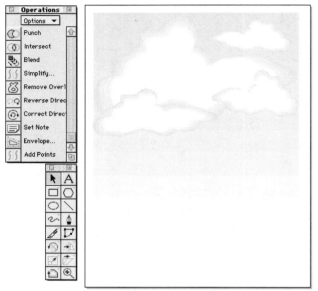

Figure 23-21: The clouds are cloned and set in a new relationship.

Step #4: Add the Sun

Create a circular sun about one-third the width of the background. Set its fill color to CMYK red (0, 100, 100, 0), and its stroke to None. Click on the original cloud shape, which is now grouped because it has been blended. Ungroup it. Click on the topmost element in the blended stack (the white cloud) and move it to the front of everything (Modify | Arrange | Bring to Front). Place the red sun behind the white cloud element, which should happen by itself once you move the sun into place.

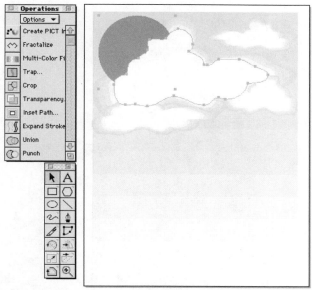

Figure 23-22: The red sun is moved into place behind the front ungrouped cloud.

Step #5: Create a Transparent Cloud Effect

Select the front white cloud in the ungrouped stack, and Shift-click on the sun object. Click on the Transparency tool in the Operations palette to display its settings dialog. Set the slider to 5, and then click on OK to apply the settings. A hazy outline of the sun can be seen through the cloud.

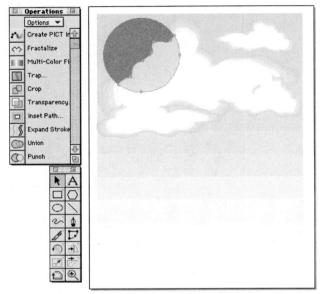

Figure 23-23: The sun appears behind the transparent cloud.

Step #6: Shade the Effect

Click on the transparent region you just created. As you can see, it is a separate object. Clone it, and move the cloned copy in the direction of the sun, so that the outermost control points of the cloned shape match up with the sun's diameter. Move this shape back one level in the stack (Modify I Arrange I Move Backward). Color this cloned shape the same red as the sun, with stroke set to None. Select the original transparent shape and the new red cloned shape, and blend them. Your FreeHand cloud graphic is finished.

Figure 23-24: The finished graphic displays the cloud fading into the sun shape.

Using xRes

xRes allows you to place one graphic over another and apply a foggy effect to the bottom graphic by adjusting the transparency/opaqueness of the top graphic.

Step #1: Create the Gradient Art

In the Gradient Options palette set the options to Blue Range gradient from the list, Folds, CMYK, and Blend. Create a new document 400 x 400 pixels in size. With the Gradient tool, click and drag from the center of the page diagonally to the right. The folded blue range gradient is rendered. Select everything, and copy the graphic to the clipboard.

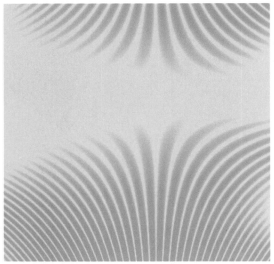

Figure 23-25: The blue range gradient is rendered to the page.

Step #2: Create an Object Stack

Open your favorite bitmap graphic or picture. Resize it so that it can be covered by the gradient you just created. Select Edit | Paste, which pastes the gradient over the graphic you just opened as a separate layer.

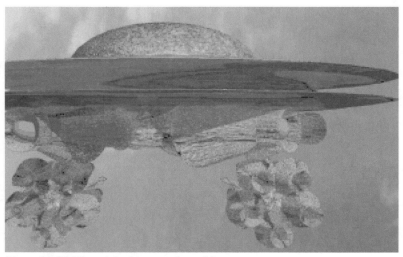

Figure 23-26: The original imported graphic.

Under the Objects palette is a slider that allows you to adjust the transparency of the selected object layer. Move this slider to the left until you reach a transparency level that shows your underlying graphic, but also displays the gradient features. Thirty-five percent is a good place to start from. Drop the object layer into place, and save the combined graphic for later incorporation into a FreeHand project.

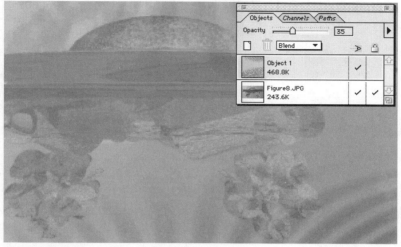

Figure 23-27: The gradient applied as a transparent layer to the imported graphic.

Using Extreme 3D

Creating a cloud background for a rendering in Extreme 3D is a snap. Just choose Render | Set Background. Locate any saved file you may have that displays a cloudy backdrop and select it. When the rendering commences, your clouds will be in place.

Step #1: Place Objects at Different Screen Depths

Use the Text tool to create a text block that reads "Foggy." Go to the Top view and duplicate it twice, moving each copy about halfway further back from the Camera view (move the duplicates towards the top of the Top View screen). Return to the Front view, and move the smallest (the farthest away duplicate) to the bottom of the screen, and move the next-largest duplicate to the middle of the screen. Apply a marble material to all of the text blocks, and render the picture. Notice that there is no discernible difference in the clarity of focus of these images, except that the farther away a text block is, the more its texture closes up.

Figure 23-28: The original rendering of the 3D composition shows everything in sharp focus. The smallest graphic is the farthest from the camera.

Step #2: Apply Global Fog

Using the Render | Global Effects dialog, you can switch on Fog. You can colorize the fog and set its depth. Select a white to black coloring, and leave the default value set for depth. Close the dialog, and re-render the graphic. Notice that now the text block farthest from the camera is muted most by the fog. If moved further back yet it would almost disappear.

Figure 23-29: The fog effect is applied to the graphic.

Water

Water is chaos. Water always breaks our expectations as to how it "should" look, and presents us with a mystery. It changes shape according to the wind, and sometimes contains all of the colors of the rainbow because of refraction. For this reason, water has always been a favorite subject of artists working in any medium.

Tip

Use the accompanying CD-ROM to load the Fish1.FH7 Project and all of the tutorial elements into FreeHand so you can more easily work through this example. You may also find some of the elements in the Parts and Pieces folder.

Using FreeHand

Water art can be developed in a realistic or stylized manner in FreeHand. In this exercise, we'll work for a stylized graphic, while making extensive use of the Blend tool.

Step #1: Create the Basic Waves

Use the Ellipse tool to place an elongated oval on the screen, longer than it is wide. Click on the Add Points tool in the Operations palette three times. The control points on an oval allow for curve shaping with Bezier curve handles, so smooth graphics result. Reshape the oval so that a silhouette of waves results at the top (refer to Figure 23-30). Delete the points at the bottom of the oval by selecting them and pressing the Delete key, resulting in a linear base for this form. Give the wave shape a one point black stroke and a CMYK light blue fill (20, 0, 0, 0).

Figure 23-30: The basic shape that we begin with results from the manipulation of an oval.

Step #2: Complete the Wave Form

Clone the wave shape, and use a dark turquoise CMYK color to fill the clone (40, 0, 40, 30). Move the clone to the left of the original shape and down, and elongate it horizontally about 20 percent (use the Resizing tool in the Toolbox). Select both shapes and blend them. Draw a rectangle across the bottom of the wave graphic to even it up, fill the rectangle with white, and remove its stroke. Group the rectangle with the wave graphic.

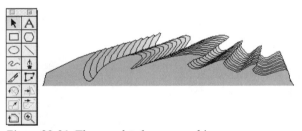

Figure 23-31: The completed wave graphic.

Step #3: Create a Gradient Backdrop

Create a rectangular backdrop for the waves. Fill it with a linear gradient that ranges from a CMYK blue at the top (100, 0, 0, 70) to a CMYK purple haze at the bottom (40, 70, 0, 0). Do not group the waves and backdrop.

Figure 23-32: The gradient rectangle is placed in back of the waves.

Step #4: Create a Fish

Use the FreeHand tool to draw the outline of a fish. Use your imagination, and set its fill color as you like, though it should stand out against the gradient backdrop you just created.

Figure 23-33: The fish.

Step #5: Multiply & Place the Fish

Resize the fish so four will fit against the backdrop and the waves. Clone it so you have a total of four. The idea is to arrange the fish in a semi-circle, with one emerging from behind the waves, while the last one reenters the water. To do this, you will need to rotate each of them to fit this choreography. The fish should be placed on top of the backdrop, but behind the waves. Use the Modify | Arrange controls to accomplish this. When you are finished, everything should be grouped and saved to disk for later use in a FreeHand project you might have in mind.

Figure 23-34: The finished graphic.

Using xRes

When it comes to applying special effects, color gradient fills, and textures in bitmap art, xRes offers a wealth of exquisite tools. In the next project, we will make special use of the gradient fill and texturizing options.

Step #1: Create the Pond

Create a new document, 400 x 400 pixels in size. Place a rectangular marquee at the bottom of the workspace, covering the bottom 40 percent of the space. Click on the Gradient tool. In its settings dialog under the Gradient Options palette, adjust the settings to the Cobalt Blue gradient, Ellipse, CMYK, and Blend. Go to the rectangular marquee, and use the Gradient tool to paint an ellipse (click and drag with the mouse) that is fairly centered within the selection rectangle.

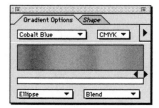

Figure 23-35: The first ripple is painted on the pond.

Step #2: Add More Ripples

Change the Blend setting in the Gradient Options palette from Blend to Maximum, and paint additional ripples in the marquee space.

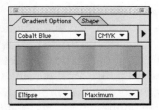

Figure 23-36: Additional ripples are added over the first one.

Step #3: Create the Sky

Choose Select | Inverse to select the area of the graphic not covered by the pond. In the Gradient Options palette, select the Sunrise gradient, Line, CMYK, and Blend. Click and drag the Gradient tool in the blank area from bottom to top to paint in a sunrise sky.

Figure 23-37: The sky backdrop is added to the scene.

Step #4: Add Elements to the Shoreline

Deselect the marquee. Using the Lasso tool, draw a silhouette that represents rocks and trees on the shoreline. Click on the Brush tool, and select the Textured and Airbrush. Set the controls for the Airbrush to a Concentration of 75 percent, a Flow of 75 percent, and a Texture of 50 percent. Choose the Rough texture from the Texture Types palette. Use the Airbrush to spray the texture within the selection, but leave some non-textured areas at the bottom. Work to leave incomplete areas at different parts of the painting, to emulate mist. Refer to Figure 23-38.

Figure 23-38: Silhouette of shoreline elements begins to take shape with the textured Airbrush.

Step #5: Add the Final Backdrop Elements

Invert the selection (Select | Inverse). Set the Airbrush controls at Concentration of 30 percent, Flow of 30 percent, and Texture of 40 percent. Lightly spray the background in back of the tree backdrop you just created. Allow it to be a little wispy. Deselect everything, and use a Smear brush with a Concentration and Flow of 100 percent (Texture set to 0 percent) to smear the places where the water meets the land. Add an orange sun to the sky. The painting is finished. Save it to a file for use as part of a FreeHand project.

Figure 23-39: The final painting is rendered.

Step #6: Darken the Graphic

If you want the entire graphic to be darkened, as if the morning hadn't broken yet, simply move the slider under the Object palette to the left. Since everything in the painting is on one object layer, the slider acts to darken the entire graphic.

Figure 23-40: A darkened version of the same painting can be generated with the slider in the Objects tab dialog.

Using Extreme 3D

Water effects in Extreme 3D can be developed with the assistance of environmental maps. Environmental maps can help create realistic reflections that reinforce our belief that we are looking at a liquid.

Step #1: Create a Faucet From 2D Elements

Select View I Orthographic perspective. Draw a series of ten circles, and rotate them in the Front view as shown in Figure 23-41. Draw a large hexagon, and move it as shown in Figure 23-42.

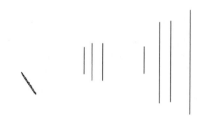

Figure 23-41: This is the Front view, showing the placement of the circles and the hexagon.

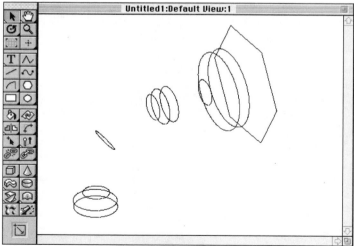

Figure 23-42: In this ¾ view, the arrangement of the 2D elements is clearer.

Step #2: Skin & Texturize the 2D Shapes

Use the Skin tool to connect the 2D shapes, and to render the resulting object in 3D. Import the Default-Chrome and Glass material to the Materials in Scene list on the left of the Materials browser, and open its Edit dialog. Under the Surface tab, select the Clouds Environment map, and set the Chrome Specular highlight to a deep yellow. Click on OK to accept the changes. Assign this material to the faucet, and do a test render.

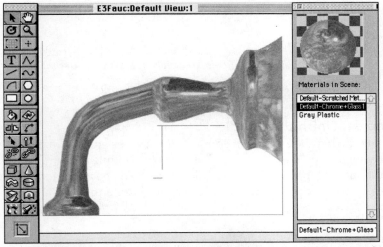

Figure 23-43: The faucet is shaped with the Skin tool, and a Chrome material is applied to it.

Step #3: Design & Render the Faucet Handle

Use the Oval tool to create two ovals to be used as the central part of the faucet handle, and skin the shapes to produce a 3D tube. Draw the handle profile with the Spline tool, and lathe it to complete one handle. Add a textured sphere as a knob, and use your own selection of material to texture it. Lock-link the ball to the handle.

Figure 23-44: The handle profile after it has been lathed, with the attached knob. The tube is to the right.

Step #4: Finish the Handle

Rotate the handle and attached knob -90 degrees on the Z-axis. Embed it partway in the tube. Mirror the handle so its double appears on the other side of the tube. Duplicate the knob, and place the clone at the top of the tube. Lock-link every part of the handle. Render it for a preview.

Figure 23-45: The completed handle, ready to be attached to the faucet.

Step #5: Attach the Handle to the Faucet

Move the handle into place on the faucet, and do a preview render to make sure everything is as you want it. When satisfied, lock-link the handle to the main faucet body.

Figure 23-46: The finished faucet.

Step #6: Render Your Environment Map

Select a background from your files, and import it into the scene (Render | Set Background). Do a final rendering with the background in place. Export the graphic to xRes, and crop the picture so that the faucet is maximized in size against the background. Save this graphic with a unique name.

Figure 23-47: The faucet graphic.

Step #7: Create the Water Drop & Apply the Environment Map

Place a sphere in the window. Open and simplify its geometry, so that you have control points and Bezier handles to manipulate. Pull up on the top control point so that the sphere becomes a teardrop. Close the geometry, and place the tip of the teardrop in the faucet's opening. Select another Chrome and Glass material, bringing it over to the list on the left of the Materials palette. Edit it, selecting Chrome and Glass as the texture type. Use the snapshot of the faucet and sky you saved in Step 6 as its Environment map. Close the Materials editor, and apply this new material to your teardrop. Render the graphic to file as a resource for a FreeHand project.

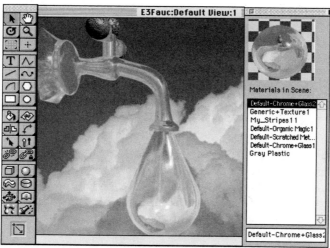

Figure 23-48: The finished graphic shows the drop of reflective water coming from the faucet. You can view this graphic from any angle and render it for an optional FreeHand resource element.

Tip

> *Extreme 3D lists three Water Material types in the Presets folder that can be brought into your project: Pool, Lake, and Ocean. These are all similar except that they address color and bump mapping in different ways to emulate the type of water indicated.*

Step #8: Use Preset Alternatives

Draw a rectangle and give it a little extrusion depth so that it will accept a material texture. Embed an object of your choice in the rectangle, allowing half of it to protrude above the rectangle. Load in the Water Presets, and move the Water-Ocean material into your project list on the left of the Materials browser. Apply the Water-Ocean material to the rectangle, and apply any material of your choice to the embedded object. Render and save to disk as a FreeHand resource graphic.

Figure 23-49: The rectangular plane has been mapped with the Water-Ocean material, giving it color and bumpiness.

Fire

Fire is one of the most sought-after effects in computer graphics. It can signify an explosion or just denote a hot topic. Smoke, either as an accompaniment to a flame or as a stand-alone effect, can also add interest to a selected graphic.

Tip

Use the accompanying CD-ROM to load the Fire1.FH7 Project and all of the tutorial elements into FreeHand so you can more easily work through this example. You may also find some of the elements in the Parts and Pieces folder.

Using FreeHand

The Blend tool is by far the most useful FreeHand tool for creating flames, with a few others vying for second place. The Blend tool allows us to create flames that vary in intensity and color.

Step #1: Create Basic Flames

Draw a basic flame shape, similar to a teardrop with a point on it. I prefer the FreeHand tool, but you can also use the Pen tool. Set its stroke to None, and target it for a gradient fill. Different materials burn with different colored flames, but there is a general similarity in that the flame's color changes from top to bottom. Duplicate your flame shape, and explore different gradient fills. A few examples are blue or green at the top to white at the bottom, red at the top to yellow at the bottom, or blue at the top to orange at the bottom.

Figure 23-50: Explore changing the gradient hues that fill a flame with color.

Step #2: Add Flames Within Flames

After creating three or more gradient flames, clone each of them and reduce the size of the clones by about two-thirds. Explore moving these smaller frames to other gradient flames as their central fire. This can lead to interesting variants.

Figure 23-51: Place the smaller cloned gradients at the base of other gradient flames for variety.

Step #3: Add Chaos to a Flame

Instead of a smooth outline, a flame can communicate its energy by having a more erratic outline. Use the Roughen tool in the Xtra Tools palette to give the edge of your flames a vibrating form.

Figure 23-52: The Roughen tool creates flame edges that vibrate.

Step #4: Blend the Blends

As long as your graphics contain the same type of blends and strokes, they can be blended again with each other. Select three flames with different blend colors but with the same number of blend colors and the same strokes (None). Shift-select each one, and click on the Blend tool in the Operations palette. After they are blended, click on the Add Points tool three times. Your graphic should resemble that shown in Figure 23-53.

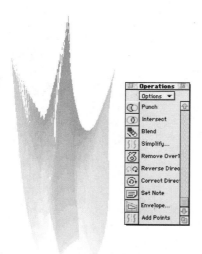

Figure 23-53: After blending three gradient flames, use the Add Points operator to give the flame some spikes.

Step #5: Add Smoke

Smoke is another element that can be generated with the Blend tool. Draw an outline of a puff of smoke with the FreeHand tool. Set its stroke to None, and fill it with a linear gradient that is set at a medium CMYK gray at the top (0, 0, 0, 40) and white at the bottom. Set the fill in the Smudge Tool dialog to black (double-click on the Smudge tool in the Xtra Tools palette to bring up its dialog box). Click on the Smudge tool, and click-drag it down over the selected smoke graphic. This adds further blurring to the smoke.

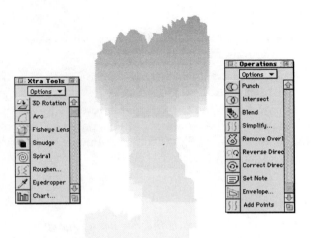

Figure 23-54: Smoke is created with the Blend tool and the Smudge tool.

Step #6: Create Explosions

Although there are any number of ways to create fiery explosions in FreeHand, this is one of my favorites. Draw an outline of an explosion with the FreeHand tool, trying to make it look fairly random. Set its stroke to None, and target it for a radial gradient fill. Design the gradient fill so that it contains several transitions of color, mostly reds and oranges and yellows, with white at the top of the gradient bar so that it fades into the backdrop. Make sure the radial type is selected and that the radial center dial is placed in the center of the target area.

When the shape is filled with the gradient, click on the Add Points tool three times. Then click on the Fractalize operator three or more times. This adds a convincing breakup to the explosion's edges.

Figure 23-55: Convincing explosions can be generated in FreeHand.

Using xRes

Unique flames are created in xRes by filling the shape with a selected multicolor gradient and gradient type.

Step #1: Apply Different Gradients

Draw a flame shape in xRes with the Lasso tool. Explore the following gradient/gradient type variations in the Gradient Options palette: Hot Pink/Folds, Hot Pink/Satin, R-O-Y/Line, Sunny Sky/Diamond, Purple Haze/Satin, Metal Burst/Satin, Mystical/Folds, and Geometric/Folds.

Tip

How far you drag the mouse and in which direction has a large effect on what the final gradient will look like in the shape. No two options work the same way, so exploration is essential with each gradient/gradient type pair.

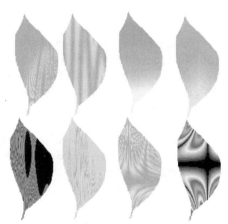

Figure 23-56: Thousands of fills are possible using xRes gradients combined with gradient types, and each one is further influenced by the distance and angle the mouse is clicked and dragged.

Step #2: Add Vibrations to Flames

Use the Ripple effect to add interesting vibrations to gradient flames. Select one or more flames and bring up the Ripple Effects dialog (Effects | Distort Ripple). Set the sliders to an Amplitude of 10 and a Wavelength of 30, and select OK.

Figure 23-57: The Ripple Effect causes the flames to vibrate.

Using Extreme 3D

You achieve natural effects in Extreme 3D by applying specific materials to objects. The materials can have adjustable levels of transparency, which makes effects like smoke possible. Though no flame or fire materials are offered as such, Extreme 3D offers a unique preset library of materials for fire effects, dedicated to Lava.

Step #1: Create a Blob of Lava

From the Top view, draw a group of circles of different sizes, allowing each to touch another circle in the group. Select all of the circles.

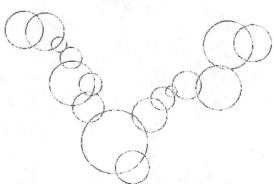

Figure 23-58: Draw a series of circles in the Top view, and select all of them.

Step #2: Use the Metaform Tool

Click on the Metaform tool in the Toolbox. In the dialog box that is displayed, click on Yes to confirm that you want to create a metaform. That's all there is to it. The 3D blobby object is created automatically from the 2D profiles.

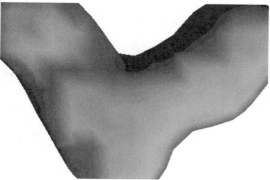

Figure 23-59: The metaformed object is created from the profiles.

Step #3: Assign the Lava Material to the Object

Open the Lava preset material library, and load it in. Select the Hot-Lava material type from the list on the right of the Material palette, and use the left-pointing arrow keys to bring it to the list on the left (the active Materials in Scene list). Assign the Lava-Hot material to your selected blobby shape.

Figure 23-60: The Hot-Lava material covers the blobby shape.

Step #4: Add Some Smoke to the Lava Object

Create four cones, and invert them. These will be our shapes for assigning the Smoke material. Use the Twist tool to deform each of them in a different way on their Y-axis, and embed them partway in the Lava blob as seen from the Front view.

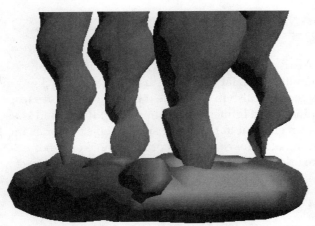

Figure 23-61: Before rendering, the smoke cones are seen from the Front view, deformed on their Y-axis and embedded in the lava blob.

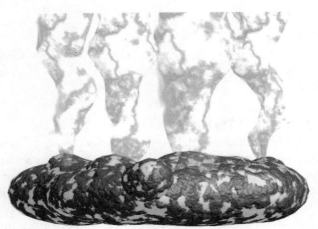

Figure 23-62: When rendered, the smoke adds a dynamic element to the lava.

Tip

Although Extreme 3D itself does not contain a Fire material, a set of fire graphics (including bitmaps, bump maps, and transparency maps) is included on the FreeHand Graphics Studio CD-ROM. The set is in the Wraptures folder from Form and Function. You can load these Fire sets into an edited version of the Mondo material, and map the fire graphics to any selected 3D object. If you need the renderings for a background, just map them to a flat plane in Extreme 3D before porting them to FreeHand.

Wondrous Woods

Wood textures are used in three major ways in computer graphics art. In a vector application like FreeHand, wood is used both as a background against which text is placed, and also to texture text blocks themselves (especially large bold headlines). In a bitmap application, like xRes, wood is used as a backdrop and as an element in rendering specific objects (for example, a bitmapped painting of a chair). In a 3D application, like Extreme 3D, wood is used as a texture or material that is applied to a selected 3D object.

Tip

Use the accompanying CD-ROM to load the Woodz.FH7 Project and all of the tutorial elements into FreeHand so you can more easily work through this example. You may also find some of the elements in the Parts and Pieces folder.

Using FreeHand

Creating a vector-based wood texture in FreeHand is useful for adding texture inside a selected text block. The main tools to be used are the FreeHand tool and the tiled fill effect.

Step #1: Create a Wood Texture

Double-click on the FreeHand tool to open its settings dialog. Choose Calligraphic Pen, Tight Fit, Fixed Width, a width of two pixels, and an angle of 135 degrees. Click on OK to apply the settings. Create a 4 x 4 ½-inch rectangle with a one point black stroke and a CMYK brown fill (0, 60, 100, 20). Click on the Calligraphic Pen (FreeHand tool). Create a dark brown CMYK fill color (0, 50, 50, 70) in the Color Mixer palette. Draw a series of striations from top to bottom in the rectangle to represent woodgrain.

Figure 23-63: The wood panel should look something like this.

Step #2: Make the Tiled Texture

Select the panel and copy it to the clipboard. Deselect the panel. In the Inspectors palette, choose Fill | Tiled. In the Tiled dialog, click on Paste In. Your paneled texture is now visible in the Tiled preview screen. Anything you draw with the tiled texture selected will contain that texture. Try it.

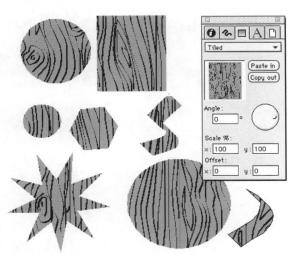

Figure 23-64: Any shape drawn with the Tiled texture selected in the Fill dialog will contain that texture.

Step #3: Add Some Handwriting in the Wood

Use the Calligraphic Pen to write some text, perhaps your name. As long as
the Tiled option is selected in the Fill dialog, whatever you do will contain that
texture. Standard text transformed to Paths, Calligraphic Pen, or any filled
image you draw now has the flavor of wood.

Figure 23-65: The wood texture fills a text block as well as a graphic.

Using xRes

xRes can apply any selected texture from its textures library to the marqueed
area selected in your workspace. Many of the xRes textures can emulate wood.

Step #1: Test the Textures

Open the Textures palette. Look closely at the textures represented as visual
swatches.

Tip

*Since there is a texture in the texture library called "wood," you might be tempted
to select it alone for a wood texture. I have found that other textures work better for
wood, however, and that the texture called "wood" in the library is too fine-grained
for my tastes.*

Use the Textured Airbrush tool (with the Texture slider set all the way to the right at 100 percent) to test spray various texture selections in your workspace. Determine which ones look like wood to your eye.

Tip

It's a good idea to create a texture swatch book to keep an available texture reference at your side. Paint one or more textures to a screen, label them, and print them out for future reference.

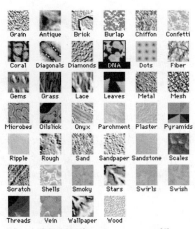

Figure 23-66: The xRes texture library.

Step #2: Create a Wood Block

Draw a rectangular marquee on the screen. Click on the Brush tool and select the Textured Airbrush and Textured. Set Concentration and Flow to 15 percent and Texture to 100 percent with the sliders in the settings dialog. Create a CMYK brown in the Color palette (0, 80, 100, 0). Set the Airbrush size and the Soft Edge to maximum (100%) in the Brushes tab of the Brush palette. Select the Onyx texture from the textures list. Use the Airbrush to gently spray it in the rectangular marquee.

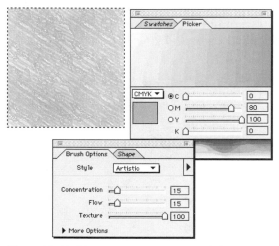

Figure 23-67: The Onyx texture creates a believable looking woodgrain.

Tip

Remember that xRes textures can be layered, so one can be used over another to provide variance and shading. This is especially useful when developing a wood texture; it helps you avoid a texture that looks too symmetrical and unnatural.

Using Extreme 3D

Extreme 3D has a separate materials Presets folder that contains a collection of wood textures. This is the main resource for developing wood looks in Extreme 3D.

Step #1: Create a Wood Sampler

If you plan to use the wood textures found in the Wood folder in the Extreme 3D Presets, it's a good idea to have a visual document to refer to for your future endeavors. Create three spheres and three cubes and paste them in place in your workspace. Open the Wood Preset, and load the six wood types to the list on the left of the Materials browser. Select each one in turn, and map it to one of the six objects on the screen. Render it at the highest resolution and save the rendering to disk. Print out the rendering in color, and keep it handy for the times when a FreeHand project calls for a wood texture.

Figure 23-68: These six objects (left to right and top to bottom) have been mapped with the six wood materials in the Presets folder: Walnut, Pine, Oak, Mahogany, Cherrywood, and Burl. Each can be further customized in the Materials Editor.

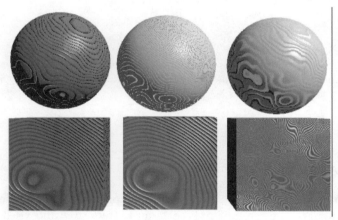

Figure 23-69: One way to emphasize the grain in all of the woods listed in Figure 23-68 is to change the map type to Spherical and to push the bump map up all the way.

Step #2: Access the Wraptures Bitmaps

A set of dozens of high-quality bitmaps from Form and Function is included on the CD-ROM, one folder of which contains woods. Use the same spheres and cubes models from the previous step to include these in your visual portfolio. Load three Generic Texture materials defaults to the active list on the left of the Materials browser. Locate your Wraptures folder on the FreeHand

CD-ROM. Edit each of the three generic Texture materials to include one of the Wraptures bitmaps: Bark, Maple, and Wood Planks.

Step #3: Set the Roughness

Set the Roughness slider to about 25 percent on each, and target a sphere-cube pair for each of these textures. Render it, save it, and print it out as a page in your wood textures resource portfolio.

Figure 23-70: The Wraptures textures that come as extras with the FreeHand 7 Graphics Studio CD-ROM include these wood bitmaps. Left to right, they illustrate Bark, Maple, and Wood Planks mapped to spheres and cubes.

Moving On

In this chapter, we have taken a series of excursions, delving into the ways that natural elements can be created in FreeHand, Extreme 3D, and xRes. In the next chapter, we will focus on graphics that depict food and drink, showing how to use all three of the Graphics Studio applications in the process.

24

Food & Drink Graphics

Food and drink graphics are important for producing menus, flyers, brochures, product labels, and Web pages about nutrition and dietary health issues. FreeHand, xRes, and Extreme 3D offer creative opportunities for stylizing and customizing art that deals with this topic. In some of the exercises, we will move from one application through the others to get to a final graphic, showing that though FreeHand, xRes, and Extreme 3D are stand-alone applications, we can also use them in a cooperative manner to generate the final result.

Graphics that depict food and drink can range from photorealism to abstracted media. Your media choice is really determined by the target project. In the case of extreme photorealistic requirements, you might simply import a photo of the subject and add highlights or remove unwanted artifacts. This would be a task for xRes. In the cases presented here, we will develop graphics that are stylized, though quite representative of the items involved. Be sure you have a snack next to you while you create these graphics, so they don't make you too hungry.

Fruits & Vegetables

Did you eat your fruits and vegetables today? Besides being a wise health choice, vegetable shapes offer unique challenges to the computer artist trying to capture their many forms. There are hundreds of types of fruits and vegetables in the world, far too many for us to cover. We will look at examples that cover a range of design issues, so that you can extrapolate on these exercises to design other selections as well.

Tip

Use the accompanying CD-ROM to load the Veggy1.FH7 Project and all of the tutorial elements into FreeHand so you can more easily work through this example. You may also find some of the elements in the Parts and Pieces folder.

Using FreeHand

The FreeHand drawing options, including both the FreeHand tool and the Bezier Pen tool, offer computer artists a way to create subtle organic forms with a minimum of effort. The gradient fill and stroke properties allow muted color to be added to these forms consistent with their nature.

Step #1: Design the Carrot

Begin by drawing half of the vertical outline of a carrot shape with the FreeHand tool. Select the drawing, and clone it. Now use the Reflect tool to place the cloned half with the original half. If necessary, drag the outline at the top and bottom of the cloned duplicate so it touches that of the original shape. Use the Join command to marry the halves.

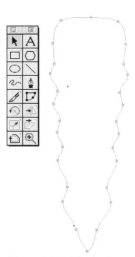

Figure 24-1: The basic carrot shape is complete.

Tip

> *Note that with different coloring, this would also suffice for a parsnip or a hot pepper.*

Step #2: Add Color

Set a color gradient that ranges from a dark CMYK orange (0, 80, 100, 0) at the top of the color ramp to a lighter orange (0, 20, 60, 0) at the bottom. Set the gradient angle to 180 degrees with a linear taper. Use the FreeHand tool to add dimensional curving horizontal lines to the carrot, emphasizing its 3D nature. Group all of the elements as one.

Tip

> *At this point, you can clone the carrot and save it as a separate graphic for the times when you want to use it without its leafiness.*

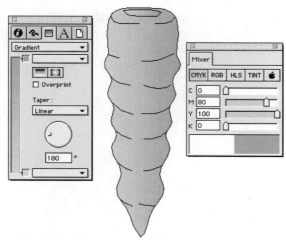

Figure 24-2: Color is added to the carrot with a gradient fill, and the carrot is given dimension with curving horizontal lines.

Step #3: Add the Greens

Draw one curved green topping that can be cloned to get the necessary quantity. Color it with a solid CMYK green (80, 0, 100, 25).

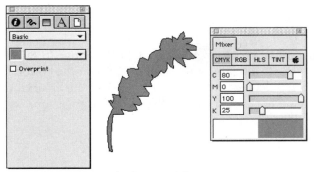

Figure 24-3: Draw and color one of the green tops.

Step #4: Multiply the Greens

Clone the top several times. Resize, rotate, and mirror some of the greens so that you have a collection that looks randomly ordered. Group all of the greens. Move the greens to their position at the top of the carrot, and use the FreeHand tool to draw some stringy roots. Group everything.

Figure 24-4: The carrot is now complete.

Step #5: Create a Bunch

Need a bunch of carrots? Simple. Just clone the carrot as many times as you need to, and resize the clones to introduce some randomness. Rotate each to give the graphic more interest.

Figure 24-5: From the one, many.

Step #6: Begin the Tomato

Create an oval, longer than it is high. Add points to it by clicking the Add Points tool twice.

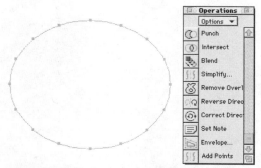

Figure 24-6: The basic tomato shape starts with an oval.

Step #7: Adjust the Control Points

Pull on the topmost control handle to give the shape a slight indentation at the top. Fill the shape with a bright CMYK red (0, 100, 100, 0). Add the tomato top by positioning a small oval and coloring it a CMYK olive green (60, 0, 100, 30). Group everything.

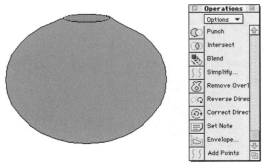

Figure 24-7: The basic tomato shape begins to form.

Step #8: Add a Highlight

Draw two concentric ovals, a large CMYK red one (0, 100, 100, 0) about one-quarter the size of the tomato and a smaller white one inside of it. Blend the two ovals. This is a movable highlight that can be repositioned to create different clones. Place the highlight on the tomato. Group everything and save the graphic to disk.

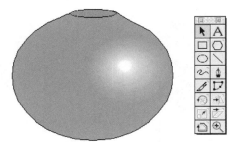

Figure 24-8: The finished tomato.

Step #9: Multiply the Tomato

To get a grouping of tomatoes, just clone, resize, and reposition.

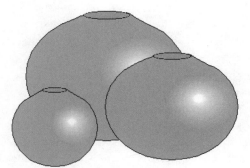

Figure 24-9: A tomato family in repose.

Step #10: Transform It into an Apple

Remember that we added several points to the tomato shape in Step #2, and now's the time to take advantage of them. Select the tomato, clone it, and ungroup the clone twice. Discard the button at the top, and resize the highlight so that it is taller than it is wide. Use the control points on the main body to shape it like an apple. Draw a leaf, clone it, and rotate the clone. Color the original leaf a CMYK green (40, 0, 60, 0) and the cloned leaf a darker CMYK green (40, 0, 60, 25). Position the leaves on the apple, and group everything.

Figure 24-10: The apple is born from the tomato.

> *Clearly, with a little reshaping and recoloring, the tomato can be transformed into a grape, eggplant, plum, orange, or many other fruits and vegetables.*

Step #11: Create a Broccoli Stalk

Use either the Bezier Pen or the FreeHand tool to draw an outline of the broccoli stalk. Make sure you include several cut ends on the sides. Use the Pen to draw ovals over the cut ends. Fill the main stalk with a linear gradient at an angle of 180 degrees, and set the color from a dark CMYK olive (40, 0, 100, 60) to a lighter hue (10, 0, 15, 10). Set the color in the ovals to a radial gradient that ranges from a top CMYK olive color (40, 0, 100, 60) to a yellow olive (10, 0, 55, 10). Add a few lines at the cut ends to give the graphic some dimension. Group and save the stalk.

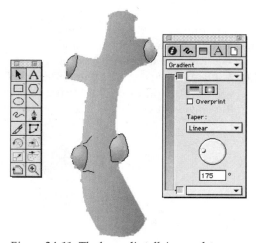

Figure 24-11: The broccoli stalk is complete.

Step #12: Add the Leaves

Draw in a leaf group with the FreeHand tool, and use a CMYK dark green color fill on it (70, 0, 60, 40). Group it with the stalk.

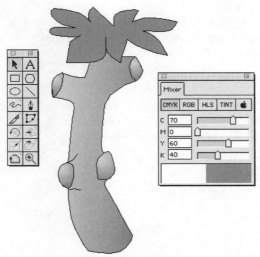

Figure 24-12: The leaves are added to the stalk.

Step #13: Add the Florets

Draw a small circle, and fill it with a gradient that ranges from a CMYK green (70, 0, 60, 40) to a light yellow (0, 0, 30, 0). Use the Duplicate command to construct a grid of evenly spaced filled circles with about 36 across and 24 down. Group all of the circles.

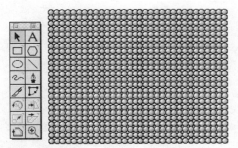

Figure 24-13: A grid of clustered buds is created.

Step #14: Distort the Cluster

It's time to add a spherical distortion to the buds to create a floret. It's not possible to apply the Fish Eye Lens effect in FreeHand because of the groupings involved, so let's do it in xRes instead. Save the grid as a TIFF file, and import it into xRes. xRes has its own Fisheye effect under Effects I Distort. Bring up the Fish Eye dialog by selecting the Fish Eye effect, and set the slider to +15. Apply the effect, and save the resulting graphic to disk.

Tip

Remember that once the bitmap is loaded into FreeHand, double-clicking on it causes FreeHand to search for an image-editing application to port the image to, which lets you select from a list of image editors present in your system.

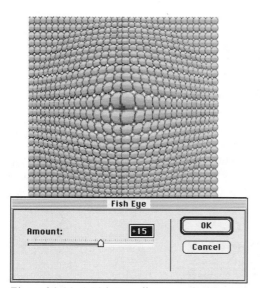

Figure 24-14: A Fish Eye effect is applied in xRes.

Step #15: Paste the Flowers inside a FreeHand Circle

Import the distorted image back into FreeHand. Place a circle over the imported graphic (with no fill and a one point black stroke). Select the circle, and select Edit I Paste Inside. The circle is filled with the bitmap pattern. Repeat this procedure to get two differently sized circles filled with the distorted bitmap pattern.

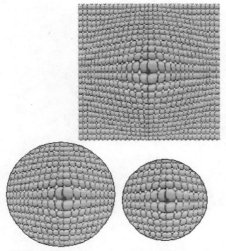

Figure 24-15: Paste the distorted bitmap into two circles.

Step #16: Complete the Drawing

Place the florets on top of the broccoli stalk to complete the drawing.

Figure 24-16: The completed drawing.

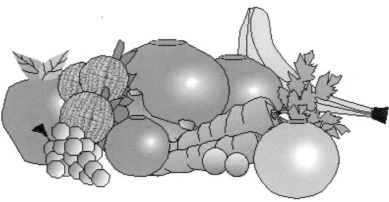

Figure 24-17: A combined vegetable composition.

Using xRes

xRes allows us to explore less formal representational graphics through the use of its extensive media tools and brushes. In all of the following xRes paintings, we will use the Basic Air Brush. In the Brush Options palette, open the More Options drop-down menu. Set Concentration and Flow to 60 percent, and Texture to zero. Under More Options, set Smoothing to 25 percent and Spacing to 15 percent, and leave the rest of the settings at their default position. We will develop a translucent painterly montage.

Step #1: Paint an Apple

Draw an apple shape, including the stem and leaves, with the Lasso tool. Use reds for the apple and greens for the leaves, and a brown stem. Work with the Air Brush and don't linger too long in one place to avoid blotches. Stay in CMYK mode so that you can darken a color by increasing its black (K) content. When you place a highlight on the apple, make sure it has a slight green component, since this is the complementary to red and looks natural. Save the graphic to disk.

Figure 24-18: The finished apple.

Step #2: Paint Some Grapes

Use the Ellipse Marquee to create an outline of a grape. Select a range of interesting purples for the Air Brush, and fill in the shape. Use a light blue color for a highlight. Duplicate the grape as many times as needed to create a bunch. Start from the bottom of the bunch and work upward when placing the grapes in the composition. Finally, select each object layer, and drop the object in place, so you wind up with only one object layer. To create the stem, use a Wet Crayon brush and a dark brown color with Concentration and Flow of 50 percent and Texture of zero. Save the graphic to disk.

Figure 24-19: The finished bunch of grapes.

Step #3: Paint an Orange

This graphic calls for the use of the Textured Airbrush. Unlike apples and grapes, oranges have a texture that can be emulated by using one of xRes's texture maps. Select the Mesh texture. Move the Texture, Concentration, and Flow sliders up to 100 percent in the Brush Options palette. As before, use the circle Marquee tool to draw the outline of the orange. You can make it a perfect circle or make it a bit shorter than it is wide. Use a range of orange colors to paint it, and make its highlight white. Paint in quick, smooth motions. After the texture has been applied to the whole orange, blot some of it out in the shaded areas by moving the Texture slider to zero and the Concentration slider to 20 percent. This allows you to overpaint the texture in selected areas with plain color. As a last step, paint a light glaze of green in the shadow areas (texture off). When finished, save the graphic to disk.

Figure 24-20: The finished orange.

Step #4: Compose the Montage

Select a background picture from your files. Choose one that's not too cluttered. My favorite backgrounds are clouds, but you can select any background you desire, or just use a color or gradient if you prefer. Open each of the graphics you just painted as separate files (the apple, grapes, and orange). Go to the apple graphic, and select it alone with a marquee (not its backdrop), and copy it. Click on your background graphic and paste the apple. The apple is now on a separate object layer over your background. Repeat this procedure for the grapes and the orange, so that each becomes a separate object layer over the background.

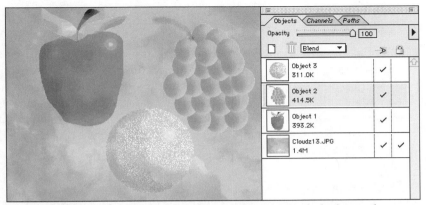

Figure 24-21: The objects are in place on separate layers over the background.

Selecting the object layer in the Objects palette allows you to determine how opaque or transparent that layer will be. You can also move the layers to alternate parts of the stack, or duplicate or delete them by copying and pasting or clearing the selected object. We want our montage to evidence layers of translucency, so explore different transparency settings for each layer, and experiment with moving selected layers to alternate parts of the stack. Do this until you have a satisfying composition, and then drop each layer into place over the background. Do not drop the layers if saving the graphic as a native xRes MMI file that preserves the layer data. Save your montage to disk as a TIFF file and a possible resource for a FreeHand project.

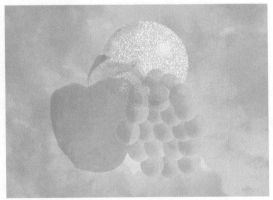

Figure 24-22: The finished montage displays interesting layered transparencies.

Using Extreme 3D

Material textures applied in Extreme 3D can greatly change the emotional content of an object. An apple, for instance, though we might recognize it by its shape, can be appreciated as a metallic or otherworldly piece of fruit. One way to make use of this option in a FreeHand document is to use the same object with different textures as a bullet that precedes a text block. Another option is to use a texture-altered food element as a spot illustration that adds interest and mystery to a page.

Step #1: Sculpt an Apple

Render a sphere to the screen. Open its geometry and simplify it, bringing up its Bezier control handles. Use the handles to reshape the sphere into an apple. Close the geometry. Draw a leaf with the Spline tool. Extrude it a bit to allow it to accept a texture, and use the 2D Reflect tool to duplicate it. Take both leaves, and place them on the top of the apple. Draw four circles in the top view. Go to the front view and set them apart vertically, altering the top circles so that they are rotated away from the bottom one, forming a curved path. Use the Skin tool to connect them, creating the apple's stem. Lock-link all of the parts to the main body.

Figure 24-23: The finished 3D apple object.

Step #2: Determine the Materials

Bring up the Materials browser. Load in the following eight Materials Presets to the active project list on the left: Clouds/Sunset, Band/Red & White, Crusty/Mud on Glass, Gradient/Red, Mold/Blue, Steel/Stripes, Tiger Stripe/ Orange, and Wire/Red. You may substitute any materials that interest you for members of this list, though the list represents a wide example of possibilities. Each of these textures can be edited and infinitely altered. For brevity, however, we will map them to the apple as is.

Step #3: Create an Apple Sampler

The materials sampler we will create would make a great graphic in a FreeHand project by itself, although you could also use it as a visual indicator of how various textures look when mapped to a 3D object. Select the apple and reduce its size so that eight apples can fit in your Extreme 3D workspace. Duplicate the apple seven times, and space the eight apples on the page in two rows of four apples each. One by one, choose the materials you loaded into the Material browser, and assign them to the apples. You can explore using the same material for selected leaves and stems, or you may want to investigate using different materials for them. When complete, render to a file as a possible resource for a FreeHand project.

Figure 24-24: A group of unique apples, any one of which is guaranteed to stop your audience in their tracks.

Step #4: Add a Bite

Go to the front view, and zoom in to get one apple on the screen. Draw a circle that acts like a bite to be taken out of the apple. Go to the top view and move the circle so that it rests in front of the apple. Return to the front view. With the circle selected, click on the Projection tool. Click on the apple, and the circle will become a cutter that acts on the apple. Access the Project tool's pull-out menu, and select the Trim tool. Click on the part of the apple that needs to be cut away, and it will disappear. Save the graphic as a TIFF file, and import it into xRes.

Figure 24-25: The circle cuts the apple away like a bite.

Step #5: Use xRes to Finish the Bite

The problem with using the cutter method in Extreme 3D on a solid object is that objects are not solid, but just a shell with empty space inside. In xRes, you can use the cut shape to draw in a solid inner surface, making it look like a real bite. Select the Lasso tool, hold down the Shift key to constrain it to a Polygon tool, and follow the shape of the bite. With the Air Brush tool, paint in the inner surface. Textures are not advised if you want to maintain a "real" look, but perhaps you want to explore using them to make the bite look unique and strange.

Figure 24-26: Thanks to xRes the apple shows the inner surface that the bite has exposed.

Burger & Soda

I live next door to a great truck stop and crave a good burger about once a month. As a staple food choice in the American diet, a graphic representation of a burger and soda is useful in giving an Americana look to a publication, as well as being used for advertisement or to visually describe a menu choice.

Tip

Use the accompanying CD-ROM to load the Burger.FH7 Project and all of the tutorial elements into FreeHand so you can more easily work through this example. You may also find some of the elements in the Parts and Pieces folder.

Step #1: Create the Top of the Bun in FreeHand

Draw an oval elongated horizontally, and click on the Add Points tool twice. Delete the necessary points and move the lower central control handle to transform the oval into a burger-bun shape. Select the radial gradient option, and move the Locate Center knob to the upper left quadrant in the radial control box. Use the CMYK sliders to set the color ramp from a toasted brown (0, 55, 100, 30) to a golden yellow (0, 15, 50, 0). Set the stroke to a one point black.

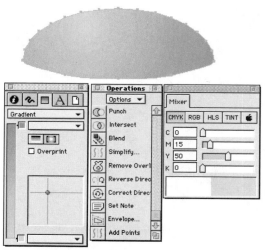

Figure 24-27: The top bun takes shape as you adjust the oval's points.

Step #2: Create the Bottom of the Bun in FreeHand

Clone the top of the bun, and use the Reflect tool to make a vertically flipped copy of the cloned element. Draw an oval that fits over the bottom of the bun, so that it looks like a 3D image (refer to Figure 24-28). Color the oval a CMYK light brownish-yellow (0, 4, 32, 6).

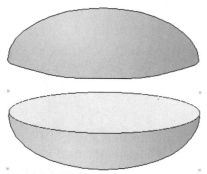

Figure 24-28: The bottom of the bun is added.

Step #3: Export the Graphic & Texturize It in xRes

Now we'll add some character to the bun, but not in FreeHand. Export the bun halves as separate bitmaps to xRes. In xRes, use the Textured Airbrush tool set at a Concentration of 13 percent and a Flow of 50 percent, with a Stars texture set at 100 percent to spray some sesame seeds on both of the buns, surfaces. For the internal surface of the bottom bun, use a Textured Air Brush with the same settings and the Sandpaper texture. This makes the inside look toasted.

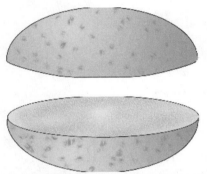

Figure 24-29: The toasted bun graphics look very realistic after treatment in xRes.

Step #4: Create the Hamburger in Extreme 3D

Now we'll craft some of the other burger elements in Extreme 3D. Here, we'll build the burger, cheese, lettuce, pickles, tomato, and onion. When we're finished, everything will be composited back in xRes.

Draw two circles in the top view, and use the Metaform tool to connect them as a 3D object. Load in the Brown Mold Preset (don't let this upset you), and edit the material as follows. In the Pattern tab: Complex with a Pattern scale of .32, Sharp pattern Transition, and an Edge Blend Bump Transition. In the Material 1 tab: Color brown (your choice of settings) and Bump slider up all the way. In the Material 2 tab: color of dark brown (your choice of specific settings) and Bump Height 1 slider all the way to the right. Accept the settings, and assign this material to the burger. Rotate the burger on the X-axis so that it seems to have the same perspective as the inside of the bun created in FreeHand. Render it and save it to disk.

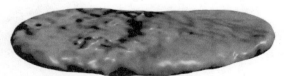

Figure 24-30: The finished burger object textured and rendered.

Step #5: Create Melted Cheese in Extreme 3D

In the Top view, draw five overlapping rectangles. Select all of them and click on the Metaform tool, and answer yes to metaforming. That's it. The cheese object is complete, and even without material has that melted look. Assign a Gray Plastic material to it, with the color changed to yellow. Rotate it in the front view on the X axis so that its angle looks right for the bottom bun. Save it to disk as a TIFF file.

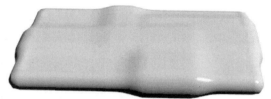

Figure 24-31: The finished cheese object.

Step #6: Add Pickles on the Side in Extreme 3D

In the right view, draw a series of ovals that will be skinned together as a pickle. Move them into place in the front view so that they form a curved path.

Figure 24-32: The pre-skinned pickle is constructed of ovals.

Step #7: Use the Skin Tool in Extreme 3D

Click on the Skin tool. Connect the ovals in a linear fashion one at a time, double-clicking on the final one. Your 3D object is formed. Load in the Bump Grn material from the Bump presets folder. Assign the texture to the pickle shape, and render. Save to disk as a separate TIFF graphic.

Figure 24-33: The finished pickle object.

Tip

It is advisable to save the pickle out in three or four different rotations, so you can use the right one for the scene later on.

Step #8: Create the Lettuce in Extreme 3D

Use the Spline tool to draw a general rectangular shape with irregular edges. Extrude it a bit so it will accept a material assignment. Open its geometry and simplify it. Move the control points around to give it a randomized 3D shape, rather like a leaf of lettuce. Use your experience with lettuce as a guide, or actually reference a real piece of lettuce. Rotate the shape so you can fit it on the bottom bun in the final composite. When finished, assign the same green material to the object that was assigned to the pickle. The only difference will be that the pattern will be Complex, and the material colors will each be a lighter green. Render it and save it to disk as a separate TIFF file.

Figure 24-34: The finished lettuce object.

Step #9: Create Slices of Onion & Tomato in Extreme 3D

Since the tomato and onion slices will be mostly buried in the burger, all that needs to be rendered as far as detail is an extruded circle, colorized the correct way for each. Create two extruded circles, coloring one bright red and the other a muted yellow. Save each to disk separately.

Figure 24-35: The rendered tomato and onion for the burger.

Tip

The first rule of 3D work is "Don't incorporate more detail than you need to." If you're not going to see the detail to appreciate it, all it will do is consume render time.

Step #10: Add a Glass of Soda & a Straw in Extreme 3D

What would a burger be without a glass of carbonated soda? Use the Spline tool to draw half a glass, and then lathe it. Make sure the inside is "empty," because we have to put contents in the glass. Map the glass with the Gray-Plastic material, and edit it as follows: use a texture map that has a little color (your favorite will do), and set the Intensity at 1.2. Under the Surface tab set the Transparency to 50 percent.

Use the inner dimensions to design the contents. As above, lathe a shape to get a 3D object. Fit the object in the glass, which will probably take a little tweaking. Use all of the views to check out the contents position. Use the Pool-Water present as a texture, and set the transparency level of the material to 50 percent. When everything is in position, lock-link the contents to the glass.

The glass wouldn't be complete without a straw. Design the straw by drawing a series of four small circles on a path that represents a bent straw in the front view. Use the Skin tool to craft the 3D object. The straw can be made hollow by selecting it and choosing Objects I Separate End, and then selecting the end caps and throwing them away. Map the straw with the Default-Stripes material in the Bands Preset folder. Recolor the materials red and yellow, and set the Pattern Type to Cylindrical. Lock-link the straw to the glass. Render the glass and straw, and save it to disk as a TIFF file.

Figure 24-36: The drink is ready to place in the finished composition.

Step #11: Create a Froth Bubble in FreeHand

A drink from a soda fountain usually has foam on it, so let's take the opportunity to show how frothy foam can be created in FreeHand.

Click on the Ellipse tool. Hold down the Shift key to constrain it to circles, and draw a series of circles resembling the one shown in Figure 24-37. Select all of them. Fill them with a CMYK slate blue (23, 0, 0, 45) to white (0, 0, 0, 0) radial gradient, and move the highlight control slightly to the upper left.

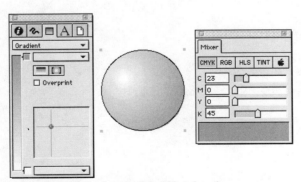

Figure 24-37: The first froth bubble takes shape.

Step #12: Create a Composition of Froth Bubbles in FreeHand

Place multiple clones of the bubbles in a configuration loosely resembling that illustrated in Figure 24-38. Change a few to vertically elongated drips as shown. Select all of the bubbles, remove the stroke, and group the arrangement as one graphic.

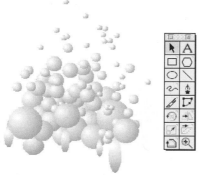

Figure 24-38: An arrangement of froth bubbles.

Step #13: Create a Series of Variations in FreeHand

Repeat this process over again any number of times you wish, creating a small collection of froth variations. Leave some without strokes and some with for variety. Save them separately to disk as TIFF graphics.

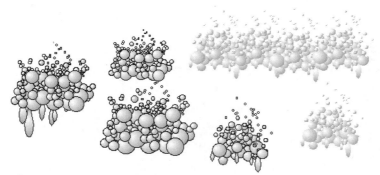

Figure 24-39: Variations on the froth bubble theme.

Step #14: Layering the Drink & Froth Graphics in xRes

The froth bubbles should be placed on the drink graphic.

Create a new xRes document, 400 x 400 pixels at 72 dots per inch (dpi). Import the drink graphic, which is automatically placed on an object layer above the background. Bring in one of the froth graphics that you saved earlier, which is placed on its own object layer. Use the slider bar in the Objects palette to give the froth a 50 percent transparency. Drop the glass and the froth layers to the background, and save the graphic as a TIFF file for placement in the complete composition.

Figure 24-40: The drink with the froth placed on it.

Step #15: Import & Place All the Elements in xRes

Now we'll use xRes to put all of the elements together in a single composition. Create a new document in xRes, 640 x 480 pixels at 72 dpi. You can leave it blank or place one of your favorite backgrounds on it. With the Rectangle Marquee tool, draw a rectangle that covers the bottom third of the picture area. Apply a metal burst Satin gradient to this area with the Gradient tool.

Figure 24-41: The initial burger backdrop.

Step #16: Bring the Drink Graphic into xRes

Open the drink graphic. Use the Wand tool on its background, and then invert the selection. Only the graphic should be selected. Copy it to the clipboard. Close it, and click on the background screen, making it active. Select Edit I Paste, and the drink graphic floats above the background on its own object layer.

Figure 24-42: The drink graphic is brought in on its own object layer.

Step #17: Bring All of the Other Elements into xRes

Use the same technique to create object layers for all of the burger parts. Try to bring them in starting with the last burger part saved because of the layering you'll have to do. If you forget, however, you can always transpose the object layers as needed.

Figure 24-43: When first brought in, the object layers will need to be fine-tuned to place the elements correctly in the stack.

Step #18: Fine-tune the Composition in xRes

Use the object layers to place everything in its proper position in the stack, and place the elements where they belong. You may want to duplicate some of the elements to make a more unique composition (It could reach the sky!). You can drop the layers in place or leave them and save the composition out in native xRes format (MMI).

Figure 24-44: One of the many possible burger compositions.

Tip

Note that saving the composition out as an MMI file preserves the layers. This allows you to build a cheese sandwich, or other delicacies with selected parts.

Bread & Alphabet Soup

Warm bread and hot soup offer respite from a cold world. Let's explore an-other series of graphics with this approach to gastronomical design.

Tip

Use the accompanying CD-ROM to load the Bread.FH7 Project and all of the tutorial elements into FreeHand so you can more easily work through this example. You may also find some of the elements in the Parts and Pieces folder.

Using FreeHand

This exercise requires a working familiarity with FreeHand's Pen tool and other tools.

Step #1: Draw Half of the Profile of a Slice of Bread

Using the FreeHand Pen, draw half of the profile outline for a slice of bread. The profile will be half of the final graphic, so make the starting and end points line up vertically.

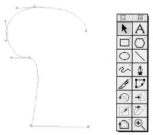

Figure 24-45: You can always adjust the control points by moving them or by manipulating the control handles.

Step #2: Complete the Profile

Clone the profile and reflect it. Select both halves and use the Join command to marry them.

Figure 24-46: The completed profile of the bread slice.

Step #3: Add Fill & Stroke

Select the profile, and add an 8 point CMYK brown stroke (0, 75, 80, 45). Use a radial gradient fill that ranges from a light CMYK yellow (0, 0, 5, 0) to a CMYK tan (0, 55, 75, 40). Move the Locate Center knob so it is set near the bottom right of the control screen. When finished, clone the slice and set the clone aside.

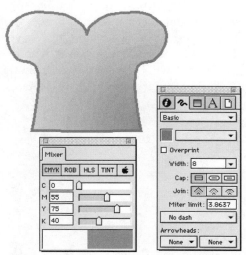

Figure 24-47: The slice of bread is completed with a stroke and a radial fill.

Step #4: Make a Loaf from the Slice

Clone the slice again and move the cloned duplicate at a 30 degree angle to the lower right of the original, about the distance you estimate the completed loaf to need. Select both graphics, and click on the Blend operator.

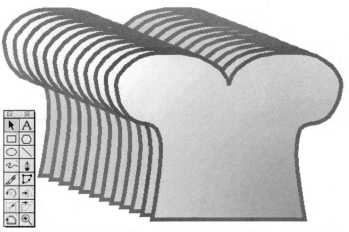

Figure 24-48: The 3D loaf is created by blending two slices, but needs more work.

Step #5: Draw Fill Panels over the Side & Top

To get rid of the spaces caused by the blend operation, it is necessary to use the Pen tool to carefully trace over the exposed side and top. As you trace over the contours, make sure that stroke is set to None and that the radial gradient fill remains operable. The only change will be to set the colors in the gradient fill to a black-brown (0, 55, 75, 85) and a dark brown (0, 30, 80, 30).

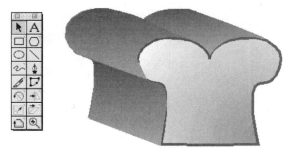

Figure 24-49: The loaf is now complete.

Step #6: Make a 3D slice

Select the slice that you cloned and put aside, and apply a 3D Rotation to it with the 3D Rotation tool so that it looks as though it is lying on its face. Double-click on the Smudge Xtra tool to bring up its settings dialog, and set the Smudge tool's fill and stroke to a dark CMYK brown (0, 55, 75, 85). While the bread slice is selected, use the Smudge tool by clicking and dragging the mouse in a downward motion, giving the bread depth when you release the mouse.

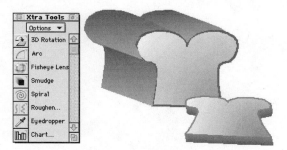

Figure 24-50: The separate slice in front of the loaf appears to have depth.

Step #7: Create a Breadboard

Create a breadboard under the bread by selecting the Pen and clicking on the four corners where the board should be. Move the resulting rectangle to the bottom of the stack, and fill it with a linear gradient that ranges from a light CMYK brown (0, 55, 75, 30) to a CMYK golden brown (0, 17, 68, 10). Set the fill angle to 130 degrees. Set the stroke to None. Use the Smudge tool to give the breadboard 3D depth.

Figure 24-51: A breadboard is created beneath the bread.

Step #8: Create a Shadow

Fake in a shadow for the loaf and the slice. Use the Eyedropper tool to select the lighter breadboard color, drag it to the Color Mixer palette, and add a 30 percent black to it. Make sure the shadow has no stroke.

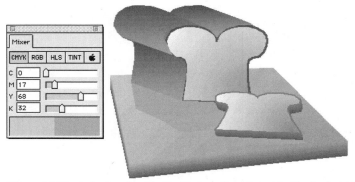

Figure 24-52: A shadow is added to the breadboard, cast by the loaf and the slice.

Step #9: Add a Knife

As a final touch, draw a knife sticking up out of the breadboard. Make sure its tip is straight and horizontal, making it seem as if it's embedded in the board. Group everything, and save the FreeHand project to disk.

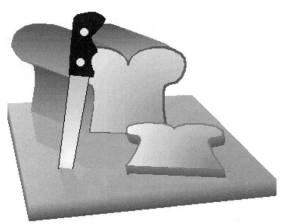

Figure 24-53: The complete composition.

Using xRes

xRes offers options that can help you develop unique spot illustrations for FreeHand.

Step #1: Import the Bread Graphic from FreeHand & Apply a Radial Blur in xRes

Import the saved bread graphic you created using FreeHand in the last exercise. Use the Wand tool to select its background, and then invert the selection. For the first spot illustration, we'll use the Radial Blur effect. When the radial blur dialog appears, set the slider to an angle of 30 degrees and three copies. Select OK to apply the effect.

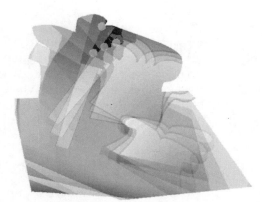

Figure 24-54: A Radial Blur spot illustration creates layered translucent abstractions.

Step #2: Add some Noise

Load in the same graphic again. Select the Add Noise effect. Move the slider all the way to the right (100 percent). Apply the effect. This transforms the graphic into a soft stippled illustration, and makes a great spot drawing alternative for cookbook art. Save the graphic to disk with a unique name.

Figure 24-55: Noise adds stippling to an illustration.

Step #3: Add the HLS Noise Effect

Use the same illustration, and select it with the Wand tool and invert the selection as in Step #1. Apply the HLS Noise effect. HLS (Hue, Lightness, and Saturation) applies a color variance to the noise, creating a painterly look like that produced by the pointillists in the late nineteenth century. When the HLS Noise dialog appears, set Hue and Lightness to 50 percent and Saturation to 100 percent. Apply the effect. Save the graphic to disk for a FreeHand project.

Figure 24-56: The HLS Noise effect creates beautiful color noise over a graphic, softening it and adding color interest at the same time.

Step #4: Emboss the Graphic

Use the same illustration, and select it with the Magic tool and invert the selection as in Step #1. Select the Stylize/Emboss effect. In the dialog, use a

Depth of 1, an Angle of +45, and a Contrast of 100. This effect adds depth and removes color, making the graphic appear as if it were stamped out of a piece of sheet metal. Use Embossing on illustrations or photos that are not too complex, and whose silhouettes are easily recognizable.

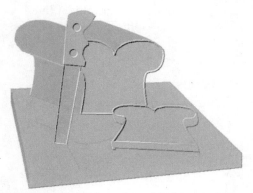

Figure 24-57: Embossed graphics have a minimum of information left after the effect is applied, greatly simplifying their content.

Step #5: Create Pop Art

The Stylize/Posterize effect creates pop art from imported graphics. Use the same illustration, and select it with the Wand tool and invert the selection as in Step #1. Select the Stylize | Posterize effect, and set the slider all the way to the left for a value of 2. Apply the effect. Pop art effects can also be used to mimic comic book art in a FreeHand project.

Figure 24-58: The Stylize | Posterize option is useful for comic book illustrations.

Step #6: Add Watercolor Washes

Computer graphics are often thought of as hard and emotionless, but they don't have to be with the right tools. Use the same illustration, and select it with the Wand tool and invert the selection as in Step #1. Select the Glass Styles brush, and set its parameters to a Concentration and Flow of 60 percent, and no texture. Paint in quick motions over your graphic. Where hard lines existed, blurred washes take their place. By toning down the Concentration and Flow, you could minimize the effect. Save the graphic to disk when you are finished.

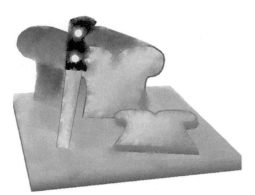

Figure 24-59: Warm bleeds and washes transform the emotional content of the graphics when you use the Glass Style brush.

Using Extreme 3D

Well, we seem to have the bread, so how about some alphabet soup to dip it in? Of course, soup needs a bowl and a spoon as well.

Step #1: Create a Bowl

Use the Spline tool to create half of the outline for a bowl in the front view, and lathe the shape on its vertical axis to complete a bowl object. Open the Gold Presets folder and load it in. Move the Gold-Smooth material to the active project list. Assign the gold material to the bowl, and render for preview.

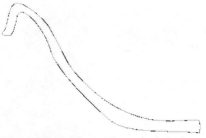

Figure 24-60: The outline to be lathed.

Figure 24-61: The bowl object after the lathing process, textured with the gold material.

Step #2: Create the Spoon

You've worked very hard to get to this project, so let's have a little creative fun. The bowl of the spoon is created the same way as the big bowl itself, by lathing an outlined shape. In the Object palette, under the Lathing tab, you will see that all lathed objects are represented by the number of degrees they have been lathed (a default of 360 degrees). Select the bowl of the spoon, and type in the number **80** in the lathed degrees space. Immediately you will see a crescent shape, much more useful for a spoon. You can revise the lathed degrees at any time in a work session.

For the handle of the spoon, explore developing a skinned object made from a number of 2D profiles. You might also opt to develop the handle by extruding a 2D shape on a path. Use whichever method meets your fancy. Speaking of fancy, let's use our gothic imagination to put some ornamentation on the spoon. These are easy to originate with the path extrude method. Capping them off with spheres or other shapes also adds to the mystery of our spoon object. Your spoon should reflect your creative explorations. The spoon in Figure 24-62 represents mine.

Figure 24-62: Creating a unique spoon gives us a chance to put a lot of the Extreme 3D tools we've learned how to use into practice.

Step #3: Place the Spoon in the Bowl

Move the spoon you created to a position inside the bowl. Check the placement in all views to make sure it is correct, and then lock-link the spoon to the bowl.

Figure 24-63: The spoon is placed in the bowl at an interesting camera position.

Step #4: Create a Liquid in the Bowl

Draw a circle in the Top view that is sized for the bowl. Extrude it a bit so it will accept a material. Select any material you like and place it on the extruded circle, as long as the material has some interest and variety. Set the transparency of the material to 75 percent, allowing the spoon to be seen through the liquid.

Figure 24-64: Placing a transparent circle mapped with a texture in the bowl makes the viewer believe it is filled with liquid.

Step #5: Add the Alphabet to the Soup

Click on the Text tool, and spell out your name. Apply the text to the screen, and extrude it so it will accept a material texture. Select each letter and color it different from the rest. Move each letter into the soup, and randomly rotate it to give the graphic interest. Find a good camera angle and render the scene. Render several views, so you can select amongst them in a suitable FreeHand project.

Figure 24-65: The finished alphabet soup scene.

The Wine Setting

In the many poster graphics created during this century, thousands center on the idea or the actual subject of wine. This can be represented as a wine glass filled to the brim with the sparkling beverage, or a tableau of a wine setting on a table in the corner, anticipating the conversation soon to pass between two lovers. Wine is both a product and a symbol, and the probability is that it will wind up in the portfolio collection that represents your best work. Here are three ways to create graphics that use wine as a central theme.

Tip

Use the accompanying CD-ROM to load the Wine1.FH7 Project and all of the tutorial elements into FreeHand so you can more easily work through this example. You may also find some of the elements in the Parts and Pieces folder.

Using FreeHand

This project will test your drawing capabilities with the FreeHand tool, and help you understand and appreciate the dynamics of cloning objects.

Step #1: Create a Grape Face

If raisins can have faces and dance in TV commercials, then grapes (the parents of raisins) can have faces, too. Draw an oval that is shaped like a grape, a little taller than wide. Give a one-point stroke to it, and use a radial gradient CMYK fill that ranges from white to purple (0, 60, 0, 30). Set the Locate Center knob to the upper left quadrant of the control area in the Fill Inspector. Use the FreeHand tool to draw a face on the grape. Group everything.

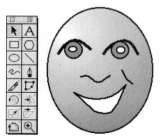

Figure 24-66: A face is drawn on the grape.

Step #2: Duplicate & Arrange the Grapes

Duplicate the grape as many times as needed to configure a bunch. Draw a stem at the top, and send it to the back of the stack. Group everything as one graphic.

Figure 24-67: A bunch of grapes greets the world.

Step #3: Create a Bunch of Bunches

You can carry this process as far as you want by simply cloning the grouped bunch. If you want to, you can hang a grouping from a vine. Double-click the FreeHand tool to display its settings dialog. Select the Calligraphic Pen with a dimension of 12 and close the dialog. Draw a vine with the Calligraphic pen and hang cloned bunches of grapes from it.

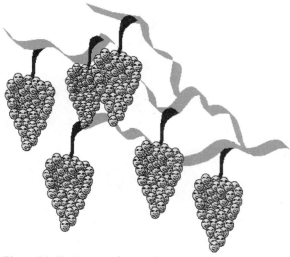

Figure 24-68: Groups of grape faces can be hung from a vine, creating an interesting border for a FreeHand page.

Step #4: Add Leaves to the Vine

You can take this stylized grape graphic one step further by adding leaves to the vine. Use the FreeHand tool to draw a leaf with a one point black stroke and a solid CMYK green fill (80, 0, 90, 30). Clone and rotate the leaf several times until you have a symmetrical grouping. Group the leaves, and clone and resize the group as many times as needed to populate the vine with leaves.

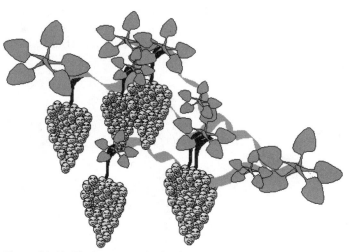

Figure 24-69: The leaves are the final touch that makes this graphic unique.

Using xRes

Next, we'll create a label for a wine bottle, using the special bitmap editing options xRes offers.

Step #1: Create the Label Background

Create a new document that is 300 x 400 pixels at 144 dpi. Fill the background with a muted yellow color. Open the final grape graphic (the vine with leaves) and also open the single smiling grape face graphic. Size the vine graphic so that it fits the width of the document (300 pixels). Use the Wand tool and the Inverse command to select only the vine graphic out of its background. Copy it to the clipboard. Click on the background screen to activate it, and select Edit I Paste. This places the vine graphic on its own object layer above the background, allowing you to reposition it. Position it at the top of the background, and drop it into place.

Repeat this procedure for the singular grape face, positioning and resizing it so that your label resembles that illustrated in Figure 24-70. Drop it into the background.

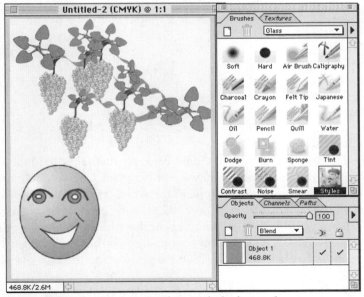

Figure 24-70: The grapes are in place on the background.

Step #2: Paint a Crown on the Grape

Use the Lasso tool to draw the outline of a crown with four spokes on the head of the grape. You can hold the Shift key down if it's necessary to add segments to the marquee. Use the Basic Airbrush with Concentration and Flow set to 50 percent and Texture to none to paint the crown a medium dark blue. Add a touch of yellow at the base. With the crown still selected, Shift-select the background with the Wand tool. Invert the selection. Paint a light brown drop shadow under the crown. Turn all selections off.

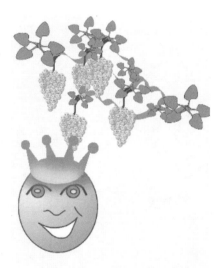

Figure 24-71: A crown is added to the grape.

Step #3: Add the Text

Change the foreground color to a dark blue. Activate the Text tool. When the text dialog comes up, select a fancy script typeface. Click on Bold and Anti-Aliased, and set the Size to 24. Type in the word "Happy," and apply the text to the screen. The word is on its own object layer, and can be positioned as needed. Before positioning the text, repeat this procedure for the words "Grape" and "Wine." Now all three words are on their own object layers, and can be singularly positioned. Position them and drop them in place.

Figure 24-72: The main text is in place on the label.

Step #4: Add the Blurb Text

Now we'll add some text to the top of the label, a little PR blurb. Repeat the methods outlined in Step #3, creating these three lines in 15 point type: "Queen of," "Happy," and "Valley." Position them and drop them into place. Add a red border around the label with the Airbrush tool by drawing a rectangular marquee inside of the label and then inverting the selection. The label is finished.

Figure 24-73: The finished label shows the added text and a border.

Using Extreme 3D

Okay. So now we have a finished product label. How about placing it on a photorealistic picture of the product?

Step #1: Create a Poster for the Background

Let's use the label graphic to create a poster that will hang in back of the actual product display. In the front view, create a portrait-sized rectangle that covers about half of the right of the screen. Extrude it a bit so that it will accept a material assignment (texture). Duplicate the rectangle, and resize the duplicate to 10 percent smaller than the original. Place the duplicate in front of the original in the Top view. Map the larger rectangle with the Satin-Gold Preset material. Map the smaller rectangle with the label art you just completed in the last exercise.

Figure 24-74: The poster displays the product label.

Step #2: Create a Product Display Surface

Create a cube on the screen that will act as the surface that the product will sit on. Elongate the cube on its X-axis (front view) by using the Stretch tool. Apply the Grooves-Khaki material preset to the cube. Render it for preview.

Figure 24-75: The cube becomes a table for product display.

Step #3: Create the Wine Bottle
Draw half of the profile of the wine bottle with the Spline tool, and lathe it to create the bottle. Use a Gray Plastic material to add a mauve color to the bottle, and load in the label as the texture to be applied.

Figure 24-76: The wine bottle profile before lathing.

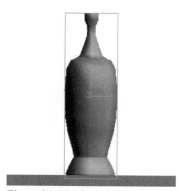

Figure 24-77: The lathed wine bottle with the material texture applied. The label is not shown yet.

Step #4: Place the Label on the Bottle

Select the bottle, and then click on the Intrinsic Texture Placement tool. At the bottom of the screen, alter the numerical indicators for material placement and size. You will have to tweak the numbers and then observe the results on the bottle to get a good feel for this. You may also have to rotate the bottle on its Y-axis (in the front view) to see the label. Incremental adjustment in hundredths and thousandths can make a lot of difference on how the label is mapped to the bottle.

Figure 24-78: Small adjustments in the parameters of the Intrinsic Texture Placement tool can accurately map the label to the bottle's shape.

Step #5: Create the Wine Glass

Draw the profile of a wine glass with the Spline tool and lathe it. Map it with a blue color and a 50 percent transparency. Set the glass on the table. Duplicate it twice, and set the duplicates in rotated positions floating above the original glass. Lathe a liquid to fit in the first wine glass, and color it with a 50 percent transparent purple hue. The scene should resemble that shown in Figure 24-79.

Figure 24-79: The wine glasses are in place in the scene.

Step #6: Create a Wall Behind the Scene

Draw a large rectangle behind the scene to emulate a wall. Leave a space in it that acts as a window behind the bottle. Load your favorite background graphic, which will be seen behind the bottle and through the window. Map the wall with whatever material suits you (as you know, I gravitate toward clouds as backdrops). When everything is in place, do a test render, followed by a group of finished renderings. Save the renderings to disk so you can select them when needed for a FreeHand project.

Figure 24-80: The finished rendering shows all elements in place. The transparent glasses add an element of mystery. The globe in the front is a Chrome sphere mapped with the poster art for effect.

Figure 24-81: Of course, you may want to port the finished 3D rendering to xRes one more time before incorporating it into a FreeHand project to add things that are best done in a 2D application, as this figure demonstrates.

Sweets

There are ten thousand sweet treats in this world, and each one can be used as a model for a great graphic. Whether used as a central theme or just as the subject of an addendum, spot illustration, candies, pies, cakes, and ice cream always attract attention.

Using FreeHand

The next time you're asked to provide a pie chart for a publication, think about this exercise. It uses a somewhat realistic pie to represent the data, an alternative that adds more interest than a cold mathematical graphic. It might not work for data that is set to represent a bank or computer company, but might be just the trick if the targeted organization is a food company or similar organization.

Tip

Use the accompanying CD-ROM to load the Piez1.FH7 Project and all of the tutorial elements into FreeHand so you can more easily work through this example. You may also find some of the elements in the Parts and Pieces folder.

Step #1: Gather Your Data

Locate and identify the data you have to use to make a pie chart. Break it down so that you can easily represent it as sections of a circle. This can best be accomplished on a sheet of paper or in xRes. If on paper, the chart can be scanned in and saved to a file. xRes roughs can be ready to export to FreeHand immediately.

Tip

The whole point in using a pie chart is to show comparative data in a way that is easy to grasp. If a section is to represent 10.1 percent, for example, rounding it off to 10 percent is okay. It will be obvious what point is being made when the 10 percent section is compared to the item that has a 20 percent slice. Pie charts work best with eight or fewer categories, so that clear labeling can be done.

You can use a calculator to make a pie chart by doing the following: Add up all of the numbers that you want to represent. For example, let's say that comes to 1500 widgets, split among six categories of widget makers. 1500 is then your total pie, so 1500 = 100%. That means that a one percent slice of the pie is equal to 1500 divided by 100, or 15. Now it's easy to just divide widget maker A's slice (let's say it's 230 units) by 15. That gives widget maker A a percentage of 15.33, or rounded off, 15 percent. If you divide up the pie into quarters, each quarter will equal 25 percent, so 15 percent can be roughed out as three-fifths of the quarter, which is fairly easy to estimate visually.

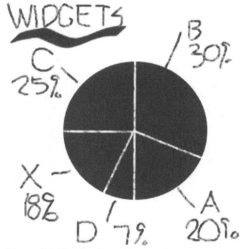

Figure 24-82: The first thing to do is to rough out a sketch of the data visually, on paper or perhaps in xRes.

Step #2: Bring the Rough into FreeHand

Import your digitized version on file or ready-made xRes rough into FreeHand so it can be used as a template for your graphic. Draw red extended lines with a two point stroke from the edge of the data demarcations outward.

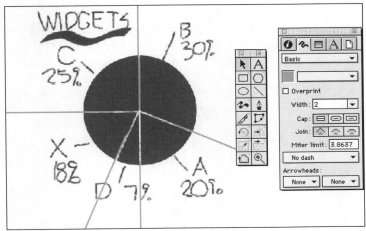

Figure 24-83: The rough file is imported into FreeHand and the red data lines are added.

Step #3: Erase the Graphic

The graphic is no longer needed, so it can be deleted or moved to a non-printing section of your document. Extend the data lines so that they meet at the center, and group them.

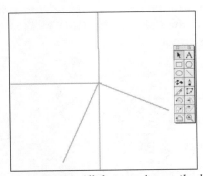

Figure 24-84: All that remains are the data lines.

Step #4: Draw a Perfect Circle

Turn on the grid. Move the center point of the data lines to an intersection on the grid. Draw a circle by using the Elipse tool while holding down the Shift key. Start the circle at the upper left corner where the grid lines meet, dragging past the data line center and to the lower right, stopping at the exact grid marker that balances the starting grid marker. You may also Opt-Shift or Alt-Shift and drag from the center of the data lines. The data lines are matched exactly to the circle you drew. Group the circle and the data lines.

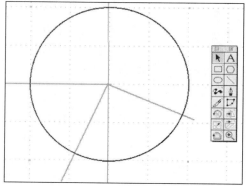

Figure 24-85: The data lines meet at the center of the circle.

Step #5: Add the Apple Pie Color

The most recognizable, and easiest edible pie to represent graphically, is an apple pie. Using the circle as your guide, draw a serrated edge with the FreeHand tool around the outer edge of the circle. Make sure the seated edged graphic is closed when you stop. Fill the shape with a CMYK apple-pie brown (0, 20, 90, 20) and a two point black stroke.

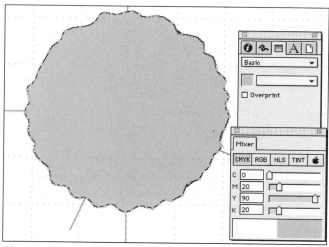

Figure 24-86: The top of the apple pie is drawn and filled in.

Step #6: Cut the Pie

With the pie selected, use the Knife tool to cut the outline where the data lines meet the serrated edge. You will see that the fill color immediately disappears, which is a good indicator that the cutting function worked. You will have to reselect all of the sections you want to cut, since these are now separated segments. Continue this process until the serrated perimeter of the pie is cut along all of the data lines. Pull the cut segments away from the circle just a little, so there is space between the segments.

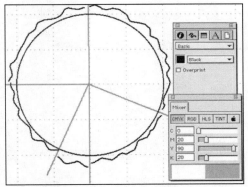

Figure 24-87: The segments are separated according to the data line template beneath.

Step #7: Complete the Sections

Using the Straight Line tool, draw in the balance of the slice edges. In each case, select the three defining perimeter lines, and select the Join command. Immediately, the slice is filled with the selected pie color. When finished, select the underlying template and move it aside. Select each slice in turn, and use the Smudge tool to give it dimension. Draw a pattern of five filled black circles. These will reinforce the identity of the pie as an apple pie. Clone the pattern, and rotate it into place on each slice as illustrated in Figure 24-88.

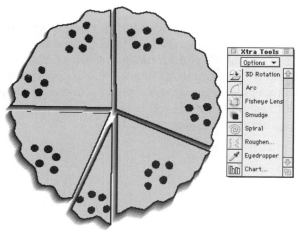

Figure 24-88: The graphic is identifiable as a sliced apple pie.

Step #8: Add the Data

Use the rough sketch as copy from which to add the data.

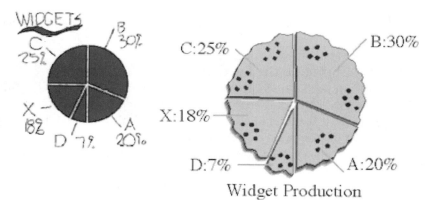

Figure 24-89: The pie chart is complete.

Step #9: Add the Accessories

Remove the data from the pie, and ungroup the slices. Draw two concentric circles, and apply a darker color or gradient to the outer one and a lighter color or gradient to the inner one. They will serve as the pie plate, so size them accordingly. Send the plate to the back of the stack under the pie. Remove one slice of pie, and duplicate and resize the large plate as a serving plate, placing it under the piece of pie. Draw a napkin with two overlapping rectangles, and add fold lines with the Line tool. Create a fork, knife, and spoon with identical "handles," using the Pen tool and the Duplication process. Draw another three concentric circles to the side of the pie. The outer one will be a top view of a cup, so use the Polygon tool to place the handle on it, and group the handle to the cup. The two inner circles will represent a beverage, so color the small inner circle a dark color and the middle circle a light color with no stroke on either. Blend them. Group the cup and the beverage. Place all of the elements and group everything.

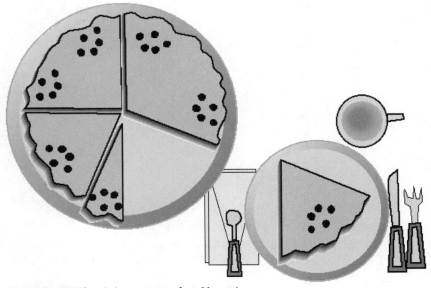

Figure 24-90: The pie is now part of a table setting.

Using xRes

I scream for ice cream, America's favorite gastronomical pastime. Let's build an ice cream cone.

Step #1: Create the Cone

Open a new document, 400 x 400 pixels at 72 dpi. Select the Lasso tool, and draw the outline of a cone on the screen. It should be about half as tall as the work area. Choose a tan color from the Swatches palette, and click on the Dots texture. Use the Textured Air Brush tool. In the Brush Options palette, set the Concentration and Flow to 50 percent, and the Texture to 100 percent. Paint the colored texture in the cone-shaped marquee.

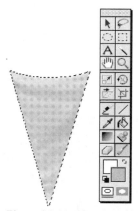

Figure 24-91: The cone takes shape.

Step #2: Give the Cone Dimension

Click on the Burn brush. Set its Concentration, Flow, and Strength to 50 percent. Use it to darken the outer edges of the cone. Deselect the cone marquee.

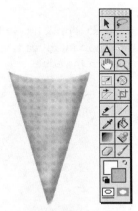

Figure 24-92: The cone gets dimension when the edges are darkened.

Step #3: Add the First Scoop

Use the Lasso tool to draw an outline for the first scoop. Select any two textures you like, and apply each one to a half of the marqueed outline (use a brown hue with the Textured Airbrush tool). As with the cone, use the Burn brush to add darkened edges for dimension.

Figure 24-93: The first scoop is in place.

Step #4: Add the Second Scoop

Draw the outline marquee for the second scoop. Select a pink hue and two different textures. Apply each one to a half of the scoop marquee with the Textured Air Brush, and use the Burn brush to darken the edges.

Figure 24-94: The second scoop has been added.

Step #5: Add the Third Scoop

Continue the same process and add a third scoop. Use the Elipse Marquee tool to draw the outline of a cherry, and use the basic Airbrush to color it red. Use the Burn brush to give it some dimension. Copy and paste it, and move the duplicates into position on the third scoop. Use the Smear tool and a size 9 brush to smear the bottom of the cherries into the third scoop. Your ice cream is ready. Save it to disk in readiness for the right FreeHand project.

Figure 24-95: The third scoop is added using Extreme 3D.

Holidays

You've eaten too much, but the aroma of fresh baked cookies melts the air. You can't resist just one…or more.

Step #1: Design a Cookie Tray

Draw half of the tray's profile, giving it a very long base.

Figure 24-96: The profile prior to lathing.

Step #2: Lathe the Profile in the Front View

Select the Lathe tool, and draw a vertical line at the end of the long profile base.

Figure 24-97: The lathed tray from the front view.

Figure 24-98: The lathed tray from the top view.

Step #3: Change the Tray's Z Dimension

From the Top view, select the tray and simplify its geometry. Double-click on the Stretch tool, select the Z-axis in the dialog, and close the dialog by selecting OK and accepting the changes. With the tray selected in the Top view, move the Stretch tool cursor up as you click and drag the mouse. You will see a new guideline that represents the changed Z dimension of the tray. Release the mouse button when the tray reaches about half of its former Z dimension.

Figure 24-99: The tray is reshaped with a shorter Z dimension, as seen in the three-quarter view.

Step #4: Shape the Handles

Go to the Top view. Hide the tray to give yourself more room to work. Draw a very complex curve and a small circle. This is the start of half of the tray's handle.

Figure 24-100: These are the basic forms that will shape the handle.

Step #5: Extrude the Circle Profile

Click on the Sweep tool, and click on the circle and then the curve. The circle is extruded along the curve forming a 3D object.

Figure 24-101: The basic handle shape is completed.

Step #6: Build the Handles

Use the Mirror tool to build the other half of the handle in the Top view, by drawing the mirror line horizontally at the lower portion of the shape. Place a sphere at the intersection points of the handle halves. Lock-link both halves of the handle to the sphere. Move the handle into place on the tray. Use the Mirror tool again to build the other handle in the Top view. This time, draw the mirror line vertically across the center of the tray. Lock-link everything to the tray.

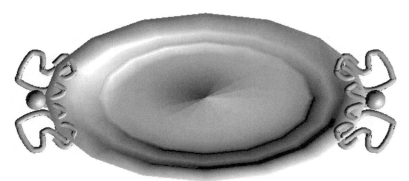

Figure 24-102: Even unrendered, the tray with handles has an appreciable 3D realism.

Step #7: Create Some Cookies

Remain in the Top view. Draw a series of shapes made from three or four intersecting circles. Select each of the circle groups in turn, and click on the Metaform tool. Respond Yes to the dialog. Each time, your circles will be metaformed into a 3D object, which will resemble bumpy cookie shapes.

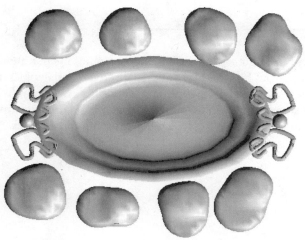

Figure 24-103: The cookies are created by metaforming 2D circles.

Step #8: Assign Materials & Move the Cookies Onto the Tray

Assign a material to each cookie. I especially recommend the Mold and Crusty Presets. They don't sound too appetizing, but they make very believable cookies. Move the cookies into position on the tray, using a random order. Render, save to disk, and import into FreeHand for a holiday brochure or card.

Figure 24-104: A tray of cookies owes its existence to Extreme 3D and a little creative energy.

Moving On

We've satisfied our appetite with a multicourse graphics meal in this chapter, creating everything from burgers and soup to ice cream and cookies. All of these graphics are perfect as elements in your next job for the restaurant 'round the corner. From here, we'll move on to animated graphics, demonstrating how FreeHand, xRes, and Extreme 3D can be used as animation engines.

25

Animation Techniques

Animations consist of a series of single frames that are played back at a speed that forces the eye to see movement. No movement really exists in animations or movies, just a slight displacement of the on-screen subjects from frame to frame. Any application that can produce single-frame graphics can produce everything you need for an animation. The only added component is software that can "compile" the single frames into an animated or movie sequence.

There are dozens of such applications on the market, and a number are detailed in Appendix D. The animation compiler application does more than just string together a number of pictures. It also deals with the issue of *compression*. Compression means that each frame is compared to the frames before and after it, so only the changes that take place are written to the file, not the entire graphic. Compression applications only write the whole graphic if the frame is denoted as a key frame. This is why a 30-frame movie or animation file is a lot smaller than the sum of the 30 individual frames. There are animation compilers that deal with vector graphics (like FreeHand) and others that deal with bitmap graphics (like the graphics produced by both xRes and Extreme 3D).

If you are using FreeHand to produce work that is printed on paper, and only that, then the whole topic of animation is probably not of primary interest to you. Publishing means more than paper output these days, however, and more often than not a publication on paper has a counterpart on the Web, or perhaps appears in CD-ROM format as well. Animation came of age on film, especially through the work of Disney and other studios. When TV came along, animation became a device used to give commercials a special flavor, a way of softening the shrill voices of the merchants. Now that we find ourselves in the age of multimedia and Web surfing, animation has become more powerful than ever for entertainment and education. It's not surprising then that an application as ubiquitous as FreeHand and the other components of the FreeHand Graphics Studio can help you create unique approaches to animation.

Tip

If you are interested in using non-animation applications like FreeHand and xRes as animation utilities, be sure to refer to Appendix D, which discusses several utilities that can be used to compile single frames into animations for either multimedia or Web purposes.

Of the three applications in the FreeHand Graphics Studio collection that are suitable for creating animations, only Extreme 3D contains the necessary tools for automating the process. Developing animations with either FreeHand or xRes requires that you record a frame each time one is ready. Frames are then saved with some indication in their name that places them where they belong in the sequence, such as adding 01 or 001 in the name for the first frame, 02 or 002 for the second frame, and so on.

File Naming Conventions for Animations

Naming conventions on the Mac OS and Windows are very different for animation, and it is important to pay attention to those conventions. For instance, on the Mac OS you can add the frame number as an extension to the file; for example, MyFrame.001, MyFrame.002, MyFrame.003, and so on. On Windows, however, you cannot add the frame numbers as an extension. Extensions on the Windows side are reserved for file type data, such as TIF, GIF, and JPG. Extensions on the Windows side must be formatted as a dot followed by a three letter extension type descriptor, such as MyFrame.TIF or MyFrame.GIF. You must fold the numerical data into the file before the extension, and the total name must have no more than eight characters. Although the eight character rule has been negated in Windows '95, it is still safer to obey for now, since so many applications haven't caught up to the Windows '95 conventions yet. An example for the tenth frame of an animation might look like MyFrm001.TIF or MyFrm010.GIF. If your animation is to be saved to a multimedia CD-ROM as single frames, follow the Windows conventions if you need both Mac and Windows compatibility, and can't include specific data for each. The Mac OS will have less of a problem interpreting the Windows file naming convention, whereas the Windows cannot digest non-Windows file naming conventions.

The method for creating animation frames in an application not designed to produce animations remains the same in all cases. It consists of altering some part of a graphic, and saving it out as a named file in the sequence, following either the Mac OS or Windows naming convention. The easiest way to do this is to save out the altered frame as you normally would, paying attention to the enumerating and naming conventions just spoken about.

There is another alternative. That is to use a screen grabbing utility (like FlashIt for the Mac OS or PaintShop Pro for Windows platforms) to grab and save the screen. Commonly, screen grab utilities allow you to surround the data to be grabbed and saved by using a definable area marquee. This is fine, as long as you are aware that all of the frames that are to be compiled later on into an animation format (like QuickTime on the Mac OS and Windows, or AVI on Windows) absolutely have to be the same exact size. If you are using a screen grabbing utility that allows you to select the size of the file with a definable rectangular marquee, the frames will not be the same size. They may be close, but if the size varies by even one pixel from frame to frame, the compilation utility will choke and refuse to cooperate. This means that using a screen grab utility to store the separate single frames will necessitate a further step, which is to double-check (and resize when necessary) all of the frames in a sequence of enumerated frames. It's better, then, to design your animated frames so that standard save processes can be used to record them to disk.

You can use various batch processing and scripting techniques to automate the process of saving out single frames in a sequence, but I would caution you against it. This is especially true if you are new to the process of developing animations in a non-animation application. Too much can go wrong and waste your time instead of saving time. Develop your single frames with as much care and finesse as possible, and then save them out to disk one by one. When it comes time to compile the animation, you'll be thankful you spent the extra time in the development process.

Using FreeHand

Because FreeHand was not designed as an animation application itself, there are several things to keep in mind if you plan to use it as a creative animation tool.

1. Make sure that the screen sizes you are working with fit the task being planned for your animation frames. If you are using FreeHand to develop an animation for use on the Web, for instance, realize that it will be some time before full-screen animations can play on the Web at their

proper speed (30 frames per second). Bandwidth is still a precious commodity, and it takes a lot of bandwidth to handle a full-screen animation. Typically, animations on the Web are about a quarter screen in size (about 160 x 120 pixels is a common size), and many are quite a bit smaller. The resolution for Web animations is expected to be 72 dots per inch (dpi), although the emerging HDTV standards may change that within the next ten years.

2. For smooth animations, movements of elements in the animation should be small from frame to frame if you want smooth playback. Within FreeHand, this means taking care (and having the patience) to move things by small increments from frame to frame as your animation develops.

3. Your FreeHand Web animations should have "safe" RGB colors (do not use a CMYK palette for animations), because RGB colors that range above the 220 mark (on a scale of 1 to 256 for each RGB channel) tend to bleed on screen. This is more true for TV than for surfing the Web on a computer, but the expansion of Web-TV alternatives means Web animators are going to have to consider the parameters of television as well as those of computer screens in the coming years. Again, the newly emerging HDTV standards will have an effect on all of this, but it's far too early to neglect the present parameters.

4. You must check the Selected objects only box when saving an animation frame to disk, and must therefore have selected all of the elements to appear in the animation on the FreeHand workspace. Otherwise, FreeHand will attempt to save the whole document to disk each time, which could result in a system crash because of data overload.

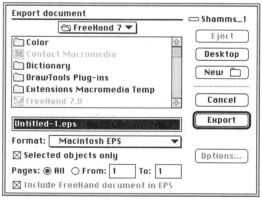

Figure 25-1: When exporting frames of your animation to disk in FreeHand, be sure to check the Select objects only.

Holes in Motion

In FreeHand, a "hole" can be thought of as an object, not just an empty part of an object. Holes as objects can be moved around like any other object, leading to some interesting visual and potentially animated effects. Holes as objects in FreeHand can be seen very clearly when you are working with text that has been transformed to a path. Letters and numbers that have separate empty parts in their design (as do the letters A, B, D, O, P, Q, R, and the numbers 4, 6, 8, 9, and 0) can be manipulated so that the spaces become objects with their own set of maneuverable properties. Once these letters or numbers are ungrouped to the point that the hole is separated from the fill space surrounding it, all sorts of animated shenanigans are possible.

Tip

Use the accompanying CD-ROM to load the Holes.mov animation for the Mac, or the Holes.AVI animation for Windows playback.

Step #1: Draw the Filled Backdrop

Draw a rectangle that is 4 inches wide by 3 inches deep on the screen. Fill it with a CMYK linear gradient that ranges from bright magenta (0, 100, 0, 0) at the top to a bright yellow (0, 0, 100, 0) at the bottom. This will be the size and background for your animation.

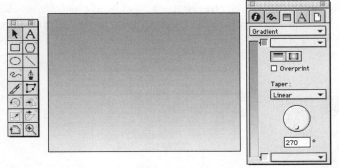

Figure 25-2: The gradient filled rectangle will be the animation's backdrop.

Step #2: Create Frame 01 of the Animation

Use the Text tool to create a text block that reads "SOS," convert to paths, and ungroup it. The letter "O" will not ungroup, because it has a hole in it. Select the "O" and use the Split command to separate the hole from the letter. Both will be filled with a solid black color by default. Select only the hole, and apply the same gradient fill as you used on the background. This represents your animation at frame 01. Group everything, and save the selected object to disk (remembering the naming conventions discussed earlier, as well as checking the Selected objects only box) as frame 01 of your animation.

Figure 25-3: The text block is ungrouped, and the hole in the letter "O" is now a separate gradient-filled object.

Step #3: Create the Balance of the Frames

Ungroup everything. Select the hole in the "O" and move its control points so it expands a little. Select everything and group it. Save this out as frame 02 of the animation. Continue this process for a total of 10 frames, each time grouping and ungrouping the hole. At frame 10 the hole should cover the background completely. Move the hole in smaller increments at the start, and larger increments from frame 6 to 10. You now have all of the frames for a 10-frame animated sequence.

Figure 25-4: Here's how the 10 frames progress from start to finish. Frame 01 is at the upper left, and frame 10 is at the lower right.

Congratulations! You have completed your first animated sequence in FreeHand. The frames can now be compiled into a compressed animation file.

ShapeMorph

This is a type of animation that FreeHand excels in because of the way that vector graphics behave. Because most computer animations are based upon bitmaps and bitmaps have a much harder time producing shape morphs (transitions from one shape outline to another) without introducing all sorts of anomalies (especially the dreaded jaggies, the stair-stepping that occurs when pixelated lines vary from horizontal, vertical, or a 45 degree diagonal), vector art is a better choice when it comes to this type of animation. Shape morphing can be defined as the transformation of one profile of a shape to another, and FreeHand offers the perfect process in which this can be accomplished: blending.

Tip

> *Use the accompanying CD-ROM to load the Morph.mov animation for the Mac, or the Morph.AVI animation for Windows playback.*

Step #1: Create the Profile Shapes to be Morphed

Use the FreeHand tool or the Pen to create two outline shapes, a bird and a fish, each facing left. This technique works best when the two elements, the source and target graphics, have recognizable profiles. Give each shape a different color, and set the stroke to a one point black on each. You can't add an eye to either drawing, because doing that would create a group, and groups can't be blended.

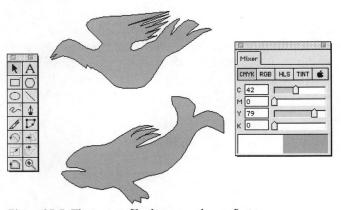

Figure 25-5: The two profile shapes are drawn first.

Step #2: Blend the Shapes

Shift-select both shapes, and click on the Blend tool. The blend produces a series of transitional shapes, each of which is a separate object. Ungroup the blended graphic twice, separating all of the elements.

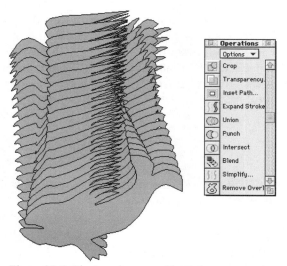

Figure 25-6: The two shapes are blended.

Step #3: Set Up the Frame

As in the last animation exercise, set up a 4 inch wide and 3 inch deep rectangle as the animation backdrop. Set another rectangle inside of it that will act as the sea, taking up about half of the larger rectangle. Color the sea with a CMYK gradient that ranges from a dark blue (60, 0, 0, 60) at the bottom to a lighter blue-green (15, 0, 30, 15) at the top. Above the sea we want to have the sky. Use a CMYK gradient that ranges from a light pink (0, 15, 10, 0) at the horizon to purple (30, 60, 0, 0) at the top. Use the Calligraphic pen tool to draw some streaky CMYK yellowish-white (0, 0, 40, 0) clouds in the sky. Place a bright CMYK red (0, 100, 100, 0) sun in the sky at the upper left.

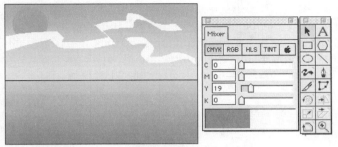

Figure 25-7: The backdrop for the animation is completed.

Step #4: Get the Pieces Ready

Create the "eyes" by drawing a small circle with a one point black stroke and a white fill. Duplicate it so you have a total of 12 pieces. This will be a 15-frame animation. Select 12 of the morphed (blended) graphics produced earlier, and set them up in an arranged order. Make sure the first is the original fish and the last is the original bird, with the others chosen from the blended series. Attach an "eye" to each of the separate 12 graphics, and group the eye to the graphic.

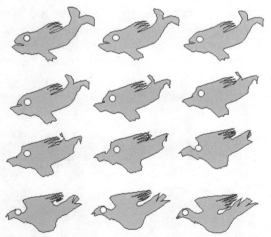

Figure 25-8: All 12 foreground pieces are ready to place.

Step #5: Creating the First Frame

The idea is to show the fish moving in the sea, and then leaving it as a transformed bird. Take the first foreground graphic (the original fish) and place it in the sea on the right. Select everything and group it. Export the graphic as frame 01 (remember to check the Selected objects only box).

Figure 25-9: The first frame of the animation.

Step #6: Create the Balance of the Frames

Use the same method to create the balance of the single frames. Remember to group the foreground to the background before exporting, and to ungroup it to use the next foreground graphic after an export is complete. You can rotate the fish as it leaves the water for even more visual interest. Frames 12 to 15 use the same graphic, the original bird shape, showing it moving more to the left.

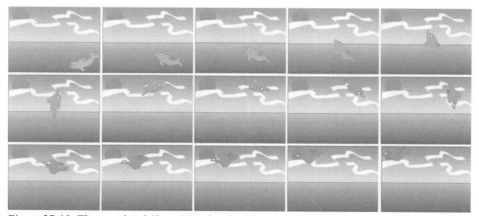

Figure 25-10: The completed Shape Morph animation.

Tip

You could take the completed FreeHand animation frames a step further and export each frame to xRes, adding splashes, foam, and other effects.

Using xRes

xRes animations, or better stated, the production of animation frames in xRes, is handled very differently than accomplishing the same feat in FreeHand. Bitmap painting applications have their own strengths when it comes to developing animation frames. Among these strengths are the following:

- The capability to work with a more diverse color palette.
- Singular pixels, which mean little to vector art, can actually become an emphasized part of the animation's look.
- Jaggies can become a focus of attention rather than an attribute to try and cover up.

Layers & Motion

The whole idea of layers in a computer graphics application was actually born in the animated film studio, Disney's studio to be exact. In the 1930s, Disney studios invented what was called the Multiplane Camera. This device allowed the animator to move several layers of foreground art against a stable background. The background, when needed, could move as well. This meant that backgrounds could be painted on long horizontal strips, so a character could go through the same motions over and over again, but since the background evidenced change, the audience wouldn't get bored.

Tip

Use the accompanying CD-ROM to load the LMtn.mov animation for the Mac, or the LMtn.AVI animation for Windows playback.

Step #1: Create the Background

Create a new document that is 900 pixels wide and 200 pixels high at 72 dots per inch (dpi). It's time for texture painting! This will be the scenic backdrop for your xRes animation. Use your creative ideas to paint a row of houses with a street in the foreground. Make the scene as colorful as you like, making it more loose and painterly than sharp edged and architectural. Use the Textured Air Brush with a Concentration and Flow of 50 percent and Texture set to 100 percent. Apply a mixture of textures to the shapes. The look should be stylistic instead of photographic. Your painting will be unique, but take a look at Figure 25-11 as one reference example. Save the painting to disk as a TIFF file with a descriptive name. Close the document.

Figure 25-11: This is one idea for working out a background texture painting for this exercise. About two-thirds of the background is shown.

Step #2: Paint a Cartoony Car

Open a new document. Make it 300 pixels wide and 200 pixels deep at 72 dpi. Paint a cartoony car, using any brush combinations and colors you want. Your car will look different from the one pictured in Figure 25-12, but you get the idea. Save the car. Use the Wand and the Inverse command tool to select only the car, and copy it to the clipboard.

Figure 25-12: A cartoony car is added to a separate document.

Step #3: Putting It All Together

Create a new document, 300 x 300 pixels at 72 dpi. Load in the background
(the 900 x 300 pixel graphic), and select all. Copy it to the clipboard. Click on
the 300 x 300 pixel document, and select Paste. The background is now floating over the 300 x 300 pixel graphic as an object layer. Select the car's background with the Wand tool, then use Inverse to select the car. Copy it to the
clipboard. Click on the 300 x 300 pixel document and select Paste. The car now
floats on its own object layer, over the 900 x 300 pixel background. Activate the
900 x 300 pixel object layer, and move the graphic so that its right edge lines
up with the left edge of the 300 x 300 pixel space. Place the car on the road.

Figure 25-13: This is the starting frame of the animation.

Step #4: Create the Frames

Move the background object layer about half an inch to the left on the screen, and move the car a little vertically for each frame. Do this for 12 frames, and save each to disk as a TIFF file. Incorporate the frame number in the name as discussed previously. After the 12 frames have been exported, load each one back into xRes to add a little puff of exhaust to the car, or whatever else you desire. Save them back to disk. When finished and after compiling the frames, the car will bounce along the road from left to right.

Figure 25-14: Four frames from the finished animation sequence.

Animated Filters

Plug-in filters drive much of the obsession for using a bitmap painting application creatively. Plug-in filters perform a wide array of magical effects on the graphics they are targeted to. xRes-native effects filters offer some very unique opportunities for developing animated sequences. This is because most of them are driven through a command dialog that allows you to set the degree and extent of the effect with a slider. Over time, a graphic can be affected by different settings of the same filter, so a gradual increase or decrease in the filter's effects can be designed. Not all of the effects in xRes are suitable for animated tasks, but those that are possible candidates for developing animations are detailed in Appendix B.

Tip

Use the accompanying CD-ROM to load the Filterz.mov animation for the Mac, or the Filterz.AVI animation for Windows playback.

The importance of taking note of the range represented by the control slider(s) in any animated xRes filter effect is that the range is equal to the potential number of different and unique frames in a sequence. A slider that ranges from 1 to 32 for instance can create its effect on 32 frames before repeating any one already generated. A slider that has a range of -180 to +180 can produce 360 different unique frames of animation. When multiple sliders enter the picture, the number of frames increases exponentially, because they can be applied singly, together, or in various combinations.

When you consider that any frame in an animation can have more than one effect applied to it, you begin to realize that a small number of effects can produce a near infinite number of unique animation frames. Here is one example of how to develop an animation using one of xRes's native filters.

Step #1: Import an Image or Photo
Load in a graphic or photo. Select all. Select Effects | Distortion and bring up the Fish Eye effect.

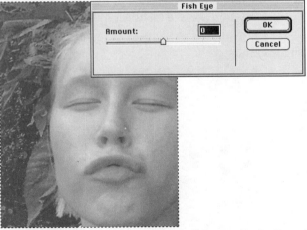

Figure 25-15: Load in your graphic, and then access the distortion effect called Fish Eye.

Step #2: Create the First & Second Frames

Save the original frame out as 001, adhering to the file naming conventions discussed earlier. For the second frame, apply a Fish Eye distortion of +10, and accept the distortion. Save the frame as 002.

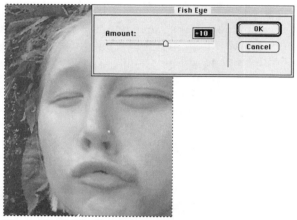

Figure 25-16: The first distorted frame is saved out with an incorporated number of 002.

Step #3: Create the Rest of the Frames

Using the same methods described in Step #2, generate a total of 10 animation single frames, tagging each with an incremental number in the file name. Frame 015, the last frame, should have an effect of +100 on the Amount slider.

Figure 25-17: An example of the Fisheye distortion is seen in these four sample frames from the animation sequence.

Using Extreme 3D

Unlike xRes and FreeHand, Extreme 3D is a true animation application, with tools and options expressly designed to help you generate animations. You need to master the use of the Animation Controls and the Score utilities to generate the animations necessary for professional work. Neither of these modules present much difficulty with a little dedicated effort. Readers who are familiar with other 3D applications should find Extreme 3D's animation controls a snap to learn.

The two most interesting and challenging uses for 3D animation applications are to be able to create and animate organic objects and logo objects. Organic objects range from human and humanoid forms to insect, animal, and even non-living forms made to act in a living way (like trees that dance and cars with movable mouths that talk). In the commercial world, animated characters often become associated with a product or service as strongly as (or sometimes stronger than) the company's logo. Cases in point would be Tony the Tiger for Kellogg or the Michelin Man for Michelin Tires.

A logo can be a text block, a corporate symbol, or any other form that represents an organization or a concept. The term "flying logos" refers to the standard process of flying a logo on screen from the distance, often with a specific spin involved, and any professional 3D software should accomplish this task with ease. The following two exercises look at both types of animations, and how to create them with Extreme 3D.

Link Dancer

Extreme 3D excels when it comes to options used to connect objects in a hierarchy. The various linking methods (free, lock, ball-joint, and watch) each have areas of specific use in developing believable animations. Of all of these, the ball-joint link is the most useful when it comes to animating characters that are to move with a degree of human movements. These do not have to be humanoid characters at all, but can range from animals to normally inanimate objects. It can be their movements that give them a degree of human understanding, and can communicate a human-like consciousness.

The ball-joint link allows parts of the subject's body to be connected so that rotations of one object low in the hierarchy (like a finger) do not disassociate themselves from their parent (for example, the hand, which is the parent of the finger). It's very important to develop ball-joint links so that they determine and display the underlying hierarchy in character animation.

Tip

Use the accompanying CD-ROM to load the Dncr.mov animation for the Mac, or the Dncr.AVI animation for Windows playback.

Step #1: Create the Figure's Head

Work in the front view, with the Perspective set to Orthographic. Draw a 2D form with the Spline tool. It can be any form you desire, though aiming for a head that can be recognized as such is desirable. When the shape is complete, lathe it into a 3D object. Create a few spheres or lathed objects for the nose and eyes. Draw a closed curve with the Spline tool, and extrude it for lips. Lock-link the parts to the head. Use the Move | Object | Center tool to move the center of the head to the bottom of the neck, allowing realistic linked motion later on. Use your imagination, but refer to figure 25-18 as one version of a possible outcome.

Figure 25-18: The head is the first part of the character to take shape.

Step #2: Create the Torso

Use a sphere to create the torso section. Adorn it with whatever shapes you think are necessary for the character you're creating. Place the head in position, and ball-joint-link it to the torso.

Figure 25-19: The torso is formed, and the head is ball-joint-linked to it.

Step #3: Create the Arms & Hands

For the upper and lower arms, lathe a splined curve, then reduce the X dimension with the Stretch tool. This gives you a thinner profile in the front view. Move the object center of the upper and lower arms to the top of the object, so that the ball-joint-links will work correctly. When finished with the upper and lower arm on one side, move them into place and use the Mirror tool to get the other upper and lower arm. Move the object center of the hand to the upper wrist portion. Draw the hand with a Splined curve, and extrude it to give it depth. Move it into place, and mirror the other hand. Ball-joint-link the parts in an appropriate hierarchy (hand to lower arm, lower arm to upper arm, and upper arm to torso).

Tip

When moving the object center of an object, open its geometry first. Then use the Object Center tool on a very closely zoomed-in view so you can see what you're doing. By default, the object center point is green.

Figure 25-20: The arms and hands have been added. This figure also has a cane.

Step #4: Add the Lower Torso & Legs

Use the same processes you just used to create the arms and hands to create the lower torso, upper and lower legs, and feet. Make sure you move all of the object centers to the top of these objects to accommodate ball-joint-linked movements.

Figure 25-21: The balance of the figure's parts are added and ball-joint-linked.

Tip

With the way that Extreme 3D's linked hierarchies operate, it's not a bad idea to place spheres at the joints that connect ball-joint-links. As various parts rotate, the spheres hide the jointed ends of moving parts.

Step #5: Use Materials to Add Color & Texture

Select any materials from the Presets library that suit the character you have developed, and edit them as necessary to provide color and texture. Save the Extreme 3D project so that you have it as a resource.

Figure 25-22: The character is painted with materials from the Presets library.

Step #6: Add the Animation

Open the Animation Controls window, and turn recording off. Set the character in a position you want for the start of the animation, and set the ending frame to 30. This will generate 30 frames of animation. Make sure zero is shown in the current timefield, and turn the recording button on by clicking on it, lighting up the red recording light.

Tip

The Animation Controls window is the easiest way to generate animations in Extreme 3D. Just a few commands need be learned, and they are intuitive. See the section in the book dealing with using the Animation Controls for a detailed discussion.

Change the current time to 10, and press Enter. This sets the animation at Frame 10. Reposition and manipulate any of the elements in the character, and set them the way you want them in Frame 10. Repeat this procedure for frames 20 and 30, each time adjusting the components that are to show movement. Having done this, you will have set key frames at frames 0, 10, 20, and 30.

Reset the Window size to 320 x 240, a common multimedia size, in the Window Setup dialog. Apply the change. Recenter the character in the new screen, and select Save to Disk. In the dialog that appears, select the Quicktime or AVI option, depending on your platform. Set quality to highest, and leave the rest of the settings as defaulted. Choose a path and a name for the animation, and begin the rendering.

When you animation is finished, you might want to break out several of the frames individually for placement in a FreeHand document. See Appendix D for a detailed look at what utilities might be helpful in this purpose.

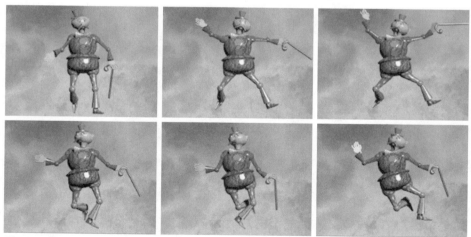

Figure 25-23: This is a collection of single frames from the author's rendered character animation.

Logo Animation

This exercise makes use of the more complex animation controls found in the Score window. The Score can be used as a stand-alone animation controller, or in concert with the Animation Controls window. We are going to add internal pulsation to the selected 3D logo, and we will also set it spinning and traveling in space.

Tip

> *Use the accompanying CD-ROM to load the Logo.mov animation for the Mac, or the Logo.AVI animation for Windows playback.*

Step #1: Import or Create a Logo

Create a logo with the Text tool. Write out a basic line of text. After it is written to the workspace, open its geometry, and alter it so that it looks more like a logo and less like text (use the control points to customize its appearance by adjusting and reshaping a few of the letters). Close the geometry. Use the Extrude tool to give it some 3D depth. Apply the Default-Scratched Metal material to it. Place it in the workspace at the upper left.

Figure 25-24: This is the logo to be animated.

Step #2: Animate the Logo

Open the Score and Animation Controls windows, and also make sure that the Object window is on screen. In the Animation Controls window, set the End number of frames to 60, meaning that the total animation will have 60 frames. Set the FPS (frames per second) to 30. At 30 fps with 60 frames, your finished animation will last two seconds (60/30 = 2).

Select your graphic on the workspace so that it has the expected red box selection indicator around it. If you have chosen to do this exercise with a text block, then select one letter in that text block. Notice that the name of the object appears in the Object window. Find that same object name as listed in the Score window (making sure that you have selected to show All Objects and All Tracks from the pull-down menus). Make sure the Animation Recording function is switched on.

Tip

Remember to have the Object window on screen while you are designing the animation. The object name is always displayed here when you click on the object on the workspace. This allows you to find that same object name in the Score window, which is vital when you need to change items that are connected to that named object (its texture, placement, size, and position).

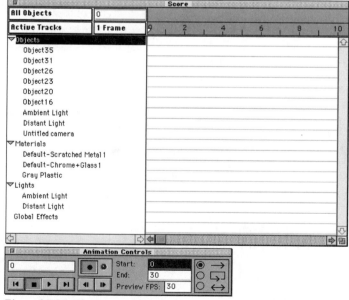

Figure 25-25: The Score and Animation Controls windows give you instant control over everything in the scene.

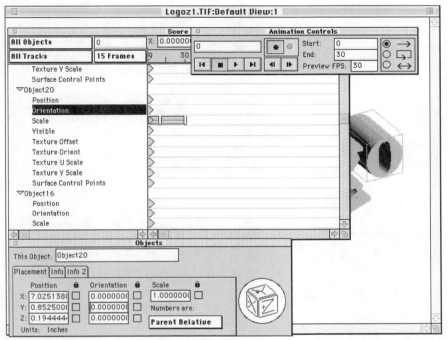

Figure 25-26: Selecting the All Tracks option gives you access to every parameter of all the listed objects, from how textures are applied to the global fog switch.

Step #3: Pulse the Graphics

In either the Score or the Animation Controls window, type in a 10 in the current time field. The number you type in is displayed in the other window, too. Press Enter, which brings you to that frame on the workspace. Now for the fun. Select any graphic element that is a part of the whole logo (or select the whole logo if you are not doing the text block process), and reduce its size to about half. Do this to as many parts of the graphic as are available as separate objects. Note that in the Score window, the action bar to the right of the Scale parameter for each object shows a solid bar that ends at the marker for frame 10, visually indicating that the scaling for that object will be animated over time.

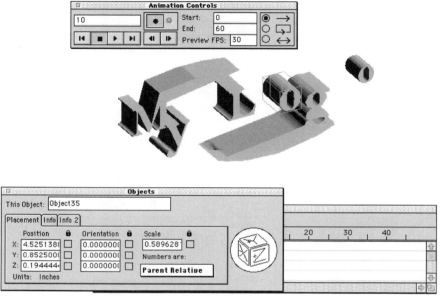

Figure 25-27: In frame 10, the logo will break up.

Step #4: Continue the Pulse

Set the current time in either the Score or Animation Controls window to 25, and press Enter. In frame 20, select all of the same elements you reduced, and enlarge them to 200 percent of the original size. This will tend to make the elements intersect each other. That is exactly what we want. Watch the Scale indicator in the Object window as you resize the selection. You can also just enter the number 200 here (200 percent), but that takes the hands-on feel away from you. I prefer manual resizing at this stage, because I can control the object interactions more effectively.

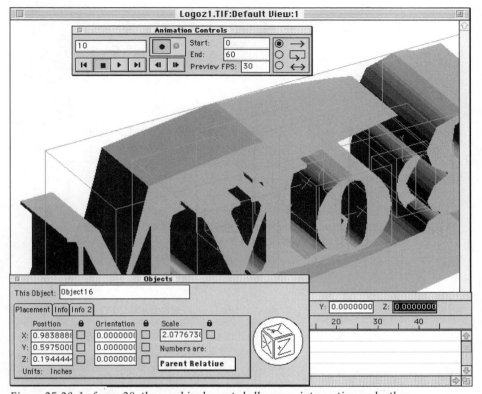

Figure 25-28: In frame 20, the graphic elements balloon up, intersecting each other.

Step #5: Continue to Frame 45

Set the current time to frame 45. Select Edit | Select All, and reset the number in the Scale area of the Object window to 1.0. This is a situation where it makes more sense to use the numeric instead of the manual option. This makes all sizes return to their original setting at frame 45, where we will leave them until frame 60.

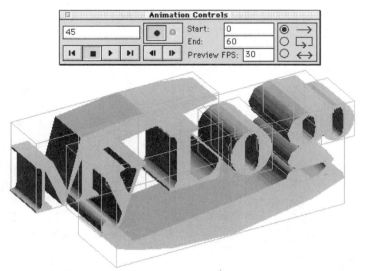

Figure 25-29: At frame 45, the elements of the logo return to their original size.

Step #6: Begin the Rotations

Set the current time to frame 0, and move the logo to the upper left of the screen, with part of it actually off the screen. In the Three Quarters view in frame 0, set the XYZ rotation angles to 90, 90, 0. Go to frame 25, and set the rotation angles to 180, 60, 0. Go to frame 45, and set the XYZ rotation angles to 30, 30, 0 (the default angles for the Three Quarters view). Return to frame 0, and select Animate I Animation path I Show. Zoom out about six times. The blue lines represent the animation path for all of the objects in the scene.

Tip

In computer animation, you can usually fake distance by making an object larger or smaller. As long as shadows aren't involved, this is a quicker way to achieve a distance effect.

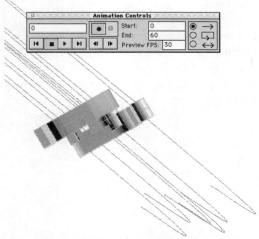

Figure 25-30: The Animation path can be seen and manipulated like any other object.

Step #7: Customize the Animation Paths

Select an animation path and open its geometry. Use the Add Points tool to add points to the path, and then move these points around. Make sure not to move the final points, or the logo will finish up in never-never land. Do this to several paths from whatever view is convenient, closing the geometry after each path has been altered satisfactorily.

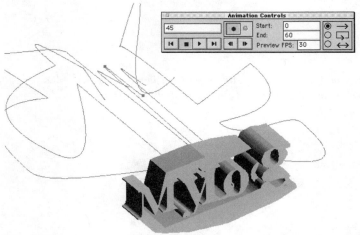

Figure 25-31: Alter the animation paths by clicking and dragging on control points and control levers.

Step #8: Render the Animation

When you think you have something interesting, render the animation at the lowest resolution and screen size possible to preview it. Especially check the last frame to see how the animation will end. This will render very quickly (turn shadows on lights off). If you are dissatisfied, alter it at the points needed. When satisfied, render it at full quality. Save the animation to disk as either a movie or single frame file.

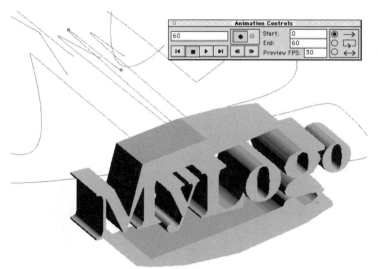

Figure 25-32: Always check the last frame. This last frame is different from the one I started with, but as luck would have it, I actually like it better.

Tip

Computer animation, like any art form, is based upon both planning and happenstance. Never stick to a structure if something better pops up.

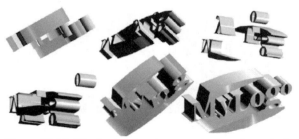

Figure 25-33: The final animation puts the logo through chaos to get to clarity.

Spin the Logo

Basic path animations are easy to configure in Extreme 3D. A path animation allows you to assign an object to a splined or primitive (rectangular or oval/circular) path, so that as the animation commences, the object follows that path in space. Here's how.

Step #1: Create a Text Block

Use the Text tool to create a text block that says "LOGO," and center the text in the workspace. Extrude the text so you can assign a material to it, and assign the Default-Marble material to it. Lock-link all of the letters to the "L."

Figure 25-34: Write the word "LOGO" to the screen, and apply a marble material to it.

Step #2: Set the Values

Bring up the Animation Controls window, and type in the number 30 as the End value. Bring up the Score window, and type in a 30 as the current time frame. Make sure that Active Object is selected. Move the selected text block a little, and you will see that the object is listed in the active list of the Score window. At the right of its Position listing, a solid bar extends from Frame 1 to Frame 30, indicating that something is being animated for this object during that time.

Step #3: Add a 2D Shape

Go to the right view. With the object still selected in the Score window, draw a circle that intersects the object.

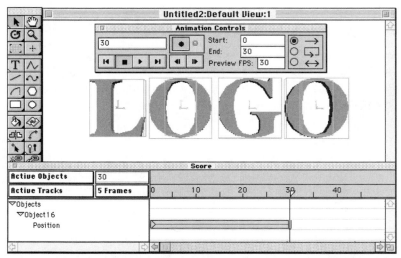

Figure 25-35: The Animation Controls and Score windows show what is occurring in the animation.

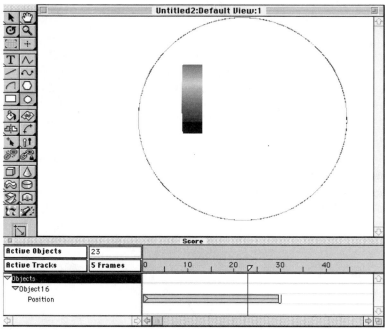

Figure 25-36: The circle is the first stage of the path.

Step #4: Convert the 2D Shape to the Object's Path

Select the Position Track in the Score window under the Object name, and select Animation | Convert the Profile to convert the profile to a path. The path will disappear, and the object will be displaced at a point along the path. Use the Animation controls to do a test of the motion. The logo is now attached to the path.

Tip

The animation path can be a rectangle or square, or even a splined curve. You can also use the path as a 2D extrusion path at the same time.

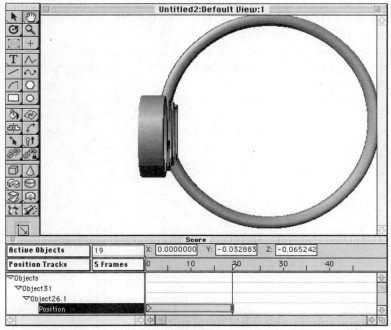

Figure 25-37: Here, the animation path has been used as an extrusion path.

Texture Animation

As far as Extreme 3D is concerned, even an object's texture is another object type that can be animated separately from whatever is occurring to the object. Texture animations targeted to text blocks make interesting animations to post to Web sites as document titles.

Tip

Use the accompanying CD-ROM to load the Txtr.mov animation for the Mac, or the Txtr.AVI animation for Windows playback.

Step #1: Write the Letter "A" & Texture It

Use the Text tool to write the letter "A" to the screen. Bring the Default-Organic Magic material into the active materials list. Select it, and click on the Edit button. Configure the Material Editor as follows: in the Pattern tab, High Pattern with a Pattern Scale of .2, a .4 Material Proportions, and Natural Blend for both the Pattern and Bump Transitions. In the Material 1 tab, a dark turquoise color and a Bump Height of .86. In the Material 2 tab, a bright yellow color and a Bump height of .95. Close the Material Editor and apply the material to the "A."

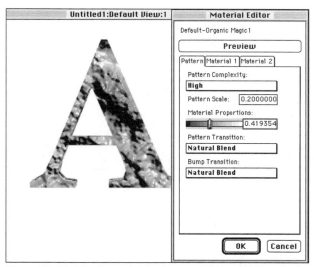

Figure 25-38: The Organic Magic material is applied to the "A."

Step #2: Alter the Texture

Bring up the Score window. Configure a 30 frame animation. Go to frame 10, and click on the Default-Organic Magic texture item in the list. Open the Material Editor dialog again for the texture. Change the texture type to "Simple," and select OK. This is the new texture setting for the material at frame 10. You will see a bar at the right of the Organic Magic item in the Score window that stretches on the timeline between frame 0 and frame 10.

Figure 25-39: The texture at frame 10 looks very different from that at the first frame.

Step #3: Alter the Texture Further

Repeat the re-editing of the texture for frames 20 and 30. Alter the settings in the Material Editor any way that pleases you, either by type, size, color, bump depth, transparency, roughness, or any combination of the settings possible. Look at the Score window under the Pattern listing for the object. Everything you have done is represented on its own timeline. You can move the key frames (the transition points for any of the changes), delete them, copy and paste them, or alter the extent of their parameters.

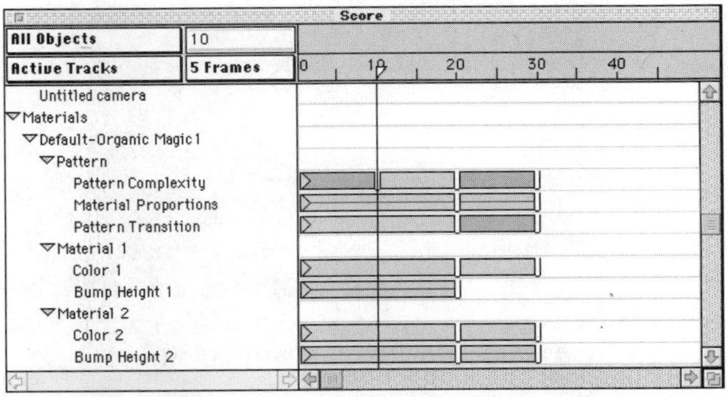

Figure 25-40: The Score timeline displays all of the associated Pattern alterations and where they take place for the selected figure.

Step #4: Record the Animation to Disk

Select the Record to Disk option, and decide whether you want to record the animation as a sequence of single frames or as a movie. If recorded as single frames, the frames will become instantly accessible as stand-alone graphics in a FreeHand document.

Figure 25-41: The finished animation frames display the animated texture.

Tip

An animation that is generated as a series of single frames presents the FreeHand user with a wealth of different views of the same subject. This can be different views of an environment like a room or a piece of machinery, or different choreographies and poses of a figure. It is also common practice in a publication to present alternate views of the same subject on different pages, or even on the same page—a vital resource in a teaching or instructional manual. Think of Extreme 3D as a potential 2D resource for FreeHand-specific uses, as well as a 3D application that can generate animations that play back as movies.

Moving On

We have covered many different ways to generate animations in FreeHand, xRes, and Extreme 3D in this chapter, and suggested where and how they might be used. In the next part of the book, we will look at the Web as an environment for creative FreeHand Graphics Studio output.

Part VI

Getting on the Web: Hands-On Exercises

26 Web Design Primer

Web Graphics

Web graphics complement the content and context of a Web page. Radical contents admit radical graphics readily, along with a wide arena for creative exploration and expression. Commercial pages generally require much stricter graphic concepts, though even these may benefit from a radically designed headline or spot graphic. Remember that millions of people surf the Web every day, so the potential for reaching a wide audience is higher than with any other display medium. The problem is that you have to reach the right audience and hold their interest. You have to invent ways to keep the audience attentive long enough so that they are exposed to the entirety of the message. This means your graphics, the mainstay of a Web page as far as immediate audience interest, have to be unique and well crafted.

In this chapter, we will explore Web graphic file formats, text uses, and Web design using color, backgrounds, and image maps. You also might be interested in exploring other books on Web design topics. Ventana offers a number of these volumes. To search out titles that might be appropriate to your interests, tap into the Ventana Web site at: http://www.vmedia.com.

Web Graphics File Formats

For FreeHand users, there are really two separate categories of Web graphics file formats. One category defines specific file formats required by Web pages in general, while the second category addresses special file formats addressed by FreeHand Shocked graphics. There is some overlap between the two.

The standard Web graphics file formats (non-FreeHand Web graphics) come in three formats:

- **JPEG:** The JPEG graphics file format has what is known as "lossy compression," meaning that there is some loss in image quality when the file is compressed too heavily. You usually won't notice this loss if image compression is set to 70 percent or higher, because present browser and transmission standards hide any artifacts. Settings below 70 percent show more and more degradation of the image. Progressive JPEG format is similar to interlaced GIF format in that it begins to display immediately when downloading commences. The progressive image gets clearer as downloading is finalized.

- **GIF:** The GIF format is the most used format on the Web. GIF graphics are bitmap graphics, and are limited to 256 colors or less. They are good for line drawings, text, and most photographic artwork (with the exception of portraiture). Because of the 256-color limitation, gradients in a GIF image (smooth blends between two or more colors) tend to show banding. Interlaced GIF files display immediately as downloading commences, and get clearer with each moment.

- **PNG:** PNG is a new upstart format, seeking to replace the GIF format. The GIF file format, however, is so pervasive on the Web that PNG has a long uphill battle ahead of it.

Shocked FreeHand graphics are handled somewhat differently. If the Web page is completely designed with vector images in FreeHand and sent to Afterburner for compression, no bitmaps are involved, because the graphics stay in vector format. These vector graphics will appear on any browser that is enabled with the Shockwave Graphics Player (new in FreeHand 7, and available for free on the Macromedia Web site). The situation changes when you place bitmap graphics on the FreeHand page destined for the Web. Shockwave graphics documents support the following file formats:

- **TIFF:** Tagged Image File Format. A very high information format previously used mostly for print graphics.

- **BMP:** Bitmapped Picture. The standard graphic format for Windows.

- **JPEG:** Joint Photographic Experts Group. JPEG files are smaller than the 24-bit graphics they reference and therefore download more quickly. You can choose how much to compress a JPEG file, but because the format is lossy, higher compression settings will cause more color information to be lost. You can usually compress a file with a setting of 70 percent and still see no discernible difference on a Web page.

- **GIF:** Graphics Interchange Format. This compact format is ideal for graphics that use only a few colors, and it was once the most popular file format for online color photos. GIF is losing some ground to JPEG. GIF images are limited to 256 colors.

The new emerging digital television codes are sure to alter what file formats are supported in the future. The expansion of Web interfaces to what is called "Web Digital Television" (a blend of computers and TV) will allow enhanced and higher resolution imagery to be used on the Web. This will also be made possible by newer transmission technologies. Shockwave will also evolve as new technologies come on-board.

Web Graphics Design Issues

There are a few easy rules for designing a Web page with FreeHand.

Design Tips for FreeHand Web Pages

It is important to adjust the FreeHand page to fit your objects:

1. Select all objects on the page by choosing Edit I Select I All.

2. Group the objects.

3. Move the group to the lower left corner of the page.

4. Note the group's width and height values in the Object Inspector.

5. Enter these values as custom page dimensions in the Document Inspector.

6. The group and the page now have the same dimensions, and the page will fit the browser page area better.

7. As a final step, you may want to ungroup the objects.

Keep FreeHand Web Graphics File Sizes Small

Until faster Web connections become a common standard, file size and the associated download time will be major considerations when designing for the Web. There are a number of things you can do to keep FreeHand Web-targeted file sizes to a minimum:

- Delete any objects that are not visible in the final graphic.
- Delete unused colors. (Choose Xtras | Delete | Unused Named Colors.)
- Delete unused or invisible layers. (Choose Remove from the Options pop-up on the Layers palette.)
- Delete unused graphics placed on the background layer.
- Simplify complex objects using FreeHand's Simplify command, which deletes unnecessary points in an object, reducing file size. (Choose Xtras | Cleanup | Simplify.)
- Limit the use of the Paste Inside command.
- Always use the Afterburner Xtra to compress your final document.

Text

The importance of text on a Web page goes beyond its necessary content. It also includes how the text is treated as an element of design. Text headlines and other selected text blocks often become graphics elements in the process. Pay attention to these basic guidelines when incorporating text on your Web pages.

Let Your Text Breathe

Text needs air to be comfortable to read. If you cram text blocks together, visitors will not read them thoroughly, no matter how important the content. Use space between paragraphs, more space than you use for paper output. Break large sections of text up into smaller paragraphs, and revise the content until you have clear statements without a lot of extraneous commentary. Most people, except for novel writers and readers, go online to gather information. Design your information in small, understandable pieces, and you'll get more visitors.

Space for Text

Space is as important as content on a Web page, and space has to be designed around the graphic elements placed on a page. Like a living organism, a page needs to have room to breathe. When dealing with an overwhelming amount of textual content information, it's always tempting to pack as much as possible into the design space. This chokes the page, making it almost impossible for a reader to get to the core of the data. Increasing the space in a document is more difficult on paper pages than it is on Web pages, because a Web page can have built-in links (URL hot spots) to other pages in a stack. A stack is a grouping of windows or pages. Each window is displayed by pressing a hot spot on another window or page. Each page in a hyperlink or Web stack can be designed so that the information has adequate breathing room, because you can link an unlimited number of pages together to hold all of the needed information (as long as you have the space on your Web server). Consequently, there is no excuse for crowding data together on a Web site.

An alternate way to give the data on a Web page more breathing space is to break the text copy into smaller chunks, and to prioritize and group these smaller elements. Always allow the first sentence of a paragraph to tell the primary information, and expound on it in succeeding sentences, allowing readers to get the primary information quickly. Place subheads (topic headings) at the top of all text paragraphs that represent new information. Headings should be rendered in a bolder typeface to stand out. This allows the reader to quickly browse the page for the exact information they are seeking, and to do it without feeling the content is too crowded.

The size of the text written to an electronic visual display screen (computer monitor and/or TV) should always be larger than it might be if you were working with a paper printout. The "point" is a standard printer's term of measurement. There are 72 points to the inch. On paper (depending on the printer), text is often readable when the point size of the type is as low as 4 ($\frac{1}{18}$th of an inch). This is not true on an electronic screen. Text on a computer monitor should be at least 12 to 14 points high ($\frac{1}{6}$th of an inch). Text displayed on television has to be even larger because of the smearing that takes place when an image is enlarged to fit the TV screen, with the minimum size being no smaller than 18 points ($\frac{1}{4}$th of an inch). As with other display data, the coming digital TV technology may allow for smaller type. Text that is too small affects the necessary breathing room of a displayed page, making it seem crowded and unreadable.

Spacing Techniques

Here are a few ways to give the text content in a Web page project more breathing space:

- Spread the text content over more than one page when necessary to avoid crowding it.
- Use links on the main page (and on succeeding pages) to connect pages and topic areas together.

- Group information into shorter paragraphs when possible, and use a bold headline for each paragraph that contains alternate content.

- Make sure that your body text is sized no smaller than 14 points, and is even larger if possible.

Adding a 3D Graphic Look to Text

Just changing the size and color of a text block can differentiate it enough from the rest of the text to create an interesting page. You can make the major headlines very large and colorful to force them to stand out from the body of the text. 2D text can also be transformed into 3D text in several ways, including a way that makes headlines pop off the page. In a sense, when you create 3D text blocks, they're perceived as both text and graphics without any picture information involved. There are three common ways that text can be given a third dimension: cast shadows, drop shadows, and extrusions. Let's look at each of these alternatives (which can also be used to give graphic elements a dimensional look).

Creating Drop Shadows

Drop shadows lie flat on the background, while the image or text that seems to project them floats at a perceived distance above the page. Drop shadows can be either solid or partially transparent. If partially transparent, the background of the page will show through them and they will look more natural.

Using FreeHand   Create the text block, and make a clone of it. Colorize the cloned text block with a light color. Now colorize the original text in a darker color, a gradient, or with a tiled texture. Place the lighter text block over the darker text block, so that it covers only part of the dark text. Save the image as a GIF file, or use Afterburner to save the FreeHand page with the incorporated shadowed text. Remove the stroke from the shadowed image, and add a 1 point black stroke to the top text block. The text will look as though it's floating above the page.

Figure 26-1: A drop shadow created in FreeHand.

Using xRes   After creating the text block, copy and paste it, which automatically places it on its own object layer. Colorize the original text block with a dark color. Colorize the pasted text in a lighter color, a gradient, or with a texture. Place the darker text over the lighter text block so that it covers only part of the light text. Drop the pasted text object layer. Save the image as a GIF file, make the background of the image transparent, and place it on your Web page. The text will look as though it's floating above the page.

Drop Shadow

Figure 26-2: This drop shadow was created in xRes.

Using Extreme 3D   Create a text block in the Top view, and extrude it a little so it accepts a texture. Create a cubic object that will receive the shadow. In the Front view, move the text so it is above the cubic object. Return to the Top view. Go to the Lights browser, and move the Distant Light so that its coordinates are X = -50, Y = 30, and Z = 35. This slants the light, so that it casts an observable shadow. In the Shadows tab of the Lights browser, turn shadows on, setting the blur amount to 5. Click OK to accept the settings, and render the scene. Save the rendering to disk, and use as a headline on a FreeHand Web page.

Figure 26-3: Using Extreme 3D, drop shadowed text obeys the real laws of light.

Cast Shadows

Cast shadows are different from drop shadows in that they seem to extend from the original image itself. Cast shadows are also called "false extrusions" because they make the text seem as if it's carved from a thick block. A "real" 3D extrusion, on the other hand, can only be accomplished in a 3D program, where the 3D text block can be turned interactively in 3D space before being painted down or saved as a 3D animation. The easiest way to create a cast shadow in a 2D application is either to use a blend or to use the drop shadow method mentioned previously, layering several darkened copies of the text block on top of each other. Then, the original lighter text is placed on top of the dark stack.

Using FreeHand   To create cast shadow effects in FreeHand you need a knowledge of the Smudge tool. Create a text block. Double-click the Smudge tool to make sure the fill and stroke settings are set to white, and close the dialog. Select your text block and click on the Smudge tool. Drag the text block about one screen inch to the lower left. The cast shadow is applied to the text block.

Figure 26-4: A common cast shadow look using the Smudge tool.

Using xRes   Unique and strange cast shadow effects can be achieved with xRes. Create a text block. Copy and paste it. This gives you two new object layers, one for each text block. Use the Resize tool to enlarge one of the text blocks to about 2 ½ times as tall as the other one. Place the larger text block under the smaller one. Assign a gradient fill to the larger text block, setting the parameters to the Sunny Day color palette with the Folds option, and an RGB Blend. Click and drag the mouse over the large text block in any direction desired, assigning the gradient as a fill. Save the graphic as a possible headline for a FreeHand Web page.

Figure 26-5: Unique cast shadow effects are possible in xRes with customized gradient fills.

Using Extreme 3D   See the following 3D Extrusion examples using FreeHand, xRes, and Extreme 3D.

3D Extrusions
You can create 3D extrusions in a 3D application or with special plug-ins in a 2D application. 3D extrusions are the most common way to add a 3D appearance to a text block. This technique is most commonly used for page headings or in subheads that stand out from body copy. Be careful not to overuse them, for example in listed data. 3D extrusions applied to long statements are very hard to read.

Using FreeHand Developing 3D extrusions in FreeHand requires the KPT Vector Effects plug-in to be installed in your Xtras folder. Create a text block and convert it to paths. Select Xtras | KPT Vector Effects plug-in, and select the 3D Transform option. In the 3D Transform dialog, set the Extrusion, Perspective, and Metallic sliders to 70 percent. Click the checkmark to apply the settings.

Figure 26-6: The KPT Vector Effects 3D Transform plug-in can help you create believable 3D extrusions in FreeHand.

Using xRes 3D extrusions can be accomplished in xRes with the help of the Emboss effect. Create a black background. Create a white text block, and drop the object layer onto the background. Go to the Effects | Stylize | Emboss dialog, and set the sliders to a Depth of 1, an Angle of +45, and a Contrast of +200. Click OK to accept the effect. Save the graphic as a headline for a FreeHand Web page.

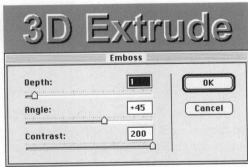

Figure 26-7: Embossed text in xRes takes on a 3D extruded look.

Using Extreme 3D Create a text block in the Front view. Select it, and click on the Bevel Extrude tool. Drag out a horizontal line about ½" long on the screen. A beveled extrusion will be assigned to your text. To emphasize the extrusion, change the Perspective view from narrow (the default) to moderate, or even wide. Render the text and save it to disk as a potential 3D heading for a FreeHand Web page.

Figure 26-8: Extreme 3D is your best bet when you need a photorealistic 3D extruded heading on a Web page.

Text on Curves

Another way to provide interest for a text block is to make the text less linear in appearance. Part of the eye strain associated with reading large amounts of text on paper or (especially) on a display screen, has to do with the monotonous unbroken line of the data. By breaking up the squareness of the text blocks once in a while, you allow the viewer to wake up, and to prepare for the next tide of data. One way to accomplish this is to take a specific text block, either headlines or interesting key words embedded in the text, and give it a twist and a less linear shape. Vector drawing program users (Macromedia FreeHand, Adobe Illustrator, Deneba Canvas, and so on) can use a variety of plug-ins that allow selected text blocks to be reshaped into infinite forms. Once this is accomplished, the modified text can be reintegrated with the original text page (dropped into place), and the whole page targeted to a Web page application. Or, the reshaped text block can be left as a stand-alone headline and placed on the Web page as a separate element.

Using FreeHand   Create a text block. Use the Pen tool to draw a curve. Select the text block and the curve, and select Text | Attach To Path. The text block is automatically attached to the curve.

Tip

When the text is attached to a curve and the curve is edited, the text block flows to the edited shape. If you need more space inside the text block to make it fit the curve better, place the text cursor between the letters and press the space bar.

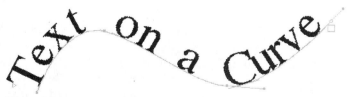

Figure 26-9: Any curve can be used to shape the text block in FreeHand.

Using xRes   Draw a circular marquee, and use the textured airbrush to paint a textured surface on it. Create a text block one letter at a time. Each of the letters is written to separate object layers. Move each of the letters so they curve around the textured circle, and rotate them so they look as though they follow the circle's perimeter. Drop all of the letters on the background. Save the graphic as a potential headline for a FreeHand Web page.

Figure 26-10: The letters are moved into place on the curve one at a time in xRes.

Using Extreme 3D   Although you can generate a text block in Extreme 3D and move and rotate all of the 3D letters to get a curved text path, there is a better alternative. Create a curved text block in FreeHand. Save it as a FreeHand file. Import it into Extreme 3D using the FreeHand Import option. It is imported as an outlined object. Use the Extrude tool to give it the depth you want. The result is a 3D object that follows the exact path that was created for the text block in FreeHand.

Tip

If you forget to remove the curved path in FreeHand, it will be imported into Extreme 3D as a curved line, which will extrude to a curved surface. You can select it in Extreme 3D and remove it there. This also opens up the possibility of drawing a series of curved lines in FreeHand, grouping them, and exporting them to Extreme 3D. Once in Extreme 3D, they can be extruded to form a lattice of 3D surfaces, or even lathed for a 3D object.

Figure 26-11: You can create text on a curve in FreeHand, save the file as a FreeHand document, and import it into Extreme 3D for extrusion.

HTML Tips

If you have experience with HTML coding, then there are a few important considerations to be aware of when configuring a Web document with FreeHand. In HTML, the dimensions of a graphic are specified by screen pixels; the number of pixels per inch and the number of points per inch are approximately the same: 72. This is why it is important to set the screen resolution at 72 dpi for a Web page.

Once you have grouped and entered the page's width and height values as outlined above, you are ready to embed the FreeHand page in an HTML document. For example, if your graphics fit on a page which measures 500 x 400 points, you can specify a width of 500 pixels and a height of 400 pixels in HTML, assuring optimum display in the browser. The HTML embed text code for that document would look like this:

```
<a><embed SRC="filename.ext" width=500 height=400></a>
```

You can also manually force the display of the FreeHand document to a percentage of its size. For example, to resize the above file to 50 percent of its original size, enter values that are 50 percent of the width and height values of the original. It would look like this:

```
<a><embed SRC="filename.ext" width=250 height=200></a>
```

Adding Toolbars to a FreeHand Graphic With HTML

You can add a toolbar to the FreeHand graphic displayed in an HTML document viewed with Netscape Navigator, a new feature of FreeHand 7. With the toolbar you can link, zoom, or pan by clicking a button. Just click the Shockwave logo to return an image to its original view.

- The toolbar can appear at the top or the bottom of an image.

- An image must be at least 85 pixels wide to display the toolbar. For greater widths, the toolbar expands to fit your image.

- The toolbar is 20 pixels in height. You must add 20 pixels to the height portion of your HTML code to display the toolbar. For example, the image below has a height of 234 pixels, but the figure entered in the height portion of the HTML code should be 254. The HTML embed tag placing the toolbar at the top of the image is:

    ```
    <a><embed SRC="filename.ext" width=244 height=254 toolbar="top"></a>
    ```

    The HTML embed tag placing the toolbar at the bottom of the image is:

    ```
    <a><embed SRC="filename.ext" width=244 height=254 toolbar="bottom"></a>
    ```

- You can manually force the display of a FreeHand document to a size other than 100 percent. For example, to display an image at 50 percent of its original size, enter width and height values 50 percent of the original values. Once you know the new image height, add 20 pixels to that figure in the HTML code for the toolbar display. The figures in your code must be proportional for correct display of the image and the toolbar. Fifty percent of the original width (500 pixels) and height (400 pixels) of the image below yields 250 x 200 pixels. Adding 20 pixels increases the height figure in the HTML code to 220.

The HTML embed tag for a resized image:

```
<a><embed SRC="filename.ext" width=250 height=220 toolbar="bottom"></a>
```

Images between 85 and 149 pixels wide can display the Shockwave toolbar, but the Shockwave logo will not be visible. When the Shockwave logo is not visible on the toolbar, press Command+Shift (Macintosh) or Control+Shift (Windows) and click to return an image to its original view.

The HTML embed tag for the image would be:

```
<a><embed SRC="filename.ext" width=85 height=155 toolbar="bottom"></a>
```

Web Color

Color on paper and color on an electronic screen have similarities and differences, and call for two slightly different design approaches. There are established basic rules of color as an element of design, and work on the Web both incorporates these principles and expands upon them.

Although colors printed on paper for a specific project are pretty much guaranteed to be exactly the same no matter how many documents are printed, the colors you use to design a Web page may not (and probably will not) be the exact colors the viewer sees. There are two basic reasons for this. Every color monitor in use displays color slightly differently. Also, many Web surfers work on systems that display only a limited Color palette; the most common is 256 colors. If you are spending weeks designing a 16 million color display page, you can bet it's going to look a lot different on the viewer's limited 256 color monitor.

The color capacities of browsers and the display card a viewer may or may not have can also have an impact. As we move towards digital Web TV in the near future, many of these issues will no longer exist, but the full implementation of the new Web display mediums will not reach their full installed potential until late in the first quarter of the twenty-first century.

Web Color Design Issues

In traditional color theory, using complimentary colors to make text stand out from the background is only one of "Seven Contrasts" considered as important by designers. The seven include: hue, light/dark, warm/cool, complimentary, saturation, simultaneous, and extension. We have already looked at complimentary colors, so allow me to present a brief description of the others, highlighting which ones are especially important when accomplishing design work for a Web page.

Hue

Hue is the simplest of the seven contrasts to understand. Hue is determined by a color's name, so using different hues means using different named colors. You might use red and purple, orange and green, or yellow and red. The most effective contrast in hue for a Web designer is between the three primaries (red-yellow-blue), because the intensity of the contrast diminishes as the hue moves away from the primaries. Surrounding text with thin black lines is also a way to accentuate the hues. See Table 26-1.

Light/Dark

The light/dark contrast differentiates between any two colors of differing light and dark values, or the same color with differing lights and darks. Light/dark contrasts are used to emulate 3D effects. The lighter an object is, the closer the eye thinks it is. The darker, the farther away. A light red text on a dark red background is very readable, while at the same time giving the illusion that two separate hues are involved. Very interesting Web pages can be created that are highly readable and interesting by using different light and dark values of just one hue. The overall result looks like a 19th-century tinted photograph.

Warm/Cool

Colors that lean towards red are called "warm," while those that tend towards blue are considered "cool." In the six-part color wheel, red-yellow-orange are considered warm. Blue and blue-purple are called cool. Green is in between, and not usually considered as one or the other, except that yellow greens are warm and blue greens cool. Reddish purple is also considered warm. A warm/cool contrast places a warm and cool color adjacent to one another. If the warm color is placed in the front, the effect will be perceived very differently than the opposite variation. It's usually considered best to make the text a warm color set against a cool background (for example, orange text against a blue-purple backdrop).

Saturation

Color saturation is adjusted by mixing a pure color hue with white to make a colder color, mixing it with black to dilute it, combining it with gray to reduce its level of intensity, or mixing the color with its complement to produce gray. Colors on an electronic display screen mix differently than paint, so altering the saturation of a color in the electronic medium calls for experimentation and exploration. A Web page designer would use the saturated color for the text and the less saturated graying background for the environment.

Simultaneous Contrast

Simultaneous contrast is not as valuable for Web page design as it is for painters. A simultaneous contrast is a contrast resulting from the close proximity of two colors, which produces a third color that confuses the perception of the other two. An excellent example of simultaneous contrast is mixing a saturated color and gray. The gray becomes tinted with the saturated color's complement. Simultaneous contrast is the result of persistence of vision, the ability of the eye to produce a complementary color on its own. Simultaneous contrasts can be distracting and disorienting, so they are not of much use when the goal is clarity.

Contrast of Extension

A contrast of extension is an expanded case of simultaneous contrast, and so it too is less valuable to the Web page designer. When a color dominates an image, it can throw off the perception of the other colors by projecting its complement on them through persistence of vision. For example, squares of gray on a field of orange will be perceived as blue instead of gray. Some exploration of extension contrast might be valuable if you want to design a page to evoke optical illusions, with a content topic to match.

Color	Temperature	Complement	Best Use	Emotional Response
RED	Very Hot	Green	Sparingly on important text, dark as a backdrop for lighter text	"Stop and look at this!" very important, fire, "Pay attention!"
ORANGE	Hot	Blue	Widely for text	Pleasant and warm, friendly
YELLOW	Warm	Violet (Purple)	Widely for text	Sunshine, happiness
GREEN	Depends on other colors it's close to	Red	Lighter for text, darker as a backdrop	Earthy, healing
BLUE	Very cold if dark, warmer if lighter	Orange	Lighter for text, darker as a backdrop	Foreboding if nothing but this color, stately if in a mix
INDIGO	Very cold when dark	Yellow-Orange	Dark as a backdrop for lighter text	Same general responses as blue
VIOLET (Purple)	Warmer as redder	Yellow	Dark as a backdrop for lighter text	Mysterious if nothing but this color, regal if in a mix
BLACK	Cold and empty	White	If absolutely necessary, use as a backdrop for light text	Black/white pages should be avoided if at all possible
WHITE	Cold and empty	Black	If absolutely necessary, use as a backdrop for light text	Black/white pages should be avoided if at all possible
GRAY	Moderates black and white to warmer	Has no direct complements	Great for use as a backdrop, or to lightly color text	The best way to achieve a pleasing balance on a Web page is with a mix of grays with other colors

Table 26-1: Color use for Web design.

Tip

Colors placed next to each other affect perception differently than colors placed against a gray background. If you want to maximize the effect of any single color, give it a lot of breathing space. Also take note that using primary colors as the dominant choices for a Web page is the way to achieve the most startling results. There are times when this is appropriate (blatant messages, children's pages, circus/ carnival themes, bright lively topics), and times when it is inappropriate (more conservative themes, commercial and business sites, "serious" topics, pages that are designed to evoke prestigious matters and events). To mute a message for a specific audience, use the primary colors more sparingly. The careful application and the conscious understatement of color is the key to good design in any medium.

When designing a Web page, remember that bright primary colors might look good on your computer's RGB monitor, but as the new Internet appliances come into being, devices that attach to a home TV set for surfing the Web, those same full strength primary colors are going to look awful. This is because the standard NTSC (National Television Standards Commission) TV transmission makes undiluted primary colors smear and blur on the screen. It's always best to darken the full strength primary colors a little when designing a Web page, just in case the page is ever viewed on an NTSC device. One caveat to remember is that this data may not apply where the standards differ from NTSC (PAL, SECAM).

Color Palettes on the Web

The separate colors in a painter's palette are chosen carefully. They change over time as the painter's personality dictates. Electronic painting also demands the use of specific palettes, some of which are tied to the way the Web transmits information, and the ways it is received and viewed. There are some limitations not experienced by non-electronic painters and designers.

The first boundary is that of the number of colors contained in the graphic's palette, its bit depth. Where a non-electronic artist can select any number of colors that the physical palette has room for, the digital artist must incorporate the demands of the computer into the palette choice. Depending upon the computer's hardware, a screen display can allow for graphics palettes that hold 2, 4, 8, 16, 32, 64, 128, 256—up to 16 million-plus colors. There is a relationship between bit depth on a computer and the number of colors contained in a palette. See the following table.

Bit Depth	# of Colors in Palette
1	2
2	4
3	8
4	16
5	32
6	64
7	128
8	**256**
9	512
10	1,024
11	2,048
12	4,096
13	8,192
14	16,384
15	32,768
16	65,536
17	131,072
18	262,144
19	524,288
20	1,048,576
21	2,097,152
22	4,194,304
23	8,388,608
24	**16,777,216**

Table 26-2: We have used boldface type to call attention to the 8-bit row of 256 colors and the 24-bit row of 16,000,000+ colors. These are the most important color palette numbers the Web page designer should pay attention to.

Computer Monitors & Color Palettes

As a Web page designer, you may be working with a monitor that has 24-bit circuitry in the connected computer. This allows you to theoretically see everything in the 16,000,000+ color rainbow that is your working palette. But what about your audience? Do they all have the same high-end window to the world that you do? While 24-bit video is economical enough and available, many Web surfers have older systems or systems that don't allow 24-bit viewing. What will they see when you post those 24-bit graphics to your Web page? Certainly not the same vision that leaves your computer. It's a lot safer to design your pages with a 256-color palette than with a 24-bit one (a 256-color palette can be displayed by 99 percent of the individuals that surf the Web).

Sites that focus upon art and photography seldom obey this convention because they require deeper palettes to display the required graphics. The expectation is that surfers who wind up at those sites will either have 24-bit viewing capabilities, or they will leave fairly quickly. There's nothing that motivates a surfer to invest in 24-bit video faster than seeing the Mona Lisa displayed in blotchy shades of green and purple. There should be a line on your Web page that reads something similar to "this page is best viewed in 24-bit color" as a courtesy to your audience.

Image Size & Color Palettes

The size of a graphic is determined by both its pixel dimensions and its bit depth. A tiny 24-bit graphic can take up more hard drive space than a graphic whose dimensions are five times as large, but that has fewer colors (lower bit depth). In Web terms, large equals time. A large graphic takes up more space on the Web server, and takes longer to download and play back (for animations) than a smaller graphic or animation (remember, when we say "smaller" we're talking about the graphic's dimension in pixels and its bit depth).

As a Web page designer, you may have all of the latest connecting devices, but a lot of the members of your surfing audience may still be using slower 14.4 modems. The size of your graphics is even more important to the surfers with slower modems who want to see your Web pages. It's not always possible to compromise image quality and limit the size of a Web graphic, but it's always worth considering. Smaller graphics color palettes usually download faster, a kindness appreciated by viewers with slower Web connections.

File Formats & Color

The file formats that you create your Web graphics and animations in also affect the overall color palettes. The first file format developed specifically for Internet and Web use was the GIF (Graphics Interchange Format), created by CompuServe. This is still the major graphics and animation file format in use today, although some legal issues may preclude its use as a standard in the future. GIF responds well to the 256-color palette limitation. JPEG is the format of choice for large photographic images embedded on a Web page, especially portraiture. PNG is a new format that is attempting to replace GIF.

Tip

GIF format images seem to show far less dithering in Netscape Navigator 2.0 and up when viewed on 256-color displays. JPEG images seem at first unaffected, but are still highly dithered when you examine them closely. A limitation of the Netscape 216 and 256 color palettes is that they contain only four grays plus black and white. Other grays can be produced with Netscape's dithering capacities.

Embedding bitmap images in a Shocked FreeHand page destined for the Web requires the bitmaps of TIFF, BMP, GIF, or JPEG file formats. xRes standalone bitmaps for Web display can be written as GIF, JPEG, or PNG. Extreme 3D allows GIF, JPEG, and PNG for stand-alone Web graphics, and adds VRML 1 and 2 for the creation of 3D worlds targeted for Web display.

Adding Color to Web Pages

Each of the FreeHand 7 Graphics Studio 2D and 3D applications has different tools and techniques for dealing with color. Each application requires the mastery of specific windows, dialogs, and tools.

Web Color Tips for FreeHand

You have to master the use of the Stroke and Fill Inspectors and the Color Mixer to control colors in FreeHand. You should keep in mind a few other considerations:

- Set the Color Mixer to RGB. The Web is addressed with RGB color just like TV, and not with CMYK.

- Work with a color-safe palette. Do not set your RGB colors to slider marks over 225. As Web TV comes into use, and before digital TV becomes the popular standard, you have to pay attention to the fact that higher RGB setting can bleed on TVs.

- Create a series of commonly used colors, and drag and drop them into the document's Color List palette before you create your projects. This will save time later. About a dozen color swatches placed in the Color List can be very handy, saving you from having to redesign the colors for fills, strokes, and gradients. Customize the colors according to your project needs. Doing this may allow you to turn the Color Mixer off, saving space on your screen.

Always save your documents out as TIFF files, and translate them to GIFs and JPEGs for the Web outside of FreeHand. Never overwrite the original TIFF file. This gives you the TIFF for printing purposes, and allows you to use better GIF and JPEG file translators than are resident in FreeHand. Select only those options you want installed. Another option is to save to AI (Adobe Illustrator) format and rasterize in Photoshop, which produces very high quality results.

Web Color Tips for xRes

xRes has a number of excellent color indexing options for addressing 256-color images, just right for Web-targeted GIF graphics.

Converting 24-Bit Images to 8-Bit Images   Many background images viewed on today's Web browsers are presented in 8-bit format, which creates considerably smaller files than images stored in 24-bit format. You can convert a 24-bit image to an 8-bit image using the indexed color mode in xRes. To convert an image to indexed color mode:

1. Open a 24-bit image. Select Modify | Color Mode | Indexed 256.

2. In the dialog box that appears, select Adaptive, Custom, Uniform 8-8-4, or Uniform 6-6-6. In most cases, select Adaptive, which creates a color index table based on the colors in your image. The Custom method creates a color index table based on the colors in the Swatches palette. Uniform 8-8-4 and Uniform 6-6-6 both load preset color index tables. Uniform 8-8-4 is based on eight shades of red, eight shades of green, and four shades of blue. Uniform 6-6-6 is based on six shades of red, six shades of green, and six shades of blue.

Transparent GIFs   You can create GIF files with transparent color in xRes. When saving to the GIF format, you can set any selected color in the 256-color palette to transparent. This allows the color or texture of the background to show through the transparent area and makes the image appear to blend into the Web page. Making the background color of a GIF image leads to page designs that are less blocky, especially when the GIF graphic is to act as a hot spot. To create a transparent GIF in xRes:

1. Open the file.

2. To change to indexed color mode, choose Modify | Color Mode | Indexed 256.

3. To open the color index table, choose Modify | Color | Color Index Table.

4. To choose the color that you wish to make transparent, click any swatch in the color index table. White and black are the most common choices for transparency.

5. To make the color transparent, click Set Matte Color in the color index table. If, at a later time, you don't want the color to be transparent, click Clear Matte Color in the color index table.

When you choose to make a color transparent, any object using that color is displayed against a background that varies depending on which indexed mode you're using. To control the background color regardless of the indexed mode, you can set the void color option. For example, you might set the void color to gray to emulate the neutral gray used in Web pages. Keep in mind that the void color does not affect the GIF image; it only affects the background of the object when you view it in xRes. To set the void color:

1. Check that the color mode is Indexed 256. If it's not, choose Modify | Color Mode | Indexed 256.

2. To open the color index table, choose Modify | Color | Color Index Table.

3. To designate a color as the void color, click the image and click a swatch in the color index table.

4. Click Set Void Color.

Creating an Interlaced Image   When saving as a GIF file in xRes, a dialog allows you to choose an interlaced option. Interlaced GIFs display onscreen progressively, much as progressive JPEGs do. Like progressive JPEGs, interlaced GIFs are useful for visitors with slower modems.

Working With the Color Index Table   xRes allows you to change the colors in the color index table and load them into the Swatches palette. This makes it easy to modify GIF images if, for example, you wish to change blue to green. To change the colors in the xRes color index table:

1. To open the color index table, choose Modify | Color | Color Index Table. The 256 colors in the indexed table are arranged in 16 rows with 16 swatches in a row.

2. Click the swatch you wish to change.

3. Use the red, green, and blue sliders in the dialog box to change the color of the swatch and click OK.

The Swatches palette in xRes stores frequently used color sets. By loading the color index table into the Swatches palette, you have easy access to these colors for painting or filling purposes. To load the xRes color index table into the Swatches palette:

1. Choose Window | Palettes | Swatches to open the Swatches palette.

2. Open the Swatches submenu by clicking the small triangle in the upper right-hand corner and then choose Load Color Index Table.

Web Color Tips for Extreme 3D

Colors are applied to 3D objects in Extreme 3D by including them in the materials textured to objects. Depending which type of material you use, colors may entail all of a texture or just a part of it. Color subtleties play an important part in creating exciting Web 3D graphics and virtual worlds.

- Never allow lights to shine directly onto objects from the front, but opt for lights that shine at an angle. This also creates more dramatic shadows.

Tip

Be careful not to set the Distant light too bright. Keep it to about a 50 percent intensity, otherwise the colors in your rendered objects will wash out. Setting over 10 percent Luminosity for an object will do the same thing.

- Use the gray plastic default material when you want nothing but a single color texture on an object. You can change the color to any hue in the spectrum, and then rename it to the hue ("Blue" instead of "Gray Plastic" for example) and save it back to the Materials In Library list on the right of the Materials browser.

- Change the specular color of a material in order to alter the light reflections away from a stark white. I use a light yellow specular color in most cases.

- Change the color of the Distant light to a muted yellow instead of a glaring white. This warms the image up, and softens the rendering to look more natural. If you want to make the rendering more machine-like, use a blue tinted light color.

- Use a light color that is tinted as a complementary to the color of the object. A red apple, for example, looks good when the light is slightly greenish.

■ When using materials that have two or more attributes that are color specified (like the swirls in the default marble material), just altering the colors produces infinite new looks. When you create new materials using this method, save them to disk to be applied in other 3D projects.

■ When you want to colorize a bitmapped texture on an object, select Composite Over Color in the Texture tab of the Material Editor. Turn down the intensity of the material to allow the color to blend with the bitmap. You can create super reflective surfaces like this.

■ Keep an eye on the preview swatch in the materials window. It will always show the color and lighting changes made to the scene.

Web Page Backgrounds

Web page backgrounds serve more than a single purpose. The most obvious is that a background can add interest to a Web page, stimulation that invites the viewer to stick around while the page is downloading, motivating the viewer to explore the rest of the page's contents once everything is onscreen. Backgrounds also serve to create an environment that enhances any page elements placed over the background, often making it more visible through color contrasts and pleasing surroundings.

Web Page Background Design Issues

What are your choices for backgrounds? You have four basic choices when it comes to creating a background for your Web page elements to rest on: a single color, a color gradient, a texture, and a pictorial backdrop. By "pictorial" we might be referring to a digitized photo (or a photomontage, a series of smaller photos), an original computer graphic bitmap, or a vector graphic. No one of these four choices works in all situations. If you have so many content elements to place on a page that choosing a pictorial background might clutter it even more, than a single color or gradient background is advisable. This is especially the case when the content placed over a background is itself pictorial.

If the content consists of numerous text blocks that you expect the viewer to read at a single sitting (which nobody ever does), then a more pictorial background composition is highly advisable. If the page has numerous interactive buttons and feedback mechanisms (like check boxes or drop-down menus, which you can add using a Web application like Macromedia's Backstage Designer), then a nice contrasting single color background or a suitable gradient might work best. (Stay away from a glaring white background if at all possible.) If it's possible to embed a collection of image maps into the background to serve all of your needs for that particular page, then perhaps the page will contain nothing but a pictorial background with hot spots. There are no hard and fast rules, only educated and informed judgment calls. You have to decide upon which type of background to use based upon the content elements that make up the intended page, as well as reflecting upon the intended audience.

The simplest background is a solid color. It conflicts less with the content placed on it. Next in line would be a color gradient, a blend between or among two or more colors. Third would be a textured background, a repeating pattern of tiled graphics. If these are muted graphics, like a company logo in a light gray color, the textured backdrop wouldn't interfere much with the content placed over it. A pictorial background, whether photographic or computer graphic in nature, tends to interfere most with foreground elements. Pictorial backgrounds therefore take the most planning to make sure that they complement the Web page and do not confuse the viewer.

If you doubt that background is perceived as a part of the content and message of a Web page, allow me to suggest a little exercise. Think of the painting of the Mona Lisa and her enigmatic smile, recognizable the world over. Does the background she is placed upon have any impact on the way we interpret her character and intent, or is it merely a random element of what we take away from the painting? Instead of the rather subtle backdrop she sits upon, allow yourself to see her image against a red volcanic sky, with sparks and fireballs raining down. Does this make any difference as to the total concept and the meaning we perceive? What if we place her against a backdrop that shows an urban street, with traffic snarled up at midday? What is she smiling about now?

Background is content, or at least a good measure of how we interpret it. If you use the wrong background graphic on your Web page, your message will not reach its intended audience. If you craft the right one, your message will be introduced to individuals that you never suspected could be reached so easily.

Creating Solid Color Backgrounds

If you use a solid color as a background for a Web page, there are some guidelines that you should follow:

- Consider making the background dark and any text content placed over it light. This makes the text more visible. The most common background color on Web pages is black, though a dark red, blue, or purple can serve just as well.

- Stay away from bright primary colors (red, green, blue) for single-color backgrounds, unless viewer irritation is your main goal. Besides, bright primary colors are best used for text blocks when needed, or for headlines, bullets, and frames.

If you have to use dark text on a lighter single color background, the best choice is gray. This will not conflict with any colors and will decrease the glare associated with a solid white background. Even a 10 percent gray can mute the effects of pure white enough to be an acceptable choice. It is seldom a good idea to choose white as a color backdrop. This cannot be emphasized too much. White allows too much screen glare to reach the viewer; as a background, it is uncomfortable physically and makes it much more difficult to pay attention to the text or foreground graphics. Dark text on a white backdrop also appears to be smaller than it actually is, further conflicting with message content. If you must use a light background color, choose one that has a muted color component, or even a light gray.

If you are going to choose a color, text will be more readable as light against dark than the other way around. Light text on a dark backdrop actually seems bigger than it is, so smaller type sizes can be used more effectively if the text is light on a dark backdrop. A dark backdrop also blocks a lot of the light from irritating the eyes. If you have minimal or no text on a page, using dark designs (framed graphics, animations, photos) on a light (but not white) backdrop is OK.

Using FreeHand

To create a solid color background for a Web page with FreeHand, do the following:

1. Draw a rectangle that matches the size of the FreeHand page, or whatever portion of it you want the background to fill (use the points rulers, since 72 points equals an inch and the Web page will be displayed at 72 dpi).

2. Use the Fill Inspector to drag and drop a color you have designed in the Color Mixer onto the rectangle, making sure that the rectangle has Stroke set to None.

3. Place the rest of your page elements (text and graphics) over the background (the background should be at the bottom of the layer stack).

Using xRes

You can add a subtle variance to color backgrounds in xRes with the Airbrush tool.

1. Create a new document, and size it according to your desired Web page dimensions (640 x 480 pixels at 72 dpi is a good choice).

2. Select the foreground color you want to use, and click on the Paintbrush tool. Go to the Media palette and select the basic Airbrush option. In the Brush Settings dialog, set Texture to None and Concentration and Flow to 50 percent.

3. Use the Airbrush to apply the color, applying it quickly in some areas while lingering for a longer application time in other areas. You will notice that the paint seems to be more opaque in the areas where you lingered during the application, while it looks thinner where the brush was moved quickly. As a Web page background, this adds a subtle interest to the backdrop that a non-varying color cannot provide. This is also a feature of xRes that cannot be duplicated with the vector methods in FreeHand.

Using Extreme 3D

Extreme 3D offers yet another variation on the application of basic color for a Web background.

1. In the Front view, use the 2D Rectangle tool to draw a rectangle that fills the workspace. Extrude it a bit so a material texture can be applied to it.

2. Bring the default gray plastic material to the Materials in Scene list on the left of the Materials palette, if it isn't there already. Select the Gray Plastic material in the list, and click on the Edit button below.

3. Make sure that the Use Texture Map box under the Texture tab is not checked. Under the Surface tab, set the color to a deep blue. Set the Specular to a bright yellow. Preview the settings. Close the Edit dialog.

4. Open the Light palette, and bring a Spotlight into the active project list on the left. Open the Edit dialog for the Spotlight. Move the light pointer so that the Spotlight is pointing at the rectangle from the upper right. Set the Spotlight color to a light red, and set the intensity of the Spotlight to 3.0 and a Source Radius of 2.75. Set the Cone Angle to 15 and Fuzziness to .5. Leave all of the other settings at their defaulted positions.

5. Click on Update Scene in the Light browser. You will see the light symbol placed over the rectangle. It is an object that can be moved like any other object. The direction the line is pointing is the direction of the light. Move the Spotlight so that it points to the middle upper edge of the rectangle, the place that a headline would be on a Web page if the rectangle were the background.

6. Render and save the image as a Web color background. The spotlighted area shows the light cone, making the rectangle lighter where the Spotlight touches it. The rectangle is a solid color with a highlighted area at the top. If you were to use this as a Web page background, you might place your main headline in the lighted area, making it seem as though a spotlight was pointing it out.

Figure 26-12: Using the spotlighted background adds a little drama to the color.

Tip

As far as the size of a Web page goes, if you create smaller graphics for background use they will automatically tile when seen with a browser sized larger than the artwork. Though there is no hard and fast rule, pages sized to 640 x 480 pixels usually work well. This means nothing to FreeHand Web pages, however, because FreeHand Web page art can be zoomed in and out in your browser.

Creating Color Gradient Backgrounds

A color gradient is a blend between two or more colors. You can use color gradients as backgrounds when the image is a JPEG, but less often when it is a GIF. Since GIF graphics are at best 256-color displays, gradients usually display severe banding when displayed in the GIF format. The user's browser, however, may still enforce a 256-color boundary on the display, just as the viewer's lower-end receiving device might. The safest bet is to use 256-color graphics throughout and where gradients are necessary, to pass them through a good dithering process first. By "good dithering process" we mean dithering that the eye sees as a blend of different colors with no obvious banding in the image.

Tip

If your gradient moves between lights and darks as most do, place dark text against the light parts of the gradient, and light text against the darker parts.

Using FreeHand
Gradients are simple to create in FreeHand.

1. Create a rectangle, sized to act as the Web page background.

2. Select the rectangle, and bring up the Fill Inspector, choosing the Gradient option. Configure the gradient with the colors you want.

3. Select the Linear gradient type, and observe how your gradient is painted to the rectangle. Explore the Logarithmic and Radial gradient types as well. Select the gradient type you like. This will be your Web page background.

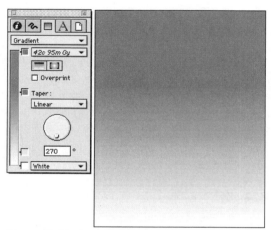

Figure 26-13: A gradient in FreeHand is configured using the Fill Inspector settings with the Gradient option.

Using xRes

When it comes to bitmap gradients, xRes is king of the heap. Gradients can be applied as a mixture of color palettes and shape types.

1. Create a new document sized to your Web page background. Draw a rectangle that fills the entire screen.

2. Click on the Gradient tool. Configure a gradient using your own choice of colors from the color list in the Gradient Options dialog. Make sure the Blend Option is selected. Select a shape type from the list. Click and drag the Gradient tool in the rectangle. Your gradient is written to the rectangle.

3. With the rectangle still selected, change the Blend option to Add. Select another color palette and a different shape, and click and drag the Gradient cursor over the rectangle again. The result is an unpredictable composite of the two gradients. Explore the settings until you achieve a Gradient rectangle you can use as a Web page background.

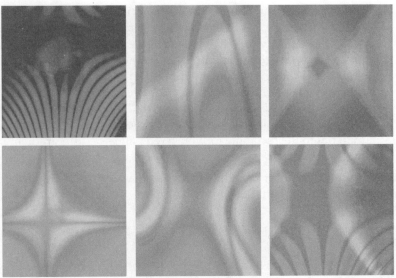

Figure 26-14: These six multiple gradient examples demonstrate the infinite variety of multiple gradients you can create as Web page backgrounds in xRes.

Tip

Text may be hard to read when placed over a multigradient Web page background. If it is, place the text in a solid color rectangle (or other shape) first. Then place the text shape over the gradient background.

Using Extreme 3D

In Extreme 3D, gradients are listed as a material type. A Gradient material group can be found in the Presets folder. All gradients can be customized, causing them to appear in a range of guises, from near-solid colors to texture-gradient combinations. Here's how to create one of my favorite textured gradients:

1. Create an extruded rectangle, sized to the correct dimensions for your Web page background.

2. Click on Select Catalog in the Materials browser, and load in the Gradient materials from the Presets folder. Five gradient materials will appear in the list to the right: blue, green, orange, purple, and red. Select any one of them and bring it over to the Materials in Scene list on the left.

3. Select the Gradient material in the Materials in Scene list and click on Edit. In the Edit dialog, set the parameters as follows: Under the Pattern tab, select the Cubic type with a Pattern Scale of .01, an Edge Sharpness of .6, and a Material Proportion of .5. Under the Warp tab, select a Turbulence of .5, and a Turbulence Scale and Bump Height of 1.0. Under the Material 1 tab, select a dark blue color and a light yellow specular color, leaving the other settings as is. Under the Materials 2 tab, select a bright yellow color and a pink specular color. Select OK to accept the settings. Apply this material to the rectangle for your Web page's texture-gradient background.

Text may be hard to read when placed over this background. If it is, place the text in a solid color rectangle (or other shape) first. Then place the text shape over the gradient background.

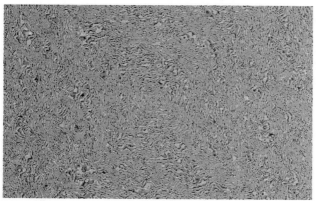

Figure 26-15: Unique Web page background texture-gradient combinations can be created in Extreme 3D.

Creating Textured Backgrounds

A textured Web page background tiles a repetitive pattern over the whole background. The tiled graphic can take on the appearance of a material (wood, cloth, metal, etc.) or can actually be an image or symbol (muted logos are common tiled textures for Web backgrounds). FreeHand, xRes, and Extreme 3D can be used to create textured backgrounds for Web pages.

Using FreeHand

You have to master the use of the Tiling option in the Fill tab of the Inspectors palette to be able to create native textured Web page backgrounds in FreeHand for shocked graphics. For a standard unshocked background, the browser itself would tile it.

1. Create or import a graphic of your choice. Copy it to the clipboard and deselect it.

2. Access the Fill Inspector, and select the Tiled option. Click on Paste, and the graphic you copied appears in the preview area of the Tiled dialog.

3. Draw a rectangle on the screen that is sized for your Web page background. It will automatically be filled with your copied and tiled graphic.

4. Adjust the X and Y dimensions of the graphic in the Tiled dialog, and also reset the rotation if necessary. This FreeHand technique is excellent for tiling logos on a Web page background.

Figure 26-16: By using the Tiled option, the graphic is automatically evenly tiled in the Web page area.

Using xRes

xRes has excellent tools for creating textured backgrounds for Web page use. A textured background can accept any images or text overlaid on it without disturbing the message or image content. Textured backgrounds offer more viewer interest than one-color backgrounds, though you do need to take care that the text is readable over the texture. The best way to guarantee this is to use a muted color, or a light gray, for the texture. Here's how to generate a textured background in xRes:

1. Determine the page size you will need. A standard size of 8" x 10" is usually acceptable; make sure it is set to 72 dpi. Open a new page in xRes that accommodates this size (set the background color to a light gray).

2. Select Windows | Palettes | Brushes to display the Brushes palette.

3. Choose either the Airbrush or the Charcoal Brush (Airbrush is the best choice), as these are the only two that allow you to use texture painting. Go to the Options pop-up menu in the Brushes palette and select "Textured."

4. Select the Paintbrush tool from the Toolbox. Go to the active screen area and start to paint down the texture. Do not remain in one area too long or the texture will be too dark. The best use of textures is to have a light muted texture with a dark text color, or a dark texture with light colored text. If the texture gets too complex, the only way to use smaller sized text will be to place it in a solid color frame on the textured background, or in some cases, to explore the possibility of placing a dark border around the lighter text.

5. After the page has had the texture applied to its surface, select the Bucket tool from the Toolbox. Select a color other than that used for your texture, and fill the areas between the texture. This gives you a two-color texture for your Web page background.

Tip

For an interesting option, you can use more than one texture, and allow the Airbrush to blend the textures as you paint. This breaks up the monotonous nature of a tiled texture. Care must be taken, however, to avoid too much complexity using this option.

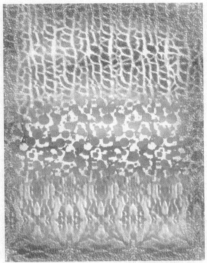

Figure 26-17: An airbrushed xRes Web page background texture provides visual interest and dynamics.

Using Extreme 3D

If you want your textured Web page backgrounds to leap off the page in 3D, use Extreme 3D to craft them. Extreme 3D's vast materials library allows you to render an infinite array of very authentic 3D textures.

1. Create a window the same size as your Web page. Draw a rectangle that fills it completely, and extrude the rectangle so it can receive a material texture.

2. Apply any material you want to, customizing it if necessary. When satisfied, save the graphic as a TIFF file, and use it as a Web page background after performing the necessary conversion.

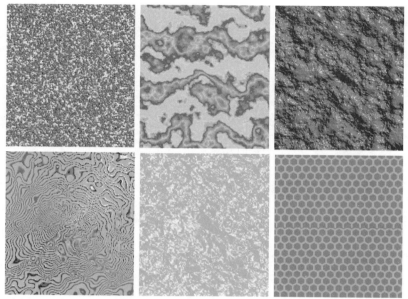

Figure 26-18: Extreme 3D has all of the textures you could ever hope for as materials presets, and every one can be infinitely customized.

Creating Pictorial Backgrounds

Using images as backgrounds, either photographic or original artwork, is becoming much more popular than using a single color. The image is the first item on the page that delivers its message, yet some Web designers prefer to use the image as a thing in itself, with little or no direct relationship to the content, except to set an emotional tone for it. Viewers will "read" the graphic long before they read the verbal content. The saying "image is everything" means that we get an instant look and feel for the emotional and aesthetic meaning before we start to decipher the text. If the image and the text conflict, the believability of the text will suffer, because the image will dominate.

Using FreeHand

This technique requires mastery of the Bitmap to Vector Translation tool and the Tiling Fill option.

1. Import a bitmap that might look interesting if tiled to a Web page background. Size it so it fits in an area about ⅟₂₀th of the page (hold the Shift key down to constrain the proportions).

2. Click on the Bitmap to Vector Translation tool, and click and drag a rectangular marquee around the graphic. The bitmap is translated to a vector drawing. Clear the original bitmap, and group the parts of the vector drawing into one unit.

3. Copy the vector drawing to the clipboard, and then deselect it. Go to the Tiled option of the Fill Inspector. Click on Paste. The graphic will appear in the preview panel.

4. Draw a rectangle that represents the size of your Web page, and it will automatically be tiled with the vector picture. Resize the picture in the Tiled dialog as needed to fill the rectangle. This is a great way to create tiled pictures for use as Web page backgrounds.

Tip

Don't be too concerned if the translation operation takes a while. A complex bitmap has to be translated one color area at a time.

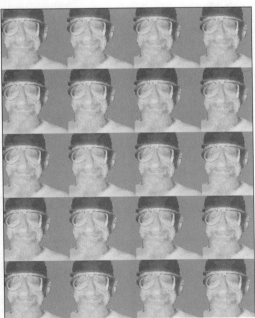

Figure 26-19: By first translating a bitmap to vector format and then tiling it, interesting pictorial backgrounds can be created for Web pages.

Using xRes

Creating photographic Web page backgrounds in xRes allows you to explore all of the diverse media tools xRes offers, with the option of transforming your photo into a digital painting.

1. Create a new page sized to the dimensions of the Web background page you need.

2. Import a photograph that is an interesting prospect for a Web page background. It will come in on a separate object layer. Resize it to fit the underlying Web page dimensions.

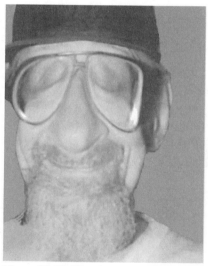

Figure 26-20: Here is our original imported photo.

3. Select the picture layer in the Objects palette, and move the slider to the left until its Opacity reads 30 percent. Select the Background in the Objects palette. Use a media brush (any one you want) to draw or paint over the outlines of the image in the photo. Add some gradient fills to areas in your painting. When you are finished, select all and copy the drawing to the clipboard. Select Paste, and the painting is placed on an object layer above the photo.

4. Turn down the opacity of the photo to 50 percent. This combines the underlying photo with the painting.

Figure 26-21: The painted representation of the photo.

Figure 26-22: The combined result of photo and digital artwork.

Tip

This technique works really well with portraiture and scenic photos.

Using Extreme 3D

Extreme 3D allows you to incorporate a bitmap texture in most of the materials it addresses. Any image you have on file can be used as a bitmapped texture component.

1. Size a screen to that of your needed Web page dimensions. Draw a rectangle that completely fills the screen, and extrude it so it can receive a Material texture.

2. Bring the default Mondo Map into the Materials in Scene list. Open its Edit dialog. Load your picture in as both a Texture and as a Bump map, activating both. Set the Bump and Texture percentages to full value. Select OK, and assign the Mondo material to the rectangle.

3. Create a sphere, make it a bright yellow, and duplicate it so that you have a total of four spheres. Align them vertically on some part of the rectangle. The 3D spheres will act as bullets for text block headings. Render, and save to disk as a potential Web page Background.

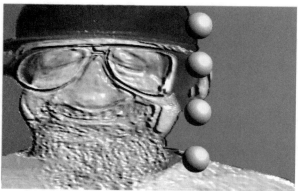

Figure 26-23: The Bump mapped texture looks like a woodcut, and the spheres act as text bullets.

Image Maps & Hot Spots

A hot spot is a section of a graphic, or an entire image, that takes you to a new site on the Web when clicked on. That site may be an alternate page in the present Web document, or, more commonly, a new URL address altogether. When a hot spot is present on a page loaded into your Web browser (Navigator, Internet Explorer, or other Netscape-compliant browsers), and you pass the cursor over the hot spot, the cursor changes from an arrow into a pointing hand. This tells you that if you click on the image or that part of the image under the pointing hand, the hot spot will be activated. Activating the hot spot will transport you to whatever page or site is indicated by the associated address embedded in that image. Text blocks can also be assigned as URL hot spots. Hot spots make Web pages highly interactive, so that the document that first appears when a Web site is accessed may be more of a doorway to a whole series of alternate and connected sites than a permanent landing space.

Image maps can be defined as a group of collective hot spots, rather like a collage that has alternate addresses attached to many if not all of the parts and pieces. Graphics designed as image maps have to be planned out carefully, with attention to the separate hot spot components as well as the overall design.

Image Map Design Issues

Image maps, which are just collections of hot spots in a larger image framework, have many of the same issues as hot spots. It's best to attach a text callout to the hot spot area of an image map to foster instant recognition that it is in fact a hot spot. When the cursor turns into the pointing hand as it passes over the named hot spot, there will be little doubt that clicking on it will transport you to the named site on the Web. You might also name the hot spot a little less specifically, like "My Favorite Web Site." That way, if your choice(s) changed over time, you could edit and change the associated URL without having to spend time altering the graphic involved. This allows you to edit and update a Web page without starting over from scratch.

Whether you are working in FreeHand or xRes to create your image maps, there are a few design suggestions to consider. These suggestions are valid for both FreeHand and xRes image map designs.

- Use a text callout in your hot spots to identify the hot area to the viewer. The only time this can be neglected is when the hot spot is an obvious stand-alone area that pops out of the background color, or on pages that consciously hide the hot spot (as in the design of a puzzle or mystery page, where hot spot access is more of a surprise than a necessity).

- Use complementary colors that set the hot spot off from the background color, either in the text callout for the hot spot or as a border around the hot spot area. Another alternative that works well is to make the hot spot a 3D graphic, which also makes it pop out of the backdrop.

- Use a JPEG file if it is to be a complex digital photo or piece of artwork, because that will show the most detail. You can also explore the possibility of using a GIF file, as long as you aren't using a human face as the dominant feature. Facial features require a lot of smooth blended gradients, and these usually break up into observable transition areas in GIF format because of the 256-color limitation. Whenever you use a JPEG, make sure it's a progressive JPEG. Progressive JPEG files display immediately as blurry images and sharpen as more data is downloaded, thereby holding the viewer's attention.

- Be careful about using a bitmap as the backdrop in a FreeHand file. Afterburner compressed and Shocked FreeHand files seen on a Web browser can be zoomed in on, and because FreeHand deals with vector graphics, you can zoom in as close as you need to see the vector elements. Zooming in on a bitmapped backdrop creates more and more jaggies the closer you zoom, which makes an ugly presentation. Better to use a solid color or FreeHand gradient as a backdrop in FreeHand Web pages.

Hot Spot Design Issues

The central design issue concerning a hot spot graphic is connective clarity with the URL. By this I mean that the graphic should somehow visually represent the URL that will be triggered. This is of course easy if you plan to use a text block as a hot spot. The word "Macromedia," for instance, can be the graphic that takes you to the Macromedia Web site. It gets a little more tricky, however, when graphic symbols without text are involved. How would you represent the Macromedia Web site URL hot spot as a graphic, without any text involved? In 99.9 percent of the cases, a text block is either used directly or folded into a symbolic graphic. That way, you needn't worry that viewers of the Web page will be confused by abstract hot spot graphics, since they will be clearly labeled.

Stand-alone URL hot spots on a Web page require fewer design conventions than do image maps. In general, you are free to experiment with any designs that come to mind as far as the content is concerned. There are, however, a few things to keep in mind:

1. Keep the hot spot small, generally less than 200 x 200 pixels. Hot spots are graphics, and graphics require download time. Even when efficiently compressed with Afterburner (for FreeHand graphics) or formatted as GIF or JPEG files (usually GIFs if they are bitmaps), smaller is better.

2. Add a callout to the hot spot. Redundancy, having both an image area and a text callout for the same hot spot, reinforces the potential activation of the hot spot. You want viewers to know what the page is about as soon as possible, so they can spend their time surfing the actual content.

3. Keep the coloring simple. Using primary colors will pop the hot spot out better, allowing the viewer to see it instantly in case they want to use it more immediately. One alternative is to use just a single bright color for your hot spot graphics, a color that stands out against the background of the page. Using a bitmap for a hot spot is OK, as long as it also contains an identifying text block in a bright color. When working with FreeHand documents, use bright vector graphics as the hot spot, placing them against a bitmap backdrop if desired.

4. Use an outline to sharpen the hot spot image. Whether the hot spot is a text block or a graphic symbol, use a dark outline (on average, of two pixels) to separate the hot spot from the background. This is true even if the background is dark, as it tends to sharpen the hot spot in all cases. It is especially true when the backdrop is lighter than the hot spot, though white backdrops are undesirable because they accentuate eye strain when viewed for too long. Adding an outline to a text block is easy. It simply means adding a defined stroke. Strokes can also be added to hot spot FreeHand graphics in the same manner. Adding an outline to a bitmap usually means drawing a defined rectangle or other shape around the bitmap. Use black or dark blue as the color of the outline (stroke).

Creating Image Maps

Image maps are the core elements that distinguish Web pages from any other medium. Only with an image map can you click on a part of a page and be transported to another Web page anywhere else in the world. You can create 2D image maps with hot spots in both FreeHand and xRes, while Extreme 3D allows you to create 3D VRML image maps.

Using FreeHand
FreeHand 7 offers new features to its URL Editing capabilities:

- The FreeHand plug-in was formerly named the URLs Xtra.
- URL Editor has better arrangement of Options pop-up items.
- New URL dialog box shows last URL created.
- Wider text fields in the New URL and Edit URL dialog boxes provide room for complex URLs.

To assign a URL to a graphic in FreeHand, do the following:

1. Select the graphic.

2. Access the URL Editor (Windows | Xtras | URL Editor).

3. Select New, Duplicate, Remove, Find, or Edit from the pull-down list. New allows you to enter a URL address in an input box. Duplicate will duplicate a URL already listed, so that you can alter it as a variant of the first address. Remove clears a URL from the list. Find will select a graphic(s) on the FreeHand page that is already connected to the selected URL. Edit allows you to edit an existing URL.

4. If you have the correct URL in the list, drag and drop it onto a graphic on the page. That graphic is now a URL hot spot on the page.

Repeat this process for every hot spot you want to configure in the FreeHand document. The entire FreeHand page will be the image map.

Using xRes

First make sure you are working in 72 dpi. If you want the graphic saved out as a GIF file for Web use, make sure that you are working in Indexed Color mode. Design your bitmap graphic. Select a hot spot area with either the Rectangle, Ellipse, or Polygon tool. Float the selection, making it appear as a separate object.

URLs are assigned to graphics in xRes from the Object Options dialog in the Objects/Paths/Channels palette. Simply double-click on the preview graphic in the Objects tab, and the Object Options dialog will appear.

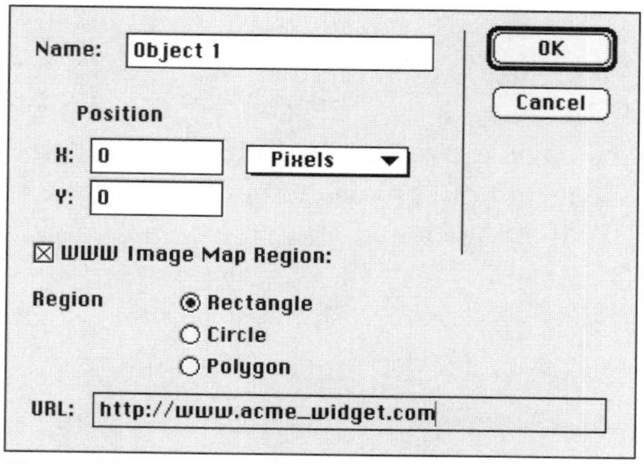

Figure 26-24: The URL Editor in xRes.

Check the WWW Imagemap Region box to bring up the settings input areas. You will see three Region radio buttons and a URL address area. Selecting the Rectangle option is the default. If you select the Oval option and the selection is a rectangle, xRes will calculate an oval area that lies within the borders of the rectangle. If you select a polygonal object layer, the exact perimeter of the polygon will be used as a hot spot for the image map.

Enter the URL data in the input area, and select OK to apply the hot spot data to the image. Save the image out as a GIF or JPEG as a image map document meant for the Web.

Moving On

In this chapter, we have presented a Web Design Primer, including detailed looks at graphics file formats, design issues based in the historical and emerging Web traditions, and using color in Web page design. We also explored the creation of Web page backgrounds in FreeHand, xRes, and Extreme 3D. Creating hot spots and URL targets was also presented in this chapter. In the next chapter, we will look at three Macromedia Web utilities important to FreeHand Web page designers: Shockwave graphics in FreeHand, and Macromedia's Flash and Backstage.

27

Macromedia Web Utilities

In this chapter, we'll look at three separate Macromedia applications for Web page creation: Shockwave, Flash, and Backstage. The last two are stand-alone applications that FreeHand users should be aware of, because they can be used as vehicles to get your FreeHand creations to the Web. Shockwave is folded into FreeHand 7, and awareness of its use is vital if you want to place your FreeHand graphics on the Web.

Macromedia Shockwave

Macromedia's Shockwave provides the capability of displaying native FreeHand graphic files within your Netscape Navigator or Internet Explorer browser. Shockwave has been a part of previous versions of FreeHand, but FreeHand 7 offers new Shockwave compatibility:

- Shockwave Graphics Player, a Netscape-compatible plug-in. This was formerly named Shockwave for FreeHand.
- Player enables font embedding in compressed documents.
- Player adds FreeHand 7 compatibility.

The Shockwave Graphics Player

The Shockwave Graphics Player is a plug-in for either Netscape Navigator or Microsoft Internet Explorer. Before FreeHand 7, this utility was called the Shockwave for FreeHand plug-in. This plug-in allows you to view (not create) FreeHand documents on the World Wide Web in a Netscape-compatible browser.

To install the Mac OS or Windows plug-in, double-click the appropriate installer in the CD\Shockwave folder. Follow the on-screen instructions. The install script will search for the browser installed on your system, and ask you whether this is the browser you want the plug-in installed to. Once installed, you can view any uploaded FreeHand document on a Web site. You will also be able to use your browser to view FreeHand Afterburner documents you have saved.

Shockwave Graphics Xtras

Two important graphics Xtras, the URL Editor and Afterburner Xtras, are installed when you install the FreeHand 7 application. Use the URL Editor Xtra to add URL (Uniform Resource Locator) hotlinks to FreeHand graphics of any shape. Use the Afterburner Xtra to import and export compressed FreeHand files. The Afterburner Xtra includes an option to embed fonts within a document and an option to lock a file to prevent it from being opened outside a browser. This option should always be used. You must use version 7 of the Shockwave Graphics Player to view compressed FreeHand 7 files or uncompressed native FreeHand files with the file extensions .fh4, .fh5, or .fh7.

Adding URLs

Tip

To add a URL, choose New from the Options pop-up. Type the text in the New URL dialog box and press Return or Enter. After adding a URL, you must apply that URL to an object before closing or resizing the URL Editor panel, closing the FreeHand document, or sending the FreeHand application to the background. URLs listed in the URL Editor but not attached to a FreeHand object will not be saved with the document.

Editing URLs

To edit a URL, select it and choose Edit from the Options pop-up, or double-click the URL. Edit the entry in the Edit URL dialog box and press Return or Enter when you are done.

Figure 27-1: URL data can be added and modified in the URL Editor dialog.

Tip

We strongly recommend that you avoid using FreeHand's Undo command when editing a URL in the URL Editor. To undo an edit, double-click the URL and manually change the URL back to its original state. If you use Undo, the URL Editor fails to reflect the Undo, even though the FreeHand object is updated with the correct URL. With an unused URL in the URL Editor the Find command cannot find any objects. If you select the object you know is linked to the correct URL, that correct text appears in the URL Editor again. You can then delete the unnecessary entries from the URL Editor.

Copying URLs

To duplicate an existing URL, select it in the URL Editor and choose Duplicate from the Options pop-up. The duplicate URL appears with the word "Copy" appended to the end of the old URL. Edit the duplicate URL as needed.

Applying URLs

After a URL has been added to the URL Editor, drag and drop the desired URL selection to an object. To apply a URL to several objects at once, select multiple objects and select a URL in the URL Editor. To remove a URL from a tagged object but not from the URL Editor, drag and drop the None entry onto the object or select the object and select None in the URL Editor.

Deleting URLs

Select a URL and choose Remove from the Options pop-up to remove the URL from the URL Editor and tagged objects.

Identifying URLs Assigned to FreeHand Objects

Choose Find in the Options pop-up to determine which objects have been assigned to a specific URL. For best results, press Tab to deselect all FreeHand objects, select a URL, and choose Find. FreeHand displays selection handles for all objects linked to the selected URL.

Assigning URLs to Individual Objects Within a Group

To select an individual object within a group, hold down Option (Mac OS) or Alt (Windows) and click to select that object. With the object selected, add a URL as you normally would.

Shockwave graphics support absolute URLs and relative URLs. Absolute URLs are URLs that include the entire path name and file name for the document. Relative URLs contain partial path names that are relative to the current folder. Relative URLs entered in FreeHand are relative to the FreeHand file's location on the server, not to the HTML file in which they are embedded. For server specific data, see the section below on FreeHand Server Connections.

Using Afterburner

Tip

You must use the Afterburner Xtra to include fonts in your document. FreeHand supports all Type 1 and TrueType fonts, but not Type 3 fonts. To embed fonts in your document, check Embed Outline Fonts in the Compress Document dialog box of the Afterburner Xtra.

The Shockwave Graphics Player normally uses the standard FreeHand file format, with an extension of ".fh7", ".fh5", or ".fh4", for viewing within a Netscape-compatible browser. It is highly recommended however, that, when creating graphics for the Web, you use FreeHand's Afterburner Xtra to compress the FreeHand file. This enables much faster document transfer over the Internet. The FreeHand 7 Afterburner Xtra differs from previous versions:

- Uses a new option to embed fonts in compressed FreeHand files.

- Every compressed FreeHand 7 file contains a broken file icon that appears when viewing these documents with version 5 of the plug-in. The icon has a link to Macromedia's web site, where you can download the latest version of the Shockwave Graphics Player.

To compress your document with Afterburner, do the following in FreeHand:

1. Open a previously saved FreeHand document, or create and save a new one.

2. Choose Xtras | Afterburner | Compress Document.

3. Type a file name in the Compress as entry field in the Compress Document dialog box.

4. Check Locked or Embed Outline Fonts, as needed. I would advise you to leave the Locked option unchecked and the Embed Outline Fonts always checked as the defaults.

5. Click OK. The compressed FreeHand file is saved to disk.

Tip

Do not open a compressed Afterburner file in FreeHand itself. If you do, you will see that it looks like a chaotic jumble of code. The compressed file is meant to be viewed in your Web browser. If you need to edit it, open the original FreeHand document file, edit it, and save it again as an Afterburner compressed file. Another alternative is to select Xtras | Afterburner | Decompress, and select the compressed file. It will be decompressed so you can edit it in FreeHand, and resave it as a compressed file.

The compressed file will have the extension ".fhc". Files compressed in this manner are automatically recognized and decompressed by Shockwave when the file is opened and viewed in your browser.

When you are exporting a FreeHand document with the Afterburner Xtra, you can lock the document so that it cannot be reopened in FreeHand in its compressed format. To lock a document, check Locked in the Compress Document dialog box. Since locked files can be viewed only in a browser (not in FreeHand), keep a copy of your original FreeHand document for later editing. It's safer to keep this option unchecked, and to use it only for security reasons.

To open an unlocked, compressed file in FreeHand, do the following:

1. Choose Xtras | Afterburner | Decompress Document.

2. In the Decompress Document dialog box, navigate to a compressed file. Only files with the ".fhc" extension are available for decompression.

3. Click Open.

A decompressed file opens as an untitled document. To name the document, choose File | Save As or File | Save. You must also save the document before you can export it again as a compressed document.

The Afterburner Xtra also embeds a small broken file icon in every compressed FreeHand 7 file. If viewing one of these files using version 5 of the Shockwave Graphics Player you will see this broken file icon, which contains a link to Macromedia's Web site. Users can click this icon to download the newest version of the Shockwave Graphics Player. Version 7 of the Shockwave Graphics Player supports FreeHand 4, FreeHand 5, and old ".fhc" files, but you must have version 7 of the Shockwave Graphics Player to view FreeHand 7 files.

Macromedia Flash

Flash is a vector graphics animation creation application. Flash was developed by FutureWave Software as the result of another one of its products: SmartSketch. SmartSketch is a stand-alone vector drawing program, akin to Macromedia's FreeHand. Through its proprietary anti-aliasing technology, SmartSketch was able to generate screen art that looked as smooth as that produced in a laser printout, as well as to grab hold of a line and turn it into a curve without the need for Bezier tools or anything else. SmartSketch is the parent of Flash, which was purchased by Macromedia from FutureWave.

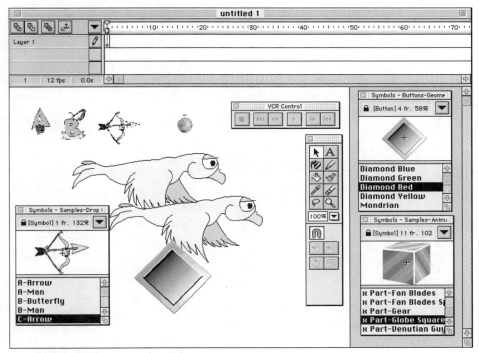

Figure 27-2: The Flash interface.

System Requirements

Flash is both Mac OS and Windows 95/NT compatible. Installation on a Mac OS system requires a 68020 processor (68040 or PowerPC recommended), with at least 5 MB of hard disk storage (10 MB suggested), a CD-ROM drive, and 8 MB of RAM (16 MB is better), running Mac OS 7.x. Windows 95/NT users will need a 486 or better PC (Pentium recommended), VGA monitor with a 256-color display, with at least 5 MB of hard disk storage (10 MB suggested), a CD-ROM drive, and 8 MB of RAM (16 MB is better), running Windows 95 or NT (3.51 or better).

Tools

The Animation palette consists of a combined Timeline Editor and Layers selector. The Toolbox has an assortment of special and unique vector drawing tools. The VCR Controller is used to preview animations, and can also be used like a jog-shuttle to move design elements into place on any selected frame.

The Symbol palette is a graphics and animation storage library that can be used within the project or accessed for separate projects.

Flash comes loaded with 20 complete animation tutorials, all stored as vector projects, which take little room on your hard drive. The tutorials include complete and detailed walkthroughs on every tool and process in Flash. You can move through the tutorials at your own speed, and back up to previous lesson pages when needed.

Drawing Features

Flash's Toolbox has a basic arrangement of vector drawing–related tools. The Pencil tool includes Straighten, Smooth, Ink, Oval, Rectangle, and Line options. Smoothing and Straightening are special options that affect how FreeHand shapes are drawn on the screen, either angular or smoothly curved. The Color palette selector, listing 228 default colors and shades, is built into the Toolbox, and customized color choices are also possible.

Symbol Palette

The Symbol palette is a library of page elements saved out with the page you're working on, though you can also call it up to place the same elements on another page. Every graphic element you use in a Flash design, animated or not, is first placed in that Page's Symbol Library palette. Any clone of is loaded from the Library palette, which is vital for Web designers, since it saves time in downloading and increases download speed.

Animation Controls

The animation controller in Flash is easy to use and mastered quickly. Elements on a page can either stay in place across the sequence; can be "interpolated" to change position, size, and rotation from targeted beginning and ending frames; or can be altered in design in a frame-by-frame process. Interpolation does not include morphing, the capacity of a shape to automatically change its outline from one configuration to another.

In addition to the standard Timeline Controller, the Animation palette also includes layer specific controls. New elements are placed on separate layers, any of which can be repositioned in the stack. Elements on any layer can appear in color, grayscale, or in single-color outlines for reshaping and stacking purposes. Layers can be made active/inactive and also locked from further editing.

Flash & the Web

Flash was designed for creating 2D animations, and includes specific tools for Web animation. Flash is a vector design application, so that animation files tend to be about 80 percent smaller than similar animations created with bitmap processes. The animation has to be saved as a proprietary animation file, a Web friendly format (not as a movie file).

The best way to save out a Flash animation if it is to be used on a Web page is as a FutureSplash Player (.spl) file. To view SPL files, you need the SPL Player plug-in, available for downloading from Macromedia's Web site. SPL animations can be written out with smoothing turned on, producing high quality anti-aliased art in a tiny file size (10 to 20 percent of what the same file would be if saved in a standard movie format).

A complete Web-associated animation tutorial (Working with HTML) guides you through the process of embedding Flash animations in your HTML documents. In addition, the documentation lists all of the necessary HTML tags, so you can customize any Flash animation for your HTML Web posting. This is also good news for Macromedia Backstage users, as it enables quick embedding of Flash animations in a Backstage document.

Flash also includes the capability to write out the animation as either a GIF animation or as a GIF sequence of single frames (so they can be edited in other suitable applications). This includes transparency recognition for invisible backgrounds. GIF animations can be incorporated into your Web pages through standard load and place means, using your Web page creation software. GIF animations can use the standard 216-color Netscape palette.

File Formats Supported

The Mac OS version of Flash can import graphics in PICT, AutoCAD, Illustrator, JPEG, and GIF formats and save graphics as PICT, EPS, Illustrator, AutoCAD, SPL, JPEG, and GIF. The Windows version of Flash can import graphics in EMF, WMF, Illustrator, EPS, AutoCAD, JPEG, GIF, and BMP formats and save graphics as EMF, WMF, Illustrator, EPS, AutoCAD, JPEG, GIF, SPL, and BMP (Windows).

Animations can be exported on Mac OS as SPL, QuickTime, Animated GIF, PICT sequence, EPS sequence, Illustrator sequence, DXF sequence, JPEG sequence, or GIF sequence. Under Windows, they can be exported as SPL, AVI, animated GIF, EMF sequence, WMF sequence, EPS sequence, DXF sequence, BMP sequence, JPEG sequence, and GIF sequence.

The FreeHand-Flash Web Connection

If you want to use Flash to get your FreeHand graphics to the Web, simply save your FreeHand graphics selections in a file format that Flash can understand. These formats include: Illustrator, BMP, GIF, JPEG, TIFF, PICT, or EPS. You can also input Flash graphics into a FreeHand Web document by saving them out from Flash in a format that FreeHand understands.

Tip

See Appendix D for a tutorial concerning transferring FreeHand Graphics Studio animations to the Web with Flash.

Macromedia Backstage Designer

Backstage Designer is Macromedia's Web design application for Windows, a program devoted to giving you all of the necessary creative tools to design a Web page with the highest interactive features available. Backstage Designer is a visually oriented application, but it also allows full HTML page editing and creation.

Though you could add FreeHand, xRes, and Extreme 3D images to a Backstage Web project (as long as they are either GIF or JPEG), a better alternative would be to use a hot spot on your main Backstage page that transported you to a stand-alone FreeHand page, crafted with Afterburner as a Shockwave document. This would give you all of the vector and bitmap assets offered by the FreeHand Web document we have discussed. It would also allow you to use Backstage Designer's exclusive HTML coding to add toolbars to selected graphics, and to perform other HTML-specific editing.

Backstage Designer comes in two editions, Desktop and Enterprise. To find out more about Backstage Designer and either edition, visit Macromedia's Web site.

Tip

*Ventana offers a comprehensive book on Backstage Designer, co-authored by the same author of the book you are reading (*Web Publishing With Macromedia Backstage Internet Studio 2*). Go to Ventana's Web site to find out the details of the Backstage book.*

Figure 27-3: Macromedia's Backstage Designer.

An alternate way to use FreeHand pages as Web backgrounds in Backstage is to first save the FreeHand page out as a 72 dpi TIFF file. Then simply import it into Backstage as a background. This allows you to use all of Backstage's text features (and even image map tools) over the FreeHand graphic.

Moving On

In this chapter, we looked at the FreeHand Shockwave and Afterburner connection, as well as presenting an overview of two external Macromedia applications important for FreeHand users to be aware of: Flash and Backstage. In the next chapter, we will walk through the creative processes involved in the creation of 10 diverse FreeHand Web pages.

28

10 Web Site Designs

Now, we're ready to apply what we learned from the tutorials in the previous chapters to comprehensive projects. As you know, FreeHand made its reputation in the print-to-paper world. Although that world still exists, publishing has gone through a number of evolutions in the last five years. When someone says they are a publisher, you can no longer assume that they are engaged in newspaper, book, or magazine publishing. Today, we have electronic publishing, multimedia CD-ROMs, and the world of the Internet, intranets, and the World Wide Web.

Visual applications like FreeHand have helped to bring about this evolution, and they function as creative tools to enhance the content involved. The Web is a special case in point; it was born from the Internet, a realm of e-mail and words. The Web still uses text as a means of expression, but like TV (the other parent of the Web), alternate forms of media expand the meaning and impact of text. If a picture is worth a thousand words, then a Web page has the potential of being worth a thousand ideas. True, there are more uninteresting Web sites than exciting ones, but this new technology is still in its infancy.

This chapter walks you through the construction of 10 unique Web sites. We will use FreeHand as the final step in their creation, and use many of the parts and pieces developed in the content tutorials presented earlier in this book. We hope that you've had the opportunity to work through these tutorials, so that you now have your own versions of their graphics. If not, however, you can still work through these Web page designs. Most of the parts and pieces these Web pages contain are on the CD-ROM that comes with this book.

Just look in the Parts and Pieces folder. Perhaps you would rather develop your own unique graphics for these pages, or you might even develop your own Web site ideas, loosely referring to the Web pages discussed here. Whatever you decide to do, these ten Web page designs should help you integrate FreeHand, Extreme 3D, and xRes into a creative resource for your own Web page designs.

Tip

Remember to include a small hot spot with the Macromedia logo on every FreeHand Web page you create. Its URL should point to the Macromedia site at http://www.macromedia.com. A small line of accompanying text should read "Download Shockwave for FreeHand." This will allow anyone without the Shockwave plug-in for their browser to get it. Without the plug-in, they won't be able to see your FreeHand Web page.

Many Web sites consist of more than one page. Many pages are linked together by hot spots that connect everything present in an interactive web, allowing you to jump from one page on a site to another. We suggest that you design separate FreeHand documents for each page on any particular site, instead of developing a multipage document in FreeHand itself for display as a total Web site. This is because FreeHand understands and displays multipage documents a little differently than a Web site does. It's best if you develop multiple FreeHand documents for each page, and connect them through hot spots. In these exercises, we will explore only one page per theme, but will suggest what other pages (or sites) might be referenced from hot spots on this main page. All 10 FreeHand documents and their Afterburner counterparts are included on the CD-ROM in the folder named "Web_10."

Winter Resort

This Web page is like that created by a winter resort that wants to expand its contact with people interested in skiing, snowboarding, and other cold weather sports. This is their main page, but as the text and hot spots indicate, other peripheral pages are available. The hot spots indicated here are not active, but you can make them active if this theme resembles a Web project that interests you.

Tip

Remember to look in the Parts and Pieces folder on the CD-ROM, as well as in the "Web_10" folder for the actual FreeHand documents.

Step #1: Develop a Palette Range for the Color List

The first thing we will do is to create a range of colors we will use for this page and place them in the Color List. Use the Color Mixer to create the following RGB hues (the numbers in parenthesis represent the red, green, and blue values, respectively): Yellow (255, 255, 0), Blue1 (0, 255, 255), Blue2 (0, 186, 255), Blue3 (0, 155, 255), Blue4 (0, 23, 255), and Blue5 (0, 0, 120). Black and White are already included in the Color List as a default.

Step #2: Create a Linear Gradient Rectangular Background

Draw a rectangle sized to the FreeHand page, leaving a slight white border around it. Go to the Fill Inspector, and select the Gradient option. Use a linear gradient at an angle of 270 degrees. In the Gradient color bar, drag and drop Blue5 at the top, Blue3 in the center, and White at the bottom. The rectangle shows a gradient fill from dark blue at the top to white at the bottom.

Figure 28-1: The gradient background.

Step #3: Open a FreeHand Document on the CD-ROM

We will use some graphics created previously. If you haven't gone through the Snowflake example in the tutorial section, open the "Snflk.FH7" document in the FreeHand folder on the CD-ROM. The name of our fantasy resort is "Mount Snowflake." Place the FreeHand graphic that says "Snowflake" at the top of the gradient rectangle. Create the word "Mount" with a yellow fill and a Blue5 stroke so that it is proportionally sized to the "Snowflake" title, and place the word "Mount" over the "Snowflake" title. Rotate the word "Mount" to the left slightly. See Figure 28-2 for reference.

Figure 28-2: Our Web page main heading is in place.

Step #4: Create a Mountain & Sun

Use the FreeHand tool to draw a mountain that extends from the title at the top down the page. Use the same gradient fill on it as the background, and set it to a one point Blue5 stroke. Draw a circle, and fill it with a radial gradient with white at the center and the yellow swatch on the outside. Set its stroke to None. Use the Roughen Xtra tool (from the Xtra Tools panel) on it to give it rays. See Figure 28-3.

Figure 28-3: The mountain and sun are added to the design.

Step #5: Add a Text Blurb

Use the Text tool to create the line "Over 100 Trails Open Day & Night." Color it yellow with a one point Blue5 stroke. With the FreeHand tool, draw a path on the right side of the mountain that follows the contour of the mountain. Select both the blurb and the path, and select Text | Attach To Path. The blurb follows the mountain's right contour.

Figure 28-4: The blurb is added to the scene.

Step #6: The Finishing Touches

Use a snowflake graphic (either one you developed from completing the snowflake graphic exercise, or the one located on the FH7 document you opened earlier), and clone it twice. Resize it so that all three fit on the left side of the page at the bottom. Left-align them. Create a line of text to be placed at the right of each snowflake. The three lines should read "Reservation Information," "How to Get Here," and "Fun for the Family." Place them next to the snowflakes, and left-align them.

Create another RGB Blue (Blue7, with values of 199, 196, 255), and place it in the Color List panel. Draw a rectangle to act as a text box. Left-align it with the bottom text lines, and size it to fit within the contours of the mountain at its base. Fill it with Blue7 and a one point stroke of Blue6. This box would act as the container for whatever body copy text you wanted to add to the main page. Perhaps the text could give a short history of Mount Snowflake.

Clone the snowflake graphic one more time, and place it in the sky to the right of the mountain. Create a line of text over it that reads "E-MAIL US." The graphics on the page are complete. Save out a separate page with Afterburner compression.

Figure 28-5: The completed Web page graphics.

Step #7: Add Hot Spots & Target Pages

Where would you place the hot spots, and where might the associated URLs lead? The E-Mail hot spot would cover the text and background snowflake in the sky, and would be best designed as a rectangle that covered this area. Three more hot spots would be configured to include each of the snowflakes at the bottom and their associated text. Each of these three hot spots would take the surfer to a separate page at the Mount Snowflake site. The Information hot spot might detail reservation costs and times, as well as special holiday pricing. The "How to Get Here" hot spot could be a detailed map of the area and the resort, and might even include airline and bus travel information. The "Fun for the Family" hot spot would include local establishments (movies, theme parks, and other family centers) that offered enjoyable and entertaining experiences for all family members. All of the associated URL data would be entered in the Xtra URL dialog in FreeHand. The last operation to be performed would be to use Afterburner to compress the FreeHand Web document for Shockwave browser display.

Tip

You will find this completed Web page on the CD-ROM in the Web_10 folder. It is named Resort.FH7; the Afterburner-compressed file is called Resort.FHC.

Child Center

For this example, you should either open the Kid's Block FreeHand document in the FH7 folder on the CD-ROM or gather the artwork you created from the Kid's Block exercise. It's important to think in terms of bright primary colors for this Web site, in keeping with the theme. We will walk through the development of the main page, and talk about possible hot spots to other pages. The name of our child center is "ABC Kids."

Step #1: Create Your Colors

Create the following RGB colors, and place them in the Color List: Green (0, 120, 0), Yellow (225, 200, 0), Blue1 (0, 0, 200), Blue2 (0, 200, 200), Red (200, 0, 0), and Orange (200, 100, 0). Draw a rectangle for the background, and color it Green with no stroke.

Select the block archway graphic that is on the imported FreeHand document (or the archway you created if you completed the KidsBlock exercises). Resize it so that it takes up about 30 percent of the top of the page, and place it over the green rectangle. Draw a yellow circle that sits in the center of the archway, and center the words "ABC Kids Inc." inside the circle. See Figure 28-6 for reference.

Figure 28-6: The top of your page should resemble this figure.

Step #2: Create the Middle of the Page

Place the large ABC block (included with the imported FreeHand page) in the center of the page below the yellow circle. Create three rectangular objects, yellow, orange, and Blue2 (no strokes), and place them as illustrated in the accompanying figure. In the yellow rectangle, write and size the text "Click Here... Kid Art" as illustrated. In the orange rectangle, write and size the text "Click Here... Books." In the Blue2 rectangle, write and size the text "Click Here... Crafts." Create arrows with 12 point white strokes and arrowheads that point from the rectangles to the appropriate face on the 3D block. Refer to Figure 28-7 as an example.

Figure 28-7: This is the center of the ABC Kids Web page.

Step #3: Design the Bottom of the Page

Now for the final part of the page. Select the 3D block, and copy it to the clipboard. Deselect the block, and select Tiled from the drop-down menu in the Fill Inspector. Click on Paste In, and the 3D block appears in the preview screen. Set the X and Y dimensions to 40 percent. Draw a rectangular area at the bottom of the Web page. It is automatically filled with the tiled 3D block. Set the stroke to None. Adjust the dimensions of the rectangle so only full 3D tiled blocks can be seen.

Deselect everything. Draw a rectangle in the center of the tiled area. Set its fill color to Blue1 and stroke to None. Create a line of text that reads "ABC Kids, Inc.: Who We Are-", with a white fill and no stroke. Place it at the top of the blue1 rectangle. This area is where you would place descriptive text concerning the history and mission of ABC Kids, Inc.

Figure 28-8: The history and mission of this organization would be placed under the heading.

Step #4: The Finished Design

Take a look at the finished design. If this was a real project, you could customize it to fit the data at hand. The history/mission section at the bottom, for instance, could be expanded or reduced in size. Other global changes could be made as well. Save out a separate page with Afterburner compression.

Figure 28-9: The finished Web page design.

Step #5: Add Hot Spots & Target Pages

Where would you place the hot spots, and where might the associated URLs lead? In this case, they are pretty obvious as far as placement. All three of the "Click Here" call-outs show you where to click. The page was designed this way to be accessible to young people as well as adults. The Art page hot spot would be a polygonal area covering the "A" side of the 3D block. The art page would have a collection of kids' art on it, digitized from the actual artwork. The Books page hot spot would be a polygonal area covering the "B" side of the 3D block. The URL it would point to would be a page of suggested readings for children, with summary biographies of books in the list. The "Crafts" hot spot would be the "C" side of the 3D block. The promotional page associated with it would be a collection of photos of children at the ABC Kids, Inc. site engaged in various crafts.

Tip

You will find this completed Web page on the CD-ROM in the Web_10 folder. It is named ABCkids.FH7; the Afterburner-compressed file is called ABCkids.FHC.

Nutrition Page

There are dozens of nutrition information pages on the Web, so this content area is obviously one with a lot of contemporary appeal. Look in the FH7 folder for FreeHand pages that contain food items to use as temporary graphics for this page, or load in your own vector or bitmap artwork as graphics content. If you completed the exercises in the food tutorials, you may want to use your xRes or Extreme 3D bitmaps as components on this page. Look in the Parts and Pieces folder on the CD-ROM for dozens of food-oriented bitmap graphics. Import 33_46 (burger), 33_57 (bread), AppleZ3, Bowl1, Burg7A (drink), Ckgz3 (cookies), Yummy, and Orange1.

Step #1: Create the Color Palette

Create the following RGB colors in the Color Mixer palette, and place them in the Color List: Orange (222, 150, 0), Yellow (255, 213, 0), Pink (255, 213, 144), Green (0, 213, 144), Blue (0, 167, 216), and Aqua (0, 114, 118).

Step #2: Configure the Background

Draw a rectangle that fills the page. Use a radial color gradient to fill it. Configure the gradient as follows: aqua at the top, yellow at the bottom. Move the Locate Center knob to the lower third of the page.

Use the Text tool to create the following page headline: Nutrition and You. Use Times Bold. Convert the text to paths. The next step requires that you have KPT VectorFX installed.

Select the text block. Open VectorFX, and set the parameters as follows: Rotate X to 24, Rotate Y to 25, Rotate Z to -4, Perspective to 80, Complexity to 60, and Extrusion to 100. Click the checkmark to apply these settings to the text block.

Figure 28-10: The page heading after being altered with KPT VectorFX.

Step #3: Place the Food Graphics

Take each of the food graphics you imported earlier and draw an oval around them. Fill the oval with white and give it a 1.5 point black stroke. Place the ovals in back of each graphic, and group the oval to the graphic. Arrange the oval graphics around the center of the page below the headline.

Figure 28-11: The graphics are arranged around the outside of the page area.

Step #4: Create a Text Block

Use the Text tool to create a centered text block that reads: Click for Caloric and Vitamin data. Place the text block over the background. Draw aqua 12 point lines to each food graphic.

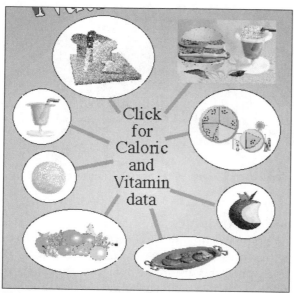

Figure 28-12: The text has been added.

Step #5: Finish the Composition

At this point, you can rearrange any of the page elements to give the page a more balanced look. You also might want to add a few lines that detail the site a bit, or perhaps even add some text around each of the food graphics. Save out a separate page with Afterburner compression.

Step #6: Add Hot Spots & Target Pages

The hot spots are pretty obvious on this page. They would be oval areas that addressed each of the food graphics. The links would detail whatever data you would like to include about the nutritional and other information.

Tip

You will find this completed Web page on the CD-ROM in the Web_10 folder. It is named Nutrit.FH7; the Afterburner-compressed file is called Nutrit.FHC.

Figure 28-13: The finished page.

Family Home Page

This is one of the fastest-growing categories on the Web. These sites function as public family albums, instantly accessible by all the members of a family and interested onlookers. One of the best uses for a family page is to document the genealogy of all family members. This is made much more readable than the same document printed to paper, because you can separate out different members with hot spots and target URLs.

Step #1: Cut Out the Main Figure

If married partners wish to design a page together, then both can be represented here. We're working with just one figure for this example. The figure we're working with is the AnimGuy created in the Extreme 3D animation tutorial (you can find his picture in the Parts and Pieces/Animguy folder on the CD-ROM). You can use any photo you prefer in this example. The first thing we want to do is to get rid of any background behind the character or photo.

Select the Pen tool. Carefully trace an outline around the image to exclude the background. Point and click with the mouse to do this, and double-click for the last point. A solid shape representing the silhouette of the figure will appear. Select the original image, and copy it to the clipboard. Now click on the shape you just drew, and Edit | Paste Inside. The image will appear inside the outlined silhouette. I prefer to have a one point stroke set to the shape, but you may select to have none.

Figure 28-14: The figure is cut away from its background with the Paste Inside operation.

Step #2: Create the Background

Create a palette of ten colors of your choice, and place them in the Color List. Draw a rectangle as the page background, and fill it with a linear gradient that has a dark color at the top and a light color at the bottom. Place your figure at the upper left, and draw a filled FreeHand voice balloon coming from the figure. Use the Text tool to create the words for the balloon, saying something like "Hi! I'm (whoever the image represents). This is my genealogy home page..." Place the text in the balloon.

Figure 28-15: The voice balloon displays the name and theme of the home page title.

Step #3: Create a Genealogical Tree

Using the colors you designed, create a series of rectangles that represent the members of your family. Create their names with the Text tool, and group each name with its rectangle. Place the rectangles in a genealogical order under the headline. Connect the named rectangles properly to show the family tree. Save the page as a separate Afterburner-compressed document.

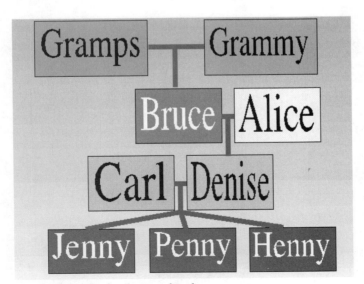

Figure 28-16: The family tree takes shape.

Figure 28-17: The completed Web page.

Step #4: Adding Hot Spots & Target Pages

The hot spots are pretty obvious on this page. They are all of the named rectangles. Each target page would display more information, and possibly visuals, of that family member and his or her personal history. Remember, Web pages are seen by anyone who surfs them, so best not to give away any family secrets.

Tip

You will find this completed Web page on the CD-ROM in the Web_10 folder. It is named Family.FH7; the Afterburner-compressed file is called Family.FHC.

UFO Interest Group

The Web is science fiction come to pass, so it's no surprise that themes like UFOs are prolific on the Web. If you created the examples in the UFO tutorials, you have all the graphics that you need for this page. If you didn't, you can find the graphics in the Parts and Pieces folder on the CD-ROM under various UFO headings.

Step #1: Import a Graphic

Import the Saucer1 file from the Parts and Pieces folder. You may have created a version of this yourself in the xRes transparency exercise. If so, use your own variation. Set it aside for the moment.

Step #2: Create the Background

Create a rectangular background, and fill it with a deep purple hue and no stroke. In the bottom third of the page, draw a horizontally centered red circle with no stroke. Center a smaller yellow circle inside it, also with no stroke. Select all three items and blend them.

Figure 28-18: The backdrop is created with a series of blends.

Step #3: Create the Heading

Enlarge the graphic that you previously imported and put aside, and place it over the top of the background. It should take up about one third of the page. Create two text blocks that read "UFO" and "World," and place them over the graphic. Color them bright yellow with a one point black stroke. Use the Smudge tool to add a shadow to the text.

Step #4: Create a Subhead

Draw a curved line on top of the graphic with the FreeHand tool, going from left to right. Create a text block that reads "UFO Sightings Around the World" in a black 36 point typeface of your choice. Select the type and the path, and then Attach to Path. The text will follow the curved path.

Figure 28-19: The top of the page design is complete.

Step #5: Add the Hot Spot Items

Import the UFO1 graphic from the Parts & Pieces folder on the CD-ROM. If you prefer, you can use your own graphic in place of this one. If you are using this graphic, perform the same Paste Inside operation on it that you performed in the previous Family page example to cut out its background. Clone the graphic twice, and place all three in a vertical alignment on the bottom left of the page.

On the right of each graphic, develop a text line. Line 1 should read "This Week." Line 2 should read "Tomorrow." Line 3 should read "Contact Us." Leave the text unconverted, and leave the color black. Set the stroke to yellow, which will draw a rectangular box around the unconverted text. Save the document as a separate Afterburner-compressed page for browser display.

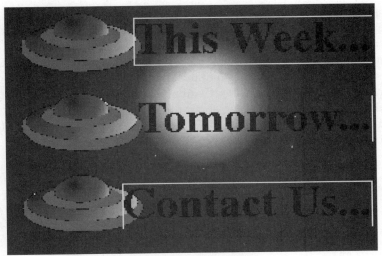

Figure 28-20: This is the bottom of the UFO page.

Figure 28-21: The completed UFO Web page design.

Step #6: Adding Hot Spots & Target Pages

The hot spots on this page would include a rectangular area that surrounds the three saucer icons at the bottom of the page and their associated text. The content of the target pages might vary, but here's what I would do. On the This Week page, I would list all of the sightings that took place all over the world during the present week. On the Tomorrow page, I would list all of the predictions people are making about those and previous sightings. On the Contact Us page, I would list all of the people at the organization, along with their e-mail addresses and other pertinent data.

Tip

You will find this completed Web page on the CD-ROM in the Web_10 folder. It is named Family.FH7; the Afterburner-compressed file is called Family.FHC.

American Heritage Group

The organization behind a site like this could range in interests from the Daughters and Sons of the American Revolution to a more commercial enterprise. For our exercise, we will structure the Web site developer as a political organization (with neither a conservative nor a liberal label) that seeks to promote awareness of our nation's heritage. As of the national elections of 1996, the Web has become a major display area for political interests. A Web page designer is likely to encounter increasing design requests from politically oriented clients well into the far future. For this exercise, open the Buntg2 FreeHand document on the CD-ROM. Also be prepared to load in the following bitmap from the Parts & Pieces folder: CandleX1.

Step #1: Create a Two-Part Background

Create the following RGB colors in the Color Mixer and place them in the Color List: Red (222, 0, 0), Blue (0, 0, 222), and Yellow (250, 241, 53). White and Black are in the Color List by default.

Create a rectangle at the top third of the document for the first part of the background. Set the stroke to None, and fill it with a radial gradient that ranges from red at the top to white in the middle to blue at the bottom. Leave the Locate Center knob at its centered default position.

For the bottom two-thirds of the page, create another background rectangle. Set the stroke to None, and fill it with a logarithmic gradient that divides the gradient color bar into blue-red-blue-red-blue-red. This will give you a blue-red striped fill.

Figure 28-22: The background is separated into two parts.

Step #2: Add Bunting & Text to the Top

On the FreeHand page you opened is a graphic with five bunting flags arranged vertically. Clone this arrangement, and place the two graphics at the top of the first background section. Space them so the radial fill can be seen. Use the Text tool to create the phrase "Keep the Light of Liberty Burning" in a script face. Convert to paths, and size it for the bottom of the upper background section. See Figure 28-23 as a reference.

Figure 28-23: The top of the page starts to take shape.

Step #3: Refine the Candle Graphic

Import the candle graphic. Select the candle graphic you imported, and copy it to the clipboard. Use the Bezier Pen to outline the candle graphic carefully, neglecting the flame and the smoke. With the outline completed and closed, select Edit | Paste Inside. Adjust the outline to block any remaining background around the candle, and then group it. The new graphic shows only the candle with no background. Draw a new flame on the wick with the Bezier Pen, and color it with a red to yellow linear gradient. Place the completed candle graphic in the center of the bunting graphics. See Figure 28-24.

Figure 28-24: The candle is added to the top of the page.

Step #4: Add the Main Web Page Heading

Use the Text tool to write "Liberty Light" in Helvetica Bold, and convert the text to paths. Resize it to fit the head of the page, so that it dominates the top section. Make sure it remains selected.

The following option is dependent upon your use of the KPT VectorFX plug-in, a separate effects package from MetaTools. Choose Xtras | KPT Vector Effects and select KPT FX | 3D Transform. Set the parameters as follows: Rotate X to 20%, Metallic to 50%, Complexity to 60%, Perspective to 100%, Extrusion to 100, Hilight Color to Light Blue, Ambient Color to Black, and Light Source to lower left. Click on the checkmark to accept the settings, which applies the effect to the heading.

Figure 28-25: The heading is modified with a 3D extrusion in KPT VectorFX.

Step #5: Add Elements to the Bottom Section
Select the graphic that shows a circular star field connected to four red stripes from the opened FreeHand document. Rotate it 90 degrees so the star field is on top. Enlarge it and place it on the left of the bottom section. Use the Pen tool to outline the red stripes, and fill them with white and a one point black stroke. Group them with the underlying graphic.

Step #6: Add More Elements & Text
Create a circle, and place it in the middle of the star field. Fill it with a radial gradient, so it has a white highlight and blends from white to red to blue. Draw a circular path around it and attach a text line to the path that reads "CONTACT." Add a line of text at the bottom that reads "Freedom is Your Responsibility!", with a yellow fill and a one point black stroke. Convert the text to paths, and resize the paths to fit the bottom of the page.

Figure 28-26: The bottom of the page takes shape.

Step #7: Add the Final Text Lines
Add the following text to the right of the bottom background: "What is the President Doing?", "What is the Congress Doing?", "What is the Court Doing?", and "What Are You Doing?!". Fill the text with yellow and no stroke. Create star-shaped filled white bullets for the text with a one point black stroke.

Figure 28-27: The bottom of the page is completed.

Figure 28-28: The finished FreeHand Web page design.

Step #8: Add Hot Spots & Target Pages

The hot spots on this page would include a rectangular area that surrounds each of the four questions bulleted at the bottom, and the bullets as well. The fifth hot spot would be the gradient circle in the center of the star field. Each of the four target pages for the star bulleted questions would present pertinent data on what those parts of the government were up to (signing and passing legislation, pending bills, court decisions, scandals, appointments, and so on). The fourth item, "What Are You Doing?!", would present information on how the surfer could act to have their voice heard. The "Contact" hot spot would hURL (sorry!) the surfer to a page that listed all of the addresses, phone numbers, and e-mail addresses of government officials.

Tip

You will find this completed Web page on the CD-ROM in the Web_10 folder. It is named Heritage.FH7; the Afterburner-compressed file is called Heritage.FHC.

Exotic Fabrics, Ltd.

The Web is the largest marketplace the world has ever known, and in the coming years it will grow a hundredfold. The move towards online shopping began at the end of the last century with the Sears catalog. Suddenly, the idea of ordering goods without being present where they were displayed caught on. The pictures of the merchandise were enough to spur the imagination and open wallets and purses. In the past few years, the same idea has given birth to remote shopping via television, and the emergence of the television shopping channels. The Web continues the process of selling merchandise and services via remote connections, allowing for more interactivity than any similar commercial transaction has ever offered, and dozens of new ways to use the Web for commerce are being crafted as you read this. It doesn't mean that this is the only way, or even the dominant way, that the Web will be used. All it means is that commerce and merchandising are on the Web to stay. Just as the country store offered a place to meet and converse as well as a way to satisfy the demands for all manner of material goods, so the Web is a place for the exchange of ideas as well as products.

Open the Chnslk.FH7 FreeHand document on the CD-ROM. If you have already created your own ChinaSilk graphics in the tutorial exercises, you are free to substitute them for the FreeHand document. Also import the following bitmaps from the Parts and Pieces folder on the CD-ROM: DragX2, DragX4, and Drgn1, or substitute your own dragon graphics.

Step #1: Design the Color Palette

Create the following RGB colors in the Color Mixer, and drag them to the Color List: Red (226, 10, 22), Yellow (255, 241, 0), Purple1 (183, 0, 193), Purple2 (183, 88, 193), Purple3 (183, 154, 193), and Blue (58, 191, 239).

Step #2: Create the Background

If you opened the Chnslk.FH7 document as suggested, you will see that the dragon is already present in the Tiled panel of the Fill Inspectors. That means anything you draw with the Tiled Fill open will be automatically filled with the dragon texture. Draw a rectangle as large as the page for your background. It is automatically filled with the dragon tiled texture. Adjust the XY scale to 50 percent, and play with the XY alignment inputs until you have a symmetrical arrangement of the dragon tiles.

Figure 28-29: The background for this Web page is a tiled graphic.

Step #3: Create the Page Head

Draw a rectangle that fits the top 25 percent of the page, and fill it with Purple3 color with stroke set to None. Use the Text tool to create the words "Exotic Fabrics" in Helvetica Bold. Convert it to paths, and expand the text block to fill the heading area. Select both the text block and the Purple3 rectangle it sits on, and join them. The text block is cut out of the purple rectangle, exposing the dragon tiles as a fill for the text. Place the small sun graphic that was imported with the FreeHand document in the center of the "O" in Exotic, and resize to fit. Create the term "LTD" in black. Convert it to paths, rotate it a bit to the left, and resize it to fit along the right side of the text block heading.

Figure 28-30: The Web page heading is in place.

Step #4: Create the Center of the Page

Study Figure 28-31 carefully as you work through this step. Create a red rectangle about one-sixth as wide as the page and two dragon tiles high, and place it on the left, flush with the page edge. Give it a one point black stroke. Inside, create a yellow text block with no stroke that reads "This Month from CHINA" as four flush left lines, and group it with the red rectangle. Create a Purple2 rectangle that extends all the way to the right of the page, starting at the right of the red rectangle, and place yellow text with a black one point stroke inside of it that reads "LUCKY DRAGON." Under that, in white text with a black stroke, create the text block "An Ancient Fabric Design."

Under the red rectangle, create three spheres, each about one dragon tile in diameter. They should be filled with a blended gradient that is white at the center, and then yellow to blue. Next to each sphere should be a text block that is yellow and enclosed by a black rectangle. The text blocks should read "Samples," "Order Form," and "Suggestions." Last, create a rectangle with one large dragon tile on the right, and place a black rectangle behind it that acts as a drop shadow.

Figure 28-31: The center of the Exotic Fabrics Web page.

Step #5: Create the Bottom Part of the Page

Study Figure 28-32 carefully as you work through this step. Clone the red rectangle created in step #4, and place it on the left of the page below the blended spheres. Create a yellow two-lined (flush left) text block for it (no stroke) that reads "Dragon Posters." Clone the purple rectangle from step #4, and fill it with Purple1 and no stroke. Create a yellow text block for it (no stroke) that reads "FREE, when you purchase 10 yards of fabric or more." You will have to convert to paths to get this text block to fit correctly. Take the three imported bitmaps, and arrange them below the Purple1 rectangle. Draw a rectangle around them with no fill and a two-point black stroke. This frames them in black, popping them out of the backdrop. Last, create a black text block that reads "We bring the World to You!" Place it at the bottom left of the page. Clone it, and color the clone with a yellow fill and a one-half point stroke in black. Offset the yellow text over the black text, creating a drop shadow that pops the text away from the backdrop. Save the page as a compressed Afterburner file for browser display.

Figure 28-32: The bottom of the page is complete.

Figure 28-33: The finished Exotic Fabrics Web page.

Step #6: Adding Hot Spots & Target Pages

There are six hot spots designed for this page. Three of them cover the spheres and their associated text. The Samples hot spot would take you to a page, or pages, loaded with diverse fabric swatches. The Order Form would take you to a page with an order form that could be e-mailed to the company. The Suggestions page would ask for surfer feedback and ideas, a valuable asset to any company in the marketplace.

The Dragon Posters would each be hot spots. Clicking on them would bring up the graphic to full-screen size (as either a GIF or JPEG file if the page was designed outside of the FreeHand arena, and as perhaps a TIFF or BMP image if incorporated as a separate FreeHand Afterburned page). One word to the wise, FREE is the best word you can use on a commercial page. With the millions of pages on the Web, FREE always stops 'em in their tracks.

Tip

You will find this completed Web page on the CD-ROM in the Web_10 folder. It is named Exotic.FH7; the Afterburner-compressed file is called Exotic.FHC.

Environmental Awareness Page

The Web allows people of like concerns to communicate across political, social, and economic boundaries like no other vehicle for contact has ever done. This means that world-wide concerns like environmental issues can be shared, and progress towards solutions can begin because of the collaboration of connected minds. There are hundreds of Web pages that deal with global issues like pollution. Let's explore one possible design for this type of page, and see how it might be constructed in FreeHand. For this example, you should import Farah1, Fishes2, Pond1, and Wocean from the Parts & Pieces folder.

Step #1: Create Your Color Palette

Use the Color Mixer to create the following RGB colors, and place them in the Color List: Blue1 (58, 191, 239), Blue2 (0, 96, 144), Blue3 (124, 209, 144), Gold (213, 191, 105), Yellow (255, 241, 0), and Red (224, 8, 42).

Step #2: Create the Background

Place the Fishes2 graphic at the bottom of the page, taking up about one-third of the total space. Place the Ocean graphic over the top two-thirds of the page. Use the Text tool to create the word "E-MAIL," and place it in the circular area of the bottom graphic.

Figure 28-34: The background is finished.

Step #3: Add the Main Graphics

Draw a rectangle at the top of the page, covering about one-sixth of the page. Fill it with a radial gradient that ranges from Blue2 to white, and set the Locate Center knob to the upper right quadrant in the Fill Inspector. Create the main heading: WATER FAQs. Create the subhead: CLEAN WATER FUND. Both text blocks are black with no stroke. Place them as seen in Figure 28-35.

Copy the Farah1 graphic to the Clipboard. Use the pen to outline the Farah1 graphic, making sure the shape is closed. Adjust it so that no background is showing. Select the outline and choose Edit | Paste Inside. The Farah1 graphic is painted into the outlined shape. Group the shape. Move the outlined Farah1 graphic to the upper left of the page.

Step #4: Create the Dripping Faucet

Create three drips coming from the faucet, each succeeding one behind the other. Shape the drips from a circle by adding points and dragging the top-most point upward. Fill them with a blend that ranges from Blue1 at the center to Blue2 to gold on the outside.

Figure 28-35: The dripping faucet is added.

Step #5: Add the Callout Text

Next to each drip, add a yellow filled rectangle with a one point black stroke. Top to bottom, create the following text blocks (black): "How Safe is Our Ocean?", "How Safe are Our Lakes?", and "ACID RAIN: The FAQs." FAQ, by the way, is an acronym for Frequently Asked Questions.

Figure 28-36: Text blocks are added next to each drip.

Step #6: Add the Final Graphic

Draw a rectangle with no fill and an eight point red stroke on the right of the page under the heading. Inside it, create a text block that reads "What is the Clean Water Fund?" Place the text inside the red border at the top. Select the Pond1 graphic and copy it to the clipboard. Draw a rectangle over it sized to fit inside the red-stroked rectangle. Select the smaller rectangle and select Edit | Paste Inside. Group the new graphic. Select the Pond1 original graphic and clear it. The Pond1 graphic is now attached to the smaller rectangle. Place the smaller rectangle inside the larger one, and align them on a common vertical center.

Figure 28-37: The finished Water FAQs Web page.

Step #7: Add Hot Spots & Target Pages

There are five hot spots in this Web page design. Three are connected to the yellow blocks, and to each of the drips that accompany them. The target pages the URLs would take you to would detail the answers to the questions being asked, and would probably include graphics and animations. The fourth hot spot is the e-mail circle area on the bottom graphic. The fifth is the picture of the pond in the red rectangular frame. This target page would detail the history and mission statement of the Clean Water Fund.

Tip

You will find this completed Web page on the CD-ROM in the Web_10 folder. It is named H2O.FH7; the Afterburner-compressed file is called H2O.FHC.

Culture & Tradition

Starting with CD-ROM multimedia and now on the Web, technology has given a voice and an image to every nation and culture on the earth. Even in the midst of conflict, all sides are represented in their own Web site. During the war in Bosnia, the Serbs, Croats, and Muslims all presented their viewpoints, history, and artistic traditions to anyone who had the means to access their Web pages. The Web has also become a repository for smaller and less well-known traditions, those more tribal than global in nature. Everyone wants to be respected for their own unique way of approaching life, their ritualistic observances, and history. Instead of being one world with one viewpoint, we are living in one world with a multitude of diverse approaches, all connected like the strands of an infinite web. In this exercise, we will put ourselves in the shoes of a tribal person wishing to talk about some of the important traditions learned from an oral tradition. This site design focuses upon the Navajo tradition, its visual designs and colors, and the practice of sandpainting.

Of course, State Chambers of Commerce and travel agencies also have a keen interest in their native populations, and they might accentuate this interest by developing a Web site around that focus (or ask you to do it). You should import the Gldtree file from the Parts and Pieces folder (unless you have created your own from the natural graphics tutorials). You should also open the FreeHand document named MosaicX1 from the FreeHand documents folder on the CD-ROM.

Step #1: Create the Web Page Heading

Select the FreeHand mosaic drawing imported with the MosaicX1 FreeHand document, and copy it to the clipboard. Go to the Fill Inspector and select the Tiled option. Click on Paste In, and the mosaic graphic is displayed in the preview window. Draw a rectangle that covers the top third of your FreeHand page. It will be tiled with the mosaic graphic. Adjust the size and position of the tile in the Tiled dialog until you have something you like.

Step #2: Add the Text Heading

Create the following text block with Times Roman: "Traditions of the Southwest." Convert to paths. Fill the text with a light blue color and a black stroke. Add a Smudged shadow, configured with a black fill and a white stroke. This makes the text look almost branded when placed on a background graphic. Place the text over the background, leaving room at the left and bottom.

Tip

Because there are so many variables that can be introduced into the color palette for this page, we will not suggest specific RGB colors. You will be asked to add colors by their hue names, and it will be left to you to customize them according to your own mind's eye.

Create a turquoise gemstone by using a blend between turquoise and white. Use the Roughen tool on the inner oval, as it produces rays of color when blended to a standard oval. Clone the gem, and resize it to about 15 percent smaller. Place it at the left of a light blue rectangle that sits at the bottom of the heading text. Create the text block "Click for Points of Interest," and place this subhead in the light blue rectangle. See Figure 28-38 for reference.

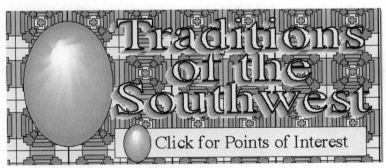

Figure 28-38: The Web page heading is complete.

Step #3: Create Mesas

The mesa is the signature of the Southwest. Use the FreeHand tool to create overlayed shapes that make up the mesa, coloring each a little differently. Give each a one point black stroke. For the first variation, select all of the shapes and blend them. This gives the mesa an etched look. For the second variation, remove the strokes from each of the shapes, and then for the third, blend them. This gives the rendering a watercolor-like look. We will use all three in this composition.

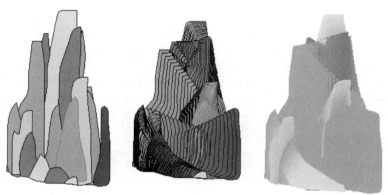

Figure 28-39: Three variations on a theme: The original outlined and filled shapes, the shapes with strokes after blending, and the shapes without strokes after blending.

Step #4: Begin the FreeHand Painting

As you follow through these steps to create the bottom two-thirds of the Web page by adding a FreeHand painting, explore your options and customize the graphic as you prefer.

Create the general divisions between ground and sky first by adding two rectangles. Fill the ground rectangle with a gradient that incorporates browns, tans, and gold. Fill the sky with a blue and white gradient. Create a gradient or blended cloud in the sky, and add a sun if you prefer.

Figure 28-40: The first part of the FreeHand painting shows the ground and sky.

Step #5: Place the Mesas in Position

Place each of the mesas, or any of your choice, on the background. You may want to clone or mirror your selections to achieve an interesting composition. Add some shadows if you prefer.

Figure 28-41: The mesas are added to the background.

Step #6: Add the Tree

Select the tree bitmap imported previously, and use the Trace tool to draw a marquee around it. After a few minutes, the bitmap painting is translated into a vector drawing. Clear away the original bitmap. Remove any of the vector sections of the tree that are background parts, and move the tree into place in the graphic (in front of the mesas on the left). Add a shadow to the tree if you prefer, and add a cloned turquoise gem at the base of the tree.

Figure 28-42: The tree and gem are added.

Step #7: Add a Sand Painting & More Gems

Select the original graphic you used as a tile fill, and click on the 3D Transformation tool. Manipulate the graphic so it appears to be receding into the distance, and place it on the ground at the lower right of the vector painting. Create three more clones of the turquoise gem, and place them in an aligned left vertical arrangement on the right: one in the sky, one by a mesa, and one over the sand painting. Save the graphic as both a FreeHand document and as an Afterburner graphic for browser display.

Step #8: Add Hot Spots & Target Pages

There are four hot spots in this Web page design, all represented by the turquoise gems in the vector painting. Their placement defines the content of the URL targeted pages. Depending upon the intention and interest of the originators of this Web site, they could lead to tourist information (weather, flora, sites, etc.), or perhaps the targeted pages might point out the sacred traditions of the native peoples of the Southwest.

Figure 28-43: The sand painting and more gems are added.

Figure 28-44: The finished Web page.

Tip

You will find this completed Web page on the CD-ROM in the Web_10 folder. It is named Trad.FH7; the Afterburner-compressed file is called Trad.FHC.

Artist's Portfolio Page

When I began my career as an illustrator, the drill was to gather all of your samples in the best leather portfolio you could afford, and make you way to every ad agency and studio within train or bus distance. Times have changed. The Web allows illustrators, animators, page designers, and other design professionals to display their capabilities and resumes to millions of viewers and potential employers/clients in an instant. Of course, you need to translate your visual samples into a format the Web understands, but that's easy enough to do in most cases. If your work is on paper or another traditional medium, a scanner is used to translate it into a digital medium. A utility program takes it the next step, translating it to GIF, JPEG, or Portable Network Graphic (PNG) file format for common Web display, or a GIF, JPEG, TIFF, or BMP for incorporation in a Shocked FreeHand document. If you are a digital artist, the process is even smoother. There are thousands of artists who have created portfolio sites on the Web, and thousands of potential contacts listed at other sites. Here is one way to craft a FreeHand Web page to act as an interactive portfolio of your work.

Rules of the Road

Unlike the other Web page designs we've looked at, there is no way to walk you through the design of your portfolio Web page step-by-step. Each Web page created to display a designer's personal talents and portfolio will be individually unique. There are, however, some general cautions to take note of when FreeHand is the vehicle for your Web portfolio design.

1. Include a picture of yourself. It can be a serious portraiture shot, or a photo you've manipulated in xRes or another image processing application. I prefer a unique manipulated photo, because it has a better chance of making visitors stop for a moment. Serious portfolio shots are somewhat boring on the Web, except for use in corporate or other contexts that demand this approach. The purpose of generating any Web site is to have one that stops the crowd of potential visitors long enough to get their attention.

2. Don't get too wordy. If your purpose is to attract surfers to your images, allow the images to speak for you, especially on the main page. Be as brief as possible, and give the audience a way of getting deeper information by using a hot spot to bring up another page. This has been done in the illustrated example by assigning a hot spot to the Resume page, a separate document that would go into detail about the resume and employment history of the artist.

3. Use JPEG images for artwork. Yes, FreeHand will allow you to use TIFF images, but TIFF requires too much bandwidth. JPEG is a terrible choice for print-to-paper options because it is glossy and adds artifacts to the image. But for Web display, a high-quality, lowest-compression JPEG (saved out at the highest JPEG setting) is fine. Web display mediums are not as fine-tuned as paper, at least not yet.

4. Include an e-mail hot spot. The whole purpose of creating a Web portfolio is to allow contacts to get back to you.

5. Have a line that tells the viewer what platforms you have experience with, and think about making this line a hot spot. This allows you to discuss in greater detail your software expertise, and also the clients you have served in the past.

6. Your images can be pirated. Know this up front. Any image data that appears on the screen can be easily grabbed by anyone with access to your Web site. The fact that it's illegal to use someone else's artwork does not prevent it from happening. So, although you will want to include your best and most representative images, realize that someone else in the world will likely download them, and maybe even use them. Add a line that tells people not to do this, and then leave your anxiety about it behind. You can always add a line that says something like, "If you would like to see dozens of other unique images, send for our catalog."

Tip

You might also want to check out the Digital Watermarking utility from Digimark. It allows you to embed copyright data in your images.

Adding Hot Spots & Target Pages

There are a few general rules for what your portfolio's hot spots should look like or where they should be placed. It's a good idea to hot spot small previews of your images, and allow the associated URL to display the same image at full screen if the viewer desires. This is a way to be kind with the audience's download time. If they are interested in seeing your image at a better resolution, allow them that choice. Always include a hot spot for your resume, and another to bring up an e-mail response dialog (check with your browser documentation and your Internet Service Provider or Web Master on how to configure your e-mail response forms).

Tip

You will find this completed Web page on the CD-ROM in the Web_10 folder. It is named Portfol.FH7; the Afterburner-compressed file is called Portfol.FHC.

Figure 28-45: One example of an artist's Web page portfolio in FreeHand form.

Moving On

Congratulations! You have worked through the entire book, and have hopefully benefited from the walk-throughs and tutorials. The material that follows in the Appendices is also meant to enhance your learning and mastery of every aspect of the FreeHand 7 Graphics Studio applications.

Part VII

Appendices

About the Companion CD-ROM

The CD-ROM included with your copy of *FreeHand 7 Graphics Studio: The Comprehensive Guide* includes valuable filters, plug-ins, symbol fonts, Xtras, and more. In addition to software, the CD-ROM contains hundreds of project images, as well as Web pages, animations, and other renderings developed for use with the book's exercises.

To View the CD-ROM

- **Macintosh PPC**—Double-click on the LAUNCHME icon after opening the CD on your desktop.
- **Windows 95/Windows NT**—Double-click on the LAUNCHME.EXE file from your Windows Explorer.

You'll see a menu screen offering several choices. See "Navigating the CD-ROM" below for your options.

Navigating the CD-ROM

Your choices for navigating the CD-ROM appear on the opening screen. You can view the software, browse the Cool Picks, learn more about Ventana, or quit the viewer.

If the viewer does not run properly on your machine, follow the following instructions for optimum performance.

For optimum WINDOWS performance:

1. Copy the LAUNCHME.EXE and LAUNCHME.INI files to the same directory on your hard drive.

2. Open the LAUNCHME.INI file in a text editor such as Notepad.

3. Find the section in the .INI file that reads:
   [Memory];ExtraMemory=400; Amount of kBytes over and above physical memory for use by a projector.

4. If your computer has enough memory to do so, delete the semicolon from the ExtraMemory line, and change the ExtraMemory setting to a higher number.

5. Save the changes to the LAUNCHME.INI file, and close the text editor.

6. With the CD-ROM still inserted, launch the viewer from the hard drive.

If the viewer still does not run properly on your machine, you can access the material on the CD-ROM directly through Windows Explorer.

For optimum Macintosh performance:

1. Copy the Launch Me file to your hard drive.

2. Click once on the Launch Me file.

3. Select Get Info from the File menu.

4. If your computer has enough memory to do so, change the amount in the Preferred size field to a higher number.

5. Close the info box.

6. With the CD-ROM still inserted, launch the viewer from the hard drive.

If the viewer still does not run properly on your machine, you can access the files on the CD-ROM directly by double-clicking on its icon on the desktop.

Software on the CD-ROM

A complete listing of the products in the Software Folder on the companion CD-ROM follows in Table A-1.

Program	Description
Andromeda Software Filters	Demo versions of Andromeda Software's Filters, including: Series 1 Photography Filters, containing ten special effects lenses; Series 2 3D Filters, offering surface wrapping, lighting and shading control, and viewpoint control for images; Series 3 Screens Filters, which convert greyscale into mezzotints, mezzograms, line screens, and patterns and specialty screens; Series 4 Techtures, offering 900 hand-rendered, realistic techtures, maps, and environments to explore and modify; and, the Velociraptor Filter, which lets you create incredibly realistic or stylized motion trails. Visit http://www.andromeda.com for more information.
Deniart Sampler	The Macintosh version of the Deniart Sampler offers sample characters from Deniart Systems' Symbol Font Library, including: Egyptian Hieroglyphics, Alchemy Symbols, Mayan Glyphs, American Sign, and Castles & Shields. Check out http://www.deniart.com to download the Windows version of the Deniart Sampler.
Extreme 3D	This demo version of Macromedia's Extreme 3D includes all the major features of the full product. You can use this demo version to get the feel of Extreme 3D, but you cannot save or export your work. Visit http://www.macromedia.com for more information.
Eye Candy	A demo of the new set of plug-ins from Alien Skin Software. Formerly known as The Black Box, these filters create special effects in seconds that would normally require hours of hand tweaking. You have probably heard experts explain complex 12-step processes for creating 3D bevels or flames. Now you can stop trying to follow those frustrating recipes and simply use Eye Candy. Version 3.0 makes professional effects even easier by giving you flexible previews and a thumbnail for rapidly navigating your image. Visit http://www.alienskin.com.
Fractal Design Detailer	Fractal Design Detailer is an amazing graphics program that lets you paint directly onto the surface of 3D models. It's the closest thing to actually holding an object in your hand and painting it! If you're a 3D artist, Detailer is a one-stop shop for creating texture, bump, and other surface maps for your 3D models. You'll enjoy

Program	Description
	substantial time savings, increased accuracy, greater control, and real-time results. If you're a 2D artist, Detailer provides the enormous flexibility of 3ºD with the compositional simplicity of 2D. With Detailer, you can easily create rendered 3D objects which become elements of your image-editing designs.
Fractal Design Expression	Fractal Design Expression combines the stylistic expressiveness of traditional artist's tools with the flexibility, speed, editability, and resolution independence of a vector-based drawing application. If you're a graphic designer or illustrator, Fractal Design Expression will change the way you think about vector-based illustration and the way you work as a computer artist. Expression's power and agility come from its exclusive Skeletal Strokes technology. For the first time ever, artists can use a single vector path to draw sophisticated, multi-element strokes or even complete illustrations. Simply select a drawing tool and a stroke style, and begin drawing.
Fractal Design Painter	Fractal Design Painter 4 is the world's leading paint program. With more than 150 unique brushes, Painter's rich set of painting tools and special effects empowers your creativity. Painter 4 now mixes raster and vector artwork, offers exciting Web features, and supports collaborative painting across a network. Painter's astounding Natural-Media® features simulate the tools and textures of traditional artists' materials. From crayons to calligraphy, oils to airbrushes, pencils to watercolor, Painter turns your computer into an artist's studio. Whether you are an experienced Painter user or you've never seen its extensive capabilities, you'll see how easily version 4 can transform the way you create!
FreeHand	This Macromedia demo allows you to explore most of the functionality of FreeHand. It includes all of the new user interface enhancements such as dockable panels and tear-out tabbed panels. Many new Xtras are included such as Bend, Roughen, Envelope, and the new Charting tool. Mac and Windows versions. Visit http://www.macromedia.com.
HVS Color for Macintosh	A demo of HVS Color, the award-winning color-reduction Export plug-in. This demo will give you an idea of the color reduction quality, but it's not unlockable, and it inserts a watermark in the center of images. An unlockable demo of the next generation HVS ColorGIF 2.0 will be available soon. Visit http://www.digfrontiers.com for more information.

Program	Description
HVS Color for Windows 95/NT	A demo of the Windows version of HVS Color. An unlockable demo of the next generation HVS ColorGIF 2.0 will be available soon. Visit http://www.digfrontiers.com for more information
HVS JPEG	A Plug-in Filter that exports superior-quality, progressive JPEGs for use on the Web and in multimedia. HVS JPEG provides the smallest size while maintaining superior graphic image quality via proprietary optimization techniques. This unlockable demo allows customers to use the full-featured product free for seven days, and may be purchased thereafter via a convenient online module. Visit http://www.digfrontiers.com to learn more.
Kai's Power Tools	A demonstration version of MetaTools, Inc.'s Kai's Power Tools 3.0. KPT 3.0 is available as a 32-bit native application extension for the Intel-based Windows 95/NT platforms, as well as for the Apple Macintosh/Power Macintosh platforms. Kai's Power Tools 3.0 is a unique and powerful collection of extensions that expand the power of image-editing applications which support the Adobe plug-in specifications. Go to http://www.metatools.com.
Macromedia xRes	If you can imagine it, you can create it fast with xRes. Macromedia xRes and Shockwave power your creativity with the next generation of image design tools. Take your work to the limit with an incredible array of creative tools, cutting-edge high-res performance, and integration with the most popular graphics programs. Publish on the Web, create art from scratch, customize your photography, and more. Visit http://www.macromedia.com.
tHreEALITY Xtras	tHreEALITY Xtras is a package of FreeHand demos, including B'box xTra 1.0, Pages xTra 1.0, Stamp xTra 1.0, and Template xTra 1.0. B'box allows you to crop and make registration marks in a snap. Pages helps you create and manage pages in an active FreeHand document. Stamp creates complex patterns and other design elements in a matter of minutes. Template will allow you to create as many templates as you need.
Vector Effects	Vector Effects increases even the most serious designer's or illustrator's productivity by streamlining complex processes and introducing new effects that would be impossible or, at best, extremely difficult to achieve in any existing vector-based plug-in or stand-alone application. Go to http://www.metatools.com.

Table A-1: Software on the Companion CD-ROM.

In addition to the software listed in Table A-1, project images and sample files are provided in the CD-ROM Resource Folder. A description of the files and their respective sub-folder names follows in Table A-2.

Folder Name	Description
Parts	A collection of well over 100 drawings and experimental paintings created as FreeHand, xRes, and Extreme 3D projects for the book.
Web-10	All of the 10 Web pages developed for the book in both FreeHand and compressed formats.
Xres	A folder containing five original xRes paintings.
Animguy	Three rendered frames of the Animguy animation in TIF and GIF formats.
FH7	This folder contains all of the FreeHand documents used in the book, plus more.
Animz	Contains all of the animations mentioned in the book's animation chapter.
Ex3D	Consists of 32 Extreme 3D project files and associated renderings.
Rocks	A folder containing seven TIF renderings associated with the natural rendering exercises in the book.
Images	This folder contains images from the following Aztech New Media Corporation collections: Floral Tapestry, which features 100 high-quality license- and royalty-free, annotated TIF photo images of exotic wild flowers; Gems, a grouping of 99 license- and royalty-free, annotated TIF photo images of precious stones, semi-precious gems, and other stones from around the world; and, Watermarks & Ghosted Backgrounds, Vol. 1, the second collection in Aztech's ArtEffects series of TIF image collections designed by David Hushion and specifically created for graphic designers. High resolution versions of these and other images are available from Aztech New Media as well. Visit http://www.aztech.com to learn more.

Table A-2: Project and Sample Images on the Companion CD-ROM.

Technical Support

Technical support is available for installation-related problems only. The technical support office is open from 8:00 A.M. to 6:00 P.M. (EST), Monday through Friday, and can be reached via the following methods:

Phone: (919) 544-9404 ext. 81

Faxback Answer System: (919) 544-9404 ext. 85

E-mail: help@vmedia.com

FAX: (919) 544-9472

World Wide Web: http://www.vmedia.com/support

America Online: keyword *Ventana*

Limits of Liability & Disclaimer of Warranty

The author and publisher of this book have used their best efforts in preparing the CD-ROM and the programs contained in it. These efforts include the development, research, and testing of the theories and programs to determine their effectiveness. The author and publisher make no warranty of any kind expressed or implied, with regard to these programs or the documentation contained in this book.

The author and publisher shall not be liable in the event of incidental or consequential damages in connection with, or arising out of, the furnishing, performance, or use of the programs, associated instructions, and/or claims of productivity gains.

Some of the software on this CD-ROM is shareware; there may be additional charges (owed to the software authors/makers) incurred for their registration and continued use. See individual program's README or VREADME.TXT files for more information.

B

xRes Animation Filter Effects

Y ou can use this appendix in conjunction with Chapters 10, 11, and 25, to determine which filters are best for creating xRes-based animations.

Radial Blur (Effects | Blur | Radial)

What it Does   Duplicates a selection from one to ten times and adds concentric blurring to the selection and the concentric copies. Angle slider sets the degree of rotation from -180 to +180 in single-degree increments.

How It Does It   Copies slider sets the number of cloned selections to be included, from 1 to 10.

HLS (Effects | Noise | Add HLS)

What it Does   Applies video noise (random visual static) to Hue, Lightness, and Saturation levels of the selection by moving any or all of the three sliders. Hue slider ranges from 0 to 100. As settings increase, multicolored speckles are added to the selection. Noise appears in the non-background parts of the selection only. Lightness slider ranges from 0 to 100. As settings increase, the amount of speckles increases over the whole range of the selection, background included. Saturation slider ranges from 0 to 100. As settings increase, the depth of speckles increases in saturated color. This slider is mainly useful as a control on the other two.

Cylinder (Effects | Distort | Cylinder)

What it Does   Applies a horizontal stretch to selected elements through the use of one slider.

How It Does It   The distortion is applied by moving the Amount slider, which ranges from 1 to 100.

FishEye* (Effects | Distort | FishEye)

What it Does   Shrinks or expands the selection through the use of one slider.

How It Does It   This distortion is applied by an Amount slider that ranges from a value of -100 to +100. The effects are very powerful at either end of the spectrum, and more subtle towards the middle.

Ripple (Effects | Distort | Ripple)

What it Does   Applies horizontal waves to the image as directed by Amplitude and Wavelength sliders.

How It Does It   Amplitude and Wavelength sliders that range from 1 to 100 apply horizontal wave distortions to the selection. This effect beaks the selection up with smooth horizontal waves, and can completely obliterate the coherence of the image. At low settings, very beautiful linear distortion patterns are introduced.

Wave* (Effects | Distort | Wave)

What it Does   Applies horizontal waves to the image as directed by Amplitude and Wavelength sliders. Similar to Ripple.

How It Does It   Amplitude and Wavelength sliders that range from 1 to 100 apply horizontal wave distortions to the selection. Though similar to Ripple, keeping the Wavelength set to low values (below 20) gives much more control over the Amplitude settings overall, and produces attractive horizontal linear screening effects.

Whirlpool* (Effects | Distort | Whirlpool)

What it Does   Applies a concentric distortion wave to a selection with an Angle slider.

How It Does It   One Angle slider that controls the concentric distortion angle and ranges from -999 to +999 controls the selection. Lower settings look like rubber sheet warping, while higher settings (above +150 or below -150) radically distort the content of the image.

Diffuse (Effects | Stylize | Diffuse)

What it Does   Breaks the image into pixels with one Amount slider.

How It Does It   With settings that range from 1 to 32, the slider applies degrees of pixel displacement. At the high settings, the result is a storm of pixel dust.

Mosaic* (Effects | Stylize | Mosaic)

What it Does   Creates larger pixel elements in the selection with two sliders.

How It Does It   Width and height sliders allow settings that range from 2 to 32. Used separately or together, they enlarge the pixel borders of the bitmap, making it seem as if the smallest picture elements are being zoomed in on. This is a new take on a vintage effect that can be generated with a video camera.

Posterize (Effects | Stylize | Posterize)

What it Does   Creates garish comic book-like pop-art colorcasts, all controlled by one slider.

How It Does It   Though the Level slider ranges from 2 to 32, the useful settings involve the range 2 to 10. The lower the setting, the more posterization occurs. The lower setting can produce interesting animated effects if applied to frames of a prerecorded single-framed movie file.

Tint* (Effects | Stylize | Tint)

What it Does   Creates duotone-related looks, and is controlled by three sliders.

How It Does It   In RGB mode, the sliders are marked Red, Blue, and Green. In CMYK mode, they are marked Magenta, Cyan, and Yellow. The sliders work together to transform the image into a duotone that combines black and whatever other color the sliders create. This is very effective when applying to just one frame of a graphic and altering the colors over time, or applied to different frames of a movie so that as the frames change, the color shifts.

Hue/Saturation (Modify | Color | Hue/Saturation)

What it Does   Three sliders affect the three components of the selection.

How It Does It   Though in traditional use, these three sliders are usually addressed in concert, as animation effects tools it is important to know how to use them singly.

Hue is also known as Chroma to computer artists. The Hue slider affects the general colorcast of the selection, and ranges from -180 to +180, where zero leaves the hue of the image as it is. Very interesting chroma effects can be applied to an image by moving the slider in either direction.

Lightness is also known as Luma to computer artists. This slider (-180 to +180) is immensely important. The zero setting leaves the image as it is. Moving the slider to negative settings results in what is known as a "fade to black" in video terms. Moving in the positive direction produces a "fade to white." Both are common transitions between diverse moving footage.

The Saturation setting (-180 to +180) is the least useful as far as an animation device. Setting it to the left removes all the hue in the image, while moving it right makes the colors more garish.

---

* An asterisk indicates that this is a primary effect for animation uses.

Appendix

C

FreeHand External Plug-in Xtras

Although there are a number of freeware, shareware, and commercial plug-in Xtras that you can use with FreeHand 7, the two most important ones from a design perspective are MetaTools's KPT Vector Effects and Extensis Corporation's VectorTools. We highly recommended that you investigate both of these plug-in applications if you are a high-end FreeHand 7 user.

MetaTools's KPT Vector Effects

Vector Effects consists of twelve separate plug-in effects for FreeHand. Each extends the creative possibilities of the FreeHand designer. A special help window is installed with these effects, giving you thorough descriptions of each plug-in. Vector Effects comes on a set of two floppy disks, and is available for both Mac and Windows.

3D Transform

This plug-in adds a 3D extruded look to your selection. You can rotate the selected graphic on any X, Y, and Z axis, add a bevel size and depth, adjust the perspective skewing, and determine the extruded depth. A quantity slider lets you add metallic and complex looks. You can also configure the apparent light source with real-time preview feedback. If the targeted selection is a text block, you must convert it to paths first. This plug-in lets you generate high-quality 3D headlines instantly and add a 3D look to clip art. You could even design a 3D scene without ever leaving FreeHand.

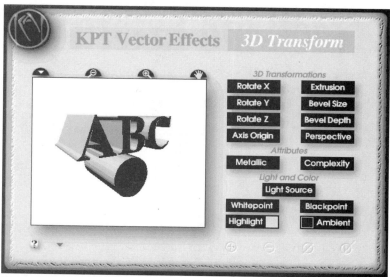

Figure C-1: The Vector Effects 3D Transform interface.

Tip

Need: *You are working on a FreeHand project that requires a metallic-looking 3D headline.*

Solution: *Open FreeHand, create your text block in the desired font, and choose Xtras/KPT Vector Effects/KPT 3D Transform. Boost the "Metallic" setting to a high setting, and preview the result with full rendering preview turned on. Export the finished text block to FreeHand, and set it in place.*

ColorTweak

This plug-in allows you to customize the color of any selected graphic in FreeHand. First, you must convert the text to paths. You can adjust the brightness and contrast or take advantage of a list of presets. The interface can be minimized so that you can work with a smaller menu of choices and see your workscreen at the same time.

Emboss

Embossed looks add interest to text blocks, and if used subtly, can also add to the distinctive look of a FreeHand document. If ungrouped after rendering, a targeted embossed selection might be blended from the darkest to the lightest cloned graphic. This softens the effect. This plug-in allows you to add embossing to any selected text block, and gives you control over the contrast, angle, and amount of the embossing.

Figure C-2: Embossed effects are a snap with Vector Effects.

Flare

Flare effects appear as overlays on the finished graphic. They do not react well when ungrouped and moved, but if left in place, they add effects like reflected light on metallic surfaces and even explosions. In computer graphics, a flare of light is something usually associated with bitmap and 3D applications, but the Vector Effects flares have been designed to address vector graphics. Though the finished flare comes in as an object, it remains invisible. Its effects, however, are visible, and display as a lighter color on the selected graphic. Vector Effects flares can be multiplied and placed in the interactive interface, and their size, halo, and flare spokes customized.

Tip

If you need to create multiple flares, keep their "arms" (spokes) at a minimum, and compose the graphic all at once by duplicating the flares in the first interface that's opened. Creating flares is a memory- and processor-intensive activity.

Need: *You are working on a FreeHand project that requires a backdrop of stars. You have to create it as a vector drawing, not as a bitmap.*

Solution: *Use the Flare Editor in the Vector Effects FreeHand plug-in menu.*

1. *In FreeHand, create a rectangle whose dimensions equal your requirements. Color it as desired (dark blue, black, magenta, or even with a gradiated fill).*

2. *Open the Vector Effects | Flare interface.*

3. *Compose a group of flare objects that shows a starry sky.*

4. *Click the Check (OK) symbol, and watch as your flares are drawn on the rectangular background.*

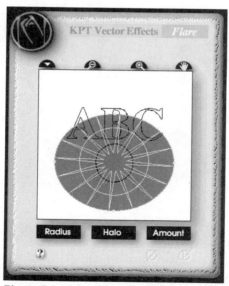

Figure C-3: The radius, halo, and the number of points in the flare's star shape can be tweaked with this Vector Effects plug-in.

Inset

Inset graphics and text add a classic look, somewhat like an engraving. With this plug-in, you control the degree to which the inset area is visible. An inset is a duplicate of the selected graphic that is sized smaller and placed over the original. The Inset plug-in lets you control the size of the inset (amount) and the way it is chiseled out of the original selection (round, beveled, or mitered). "Chiseled" is the word to remember, because the final look is like a text block carved out of granite in the classical style. Insets can also be colorized, producing a multicolored outline text block.

Figure C-4: The Vector Effects Inset plug-in interface.

Neon

This effect is like combining an inset with a blurry stroke, and is best appreciated when the selection is not too large. Used sparingly, you can make text blocks shine with an electric personality. The best thing about the neon glows you create with Vector Effects is that you can customize and preview them in real time from the Vector Effects/Neon interface. You can change only the amount and brightness of the Neonized text; the effect is more like outlined text than neon.

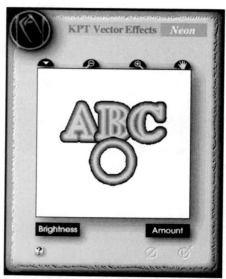

Figure C-5: With the Neon plug-in, you control the brightness and the amount of the effect.

Point Editor

The Point Editor adds control points and Bezier capability to all selected elements. The difference between the Vector Effects usage of this capacity and that offered within FreeHand is that the plug-in controls are separated from other elements that are near the selection on the page, and the numeric controls are more apparent and available.

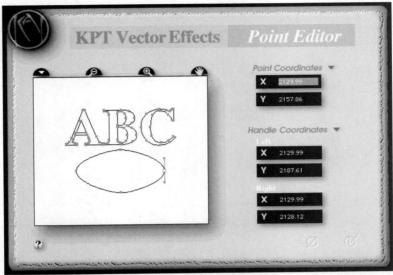

Figure C-6: Both handle and point coordinates can be modified with the Vector Effects Point Editor.

Resize & Reposition

Though not one of the most spectacular Vector Effects plug-ins, this option allows you to manipulate two of the most common needs in a FreeHand document at the same time, and to do it with exacting precision. Selected graphics can be resized and/or repositioned with pinpoint accuracy via numerical input.

ShadowLand

A whole world of diverse shadow features awaits you in Vector Effects ShadowLand. In addition to normal shadows, you can generate effects like vortex shadowing, while controlling the apparent distance of the shadows from the original selection. You can also generate flying logo effects and resize the most distant ghosted logo graphic to emphasize the effect. Use this effect as a background graphic for a whole page, and overprint it with body copy.

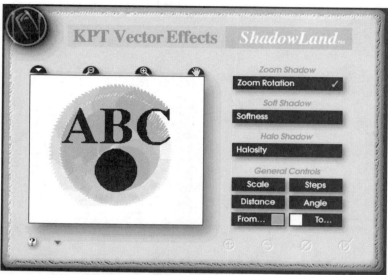

Figure C-7: The ShadowLand effects are spectacular.

Sketch

This plug-in allows you to dispense with the computer look of a selected graphic and substitute a more loosely configured pen and ink style. It works well if used with discretion for text blocks, and gives selected clip art an almost Zen drawing feel.

Figure C-8: The Sketch plug-in transforms your selection into a more hand-drawn approach.

Tip

Need: *You are working on a FreeHand project that requires that the text be altered so that it appears more childlike.*
Solution: *Create the text in FreeHand, and use fairly low settings with the Vector Effects Sketch plug-in to generate the effect.*

Vector Distort

This distortion plug-in offers great exactness, which lets you control the finest aspect of warping and even fisheye lens transformations. Sliders allow exacting percentage modifications of all of the parameters.

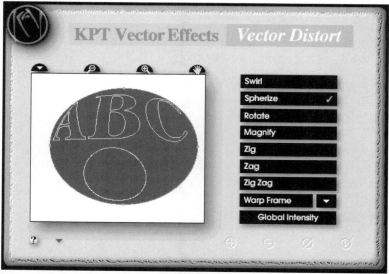

Figure C-9: Definitive warping, like making the selection appear as the surface of a sphere, is easy with this plug-in.

Warp Frame

This effect is sometimes called "rubber sheet warping," because it looks as though the contents are being stretched on a rubber sheet. It's great for mimicking effects like flags and emblems on stretched cloth. You can apply vector distortions to the whole selection or to any part of it. You can manipulate the text using a selection of options: Swirl, Spherize, Rotate, Magnify, Zig, Zag, ZigZag, Warp Frame, and the Global Intensity of the effect. The number of possible effects here is close to infinite, and the results often lend a warmer organic look to the text block.

Figure C-10: With the Vector Effects Warp Frame plug-in, push and pull the frame any way imaginable, and the content follows suit.

Extensis VectorTools 2 (Mac)

Known as DrawTools in previous editions, VectorTools is a set of nine high end plug-ins for FreeHand and Illustrator. Unlike Vector Effects, VectorTools appear as configurable dialogs on the FreeHand document screen, instead of interfaces on separate workscreens. All of the VectorTools dialogs (except VectorTips, a series of FreeHand help screens authored by Olav Kvern) come as dialog roll-ups, so placement on a crowded FreeHand document is more than manageable. VectorTools ships on a CD-ROM with other Extensis products, and requires a user serial number to access in FreeHand. VectorTools requires Mac OS 7.5 or later.

VectorTools contains several hot keys for displaying and hiding palettes, as well as other keys needed for actions within each of the individual VectorTools components. You can view the current keys by choosing Vector Tools | Hot Keys. The Hot Keys dialog box will appear. Change any of the hot keys by highlighting the command to change then pressing the new command:

Show/Hide Edit VectorBars	Option-Control-B
Show/Hide SmartBar	Option-Control-M
Show/Hide VectorLibrary	Option-Control-L
Apply Library Item to Document	Option-Control-Shift-L
Insert New Library Item	Option-Control-Command-L
Show/Hide VectorStyles	Option-Control-O
New Style	Option-Control-Shift-O
Show/Hide VectorNavigator	Option-Control-N
Manually Refresh VectorNavigator	Option-Control-R
Show/Hide VectorMagicWand	Option-Control-W
Show/Hide VectorFrame	Option-Control-F
Apply Last Frame	Option-Control-Shift-F
Show/Hide VectorTips	Option-Control-P
Show/Hide VectorShape	Option-Control-S
Show/Hide VectorColor	Option-Control-C
Show/Hide VectorTypeStyles	Option-Control-T
Show/Hide VectorCaps	Option-Control-K

VectorNavigator

VectorNavigator provides a complete view of the artwork within a document in a resizable floating palette, indicating the main screen view with a red box. The palette can also be used to navigate within the FreeHand document.

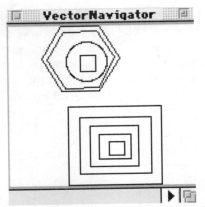

Figure C-11: The VectorNavigator interface.

VectorTips

VectorTips is a scrolling dialog box from Olav Martin Kvern that provides more than 200 handy time-saving tips.

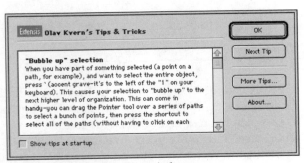

Figure C-12: The VectorTips window.

VectorLibrary

VectorLibrary provides quick storage and access to any object within Illustrator and FreeHand. Text, paths, and raster images can be stored and retrieved using the VectorLibrary palette by dragging and dropping or through the use of a key command. Your VectorLibrary is a great place to store commonly used logos, addresses, images, or other objects. You can easily share library items between computers using the import and export function. FreeHand 7.0 currently has a limitation that requires the VectorLibrary palette to be partially off the edge of the document window in order for objects to be dragged into the palette. This only affects dragging into the palette, not dragging from the palette to the document. You can also select the object you want to place in the library and then either click the Add button in the VectorLibrary palette, or press Command-Option-Control-L.

Figure C-13: The Extensis VectorLibrary adds a much-needed attribute to FreeHand.

VectorMagicWand

VectorMagicWand features a tool for selecting paths that are similarly filled, stroked, or sized. The VectorMagicWand tool is purely a selection tool. It allows you to focus completely on selecting without having to worry about accidentally "nudging" a selected piece of art. In addition to being on the VectorMagicWand palette, the VectorMagicWand tool is always available within the Xtra Tools palette. The VectorMagicWand palette lets you access the VectorMagicWand tool and controls how the VectorMagicWand tool works by allowing you to modify selection attributes and tolerances.

VectorColor

VectorColor brings interactive color management and control to FreeHand. Instead of working with FreeHand's color filters, you can modify artwork in real time using the VectorColor palette–based components. VectorColor is a palette that combines five functions: Edit Curves, Brightness/Contrast,

Multitone, Grayscale, and Randomize. Each function is a full-featured component. The VectorColor palette contains all five color editing functions (or "modes"). The mode last used when the palette was closed is displayed the next time it is opened.

VectorShape

The VectorShape palette is a set of effects that provides unique distortion capabilities within FreeHand. The VectorShape palette easily creates 3D effects by projecting artwork onto geometric shapes, including spheres, cylinders, cones, free projection, and more. All of the effects are completely customizable, and presets can be saved so they can be applied to other objects.

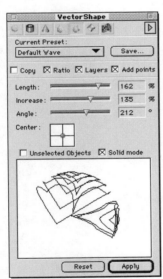

Figure C-14: If you are a FreeHand designer, VectorShape is a must.

VectorFrame

VectorFrame automatically frames selected items quickly and precisely, with the stroke and fill of your choice. Individual objects, groups, or all selected objects can have a frame applied via VectorFrame. In addition, the frame can be dynamically offset on-screen. Any object you can select in Illustrator or FreeHand can have a frame applied to it, including paths, images, and text objects.

VectorTypeStyles

VectorTypeStyles provides a quick and easy method for applying several character modifications with one click within FreeHand. For instance, to change selected type to Times, Bold, Underlined, 18 pt., with 6 pt. leading would normally require several steps in FreeHand. VectorTypeStyles allows you to make these changes with one click after configuring it as a style.

VectorCaps

VectorCaps provides a quick and easy way to set the case style for selected text. Using VectorCaps, you can convert text to lowercase, ALL CAPS, Sentence caps, Title Caps, and raNdOmCaPs.

Appendix

D

External Animation Utilities

Although your Extreme 3D animations can be controlled and generated from within Extreme 3D, xRes, and FreeHand, animations need to be composited outside of their native environments. There are a number of excellent commercial animation-compositing applications for Mac OS and Windows systems, and a fair number of shareware utilities as well. These applications can help you create movies from single-file sequences for either multimedia or Web use. Though we can't mention all of the animation utilities available, the following listing includes those that are proven and popular.

DeBabelizer & DeBabelizer Pro

DeBabelizer for the Mac OS and DeBabelizer Pro for Windows can help you in creating animations and with file format translation.

DeBabelizer (Mac) and DeBabelizer Pro (Windows 95 and NT 4.0)
Equilibrium
Three Harbor Drive, Suite 111
Sausalito, CA 94965
(415) 332-4343
http://www.equilibrium.com

DeBabelizer for the Mac OS

The new "Code GIF in/out" plug-ins (vital for your animations for the Web) can be downloaded from the DeBabelizer Web site. Download version number 1.1 or higher of the GIF reader/writers.

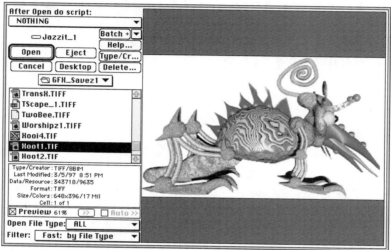

Figure D-1: The DeBabelizer interface.

The 1.1 GIF Reader

This reader will open interlaced and non-interlaced GIF files. It handles GIFs with multiple pictures if you check that option in the GIF Open Option dialog box. If you only have single-picture GIFs and want them to open quickly, don't use the GIF multiple picture option. It handles GIFs with a transparency index and will skip over other (non-transparency) "GIF89a" extensions. GIF Reader handles multiple images better: it sets the frame ULC (upper left corner) offset correctly for each image, sets the transparent color correctly for each image, sets the delay time between frames correctly for each image, and may be a tiny bit faster in handling multiple images.

The 1.1 GIF Writer

For single-image GIF files, this plug-in will write interlaced and non-interlaced GIF files. You can choose interlaced or non-interlaced from the GIF submenu in the Save Formats pop-up menu. It will write the transparency index to the GIF file if you choose the Transparency option in the GIF submenu. For multiple-image GIF files (GIF animations), the plug-in will write a "moving" GIF file (referred to as "animated GIF"), which is simply a GIF with multiple pictures indicated in the file header data. To write an animated GIF file, choose the Custom GIF option from the GIF submenu in the Save Formats pop-up menu. This will bring up the GIF Save Options dialog box. A local color table will be written for each additional image in a GIF file which has a different color table than the first image in the file.

DeBabelizer Pro for Windows

When you need to create movie files (AVI), DeBabelizer Pro separates the data into three dialog categories: Image Info (the same items as in image file properties), Movie Info (frame rate and length, color depth, separate streams, palette changes, and whether recompression settings are desired), and Palette Info (showing all of the color index numbers and RGB/HSV settings alongside representative color swatches, a uniquely useful item for Web designers because of the need to address Web palette formats).

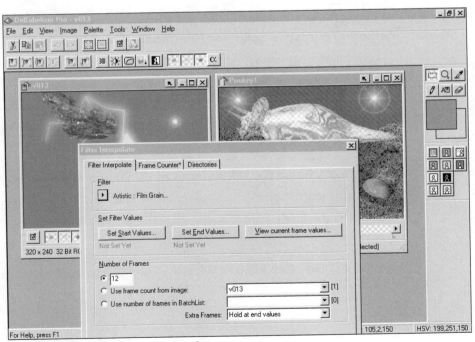

Figure D-2: The DeBabelizer Pro interface.

Batch List Processing

DeBabelizer also excels at creating batch lists for image processing. For the Web designer, this means that you could set up a batch of RGB images for translation to 256 colors, or to the special Netscape or Explorer palettes. The whole image list would be translated automatically while you take a donut break.

Filter Animations

Here's how to use DeBabelizer Pro to create animation sequences from xRes or FreeHand bitmap graphics. First, locate your xRes filters in DeBabelizer filters preferences, so DeBabelizer Pro knows where to find them. DeBabelizer allows you to locate and incorporate your filter listings for application purposes. Load in a picture saved out from xRes or a FreeHand graphic saved out as a bitmap. Then select Tools | Filter Interpolate or its icon equivalent, and then select the filter you want to apply. If the filter is adjustable, its interface is displayed. You then set the starting and ending data (how much the filter will affect the frames at the start and end), and DeBabelizer interpolates the intervening frames to create an animated sequence of filtered images. Import one graphic frame and create a series of filter-interpolated animation frames by doing one of the following (Equilibrium plans to develop an easier one-step AVI module in a future release):

Method #1: Create a Script for Filter Animations

1. Open an image file.
2. Apply a filter interpolation to the image.
3. Save the image (with an enumerated extension, 000, 001, and so on).
4. Close the saved interpolated image, and start processing the next image by going to step #1.

Method #2: A Batch List With Clones of the Image Any Number of Times

1. Add as many frames as necessary to the Batch List (called batch iteration).
2. Apply the filter script with varied settings to each instance of the cloned image.

Method #3: The DeBabelizer Wizard
The DeBabelizer Wizard can help you create a Batch List for Filter Interpolations.

Tip

Each of these methods produces single-frame image files that should be saved as a frame sequence with extension numbers in order. Then you can tell DeBabelizer to transform the single files into an AVI movie.

The GIF Save Options Dialog

This DeBabelizer Pro utility allows you to translate your xRes, Extreme 3D, and FreeHand bitmap-saved graphics into GIFs, and provides many options not found in FreeHand Graphics Studio modules. Selecting the Interlaced checkbox saves the GIF as interlaced. Select the Set Image Offset checkbox to save the current image's upper left corner offset from some imaginary screen. If unchecked, a zero value is stored for this offset. Some formats, such as PICS and Wavefront files, use this value, so when DeBabelizer reads them in it remembers these values for possible use. These values can be also set explicitly by selecting Edit | Offset.

Transparency & Background Color Options for GIFs   DeBabelizer maintains a background color which can be set and examined from the Palettes | Dithering Options and Background Color menu choices. You could also think of this background color as a transparency color; you turn on that effect by selecting Edit | Selection Transparency | Background Color. Turn on the transparency option for the GIF reader by selecting Misc | Preferences | Readers | GIF. If a GIF file has a transparency index, the File Type line in the File Info window in the Open dialog displays (Trans Index=XX), where XX represents the transparency index.

Macromedia Flash

Flash can load in your xRes, Extreme 3D, or FreeHand graphics files as long as they're in one of the following formats:

- For the Macintosh—PICT, Illustrator, AutoCAD, JPEG, or GIF.
- For Windows—EMF, WMF, Illustrator, EPS, AutoCAD, JPEG, GIF, and BMP.

The Animation Controller in Flash is very easy and intuitive to use. Elements on a page can stay in place across the sequence, can be interpolated to change position, size, and rotation from targeted beginning and ending frames, or can be altered in design in a frame-by-frame process. Interpolation does not include morphing. Morphing would let you automatically change from one shape to another. Making changes from one frame to the next by hand is called Keyframing in Flash.

In addition to the standard Timeline Controller (like that found in Extreme 3D), the Animation palette also includes layer-specific controls. New elements are placed on separate layers, any of which can be repositioned in the stack. Elements on any layer can appear in color, grayscale, or in single-color outlines for reshaping and stacking purposes. You can make layers active or inactive and also lock them to prevent further editing.

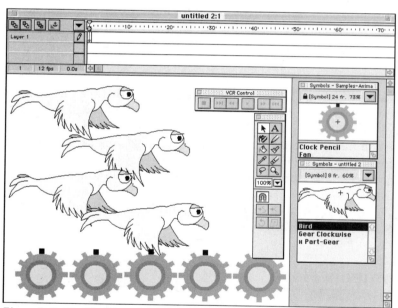

Figure D-3: The Flash interface.

Web Ready

Flash was designed for 2D animation and also provides specific tools for Web animation. Flash, like FreeHand, is a vector design application, so that animation files tend to be about 80 percent smaller than similar animations created with bitmap processes. To take advantage of the vector parameters, the animation has to be saved in a specific vector format (not as a movie file). The best way to save a Flash animation for use on a Web page is as a FutureSplash Player (.spl) file. Your Web site visitors need the SPL Player plug-in to view SPL files; the plug-in is available for downloading from Macromedia's Web site. SPL animations can be written out with smoothing turned on, producing high-quality anti-aliased art in a tiny file size (10 to 20 percent of what the same file would be if saved as a standard movie format, if the content is all vector art).

As an alternative to writing out the animation as a SPL file, Flash supports all of the GIF animation file formats. This includes the capability to save the animation as either a GIF animation or as a GIF sequence of single frames (so they can be edited in other suitable applications). This includes transparency recognition for invisible backgrounds. Any standard Web browser can read GIF animations. You incorporate them using standard loading and placing methods in your Web page design software (like Macromedia's Backstage Designer). GIF animations can use the standard 216-color Netscape/Explorer palette.

Animations can be exported to the following formats:

- For the Macintosh—SPL, QuickTime, Animated GIF, PICT sequence, EPS sequence, Illustrator sequence, DXF sequence, JPEG sequence, and GIF sequence.

- For Windows—SPL, AVI, Animated GIF, EMF sequence, WMF sequence, EPS sequence, DXF sequence, BMP sequence, JPEG sequence, and GIF sequence.

GIFmation (Mac & Windows)

GIFmation™ 2.0 is from BoxTop Software. You can import your saved FreeHand 7 Graphics Studio GIF files into GIFmation for GIF animation compositing for Web display.

BoxTop Software, Inc.
One Research Boulevard/Suite 201
Starkville, MS 39759
voice (601) 323-6436
fax (601) 324-7352
http://www.boxtopsoft.com
ftp://ftp.boxtopsoft.com/pub/
info@boxtopsoft.com

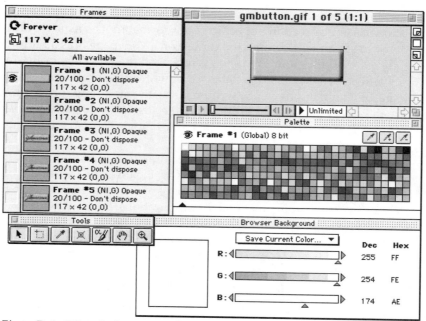

Figure D-4: GIFmation's main interface display.

The Document Window

The Document window acts as the image editing window and the animation preview at the same time. You can open multiple Documents; each will have a separate Document window. The Document title, current frame number, total number of frames, and the zoom level are displayed (in that order) in the title bar of each Document window. There are two main groups of controls in the Document window. Controls for animation preview and navigation are along the bottom left of the Document window, and controls for onion-skinning are along the upper right side of the Document window.

Onion-skinning means you can see previous frames when drawing the current frame. Onion-skinning controls consist of three buttons (from top to bottom): Onion Skin Next, No Onion Skinning, and Onion Skin Previous. When the Onion Skin Next button is on, the next image is visible through the current image. When Onion Skin Previous is on, the previous image is visible through the current image. This provides a visual aid for the positioning and alignment of images. When the No Onion Skinning button is on the current image is opaque and no images are visible through it.

The controls for previewing your animation and navigating through the animation frames while editing are the Stop button, the Play/Pause button, the Frame slider, the Step Back button, the Step Forward button, and the Speed menu. The logical screen size is the area within which all images in a GIF animation must render. It is a global file parameter that applies to the whole animation. Images in your animation cannot extend outside the area of the logical screen size. The Document window also serves as the animation preview. When an animation is playing you can use most editing commands to make changes to the animation on the fly. For example, you can change delay times and other frame settings without stopping the animation.

The Frames Floating palette provides a display of all set frame parameters and another means of navigating through your animation. Most importantly, the Frames Floating palette is where you select and deselect frames while editing your animation. Only one frame can be visible in the Document window at any given time.

You can set a browser or browser set against which compatibility is checked. If you select settings that will not work as expected in the selected browser or browser set, they are rendered as red and the Caution button is displayed in the Frames Floating palette. Click the button that displays the chosen browser compatibility setting to display a dialog where you select which browser to check compatibility with. You can also choose no compatibility checking or a global setting to check for compatibility with all browsers. Click the Caution button to display explanations of which settings are incompatible and the browser behavior that can be expected with those incompatible settings.

The total number of frames in your animation is shown at the bottom left of the Frames Floating palette. A Trashcan button at the bottom right of the Frames Floating palette can be used to delete selected frames.

Ulead's GIF Animator (Windows Only)

GIF Animator from Ulead is a stand-alone GIF animation compositor for Windows systems.

Ulead Systems
http://www.ulead.com

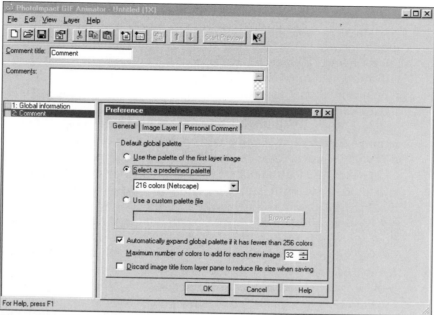

Figure D-5: GIF Animator's main interface display.

By default, GIF Animator supports the following file formats: GIF, JPEG, and BMP. Save your xRes or other files in one of these formats to use GIF Animator's capabilities. If, however, you have the full version of Ulead PhotoImpact installed on your machine, then GIF Animator will update itself automatically to use the file format support extensions (FIO) included with PhotoImpact. If you don't have Ulead's PhotoImpact, then you can download free FIOs to add to the GIF Animator FIO folder (located in the GIF Animator directory) from the Ulead Web site.

Attributes

Preferences establish the default global palette settings of every new animation, and whether or not to remove the title information when saving the file. When selecting a palette, consider the cels you want to use. If they all share the same color scheme, then choose "Use the palette of the first layer's image." This will remove the palette from all the following image layers and they will depend upon the global palette for their colors. Since they all have the same palette anyway, doing this won't affect their display quality, and it helps to reduce your overall file size. Otherwise, you can select a predefined palette of standard display colors. That means if you choose a 16-color palette, then the same 16 colors are displayed on every monitor. This means that you don't have to worry about your palette containing colors that may appear wrong on monitors that don't support them. For example, you might do all your graphics work on a 24-bit color monitor, but the surfer on the other side of the world might be stuck using a 16-bit color monitor. If you used 24-bit color to save your work, it will not appear the way you intended on the surfer's 16-bit color monitor. You can also choose a palette you have used and saved before, if you have a custom palette from another animation you created and you want to use the same color scheme in your new animation.

Exporting GIF Animator Images

You can export images in two different ways—as a new animated GIF file or as a sequence of separate GIF files. To export a group of images as a new animation:

1. Select the images you want using your mouse while holding down the Ctrl key (to select a range of non-sequential image files) or the Shift key (to select a range of sequential image files).
2. Select 'As a single file' under 'Export multiple images:'.
3. Click OK.
4. Name your new file and click Save.

Exporting a Group of Images as a Sequence of Files

1. Select the images you want using your mouse while holding down the CTRL key (to select individual image files) or the SHIFT key (to select a range of image files).
2. Select 'As a sequence of files' under 'Export multiple images:'.
3. Click OK.
4. Choose a name to be shared by the files and click Save.

Images exported as part of sequence will all have the same name but be numbered according to their order in the original GIF animation. For example, if you were to choose FIRE as the shared name, then the new files would be named FIRE.GIF, FIRE001.GIF, FIRE002.GIF, and so on.

PhotoGIF

PhotoGIF™, also from BoxTop Software, is a file format plug-in for Adobe Photoshop 3.0 and above that provides capabilities for creating and editing highly optimized, Web-ready GIFs and GIF animations. For FreeHand Graphics Studio users, original art can be created in xRes and ported to Photoshop for PhotoGIF processing. Except for facial portraits, where banding might occur because of the limited color palette of a GIF file, PhotoGIF images are comparable to 24-bit graphics.

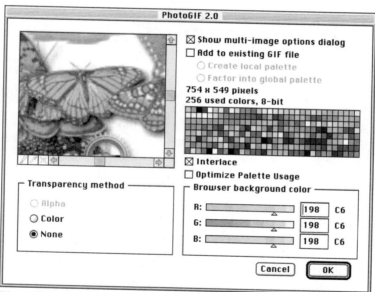

Figure D-6: The PhotoGIF interface.

Its key features include:

■ Creation of high-quality, small GIF files. It uses advanced proprietary techniques for quantization, palette usage optimization, and compression enhancements resulting in superior image quality while saving up to 50 percent in file size.

■ Advanced color reduction capability. PhotoGIF utilizes new color reduction technology that improves both image quality and compression when using custom or fixed palettes such as the Netscape palette. It also provides true super palette capability for GIF animations.

- Complete support for multiple image GIF animation files. PhotoGIF allows you to create and edit GIF animations directly in Photoshop with complete control over palette usage, background color, looping, logical screen size, image position, delay times, and disposal methods.

- Transparency tools. Transparency can be set by color or from any alpha channel in the working image. A preview with advanced transparency tools including eye dropper, color picker, touch up brush, and automatic halo removing edge tool allow perfect transparency every time.

- Preferences. Gives you the capability to speed up your work. Every aspect of opening and saving files can be easily configured through preference settings and customized for individual work habits to speed use and simplify working with large numbers of images.

Corel's PhotoPaint (Windows)

Corel Corporation
1600 Cerling
Ottawa, Ontario, Canada K1Z 8R7
613-728-0876
http://www.corel.com

Windows users of the FreeHand Graphics Studio might want to consider generating original art in xRes and porting the results to Corel's PhotoPaint 7+ or Adobe for developing filter animations. PhotoPaint has a different series of filters than xRes offers, and some might be closer to what you need to see happening in the animated image. What PhotoPaint really offers the animator, however, is a fully featured animation controller for developing 2D filter animations. All that's necessary is that you alter the way an effect is being applied from frame to frame in one or more ways, saving each file out in a sequential manner or as a movie (AVI or QuickTime) file. It offers full preview and playback controls, as well as control dialogs that allow you full control over each filter aspect.

Figure D-7: The Corel PhotoPaint 7+ Animation Controller window.

PhotoPaint is a high-quality post-production tool for video animation. Just import your single xRes or FreeHand bitmap-saved frames, and use any of PhotoPaint's image enhancement tools to paint on each frame, or use an image processing filter. Use the VCR controls to preview any frame or initiate a playback. It's best to translate your movie frames to 256-color mode unless you plan to record them as single frames with suitable hardware. The finished movies can be saved out in AVI, QuickTime, or MPEG formats.

In addition, PhotoPaint offers you lens objects, including brightness-contrast-intensity, hue-saturation-lightness, tone curve, sample/target balance, threshold, level equalization, posterize, gamma, color balance, replace colors, invert, and desaturate. Corel's Lens Object application of these features is like nothing that you've ever seen before. All of these effects are applied to a separate object layer that can be resized, rotated, and moved around. Since this is a separate object layer, it can also have opacity adjusted. When you're satisfied with the composition, just paste the lens object into the background layer. This attribute can be used to create interesting titling and logo animations by itself. Using lens object techniques on an imported xRes graphic results in unique animated sequences.

Browsers Supporting GIF Animation

Very soon, GIF animations will be supported in the current versions of all graphical browsers. The following list of browsers currently support GIF animation:

Macintosh

- Netscape Navigator 2.0 and later
- Microsoft Internet Explorer 2.1 and later
- Apple CyberDog 1.2 and later

Windows

- Netscape Navigator 2.0 and later
- Microsoft Internet Explorer 2.0 and later
- Opera 2.1 and later

Index

VENTANA

Macromedia Director 5 Power Toolkit

$49.95, 552 pages, illustrated, part #: 1-56604-289-5

Macromedia Director 5 Power Toolkit views the industry's hottest multimedia authoring environment from the inside out. Features tools, tips and professional tricks for producing power-packed projects for CD-ROM and Internet distribution. Dozens of exercises detail the principles behind successful multimedia presentations and the steps to achieve professional results. The companion CD-ROM includes utilities, sample presentations, animations, scripts and files.

The Comprehensive Guide to Lingo

$49.99, 700 pages, illustrated, part #: 1-56604-463-4

Master the Lingo of Macromedia Director's scripting language for adding interactivity to presentations. Covers beginning scripts to advanced techniques, including creating movies for the Web and problem solving. The companion CD-ROM features demo movies of all scripts in the book, plus numerous examples, a searchable database of problems and solutions, and much more!

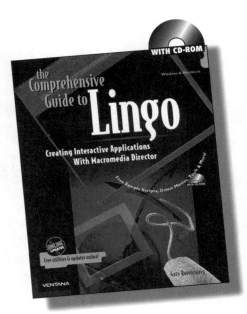

Shockwave!

$49.95, 400 pages, illustrated, part #: 1-56604-441-3

Breathe new life into your web pages with Macromedia Shockwave. Ventana's *Shockwave!* teaches you how to enliven and animate your Web sites with online movies. Beginning with step-by-step exercises and examples, and ending with in-depth excursions into the use of Shockwave Lingo extensions, Shockwave! is a must-buy for both novices and experienced Director developers. Plus, tap into current Macromedia resources on the Internet with Ventana's Online Companion. The companion CD-ROM includes the Shockwave plug-in, sample Director movies and tutorials, and much more!

VENTANA

The Director 6 Book

$49.99, 560 pages, part #: 1-56604-658-0

Macintosh, Windows 95/NT
Intermediate to Advanced

Raise your standards—and your stock—as a multimedia specialist by harnessing what's new in Macromedia Director 6. This professional-level guide focuses on key techniques for creating, manipulating and optimizing files. Your projects will look, sound and play back better and more consistently than ever.
Provides:
• Undocumented tricks for Director 6.
• Tips for moving from Director 5 to 6.
• Issues and answers for cross-platform presentations.
• Techniques for integrating Director 6 with JavaScript, CGI and Shockwave audio.

The CD-ROM includes more than 50 sample Director movies with code included, plus Macromedia and gmatter Xtras, shareware and more.

The Lingo Programmer's Reference

$39.99, 500 pages, part #: 1-56604-695-5

Windows 95/NT, Macintosh
Intermediate to Advanced

The Ultimate Resource for Director Professionals! High-level mastery of Lingo is the only route to real Director expertise. This comprehensive reference goes beyond tutorials and simple listings to provide thorough explanations of every aspect of Lingo, supported by practical examples, professional tips and undocumented tricks. Includes:
• What's new in Director 6, property lists for sprites and other objects, and a JavaScript reference for Lingo programmers.
• In-depth discussions, including types of parameters to pass to properties, commands, functions and type of data returned.
• Encyclopedic listing, extensively cross-referenced for easy access to information.

The CD-ROM features a searchable, hyperlinked version of the book.

VENTANA

The Mac OS 8 Book

Maximize your Mac with this worthy successor to Ventana's bestselling *The System 7.5 Book*! Comprehensive chapters cover installing, updating, third-party add-ons and troubleshooting tips for Mac OS 8, along with full instructions on how to connect to the Net and publish on the Web with Mac OS 8.

This thorough look at what's new also provides a complete overview of all commands and features, including

- High level of backward compatibility.
- Increased performance, stability and ease of use.
- Streamlined and enhanced programming model to simplify the job of writing software for the Mac OS 8 platform.
- Technologies that enable users to add new features to their software that were impossible or inconvenient to add with earlier System 7 generations.
- User interface themes.
- V-Twin searching and indexing technology.

The Mac OS 8 Book

Getting the most from your Macintosh operating system

Mark R. Bell   VENTANA

Plus—online updates for up-to-the-minute patches and fixes for Mac OS 8, as well as updates to the book.

part #: 56604-490-1
658 pages $29.99

VENTANA

FreeHand 7 Graphics Studio
The Comprehensive Guide

R. Shamms Mortier
$49.99, 800 pages, illustrated, part #: 679-3

A master class in cutting-edge graphics! Express your
creative powers to the fullest in print, on the Web, on
CD-ROM—anywhere sophisticated imagery is in
demand. Step-by-step exercises help you master each
component—Freehand 7, xRes, Fontographer and
Extreme3D—with professional guidelines for using
them separately, together, and in partnership with third-
party products.

CD-ROM: Sample files, sample web pages, free Xtras,
plug-ins & more!

For Windows, Macintosh • Intermediate to Advanced

Web Publishing With Macromedia Backstage
Internet Studio 2

R. Shamms Mortier, Winston Steward
$49.99, 448 pages, illustrated, part #: 598-3

Farewell to HTML! This overview of all four tiers of
Backstage Internet Studio 2 lets users jump in at
their own level. With the focus on processes as well
as techniques, readers learn everything they need to
create center-stage pages.

CD-ROM: Plug-ins, applets, animations, audio files,
Director xTras and demos.

For Windows, Macintosh • Intermediate to Advanced

VENTANA

To order any Ventana title, complete this order form and mail or fax it to us, with payment, for quick shipment.

TITLE	PART #	QTY	PRICE	TOTAL

SHIPPING

For orders shipping within the United States, please add $4.95 for the first book, $1.50 for each additional book.
For "two-day air," add $7.95 for the first book, $3.00 for each additional book.
Email: vorders@kdc.com for exact shipping charges.
Note: Please include your local sales tax.

SUBTOTAL = $ _____

SHIPPING = $ _____

TAX = $ _____

TOTAL = $ _____

Mail to: International Thomson Publishing • 7625 Empire Drive • Florence, KY 41042
☎ **US orders 800/332-7450 • fax 606/283-0718**
☎ **International orders 606/282-5786 • Canadian orders 800/268-2222**

Name _____

E-mail _____ Daytime phone _____

Company _____

Address (No PO Box) _____

City _____ State _____ Zip _____

Payment enclosed ___ VISA ___ MC ___ Acc't # _____ Exp. date _____

Signature _____ Exact name on card _____

Check your local bookstore or software retailer for these and other bestselling titles, or call toll free:

800/332-7450
8:00 am - 6:00 pm EST